CELTIC

THE OFFICIAL ILLUSTRATED HISTORY

1888-1995

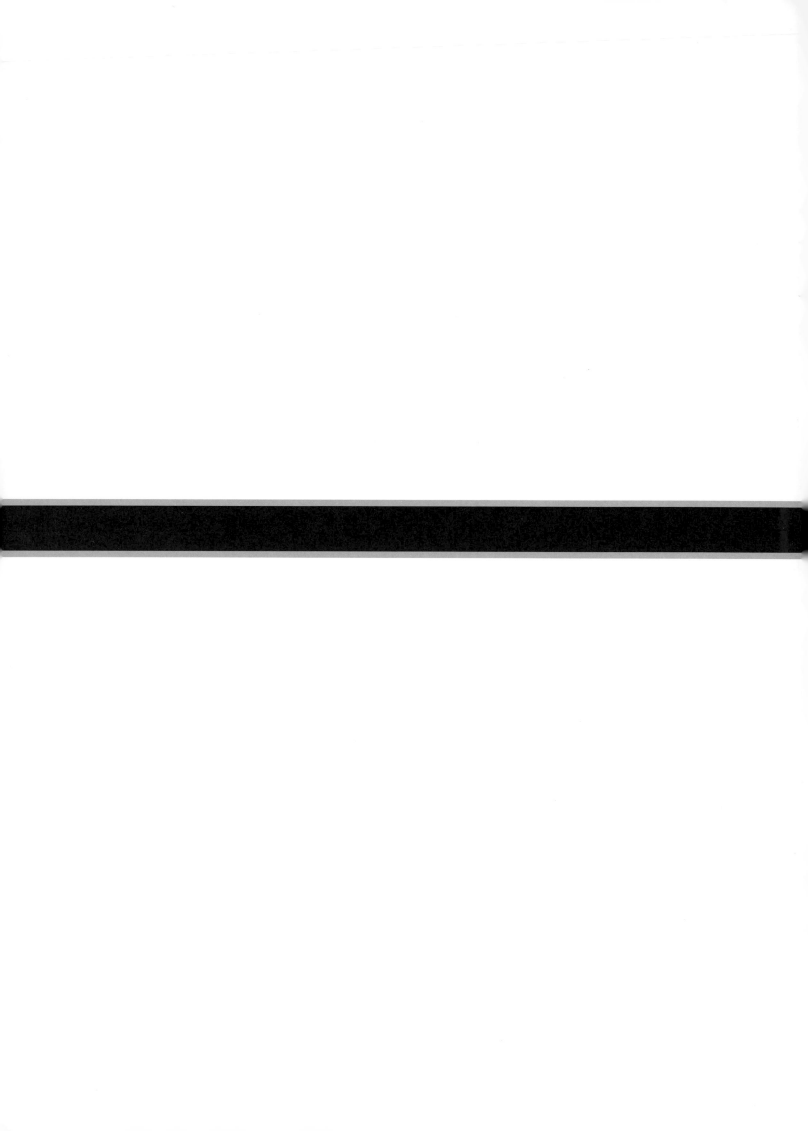

CELTIC

THE OFFICIAL ILLUSTRATED HISTORY

1888-1995

FOREWORD BY PAUL McSTAY

GRAHAM McCOLL

HAMLYN

Acknowledgements:
The author would like to thank the following representatives of Celtic past and present for giving me so much of their time in interviews: Tommy Burns, John Divers, Tommy Gemmell, Stuart Gray, David Hay, John Hughes, Jimmy Johnstone, Murdo MacLeod, Paul McStay, Charlie Nicholas, Andy Walker. I would also like to thank the following individuals who assisted greatly in researching and producing this book: Jack Murray, John Bonner and Kevin Donnelly for providing background material and illustrations; Rona Leggat and Claire McGhee at Celtic for help in arranging interviews and match tickets; Peter McLean, Public Relations Officer at Celtic, for proofreading the text; George Sheridan for supplying statistics; Mike LeBihan for designing the book; Maria Gibbs for Picture Research. I would also like to thank Rab MacWilliam of Reed Books for his help throughout the twelve months it took to bring this book to life. The newspaper archives of the Mitchell Library in Glasgow proved to be an invaluable source of information. Back numbers of the following newspapers helped greatly in my research: the Celtic View, the Daily Record, the Sunday Mail, the Glasgow Herald, Scotland on Sunday, the Guardian, The Independent, The Scotsman, the Weekly News, the Weekly Record.
The following books also provided useful background material:
An Alphabet of the Celts by Eugene MacBride & Martin O'Connor with George Sheridan (Polar Publishing, Leicester, 1994), **Celtic** by Sir Robert Kelly (Hay Nisbet and Miller Ltd, 1971), **The Celtic Football Companion** by David Docherty (John Donald, Edinburgh, 1986), **The First 100 Years of the Scottish Football League** by Bob Crampsey (The Scottish Football League, Glasgow, 1990), **Back to Paradise** by Billy McNeill with Alex Cameron (Mainstream, Edinburgh, 1988), **The Ultimate Encyclopedia of Soccer** General Editor Keir Radnedge (Hodder & Stoughton, London, 1994), **The Story of Celtic** by Gerald McNee (Stanley Paul, London, 1978), **Paradise Lost** by Michael Kelly (Canongate Press, Edinburgh, 1994), **Celtic, A Century with Honour** by Brian Wilson (Collins Willow, London, 1988), **The Glory and the Dream** by Tom Campbell and Pat Woods (Mainstream, Edinburgh, 1986).

First published in Great Britain in 1995
by Hamlyn, an imprint of Reed Consumer Books Limited
Michelin House, 81 Fulham Road, London SW3 6RB
and Auckland, Melbourne, Singapore and Toronto
Produced and designed by Brown Packaging Limited
255-257 Liverpool Road, London N1 1LX

Copyright © 1995 Reed International Books Limited

ISBN 0 600 58707 X

A catalogue record for this book is available from the British Library
Printed in Great Britain

Picture Acknowledgements:

Allsport / Hulton Deutsch 72 below right, 76 top, 77 top right, 81, 83, 84, 85, 89, 91 below, 94 top, 98 top left, 99 top right, 100 top, 101 below, 103 below, 106 top, 132
John Bonner 49 top, 64, 70 top right, 70 centre right, 71 below left, 71 centre left, 72 top, 76 centre right, 76 below right, 77 top left, 78 below, 79 top, 80 below, 82 below, 88 below right, 88 centre right, 93 top, 94 below, 97, 98 below right, 99 below left, 100 below, 101 top
Celtic FC 8, 10, 11, 14, 22, 26, 27, 29, 52, 72 below left, 73, 79 below, 90 below
Celtic View 126 top, 128, 135 below, 135 top, 144 top right, 151 top left, 151 below, 151 top right, **/D.Gillespie** 121 top right, 121 top left
Colorsport 116, 118
D.C.Thompson & Co. Ltd. 74, 82 top, 87, 109, 126 below
Kevin Donnelly 90 top, 93 below, 95, 102 below, 103 top left, 103 centre left, 106 below, 114
Empics 141 below, **/Peter Robinson** 110, **/Neal Simpson** 6
The Herald and Evening Times, Glasgow 30, 34, 43, 46 top left, 47 below, 47 top, 49 below, 50, 53, 54 left, 54 right, 55 below right, 55 below left, 57, 58, 60, 62 right, 65 top, 65 below, 66, 67, 68, 70 below, 71 top, 78 top, 80 top, 86, 88 below, 91 top, 92, 99 left, 102 top, 104 top left, 104 top right, 105, 107 below, 107 top, 111, 112, 115, 120, 122, 123 below left, 123 below right, 124 top, 125 top, 125 centre, 125 below, 129, 130, 134 top, 136 top right, 136 top left, 138, 140 top, 142, 144 top left, 145, 146 below, 146 top, 147, 150 top, 152 below, 153 centre, 153 below, 153 top, 154 top, 155 top, 158
Graham McColl 55 top, 63, 123 top, 124 below, 134 below, 136 below, 139 below, 139 top, 140 below, 141 top, 150 below, 152 centre right, 152 top right, 154 below, 155 below left, 157
Jack Murray 12 below, 12 top, 16, 18, 19, 21, 24, 25, 28, 32, 33 centre left, 33 below left, 33 top, 36, 37 top, 37 centre, 37 below, 40, 41, 44, 45, 46 top right, 48, 61, 62 left
Popperfoto 96
Professional Sport /Tony O'Brien 148, 155 below right, 156
Scotsman Publications Ltd 108

Thanks to the Scottish Football Association and the Scottish Football League for the reproduction of match programmes and to the staff at the Herald and Evening Times, Glasgow, for their help with picture research.

Contents

FOREWORD   **7**

CHAPTER 1
A Grand New Team   **8**

CHAPTER 2
Maley's Maestros   **20**

CHAPTER 3
Triumphs and Tragedies   **34**

CHAPTER 4
A Golden Era Ends in Style   **50**

CHAPTER 5
Glimpses of Greatness   **58**

CHAPTER 6
European Adventures   **74**

CHAPTER 7
Return to Splendour   **112**

CHAPTER 8
Celtic Enter a New Age   **132**

CHAPTER 9
A Promising Future   **148**

FACTS AND FIGURES   **159**

INDEX   **207**

FOREWORD
by Paul McStay

In common with many Celtic supporters, I became aware that Celtic had a great history almost from the moment I was old enough to kick a ball. In my own case, there was extra spice in the tale because two of the club's most distinguished servants during the first half of this century were relations of mine: my great-great-uncles Willie and Jimmy McStay. I have also been very fortunate in that my brothers Willie and Raymond have been on the club's playing staff during my time at Celtic Park and I was more pleased than anyone when Willie recently became the club's youth development officer.

So when people describe Celtic as a family club, I understand immediately what is meant. I also, like many Celtic fans, feel as though the great players I have watched and heard about are like members of an extended family: the Celtic family.

This club was created by people who were determined to provide funds for charitable causes. That ensured that Celtic would always possess a special kind of spirit. Throughout the club's history this spirit has helped Celtic through some difficult times and made the good times extra-sweet.

I have been particularly happy during my own career at Celtic, especially during the centenary year of 1987-88 when the Celtic players were spurred on to great achievements by the knowledge that it was a hugely significant time in the club's history and by the importance that celebrating that year in style held for the fans. It helped, of course, that many of the players, then as now, were fans themselves. That gave them an extra determination and resolution without which certain matches would not have been won. On other occasions down the years, that Celtic spirit has manifested itself to give us that bit extra and those moments will always live with me and, I know, thousands of others among the Celtic support for many long years.

There have been some difficult moments for Celtic in recent times but once again the future is looking extremely bright. One of the valuable lessons that can be gained from Celtic's history is discovering how the club has come through bad times before and has eventually become better and stronger for it.

This book provides a celebration of all of the great moments in the Celtic story. It brings alive the characters and events that have made Celtic one of the world's greatest clubs, a club that has given enormous pleasure to people in all corners of the globe and which will continue to do so in the future. Everyone at Celtic Park is looking forward to writing the next chapter in the club's history and we are confident it will be as exciting and enjoyable for Celts everywhere as the nine that are in this book.

From its beginning, Celtic football club was a runaway success. It quickly fulfilled its purpose of providing money for charity and did so by winning Leagues and Cups in superb style.

1 A Grand New Team

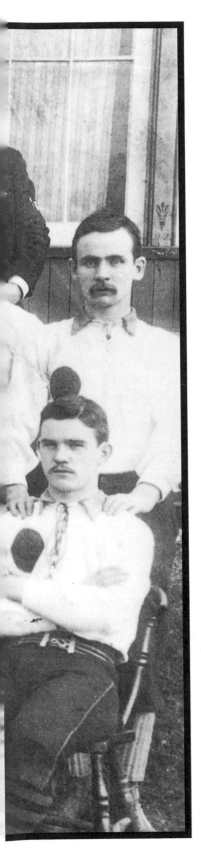

The first Celtic team. Neil McCallum, scorer of the club's first goal, is seated second from right in the front row.

The individuals who brought Celtic football club into being were late starters. By the time Celtic played their first fixture on 28 May 1888, Rangers had been in existence for 15 years, Hibernian for 13 and Queen's Park, Scotland's oldest club, had been playing since 1867.

Yet when it came to timing, Celtic's founders could not have picked a better moment. The club was founded just in time to participate in the first season of the Scottish League, which kicked off on 16 August 1890. A crowd of 10,000 watched Celtic's home match with Renton, who had not long before described themselves as 'champions of the world' after their victory over FA Cup holders West Bromwich Albion. On that first day of organised League competition, the Celts lost 4-1 to Renton but the new club would go on to win the League, at just the third time of asking, in 1892-93.

Nor, once they had made their well-timed entry on to the Scottish football stage, could Celtic be accused of timewasting. Their first major trophy, the Scottish Cup, was captured at just the fourth attempt, in 1892, with the team already playing the type of attractive, attacking style that would become the club's instantly recognisable calling card down the decades. And Celtic's first home games were played at a ground that had been created from scratch inside six months and where they had drawn sizeable crowds from day one – the attendance for the Renton match on that first League card was more than double Rangers' attendance for their home match with Hearts on the same day.

In April 1889, less than a year after the club had played its first match, two Celtic players, James McLaren and James Kelly, had starred in Scotland's 3-2 victory over England at the Kennington Oval in London. Left-half McLaren, nicknamed 'The Auld Gineral', got the winner with the last kick of the game, a 20-yard volley.

It would be misleading to say that all of those early achievements combined to give Celtic the type of start the club's founders had dreamed of, because these men were not dreamers. Celtic's successes, then as now, were built on a worldly romanticism – a realisation that even the best intentions and ideals are useless unless backed up by hard work and a practical attitude.

Walfrid's inspiration

If looking for an individual who would perfectly fit the description of worldly romantic it would be necessary to go no further than Brother Walfrid, the man whose imagination and inspiration was largely responsible for bringing the club into being. As leader of the teaching institute the Marist Order in Glasgow, he had witnessed the poverty and despair that was the lot of the Irish immigrants in the city's East End.

Crowded into slums, they were discriminated against and hated by the locals because of their willingness to take work at rates of pay that undercut those of the native Clydesiders and because of the foreignness of their Roman Catholic religion. It was a life that was only a slight improvement on their probable fate had their families remained in Ireland to become victims of the Great Potato Famine of 1845 which had seen tens of thousands of Irish emigrate, purely for survival, to America and Britain. Cruel caricatures of the Irish in some sections of the Scottish press cast them as ignorant, backward and stupid.

Faced with such barriers, their chances of proving themselves the equals, or betters, of the Scots appeared almost non-existent.

Brother Walfrid was concerned with both that community's spiritual needs and its even more pressing temporal ones. The Poor Children's Dinner Table, which he had instituted when headmaster of Sacred Heart school in Bridgeton in conjunction with one of his colleagues, Brother Dorotheus, was a charity that, for a nominal sum, provided meals for the hungry, ragged Irish-Catholic children of the East End.

Football for the community

Walfrid had been given food for thought at a post-match reception in Glasgow for the victorious Hibernian team after their 2-1 win over Dumbarton in the 1887 Scottish Cup final. The Edinburgh side had been founded by an Irish cleric, Canon Edward Hannan, and at one time had been composed entirely of practising Catholics. The club received great support from the Irish-Catholic communities in both Glasgow and in the capital.

On that happy occasion, Hibs' secretary John McFadden, cheered by the convivial company, scored what has to be one of the earliest and worst own goals in Scottish football history when he exhorted his west coast friends to start their own club in the image of Hibs. It was a suggestion that would eventually cause his own club to explode from within – a large percentage of Celtic's early sides was composed of players who had been tempted away from Hibs.

McFadden's suggestion provided Brother Walfrid with the idea of achieving two aims simultaneously. A football club in Glasgow would give his parishioners something that was truly their own and which, if successful, would provide them with pride and belief in themselves. He also planned for it to provide practical help, with the financial profits going to the Poor Children's Dinner Table and other deserving charities.

He urged leading members of the East End parishes of St Mary's, St Alphonsus' and St Andrew's to think hard about starting a football club. Two men, prominent among the parishioners of St Mary's, John H. McLaughlin and John Glass, supplied most

of the drive and businesslike nous that was needed to get the enterprise off the ground.

On 6 November 1887, at the parish hall of St Mary's, John Glass presided as chairman over a meeting that would have enormous repercussions for the Catholic community of Glasgow and, indeed, Scotland as a whole. The idea of a Catholic football club had been conceived nine months previously at the reception for Hibs at the same venue. At St Mary's Hall that Sunday afternoon in November Celtic FC was born.

It was a healthy infant, with bright prospects and enormous potential, and with a large extended family watching carefully over its every move. On the advice of Brother Walfrid it was christened Celtic, a clever name that immediately provided it with both an Irish and a Scottish identity. But it had been born homeless. Steps were immediately taken to put that right.

A patch of land to be used for the club's new ground was rented at a cost of £50 a year. It was situated adjacent to the Eastern Necropolis, and within a corner kick of the modern Celtic Park. The feeling that the

John McLaughlin (above) and John Glass (opposite), the two men who did most to ensure that Celtic was built on solid foundations. Publican McLaughlin was the club's treasurer when it produced its first, hugely successful, balance sheet in June 1889. In 1897 he would become the club's third chairman, after Glass and Dr John Conway.

terracing that had been sculpted into shape from the earth found on the site.

The opening match at the ground, surprisingly, did not involve Celtic. Hibernian and Cowlairs (a club that played in the Springburn area of Glasgow), two of the finest Scottish sides of the time, played out a 0-0 draw on 8 May 1888 in front of a healthy crowd of 5,000. The ground's owner, however, was dissatisfied at the alterations that had been made to his land by the club. Prior to the Hibs v Cowlairs game he had warned Celtic that he was on the verge of taking them to court but the committee replied that they would take out their own action against him.

A quiet beginning to a great rivalry

The Celts stepped out for the first time three weeks later, on 28 May 1888, for their opening fixture, a friendly. Uncannily, their first opponents were Rangers. It would be several decades before the sectarianism that has heated the relationship between the clubs would emerge so the choice of Rangers rather than any other Scottish club can be put down to friendliness rather than rivalry. Their relationship at that point was cordial: at one stage John McLaughlin played piano with the Rangers Glee club. And in the early stages of Celtic's existence their players and officials would share the same railway coach on their New Year visits south of the border to play prestigious friendly matches.

For that first game, the Celtic players took the field in white jerseys with green collars and with a badge on their breasts that featured a red Celtic cross. The first Celtic side was: Dolan, Pearson, McLaughlin, Willie Maley, Kelly, Murray, McCallum, Tom Maley, Madden, Dunbar, Gorevin. Rangers had sent their reserve team and after 10 minutes Neil McCallum scored Celtic's first-ever goal.

The Celts notched up a stylish victory and a scoreline that would have been welcome in any future encounter with their cross-city rivals – 5-2. Admission was sixpence, with women, who made up a sizeable proportion of football crowds in the early days of the game, admitted free. The attendance was 2,000, highly respectable in those days.

Before Celtic entered into serious competition in the 1888-89 season, three friendlies gave them their first clean sheet (1-0 against

Irish-Catholic community had for the new club was harnessed to create the club's first home. Despite their tough lives working long hours in manual labour or trudging the streets in search of employment, they provided, free of charge, their best efforts to construct a ground for their club.

For a club to build their own ground, confident of the club's success before a ball had even been kicked, was something that had never been seen before. But as immigrants who had to fight tooth and nail for every concession, the movers and shakers who were behind Celtic knew that they couldn't take for granted the luxuries afforded the locals.

As with everything else about Celtic, the reasons behind their streamlined approach to creating a new ground could be traced back to the original purpose behind the club's existence. This was no mere leisure activity – a people's pride was at stake.

Inside six months, the new ground was ready for football. Located beneath a main stand were changing rooms for match officials and players while the standing spectators watched the game from a bank of

popular Catholic outfit Dundee Harp in front of 6,000), their first draw (3-3 with another Catholic club of the time, Mossend Swifts), and their first defeat (from Clyde).

Two great club servants sign up

Tom and Willie Maley, both of whom had featured in the debut eleven, were relied on by the Celtic committee to find the best players and put out the best team. Tom Maley, a winger, had been an early target for the club's hierarchy. He had the footballing pedigree from his time with Third Lanark and Hibs and he had the Catholic pedigree and good character that was so important to the founders of the club.

One evening in December 1887 three Celtic representatives, Brother Walfrid, John Glass and Pat Welsh, had visited his home in Cathcart on Glasgow's South Side. Welsh had brought the Maley family to Glasgow in 1870 in gratitude for Maley senior, at the time a soldier in the British army, showing mercy on him when he had been a fleeing rebel in Dublin three years earlier. Maley senior, a native of County Clare, had even helped smuggle the young Fenian out of Ireland.

Tom was out, but Willie was not and, after an enjoyable evening's chat, Walfrid invited Willie to try out for Celtic as well.

'I was at home when the deputation arrived,' said Willie. 'Tom was at Pollokshaws at the home of his wife-to-be. I had a long talk with the visitors. My father gave them his hearty support. I was asked to throw in my lot with Celtic. My reply was that, although I had played a few games with Third Lanark's second string, I was still a junior. That didn't matter and insistence on my joining was so strong I agreed.'

Willie, despite being more committed to athletics than football at the time of that meeting, went on to become the club's match secretary and secretary-manager. Walfrid's judgement that first evening was borne out in style: during his years as secretary-manager between 1897 and 1940, Willie Maley guided the club to some of its greatest triumphs.

Tom Maley had played with Hibs and he used his contacts at that club to entice several players to swap coasts for the purpose of playing football. Following their Scottish Cup triumph over Dumbarton, the Edinburgh

club had won the Association Football Championship of the World by beating England's 'Invincibles', Preston North End, 2-1 in the summer of 1887, so it was a good place to look for talent.

From Easter Road came James McLaren, one of the scorers in that Preston game, John Coleman, Mick Dunbar, Paddy Gallagher, Willie Groves and Mick McKeown. Pleading innocence, Celtic claimed that the Hibs players had approached them first because of the Edinburgh club's monetary worries but few observers of the Scottish football scene were convinced. This episode caused so much upset in Edinburgh that, when Celtic played their first game in that city, furious Hibs fans who had invaded the pitch to confront Celtic players had to be restrained and then forced back by mounted police.

James Kelly of Renton, who was the the most accomplished centre-half in the whole of Scotland, was wooed away from that club by the incessant efforts of John Glass. A speedy competitor who never knew when he was beaten, the Scottish international's decision to commit himself to Celtic rather than Hibs, who were also in the hunt for him, showed that Celtic were of sufficient stature to be ready to join the big boys. It was also the beginning of the Kelly connection with the club; both he and his son, Robert, would later hold the position of Celtic chairman.

Celtic's single-mindedness in acquiring the best players available was a vital ingredient in the club's vigorous battle to have themselves taken seriously. Sometimes pure persuasion was all that was necessary to obtain the services of a player. Sometimes the club's representatives had to employ somewhat underhand tactics.

At that time, footballers in Scotland were nominally amateurs but that didn't mean they weren't paid. Payment would be either illegal or, if it was felt that it was necessary to get round the rules, described as for 'lost time', that is, for time spent on football at the expense of the individual's work (although the sums meted out were usually far in excess of those the individual concerned would have received from his 'day job'). The men on the Celtic committee, having had to fight hard for everything they had acquired in the harsh, unforgiving, Protestant-dominated jungle of Glasgow's business world, were unwilling to allow the finer points of amateurism to get in the way of their ambitions

for creating a truly great club. It would have been unnatural for them to have stored a great deal by the Corinthian spirit in football when Irish-Catholics had found an equivalent sense of fairness was conspicuous by its absence when it came to the more vital aspects of everyday life.

Undercover raids and cross-border snatches

Celtic became renowned for their audacious recruitment policy. Full back Jerry Reynolds was poached hours before a Cup match against Queen's Park when he was visited at home in Carfin during the wee sma' hours by John Glass and Dan Malloy. They persuaded him to leave his local club, Carfin Shamrock, for Celtic. But just to ensure that none of the locals had the opportunity to change the player's mind they crept out of Carfin that very night to a cab whose driver they had ordered to wait just outside the village.

John Madden, who had figured in the first-ever Celtic team, had signed for Sheffield Wednesday in 1892 when, by sheer coincidence, he came across John Glass and Willie Maley at Sheffield railway station. Glass, the great persuader, convinced Madden that he should remain at Celtic and immediately whisked the player off on tour with the club, with a few bob in his pocket to help him along on the journey.

In an even more daring episode, two Celtic committee men were despatched to Nottingham in October 1892 to recover Sandy McMahon, who, along with Neil McCallum, had signed for Forest in June of that year. McMahon was being kept under guard at a Nottingham hotel precisely because the Midlands club expected Celtic to try to get their player back.

Despite that, the Celts' representatives managed to draw him into conversation and offer him a better deal than the English club. They obtained his agreement to return with them to Glasgow. The only problem that remained was how to get him away from his guards. The solution wasn't subtle but it was effective. The two Celtic men and the player simply bolted for the door, sending hotel furniture and fellow guests flying in their wake, grabbed a cab and made for the station, jumping aboard the first train they saw, which was just about to leave.

The most blatant example of Celtic riding roughshod over the rules of the day came with the capture of Dan Doyle in 1891. The left-back had won a Championship medal with Everton that very year, had just been made captain of the club and was enjoying professional status with them. Yet he was willing to give all that up after receiving an offer of a game from supposedly amateur Celtic. The episode moved the Football League to blacklist Celtic for a short period and Everton took out a High Court action on the grounds of breach of contract.

Without those players, though, Celtic would have struggled to make such a sudden splash. Doyle and Reynolds, the two full-backs, complemented each other perfectly. Reynolds's strength and power in the air was unsurpassed while Doyle, decisive and direct in his tackling, could pick out players in the opposition penalty box with incisive passes from inside his own half of the field. 'Dan Doyle! The inimitable Dan. A sure two-footed back. Splendid with his head. A mighty quick thinker... Doyle was seen at his best on the football field when the tide was going against his side,' said former team-mate Willie Maley.

McMahon, who was nicknamed 'Duke', possessed the unusual combination of intricate dribbling skills and powerful, accurate heading and shooting, and was to spend a dozen years at Celtic.

In 1890 the SFA mounted an investigation into clubs' finances. Celtic handed in their books a week late with an elaborate sicknote that would have been beyond even the most imaginative of schoolboy absentees. They explained that there had been fever in their secretary's house. They had held back delivering the books for fear of passing infection on to the good gentlemen of the SFA. They had thought it best to enlist the help of the sanitary authorities to disinfect the books before delivering them, causing an unfortunate delay. It was another example of the club's intention to protect their interests in the face of interference from authority, either by devious or direct means.

The first competitive games that Glasgow Celtic played during season 1888-89 were in the grandly-titled World Exhibition Cup, a tournament for clubs in the Glasgow area. They defeated Dumbarton Athletic and Partick Thistle before losing 2-0 to Cowlairs in the final. Years later, Willie Maley remembered that 'our Celts were jeered at and

THE GLASGOW TEAMS SERIES.

"PLAY UP CELTS"

insulted in disgraceful fashion'. Those on the end of that type of discrimination either lie down to it or decide to show what they're really made of and use it to spur them on. There was never any likelihood that Celtic would opt for anything other than the latter course of action.

The Glasgow Cup, a more prestigious tournament, produced wins by 11-2 over Shettleston and 6-1 over Rangers before a 2-0 defeat at the hands of Queens Park, the one truly amateur side in Scottish football, then and now. The captivating style of play that has characterised Celtic sides down the years was in evidence even in the club's infancy. The side was geared to attack, the forwards' clever passing moves dovetailing neatly with inspired individualism.

Thirty goals, scored in five games against Shettleston, Cowlairs, Albion Rovers, St Bernards and Clyde, powered Celtic to their first Scottish Cup quarter-final in their first season. There, they squeaked through at East Stirlingshire by 2-1 and in the semi-final a 4-1 win, which featured three goals from one of the first great Celtic crowd-pleasers, Willie Groves, disposed of Dumbarton, a club that had appeared in the Scottish Cup final four times during the 1880s.

Groves was a neat player, nimble in his avoidance of the heavy challenges of defenders, quick off the mark and with fantastic ball control. He also had the experience of being a Cup-winner, having been a key member of the Hibs side that had beaten Dumbarton in the 1887 final.

Celtic in 1890-91. Back row, left to right: M. Dunbar, J. Anderson (trainer), Jerry Reynolds, Boyle, Bell, McKeown, committeeman J. O'Hara, Kelly. Middle row: Linesman P. Gallagher, Donan, McGhee, W. Maley, T. Maley. Front row: Madden, Coleman, Dowds, McMahon and Campbell.

Third Lanark awaited Celtic in their debut Scottish Cup final on 2 February 1889. It had snowed on the morning of the game, making conditions tricky, but in front of a crowd of 18,000 at the second incarnation of Hampden Park, Third Lanark won 3-0. After receiving the officials' report on the difficulties caused by the weather, though, the SFA decided there had to be a replay. A week later, Celtic made much more of a match of it, being edged out by the odd goal in three.

Celtic's quick and dramatic impact on football

The new club had made an immediate, dramatic mark on Scottish football and was rapidly becoming the number one hope as far as football-minded Irish-Catholics were concerned. There had been various other clubs around Scotland that had attracted the support of the Catholic population but none had managed to match the momentum of the Bhoys from the East End. At the end of the 1888-89 season the club presented Catholic charities with £421.

'An extraordinary fact in connection with the start of Celtic,' said Willie Maley, looking back in the year of the club's golden anniversary, 'is that not a man among the founders knew anything about the practical side of football. None had ever played the game. Some, perhaps, had never seen a match. Yet in the first year of the club's life Celts were within an ace of winning the Scottish Cup.'

Celtic's first fixture list, reproduced as part of their membership card for the 1889-90 season, makes interesting reading. The club's patrons are named as His Grace the Archbishop of Glasgow, the clergy of the East End parishes and Michael Davitt Esq., Dublin. Davitt was an Irish nationalist politician who, on 18 August 1879, had founded the Irish Land League, which called for that land to be returned to the Irish people.

Virtually the entire fixture list is composed of friendly matches, with the exception of two Cup ties in September, a Glasgow Cup match with Victoria and a Scottish Cup tie with Queen's Park. Among the friendlies are home and away games with top English clubs of the time such as Preston North End and Blackburn Rovers while trips to Sunderland and Everton are pencilled in alongside matches with local sides like Vale of Leven

and Abercorn, a club from Paisley that became defunct in 1921.

Two early knockouts from those Cup competitions, therefore, and Celtic would have been playing friendlies from late September through to April. There were several blank Saturdays on the card; November, for example, promised only a home fixture with Cambuslang. The list ended with a home match on 1 March followed by seven away games in succession. It made for a lop-sided, uneven season but it was the way in which the established Scottish clubs had been conducting their business for some years.

While Celtic's early history is peppered with games in such competitions as the Charity Cup and the Glasgow Cup, both of which could sometimes produce sizeable crowds, they were lesser tournaments simply because entry was limited to the Glasgow clubs. It was the Scottish Cup that every club wanted to win more than any other trophy.

That 1889 Scottish Cup tie at home to Queen's Park was a clash of old and new. The amateurs were determined to put the nouveau riche upstarts in their place and a crowd of 25,000, the biggest at that time for a game in Scotland, saw the game end in a 0-0 draw. Celtic did have a goal ruled out and the game was interrupted by a series of encroachments by the crowd on to the pitch as a result of their numbers testing the new ground's ability to cope to the limit.

The area had been so congested beforehand that the visitors had been unable to gain access until some Celtic representatives guided them through neighbouring gardens into the ground. The replay saw one of the final triumphs for amateurism in Scotland, Queen's Park winning 2-1 at Hampden.

The following season, Celtic entered a new competition, the League Championship, which, in its earliest days, was considered inferior to the Scottish Cup. The appointment of Celtic committee member John H. McLaughlin as the first secretary of the League was significant as it showed that the club's businesslike approach on and off the field had been noted and acknowledged by their fellow clubs.

Throughout his five-year spell in the post McLaughlin's impressive organisational skills and way with words helped establish the League as a bona fide competition in the face of serious opposition from the then Scottish football establishment. His conduct was of the type that would go some way to gaining Celtic, and the Irish-Catholic diaspora in Scotland, widespread acceptance.

At the first meeting to discuss the formation of a League, at Holton's Hotel, Glasgow on 20 March 1890, McLaughlin had cited the newly-formed English League as an example of the benefits of such a competition. In the south, it had made for greater interest in football and allowed for a more relaxed, expressive style of play than did the hurly-burly of Cup competitions.

McLaughlin fights for a better future

The club that had opposed the formation of a League most strenuously was Queen's Park. Their secretary, Mr J. McTavish, believed, correctly, that it was a threat to the then amateur status of Scotland's football clubs. He also anticipated, again correctly, that the new set-up would lead to the extinction of many of the small-town and village clubs who were then in existence and who existed on a diet of friendlies and Cup matches.

Mr McLaughlin's point of view was equally accurate: 'You might as well attempt to stop the flow of Niagara with a kitchen chair as to stem the tide of professionalism.' He was the prime mover behind the motion to acknowledge and accept professionalism that was finally accepted by the SFA in 1893, using all his debating skills and cleverness to have the idea accepted.

A new era was beginning for Scottish football and, despite the fact that it was only a few years old, Celtic FC was about to experience its second major upheaval (the first had been moving to a new ground in 1892). The club that had been founded to provide alms for charity was advancing rapidly down the road to becoming a limited company.

One of the main reasons for McLaughlin favouring open professionalism was that it would give clubs greater control over players, and by the early 1890s Celtic were providing their players with diet sheets and laying down a strict training regime. A code of conduct ensured that, in Willie Maley's words: 'The player who cannot conduct himself on and off the park has no peg for his suit at Celtic Park.' On Christmas night in 1893 Celtic played a match with Clyde under artificial light. The experiment was unsuccessful but it

was further evidence of Celtic's willingness to embrace new developments. It would be the 1950s before floodlighting had developed to the extent that senior matches in Scotland were regularly played under artificial light.

Against such a background Celtic became champions in 1893, 1894 and 1896, a season that also saw them gain their record victory, to date, of 11-0 in the game with Dundee on 26 October 1895.

Celtic's highly disciplined, professional approach had been vindicated. The early 1890s had seen a first Scottish Cup clash, and win, by 1-0, over Rangers in September 1890, thanks to a superb solo run and goal by Willie Groves. But that year's Cup run ended with a 3-0 defeat at Dumbarton on a tricky, frozen pitch. Celtic's first League campaign saw them finish third out of the eleven clubs who

Sketches of the Celtic side, set out in 2-3-5 team formation, that triumphed in the Scottish Cup final with Queen's Park in 1892, to win the club's first major trophy.

had participated, behind Dumbarton and Rangers, who shared the title. That was despite the handicap of having four points deducted for fielding an ineligible goalkeeper, Jamie Bell, in the 5-0 away win over Hearts. James McLaren had been the stop-gap goalkeeper in the club's first-ever League fixture, against Renton, the previous week.

Rangers barred the way in the 1891-92 Scottish Cup, this time at the semi-final stage. In an enthralling game, Celtic were 4-0 up at half-time, before letting it slip to 4-3 in the second half. A winner at the death made for a final score of 5-3. In the final, Queen's Park waited, hoping to teach the young upstarts another lesson. Close to 40,000 (with 20,000 locked out) packed Ibrox to witness a game that had been the focus of tremendous press attention in the days beforehand.

There were snowfalls on the day of the game, 12 March 1892, making conditions underfoot extremely difficult for the players. Unfortunately, the crowd, many of whom had entered illegally, made frequent incursions on to the pitch, forcing the two captains, in mid-match, to tell the referee that they would afterwards be requesting that the game be replayed in more suitable circumstances.

It was a common arrangement at the time and it was also accepted that the game that was in progress, even though almost certain to be replayed, should be played to a finish. Celtic ended up as 1-0 winners but the SFA accepted the clubs' demand for a replay, setting a date of 9 April.

With admission prices increased to two shillings from one, the crowd was reduced to 23,000. At half-time, despite a sterling performance by centre half Kelly, Celtic were one down. But within six minutes of the second half they had equalised through Johnny Campbell and soon Campbell, one of the first great Celtic forwards, had put them ahead. Sandy McMahon exhibited his dribbling skills par excellence before slotting home the third midway through the second half and with quarter of an hour remaining a Kelly free kick caused such panic in the amateurs' defence that Sellar put through his own goal. Celtic weren't finished: as the seconds ticked away McMahon put the sheen on a polished victory with a courageous header. The win had been masterminded by Willie Maley's fine display at half-back. Wild celebrations at the capture of the club's first major trophy ensued throughout Scotland's

Irish-Catholic enclaves. That 1891-2 season had also seen an improvement in the League, the Celts ending their fixtures in second place behind Dumbarton, the first outright winners. The Celtic team in the Scottish Cup final was: Cullen, Reynolds, Doyle, Gallagher, Kelly, Willie Maley, Campbell, Dowds, McCallum, McMahon and Brady.

Chasing the first double

The next two seasons saw Celtic win the League Championship and narrowly fail to become the first double-winning side in both years. In the 1893 Scottish Cup final, against Queen's Park, it was Sellar, the man whose own-goal had helped Celtic to victory the previous year, who would play a crucial role, this time, decisively, in his own side's favour. Again, a dreadful playing surface at Ibrox resulted in the originally-scheduled final ending up as a friendly with the same result as the previous year, a 1-0 win for Celtic.

A fortnight on, the real thing saw a Sellar double put his side two up in half an hour. The second goal met with heated protests from the Celtic players who were adamant that the ball had not passed between the posts (the final had been played without goal-nets in place, much to Celtic's chagrin). It was a proverbial kick in the teeth for the Celts whose Willie Maley had experienced the real thing minutes earlier when he felt the full force of a Queen's Park boot and had to leave the field to have four teeth extracted.

That double blow, together with several other injuries sustained throughout the team, only served to spur the Celts on as the second half began and they soon got a goal back through their inside-right, the model professional Jimmy Blessington. But despite tremendous efforts on their part, including throwing full-back Dan Doyle into attack, they couldn't get the equaliser. The following year the final was a less close-fought affair, Rangers taking the trophy with a 3-1 win.

In 1892, the club had made the short journey across Janefield Street to the site of its present home, when the landlord had attempted to increase the annual rent from £50 to £450. The proposed new site – a flooded brickfield – wasn't ideal and it took 100,000 cartloads of earth to bring it up to scratch. As with the original ground, the hard graft that went into the enterprise was pro-

vided by selfless volunteers from the Irish-Catholic community.

On the Janefield Street side of the new ground, where the 'Jungle' would be situated in later decades, a magnificent new stand was erected that ran almost the full length of the field and which could hold 3,500 spectators. To the stand's right, a stylish pavilion had been constructed that contained dressing rooms, a players' lounge and administrative facilities for the club.

One witness of a philosophical mind, bearing in mind that the previous ground had been adjacent to the Eastern Necropolis, remarked that it was like 'moving from the graveyard to Paradise'. This most appropriate of nicknames for the ground, considering the club's religious origins and the temporary heaven it provided for those oppressed by their everyday hell, stuck.

As they toiled, surely not even those who had inherited the great Irish creative talent for storytelling would have imagined that seven decades on their club would be led to some of its greatest successes by a Protestant, Jock Stein. He would pause to pay tribute to

their efforts: 'The people who formed this club looked very far ahead… they built a ground to accommodate 70,000. I don't think we'd be as clever as to look as far ahead as those people did in those days.'

One feature of Celtic's new home that was to play an important part in the club's future was the cycling track that, along with a running track, separated the terracing from the pitch. The Glaswegian love of cycling was already well-established in the late 19th century and sports days that featured cycle races were enormously popular and profitable for several clubs. In 1895 the Scottish Cyclists' Union had offered Celtic £500 to hire Celtic Park for their World Cycling Championship.

The event was not scheduled to take place until two years later but in order to bring the cycling track up to international standard it was projected that Celtic would have to spend £900 on alterations. Once it had a top-class cycling track the club would then become one of the choice venues for staging other money-making meetings. It was to be this non-footballing matter that would finally bring to boiling point an internal crisis at

During the early years of organised football, brake clubs, as supporters' clubs were then known, became enormously popular. Their members would follow their team in carriages known as brakes, and, like modern supporters' clubs, tended to favour one particular player. This, one of the first Celtic brake clubs, was, as its ornate banner shows, dedicated to Tom Maley.

Celtic that had been simmering throughout much of the 1890s.

The committee decided that they would use this issue to make a stand and stated that they would not authorise the spending of money on the cycling track unless the club became a limited company. At a meeting in St Mary's Hall on 4 March 1897 the membership agreed to pass that motion and finally put an end to a rift that had plagued the club throughout the 1890s when at each AGM the membership would be split between those who wished the club to become a limited liability company and those who wished to pay cash rather than lip service to the club's charitable origins, which already appeared to be part of a sentimental past. As donations to charities decreased – and in the case of the Poor Children's Dinner Table disappeared altogether – so payments to club officials and players had gradually increased.

In addition, the same year as those cycling Championships took place, 1897, the Celtic committee paid their landlord £10,000 to become owners of Parkhead. The ground had also become the regular venue for the biannual Scotland v England international, which Celtic staged five times between 1894 and 1904 – a prestigious appointment and a highly lucrative one. The club's progressive approach had seen it becoming more and more professional with each passing season – its establishment as a limited liability company was simply a matter of formalising the club's natural evolution and paving the way for further progress. Had Celtic decided to remain a purely charitable institution, it's likely they would have gone on to become an endearing eccentricity, in the manner of Queen's Park, whose supporters brought out books to read at half-time. Celtic might have become known as the club whose supporters brought out the collection plates at half-time.

Celtic enter a new era

With a glorious first decade behind it, and the club now appearing to have been placed on a sound footing, greater glories beckoned. Brother Walfrid's aim of providing cash for charity had gone west around the same time as he himself had taken up a new posting in England in 1892.

But the other aim of the club's founders, of establishing an institution that would give the Irish-Catholic community successes they could share in and that would repay them for their efforts in creating their club, had been entirely fulfilled. On a visit to England in the 1890s the club's reputation was such that it had been billed by the locals as 'The Greatest Team on Earth'. Taking into account the circumstances of the club's foundation and the rapid progress that had been made in its early years, this was no more than a fair description of Celtic. The club's reputation had been established. Now it had to live up to it.

The Celtic squad in 1894, after bringing home the League Championship for the second year in succession. Back row, from left: Curran, McArthur, Blessington, Cullen, T. Bonnar (trainer), T. Dunbar, Campbell, Jerry Reynolds, Mr P. Gallagher (linesman). Middle row: Cassidy, Madden, Kelly, Doyle, W. Maley. Front row: Divers, McMahon (captain), McEleny.

Willie Maley became Celtic's first manager in 1897. He focussed on young, local talent at the expense of established stars. That policy was to pay enormous dividends in succeeding years.

2 Maley's Maestros

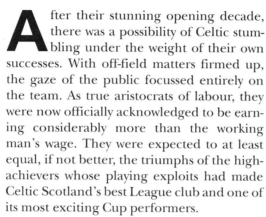

After their stunning opening decade, there was a possibility of Celtic stumbling under the weight of their own successes. With off-field matters firmed up, the gaze of the public focussed entirely on the team. As true aristocrats of labour, they were now officially acknowledged to be earning considerably more than the working man's wage. They were expected to at least equal, if not better, the triumphs of the high-achievers whose playing exploits had made Celtic Scotland's best League club and one of its most exciting Cup performers.

One thing in Celtic's favour was the style of play that was prevalent in the early decades of the game. Most clubs were more interested in winning through their own positive efforts than in stifling the opposition. Defensive duties were certainly attended to, revolving around a back two consisting of of two full-backs. A centre-half and two half-backs operated in what would now be recognised as the midfield, sometimes defending, sometimes providing service for the forwards. James Kelly was one centre-half who was as interested in contributing to the attacking side of the game as to its defensive aspect.

The typical team formation at the turn of the century featured five forwards: two wingers, an inside-right, an inside-left and a centre-forward. Celtic's traditional penchant for employing unpredictable wingers and inside men with minds of their own was already established. And the Irish aptitude for spontaneous invention, with which the club was imbued, gave Celtic an extra edge.

After claiming the title in 1896, however, certain players had become too carried away with themselves for the Celtic committee's liking. After press reports of Celtic's play as

being over-aggressive in the defeat by Rangers in the Glasgow Cup final of 21 November, full-back Peter Meechan, half-back Barney Battles and forward John Divers refused to take the field for the match with Hibs the following week. They wanted the representatives of the *Glasgow Evening News* and its sports paper *Scottish Referee* to be removed from the Parkhead press box. Willie Maley got stripped and played even though he had officially retired and, having drafted in a reserve, Celtic played with ten men until another reserve arrived at Parkhead in time for the second-half.

The whole team had felt aggrieved by the previous week's reports but the three who had taken direct action were dealt with severely, being immediately suspended and having their wages slashed. Meechan was moved on to Everton in January 1897 while Battles went to Dundee and Divers to Everton on the same day, 1 May 1897.

That same year, John McLaughlin took over as chairman from John Glass who had been in the position since 1890, when he had succeeded Celtic's first chairman Dr John Conway. On 3 April 1897, a month after the club had been established as a limited company, Willie Maley was appointed the first secretary/manager of Celtic, with an annual salary of £150. An accountant by profession and a stern man, in the mould of the Victorian paterfamilias, Maley's steady hand on the tiller would guide Celtic through some choppy waters in forthcoming decades.

In the meantime, the final days of the old century were seen out in a winning way while the new one was welcomed in with further celebrations. In February 1898, Barney Battles was a member of the Dundee team that

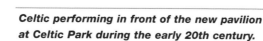

Celtic performing in front of the new pavilion at Celtic Park during the early 20th century.

did Celtic an enormous favour by beating Championship rivals Rangers in a League match at Ibrox, a result that went a long way towards Celtic, who were unbeaten throughout the League programme, winning their fourth title in Maley's first full season as secretary/manager. Sandy McMahon was still going strong and Johnny Campbell was enjoying his second spell with Celtic after Tom Maley had persuaded him to return home from Aston Villa for the beginning of the 1897-98 season.

Early Cup exits

In January 1897, Celtic had suffered one of the biggest upsets in Scottish football history when they were put out of the Scottish Cup in the first round at Arthurlie. The following year, by coincidence, the first round Cup draw took Celtic to Arthurlie again. This time Celtic won 7-0 but they went out in the next round to Third Lanark.

Celtic took the trophy for the second time with a 2-0 win over Rangers on 22 April 1899. Erstwhile rebels Battles and Divers had been welcomed back to Celtic in October 1898 and Divers was centre-forward in the Cup final. But it would be a goal apiece from Sandy McMahon and winger Johnny Hodge that settled the game in Celtic's favour.

The following season, Hodge scored the opening goal in a masterful display of attacking football from Celtic that propelled them to a 4-0 victory over Rangers in the Scottish Cup semi-final replay after a 2-2 draw. McMahon chipped in with two goals and winger Jack Bell got the other. In the final, 'Duke' McMahon, playing in lordly fashion, inspired Celtic to a 4-3 win over Queen's Park. McMahon scored his seventh goal of that year's competition in the final, with Divers getting two and Bell the other.

'To look at McMahon as he came out to play,' Willie Maley reminisced, 'one would have been pardoned for thinking he was an absolute misfit. His big, ungainly form, his

Celtic's Scottish Cup winners of 1899. Back row, left to right: Friel (trainer), Campbell, Hodge, McMahon, Divers, King, W. Maley (secretary/manager). Middle row: Bell, Marshall, Storrier, Welford, Battles. Front left is the goalkeeper, McArthur.

toothless upper jaw – Sandy wouldn't have an artificial set – his enormous feet. How could this fellow play? Then would come the great surprise. McMahon on the ball was a treat. Standing almost six feet, with back slightly bent and arms spread out like wings, away he would go weaving and swerving his way through the defence, and co-operating with Johnny Campbell with the precision of a machine. He was the best header of a ball ever I have seen... when a ball came across to Sandy he could almost hold it with his head. And he could direct the ball in any direction he pleased with the greatest of ease.'

The scoreline in the 1901 Scottish Cup final was the same but Celtic were on the wrong end of it, losing 4-3 to Hearts, after keeping four clean sheets on the way to the final. The run included a 1-0 win over Rangers. Scottish international goalkeeper Danny McArthur, who suffered severely throughout his 11-year career with Celtic from the type of heavy challenges from forwards that were then part of the game, was blamed for each of the goals. Hearts' late winner came after Celtic had clawed their way back into the game to make it 3-3.

In 1902, Celtic lost the Cup final 1-0 to Hibs, a game that was staged at Parkhead because the first Ibrox disaster had taken place shortly beforehand at a Scotland v England match and it would be the following year before the new Hampden Park would be opened. That year Rangers won their fourth League title in a row.

The 'Old Firm' of Celtic and Rangers were rapidly becoming established as the two dominant forces in Scottish football but some of the players who had done so much to help establish Celtic's reputation during the 1890s were coming to the end of their careers. Great club servants such as Danny McArthur, Sandy McMahon, who had been at Parkhead since 1890, and Johnny Campbell, who had given ten years of his footballing life to the club, had now passed the age of 30. An injection of new blood was needed to rejuvenate the body Celtic.

One young blood who would do much to boost and sustain the Celtic esprit de corps over the next decade-and-a-half was already on the premises. Jimmy Quinn was the mightiest of centre-forwards at a time when might was right. Born in the Catholic stronghold of Croy (sometimes known as 'the holy village of Croy') in 1878, Quinn was a battering ram

with brains, a man who possessed physical presence and skill in equal measures. He was a powerful header of the ball, with a strong pair of shoulders that came in handy for fighting off the industrial-strength challenges that were one of the dominant features of Scottish football, and he was also immensely talented when it came to keeping possession on the ground.

The mighty Quinn

Jimmy Quinn had provided Celtic with highly visible evidence of hope for the future just three months after joining the club. In the 1901 Cup final with Hearts, the 22-year-old, who played his first games on the left wing, went bobbing and weaving past no fewer than six Hearts players on the left before nimbly manoeuvring himself into position to crack home a shot for the first of his many Scottish Cup final goals.

Quinn's appearance in the Celtic team was no accident. Willie Maley had embarked on a policy of scouting for young talent in preference to buying proven stars from clubs in Scotland and England. Quinn had been picked up from the junior ranks.

On his way to watch Quinn for the first time, Maley bumped into Rangers manager Willie Wilton going to a game in Falkirk. Not wishing to let Wilton know about Quinn, the quick-thinking Maley told him he was going to the same game as the Rangers man. At half-time, and genuinely bored with the game, Maley made his excuses and left. Before the game, he had surreptitiously managed to arrange for an old contact from the Celtic Sports days, former cycling champion J. McLaren, to be waiting for him in a cab to whisk him off to the game at Stenhousemuir in which Quinn was playing.

Just as Maley arrived, though, Quinn was limping off the pitch. 'The lad limped to the Plough Inn, the place in which the players had their dressing-room. I followed. Quinn, I saw, was a young man of fine physique, strong on his legs, broad shouldered, deep-chested.'

It took a good deal of persuasion on Maley's part to convince Jimmy, who was naturally diffident, that he would be able to make the grade at senior level.

'I called on Quinn at his home in Croy,' he said. 'I did so because information had reached me that other senior clubs –

Sunderland and Manchester City – were after him. Father, mother, brother Peter and Jimmy himself received me. I joined them in a cup of tea. Then, fingering my registration form, I asked Quinn if he would not sign for Celtic? Quick and curt was his reply: "No, Mr Maley. I don't want to leave the juniors."

'I almost exhausted my persuasive powers. Always the same "No." I turned to his dad – "Jimmy maun please hissel'," was what I got. And brother Peter added: "You've said it, faither."

'Even then I did not altogether despair. I tackled Quinn again. His reiterated negation had begun to get on my nerves.

'"Look here Jimmy," said I. "I want to prove to my directors that I have done my duty. If you will give me your signature on this registration form it will be proof, and it will not necessarily bind you to play for Celtic." Quinn puzzled over this in silence for a minute, and then declared his willingness to sign, on condition that I did not lodge the form with the SFA without his consent.

'"That'll be all right," said I. You see, I wanted Quinn, and trusted to his speedy change of mind to rectify what at that moment was an absurd position. Then he took pen in hand and wrote his signature on the dotted line. I felt immensely relieved. On pocketing the form, I shook hands with all, paid Jimmy and Peter £2 each for "time lost", waved my farewells, and was off to Glasgow. Next morning I reported to my directors.

'In January 1901, Celtic went into special training at Rothesay. I invited Quinn to join us and have a good time. He accepted, and enjoyed himself thoroughly. Before we returned home I asked him to sign another form. He signed gladly. He got £20 for signing, and his pay contract was £3 10s per week. Without delay the form was lodged with the SFA, and the collier lad was ours.'

Maley's persistence, persuasion and, above all, instincts were to be proven correct. He had never, after all, seen Quinn play in a match at the time he signed him.

The new side was beginning to take shape and the new faces were soon wearing a new Celtic strip – in 1903 hoops replaced stripes on the club jersey. The stadium had also taken on a different guise when, in 1898, one of the directors, James Grant, had, with the club's blessing, built a stand on the opposite side of the park to the one that was already in existence. He had the agreement of the rest

The 1901 Exhibition Cup was originally put up as a one-off trophy, and was won by Rangers. It was removed from the Ibrox trophy room the following year and put up as the prize in a tournament that had been organised to benefit victims of the first Ibrox disaster. Celtic carried it off for good after victories over Sunderland and Rangers.

of the board to run the new creation as his own profit-making enterprise. It was a luxurious place from which to watch football – once its patrons had reached their seats, that is.

One of the many complaints about the new stand was that there were too many stairs to negotiate before reaching the spectating area. Another aspect of its luxury was windows that could be closed to keep out the rain. In the damp West of Scotland climate they were frequently in use but when closed the condensation that was created hindered the onlookers' attempts to follow the game.

Endless success

And those who turned up at Parkhead at that time would not have wished to miss a second of the action as Celtic pursued trophies with renewed life and vigour. In 1904 the Scottish Cup came back to Parkhead and from then until 1917 the Celts would go only one season without landing either the Cup or the Scottish League title.

Celtic had been invited to provide the opposition for Queen's Park in the official opening match at the new Hampden Park, on 31 October 1903. They lost that friendly 1-0 but they were back within six months for the Scottish Cup final with Rangers. Willie Maley had suffered some soul-searching in the previous couple of years when he had had his doubts over whether the policy of concentrating on signing young, untried players with Scottish clubs was going to bear fruit. But the particular batch of fresh home produce that helped win the Cup for Celtic in thrilling fashion that day would go on to harvest success after success for the club.

Of the forwards, Peter Somers and Jimmy McMenemy had signed from Hamilton Academicals and Rutherglen Glencairn respectively. Winger Davie Hamilton had arrived from Cambuslang Hibernian and Jimmy Quinn from Smithston Albion. Junior-international goalkeeper Davie Adams had been signed from Dunipace Juniors, centre half Willie Loney from Denny Athletic and full-back Donnie McLeod joined Celtic from Stenhousemuir. The side did benefit from the leadership of an experienced captain in the person of 30-year-old left-back Willie Orr, who had been signed in 1897 from Preston North End and had been a member of Celtic's 1898 title-winning side but this was essentially a young team, inexperienced in playing at a high level, and with the bulk of the players in their early twenties.

In the final, watched by a then Scottish Cup record crowd of 65,323, Jimmy Quinn was in typically exuberant form, his first-half double getting Celtic back on level terms after Rangers had taken a 2-0 lead in only 12 minutes. With seven minutes remaining of the match, Quinn scored the winning goal. It was the first hat-trick in a Scottish Cup final. It would remain unequalled until 1972 when another popular Celtic striker, Dixie Deans, got three in the 6-1 win over Hibs.

It had been a sweet success for Willie Maley. 'The enthusiasm of youth, and the never-say-die spirit to conquer, coupled with harmony in execution, sent Celtic rioting home to a wonderful victory,' was how he summed up the match. A week later, brother Tom was manager of Manchester City when they beat Bolton Wanderers 1-0 to win the FA Cup. City had also been runners-up to Sheffield Wednesday in that year's English League Championship.

Willie Maley had been vindicated in his policy of opting for youth. The team had cost Celtic a mere £200 to assemble. He enjoyed some assistance in team selection and certain aspects of coaching from two former players who had lined up alongside him in the first-ever Celtic team and who by 1904 were successful businessmen and had taken places on the Celtic board of directors: Mick Dunbar and James Kelly.

A controversial sending-off

The 1904-05 season saw the competition between Celtic and Rangers stiffen even further. A controversial Scottish Cup semi-final at Parkhead saw Celtic lose 2-0 to Rangers. Jimmy Quinn, who was on first-name terms with most referees, was ordered off eight minutes from the end for what the referee, Tom Robertson, saw as his kicking the Rangers player Alec Craig in the face.

Sections of the crowd invaded the pitch towards the end of the match. The referee managed to restart the game but was forced to abandon it after a second pitch invasion. It was the second occasion that season on which a game between Celtic and Rangers had been abandoned because of the crowd intruding on the pitch. Celtic conceded the tie.

Craig later stated that Quinn had not kicked him in the face, but the SFA stood by their man. Quinn had to serve a four-week suspension that could have been fatal to Celtic's title hopes in a season when the Glasgow rivals kept the race for the flag alive to the last kick of the ball. Both of them finished their League fixtures with 41 points. As was laid down in the rules of the time, when two clubs were tied on points the winners of the Championship would be decided by a play-off. Hampden Park hosted a 2-1 win for Celtic which began one of the greatest League-winning runs in world football.

The players who had won the Scottish Cup in 1904 formed the core of those title-winning sides. One star addition was Alec McNair, a versatile player who was signed from Stenhousemuir within weeks of that final. He was made the side's regular right-back early on in his Celtic career and in a 21-year stay at Parkhead he would make 604 appearances for the club, rarely falling below the high standards of play that he set himself. Perhaps one of the reasons for his playing longevity (he appeared in the 1923 Scottish Cup final at the age of 39) was that in his

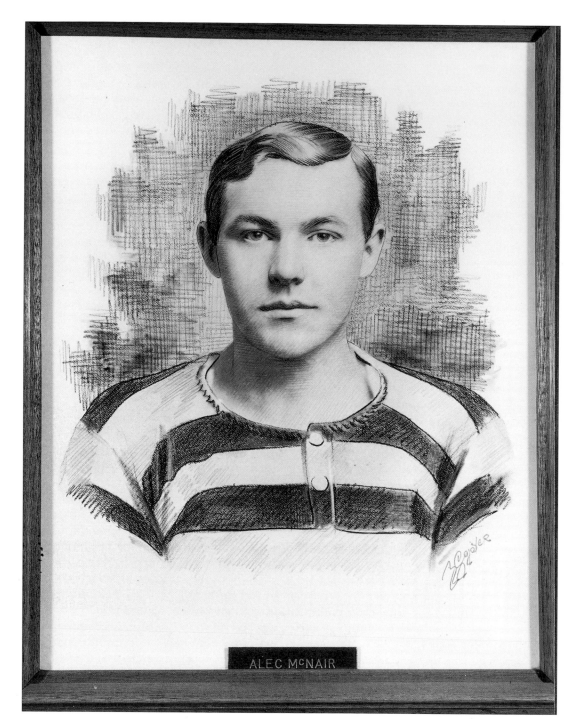

ALEC McNAIR

Alec McNair, who gathered 11 well-deserved Championship medals during a 21-year spell with the club. His cool, calculating play at right-back added a new dimension to defending in Scotland. He played on his wits, disarming opponents through anticipation and intelligence rather than muscle.

defensive duties he relied on brains rather than brawn to dispossess and disarm his opponents. 'The Icicle's coolness under pressure was an invaluable element in protecting the attacking advantages that his more inventive team-mates would create.

In 1904 the spanking new stand that had been built when Celtic had moved to the new ground in 1892 had been gutted in a fire. The club took the decision not to replace it with seated accommodation but to instead make that side of the arena a covered enclosure for standing spectators.

From then on, it gradually developed into the habitat of comedians manqué, barrack-room lawyers and street philosophers. Only the fittest of wits survived and thrived in the part of Parkhead that became known as 'the Jungle'. Shortly after the fire, Celtic bought the stand on the opposite side of the ground from James Grant for whom its drawbacks had proved a recipe for economic disaster.

JIMMY MCMENEMY

Jimmy McMenemy, like Alec McNair, was another long-serving Celt who favoured the cerebral approach to football. His son John would also go on to play for Celtic. Jimmy himself would return to Parkhead as a trainer after his playing days were over.

Celtic retained the title in the 1905-06 season and Scottish football was to see its first double-winning side in the following year. The Celts started the League season with six successive clean sheets, and that run was only ended by an Aberdeen goal in the final minute of the seventh game.

That season, Celtic brushed off the challenge of Dundee in the League, with the ease of a farmer snapping a scrawny chicken's neck. They then comprehensively defeated Hearts 3-0 in the Scottish Cup final in front of a crowd of 50,000 at Hampden.

Willie Orr's penalty had opened the scoring in that match. At the end of the previous season Orr had passed on the honour of being captain to Jimmy Hay. Hay, who alternated between left-half and left-back, was a typically skilful member of the side.

An honest man of Ayrshire, he was a fierce competitor who was instantaneously transformed into a creative artist once he had won possession of the ball. He remained as captain while Celtic landed the remainder of their six titles in succession. Hay's drive and ambition inspired his team-mates and was also noticed by the international selectors, who made him captain of Scotland.

The brains of the team

Inside-forward Peter Somers, who got two goals in the 1907 Scottish Cup final win over Hearts, was a footballing brainbox who produced answers to attacking queries at speed and who used his sharp brain to gee up team-mates and wind up opponents with a steady succession of smart one-liners.

Fellow inside-forward Jimmy McMenemy, who stayed with Celtic for 18 years after joining them in 1902, was a master-strategist nicknamed 'Napoleon'. His average scoring rate was close to a goal in every three games and was a healthy supplement to Jimmy Quinn's work in front of goal. Winger Davie Hamilton was another player who gave lengthy service to Celtic, in his case from 1902 to 1912. He tended to veer between providing the unexpected and the unwanted but his positive contributions included a considerable number of goals.

This glittering forward line was completed by Alec Bennett. He scored the only goal of the League match against Rangers at Ibrox in April 1908, when Celtic completed a back-to-back double of Scottish League and Cup. That season, they also collected the Glasgow Cup and the Charity Cup. It was the first time that any team had captured all four of those trophies in a single season. Bennett had also produced two goals a week earlier, in Celtic's 5-1 rout of St Mirren in the Scottish Cup final, with 55,000 in attendance. On a bright spring day, Quinn, Somers and Hamilton also got on the scoresheet.

Bennett was another who garnered a respectable hoard of goals for Celtic and the ability of all five Celtic forwards to send goal attempts raining in from every conceivable angle was a major factor in the club's flood of successes. It wasn't a side that launched itself thoughtlessly into attack, however. The goals came after clever, patient, probing play had eased open opposing defences. But within a few weeks of that 1908 double the team suffered its first major blow, when unpredictable winger Bennett signed for Rangers.

Dundee were Celtic's closest rivals for the 1909 Championship but the flag remained at Parkhead after a preposterous end to the season that saw Celtic forced to play their final four games in five days. They managed to take the title, although it went to the final game, played at Douglas Park on a Friday. Goals from Hamilton and McMenemy gave the Celts a 2-1 win over Hamilton Accies and 51 points to Dundee's 50.

Celtic had reached the Cup final again that year but their chances of obtaining a third double in a row were to be obliterated in the most notorious Scottish Cup final in history. Against Rangers at Hampden Park on 10 April, with a record-breaking 70,000 watching, the two teams fought each other to a standstill, the game ending in a 2-2 draw. Jimmy Quinn had scored the opening goal after half an hour and Celtic also owed their equaliser to him when Rangers' goalkeeper Rennie, in an attempt to get out of the way of a Quinn shoulder-charge, inadvertently carried the ball into his own goal.

The Hampden Riot

Many supporters went along to Hampden for the replay the following Saturday afternoon believing a newspaper rumour that there would be extra-time in the event of a drawn match. As in the first game, it was Jimmy Quinn who brought Celtic back on level terms and the match ended in a 1-1 draw. At the end of the 90 minutes, some players remained on the pitch as if awaiting extra-time but after a few minutes they headed for the changing rooms.

It eventually became clear to the 60,980 on the terraces that the teams were finished for the day. Some punters' actions then ensured that, regardless of what was written in the rule book, there would be no second replay. The more volatile elements in the crowd, angry in the belief that they had been done out of 30 extra minutes' play, invaded the pitch. The final result of the 1909 Cup final was to be the Hampden Riot.

Celtic and Rangers fans, in a scenario unimaginable in modern times, became united in their fury and took their revenge on symbols of authority rather than on each other. Payboxes, the antecedents of turn-

stiles, were burned, and a measure of the fans' upset was that whisky was reportedly used to stoke the fires. Other fires were lit inside the ground. When members of the fire brigade, around 100 of them in total, arrived, they were attacked and had their hoses sliced open. Officials and police were attacked with stones and bottles and were confronted by some fans brandishing iron railings as the violence went on and on. The dismembered goalposts were even used as weapons. It would be eight o'clock on the evening of the match before order was finally restored.

In the wake of the 1909 Cup final's funeral pyre, Celtic and Rangers officials jointly announced that, in the light of the events at Hampden, neither of the clubs wished to have a second replay. The SFA decided to withold the 1909 Scottish Cup and the two clubs were instructed to pay compensation of

£150 each to Queen's Park for the damage caused to their stadium.

It was an inglorious end to Celtic's quest for a glorious hat-trick of doubles and the SFA must have breathed a collective sigh of relief when it was Dundee and Clyde who reached the final (a match that did go to a second replay) the following year. Clyde had knocked Celtic out at the semi-final stage. Jimmy McMenemy was missing after having taken a bruising from the Welsh team in an international match at Kilmarnock shortly beforehand. Celtic were also without goalkeeper Adams through pneumonia and, in a friendly gesture, Welsh goalkeeper Leigh Roose offered his services on loan from Sunderland for the semi but he couldn't prevent Clyde winning 3-1.

James Kelly succeeded John McLaughlin as chairman in 1909 and Celtic claimed their

sixth League title in 1910, by a short head from Falkirk. The following year, the other Scottish League clubs presented Celtic with an ornate silver shield, featuring the names of all the players who had represented the club in League games from 1904 to 1910, to mark their run of six titles in a row.

While Celtic were not exactly a spent force, for the next three seasons it was Rangers who took the League flag. The players who had given Celtic new life were now seasoned professionals. Some left the club, although the mighty Quinn and Alec McNair were among those who remained. There was

plenty of spirit at the club but once again it needed rejuvenation, another change of blood. Just as Jimmy Quinn had burst on to the scene almost a decade before, so another youngster who was to become a Celtic legend now skipped on to Scottish football's stage.

Patsy Gallacher, Donegal-born and picked up from Clydebank Juniors, weighed under 9 stone and was 5ft 5in tall but he was a man of substance. In common with Jimmy Quinn, he made his debut in a victory over St Mirren although unlike Quinn he didn't score.

Gallacher was an individualist who personified the type of improvisational skills that set

Celtic in 1908. Back row, from left: Directors White, Kelly, Colgan, McKillop, Grant, Dunbar. Middle row: W. Maley, Young, Somers, McMenemy, Adams, Mitchell, Weir, R. Davis (trainer). Front row: Hamilton, McLeod, Loney, Hay, Quinn, McNair.

Celtic apart as a club where self-expression in a player is something that is not so much encouraged as expected. A one-man variety show, impossible for defenders to pin down, this wiry little man would duck and dive past his opponents, following the scenic route marked out on his own personal route-map to goal. Once he arrived at his destination he would be an unwelcome visitor because, despite his slight build, he could get in where it hurted and he did more than his fair share of hurting – 187 goals in 432 League games.

Sir Robert Kelly, the Celtic chairman from 1947 to 1971, noted in his study of the club: 'Anyone who treated Gallacher badly got his own medicine back. Nor did it matter what the size of the opponent was; the bigger they were the harder they fell to Gallacher.'

Patsy was naturally fit and once he was an established star in the Celtic team he was indulged by Willie Maley, who allowed him to adopt a take-it-or-leave-it attitude to training. Patsy would usually leave it. Maley saw training as a matter of exercise for those players who needed to keep their weight down. As this didn't apply to Gallacher, Maley was happy if Gallacher didn't move a muscle from one game to the next.

He was also, unlike Jimmy Quinn, not backwards about coming forward. Once Gallacher had seen that he could captivate the crowds, he got himself on the best of terms, financially, at Celtic Park. A team-mate once told Gallacher that he too was going to seek out a personal deal to get what he was worth. Gallacher's answer hit the mark as surely as one of his on-the-field strikes, telling the player in question that he'd be best not to bother unless he wanted to be going home with a lighter wage packet in future.

A similar sense of pragmatism saw Patsy turn Celtic down the first time they asked him to join the club. 'I got a request from Parkhead to come and play against a team of soldiers from the district,' he remembered. 'I answered the call, and the game which followed resulted in a five to nothing win for the Celts, three of the goals being scored by yours truly. The Celtic directors thought the matter over… and evidently came to the conclusion that though I was small I could score goals. That settled it, and I was asked to sign on and stop work right away.

'However, I had just completed about three out of a five years apprenticeship as a shipwright, so… there was nothing doing.'

It was agreed that Patsy would finish his apprenticeship before he signed for Celtic and what he described as 'a glorious experience' for 'the most remarkable football team that Scotland has ever had'. The 18-year-old inside-right arrived in the first team, at that time Scottish Cup holders, shortly before Christmas 1911. Celtic had captured the Cup with a 2-0 win over Hamilton in the replayed final after a 0-0 draw in the first game. Jimmy Quinn and centre half Tom McAteer, who had captained Clyde in the previous year's final, were the scorers. In April 1912, Celtic successfully defended the trophy, defeating Clyde 2-0 in the final with McMenemy and Gallacher scoring the goals that took the Cup to Parkhead for the eighth time.

Maley the master builder

Almost imperceptibly, Willie Maley had started rebuilding the team, filling in the cracks that had begun to appear in the first great side that he had created. Andy McAtee was another of the bright new pupils at Scottish football's most distinguished finishing school. Signed from Mossend Hibs in 1910 aged 22, the winger stood at only 5'7" but possessed a powerful pair of thighs that provided him with the type of acceleration that most motor vehicle owners of the day could only dream about. Those quadriceps also ensured that his shooting was of military precision and power.

After their first season for a decade without winning the Scottish League or Cup, 1912-13, Celtic made up for the loss with their third double the following year, the last before the outbreak of World War I in August 1914. It was another find, 21-year-old centre-forward Jimmy McColl, who had been spotted playing for St Anthony's juniors, whose double after just ten minutes of the replayed Scottish Cup final provided the impetus for the 4-1 victory over Hibs. The first game had ended in a 0-0 draw. Winger Johnny Browning got the other two.

Just as had been the case a decade previously, Maley's new side was youthful as well as useful, with guidance being provided by some old faces. Once again, the new faces were, in the main, drawn from the junior game. Browning was 22 when he signed for Celtic from Vale of Leven; left-back Joe Dodds was brought from Carluke Milton

Rovers at the age of 20; centre-half Peter Johnstone was 19 when he signed from Glencraig Celtic; left-half John McMaster was Celtic's second signing from Clydebank Juniors in successive years, following Patsy Gallacher, and was barely 20 when he made it to the big time.

Expert tuition for Celtic's youngsters

In their early days at Celtic these youngsters must have benefited immeasurably from being helped along by the familar figure of Jimmy Quinn, while Jimmy McMenemy and Alec McNair would see the job through to the end, cultivating Maley's hand-picked crop of prospects through the remainder of the decade. Right-half 'Sunny Jim' Young, the tireless 32-year-old captain of that 1914 team, was another who had joined the club as a youngster over a decade previously and who was now enjoying further heady success, this time in a senior role.

McColl had the role of apprentice along-side the master craftsman Jimmy Quinn at Parkhead during the 1913-14 season even though Quinn, by then weakened by the knocks he had taken down the years, only managed a handful of games. McColl then took over from the great man and was centre-forward as the Celts made it four titles in a row by winning the flag during seasons 1914-15, 1915-16 and 1916-17.

In common with Gallacher, McColl was slim and wiry but he was big enough to get 123 goals in 169 appearances for Celtic. 'The Sniper' could hit the target from the unlikeliest of positions.

Goalkeeper Charlie Shaw was a rarity for the Celtic fans in those years, a purchase from an English club. Born in Twechar, Dunbartonshire, Shaw had been in London for six years when Willie Maley signed him from Queen's Park Rangers in 1913 for £100. He was 27 years old when Celtic brought him out of exile. An inspirational figure, he became captain of the side in 1916 and would remain with Celtic until he was three months off his 40th birthday.

On 30 January 1915, Jimmy Quinn, by then 36 years old and having been dogged by serious knee trouble for several years, played his final game for Celtic. A powerful reflection of the affection in which the player was held by the Celtic support is that when he was suspended after being sent off against Rangers one Ne'erday several years earlier, Celtic supporters far and wide had collected a total of £277 to show their support for the centre-forward, who had been handed down a lengthy suspension. This was at a time when the average Scottish First Division player was earning approximately £3 a week. Jimmy Quinn scored his final goal for Celtic on 26 December 1914.

Jimmy Quinn (left) led the Celtic line with gusto during the early part of the new century. His unflinching pursuit of goals in the face of desperate attempts to stop him made him a clearly identifiable object of the Celtic supporters' affections.

Opposite: The team that triumphed in the 1914 Scottish Cup final with a 4-1 replay win over Hibs. Back row: W. Maley (secretary/manager), McMaster, Dodds, Shaw, McNair, Johnstone, McColl, Quinn (trainer). Front row: McAtee, Gallacher, Young (captain), McMenemy, Browning.

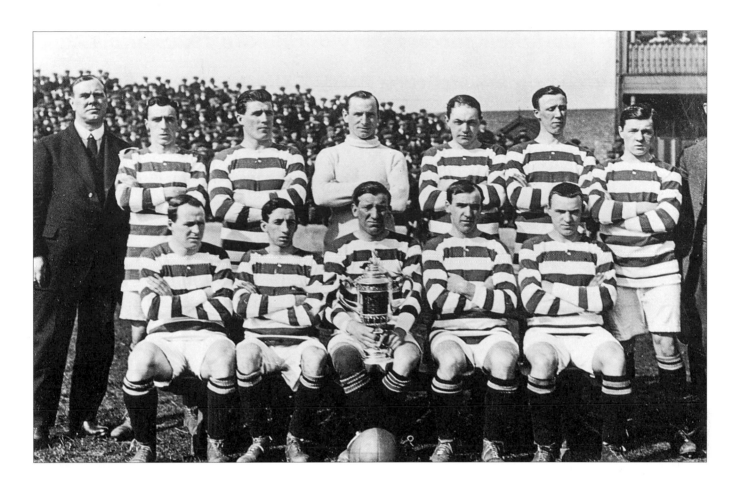

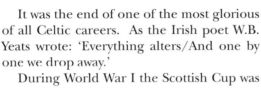

It was the end of one of the most glorious of all Celtic careers. As the Irish poet W.B. Yeats wrote: 'Everything alters/And one by one we drop away.'

During World War I the Scottish Cup was abandoned and players' wages were reduced to a maximum of £2 a week. However, League competition would be continued, although footballers had to help with war work and matches could only be played on Saturdays and public holidays. Football was judged to be good for morale: news of the game gave the poor souls stuck in the trenches a glimmer of relief from the horrors of war, while the large assemblies that were found at football grounds provided the perfect opportunity for the army to stage recruitment drives in front of a captive audience. Several players who had worn Celtic's colours volunteered for action. Some of them did not come back.

A new chairman, Tom White, had been appointed in 1914. Just as the war was not over by Christmas, as some commentators had earlier predicted, neither was the Scottish League Championship. Hearts maintained pressure on Celtic through-out the season but by the end Celtic were four points ahead of them. The following year Celtic finished 11 points clear of nearest rivals Rangers and they were ten points ahead of second-placed Morton as the 1916-17 season came to a close.

A marathon effort

The final home game of that season, on 21 April 1917, had seen Kilmarnock beat Celtic 2-0 – Celtic's first defeat in the League since 13 November 1915. They had set a Scottish League record of 62 matches unbeaten and it would be a further six months before they would lose an away match in the League.

When hostilities ended in Europe that November, Celtic were no longer Scottish League champions. They had narrowly failed to make it five in a row, losing their title to Rangers by a single point. As Europe settled to an uneasy peace, Glasgow was about to witness the resumption of an ideological struggle that, in terms of passion, intensity and bitterness, could rival any continental dispute over crowns or territories.

Celtic continued their success story during the 1920s and 1930s. Players such as Jimmy McGrory, Patsy Gallacher and John Thomson became established as Celtic immortals.

3 Triumphs and Tragedies

In the first year after World War I, business appeared to have resumed as usual for Celtic. Several important players had been posted missing during 1918, after conscription had been introduced. Rangers, strangely, weren't affected as badly as Celtic in this respect. Celtic's 1918-19 League title was captured, albeit by just one point from Rangers, by a team packed with old favourites from the side that had won four titles in succession during the war and who had volunteered for postwar action with the Celts.

A 2-0 win at Ayr in May 1919 wrapped things up. Andy McAtee opened the scoring in the first half and in the second provided the cross from which Adam McLean made it 2-0 and Celtic's Championship. A light-hearted moment saw a Celtic fan run on to the park to try to plant his flag beside Charlie Shaw's goal but he was thwarted by local officials. One Celtic brake club didn't turn up until after half-time but it didn't seem to matter much to the members – celebrations were the order of the day.

The next time Celtic tied up the title, however, there was little singing or dancing on the streets of Greenock, where they finished the task. After two years of Rangers taking the flag, Celtic faced a tough fixture against Cup-holders Morton on the final day of the 1921-22 season. Before the game, played in front of 23,000, Celtic were a point ahead of Rangers, who travelled to Shawfield to play Clyde on the same afternoon.

Alec McNair and Charlie Shaw were outstanding that day and 34-year-old left-back Joe Dodds had what was probably his finest game in a Celtic shirt, winning everything he went for in his usual enthusiastic fashion. Despite that, by half-time Celtic were on the

ropes and a touch fortunate to be only 1-0 down. The players were also fortunate to be inside the dressing room rather than outside. Some of the Morton fans, who had had weapons passed over the perimeter wall to them, began charging the Celtic contingent.

When the players did re-emerge they helped the police by persuading the crowd to stay on the terraces. Even the referee, Peter Craigmyle, chased one intruder off the pitch. About a dozen injuries were treated in the pavilion. Most of the lovingly-crafted banners that belonged to the Celtic brake clubs had been captured by their adversaries. Some banners were also taken away by the police.

The title seemed to be slipping away from Celtic, whose concentration on getting an equaliser couldn't have been helped by the scenes around them. But with just six minutes remaining, John 'Jean' McFarlane's cross was palmed away by Morton goalkeeper Edwards. As the Morton defenders struggled to clear the loose ball, Andy McAtee got the nod to equalise. His header looped beautifully over the helpless Edwards.

It was a dramatic ending to what had been, in purely footballing terms, a great match. Rangers had drawn 0-0 at Clyde and the title flag could once again be embroidered green.

Green with envy, however, the Greenock contingent couldn't let the Celtic fans leave without a big send-off. At the end of the game, they were rushed again and more of their banners were captured and burnt in a bonfire in the street. All along the route from the ground to Cartsdyke station the trouble continued. Bottles and stones were thrown and shop windows smashed. Outside the station, one huge final battle took place with the Celtic fans standing targets.

Jimmy McGrory (third left), the greatest goalscorer in Celtic's history, leads his teammates in training at Celtic Park.

Anti-Catholic feelings

The part of Greenock where much of the fighting outside the ground had taken place was populated largely by Protestants. Those scenes were of a type that was becoming more and more common as people of Irish-Catholic origin in Scotland found attitudes hardening against them.

Shortly before the war, the Belfast shipbuilding company Harland & Wolff had established a yard on Clydeside and Protestants from the North of Ireland had been brought over to Scotland to work in it. At that time the whole island of Ireland was part of the British Empire, but on 1 May 1916 a man walked into the main post office in Dublin, waited quietly in the queue for stamps, then drew a gun on the counter-clerk and declared that Ireland was now a republic.

So began a bitter and bloody five-year struggle between Irish Republicans and the British army that at one stage led to martial law in Ireland and which ended in the formation of the Irish Free State on 6 December 1921. Twenty six counties in the generally Catholic South became independent while six counties in the largely Protestant North remained part of the United Kingdom.

Those Northern Irish Protestants who were in Glasgow felt this attack on British authority more keenly than their fellow Protestant Scots. But in the years after World War I, years of fear and insecurity when not just Scotland but the whole of Europe was in a deeply unsettled state, it didn't take much to persuade Scottish Protestants of the menace of the Catholic presence. Celtic was the biggest and most clearly identifiable target for sectarian hatred.

Unlike Celtic, Rangers, in their earliest years of existence, had never been anything other than a footballing institution. Initially, they had lagged behind Queen's Park but with the arrival of regular League competition and professionalism they soon became the only West of Scotland club with the means to challenge Celtic on a regular basis.

Celtic's strong Irish-Catholic identity understandably made it difficult for most non-Catholic Scots to identify with them – even though Celtic's doors were always open to Protestant players – and so those wishing to follow a successful team turned to Rangers. Significantly, however, it wasn't until the 1920s, that decade of political tur-

moil, that Rangers' unwritten policy of refusing to have Catholics on their staff became established.

During the 1920s the Scottish League Championship flag did not leave Glasgow. In 1919-20 the fight for the title again went to the last week of the season but in their third-last League match Celtic couldn't keep the pressure on Rangers, failing to beat a Dundee team that at one stage had only nine men on the field due to injuries.

That season had seen a new addition to the side in centre-forward Tommy McInally, who scored a hat-trick on his debut, against Clydebank on the first day of the season, and who followed that up with another in the next game, against Dumbarton, as Celtic began the League campaign with nine straight wins. At his best McInally was rated as being as effective as Jimmy Quinn but he was a maverick, a player who only gave his best when the mood took him. Willie Maley did his best to chivvy him along but by 1922 his patience had run out and McInally was transferred to Third Lanark.

Celtic beat Rangers in the Ne'erday match of 1921 at Ibrox thanks to a Joe Cassidy double, but ended up ten points behind them when all the fixtures had been completed. Willie Maley was involved in making arrangements for the 1921 Cup final but only as its host – Parkhead was the venue for Partick Thistle's 1-0 win over Rangers.

After winning the Championship in dramatic style in 1921-22, Celtic fell away badly in the next season's League competition. They were eighth at Christmas and although their form improved in the new year they still ended up well off the pace.

Patsy Gallacher had been injured midway through the season and the Celts missed him badly. While he was absent, an 18-year-old filled his inside-right jersey for the match against Third Lanark on 20 January 1923. The debutant was Jimmy McGrory, and few who watched him struggle to keep up with the flow of the game in that 1-0 defeat could have guessed the impact he would make on 20th century football.

He played just three games that season although he scored in one of them, the 4-3 defeat by Kilmarnock. The following season he was farmed out to Clydebank before beginning 1924-25 as Celtic's centre-forward. And that was where he would stay for the next

Scottish champions Celtic prepare to face Sparta Prague on tour in 1922. The players in the front row are (from left to right): McFarlane, Cringan, Gallacher, Cassidy, McAtee. Behind them are (clockwise from top left): McMaster, McNair, Gilchrist, Willie McStay, McLean and goal- keeper Shaw. Willie Maley is behind Cringan and Gallacher.

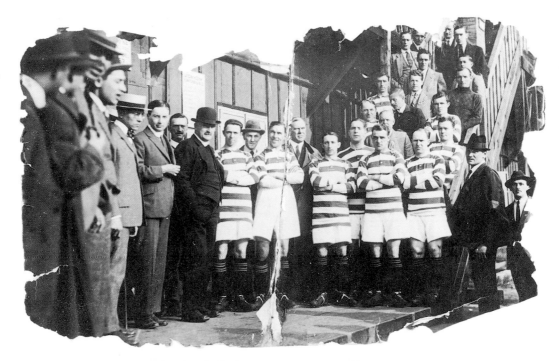

The Celtic party enjoying continental travel during their 1922 visit to Europe. In Germany they played a game in Berlin that ended in a 1-1 draw. The three matches in which Celtic participated on that year's trip drew an average crowd of 30,000.

A relaxed Celtic group picture from the 1922 tour. The two matches in Prague, though, against Slavia and Sparta, were tough, tense occasions. Willie McStay and Johnny Gilchrist were sent off against Sparta.

13 years, in a club career that eclipses those of all other British goalscorers: his 550 goals in first-class football remains a British record. Of those, 472 hit the nets of Celtic's opponents in the League and the Scottish Cup and the most notable aspect of that – the one that makes him unique – is that he got them playing fewer games than the number of goals he scored – 445 appearances in total.

McGrory's glory

By the end of his career with Celtic Jimmy McGrory's record included five goals in matches against Aberdeen, Dundee United and Clyde in season 1926-27, eight goals in one game against Dunfermline Athletic in 1928 and seven hat-tricks in League games in 1935-36, including three goals in three minutes against Motherwell. He was only capped seven times by Scotland but he scored in six of those games. Hughie Gallacher of Airdrie, Newcastle and Chelsea was usually preferred to him at international level but it seems strange that both of those outstanding talents couldn't be accommodated in the same side by the Scotland selectors.

Jimmy McGrory was a wonderful centre-forward: powerful and accurate with his head, mobile, capable of distracting defenders to create goal chances for his team-mates, aware of everything that was going on around him and interested in only one goal, the next one. He also possessed the ideal physique for a striker, with the type of upper-body strength that looked as though he would be able to compete in a tug of war as a one-man team, and a mental attitude that placed the cause of Celtic above all else.

But at the time of McGrory's debut Celtic were ailing and looking as though the team might even benefit from trying one of the quack cures that were hugely popular during that era. Instead, they turned to a traditional remedy. The Scottish Cup, which had been suspended during the war years, had been resumed in 1920 but it took Celtic until 1923 to make a Cup comeback.

The first round was hurdled with a 3-2 win over Second Division Lochgelly United with all three goals scored by the quick-thinking centre-forward Joe Cassidy. He also scored all four as the Celts defeated Hurlford of the Western League in the following round. Another favourable draw for the next round

saw Celtic at home to East Fife and again Cassidy did the honours by scoring both goals in the 2-1 win.

For the quarter-final with Raith Rovers, a 30,000 crowd at Parkhead saw Patsy Gallacher's tricky run and cross set up the only goal of the game, Adam McLean scrambling the ball over the line 19 minutes from the end. Cassidy had failed to hit the target in that match but he made up for it in the semi-final with Motherwell at Ibrox. The 71,506 who attended – 18,347 of them entering at the unemployed gate – saw him open the scoring in the first minute when Motherwell captain Craig Brown stumbled trying to cut out a through ball from Celtic centre-half Willie Cringan and gave Cassidy a clear sight of goal. Midway through the second half Patsy Gallacher was fouled and Andy McAtee's free-kick was deflected into the Motherwell net to make it 2-0.

Celtic's tenth Scottish Cup

On 31 March, in front of 80,100 at Hampden, Celtic defeated Hibs 1-0 in the 1923 Scottish Cup final, with none other than Cassidy getting the only goal of the game with a 64th minute header. Hibs felt unfairly done by: they had had claims for a penalty turned down. But Willie Cringan, who held Celtic together in both the semi and the final, said afterwards: 'I think everyone will admit we were the better team. I honestly don't think there was any justification for even a claim for a penalty. The ball bumped up suddenly and hit me on the arm. If I helped in any way to win the Cup, the credit is not mine. It goes to our assistant trainer Eddie (McGarvie) for the great skill and trouble he exercised in getting my leg fit.'

Charlie Shaw and Alec McNair were still part of the Celtic side in that final even though they were fast approaching their 40th birthdays. Both would leave the club in 1925, McNair to manage Dundee, the adventurous Shaw to try his luck in the USA, where there appeared to be a growing interest in soccer. Left-back Willie McStay also went Stateside that summer looking for better conditions than were available at Celtic but he was back in time for the following season when he would become captain. His younger brother Jimmy was at right-half in the Hibs Cup final but Willie Cringan was transferred after a wages dispute early in the 1923-24 season and Jimmy took over from him at centre-half. He proved just as dependable as his predecessor. Both McStays would give Celtic tidy, steady service at the back for the rest of the decade.

Left-half John 'Jean' McFarlane had joined the club in November 1919 and could be relied on to enliven most Saturday afternoons. He was a delightful player to watch, always inventive, and his perceptive passing could rip apart opposing defences as quickly and joyously as a child opening presents on Christmas morning.

The combination of Andy McAtee and Patsy Gallacher on the right was potent as ever and Cassidy at centre-forward had worked well with them. Adam McLean was one of Celtic's greatest left-wingers although he played at inside-left in the Cup final with Hibs to allow Paddy Connolly to play on the left wing and it was Connolly's cross that set Cassidy up for his header.

Both McLean and Connolly had been snapped up in time-honoured fashion by Maley from junior football but both would also finish playing their days with the club on less than friendly terms, because of wage disputes. Maley the stern Victorian, backed by a thrifty board, took a dim view of players who asked for more money. During the autumnal years of Maley's spell in charge of the club, this tale would be told over and over again.

A frustrating season

The 1923-24 season was almost instantly forgettable. After six games Celtic had just six points and were in the lower half of the table. Typical of their erratic form was the sixth match of the season, at Ayr, where McAtee and Gallacher put them 2-0 up after only eight minutes. Yet the match ended in a 4-2 win for Ayr. Celtic possessed some huge talents but opposing sides were becoming better organised and more resilient, particularly in the half-back line.

The defence of the Scottish Cup ended in the first round thanks to a defeat from Kilmarnock, memorable only for the unusual sight of Patsy Gallacher at centre-half after Willie McStay had left the field injured. Both Shaw and McNair looked shaky that day and both were phased out early in the following season, with Shaw replaced by Peter Shevlin, a £120 purchase from St Roch's Juniors.

Cassidy had been a regular scorer for Celtic but in August 1924 he was sold to Bolton Wanderers. Jimmy McGrory became the focus of the team's efforts and early in the season Celtic were briefly top of the League. But an unlucky 1-0 defeat at home to Rangers in October and a knee injury that sidelined McGrory for two months saw Celtic out of contention in the League by the turn of the year. Gallacher was still in top form but on the eve of that defeat from Rangers he admitted: 'I'm beginning to think if we don't buck up Rangers will soon have as many badges as the old Celtic team had.'

A successful ex-Celt

During this period Airdrie, managed by former Celt Willie Orr, finished runners-up in the First Division four times and won the Scottish Cup. Hughie Gallacher was the Airdrie star and he, like Alec James of Raith Rovers and later of Arsenal, testified to having learnt much through watching Patsy Gallacher from the Parkhead terraces when they were youngsters. Orr's talents might have freshened things up at Parkhead if he had been added to the backroom staff there but in the summer of 1926 he moved south to become manager of Leicester City.

In the first round of the Cup in January 1925, Gallacher was in brilliant form, inspiring Celtic to a 5-1 win over Third Lanark. Patsy got one himself and McGrory the other four, his first goals after being almost three months absent through injury. The final goal saw Gallacher and McGrory weaving through the Thirds defence together like two kids in a cornfield before Gallacher set McGrory up for a shot that smacked off the stanchion and came speeding back out.

Two moments of inspiration from Patsy gave McGrory two more goals in the next round for a 2-1 win over Alloa. Celtic's next opponents were Solway Star. Inside-forward Alec Thomson, with a header, and McGrory, with a low drive, put Celtic through. In the quarter-final St Mirren were finally beaten by a McGrory goal after two replays. With the seconds ticking away in the second game, a St Mirren player was tripped inside the penalty area. Aberdonian referee Peter Craigmyle, a law unto himself, awarded a free-kick just outside the box. The St Mirren players, instead of taking the kick, continued protesting and

glaring at Craigmyle who, instead of arguing back, simply blew for time-up without the kick having been taken.

In the midst of that Cup run Celtic had beaten Dundee 4-0 in their finest performance of the season up to that point but this was to be eclipsed in the semi-final. Patsy Gallacher had expressed a desire earlier in the season to meet Rangers in the Scottish Cup. His wish was granted although it looked like a death wish as far as Celtic's Scottish Cup ambitions were concerned. Rangers were pushing on towards their third successive title and they had beaten the Celts comprehensively in the Ne'erday meeting at Ibrox. Celtic's League form was mediocre and they had just squeezed through against St Mirren the Monday before the semi-final.

There were 101,700 at Hampden Park for the semi and the running track was crammed with fans who had spilled over from the terraces. Many spectators didn't get in until after half-time. It was a typically scruffy Cuptie during the first half hour. Then Celtic's elegant, intelligent right-half Peter Wilson found Connolly on the right wing and McGrory met his cross for the opening goal. As Celtic increased the pressure before

half-time, Rangers' Dixon almost sliced the ball past his goalkeeper Robb.

With 62 minutes gone, a Connolly corner found McLean's head for the second and five minutes later Connolly again bamboozled the Rangers defence as he took a pass from McGrory and returned the compliment for the centre-forward, playing his best game for the club up until that point, to make it 3-0. An Alec Thomson header made it four and with just a few minutes remaining McLean capitalised on a mistake by Robb to bury a low drive past the despairing goalkeeper.

The tormentors of Rangers

Gallacher, Thomson, McGrory, Connolly and McLean had shown Rangers and their supporters that creativity could still win the day. Equally importantly, Jimmy McStay had been outstanding at centre-half, ensuring throughout that Celtic suffered no breach of security at the back.

The final, on 11 April, paired Celtic with Dundee and after their 4-0 League triumph over the Dens Park side a few weeks earlier and their stunning victory over Rangers, it

Celtic Park, featuring the new stand that was built in 1929. It replaced the James Grant stand, which had been demolished earlier that year. In 1971, when another new stand was put in place the imposing facade was retained.

was Celtic who went into the match as favourites. Again the tables appeared to have been turned when Dundee took a 1-0 lead after half an hour. In the second half, some desperate defending from the Taysiders kept Celtic at bay but just as deflation was beginning to spread among the green-and-white masses on the terraces, Patsy Gallacher, as so often before, produced a moment of pure elation, a gem that was hallmarked Celtic.

Taking possession of the ball just inside the Dundee half, he rolled past challenge after challenge, sometimes appearing in danger of toppling over as he swerved and swayed dangerously close to the ground. No Dundee boot or body could stop him completely as he veered, surefooted as a young deer, towards their goalmouth. Finally, a heavy, desperate Dundee tackle grounded him inside the six-yard box. Patsy hit the turf and for an instant his brave effort seemed at an end. But Patsy had not yet parted company with the ball, which remained between his feet. A quick somersault and both Patsy and the ball ended up entangled in the Dundee net for the most unorthodox goal in a Scottish Cup final.

In his book *Celtic*, Sir Robert Kelly commented: 'The Dundee players an hour after the match were still hardly able to credit that this goal had been scored. There had been something magical, out of this world, about it, they said. It was the greatest feat of skill and determination they had ever seen on a football field.'

With a few minutes remaining, Jimmy McGrory got the winning goal with a diving header from McFarlane's free kick. Along with Patsy Gallacher, both of the McStays, McFarlane, Wilson and the left-back Hugh Hilley were outstanding in a match that emphasised Celtic's special relationship with the Cup. It was their 11th victory in the tournament and that made them record-holders, with one more win than Queen's Park.

In the close season, Gallacher travelled to the USA where, with Charlie Shaw in goal, he played for New York's Hibernians against Brooklyn Wanderers in a game billed as: 'The only authorised appearance in Greater New York of the World's Greatest Soccer Player, Patsy Gallacher'.

That close season, the offside rule was changed. For a forward to be onside, only two defenders now had to be between him and the goal instead of the previous three. It was a rule change that looked likely to suit attacking teams such as Celtic. Willie McStay, although a defender, embodied the Celtic philosophy, and said: 'I think the back who stoops to play rotten offside tactics is only killing the game. I won't say it is want of ability to beat his man that makes him do this. To me it seems rather like a man slinking out of the back door in preference to meeting his opponent. If all backs were to adopt the same tactics that they do in England, it would kill football entirely. Spectators would get sick of it, and when all is said and done you must please the spectators.'

The return of McInally

Another boost to Celtic for season 1925-26 was the return of a supposedly more mature Tommy McInally to assist McGrory from inside-left. That season, he fulfilled his full potential, using all his cleverness to conduct the Celtic forward-line in sweet, flowing symphonies. Celtic started in the manner to which their fans would become accustomed, with McInally and McLean immediately hitting it off on the left and McGrory getting a hat-trick in the opening day 5-0 win over Hibs in front of 20,000 at Celtic Park.

Gallacher was suspended for the first fortnight following indiscretions the previous season. He was also troubled by a knee injury and would make only one appearance in League and Cup during 1925-26. Celtic lost 5-1 at Airdrie in October and there was a further setback when they lost the first Old Firm clash a fortnight later. But by the time their meeting with St Mirren came around in early December it was a clash of the top two.

In front of 27,030 at Love Street the pace was unrelenting. Jimmy McGrory battled all afternoon in a direct head-to-head with Saints goalkeeper Jock Bradford. In one incident he slammed into Bradford with such force that he knocked his cap into the net. The reaction of many in the crowd showed that they thought it was the ball.

In the second half Adam McLean's corner was driven home through a crowd of players by Alec Thomson for the opener. After that, Celtic really took control with McInally spreading things out from midfield and proving a persistent irritant to the St Mirren defence with his long-range shooting.

The second goal came when Connolly, back on the field after receiving treatment for an injury, crossed for McGrory to head past his doughty opponent between the Buddies' posts. The goal was a fitting testimony to McGrory's perseverance, skill and energy that afternoon. The two McStays and Hilley were resolute in defence.

The title returns to Celtic

That win meant Celtic nudged ahead of St Mirren on goal average. The following week the Celts signalled that they were serious in their intentions towards the title with a superb 3-2 win over Airdrie after being 1-0 down in front of 22,000 at Celtic Park. Willie Orr's side ended up as Celtic's closest challengers for the title but they were still eight points behind in the final League table.

In the Cup, Celtic's run to the semi-final saw them score 19 goals in their four ties against Kilmarnock, Hamilton Accies, Hearts and Dumbarton with just one conceded. At Tynecastle in the semi with Aberdeen, 24,000 paid £915 and saw two goals that summed up Celtic's season. For the first, McInally cheekily flicked the ball over his shoulder before calmly placing the ball in the net. The second was a classic McGrory header.

In the final against St Mirren on 10 April, in front of 98,620 at Hampden, Celtic had most of the possession but lacked their usual verve and Peter Shevlin was at fault for both St Mirren goals as Celtic went down 2-0. It was an unfortunate ending to what had been, overall, an exciting and enjoyable season.

The summer of 1926 brought the departure of Patsy Gallacher at the age of 33. Appropriately, it was an episode full of twists and turns. In the club's yearbook, *The Celtic Football Guide*, published in the 1926 close-season, Willie Maley stated that Patsy Gallacher had retired. Gallacher, however, insisted publicly that he was fit as a fiddle and on 18 August, following a benefit match for Jimmy Quinn, he met the Celtic directors in Maley's Bank restaurant to discuss signing with the club for another season. They were unconvinced of his fitness and offered him only the minimum wage. When he refused to accept, he was made available for transfer and Falkirk were quick to snap him up for £1500. Patsy proved how much he had left in his legs by starring there for a further six years.

On 23 October Jimmy McGrory looked to be heading for the record books – his head produced four of Celtic's six goals against Aberdeen, his boot a fifth. The record individual score in a Scottish First Division match was six and Jimmy looked to have equalled this with a header in the closing minutes but he was given offside.

On Boxing Day 1926 Celtic were a point behind leaders Motherwell with two games in hand. But on Ne'erday the champions lost 2-1 at Ibrox. That result brought Rangers level with them and by the end of the season the Celts were seven points behind their Old Firm rivals, who took the title.

In Peter Wilson and 'Jean' McFarlane Celtic possessed two highly creative halfbacks but they were often overcome by the more brutal forces who roamed the middle of Scotland's football fields. One bright spot that season was Jimmy McGrory creating a new individual First Division scoring record with a total of 47 goals.

In the 1927 Scottish Cup, Celtic ran up a tally of 19 goals in beating Queen of the South, Brechin City, Dundee and Bo'ness to reach the semi-final, where Falkirk and Patsy Gallacher awaited them. In front of 73,000 at Ibrox, a Connolly cross found McLean in front of an open goal and the winger knocked home the only goal of the game. The match at Dundee, which Celtic had won 4-2 in front of 37,447, had been Celtic's best of the season. They showed on that occasion that they still had the most inventive forward line in the country.

A shocking start to the final

There was an early surprise for the 80,070 at the final when Second Division East Fife took a seventh minute lead. A minute later Celtic equalised when Connolly's cross took a deflection off East Fife's Robertson. Ten minutes from half-time McLean whipped the ball past East Fife goalkeeper Gilfillan to put Celtic ahead. One minute after the break Connolly completed the scoring when he drew Gilfillan from his goal before carefully placing the ball past him.

The following year McInally was the one Celtic forward who was a success in the Scottish Cup final debacle when they lost 4-0 to Rangers, a result that put the seal on a troubled campaign. McInally had been

Patsy Gallacher (left), one of the greatest entertainers ever to grace Celtic Park, up to his usual tricks in a match with Hearts. A master of the unconventional, Patsy had a multitude of means by which he would wrongfoot opponents.

suspended by the club midway through the season 'for a breach of training rules'. He kept fit on his own by pounding the roads around Barrhead and Paisley.

With what looked like almost calculated perversity, that Rangers game was one of his few useful performances that season. In May 1928 he was transferred to Sunderland, and a few months later was followed to the same club by Adam McLean.

Although there were frequent rumours afterwards that one of Maley's favourite prodigal sons would be returning to his spiritual home, the dapper McInally had woven the last of his sophisticated patterns in a Celtic jersey. Even more sadly, for those Celtic supporters who appreciated that talent has to be accompanied by application, was the loss of the influential McLean – even though the player's financial argument with the club could have been easily resolved.

Jimmy McGrory had set a world record for the number of goals by an individual in a single game on 14 January 1928 when he stuck away eight of Celtic's nine in the win over bottom club Dunfermline. Three of them came in the first nine minutes of the match and it was Alec Thomson who interrupted him to get the fifth. Two fans ran on to the park to congratulate the centre-forward. One shook McGrory by the hand, the other was intercepted by the referee.

Yet while passing through London on the way to Lourdes in the summer of 1928, Willie Maley, on the advice of the Celtic directors, took McGrory to meet Arsenal manager Herbert Chapman with a view to selling the player to the Highbury club. McGrory, who wished to play for Celtic and no-one else, made it clear he had no interest in a move.

On the way back Chapman met the Celtic pair once again. McGrory, as a ploy to put the Gunners' boss off for once and for all, plucked a ridiculously high signing-on fee out of the air, and any possibility of a deal was immediately off. Unknown to him, though, he would be secretly punished by the Celtic board, being paid, for the rest of his career, less than the other players. It was a shoddy way to treat one of the club's finest servants but it was indicative of the philosophy that appeared to hold sway at Celtic, of rearing players then selling them off like prize cattle, regardless of the individual's wishes. The support was growing restless in the face of these dealings and of persistent rumours of player unrest over terms and conditions.

One positive aspect of the late 1920s was the discovery of a new goalkeeper who seemed to get better with every game. John Thomson had been signed from Wellesley Juniors in 1926 at the age of 17 and had been Celtic's undisputed number one from 1927 onwards. The 1928-29 League season was again disappointing with the Celts never in contention for the title. The Cup brought a 1-0 defeat by Kilmarnock in the semi-final.

McGrory's injury worries

Two Jimmy McGrory solo efforts opened Celtic's League account in August 1929, in a 2-1 win over Hearts. But the centre-forward had injury problems throughout that season, missing a dozen games and, in those days before substitutes, being carried as a passenger during another five. Again Celtic finished as also-rans in the League and the Cup.

In January 1930, the figure of Herbert Chapman was once more casting a long shadow over Celtic Park. This time he was at the Ne'erday match with Rangers although he said afterwards that McGrory hadn't impressed him. The following month it was rumoured that Chapman had described John Thomson as the world's best goalkeeper and that he wanted to take him to Highbury.

Celtic's standing in the League had improved by the end of 1930. They were a point clear of Rangers and they had found a new forward, Peter Scarff, signed from junior club Linwood St Conval's. Scarff could deputise for McGrory whenever the wounds of battle caught up with the centre-forward, and he could also play alongside McGrory at inside-left. Scarff had scored 19 goals in League and Scottish Cup the previous season and he was to surpass himself in 1930-31. Huddersfield Town, one of England's top clubs, were interested in signing him, but the Celtic board turned down their approach.

The club was now also running a reserve team, the absence of one in the 1920s having

John Thomson, one of Celtic's greatest goalkeepers, with the Scottish Cup during the club's 1931 close-season tour of America. A great sportsman and athlete, Thomson was, at the age of 22, already established as the Scottish international goalkeeper.

given them an unwelcome distinction and disadvantage among the top Scottish clubs of the day. The fans sensed a sea-change in Celtic's fortunes and began to get carried away by a new wave of players such as the left-winger Charlie 'Happy Feet' Napier, inside-forward Bertie Thomson, right-half Chic Geatons and right-back Willie Cook. All had been signed from junior clubs.

After a 2-0 win over Rangers in September 1930, thanks to two crisply-taken goals from Alec and Bertie Thomson, Willie Maley stated that the old Celtic spirit had returned but he dismissed as 'bunkum' suggestions that Rangers were finished as title contenders. He was entirely right. Celtic lost the return match on a dreadful Ibrox pitch on Ne'erday and stuttered through the second half of the League season before ending up two points behind their table-topping Glasgow rivals in the final reckoning.

McGrory had landed five goals in the 9-1 victory over East Fife at Celtic Park on 10

January. Even then, an arm injury late in the first half had forced him to go to outside-left, with Scarff taking over at centre-forward, scoring three goals and eclipsing McGrory's overall performance. Bert Thomson, with a raking diagonal volley, got the other.

The following week, in the first round of the Scottish Cup, at East Fife, it was a different story. In front of 9,000, the Fifers took the lead in the 38th minute and their defence determinedly snubbed McGrory's scoring attempts time after time. Eventually, Celtic's overall superiority told with goals from Napier and Scarff.

Fourteen further goals, against Dundee United, Morton, Aberdeen and Kilmarnock, took Celtic to the 1931 Scottish Cup final, where they faced Motherwell, then enjoying the most successful period in their history. With a minute left to play, almost everyone in the 105,000 crowd at Hampden believed that the 'Well were about to get their hands on their first major trophy. Bertie Thomson appeared to have been shepherded out of harm's way into a corner of the field. Even when he managed to wheel and send over a cross there didn't seem to be much danger for the Motherwell defence to worry about... until their centre-half Alan Craig flew at the ball and headed it past his own goalkeeper, McClory, for Celtic's equaliser.

The first half had belonged to Motherwell and they could have been four instead of two ahead by half-time, although Celtic were somewhat unlucky in that one of 'Well's goals had been deflected past Thomson by Jimmy McStay. In the second half the indomitable Celtic spirit fought back to save the day. With 10 minutes remaining, Napier's free-kick was poked away with panache by McGrory to be followed by Craig's own goal. It had been an enthralling game, with Willie Cook, Jimmy McStay and Bertie Thomson outstanding for Celtic. Surprisingly, John Thomson, by then established as the Scottish international goalkeeper, had a nervous afternoon, fumbling the ball several times, although he was blameless for both goals.

Jimmy McGrory gave Motherwell credit for the way they had played but said: 'Things might have taken a turn had we been given even one of the two penalties we claimed. It was a clear case of "hands" each time. We can win the replay.' Chic Geatons added his opinion: 'I think that we deserved a draw for our uphill fight. Our lucky goal was surely balanced by Motherwell's second counter. Football is a 90 minutes game.'

In the replay, a bad-tempered tussle, two goals from Bertie Thomson and two from McGrory gave Celtic a 4-2 win. Afterwards, the team were cheered through the streets on their way to a reception at the Bank restaurant. One fan, in his eagerness to clasp a player's hand, smashed a window on the team bus. Another player even made front-page news by getting a kiss, during which he lifted the lassie off her feet.

A tour of the New World

A party of 17 players took the Cup with them on a close-season tour of North America, where they were described as 'the all-Irish Glasgow Celtics'. John Thomson was in impressive form throughout the 13-game odyssey, which featured matches in New York, Chicago and Montreal. Some of the refereeing left a lot to be desired and at the final whistle in a brutal encounter with Pawtucket Rangers, four Celts attacked Sam Kennedy, a former Clyde player.

Holding court at the Bank restaurant on his return, Willie Maley said, when asked for his most vivid memory of the United States: 'A desire to get out of them. I do not think there is one among our party who is not jolly glad to be back once more in bonnie Scotland.' There were positive aspects to the tour, though. Celtic received great receptions in Montreal, Toronto and Philadelphia and one original member from 1888 travelled 500 miles to see the team play.

Five wins in six games gave Celtic a great start to the 1931-32 season and in the sixth of those games, a 6-1 win over Hamilton Accies, John Thomson was magnificent. One newspaper ran a regular poll at the time to gauge the popularity of Scotland's top players and Thomson was the top Celt, consistently getting twice as many votes as Jimmy McGrory. So the Celtic fans were perturbed by fresh rumours of the 22 year old going to Arsenal.

A week later Celtic were to suffer their greatest tragedy.

There were 75,000 at the first Old Firm meeting of the 1931-32 League season, on 5 September, a game spattered with bruising

JAMES McGRORY.

PETER WILSON.

tackles from the kick-off. The sectarian-based gang warfare that had developed in Glasgow during the Depression was, for the duration of the afternoon, transferred from the streets to the Ibrox terraces.

The John Thomson tragedy

Little constructive football was played but in the 50th minute a rare scoring chance fell to Rangers' Sam English, who was taking part in his first big match. With no defensive cover in sight, the forward went straight for John Thomson's goal. The goalkeeper left his line and, as English shaped to shoot, Thomson dived at his feet. The ball rolled wide of goal and Thomson lay prone on the turf.

The trainers, doctors and managers of both teams immediately rushed on to the pitch. Certain elements in Rangers' notorious Copland Road end cheered and waved flags at the sight of a stricken opponent and, to his eternal credit, the Rangers captain Davie Meiklejohn immediately went behind the goal and signalled for silence. Sadly, his efforts weren't fully successful.

It was immediately obvious that Thomson's injury was serious. Blood had been spurting from his head and he was taken off the pitch on a stretcher with his head heavily bandaged. Left-half Chic Geatons took his place for the remainder of the game, which ended in a 0-0 draw. In the dressing room, a depressed fracture of the skull was diagnosed and John Thomson was taken to the Victoria Infirmary. His father and mother were

quickly summoned from their home in the mining village of Cardenden, Fife, and arrived shortly before he passed away at 9.25 pm on that Saturday evening.

On the Monday, his coffin went from the Victoria to Cardenden. A memorial service was held on the Tuesday in Trinity Church, Claremont St, Glasgow. Davie Meiklejohn read the lesson. So many people wished to attend that an overflow service had to be held. On Wednesday 9 September, the day of John Thomson's funeral, a special train, packed with mourners and with two carriages crammed with floral tributes, left Glasgow's Queen Street station for Cardenden. There was glorious sunshine and 30,000 people packed both sides of the funeral route six-deep. Every prominent individual in Scottish football attended.

Before Celtic's next match, at home to Queen's Park the following Saturday, pipers played a lament, a bugler sounded the last post and the band played 'Lead Kindly Light'. The crowd stood with bowed heads in an unbroken two-minute silence and the players, who entered the field in single file, stood and faced the stand. Across Scotland, there were gestures of respect at the other matches played that day.

The Bing Boys, John Thomson's first football team, for whom he played aged 13, formed a committee to erect a memorial for a man who had died as he had lived, doing what he did to the best of his ability. Willie Maley's memorial card to him read: 'They never die who live in the hearts of those they leave behind.'

On 5 September 1931, Celtic suffered the saddest day in the history of the club. In a match with Rangers at Ibrox, the Rangers centre-forward Sam English, in shooting for goal, accidentally kicked the Celtic goalkeeper John Thomson on the head. Anxious players of both sides immediately gathered round the injured Thomson but he had suffered a fractured skull and was whisked off to hospital. Within hours, the goalkeeper was dead.

A pall hung over the rest of the season and Celtic fell away listlessly in the League. They would not mount another challenge for the title until 1934-35, when they would finish three points behind Rangers.

On 9 December 1933, further tragedy was to hit Celtic with the death of Peter Scarff, who played in that game at Ibrox, from tuberculosis at the age of 25. Four years later, Bertie Thomson, who had by then left Celtic, passed away at the age of 30 as the result of a heart condition.

Motherwell extracted revenge for the 1931 Cup final by beating Celtic 2-0 in the third round of the 1932 tournament but a hat-trick of Cup encounters between the clubs was completed in the 1933 final.

On their 1931 North American tour Celtic had failed to score in only one of their 13 games and that was against Fall River whose goalkeeper, Joe Kennaway, had moved Willie Maley to compare him to John Thomson. In the wake of the tragedy of September 1931 Kennaway had been sent for and the

Celtic captain Jimmy McStay leads the mourners at John Thomson's funeral in the village of Cardenden, Fife.

Canadian would be Celtic's first-choice goal-keeper for the remainder of the 1930s.

In the 1933 Scottish Cup final, attended by 102,339, he played what he himself considered his finest game for the club. One incredible save in the 27th minute saw him stretched out on the ground but still able to turn Stevenson's shot over the bar. At half-time the score was 0-0 but two minutes after the interval Bertie Thomson's trickery got the 'Well defence in a muddle and after the ball had ricocheted off two of them it fell nicely for Jimmy McGrory to stab it into the net from close-range. Near the end McGrory came close to making it two, his shot going just the wrong side of the post. Celtic were dominant throughout and deserved winners.

One of the most unusual games ever to be played at Celtic Park took place the following autumn when a Peruvian/Chilean select arrived to play a friendly. In those days, clubs were just beginning to come out of their

CELTIC "A" TEAM—Alliance Champions, 1933-34.

In the 1930s the Celtic reserve team was successful both in its own right and in nurturing players in readiness for the first-team. This picture was taken outside the main door at Celtic Park. When a new facade was erected in 1988, the decorative stained-glass window above the door was preserved. It now resides on display inside the stadium.

shells as far as meeting European opposition was concerned so a visit from a South American outfit was a real novelty. Fourteen tourists took the field before the match, three retiring to the touchline before kick-off. The three spare men donned overcoats with the innovative idea of replacing injured team-mates, although they were not called upon on this occasion.

The South Americans played like gentlemen, skilful on the ground if ineffectual in the air. The visitors' forwards never charged the goalkeeper, and their trick of opening their legs to let the ball go through them was another piece of invention that was new to Scottish onlookers. Goalkeeper Valdiviesa was particularly impressive and he jumped up and down on his goal-line when Celtic were awarded a penalty. He saved the spot-kick and the rebound but Celtic finished 2-1 winners. It had been an interesting glimpse of a different approach to the game and afterwards both parties retired to the Bank restaurant for a convivial civic reception.

The players of the Peruvian/Chilean select and Celtic before one of the most exotic matches Parkhead has seen.

Cup-holders Celtic lost 2-0 away to St Mirren in the 1934 Scottish Cup quarter-final and the next year went out at Aberdeen at the same stage of the tournament. The potential of the team of the early 1930s had never been fully realised but there were mitigating circumstances that only the hardest-hearted observer of events would fail to concede.

By 1935, Celtic had another new group of promising young players. The introduction of Jimmy McMenemy, who had been coaching at Partick Thistle, as trainer early in that year did much to help them along. Willie Maley was, after all, 66 years old. McMenemy knew all about combining artistry and effort to best effect and, above all, about how to get results the Celtic way. Alec McNair, recalling their playing days, said: 'Apropos our carpet play, I remember once when Willie Loney lobbed a ball to McMenemy, Jamie asked: "Do you think I brought a ladder?"'

Despite all that had happened in the previous few years the future looked promising. Once again, however, Celtic's support were about to see the sky blackening almost as soon as a bright new dawn had arrived.

Celtic celebrated their golden jubilee by winning the League and the Exhibition Cup. Two years later, secretary/manager Willie Maley resigned and Celtic entered an uncertain future.

4 A Golden Era Ends in Style

Between the two world wars, football in Britain changed considerably. The alteration in the offside law that the International Board ordered in 1925 had left many teams vulnerable at the back. Managers and coaches began looking at ways to shore up the gaps which had begun appearing in their defences. The most successful solution was the one put into action by Herbert Chapman. Before his arrival at Arsenal, the Londoners had won nothing. In the 1930s they won the English League five times and the FA Cup twice. They did this largely through a new defensive sophistication that was soon being imitated throughout Britain.

To fill the hole in the middle of the defence, the centre-half moved back to between the two full-backs and began concentrating fully on his defensive duties. The other main development was that the two inside-forwards were required to tackle back when necessary rather than thinking entirely of creating and scoring goals. It made for less space in key areas of the field and players, more than ever, had to fight for the right to express themselves.

Celtic would never forget their traditions, but flexibility, adaptation and innovation have always been part of them. By the mid-1930s Celtic had a side that was just right for the times. Another array of excellent entertainers had been assembled at little expense to provide assistance to the magical McGrory but their efforts were underpinned by a supporting wall of defence that was able to withstand all sorts of pressure.

Bobby Hogg was another of Celtic's cool, calculating right-backs while his counterpart on the left, Jock Morrison, was relishing his arrival in the spotlight after several years of waiting in the wings before displacing Peter McGonagle, who had given Celtic a decade of blood, sweat and cheer. At centre-half, the rugged Willie Lyon had taken over from Jimmy McStay, who had been an old-style centre-half in his desire to get forward at every opportunity. The half-backs, meanwhile, Chic Geatons and George Paterson, were tough, physical, wordly players, well aware that possession had to be earnt before it was spent in the pursuit of more pleasure for the Celtic support.

And in the second half of the 1930s there was a lot of pleasure to be had at Celtic Park. Four days before Christmas 1935, 40,000 were there to see Jimmy McGrory equal then pass the British League-goals record of 364. He did it in typical style, with a hat-trick in the 5-3 win over Aberdeen. Two of the goals were classic McGrory: piledriving headers from the edge of the six-yard box.

The centre-forward was ably assisted that day by inside-right Willie Buchan, who had taken over from Alec Thomson the previous season. Buchan also scored, making it 3-0 on half-time. A player of endless imagination, conjoined with an industrious approach, Buchan would be constantly involved in a game from the first to the final minute, seeking out opportunities to put his ideas and inventiveness to work. The final goal that afternoon was scored by Frank Murphy, also enjoying his second season in Celtic's first-team. The lithe left-winger sped away from midfield then crashed an unstoppable shot past Dons goalkeeper Smith.

A poem in the *Sunday Mail* summed up the day: 'A Celtic fan cried, in a pause/Where Parkhead's fog hung hoary/"We dinna need yer Santa Claus/While we ha'e Jimmy

The record crowd for a European club match, 146,433, packs Hampden to watch Celtic and Aberdeen contest the 1937 Scottish Cup final.

McGrory".' That victory over Aberdeen, as well as giving McGrory a personal milestone, left Celtic two points behind the Pittodrie club with a game in hand as the League Championship race increased in intensity.

For the second season in succession, Celtic reached the halfway mark as serious title contenders. Although they narrowly lost the Ne'erday game 4-3 to Rangers, Celtic had the victory that really mattered. They won their first Championship in a decade, finishing five points clear of both Rangers and Aberdeen, who shared second place. Celtic had a total of 115 League goals to their credit.

Four days after the end of the season, the 'A' Team completed a double of sorts for Celtic when they won the Second Eleven Cup with a sparkling performance in front of 22,000 at Parkhead. Among the youngsters in the side that defeated Motherwell reserves

4-2 was a talented 24-year-old inside-left, John Divers, who could not get a place in the top team because of the presence of one Johnny Crum, a light, lissom forward who provided Jimmy McGrory with silver service during the twilight days of his career.

Another who had come into the side in the 1934-35 season was Jimmy Delaney. In a team crammed with talent the slim right-winger took the eye more than any other individual with his calculated, efficient artistry. An utter gentleman both on and off the field of play, Delaney coaxed results from the ball through delicate persuasion.

A working man with aristocratic bearing, Delaney was tall for a winger at 5ft 11in but he was quick as a whippet. His accuracy, vision and understanding of the game was as close to a thing of refinement and beauty as Scottish fans had seen up to that point.

Celtic with their 15th Scottish Cup, captured after a 2-1 win over Aberdeen in 1937. Back row, from left to right: Geatons, Hogg, Kennaway, Morrison, Buchan, Paterson.
Front row: Secretary/manager Willie Maley, Delaney, McGrory, Lyon, Crum, Murphy, trainer Jimmy McMenemy.

Apart from the Ne'erday game, the only home defeat Celtic suffered that season was to St Johnstone in the second round of the Scottish Cup. The following year, when they reached the final, Celtic and their fans were to help make British football history.

Europe's record crowd

En route, Celtic defeated Stenhousemuir, Albion Rovers, East Fife, Motherwell and Clyde. When their sale was announced, tickets for the final were slightly more expensive than the public had expected. The price of stand seats ranged from five shillings to ten shillings and sixpence while the terracing was a standard one shilling all round. Despite the extra expense, when tickets went on sale to Glaswegian supporters at Lumley's in Sauchiehall Street and the Sportsman's Emporium in St Vincent Street they were quickly snapped up.

The match between Scotland and England the previous week had attracted a record international crowd of 149,414. Jimmy Delaney had been on the right wing and Scotland had won 3-1. The Scottish Cup final caught the public imagination to the same degree. It was to be contested by Aberdeen, who were on course to finish second in the League, and third-placed Celts. League matches between the two sides had been very tight with each gaining a narrow victory over the other. The standard of play at Parkhead had remained comparable to the previous season but injuries to McGrory had weakened them at several stages and his presence and goals had been badly missed.

The official attendance was 146,433, a figure which stands to this day as the highest for a match between two European clubs. The game generated receipts of £11,000. An estimated 20,000 who would have liked to have contributed to the coffers were locked out.

Those inside were given their money's worth by Celtic's youthful adventurers. They rose to the occasion with a wrinkle-free performance. The Dons, in their usual pre-war black and gold jerseys, looked nervous. Willie Buchan was Celtic's star man with his smooth, eye-catching passing. Johnny Crum probed for openings studiously and methodically. McGrory, who hadn't missed any of the matches in the Cup run, compensated for his declining physical powers with intelligent positioning, dummies and decoy runs. He was not fully fit but he insisted on playing.

With 11 minutes gone, Buchan's shot took a deflection off a defender, Aberdeen goalkeeper Johnstone got to the ball but couldn't hold it and, when the ball squirmed from his grasp, Johnny Crum was in place at Johnstone's right-hand post to sweep it over the line. Within a minute, however, Aberdeen had equalised through Armstrong.

After half-time, Celtic had to withstand a spell of Aberdeen pressure as the sizeable northern contingent present roared them

Jimmy McGrory's goalscoring feats came to an end in 1937 when he retired from the game. He was the complete jersey player, having given everything he had for Celtic. There had been opportunities for him to earn greater financial rewards elsewhere but Jimmy was never tempted to leave Parkhead.

Two of the players who gave Celtic fans great hopes for the future in the late 1930s: Malky MacDonald (far left) and John Divers (left). MacDonald's versatility enabled him to play at full-back, centre-half or half-back. Divers was an intelligent inside-forward. Both were in their prime in the late 1930s. When World War II ended in 1945 they had lost what could have been the best six years of their careers.

on. But with 20 minutes remaining, McGrory, who had taken a knock earlier in the match, controlled a pass on his chest while under pressure, glimpsed Buchan making a run into the penalty area and sent the ball into his path. The inside-right's 12-yard shot struck the foot of a post, rolled across then over the line to spark off celebrations that rocked the massive Hampden terraces.

At the time, the trophy was not presented in front of the public. In the Hampden pavilion afterwards, chairman Tom White was asked to accept the Cup. 'Ladies and gentlemen,' he intoned, mimicking a strained voice, 'I am tired. I am very tired, taking this Cup from Hampden for my club.' White handed the trophy to the team captain Willie Lyon who, with a coat concealing his strip, had been brought into the room by Willie

Maley. The Cup was then taken away to be decorated in Celtic's colours. Jimmy Quinn, Alec McNair, Patsy Gallacher, Joe Dodds and Johnny Browning all joined the man they knew as 'Boss', Maley, at the Bank for the celebrations that evening.

Jimmy McGrory, bruised and battered by years of punishment, played his last match, at the age of 33, on 16 October 1937 in a home fixture with Queen's Park. He went out in fitting style for one of the all-time Celtic immortals, scoring in the 4-3 win.

The main focus of interest before the match had been how Buchan would perform at inside-left. That was just one permutation in a season that saw Joe Carruth come in at centre-forward against St Johnstone the week after McGrory's final game and score a hattrick. For the second half of the season,

though, it was the nimble Johnny Crum who was at centre-forward, the first Celtic front man to rely entirely on anticipation, timing and guile rather than physical strength and power. His place at inside-left was taken by John Divers and he struck up an immediate understanding with Crum. A less welcome change was the departure of Willie Buchan to Blackpool in November 1937 for a fee of £10,000 but again Celtic had a suitable replacement in reserve in the shape of the combative Malky MacDonald. Although they all had standard recognised positions, the members of the Celtic forward line could interchange places at will, making them infinitely unpredictable and difficult for heavy stoppers to pin down.

On 6 November, a forward line of Delaney, Buchan, Carruth, Crum and Murphy concocted a 6-0 victory over Partick Thistle at Celtic Park. Celtic were clever, fast and strong and they would go on to take the title, finishing three points clear of Hearts. That season also saw Celtic's record home attendance when 92,000 turned up for the 3-0 win over Rangers on Ne'erday.

There would be two further celebrations for Celtic at the end of that season. To mark the Empire Exhibition in Bellahouston Park, Glasgow, an eight-club tournament featuring some of the most illustrious names in British football was held at Ibrox Park. Celtic, Aberdeen, Hearts and Rangers represented Scotland. Everton, Sunderland, Brentford and Chelsea were the English visitors.

Fine exhibitions of football

The opening game of the tournament, on 25 May, saw Celtic and Sunderland battle to a tight 0-0 draw in front of 53,976 spectators. In the replay the following evening, Sunderland scored first but Celtic's forwards were in the mood. Crum equalised before Divers twice picked his way carefully through the English side's defence for the second and third. A tense match with Hearts in the semi-final ended in a 1-0 win for Celtic. A goal midway through the second half by Johnny Crum pleased most of the 48,000 who were there.

Everton had beaten Rangers and then Aberdeen to reach the final. They were the coming team in England and would go on to

Joe Kennaway (far right) and winger Jimmy Delaney (right) made an immense contribution to Celtic's League and Cup successes of the 1930s. Kennaway, a native of Montreal, brought an unorthodox approach to goalkeeping. Delaney signed for Manchester United in 1946, seeking financial security that was not available at Celtic. He was Matt Busby's first signing as United manager. Busby rated him his best signing of all.

take the English First Division Championship the following season. Ex-Celt Willie Cook was their right-back and they had outstanding English internationals in centre-forward Tommy Lawton and right-half Joe Mercer. Their side also featured two former Rangers players, Alec Stevenson and Torry Gillick.

A great day for Celtic

The game lived up to its potential, 82,000 fans seeing a sophisticated display of football played at an extraordinary pace. The score was 0-0 at the end of 90 minutes but in injury time Divers topped off the season the way he'd spent so much of it, laying on a chance for Johnny Crum to send a clean-cut 15-yarder into the Everton goal. It was all Celtic needed to bring home the Empirex trophy.

It provided the perfect hors d'oeuvre for the 50th anniversary dinner that was held at the Grosvenor restaurant in Gordon Street the following Wednesday, 15 June. Jimmy Quinn, by then 59, and with snow white hair, was a guest of honour, as were Jimmy McGrory and Tommy McInally. Tom White made a gift of 2,500 guineas to Willie Maley and said: 'When your time comes to be called, and you look down on the Celtic ship you have served and loved so well I do trust it will not be to see it buffeted about by Clyde.'

A year later, Clyde won the Cup. Celtic slipped anchor from the prize berth to second place in the League and begin one of the choppiest passages in their history.

John Divers scored Celtic's final peacetime goal in the 1-0 win over Clyde on 2 September 1939. The following day, war was declared on Germany. League competition was suspended. The government soon allowed football to resume but the Scottish League remained in suspension. Regional Leagues were run by the clubs themselves.

During season 1939-40 Celtic played in the Regional League (Western) and from 1940-46 in the Southern League. The Scottish Cup was suspended but the Southern League Cup, served as substitute from 1940-41 to 1945-46. Another new tournament, the Scottish Summer Cup, also began. Celtic failed to win any of these competitions. They were often to be found close to the bottom of the League table although they were runners-up in the Southern League in 1944 and 1945. By then Celtic had a new manager.

On Ne'erday 1940, after a 1-1 draw at Ibrox, the news had been released that Willie Maley had resigned. He had handed in his notice in mid-December. Eighteen months previously, at the time of the golden jubilee dinner, rumours had circulated that the manager was about to go. Desmond White, chairman Tom's son, had retired as Queens Park's goalkeeper and it was known he was keen on having the job of secretary at Celtic.

Maley, who was still secretary-manager – of the then League champions and Empirex trophy holders – would have been in a strong enough position to resist any efforts to make him relinquish his duties. Eighteen months on, Celtic were in a less healthy position. On 4 January 1940, it was announced that Desmond White was Celtic's new secretary.

The Celtic directors had been in dispute with Maley over a taxation arrangement on the gift of the 2,500 guineas he had received in June 1938. In addition, they apparently objected to the use of Maley's Bank restaurant as a meeting place for Celtic players because of its raffish clientele. Yet the Bank had been the unofficial social club for Celtic players and directors for many years. The underlying problem seems to have been that the directors saw Maley as having too much power inside the club. They were no longer prepared to tolerate such a situation once his managerial talents showed signs of slipping.

Maley was furious over the way in which he had been eased out of his post. He was 71 years old, however, and although it does appear a shabby way of removing a manager who had moulded many excellent sides, it's difficult to envisage the stubborn Maley having left the club in any other way. Maley had supervised the departure of a host of good Celtic men because of petty financial fights with the club; he had little reason for complaint when the same thing happened to him. Jimmy McMenemy left along with him.

Through sheer strength of will, opportunism and ruling with a rod of iron, Maley had made Celtic the most successful and attractive club side in Scotland.

Jimmy McGrory had achieved some success as manager of Kilmarnock. He appeared almost certain to become Celtic's second manager. But on 16 January Jimmy McStay became Celtic's new boss. He had been performing miracles on an almost non-existent budget at Alloa Athletic after a previous spell managing in the Irish Free State.

Jimmy McStay in the manager's office at Celtic Park. He had little opportunity to do himself justice as Celtic manager, being restricted by the constraints of wartime football. His removal by the board to make way for Jimmy McGrory was one of the least dignified episodes in Celtic's history.

By then, Clydeside was working overtime to help with the war effort. Amidst stories of real massacres, tragedies and disasters, football was relegated to the second division of most people's preoccupations.

In March 1940, Jimmy Delaney was close to fitness after suffering a severe arm injury that had kept him out of football for almost a year. He said of Celtic's poor form at that time: 'I don't think they're so far out as some folk imagine. Of course, the war and the fact that many of the boys are now doing heavy work during the week has upset things.'

Delaney was due to register for military service; Joe Kennaway had returned to North America at the start of the war; Jock Morrison was helping out down the mines and had to retire from football in 1941; Willie Lyon enlisted in the army in May 1940; George Paterson joined the RAF, as did Frank Murphy; in early 1940 Chic Geatons was injured and out for some time after somebody dropped a length of tubing on his feet at the cable works where he was employed.

Scotland's clubs carried on through the war years but most were like ragged armies as they limped through the no man's land of the regional Leagues. Guest players, who were stationed in Scotland, turned out for local clubs. Matt Busby spent time at Hibs. Stanley Matthews turned out for Rangers and Morton, where he formed a fine understanding with Johnny Crum, who had been transferred in 1942. Tommy Lawton also played for the Greenock side. But these were loose, inconsistent arrangements. Celtic believed in sticking with their own talent: the players who would be in place whenever normality returned.

McStay is sacked

Jimmy McStay was a gentleman, a man without an enemy. The Celtic directors were pleased to have to deal no longer with a headstrong individual such as Maley. The board began to take more of a hand in team selection and signings. But in July 1945 Jimmy McStay was removed from his post.

McStay seems to have been a stop-gap manager for wartime, although he himself was unaware of this. In *Celtic*, Sir Robert Kelly said: 'His appointment came in time of war when football was at sixes and sevens and Celtic were having a doleful period. In any case, we had already earmarked the man who we hoped would become the Celtic manager. He was Jimmy McGrory.'

McStay told the *Sunday Mail*: 'I can only assume that the Chairman and his directors felt that a change in managership might bring a change in the team's fortunes. And I want to wish my old colleague, Jimmy McGrory, every possible good fortune. At the same time, I must confess I was deeply hurt over the whole thing. No hint of a change had been given me when I prepared to leave for two weeks' holiday. I made up the groundsmen's wages just before I left and went down to Ayr with my family.

'You can imagine my feelings when, a few days later, I picked up a paper and read that I was likely to lose my job. It was obviously not just a rumour, so when I returned I called on the chairman, Mr White, who asked me to hand in my resignation. I did so, of course, but the whole affair has caused me much unjustified embarrassment.'

As the war ended, many football people, particularly those who had been part of the promising Celtic side of the late 1930s, could justifiably believe their careers had become casualties of war. But as John Divers would often remark, although the war had disrupted his and others' playing careers, it had ruined a lot more for a lot more people.

There wasn't much for Celtic fans to cheer about in the years following World War II. Yet in that barren period seeds were sown that would bring Celtic great success in future years.

5 Glimpses of Greatness

Before post-war League and Cup competition got underway again, Celtic suffered a shock to the system from which it would take them years to recover. Jimmy Delaney, who had almost singlehandedly carried the team during the war, was transferred to Manchester United in February 1946 after 13 years with Celtic. At Old Trafford he joined up with an old friend from Scottish international duty, Matt Busby, who, as one of the first tracksuit managers, would join in training sessions. The contrast with Celtic was enormous. While Busby was in among his players trying out new ideas, at Celtic Park Jimmy McGrory had a more traditional approach to the job, behaving like a distinguished figurehead in the mould of Willie Maley, but without the bark or the bite.

Some players saw the need for new, radical ideas if Celtic were to regain their rightful place in Scottish football. Shortly after the war, George Paterson told the *Sunday Mail*: 'I am convinced the nature of my RAF work has prolonged my playing life.

'The old notion of being satisfied with a few laps of the field, with perhaps a few sprints thrown in is of no use in modern football. Players should train more often. I do P.T. every day and feel nothing but benefit from it. I even do light exercise some Saturday mornings before a game.

'Football is going to be streamlined. We shall see soccer commandoes, hard as nails from head to feet. I play five games a week from Monday to Friday, each game of half-an-hour. Enough to make the old-timers turn in their graves, perhaps. But why not? The trouble with half the players today is lack of ball control. Let them play with it till they can make it talk, then they'll make the fans talk.'

It would be long after Paterson's time at the club – he moved to Brentford in October 1946 – before such ideas were to be contemplated at Celtic Park.

As post-war Britain reeled under rationing and other privations, Celtic fans found their sport reflecting reality only too well. They had to get by on scraps of goodness in the hope that one day things would get better.

After the first, unofficial, post-war season, when Celtic came fourth, League competition, under the official auspices of the Scottish League, was finally restored for 1946-47. At Celtic's first official post-war League match, 35,000 turned up at Parkhead only to see a Morton side with John Divers at inside-right win 2-1. Divers, who was on loan at that time, would complete his full transfer to Cappielow the following month. Only Bobby Hogg of the glorious side of the late 1930s remained in the Celtic line-up.

That result against Morton was no isolated occurrence. In the first seven seasons after the war, Celtic's best position in League Division A, as the First Division was temporarily known, was fifth, in 1949-50. The only time the club was involved in an exciting finish to the season during those years was in 1948 – when they went to Dundee for their final League game needing a win to be sure of avoiding relegation.

There were 31,000 inside Dens Park that day and Patsy Gallacher's sons, Willie at inside-left for Celtic, Tommy at right-half for Dundee, faced each other. Celtic took the lead in the 14th minute when right-winger Jock Weir, a £7,000 signing from Blackburn Rovers two months previously, finally got the ball in the net after some desperate Dundee defending. The home side then went 2-1 up

Willie Fernie strokes a 90th minute penalty into the Rangers net for the final goal in Celtic's 7-1 victory in the 1957 League Cup final.

but Weir scored another two untidy goals for his hat-trick and Celtic's ticket to safety. Celtic finished 12th out of 16, four points off second-bottom-placed, relegated Airdrie.

Celtic's record in the Scottish Cup and the League Cup – a peacetime continuation of the Southern League Cup – was equally abysmal. Up until 1951 the best they managed was a semi-final appearance in the 1948 Scottish Cup. Eight goals without reply in

three matches set them up for a semi with Morton. In front of 80,000 the Cappielow side snatched it with the only goal of the game during extra-time, the Greenock side's fitness proving superior to Celtic's.

One of the more notable members of the side in those immediate post-war years, goalkeeper Willie Miller, left the club in August 1950 but he was succeeded by a more than competent custodian, George Hunter, whose

Irishman Charlie Tully, who joined Celtic from Belfast Celtic in 1948, brightened up the gloomy post-war years with a host of mischievous tricks that never failed to delight the fans.

confident performances did much to bring Celtic their first major post-war trophy, the 1951 Scottish Cup.

There were other signs that Celtic were, at last, beginning to get a team together. Alongside Weir in the forward line for that final were the crafty inside-right Bobby Collins and John McPhail, a centre-forward in the Jimmy Quinn mould who could run from deep at defenders, outmanoeuvring them with a magnificent body-swerve and who was increasingly being used as a spearhead after a lot of chopping and changing of his position. On the left wing, Celtic had two Irishmen, Bertie Peacock at inside left, and Charlie Tully outside him. Peacock, like Collins, combined guile with toil and had a blistering shot. The sturdy, red-headed figure of Bobby Evans at right-half fetched and carried for the front men with aplomb.

Tully the crowd-pleaser

But it was Tully who was the fans' favourite; an impudent individualist who could make defenders look less mobile than traffic bollards. Like his fellow Irishman Oscar Wilde he appeared to believe that consistency indicated a lack of imagination although he was marvellously consistent on one occasion, a 1953 Cup-tie at Falkirk, when he scored direct from a corner and, on being ordered to retake the kick, scored again.

In the years after the war, fans, desperate for diversion after blackouts and blitzes, attended football in enormous numbers. On their run past East Fife, Duns, Hearts, Aberdeen and Raith Rovers, Celtic were watched by a total of 280,000 people and there were a further 131,943 at Hampden Park on 21 April to see another in the Celtic v Motherwell Cup final series. Yet again Celtic were to emerge as victors, an undistinguished game producing a goal of the highest order after 12 minutes. John McPhail nicked the ball neatly between two defenders just outside the 18-yard box and let it bounce once before controlling it and scooping it over the diving Motherwell goalkeeper Johnstone. It was the only goal of the game and it gave Celtic their first major trophy in 13 years.

Celtic toured North America that summer, playing nine matches and visiting New York, Philadelphia, Toronto, Detroit, New Jersey and Montreal. They took the Cup with them

Celtic fans took the stylish battler Bobby Evans (above right) to their hearts. A half-back of consummate skill, he was captain of the side when they won their first League Cup trophy in 1956.

and before each match John McPhail showed it to the fans. On their return, the Celtic players were mobbed at Glasgow Central Station by frenzied followers, many of them female.

Celtic made one of their most important signings ever on 4 December 1951. Assistant trainer Jimmy Gribben suggested a player whom he thought could do a job for the club and his advice was acted upon. The man in question, Jock Stein, joined a side struggling in the lower half of the First Division.

Few observers of the Scottish game at the time thought of Stein as a man touched with the elixir of success. He had spent a year playing non-league football in Wales for Llanelly after eight seasons as centre-half for perennial strugglers Albion Rovers in his native Lanarkshire. His arrival was to be followed by a revival of Celtic's fortunes that was to be no mere coincidence.

The enduring image of Jock Stein as a player is not one of any exceptional doings with the ball at his feet. Rather, it is of Stein overseeing matters in his own penalty area, ideally-positioned, watchful and ready to tidy up should the ball escape the control of his

Willie Fernie (far left) holds the Coronation Cup, one of Celtic's most famous successes. Before the tournament began there had been some controversy over Celtic's inclusion in the eight-team tournament because of their poor standing in the League at that time. Their winning performances quietened that particular debate.

John McPhail (left) was a Celtic centre-forward in the classic mould. His goal in the 1951 Scottish Cup final ended the club's longest-ever run without a trophy – 13 years. That won him a special place in the affections of a generation of Celtic supporters.

goalkeeper Johnny Bonnar or another defender. Stein admitted he was a limited player but his sense of being in control of any given situation was just what Celtic needed.

The Cup-holders were knocked out in their first game in defence of the trophy, after a replay at Third Lanark. They had achieved their best showing in the League Cup up to that point by reaching the 1951 semi-final where they were beaten 3-0 by Rangers although Charlie Tully and centre-half Alec Boden both struck the bar.

One of Celtic's most memorable successes capped the 1952-53 season even though they

finished eighth in the League, managed to reach only the quarter-finals of the Cup and failed to qualify from their four-team section in the opening stages of the League Cup.

The escape clause out of another unremarkable year for Celtic was provided by Queen Elizabeth II's coronation. The footballing community celebrated the occasion with another eight-team 'British Cup' similar to the one that had been played during the Empire Exhibition 15 years earlier.

The Coronation Cup featured the cream of British football and in the first round, in front of 59,500 at Hampden Park, Celtic

defeated the newly-crowned English champions Arsenal. The match ended 1-0 in Celtic's favour thanks to a 23rd minute goal by Bobby Collins direct from a corner but dozens of shots rained in on the English goal and only a combination of fine goalkeeping and luck let the Gunners off lightly. Five days later, 73,000 were at the same venue to see Bertie Peacock in dazzling form and a force-nine strike from him and another from Neil Mochan defeated a star-spangled Manchester United side 2-1. Both of those goals had been set up by Charlie Tully.

There were 117,060 at the final on 20 May to see Celtic take on the finest team in Scotland during the early 1950s, Hibs, featuring their Famous Five forward line of Smith, Johnstone, Reilly, Turnbull and Ormond. It was a much closer affair than the games against the English teams, although Celtic had the initiative in the first half and a 35-yard stunner from Mochan put them ahead after 28 minutes.

The second half belonged to Hibs – as well as Celtic goalkeeper Bonnar and now-captain Stein. The inventive Hibees had scoring attempts from all sorts of angles but they couldn't find a solution to beat the Celts' last man while Stein ensured that calm rather than panic broke out among his team-mates as the pressure increased. Three minutes from the end, inside-right Jimmy Walsh crowned Celtic's Coronation Cup victory with the second goal.

It was a notable achievement but even after Celtic's scintillating play in that tournament the club's enormous success in the following season was to be a huge surprise even to the most supreme optimist. That was in spite of their beginning the 1953-54 fixtures by finishing bottom of their League Cup section table and suffering a 2-0 defeat at Hamilton in their opening League match.

John McPhail was back as the regular centre-forward in the early part of that season but he was plagued by weight and fitness problems and managed only four League goals. He was replaced in the new year by the enthusiastic but limited Sean Fallon. Fallon managed five League goals but the top scorer was Neil Mochan with 20, while the sweet-moving, athletic inside-right Willie Fernie chipped in with ten, as did Bobby Collins.

In a title clash on 6 February before 47,519, Celtic lost 3-2 to Hearts in Edinburgh and by the end of that month Celtic were seven points behind the Tynecastle side, who led the League. The Celts had three games in hand but only an outstanding effort would win the title and that's exactly what Celtic came up with. They won their remaining eight League games, scoring 27 goals and conceding just two. They outthought opponents on the flanks thanks to the intricate work of Collins, Fernie, Tully and Mochan. Bobby Evans and Bertie Peacock kept the whole enterprise ticking over nicely with astute interventions from the middle of the field while the value of Stein's steadying presence was inestimable.

In the Scottish Cup, away victories at Falkirk, Stirling Albion and Hamilton Accies took Celtic to the semi-finals where they met their old Cup rivals Motherwell. After a replay, Celtic were in the final to face an Aberdeen side who had beaten Celtic three times already that season and who had scored eight goals in the process.

Fallon was at centre-forward for the final, but there was no place for Bobby Collins, kept out of the side by the exciting 21-year-old right-winger John Higgins. Five minutes after half-time, most of the 129,926 present were in a state of delight. Mochan cut in from the right and sent in a cross-shot that caught Aberdeen centre-half Young on the hop – the ball flew off his foot and into the net.

An unlikely Cup final hero

As in the 1937 final, however, the Dons equalised inside a minute, through Buckley. With 63 minutes gone, one of the many inspired moments that Willie Fernie provided for Celtic down the years gave them the Cup. His lung-bursting run from his own half took him to the goal-line from where he reviewed the situation before crossing into the middle for Fallon to nudge the ball past Martin. It was Celtic's first double since 1914.

Aberdeen lost both of their League games to Celtic during the following season but the Dons still deposed the champions, finishing three points clear of the Celts. Celtic made another Scottish Cup final appearance. A double from John McPhail, in only his seventh game of the season, had seen off Airdrie in the semi-final replay and his talismanic presence enthused the Celtic fans among the 106,234 who made their way to Hampden for the final with Clyde on 23 April.

He and Tully were in fine fettle on the day but it was another devastating pass from Fernie that set up inside-left Jimmy Walsh for a well-taken opener after 38 minutes. There should have been further goals for Celtic, but it was typical of the afternoon when a low cross from Tully that only needed a nick from McPhail or Walsh was completely missed by both players. With two minutes remaining, one goal looked enough. But a corner from Clyde's Archie Robertson was misjudged by both Bonnar and left-back Frank Meechan at the near-post and the ball slipped over the line. In the replay a goal from Ring shortly after half-time gave Clyde the Cup.

Celtic reach another final

Further disappointment followed as Celtic dropped to fifth place in the League the following season and failed to qualify from their League Cup section yet again. The Scottish Cup semi-final provided an opportunity to get even with Clyde, which was taken with a 2-1 win through a penalty from right-back Mike Haughney and a goal from centre-forward Jim Sharkey, who had capitalised on a bad back-pass after just two minutes.

Sharkey was missing from the line-up in the final after word of a breach of discipline at Seamill had reached the ears of Robert Kelly who had taken over as chairman in 1947 on the death of Tom White. Kelly regarded team selection and discipline as part of his duties. Bobby Collins had been dropped from the previous season's replayed final, allegedly because Kelly had disliked an over-physical challenge on the Clyde goalkeeper in the first game.

Celtic were also without Jock Stein for the 1956 date. He had suffered an ankle injury at the beginning of the season, and Collins was also missing, this time through injury. The inexperienced 19-year-old Billy Craig was on the right wing with Haughney, the team's regular right-back, drafted in at inside-forward in Sharkey's absence. It was a team selection that reflected the chairman's wishes but it puzzled most of the 132,842 who had paid their hard-earned money to see the final. An accomplished Hearts side ate Celtic up, a 3-1 win taking the Cup to Tynecastle.

Hopes of Celtic improving on their dreadful League Cup record all but disappeared when they were drawn in a tough-looking qualifying section with Aberdeen, Rangers and East Fife, then also a First Division side. But after an away win at Aberdeen, clever goals by Collins and Tully gave Celtic a 2-1 win over Rangers at Parkhead and the return at Ibrox ended 0-0, two scorelines that didn't so much flatter Rangers as do a public relations job for them.

Home and away victories over East Fife and a 3-2 defeat of Aberdeen set Celtic up for a 6-0 quarter-final defeat of Dunfermline at Parkhead although they lost the meaningless return 3-0. The semi-final at Hampden paired them with Clyde. There, new signing, centre-forward Billy McPhail, signed on the very day his older brother John had retired, 5 May 1956, got the double that defeated his old club.

The League Cup was still very much a secondary tournament, and that was reflected in the size of the crowd for the final between Celtic and Partick Thistle: 58,794. The honours went to Thistle who limped through extra-time with only ten men. There were even fewer spectators, 31,156, at the midweek replay but they saw Celtic pick up their first League Cup after another Billy McPhail double had sent them on their way. Evans, still plying his trade with intelligence and insight in the middle, set Collins up for the third and final goal, and the inside-right ended any Thistle hopes of a comeback with a crisp, low shot. The following year, Celtic would win the League Cup a second time but while their first triumph in the tournament had been relatively low-key, their second would produce a result that would reverberate around Glasgow for decades to come.

After topping their League Cup section ahead of Hibs, Airdrie and East Fife, Celtic ran up a 9-1 aggregate against Third Lanark in the quarter-final. The semi was at Ibrox and, while Rangers fans may not have enjoyed hearing that Celtic had won 4-2 against Clyde on their home ground, they were to enjoy the final a great deal less.

It was an ageing Celtic team, with several players hovering around the age of 30, who took the field at Hampden Park on 19 October 1957 for the League Cup final

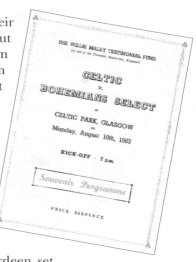

Celtic captain Jock Stein (centre) ensures that everything is under control in the 1954 Cup final with Aberdeen.

The opening goal for Celtic in the 1954 final. The ball has just been deflected off Aberdeen centre-half Young's foot and past his confused goalkeeper Martin. The match ended with Celtic 2-1 winners.

against Rangers. Rangers were the League champions and favourites for the match. The previous week Celtic had put on a dreadful display in the 1-1 home League match with Raith Rovers and in the days before the final greater excitement was generated by the press in Rangers' forthcoming European Cup tie with AC Milan.

Celtic had, however, beaten Rangers twice in Cup encounters the previous season and had won the first Old Firm clash of 1957-58 at Ibrox four weeks previously. The third goal in that 3-2 win had been scored by Sammy Wilson, in his first season with the club. He had also scored the first in the 4-2 defeat of Clyde. The 25-year-old repeated the feat in the final, scoring the first goal after an opening 20 minutes in which both Collins and Tully hit the woodwork.

Wilson had established a useful partnership with Billy McPhail. The centre-forward nodded the ball down to him in the 23rd minute and Wilson, on the penalty spot, leaned back and sent a cute right-footed volley into the corner of the Rangers net. Celtic were on a higher plane than their opponents and, after Wilson's opener, Bobby Collins saw his 30-yard free-kick rebound from the bar.

A minute from the interval Neil Mochan made it two. Again Billy McPhail provided the service and Mochan cut in from the left wing, brushed off two Rangers defenders and his unstoppable left-foot shot from the edge of the six-yard box flew between Niven and his near post.

Rangers could consider themselves lucky to be going in just 2-0 down at half-time but that was when their luck ran out.

Eight minutes after the interval, a lofted pass from just outside the Rangers penalty area found McPhail on the edge of the six-yard box and the centre-forward jumped with the poise, balance and grace of a gymnast to rise above two Rangers challenges and guide the ball into the net. Simpson got one back for Rangers but if they thought they could get away with a respectable scoreline they were soon disabused of the idea. McPhail's second, when he forced a loose ball over the line, was less picturesque than his first, but it was equally welcome.

Mochan made it five with another left-foot shot, and McPhail got his hat-trick with the best goal of the game, heading the ball neatly round Rangers centre-half Valentine, controlling it quickly and sending it past Niven.

Bertie Peacock, Celtic's industrious left-half, makes a clearance in the 1955 Cup final with Clyde. Jock Stein (far right) and Bobby Evans (centre) are his watchful team-mates.

A hail of bottles poured down from the Rangers end of the ground after Celtic had been awarded a 90th minute penalty. Willie Fernie, playing the greatest game of his life, passed it into the net for a scoreline that will live in the hearts and minds of Celtic fans as long as the club exists: 7-1. That it came in a Cup final and remains the record score for such a match makes it all the sweeter. Charlie Tully, asked the time afterwards, said: 'The only time I know is seven past Niven.'

It proved to be the last hurrah for players such as Tully, Evans, Peacock, McPhail, Mochan and Fernie. But what a way to be remembered!

An exhilarating Scottish Cup run in 1957, which included a 2-0 win over Rangers after a 4-4 draw at Parkhead, ended at the semi-final stage with a 3-1 defeat from Kilmarnock after a 1-1 draw, the two games being watched by a combined attendance of 186,000. Celtic would reach the semi-final stage again in 1959 and 1960 but would suffer heavy defeats each time and it was not until 1961 that they were to reach another Scottish Cup final.

The 1956-57 League Championship had ended with Celtic in fifth place in the First Division, and for the remainder of Jimmy McGrory's time as manager they would not be realistic contenders for the title, never finishing higher than third in the table, and a poor third at that. After a semi-final appearance in 1958, Celtic's League Cup form would return to normal: in the five seasons from 1959 to 1963 they would fail to qualify from their section.

Celtic's lack of leadership

The players at Celtic Park would not see Jimmy McGrory from one Saturday to the next, unless they had to discuss some administrative matter with him. John Divers, the son of the inside-left in the great team of the late 1930s, signed for Celtic, like his father as an inside-left, in July 1956, and remembers the era well. 'In those days people would put an old grey sweatshirt on and train by running round the park and up and down the terracing steps. If people asked for a ball they were told, "No, no, no, Patsy Gallacher didn't train with a ball. What was good enough for Patsy Gallacher is good enough for you."

'But it was a period when society was changing and people were beginning to challenge

Celtic fans in happy mood at Hampden Park for the 1955 Cup final. The mid-1950s brought them plenty to cheer but another bleak spell would follow as Celtic entered a period of confusion.

authority. The players would complain that we went from Saturday to Saturday and never touched a ball, which was true. Duncan MacKay, who was a magnificent athlete with a great touch, wanted the ball to play all the time, and said to the management, "This is ridiculous – Joe Davis doesn't run round a snooker table when he's practising for snooker matches."

'Jimmy McGrory was a very quiet man. I always found him a very decent man but we did not talk tactics. In later years I would meet Rangers players such as Jimmy Baxter and Davie Wilson and talk to them about football and they'd say to me, "We used to play 4-2-4." So there was tactics at Rangers. Celtic used to just go out on the park.'

John Hughes, who signed in October 1959, and who would be a prolific goalscorer for the club during the following decade,

says: 'It was a nightmare. I was there as a big raw laddie and basically you didn't get any help at all. I just made a lot of mistakes and nobody said anything. Players are playing all the time now at 17 but if you go back to 1960 that wasn't the case and I was in there at 17. I played centre in a bad Celtic team and scored 32 goals one season. I often feel that if I had had some guidance in the early years I'd have been a far better player.

'I got this tag of being up and down, that I could be a nightmare or good. A lot of that was because of the fact that nobody was saying, "Look, you'll need to come back and work on this" or "You're doing the wrong thing, try and do this." No, you were thrown into a thing where you had no help.

'Jimmy McGrory was too nice to be a manager. He couldn't say to you, "Look, you just get this done" or "You're not doing this".

A unique talent arrived at Celtic Park in the late 1950s, the one and only Jimmy 'Jinky' Johnstone. Even before his debut in 1963, those inside the club were becoming amazed by his skills. He would go on to become one of the world's greatest players.

'He just wasn't that kind of man. Sean Fallon used to lock him out of the dressing room at team talks, wouldn't let him in. He gave the team talks. It was very amateurish, there was no real thought going into things.

'Jimmy McGrory didn't contribute. When I got into the first-team I was getting about £7 a week and the others were getting £12 a week. I went to see him and I said, "They're getting £12 and I'm getting £7." He said, "I know, but you're only a boy." I said, "But I'm doing the same job as them." "I know, but you're too young yet to get that kind of money." That was the kind of thinking that made it just a shambles at that time.'

Stein's first coaching post

Things were far from shambolic at reserve-team level: players who had switched from first-team to reserves found the second-string set-up invigorating. Jock Stein had taken over there in the summer of 1957 after his ankle injury forced him to retire as a player. 'When Big Jock took charge of the reserve team you did everything with the ball – which was revolutionary,' says Divers. 'He was dealing with talented guys, he was tactically aware and he could motivate people. That whole combination produced success for the reserve side.

'Duncan MacKay was a hardworking but ordinary midfield player for Celtic Reserves. Before he left Big Jock had turned him into an attacking, pacy right full-back. In those days if a full-back kicked the ball right out of the park he thought he'd done a job. That showed how far he was ahead of his time: having attacking full-backs. Jock left, Dunky's star dimmed at Celtic Park and he drifted out of the game. Many people think that if Big Jock had stayed he'd have been the Celtic right-back. Big Jock really admired him.'

The Celtic supporters who turned up for home games in the late 1950s were the first to set eyes on a new, natural talent, although he wasn't on the field of play. Jimmy Johnstone had arrived at Celtic Park but for the only time in his exceptional career he could be easily overlooked by the paying audience. 'I was about 13 and playing with the Boys' Guild in Viewpark and Manchester Utd were wanting to sign me. John Higgins, he was the chief scout at Celtic Park at the time, said he'd like me to come in so I went on to the ballboys' staff for matches at Celtic Park.

'But it got to a certain time when I was missing out on my Saturday football with the Boys' Guild and I chucked it. Immediately, Celtic were right in and they took me on for a Tuesday and a Thursday for training. They put me out to Blantyre Celtic for a couple of years just to get a bit of strength about me. All this time I was working and working and working at the game, different aspects, the bits I was weakest at.

'For instance, I could get past a player and after another ten yards he'd be back to me again. I didn't have the strength so my father gave me his pit boots, he was a miner all his days, and I used to play in them for maybe half-an-hour every night. I used to do 50 yards, 100 yards sprints with these and it ended up that players weren't catching me. After about seven weeks I really began to feel the benefit when I took them off.

'As a youngster I'd get cones and milk bottles as well and go in and out of them at pace. I saw Stanley Matthews in the Cup final and I thought right away that was what I wanted to do because I got carried away with it. And I still am today when I see somebody going up to somebody and taking them on.

'My routine was I ran home from school, about two miles, over parks and up bings, into the house, got the t-shirt on and the jeans, no shoes or anything on my feet. I got the milk bottles out, shoved all the furniture back, and just went in and out of them. The woman down the stairs, God love her, put up with it for five years. And when you were downstairs and you heard somebody just walking across the roof you'd have thought they were coming through it. To put up with that for five years... and they were Rangers supporters too! I'll never forget her for that. I owe her a lot for never complaining.

'After an hour and a half there, I'd go into the street and just run up and down hitting the ball off the fence, the kerb, sprinting and twisting and turning, then I'd go into the school and it had about a 100-yard wall and it was ideal. I used to go up and down it just playing one-twos. One side with my left foot, turn, come down the other side with my right foot. Then I'd hit the ball off the wall and practise trapping it and controlling it.

'It would get dark but your eyes got accustomed to it. I used to sleep with the ball. The first thing I'd do every morning was see if it was there. Football was your outlet, you had nothing else, so that's how I think you unconsciously developed all these skills.' Johnstone would make his first-team debut in 1963, and his purposeful meanderings on the wing would almost immediately capture the hearts of the club's supporters.

Stein's team faces Celtic

It was inevitable that Jock Stein would get his chance to try out his ideas as a first-team manager but he had to leave Celtic to do so. Just over a year later, as manager of Dunfermline Athletic he was to take the Fife club to their first Cup final where he would meet his old club. Celtic had scored 19 goals in the 1961 tournament, defeating Falkirk, Montrose, Raith Rovers, Hibs and Airdrie.

The 17 year old John Hughes, ending his debut season, was unlucky not to score in the final but Denis Connachan, in Dunfermline's goal, was in inspired form and the 113,328 in attendance were thoroughly entertained even though they didn't see any goals. Four days later, Celtic again had most of the play and Connachan was again outstanding. This time there were goals: both for Dunfermline. Celtic had shown themselves to be a team with a superior quality of individual player but hadn't matched Dunfermline's team-

work – and that was what had sent the Cup to East End Park rather than the East End of Glasgow. Jock Stein had started working his special magic at Dunfermline and would do so continually for the next four years before moving on to do the same at Hibs.

Two years later Celtic were again in the final, this time with Rangers, a game that again needed a replay and a tie watched by a total of 250,000. In the first game, Rangers' Brand opened the scoring two minutes before half-time but Bobby Murdoch equalised almost immediately, side-footing the ball into the net after John Hughes' shot had been stopped on the line.

The outstanding individuals in a determined performance from Celtic were Billy McNeill, goalkeeper Frank Haffey and, at outside-right, Jimmy Johnstone. Eleven days later, the winger was inexplicably dropped for the replay. Bobby Craig, an inside-right signed from Blackburn Rovers a year previously, had performed poorly before the final, but incredibly he was brought in to replace Jimmy Johnstone on the wing. He floundered against Rangers, as did the rest of the Celts, and the side were beaten 3-0.

Looking back, Jimmy Johnstone says: 'I got dropped for the following game. With no

Celtic players leave the Parkhead pitch in happy mood after the 3-0 win over MTK Budapest in the first leg of the semi-final of the European Cup-Winners' Cup in 1964. It was only Celtic's second venture into Europe and they were almost in a final. In Hungary, however, their lack of European experience would be exposed and would lead to an unexpected defeat.

Jock Stein returned to Celtic Park as manager in early 1965 and quickly brightened the whole place up. He made the players feel good and livened up training. His weekly talk-ins encouraged the players to express themselves and helped them feel important. Back row, from left to right: Stein, Hughes, Chalmers, Young, Auld, McNeill and Clark. Front row: Lennox, Gemmell, Murdoch and Fallon.

disrespect to anybody, I don't think that Jimmy McGrory was very influential. I think it was really the man above him, Bob Kelly, who was the man who ruled everything. If somebody had had a good game and had been dropped and someone else was brought in we used to say, "Old Bob must be wanting to see what he's like."

'Even in the Cup final I thought that was the reason. I feel it wasn't Jimmy McGrory's decision. I think the decision to put Bobby in came from the top and I think I was the youngest so that's how it worked out. Amazing, but these were the kind of decisions that were made.'

The following year, Celtic finally got out of their League Cup rut, reaching the 1964 final against Rangers. Robert Kelly's decision in the late 1950s for the club to concentrate on youth was finally coming good. Kelly Kids such as Jimmy Johnstone, Tommy Gemmell, Billy McNeill, Stevie Chalmers and John Hughes were showing great promise.

'It was the first time in my playing career that Celtic started a game bookmakers' favourites to beat Rangers away from Celtic Park,' says John Divers. 'There was a feeling among the bookies that a change was about to occur. No matter what the results had been in the previous two or three weeks

Rangers had always previously been favourites to beat Celtic at Ibrox or Hampden Park. With hindsight you look back and see the bookmakers were sensing the change.'

On the day, Celtic were just edged out. Rangers were already two goals ahead when Jimmy Johnstone pulled one back with 21 minutes remaining, the signal for avalanche after avalanche of noise to come sweeping down the Hampden slopes as the Celtic and Rangers fans roared on their men. But for Celtic it was not to be.

An impressive set of floodlights had been installed at Parkhead in 1959, creating the perfect stage for glamorous midweek European matches. But the club's poor domestic record meant they missed out on the earliest days of European competition, making their debut six years after Hibs had become the first British club to play in a European tie. In their first European game, in the Fairs Cities Cup in September 1962, Celtic had the most unlucky draw possible, against Valencia, the holders. The first leg was in Spain and although Celtic lost 4-2, they had a Stevie Chalmers effort ruled offside and two strong penalty claims turned down.

There were 45,000 at Parkhead for the return but it proved a damp squib as the Spaniards eased into a 2-1 lead with ten minutes remaining. A late goal from Pat Crerand gave Celtic a draw and it was some consolation that Valencia proved themselves good enough to retain the trophy, beating Stein's Dunfermline and Hibs on the way.

Excitement in Europe

The following year, Celtic came close to winning a European tournament at just their second attempt. A 10-1 aggregate win over Basle of Switzerland and by 4-2 over Dinamo Zagreb of the then Yugoslavia, took Celtic into the Cup-Winners' Cup quarter-final where they faced Slovan Bratislava, the Czechoslovakian Cup winners.

The first leg was typical of Celtic at that time: plenty of clever individualism but a lack of integrated team play. After 90 minutes when they had had most of the ball, they had only managed one goal, a Bobby Murdoch penalty. In the second leg, another moment of individualism put Celtic into the semi-final. John Hughes picked the ball up 60 yards from goal and used his tremendous power and pace to beat off every challenge he faced. As goalkeeper Schroif advanced to meet him he switched from power to preci-

sion and flicked the ball over his opponent for the only goal of the game.

In the semi Celtic were drawn against Magyar Testgyakorlok Koere, better known as MTK, of Budapest. Jimmy Johnstone and Stevie Chalmers were the heroes in the first leg, two goals from Chalmers and one from Johnstone being just reward for their efforts on an evening when Celtic appeared to have reached the final before the second leg had been played. But Celtic were to find that playing it off-the-cuff was not quite enough against the better sides in Europe. Without a real strategy for retaining the lead, the naïve Kelly Kids were crushed 4-0.

Celtic were back in the Fairs Cup in 1964-65 but after eliminating Leixoes of Portugal they were outmanoeuvred by Barcelona, losing 3-1 on aggregate.

Victory in Europe seemed as far away as ever and, just as alarmingly, it was beginning to look as though the Kelly Kids would always be nearly men in the games that really mattered. Without action to stem the flow of failures, it appeared likely that Celtic would haemorrhage players. The half-back pass-master Pat Crerand had moved on to

Manchester United in 1963, after a stand-up argument with coach Sean Fallon. By early 1965 there was talk that the outstanding centre-half Billy McNeill was also dissatisfied and would be following him south.

Stein returns to Celtic

It was then that Robert Kelly met Jock Stein for lunch and gave him something to chew over – the chance to manage Celtic.

The announcement of Stein's appointment was made on 31 January 1965. After guiding Hibs to the Cup semi-final Stein took over at Parkhead on 9 March. Robert Kelly appointed Sean Fallon as his assistant. Jimmy McGrory became Public Relations Manager. After his original proposal to Stein, Kelly had later suggested that Stein and Fallon become joint managers of the team. Stein refused to contemplate such an idea.

'I've got a vivid memory from 1965,' says John Divers, 'when it was announced that he was coming back from Hibs, of Billy McNeill saying, "Oh that's fantastic! Wait and see how things change now!" Big Billy was right – they literally changed overnight. Within six weeks they won the Scottish Cup.'

Stein's first conjuring trick produced Celtic's first trophy for eight years. Three special goals in the Scottish Cup final of 1965, played in front of 108,800 at Hampden, showed that there was a new spirit at Celtic.

Dunfermline took the lead after quarter of an hour but with 31 minutes gone Bertie Auld had the Celts level when he waited for a high ball to drop in front of goal before heading it over the line. In doing so he had risked serious injury from desperate defenders. Auld got Celtic's second equaliser when he fought his way through a crowded penalty area and smacked a Bobby Lennox pass past goalkeeper Herriot.

With the minutes ticking away, it would need a special effort to win the Cup. That piece of inspiration came from a man who would do the same thing on several occasions in the future: Billy McNeill. With nine minutes remaining, the captain, who hadn't scored up to that point in the season, soared then swooped like a majestic bird to head Charlie Gallagher's corner with the perfect combination of force and accuracy. The ball kissed the net and the celebration champagne could be broken open at last. King Billy, in true regal fashion, had launched Celtic's voyage into a new era.

Three goals that signalled the beginning of a brave new world at Parkhead. Bertie Auld (left) heads the first goal against Dunfermline in the 1965 Cup final. The same player (centre) has just sprinted through the Dunfermline defence to knock home the second. And Billy McNeill (right) towers above Bobby Lennox and the Dunfermline backs to head the winning goal that gave Celtic their first trophy for eight years.

In the 1960s and 1970s, Celtic scaled heights of performance which few British teams have equalled. They played a brand of positive, attacking football that took Europe by storm.

6 European Adventures

Ten years after Billy McNeill scored the winning goal against Dunfermline in the 1965 Cup final he was to make his final bow as a Celtic player, chaired round Hampden Park on the shoulders of his team-mates after another Scottish Cup win, over Airdrie. In the decade between those two games, McNeill had captained Celtic to the greatest series of successes ever strung together by a Scottish football club.

They had become the first side from Northern Europe to win the European Cup and the first to do so with a team composed entirely of players from the country they represented. They had reached a second European Cup final and had come agonisingly close to a further two. They had won their domestic title a world record nine times in succession, as well as capturing a plethora of other prizes. They were Britain's best and one of the most exciting sides that Europe has ever seen.

Jock Stein's teams allied sophistication with strength, subtlety with explosiveness and graft with glamour. They could match the toughest for toughness but the dominating element in their play was a passionate need to provide captivating moments of attacking football, moments that combined speed and precision in their execution.

In almost every game they played they produced cameos that their supporters could take away with them and carry in their memories as souvenirs of Celtic's excellence. And it was through that irresistible zest for the good things in the game that they would most often overwhelm opponents.

Before they could embark on their exotic European jaunts, they had to clean up at home and, in Jock Stein's first full season in

charge at Celtic, Rangers found their dreams of dominance gradually disappearing into a vacuum. In Stein's first Old Firm League game as Celtic's manager an injury to Billy McNeill badly handicapped Celtic in the second half at Ibrox. They subsequently put Rangers' defence under severe pressure but couldn't add to John Hughes' 18th minute penalty, losing 2-1.

Five weeks later, Glasgow's big two met again, in the final of the League Cup at Hampden Park, with 107,600 intrigued onlookers who were keen to know just how far Stein's new broom was going to sweep. Celtic had got there on a first-class ticket, carefully negotiating a difficult section that pitted them against the two Dundee sides and Motherwell and following that up with a 12-1 aggregate win over Raith Rovers in the quarter-final and a 4-0 victory in their semi-final replay against Hibs at Ibrox.

They had also been running on a full tank in the League. After their defeat at Ibrox on 18 September they had clocked up 16 goals in three League wins, including a 7-1 rout of Aberdeen. The League Cup final was to produce another victory. Celtic's first goal came courtesy of an 18th minute John Hughes penalty after McKinnon had jumped like a basketball player to handle the ball. Ten minutes later, Jimmy Johnstone was tripped inside the box by Rangers' left-back Provan, a player Jinky would torment time and time again over the next few years. Yogi Bear scored his second penalty.

'I always put my penalties in the same place, to the goalkeeper's right,' he says. 'But Greig spoke to Ritchie before the first penalty, I could see him speaking to him, so I changed it. It wasn't a particularly good

The sweetest moment in Celtic's history. Stevie Chalmers scores the winning goal in the 2-1 European Cup final victory over Inter Milan.

penalty – it wasn't in the corner, it was about two feet from the corner, and Ritchie half got to it– but it went in and that made it a good one. The second one I hit where I normally put them and he got his hand to it but he didn't stop it. I'm proud of scoring those goals because you're under a lot of pressure taking a penalty, especially against the Rangers. I was quite chuffed with myself after that.'

Rangers are humbled

By the end of 1965, the Old Firm shared the lead at the top of the Scottish First Division, level on points. On 3 January 1966, Celtic lost a goal to Rangers after just 90 seconds. After 90 minutes they had compensated for that loss with five goals of their own, a fair indication of how things would balance out in Celtic's favour during the following decade.

Stevie Chalmers, an ever-alert individual with the reflexes and speed of a cat, pounced for a hat-trick, exploiting gaps that had been opened up around the Rangers goalmouth by Celtic's ceaseless running and invention. Bobby Murdoch got his weight behind a 30-yard shot and Charlie Gallagher met a Hughes cut-back on the edge of the area to crash one in off the underside of the bar.

The Championship was far from over. During the next two months Celtic lost at Aberdeen, Stirling Albion and at Hearts, a game in which Celtic were handicapped from the start: they had arrived home late the previous evening after severe flight delays on the long and winding return trip from playing Dynamo Kiev, in Tbilisi, in the European

Cup-Winners' Cup. Celtic had fallen victim to a lethal combination of Soviet bureacracy and bad weather during their flights in and out of the Soviet Union, and after flying back to Glasgow via Stockholm they rushed to Parkhead for an 11pm seven-a-side loosening-up match, watched by a welcoming party of 500 fans who cheered their every move. Celtic had been representing Scotland in Europe; the Scottish League still insisted that they play their League match, regardless of their two days of travel.

But those defeats were the final slip-ups in a season that ended with Celtic clinching their first Championship for 12 years with a 1-0 victory at Motherwell on the final day, Bobby Lennox sidefooting the ball over the line from a Jim Craig cut-back in the 89th minute of the match.

The Scottish Cup final was an anti-climax. In the first game, a Billy McNeill header came crashing off the bar as the sides battled to a 0-0 draw. Celtic outplayed Rangers in the replay but failed to convert the credit with which they ended the game into the hard currency of goals and lost the trophy to a Johansen strike.

In the Cup-Winners' Cup they had brushed off the challenge of the Dutch side Go Ahead Deventer in the first round, winning 6-0 in Holland and 1-0 at Parkhead and had followed that up with a similarly uncomplicated 3-0 aggregate win over Aarhus of Denmark.

The quarter-final looked to have thrown up a more difficult proposition, Dynamo Kiev, making history that season as the first representatives of the Soviet Union to play in European competition. Stein rated them so highly that he believed that if Celtic won the tie they would win the European Cup-Winners' Cup.

In front of 64,000 at Parkhead Celtic gave themselves a strong power base for the second leg with a 3-0 victory. Bobby Murdoch, on whose broad shoulders Stein was placing more and more responsibility, controlled the game in midfield and scored two second-half goals: the first an unstoppable shot, the second a more straightforward affair after Jimmy Johnstone had given him the ball in front of goal. Tommy Gemmell had opened the scoring with one of his specialities – a

Tommy Gemmell restrains one of the Rangers supporters who invaded the field at the end of the 1965 League Cup final. Celtic had been parading the trophy in front of their fans. Laps of honour were subsequently banned.

Joe McBride was Jock Stein's first signing for Celtic for a fee of £22,500 from Motherwell in June 1965. Stein's judgement was to be completely vindicated as the forward went on to become Scotland's top scorer for the 1965-66 season with 43 goals.

long-range drive. In the second leg, in Tbilisi because Kiev was unplayable in January, right-back Jim Craig was sent off along with Kiev left-winger Khmelnitsky as the tie turned nasty. But Celtic fought their corner for a 1-1 draw and a place in the semi, left-back Gemmell planting another long-range shot past goalkeeper Bannikov after a cut-back from Hughes had set him up nicely. There was a pronounced difference between this game and the MTK semi-final two years previously, Celtic using disciplined defence to keep the Kiev tie under control.

English Cup-winners Liverpool, managed by Stein's friend Bill Shankly and with the Scottish internationals Tommy Lawrence, Ian St John and Ron Yeats in their side, were the visitors to Parkhead for the semi. It was a clash of the champions-elect in England and

Scotland and 80,000 packed Parkhead for an absorbing match in which Celtic electrified the crowd with their incessant attacking. Six minutes after half-time, Bobby Murdoch was first to a loose ball on the right wing, glided to the goal-line and sent a dangerous cross into the six-yard box. Centre-forward Stevie Chalmers got a touch to it, as did goalkeeper Lawrence, before Bobby Lennox, lean and quick, darted in between three Liverpool defenders to whip the ball into the net. A flurry of further goals looked to be on the cards for Celtic but they didn't materialise.

Stein said afterwards: 'It was suggested that we weren't good enough to be in the same tournament as Liverpool. This result has proved we are.' Referee Rudi Gloeckner of East Germany said: 'It was a very sporting game. Celtic had the chances to win. I thought they played very well and their fans were the best I have ever come across.'

Two Liverpool goals midway through the second half in the return at Anfield put the Celts on the back foot but McNeill, Clark and Simpson were outstanding in defence. Near the end, Lennox appeared to have won the tie for Celtic. He had the ball in the net but he was given offside. Stein was furious: 'It wasn't Liverpool who beat us. It was the referee. Bobby Lennox was onside. It was a perfectly good goal.' Robert Kelly added: 'It was a very, very bad decision.' Referee Josef Hannet of Belgium refused to comment, citing his poor command of English; a strange choice of official for UEFA to have in charge of a match involving two English-speaking sides.

'There was no way Bobby's goal was offside,' says Tommy Gemmell. 'If that goal had stood we would have been into a European final in Jock Stein's first full season. We should have buried them at Celtic Park. We played very well there apart from putting the ball in the pokey hat. The actual final was played at Hampden Park so that would have suited us fine.'

A successful start to the Jock Stein era

Stein had expertly steered Celtic through a busy season that saw them reaching the latter stages of all four of the major competitions in which they were involved, winning two trophies and getting within touching distance of the other two.

'He was terrific at getting people to play in the position he thought they were best suited for and to do it at 100% of their ability for themselves, for Jock Stein and for the support,' says John Divers, who observed Stein work his transformation of Celtic at close-quarters during that season.

'People had specific roles. He would say, "You have a role and it might not be appreciated by the supporters on the terracing but it's what I want you to do and if you do it the way I want you to do it that's fine."

'He would tell people to do things which would not be glamorous but if someone did that type of job properly he would make a point of congratulating them after the game. They might get four out of ten in the newspaper but they'd have done what big Jock had wanted them to do.'

'He made the thing professional and he made you feel good. He just changed the whole thing,' says John Hughes. 'He had been to Italy to observe Helenio Herrera and he was the first man to introduce tactics such as 4-2-4, 4-3-3, that kind of thing.'

One of the greatest beneficiaries of Stein's arrival was Jimmy Johnstone, who was now being given free rein to practise his skills in training. Stein encouraged camaraderie and loved games of one-touch and two-touch football but he was also happy to let players practise on their own or in pairs.

'We worked with the ball all the time,' says Johnstone. 'Big Jock was a great believer in that. As soon as the training started, the first day, all the balls were out. That is the secret: work with the ball all the time. Maybe seven or eight exercises with it, volleying it from both sides, crossing it, heading it… My main thing, I used to do it for ages and ages, was just to run with the ball. The way I'd discipline myself was by putting myself in a match situation, imagining there was somebody chasing me and I was trying to shake them off and that there was somebody in front of me and I was trying to go by them. You knew when you'd done it properly; you'd get the right feeling. But if you didn't you'd go back and do it again and again.'

'I was told by the management people before Jock Stein came that if I crossed the halfway line I wouldn't be in the team,' says Tommy Gemmell. 'I'd heard that Jock liked attacking full-backs so when he came I thought, "This is going to suit me." When he arrived at first I went crazy and did too

Bobby Lennox makes it 3-1 in Celtic's second round European Cup tie against Nantes at Parkhead on 7 December 1966. Lennox, Celtic's top scorer since World War II, scored a host of great goals from inside the six-yard box, sometimes creating the chance himself, sometimes snapping on to the ball after a fumble from the goalkeeper or a rebound from the woodwork, sometimes connecting with a cross after arriving late at the near post.

much attacking and not enough defending and he gave me a wee fright in the early weeks and left me out of a couple of games. There was plenty of ability there but we needed somebody to give us guidance and he was that somebody. His leadership welded us into a team.

'Various players were good at different things. Bobby Murdoch and Bertie Auld, for example, were good at getting the ball and knocking it around and passing well. Wee Jinky, of course, was good at taking players on and opening up defences. We had myself and Jim Craig overlapping and Big Yogi rumbling them up up front. Big Billy was brilliant in the air, wee Bobby Lennox and Steve Chalmers had great pace up front.

'Everybody was asked to do what they were good at and when you get the chance to express yourself the best comes out in you. We were also very friendly off the park as well as on the park and that makes a big difference. When you're all pulling together it's like having an extra man.'

Stein could also be ruthless if he thought it was required. One talented individual, highly rated by the manager, was being paid first-team money in the reserve team. The player in question, believing Stein wasn't at one particular reserve match, as he hadn't travelled

on the team bus, decided that the game wasn't worth the effort. At the interval Stein turned up in the dressing room and inquired as to whether the individual concerned had an injury. When the answer was no, Stein said: 'Go out and enjoy yourself. This'll be the last time you'll wear a Celtic jersey.'

A productive tour

After winning the League, Celtic went on a close-season tour to Bermuda, the USA and Canada. They were away from home for five weeks and played 11 games. They defeated Tottenham Hotspur twice and drew with them once, drew with Bologna and Bayern Munich, defeated Atlas of Mexico and thumped various local selects.

Stein tried out various things, including moving Bertie Auld, who had been playing as a left-winger, into midfield. During the previous season he had successfully converted John Hughes from a centre-forward into a left-winger, believing, correctly, that the extra space on the flank would give the powerfully-built Hughes more room to turn in.

'Being away for five weeks we were living out of each other's suitcases so we got to know each other very, very well and that increased the team spirit,' says Tommy

Billy McNeill (second right) watches his last-minute header sail into the net against Vojvodina, a goal that put Celtic into the European Cup semi-final in the most dramatic style imaginable. McNeill was a magnificent athlete, unbeatable in the air, and an individual of stature. As club captain he was greatly relied on by Jock Stein.

Gemmell. 'We had all been born within 30 miles of Glasgow so we all had the same sense of humour and we were always creating laughs and doing wind-ups on each other. Jock was trying to make us one big family and he succeeded. We were also hungry for success. We'd never had success so we wanted to win things. And once you start winning things it becomes a habit and you don't want to stop winning.'

Over the following seasons, winning was to become not so much a habit as a way of life.

The challenge of Europe

After capturing the 1965-66 Championship, Jock Stein had told Ken Gallacher of the *Daily Record*: 'It is up to us, to everyone at Celtic Park now, to build up our own legends. We don't want to live with history, to be compared with legends from the past. We must make new legends and our League Championship win is the first step towards doing that. The greatness of a club in modern football will be judged on performances in Europe. It is only in the major European tournaments that you can really get a chance to rate yourself alongside the great teams.'

Celtic's first European Cup tie took place at Parkhead on 28 September 1966. Their opponents were FC Zurich and the 50,000 who turned up saw Tommy Gemmell become the first Celtic player to score in the European Cup. Fists had flown at several stages and the Celtic players in general, and Jimmy Johnstone in particular, were frequently hacked down on an evening that was frustrating until the extra dimension that Gemmell gave Celtic was fully exploited. Hovering 40 yards out, he took a John Clark pass in his stride and walloped the ball past Zurich goalkeeper Iten.

Five minutes on, in the 69th minute, Joe McBride, who had missed chances earlier in the game, added the second. A week later, on the eve of Stein's 44th birthday, Celtic completed the job. The Swiss had to come out and open things up if they were to get anything out of the tie and their attempts at expansiveness gave Celtic the room in which to play. After 22 minutes Gemmell, from the left wing, scored an identical goal to the one at Parkhead. Chalmers made it 2-0 shortly before half-time and Gemmell completed the formalities with a penalty. 'We won easily,' said Stein, 'because we were allowed to play football tonight.'

The following Saturday, in front of 43,000 at Easter Road, Celtic's slick play overpowered Hibs in a League match and the Glasgow Bhoys ran out 5-3 winners with McBride scoring

Willie Wallace makes it 2-0 for Celtic in the 1967 Scottish Cup final. A goal from Wispy either side of half-time gave Celtic a 2-0 victory over Aberdeen. Both goals came from similar moves. Johnstone for the first and Lennox for the second, reached the goal-line and turned the Dons' defence with speedy cut-backs that Wallace met first-time.

Jimmy Johnstone (left) watches as Bobby Lennox's shot is deflected on to Rangers goalkeeper Martin's left-hand post. Jinky was on to the rebound in a flash for the opening goal in a 2-2 draw at Ibrox on 6 May 1967 that brought the Championship to Parkhead. Inter Milan manager Helenio Herrera was among the 78,000 looking on as Johnstone got both goals, the second a 20-yarder that found the top corner of Martin's net.

four times. It would be Hogmanay before they would suffer their first defeat of any description that season, 3-2 to Dundee United in a League match at Tannadice. In terms of movement, thinking, anticipation, imagination and technique, Celtic were light years ahead of any team in Scotland.

Another Old Firm victory

At the end of October, they had successfully defended the League Cup in a tremendous Old Firm game watched by 94,532. There was only one goal, but it was one to savour. Auld's clever lob to the the right-hand side of the penalty area was reverse-headed by McBride and Lennox, arriving with the speed of a hare, steadied himself to drive the ball, on the run, past Martin before the goalkeeper could blink. Celtic had amassed a total of 35 goals in their ten ties.

Before Celtic discovered the identity of their next opponents in the European Cup, Stein said: 'I'm not boasting but I have no fear of the draw. It doesn't really matter who we get. We must be just as good as anyone. I feel we can beat the big shots.' The draw produced an uncomplicated trip to France to play Nantes, a challenging game but not one to overawe anyone at Celtic Park. Celtic flew into the French industrial port to find the

locals and their sporting press writing off their own side's chances and raving about Joe McBride's scoring exploits.

The first leg took place on St Andrew's Day and gave Scotland reason to have pride in their European Cup representatives. Nantes opened the scoring in the 14th minute through Magny but Celtic remained confident and competent. Ten minutes later, Lennox set up McBride. He showed that the stories that had been reaching France about him hadn't been exaggerated by equalising with a powerful shot.

Auld was catching the eye in midfield with his smooth style but it was an inch-perfect pass from Bobby Murdoch that put Lennox in for the second. He shook off two defenders before sending a close-range shot past Castel. It was a sporting encounter, with the French doing their best to make a game of it, but a blunder by their centre-half Budzinski gave Stevie Chalmers a tap-in and Celtic what looked to be an unassailable lead.

The day before the return at Celtic Park, Jock Stein signed Willie Wallace from Hearts for £30,000. Future events would make this move look as though Stein had second sight. The following evening, a run and shot from Johnstone, a header from Chalmers and Lennox's close-range shot from a Johnstone cross gave Celtic a 3-1 victory over Nantes and a place in the European Cup quarter-final.

The town of Novi Sad, just north of Belgrade, was Celtic's next stop in the European Cup. There, on 1 March, they faced Vojvodina, the Yugoslavian champions, and a challenge that was a couple of grades higher than those Celtic had faced up until then in the tournament. A slip by Tommy Gemmell, followed immediately by another one by sweeper John Clark let Stanic in for the only goal of the game in the 69th minute of a tight match. 'We shouldn't have lost,' said Stein. 'but we know we're a better team than Vojvodina and there's no reason why we shouldn't win next week.'

Over two months earlier, Celtic had been severely handicapped for the quarter-final. Joe McBride's knee had given way in a match at Aberdeen on Christmas Eve and that cartilage injury would keep him out of action for the remainder of the season. McBride was strong, able to withstand the sternest challenge, unbeatable in the air, clever at laying the ball off: the perfect all-round penalty-area goalscorer.

He had been top scorer in the Scottish First Division at the time of his injury, with a haul of 35 goals just halfway through the season, and he remained so despite not playing another game. Although he eventually recovered from his injury, McBride was never again central to Stein's plans and was transferred to Hibs in 1968.

Willie Wallace, who had been signed to add more all-round firepower to the Celtic forward line, became a more than suitable replacement for McBride but he was ineligible for the Vojvodina tie. Speedier than McBride, although not as prolific a scorer, Wallace was a similar type of player, the fly in the ointment for defences everywhere.

Vojvodina took charge in the first half at Parkhead, expertly slowing the game down, eluding Celtic with their crisp, accurate passing and coming close to scoring with a couple of crisp breakaway moves. For the second half, John Hughes was switched to the right wing, where he perfectly complemented Jimmy Johnstone, and the little and large double act began to pick away at the Vojvodina defence.

With almost an hour gone, goalkeeper Pantelic fumbled Tommy Gemmell's cross and Stevie Chalmers nipped in for the equaliser. Celtic proceeded to throw their entire collective weight behind the search for the winner but Vojvodina refused to crumble under the resultant pressure. Corner after corner sailed into their penalty area but everything was dealt with

Tommy Gemmell's shot from just outside the penalty area flies past Inter Milan goalkeeper Giuliano Sarti for the equaliser in the 1967 European Cup final. The Italians were a well-drilled defensive side but Celtic had too much guile for them.

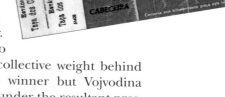

Despair sets in among the Inter players after Gemmell's goal. Goalkeeper Giuliano Sarti was the Italians' star that day, with a series of fine saves. He made such an impression on the Celtic players that in later years he would be their guest in Glasgow for functions to commemorate their 1967 European Cup win.

steadily by the resilient Yugoslavs. In the final minute, with a play-off at a neutral venue looming, Celtic were awarded another corner. Inside-forward Gallagher appeared ready to play the ball short but left-back Radovic raced out to cut off that option. Instead, Gallagher sent the ball sailing high into the night air and Billy McNeill made 75,000 Celtic fans go crazy with delight as another of his majestic headers hit the net. Celtic were in a European Cup semi-final.

'We thought Vojvodina were the best side we played in the European Cup that year,' remembers Tommy Gemmell. 'They had class. Every one of their players looked comfortable on the ball, they held possession well and they showed a lot of good teamwork. They gave us our hardest two matches in all my years in Europe.'

The semi-final paired Celtic with Dukla Prague, the Czechoslovakian army side. The first leg, at Parkhead, was unusual in that the away team were prepared to take the game to Celtic almost as much as Celtic took the game to them. The Scots quickly got to grips with the situation and took the lead in the 27th minute. Bertie Auld won a challenge in midfield, advanced and sent the ball round another defender and on to Willie Wallace; his shot was blocked and the ball went spinning into a gap in the penalty area. Jimmy Johnstone quickly assessed the run of the ball, chested it down and expertly timed a volley that left goalkeeper Viktor clawing the air as the winger hurdled him.

A minute from half-time, however, Dukla, playing attractive, studied football, equalised through Strunc after the Celtic defence had got themselves into a tangle on the edge of their own area.

Wallace's well-timed intervention

The Czechs were of a similar calibre to Vojvodina and were only 45 minutes away from a result that would leave them in control for the second leg. But a couple of inspired moments from Willie Wallace, who was making his European debut for Celtic, were to move the Parkhead side closer to the final in Lisbon. In the 59th minute a high, looping ball delivered from Gemmell on the halfway line caught the Dukla defence on the turn and Wallace stole in to prod a first-time, right-footed volley past Viktor from the edge of the six-yard box.

Six minutes later, Dukla gave away a free-kick close to their penalty area and directly in front of goal. Bertie Auld, crafty as ever, made to take it but then stopped as if to steady the ball. The defensive wall waited for him to step back for a run at the ball but he surprised them by tapping it sideways to Wallace whose 20-yard shot left Viktor in its slipstream.

Just as the first leg had been unusual in that Dukla had opted to attack in Glasgow, so the return in Prague saw a departure from tradition with Celtic adopting a thoroughly negative approach and packing their own penalty area. Dukla had a succession of half-chances and the Celtic players knew that all it needed was for the Czechoslovakians to pop one away and they would have hit Celtic like a ton of bricks. Celtic used delaying tactics and were willing to hold on to possession in harmless areas of the field with little intention of making scoring opportunities.

A hard lesson for Celtic in Czechoslovakia

Dukla had several players coming to the end of their careers, such as the brilliant midfielder and former European Footballer of the Year Josef Masopust, then 36, and in the last half hour these players tired. 'As soon as we snuffed him out it snuffed them out,' says Tommy Gemmell. 'It was a nerve-racking game.' There was a collective feeling afterwards among the Celtic party, including Jock Stein, that playing in that fashion had been entirely unsuited to Celtic. And although Celtic played in a calculated way in future European ties, they never again played in such a stultifying fashion.

But it had done the trick. Celtic were in the European Cup final where they would face the mighty Inter Milan, twice winners of the trophy and world club champions in 1964 and 1965. Tickets were available from the SFA with the highest price being two pounds, seven shillings and sixpence and the lowest ten shillings.

In between the European Cup semi and the final, Celtic tied up the Scottish Cup and the Championship, playing within themselves in defeating Aberdeen 2-0 in front of 126,102 in the Hampden final on 29 April. The following Wednesday, Dundee United, the only Scottish club to beat Celtic all season, won the League game at Parkhead 3-2 but at Ibrox three days later a 2-2 draw gave Celtic the title.

A week before the European Cup final, at the Cafe Royal in London, Jock Stein was named Britain's Manager of the Year for the second successive year. The Monday before the game, after a weekend with their families, Celtic trained at Parkhead. The previous week had been spent at Seamill, and Stein had kept his squad fresh with a combination of hard work and relaxation. On the Tuesday they flew to Lisbon, where Celtic fans were already teaching the Latins a few lessons in how to create a carnival atmosphere.

There were 12,000 Celtic supporters in the National Stadium, the most romantic setting

there has ever been for a European Cup final. Situated in woods six miles to the west of Lisbon, one side of the stadium was tree-lined, with a trim hedge on either side of a tiny grandstand. The opposite side of the ground was crowned by a stylish row of columns rising up from a marble rostrum where the winning captain would receive the trophy. Celtic would do the setting justice.

The match kicked off on Thursday 25 May at 5.30pm in front of a full house of 56,000. A running track and an eight feet deep moat were situated between the pitch and the spectators. The team that took the field that day can now be recited like a mantra by Celtic supporters: Simpson, Craig, Gemmell, Murdoch, McNeill, Clark, Johnstone, Wallace, Chalmers, Auld and Lennox.

After seven minutes, Craig challenged Inter's Cappellini, who was veering away from goal, just inside the penalty area. The Italian went down and referee Kurt Tschenscher of West Germany pointed to the penalty spot. Sandro Mazzola sent Ronnie Simpson the wrong way with his spot-kick.

'It suited us ideally them getting the penalty kick so early in the game,' says Gemmell, 'because at that time the Italians' motto was, "If you score get everybody back." Inter were a tremendous side, they just oozed class, but they played like we tried to play in the second match against Dukla and there wasn't a side in the world could afford to give us as much of the ball as they did without

The experienced Ronnie Simpson (above) in the Celtic goal exerted a commanding presence in the European Cup final. Here Billy McNeill and Jim Craig watch him smother a rare Inter attack. Simpson, 36 at the time of the final, was considerably older than the other players and was nicknamed "Faither". As a youngster, he had played in the 1952 and 1955 FA Cup finals for Newcastle United.

Billy McNeill (opposite) receives the European Cup from the president of Portugal. McNeill had to battle through crowds on and around the pitch to receive the trophy.

being beaten. Because if you take out Ronnie Simpson and John Clark, every other player was a potential goalscorer.

'We had nine potential goalscorers and they gave us the ball.'

Stein's men fulfil their manager's promise

Stein had promised that Celtic would attack with passion. Any Inter players who believed that this was the usual pre-European tie bluff must have been severely shocked as the Celts came at them time and time again. Like a swarm of green-and-white wasps they buzzed ceaselessly around the Inter penalty area, stinging the Italian defence with venom, kept at bay only by a stunning display of goalkeeping by Giuliano Sarti.

Jimmy Johnstone remembers: 'After the first 20 minutes I was thinking, "Are these guys kidding us on? When are they going to start to play? Because we were running them ragged. We could have beaten them 10-0. Sarti had a game that was unbelievable. At half-time we knew we could win, even though we were down 1-0, because of the amount of chances we had made.

'Another thing was the temperature – we'd never played in that in our lives and these guys were used to it. It was about 75 degrees; it would have burned a hole in your head. We felt the heat but it didn't affect us. I think we were all so carried away that it didn't matter about the heat or anything. The crowd was behind us as well and everybody was motivated. It was a great occasion.'

Celtic themselves had two serious penalty claims turned down but in the 63rd minute Tommy Gemmell, on the edge of the 18-yard box, cottoned on to a Jim Craig cut-back and the ball went thundering past Sarti. It was one of the most spectacular and best-deserved goals in all European Cup finals.

'I should actually have had my behind kicked,' says Gemmell, 'because I shouldn't have been there in the first place. The golden rule was that if one full-back was up the other one should be round covering central defence and it was Jim Craig who cut the ball back for me. But there was no need because they only had one player in our half, as against our two defenders. If they'd had two, I would have had to have stayed back.

'If you look at the game on film you'll see there's an Italian defender comes out to attack the ball as Jim Craig squares it to me

A tearful Bobby Murdoch (second left) is congratulated by Celtic fans and physiotherapist Bob Rooney (third left) on the pitch at the end of the European Cup final. One of Jock Stein's initial decisions as Celtic manager was to switch Murdoch from the forward line to midfield. Murdoch's perceptive passing and strong tackling were vital to most of Celtic's successes during the Stein era.

but he stops and half turns two yards from me. If that guy had taken one more pace he could have changed the whole course of Celtic's history. They could have broken away and scored a goal and I would have been castigated because there was no way I should have been there in the first place. Sometimes rules are made to be broken.'

That was a symbolic moment. The player who had been attempting to block the shot had been the Inter captain Armando Picchi. As the sweeper of the side he had been the cornerstone of Herrera's employment of *catenaccio*, the stifling defensive system perfected in Italy that had been squeezing the life out of the European game during the years prior to the 1967 final. Gemmell's shot left Picchi flailing in its wake. A new order in European football was established at that very moment.

'The big problem was getting the breakthrough,' adds Gemmell. 'As soon as I scored that goal the Italian players' heads went down. They didn't want to know after that. They knew the writing was on the wall.'

Celtic continued to press and with five minutes left Stevie Chalmers, positioned in front of the Inter goal, diverted a Bobby Murdoch daisy-cutter past Sarti. 'I made a run down the left-hand side,' says Gemmell. 'Bertie knocked it out to me. A defender came to me and then another defender went

behind him. I just did the wee Ali-shuffle and knocked it back to Bobby Murdoch who had a shot at goal, which was going past, and Stevie slid it into the net.

'That wasn't an accident. We did exactly the same thing in training every day of the week: players going down either side, cutting it back to midfield players supporting front players, hitting it and the front players always trying to deflect it. It was no fluke; even if Bobby's shot had been going in Stevie would still have deflected it.'

Gemmell had twice crossed the half way line to triumphant effect: there was no way back for Inter.

Stein said: 'We won and we won on merit. This win gives us more satisfaction than anything. I can still hardly believe that it's true. To say I am proud of them is a complete understatement of the case.'

Helenio Herrera was gracious in defeat: 'We can have no complaints. Celtic deserved their victory. We were beaten by Celtic's force. Although we lost, the match was a victory for sport.' The match in Lisbon remains one of the most memorable in the history of the European Cup.

There were an estimated 40,000 at Parkhead the following evening as a lorry, with green and white trimmings, carried the Celtic squad round the running track to

Another big game and another vital goal from Billy McNeill. His header arcs over the Racing Club goalkeeper Cejas and central defender Martin for the only goal of the World Club Championship first leg between Celtic and the South American champions.

display the European Cup to the supporters. It had been the greatest single triumph ever attained by a British club.

In Lisbon, Celtic leapt from being a great Scottish club to being a great European club. The manner of their victory, through spirited, all-out attacking football, was also important. It endeared them to football fans across Europe and beyond. Celtic's wonderful football that day places them among the cream of the 20 clubs who have been European champions, those sides who have won their finals in the style that Real Madrid established as the benchmark for the European Cup in its earliest days.

Celtic had never been just another club; now the continent of Europe had become fully aware of that fact.

A bracing start to the season

Few events concentrate the Glaswegian mind more than an Old Firm clash so there was little chance of a feeling of anti-climax setting in at the beginning of the 1967-68 season. Celtic had not one but two encounters with Rangers to deal with that August in a difficult League Cup section that also featured Aberdeen and Dundee United.

A total of 330,000 people watched Celtic's six sectional games in which they won home and away against the north-eastern teams and

drew the first game with Rangers, 1-1 at Ibrox. The return at Parkhead was a thriller. Rangers took the lead through Henderson only for Celtic to recover in the final 12 minutes through close-range efforts from Wallace and Lennox and a Bobby Murdoch 20-yard special.

The defence of the European Cup saw Celtic paired with Dynamo Kiev. The first leg at Parkhead drew a 54,000 crowd who saw a shambolic performance from the European champions as they stuttered to a 2-1 defeat with Bobby Lennox getting Celtic's counter.

Things worsened in Kiev. Bobby Murdoch was sent off in the 57th minute after throwing the ball in disgust at a foul that was awarded against Jim Craig. Murdoch had earlier been booked for dissent and he was in tears as he made his way to the dressing-room, his jersey covering his head.

But three minutes later the 85,000 Ukrainians present were stunned when a battling Celtic side levelled the overall score in the tie. Kiev goalkeeper Zanokov was penalised for taking too many steps with the ball and Bertie Auld's free-kick was slipped into the net by Lennox. Celtic had a John Hughes goal ruled out but with a minute left Kiev took the tie with a goal from Byshovets.

Disgust at the Argentinians' antics is written all over the faces of the Celtic players during the World Club Championship first leg against Racing Club in Glasgow. The previous year England manager Alf Ramsey had described the Argentinian team as 'animals' during the 1966 World Cup. That created simmering resentment in Argentina and was very much in the Argentinians' minds as they visited Britain for the game with Celtic.

'Between the final and the first round the following season we started to realise, "Hey, we're the champions of Europe!"' says Jimmy Johnstone. 'And we were given huge respect because of it; we had people coming from all over the world wanting to know about our players. We got all this adulation and it hit us. Losing to Kiev was a wee bit of a let-down but afterwards we picked ourselves up and thought, "Come on, it doesn't go on forever. Let's get back to the basics again." That's when we became a good team again. Maybe getting knocked out at that stage did us the world of good.'

Rather than dwelling on the Kiev defeat, Jock Stein preferred to look forward to the next big challenge, the two-legged match for the World Club Championship with the South American champions Racing Club of Argentina. 'I know the boys can rise to it. They're disappointed about the match with Kiev. But this is something new, something bigger than anything we have been involved in. That's the tonic they need.'

Instead, it was to be a sickener. Before the first leg, in Glasgow on 18 October, the hype was amazing. The game was billed as being bigger and more prestigious than the European Cup final. Prime Minister Harold Wilson was at Hampden and the match was televised live throughout Europe and South America. Celtic were to have tea at half-time while Racing had ordered coffee and Russian tea. On the field, matters were a great deal less civilised. Racing were on a bonus of £1500 a man to win the World Club Championship, the same bonus Celtic had received for winning the European Cup final. But Racing didn't care how they got it.

'The worst thing was they spat on you all the time and they were kicking lumps out of you. We had never experienced anything like that before,' says John Hughes. Celtic still managed to win. As Hughes went to take a corner, Billy McNeill advanced into the Racing penalty area and found himself being pushed and jostled as he waited for the ball to come over. The Celtic captain turned back, appearing to have become disheartened by the Argentinians' tough treatment.

They momentarily ignored him and as Hughes' corner came over McNeill sent a

towering header over the stranded goal-keeper Cejas. It had been a trial of mental strength and Celtic had managed to keep their collective cool in the face of extreme provocation. They knew they would face an even greater ordeal in Buenos Aires.

Back to domestic matters

In the quarter-finals of the League Cup Ayr Utd were beaten on a crushing 8-2 aggregate and in the semi Celtic were in masterful form as they beat Morton 7-1, setting them up for the final with Dundee. A crowd of 66,600 saw an attractive match with both teams playing enterprising football. Two goals from Chalmers, and one each from Hughes, Lennox and Wallace made it 5-3 to Celtic. They then flew out to Buenos Aires for a different sort of game.

When they reached the Argentinian capital, Celtic were given an ecstatic welcome by thousands of fans. An attractive woman greeted Jimmy Johnstone with a kiss and in the build-up to the game Argentinian fans continually offered Jinky sweets, flowers and footballs. The atmosphere inside the Avellaneda stadium was markedly different. There were 1,000 policemen on duty and the pitch was guarded from the fans by a 20 feet deep moat. The worst hooligans, however, were on the pitch, wearing the blue and white striped shirts of Racing.

Stein brought in defender Willie O'Neill for John Hughes. 'We were up in the stands,' says Hughes, 'and they were peeing on us. You would turn round and they'd just be roaring at you. Ronnie Simpson got hit by a missile while he was warming up and we still think it was one of the photographers because behind the goals there was this big wire mesh. For somebody to throw something that distance that would go over the mesh, over the crossbar and just dip to hit Ronnie was almost impossible. So we're pretty sure it was one of the photographers.'

John Fallon came in for Simpson, who was led from the field with a gash in his head that required several stitches. From the kick-off, Celtic sprang into attack. Jimmy Johnstone, who was in the mood to tango, was denied what seemed a clear penalty against him. Then, midway through the first half, Johnstone slalomed through the Racing defence and was brought down by Cejas. This time the referee gave the award.

Celtic had been worried that if they scored early on it would provoke the Argentinians' fury but Tommy Gemmell showed no fear of the consequences as he lashed the ball straight into the middle of the goal. Ten minutes later Racing equalised with a header from Raffo and four minutes after half-time Cardenas levelled the aggregate. Johnstone had had a goal disallowed, for no apparent reason. And in contrast with Glasgow, Celtic

Great excitement was generated by Celtic's European runs. Here fans queue for tickets at Parkhead for the 1969 European Cup quarter-final with AC Milan.

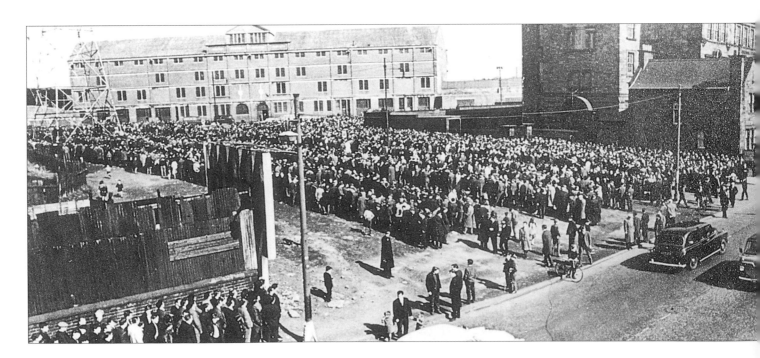

Robert Kelly with Jock Stein. Celtic chairman Kelly was a remote but respected figure.

Stevie Chalmers (below) scores Celtic's fourth goal against Rangers in the 1969 Scottish Cup final with typical style. Chalmers' cool finishing and tireless work were vital components in a variety of Celtic victories.

had reached their dressing-room at half-time to find the water supply had been cut off.

A play-off was scheduled for three days later, 4 November, in Montevideo. Stein said: 'The way I feel right now, I want to take the players right back to Scotland and not go to Uruguay. What a disgusting way to treat a player before the ball was even kicked.' Racing officials had shown little sympathy for Simpson's plight before, during or after the match. Robert Kelly was also contemplating walking out in disgust at Racing's 'controlled ruthlessness' but the SFA secretary Willie Allen intervened to persuade the club's officials to go through with the game. UEFA and FIFA took no action.

Celtic's patience had been tested to the limit and before the play-off Jock Stein said: 'The time for politeness is over. We can be hard if necessary and we will not stand the shocking conduct of Racing.'

Near the end of the first half, Rulli chopped Johnstone down and was sent off. As Racing began a brawl, Paraguayan referee Rodolfo Osorio called for the police. After a semblance of order had been restored, the referee sent off Basile and the innocent Lennox in a case of mistaken identity. Osorio had clearly lost control.

Jimmy Johnstone was sent off after retaliating against the umpteenth foul on him – a neck-high tackle – and John Hughes was sent off for kicking Cejas. With a minute remaining, Auld was ordered to leave the field after

taking a pop at Raffo but Bertie capped the farce by refusing to leave the pitch. In the midst of the anarchy, Cardenas had scored the only goal of the game shortly after half-time to give Racing a tarnished World Club Championship.

'We were unfortunate to lose the third game,' says John Hughes. 'The crazy thing about these guys was that they could play a bit too! In the third game Bobby Murdoch was

running about daft. He was kicking everybody. After that we called him "Chopper". Big Jock used to go crazy about that – "Never mind the Chopper," he'd say.'

Celtic had been the first European victims of Argentinian violence in the World Club Championship, a tournament that would produce similar scenes over the next three years in matches between Argentinian sides and the European champions.

By the 1970s the competition had become thoroughly devalued and it has never fully recovered from the blows inflicted on it by Racing in 1967.

In their second League fixture of the 1967-68 season, at Ibrox, Celtic had lost 1-0 but that was to be their one and only League defeat. They became the first club to win the title three times in a row since 1935, scoring 106 goals and conceding just 24 in the process. It was the best record in the League during Stein's years.

Having established their indisputable right to be at the head of the table in Scotland, Celtic were once again hungry for another slice of action in the European Cup. They warmed up by winning all six games in their 1968 League Cup section, easily defeating Rangers, Partick Thistle and Morton home and away, scoring a total of 20 goals and conceding just two.

The quarter-final brought the Second Division side Hamilton Academicals to Parkhead and Bobby Lennox and Stevie

Chalmers helped themselves to five goals each in a 10-0 win. Stein rested some of his first-team players for the second leg, a game in which a 17 year old named Kenny Dalglish made his debut as a substitute. He impressed immediately, showing some clever touches and linking well with the 19-year-old George Connelly, who had also just broken into the team. Other youngsters giving the select 4,000 crowd a glimpse of the future that night included Lou Macari and David Hay.

Another tough European assignment

In the first round of the European Cup, Celtic faced first-class opposition in French champions St Etienne and returned to Glasgow trailing by 2-0 in the tie. At Parkhead, 75,000 saw how good the French were for themselves and the game was scoreless until shortly before half-time when left-back Camerini challenged McBride inside the penalty area and conceded a spot-kick. 'They were throwing clods of dirt on the ball and all that sort of stuff, you know, delaying tactics, so I went up and I was taking these clods away from the ball and I said to myself, "You've got to score this one,"' says Tommy Gemmell. 'I did and we came out and slaughtered them in the second half.' Celtic, and especially Johnstone, moved into top gear in that second period. Right-back Jim Craig

Bertie Auld, Celtic's meticulous midfield craftsman, sends a superb left-foot shot into the Fiorentina net in the 1970 European Cup quarter-final.

scored his only European goal with a blazing shot after he had been fed by Johnstone. Chalmers and McBride made it 4-0.

St Etienne were a fine side but Celtic had shown they were back to their European best. Their attacking play had been fast, flowing and irresistible. Clyde had been beaten 1-0 in the League Cup semi-final in between the visit of St Etienne and that of Celtic's second round opponents, Red Star Belgrade, a match that was to provide another batch of memorable moments.

Three minutes into the first leg, Bobby Murdoch found Jimmy Johnstone with a free-kick, latched on to the return, and, as he entered the Red Star area, hammered an unstoppable shot past Dujkovic. Lazervic equalised, however, and by half-time Red Star were the superior side. It needed something special to get Celtic going again. Stein, the master psychologist, had already formulated a plan.

'I'd had a fright coming back before the rest of the boys from the American tour in 1966, to get married,' says Jimmy Johnstone. 'The plane fell I don't know how many feet out of the sky. It was horrific. It was just a wee bit of turbulence and all the meals were getting put out by the stewardesses when without warning the whole thing just fell. All the food was suspended in the air and there were children and stewardesses thrown everywhere. You should have seen the mess of the plane after it. I hated flying because of that.

'At half-time in the Red Star game, big Jock said, "If we win by four clear goals you won't need to fly to Belgrade." That was the spark, that was definitely what spurred me. I was everywhere looking for the ball in that second-half. That was great psychology.'

Two minutes into the second half, Johnstone pounced on a loose ball to make it 2-1. From a Johnstone cross, Lennox knocked in the third. Johnstone supplied Wallace with the chance for the fourth. And Johnstone was unstoppable as he snaked through Red Star's defence before firing home a jet-paced shot. It was a brilliant individual performance and it ensured his feet would remain firmly on the ground.

Tommy Gemmell says: 'Wee Jimmy was absolutely magnificent that night. We were four clear goals up and with two or three min-utes to go they had a corner kick on the left-hand side and guess who cleared it with his head, six yards out – wee Jimmy!'

'When we got out to Belgrade they were all looking for him,' says John Hughes. 'They couldn't believe we'd leave someone of his calibre at home. They thought we had him in the hamper.' Celtic coasted to a 1-1 draw.

Stein the motivator

'Big Jock's biggest attribute was man-management,' says Hughes. 'He could drop you, then he'd come and put his arm round you and say, "Come on, big man, I'm playing you tonight, you can do it for me." And you would do it for him.

'I remember I was out injured and we went to play AC Milan in the European Cup at the San Siro. I hadn't played for about six weeks and I needed games. And the day before the game he came and said, "I want you to play tomorrow." I said, "You're joking." But I did and we got the result. He made you feel that you could do it. He would say, "I wouldn't be asking you to do it if I didn't think you could do it." Then all of a sudden you'd think, "I could do this."'

That game, the 1969 European Cup quarter-final, had generated record receipts in Milan of £136,000 from a crowd of 81,000 and Milan were on £1,000 a man to win. The game was played in a snow blizzard but Celtic, now tactically sophisticated in handling European away legs, were surefooted throughout and obtained a 0-0 draw. Ronnie Simpson had dislocated his shoulder in a Cup tie with Clyde a week earlier and his replacement, John Fallon, made a series of fine saves. Hughes went on some spectacular runs and one saw him beat four players only for goalkeeper Cudicini to save. At the back, McNeill was in commanding form.

Throughout the match Celtic had looked comfortable with a combination of a holding game and counter-attacking. The Italian side, featuring world class stars such as Gianni Rivera, Karl-Heinz Schnellinger and Kurt Hamrin, had been outthought and out-fought in midfield. Their manager Nereo Rocco, a master of *catenaccio*, congratulated Stein on his superb tactics.

Celtic were firm favourites for the return and some Celtic fans had already booked charter flights to Madrid for the final itself.

But after 11 minutes Jim Craig's throw-in saw McNeill struggle to control the ball and Pierino Prati whipped it away from him, sped towards Fallon's goal as if drawn there by a magnet and put Milan ahead. It was Milan's only chance but it was the only one they needed. Celtic created a host of scoring opportunities but couldn't put the ball in the net. The only consolation was that if Milan hadn't won the European Cup that year Celtic almost certainly would have.

'That was the hardest game we have ever played in,' said Rivera afterwards, 'and certainly it is the best victory we have ever had. It can only be beaten if we win the final in Madrid.' They would go on to do so, Prati getting a hat-trick in their win over Ajax.

'Everybody loved European nights at Celtic Park,' says Tommy Gemmell. 'Two weeks before the game you couldn't get a ticket. And 15 minutes before kick-off there would be no queues at any turnstiles. We'd go out to loosen up three or four minutes before

we normally would, just to soak up the atmosphere, which was always incredible. And the reception we got when we came out would frighten any side. The Celtic supporters were out of this world; I've still to find supporters to better them. I loved playing at night especially when the ground was dewey and wet. You could fire the ball around and it was great for long-distance shooting: the goalkeeper was always liable to fumble things and inevitably you'd have Bobby Lennox there to tap it into the net.'

Celtic had little time to dwell on the misfortune against Milan. Ten days later they defeated Morton 4-1 in the Scottish Cup semi-final and on 5 April they faced Hibs in the League Cup final, a game postponed from the autumn after a fire at Hampden. Before the match, Stein said: 'This is a very important month for us and the players know it. Within the next four weeks they could lift as many medals as other players take a lifetime to get.'

Bobby Murdoch (the third Celt from left) wheels away as his shot hits the back of the Leeds United net for Celtic's second goal in the 1970 European Cup semi-final at Hampden Park.

Celtic had too many ideas for Hibs to cope with and they strolled to a 6-2 win that featured a Lennox hat-trick and one each from Wallace, Auld and Craig, every goal a gem. They won the title at a canter, finishing up five points clear of second-placed Rangers. But the biggest treat on the domestic front that season came in the Scottish Cup final. All 134,000 tickets had been sold a week in advance of the game and there were some further spectators after just two minutes when Billy McNeill rose unchallenged to meet Bobby Lennox's corner. Five Rangers defenders stood and watched as the ball sailed into the net.

The second arrived a minute before half-time when Lennox ran 30 yards, eluded Mathieson's tackle, and bent the ball round Martin. As Rangers waited for the half-time whistle, George Connelly, making his first appearance in the Scottish Cup, intercepted Greig's pass, dummied Martin with ease and sent the ball into the unguarded goal.

The final goal was a masterpiece in the art of teamwork. Tommy Gemmell, situated on his own goal-line, volleyed the ball forward as far as Bertie Auld who nodded it back to Bobby Murdoch, just outside the Celtic penalty area. Murdoch, with a first-time left-footed pass returned the ball directly into the path of the running Auld who lifted it on to Stevie Chalmers. The swiftness of the move had caught Rangers out and Chalmers had space to run into in the Rangers half. As he entered their penalty area, he made as if to pass but instead flicked the ball neatly and sweetly past Martin.

Rangers, as they had done so often, had tried to pummel Celtic into submission but they had found themselves involuntarily indulging in some shadow boxing. Even the 4-0 scoreline did not do enough to express how far ahead of their rivals Celtic were, even without the suspended Johnstone and the injured Hughes. That year Bobby Murdoch – 'the finest player in Britain' according to Stein – had been named the Scottish Player of the Year. Ronnie Simpson had won the award in 1967 and Billy McNeill in 1965. As the swinging sixties drew to a close there was no sign of Celtic's golden period ending.

It was becoming a pleasing habit for Celtic to begin the season by finishing above Rangers in their League Cup section and the start of the 1969-70 season saw that new tradition maintained. Celtic experienced a couple of tough matches against Aberdeen in the quarter-final but they got through on a 2-1 aggregate and then overcame a spirited Ayr United after a semi-final replay.

The final was another difficult game, against St Johnstone, but in front of 73,067 Celtic held on to the advantage given them by Bertie Auld's second-minute goal for their fifth consecutive League Cup.

An hour before kick-off Stein had sprung a surprise, replacing Tommy Gemmell with David Hay. Gemmell had been sent off the previous midweek playing for Scotland in West Germany and had not been present when the team was announced.

Afterwards, Stein reminded the player of Robert Kelly's strong feelings on discipline but Gemmell, who asked for a transfer after the incident, retorted that if Rangers had been Celtic's opponents that day Stein would have made sure he was in the side. The matter blew over after some months but it was a sign of increased competition for places as a new wave of players jostled in the queue for first-team places.

More European glory

The first round of the European Cup had produced a 2-0 aggregate win over Basle and the second round paired Celtic with Benfica, a team packed with Portuguese internationals including the great Eusebio, who had been one of the outstanding players in the 1966 World Cup. There were 80,000 inside Parkhead to see another inspired Celtic performance. After just two minutes, Bertie Auld tapped a free-kick to Tommy Gemmell and from a distance of 25 yards the full-back launched himself at the ball to send another of his specials roaring past Henrique.

Hughes had a goal disallowed but just before half-time Willie 'Wispy' Wallace went flying down the right flank of the Benfica penalty area. Such was his momentum that he appeared certain to run the ball out of play but he balanced himself for an incredible shot on the run from the tightest of angles and Celtic were two ahead. Midway through the second half, Harry Hood, signed from Clyde the previous season, scored with a header to make it 3-0.

In Lisbon, Fallon made some outstanding saves early on, including one from Eusebio,

Feyenoord goalkeeper Pieters Graafland deals with a Celtic attack in the 1970 European Cup final. It was a sad night for Celtic, who were a pale shadow of themselves in the 2-1 defeat. Tommy Gemmell's goal, however, makes him one of only 10 players to have scored from open play in two European Cup finals. It places Celtic's extraordinary full-back in the company of players such as Alfredo Di Stefano, Ferenc Puskas and Hector Rial of Real Madrid.

who was playing with a heavily strapped thigh, but the striker pulled one back before half-time, and Graca got a second. Celtic held on to their narrow advantage until, several minutes into injury time, Diamentino levelled the aggregate. Extra-time produced no further scoring and in those pre-penalty-shoot-out days Billy McNeill found himself deep in the bowels of the Stadium of Light settling the outcome on the toss of a coin. Dutch referee Louis van Raavens' two-and-a-half guilder piece landed sunny side up as far as Celtic were concerned and they were in the quarter-finals once again.

McNeill said: 'I didn't think we would carry the luck in that toss because it was the second one I had faced. The first time the referee asked us to call to see who would spin the coin. I called heads and won that one. When I spun the coin I couldn't believe that I would win again. But I did and it was the greatest relief of my life.'

The quarter-final with the Italian champions Fiorentina brought the best out in Celtic.

Bertie Auld was immense as Celtic pulled and stretched the Italians all over the field like an expert team of sadistic masseurs. After half an hour, Auld scored one of the classiest goals in all Celtic's European runs. As a Hughes header reached him on the edge of the Fiorentina penalty area he controlled the ball on his left instep and steadied himself carefully. He then waited cheekily for the Italian defenders to come at him before scooping the ball low into the corner of the net. A Carpenetti own-goal and a close-range Wallace header made it 3-0.

'We toyed with them at Celtic Park,' says Tommy Gemmell. 'Bertie, myself and Willie Wallace got the ball halfway in their half when we were 3-0 up and we had about 20 consecutive passes, just knocking it in a triangle. None of the Fiorentina players were coming out to get the ball. Next thing I hear Big Jock screaming in my ear from the Jungle side; he'd come out the dugout and gone right round behind the goals and halfway round the track – and the angrier he got the more his limp was emphasised. He was telling us in the strongest language to get the ball moving. He said, "It's all right for you three, you can knock it around. But what if we get it into our half and someone who can't do that tries it and we lose a stupid goal?" '

Beating the Italians at their own game

In the return Celtic held their lead in a vice-like grip. 'It was one of those games,' says David Hay, 'when you were never under serious pressure of losing the tie on aggregate. We never sat back in defence but we were never as attack-minded as we had been at Celtic Park. We were comfortable with our defending and we had control of the game. There was never any onslaught when we felt that if they scored then we'd really be under pressure.' The Italians won the match 1-0 but Celtic had won the tie. Stein said: 'The team played exactly as I wanted. It was a studied game, a thoughtful game. And we did what we came to Florence to do – we reached the semi-finals. Everyone did their job tonight. I was proud of the entire team.'

Feyenoord of Rotterdam, Leeds Utd and Legia Warsaw were the other semi-finalists. Jock Stein wanted his side to be drawn against Feyenoord in the semi and hoped then to meet Leeds in the final in Milan. Instead, it was Leeds who came out of the hat, a side crammed with English, Scottish, Irish and Welsh internationals, including striker Allan Clarke, who had been Britain's most expensive player, when he was signed from Leicester City for £165,000 in 1969.

'Leeds were being hyped up by the English press to be unbeatable,' says John Hughes. 'There was no messing about with them. It was "Leeds will win 4-0", there was no 1-0: we were turning up just for the sake of making a game of it and Leeds were going to wipe the floor with us. Jock used all that, he came in on the morning of the game, brought the papers in saying, "What about them? Eh? What about them?"'

In the first leg Leeds wore their usual white socks and the Celtic team were informed close to kick-off that they'd have to wear Leeds' change socks – coloured orange. Stein came into the dressing-room and told the players he had never seen the Leeds manager Don Revie looking as nervous before a game as he did that night.

It didn't take long for Celtic to establish a grip on the tie. With less than a minute gone, a probing ball from Bertie Auld had the Leeds defence in a state of confusion and George Connelly's 15-yard shot took a deflection that left Gary Sprake, the Leeds goalkeeper, wrongfooted. It was the end of the scoring that night but Celtic were well on top throughout with Jimmy Johnstone's twisting and turning leaving Leeds' left-back Terry Cooper dizzy.

Leeds were tough and methodical, with the occasional touch of flair, but that would never be enough to beat that particular Celtic team. 'They thought they were invincible,' says Tommy Gemmell. 'And at that time in England they were. We never thought they were invincible. We thought we were invincible. We would have been happy to come away from Elland Road a goal down; coming away a goal up you were doing handstands.'

The second leg, at Hampden, was to make football history, the attendance of 136,505 still a record for a European Cup match. Thousands more were believed to have seen the game by deciding to waive the formalities of the turnstile entrance. Jock Stein's programme notes showed how he felt about the game. 'Tonight San Siro Stadium is our goal – San Siro and a second European Cup victory for tonight the victors must indeed be favourites for that honour.'

Leeds went ahead through their Scottish international midfielder Billy Bremner after 14 minutes when he sent a long-range shot past Celtic goalkeeper Evan Williams, who had been signed from Wolves the previous autumn. But that setback didn't break Celtic's stride for an instant and once again they rolled over the English champions.

Two minutes after half-time David Hay played a short corner to Bertie Auld and his curled cross to the near post was met in exhilarating fashion by the diving John Hughes who had left his marker Jack Charlton for dead. His glancing header gave Sprake no hope of saving.

'I was up against Jack Charlton that day and I had always played well against him in various games down the years. So Jock played me at centre,' says Hughes.

Sprake then went over on his ankle and was replaced by substitute goalkeeper Harvey whose first touch was to help the ball into his own net. A swift Celtic move swept the length of the field to Johnstone and his cutback was met by Bobby Murdoch for a goal that established beyond all reasonable doubt that Celtic were the finest team in Britain. 'We played Leeds off the park in the two games even though there were tight scorelines,' says David Hay. 'We played exceptionally well.'

More domestic honours

Despite their external commitments, Celtic won the League Championship by the biggest margin of the Stein years, finishing 12 points clear of Rangers. The Scottish Cup was to prove a disappointment, leaving Stein seething at Bobby Davidson's refereeing as Aberdeen won the final 3-1.

Feyenoord were to be Celtic's opponents in the 1970 European Cup final in Milan. Professionalism had only been introduced in Holland in 1957, their club sides had never won anything in Europe, and their national sides had more often than not been complete pushovers. Sadly for Celtic, the breakthrough that began the unending run of modern Dutch footballing success was to be achieved at their expense.

'It was Inter Milan and us in reverse,' says Jimmy Johnstone. 'Dutch football hadn't been heard of. We got off the bus first and, I'll always remember it, they were in already and we were walking down to the dressing-rooms, though big, open-wide corridors. Their dressing-room was next door to ours and they were all out watching us, and they were kind of overawed, pointing out this one and that one among us. I think our heads went a bit and we became over-confident. We underestimated them. We were the Celtic, we had won the European Cup and we honestly thought that we were just going to go out there and lift that trophy again.'

'Strangely enough,' remembers David Hay, 'it wasn't the same team that beat Leeds that played in the European Cup final. The strength of the team was the midfield, although wee Jimmy was exceptional in both the Leeds games. George Connelly was left out and Bobby, George and Bertie had exerted a stranglehold on Billy Bremner and Johnny Giles, which was where the strength lay in the Leeds team. We went 4-2-4 in the European Cup final and part of their strength was in the midfield with a guy called van Hanegem.'

Tommy Gemmell adds: 'Big Jock said, "There's a guy plays left side of midfield, he's all left foot, he plays a bit like

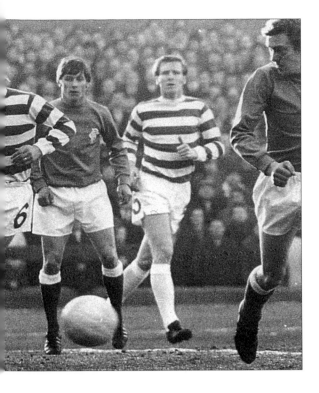

Bobby Murdoch (above) was transferred to Middlesbrough in 1973. He would be hugely influential there, helping to bring on the young Graeme Souness, among others. John Hughes (above right) was an exciting winger, who could combine strength with subtlety to great effect.

Jim Baxter. But after about 20 minutes you won't see him, he just fades out of the game. He's got good ability but that's it." We'd played 90 minutes plus extra-time and this guy was still controlling the game: van Hanegem, who went on to get over 100 caps for Holland. And their centre-forward Kindvall could catch pigeons. Jock's team-talk made us think that we were playing a second-rate side. We went out mentally unprepared.'

'There was all sorts of talk about money problems' says John Hughes. 'But I can't honestly remember money being a factor. The biggest factor for me was that he went to see Feyenoord and he gave us the impression that all we had to do was turn up to win.

'He said that their midfield players were slow and that Kindvall, the centre, wasn't very mobile. At that time Dutch football was emerging and the year before AC Milan had beaten us and played Ajax in the final. He told us that five Ajax players had collapsed with nerves in the dressing-room before the final. Milan had cuffed them 4-1. He said, "This team will be the same, they'll all be panicking."

'It just didn't work out like that. They were tremendous. Football is not like a tap – once you get out and into a particular mode and realise it's not good enough you can't say, "Wait a minute here,

we'd better change this." You can try but I think it's all about preparation. I remember telling people before the game, "I think we'll win 3-0 or 4-0," because that was the attitude.'

A late change of mind

'Latterly, the day before the game, he realised what was going on and he tried to gee us up, he tried to change it but it was quite difficult. In the weeks approaching it your attitude's there and it's difficult to change it at the last minute. I think that was all a result of the Leeds game because I think once we'd beaten them Jock thought it was just a matter of course. They were just a far better side than we anticipated.'

'Even the Celtic fans were caught cold,' says David Hay, 'because unlike Lisbon where they were in the majority there were a large number of Feyenoord fans and although they never outsang the Celtic fans they outnoised them with their klaxons. Maybe that affected us when we walked on to the park, as well.'

In Glasgow, bookmaker Tony Queen, a friend of Stein, had offered the punters a bet on Feyenoord, giving the Dutch a goal of a start, and still making Celtic 6-4 on to win with Feyenoord 9-4 against.

The Dutch had appeared to have problems even before the game began. Their

David Hay's distribution and sharp tackling in the Celtic midfield were badly missed after he was transferred to Chelsea in the summer of 1974.

goalkeeper, Eddie Pieters Graafland, hadn't played in a competitive game for a year and the man he replaced, Eddie Treytel, made his feelings on the matter public. Seven Lisbon Lions began the game, which kicked off at 9pm on 6 May. Celtic weren't helped by an injury to central defender Jim Brogan in the opening minute that kept him in pain throughout the match but in the opening stages they looked out of sorts.

With half an hour gone, Celtic were awarded a free-kick after a foul on Wallace a yard outside the box. Bobby Murdoch's natty back-heel was met by Tommy Gemmell and the Dutch defensive wall disintegrated in the face of his shot. The Italian referee Concetto Lo Bello, positioned behind the wall, moved across Pieters Graafland's line of vision, unsighting him briefly, and the ball went hurtling into the net.

Celtic remained sluggish, though, and the Dutch took just three minutes to equalise. Israel was left free on the edge of the six-yard box to lob Evan Williams with a header that went in off a post. Wim van Hanegem and the 24-year-old Austrian Franz Hasil began laying down the law in midfield as the Dutch moved the ball around delightfully, every player displaying a sharp first-touch and an ability to create space for themselves and their teammates. As the game went on, their defence got stronger and stronger.

Hasil struck a post and Williams, Celtic's best player, made some accomplished saves. The match moved into extra-time, the most entertaining period for the 53,000 present, a

crowd that included 20,000 Scots. Almost immediately John Hughes had an excellent chance to put Celtic ahead again but he knocked the ball against Pieters Graafland.

Feyenoord's killer blow

Four minutes were remaining, and a replay looming, when a long, high ball put the back-tracking McNeill, on the edge of his area, in trouble. The centre-half stumbled as he ran backwards and attempted to stop the ball with his hands. He half-succeeded but the ball travelled on to the Swedish international Ove Kindvall who extended a leg to flick the ball over Williams for the winner.

Afterwards, van Hanegem sported a Celtic supporter's bunnet but he was the only person wearing green-and-white who could be satisfied with the night's work. The biggest disappointment, bigger than losing the game, was that Celtic hadn't played as they had shown they could during their magnificent run to the final. A convincing performance ending in a defeat would have been painful but almost acceptable.

A problem-plagued tour of America followed hard on the heels of the defeat in Milan, with Jock Stein returning home early for talks with the unsettled Jimmy Johnstone and, in his absence, Tommy Gemmell and Bertie Auld being sent home for a breach of discipline. That summer,

though, Johnstone pledged his future to Celtic and Gemmell withdrew his transfer request. There was further cause for optimism early in the season when another youngster from the late-1960s Celtic youth movement nicknamed the 'Quality Street Gang' graduated to the first-team. Danny McGrain, a pacy, overlapping full-back with the flair of a forward, would give the club two decades of service of unfailingly high quality. He was flawless in all aspects of his game: as a hard-tackling defender, in his distribution of the ball and in supporting the front players with his runs to the opponents' touchline.

David Hay remembers those days fondly: 'We were just delighted to be young boys playing with Celtic, training with exceptional players almost every day. That brought us on as much anything.

'We used to watch them play as well and you saw them being successful. All that rubs off on you and I think that generated an element of, not arrogance, but confidence. We always felt we could beat anybody. We were also an extremely close group of people; we'd help our team-mates as much as possible.

'Shortly after I'd gone full-time I'd get an odd game in the first team because that was the way Jock Stein worked. He would break you in and then take you back into the reserves. When you look back on it you realise it was clever because your progression was right. He'd throw maybe myself into the first-team so your mates would be wishing you the best but they'd always want to be there as well so for every one that was in the first-team there'd be four wanting to be there. So there was always that edge of competition for us to get into the first-team.

'The reserve team would be strung together by players like Bertie Auld, Joe McBride or Stevie Chalmers. So you had that element of experience in among you as well. Sean Fallon, who took the reserves, takes a lot of credit as well and Willie Fernie would also help out. We used to play Rangers reserves and beat them by maybe five and six goals.

'I think one season Kenny, Louie Macari and Victor Davidson scored maybe 30 goals each in the reserves. I think whoever dubbed us the Quality Street Gang was probably right although I don't know who were the soft centres and who were the hard ones. Nobody ever got round to comparing us to the actual

George Connelly's efficient passing in midfield was one of the most enjoyable aspects of Celtic's early-1970s play. He was named Scotland's Player of the Year in 1973 but was finding it difficult to cope with the pressures of top-class football. In 1976, after several years of off-field problems, he was given a free transfer.

sweet – maybe Quality Street should have sponsored us. It was a great time.'

There was a new challenge in the League from Aberdeen and by Christmas they had a one-point lead over Celtic with, even at that early stage, no-one else in contention. The League Cup final had brought a 1-0 defeat from Rangers. But Celtic had enjoyed an easy ride in the early rounds of the European Cup, aggregates of 14-0 over Kokkola of Finland and 10-2 over Waterford of Ireland putting them in the quarter-finals where they were to face Ajax Amsterdam.

Celtic face Johan Cruyff

Three superb Ajax goals late on in the first leg in Holland, one from Johan Cruyff, left Celtic in trouble for the second leg. Jimmy Johnstone's close-range goal after 28 minutes gave them hope but although they went close on several other occasions Ajax held out. It was the third year in succession that Celtic had lost to the European Cup winning side.

'We were doing well up until about the last 20 minutes of the game over there,' remembers Jimmy Johnstone. 'Then everything just fell about us due to Johan. I couldn't have seen us beating them at that time because they were superb. Cruyff was running the show. Every time he got the ball it was absolute mayhem. His pace was electric.'

On 29 April 1971 Celtic equalled the feat of the six-in-a-row team from the early days of

the century with a 2-0 win over Ayr Utd, a match played at Hampden Park because of ground alterations at Parkhead. After the game, Stein announced that the following Saturday, 1 May, his Lisbon Lions would play for the final time. There was no stand in operation at Parkhead and the players carefully made their way through the rubble of the seating area from which so many great games had been witnessed.

A crowd of 35,000, paying 30p a head, saw a hat-trick from 'the buzz-bomb' Bobby Lennox, two goals from Willie Wallace and one from Stevie Chalmers as Clyde succumbed 6-1. Five days later, Bertie Auld joined Hibs on a free transfer while Ronnie Simpson had already announced his retirement due to his recurring shoulder injury. John Clark and Stevie Chalmers left for Morton soon afterwards. Within a year, Jim Craig, Tommy Gemmell, John Hughes and Willie Wallace would also have departed.

It had been the greatest side in Celtic's history, glued together by the painstaking efforts of Stein. Most teams, at home or away, would be happy to be 2-0 or 3-0 down to Celtic at half-time. To them, that would be containing Celtic. 'Any team that came to Parkhead would play with eight defenders,' says John Hughes. 'That was normal for us. We broke them down because we had the players to break them down.'

'I've seen us in the dressing-room before playing a particular side such as Motherwell or Hibs or Hearts or whoever it might be,' says Tommy Gemmell, 'and we'd actually be saying to each other, "What do you think – 3-0 or 4-0?" We knew we could go out and if we played we'd take three or four goals off them without any problem. That's how confident we were. And invariably we got the results we were looking for.

'We got progressively better and better. Big Jock wouldn't change the back four unless he really had to through injury or suspension or severe loss of form. If you were off-key a little bit he would persevere with you. It was basically the same in the middle of the park. He would normally play Bobby and Bertie – we were playing a 4-2-4 system at that time. But he would chop and change the front players depending on who we were playing. When you're playing together as often it makes it easier and easier on the teamwork side of things.'

It had also been a team in the great Celtic tradition in that it had been assembled at next to no cost. Ronnie Simpson had signed for Celtic shortly before Stein's return for a knockdown price from Hibs. Bertie Auld had cost £12,000 from Birmingham City and Willie Wallace had been bought from Hearts.

The rest had been signed straight from school, or from amateur or junior teams. It had been one of the finest achievements in world football history for Stein to mould those players into one of the greatest club sides that Europe has ever seen.

Jimmy Johnstone feels the full weight of an Inter Milan tackle in the 1972 European Cup semi-final at Parkhead. Inter killed that game as a spectacle with their negative tactics but they would be comprehensively beaten by Ajax in the final. Celtic would have made worthier opponents for the Dutchmen.

On 8 May 1971, the Old Firm came face to face in the Scottish Cup final, their first encounter since the tragedy of the Ibrox disaster on 2 January when 66 people had lost their lives after terrible crushing around an Ibrox exit. Bobby Lennox's 40th minute goal was levelled three minutes from time by Derek Johnstone. In the first game Rangers right-back Alex Miller had suffered a broken cheekbone. In his place for the replay was young reserve Jim Denny. 'Jim Denny was thrown in at the deep end,' says Jimmy Johnstone. 'Before the game Big Jock said, "You know where you're going, don't you?"'

There were 103,332 at Hampden for the replay on a balmy spring evening and, from the off, Jinky went past Denny a couple of times and the player was left reeling for the rest of the game. 'When you see the defenders getting tackles in and winning balls in the air,' he says, 'you get a bit of confidence and you start to think it's your day. I think it works the same for them when they see you going by defenders and skinning them.'

Rangers' vigorous approach had brought them the draw in the first game but Celtic were back at their sophisticated best in the second match. And after 24 minutes Lennox's corner was deflected into Macari's path by Greig. The ball was moving quickly but the little striker showed swift reactions to tuck the ball into the corner of McCloy's net. Within a minute, Celtic had scored a second goal. Jimmy Johnstone was brought down by McKinnon

and Harry Hood scored with the resultant penalty. Celtic won 2-1.

Robert Kelly passes away

On 20 April 1971, the seriously ill Sir Robert Kelly, who had been knighted in 1969, became club president, succeeded as chairman by Desmond White. Later that year, Robert Kelly died after a long illness. He had striven continuously to do the right thing for Celtic. In the autumn of 1968, for example, after Soviet tanks had crushed support for the elected government in Czechoslovakia, he had moved that Celtic withdraw from the European Cup after being drawn against Ferencvaros, representatives of the then Soviet satellite Hungary. UEFA made the draw again to keep western and eastern clubs apart. Consequently, the Warsaw Pact countries scratched from the competition.

In 1952 he had stood equally firmly, and successfully, in opposition to the SFA when elements within that organisation attempted to impose a ban on Celtic flying the Irish flag at Parkhead. He had organised Celtic parties to go to World Cup games and international and club games outside Scotland during the 1950s and one of the main beneficiaries of this refreshing look at other methods and approaches had been the young Jock Stein.

Robert Kelly had been a visionary with blind spots but a man who, of all Celtic's modern-day chairmen, had made the most dynamic contribution to the club.

Billy McNeill opens the scoring in the 1972 Scottish Cup final after only two minutes. A Dixie Deans hat-trick and a double from Lou Macari in the 6-1 win made it a record score for a 20th century Scottish Cup final. Two years later, Deans got another hat-trick in the 6-3 League Cup final win over the same club.

they finished ten points clear of their closest challengers, Aberdeen.

More continental jaunts

Celtic defeated BK 1903 Copenhagen 4-2 on aggregate and Sliema Wanderers of Malta 7-1 to reach the quarter-finals of the European Cup. That took them to Budapest where film stars Richard and Liz Burton found themselves sharing the Duna Intercontinental Hotel, overlooking the Danube, with Celtic supporters. Murdoch, Hay, Dalglish and Hood were the stars in midfield against the Hungarian champions Ujpest Dozsa as Celtic conjured up a performance that was as glittering as any Hollywood production.

From a Brogan cross, Horvath headed into his own net after 19 minutes but the same player equalised for Ujpest midway through the second half. Celtic continued pressing, as they had from the start, and after Dalglish's shot was stopped by a defender Macari stole in to squirt home the winner. 'At this level and when you consider the age of this team of ours, it is probably Celtic's best European Cup display since Lisbon,' said Stein, who always weighed his words carefully. The Burtons threw a £5,000 post-match caviare and champagne party for 130 fans. Liz sported a Celtic tammy and scarf.

Ujpest were a more than useful side, however, and after just five minutes at Parkhead they had levelled the tie on aggregate

On 1 September 1971, Jimmy McGrory opened the new stand at Parkhead and, in front of 60,000, the occasion was celebrated with a 3-0 win over Nacional of Uruguay, the South American champions. The fans saw a potent blend of old and new. Bobby Lennox scored the first. Then an incisive long pass from the Celtic half by Connelly found Lennox who teed the ball up for the 20 year old Dalglish, starting his first season as a regular in the side, to thump the ball off the bar. Midfielder Tommy Callaghan, a purchase from Dunfermline, headed in the rebound. Five minutes from the end Kenny Dalglish was fouled just outside the penalty area, Murdoch took the free-kick and Lennox headed in the third.

The League Cup final found Celtic, without Billy McNeill, on an off-day, losing 4-1 to Partick Thistle. In the First Division, though,

was no way to win a European Cup tie. Sandro Mazzola scored the first penalty then John 'Dixie' Deans, a popular striker signed from Motherwell six months earlier, took Celtic's first and sent it over the bar. The other eight players all scored and Inter were in the final in a manner that, in practice, had proved almost as unsatisfactory as the toss of a coin. The extrovert Deans soon recovered and within weeks had emulated Jimmy Quinn with a hat-trick in the 6-1 Scottish Cup final win over Hibs.

A return visit to Ujpest

Ujpest Dozsa were to make a swift return to Celtic Park, being drawn to go there in the second round of the European Cup after Celtic had beaten the Norwegian side Rosenberg Trondheim on a 5-2 aggregate.

There were 55,000 fans at Parkhead and they saw an engrossing game. Bene opened the scoring for Ujpest after 20 minutes but four minutes after half-time Dalglish locked on to a searing pass from Connelly to equalise. Celtic began to move the ball around with style and, after they had been denied a good claim for a penalty, substitute Lennox curled a cross into the area and Dalglish headed neatly past Szentmihalyi.

Three goals for Ujpest in a 15-minute period early in the first half in Budapest virtually killed the tie, although a Billy McNeill header was cleared off the line and a Dalglish shot hit the bar. Celtic had gone out to defend and there was no way of changing their plans midway through the match. There was further disappointment in December when Celtic lost the League Cup final 2-1 to Hibs and in May when Rangers beat them 3-2 in the Scottish Cup final.

A week prior to that game, on 28 April, Celtic had once again won the League title. On that final day of the 1972-73 season they faced a difficult game at Easter Road, needing a single point to make sure of the Championship. A double from Deans and a goal from Dalglish gave them their eighth title. 'Class told in the end,' said Stein after a run-in that had seen Celtic score 23 goals and lose just one as they took full points from their final seven games.

Ten months later, Celtic faced Hibs, one of the few Scottish sides consistently able to give them a testing game, at Easter Road, in

At the end of the match with Atletico, police had to separate players from both sides. Fists had flown after an Atletico player had attacked Jimmy Johnstone on the running track as the teams were leaving the field. Blows were also exchanged in the tunnel as the Celtic players, after ninety minutes of incessant provocation, finally lost their tempers.

through Dunai. The Hungarians then began to run the match with their controlled, flowing football but after the half-time break Jimmy Johnstone eased the pressure on the team and the 75,000 fans with an old-style performance. Midway through the second half, Connelly's through ball ripped into the Ujpest defence. In the resultant confusion Maurer tried to find his goalkeeper and Macari darted in to divert the ball high into the Ujpest net.

The semi-final paired Celtic with Inter Milan but few memories of the 1967 European Cup final were to be jogged by this game. In the San Siro stadium, George Connelly stole the show as Celtic held the Italians to a 0-0 draw. In the return, in front of another 75,000, Celtic, missing the injured Hay and McGrain, threw everything at the Italian defence but they packed their penalty area, did nothing positive, played for penalties, and got them.

'They were great ones for just stopping and body-checking,' says Jimmy Johnstone. 'And they got away with it because they were so professional it didn't look like a foul. They were pulling and holding and all the rest of it, stopping your momentum. They're past-masters at it. It was so frustrating to play against.'

UEFA, at a meeting in Milan before the 1970 European Cup final, had decided to replace the toss of the coin with penalties. Robert Kelly had been one of the prime movers behind the change after the Benfica match that year, believing that a toss of a coin

Harry Hood, a consistent goalscorer for Celtic in the early 1970s, opens the scoring in the 1974 Scottish Cup final win over Dundee United. Steve Murray and Dixie Deans got the other goals in Celtic's 3-0 win.

another League fixture. A win would put the Glasgow side five points clear of their Edinburgh rivals in the Championship and would almost certainly ensure them their ninth title in a row.

Nine titles in a row

With 48,000 fans watching, Kenny Dalglish, the Motown-loving Glasgow boy whose moves were sharper than a Smokey Robinson two-step, inspired Celtic to a 4-2 win. It was a victory as memorable as any with which they had graced the Scottish League during those years. After 75 seconds, Deans swept on to a Black passback to stab home the opening goal. Duncan equalised but Dalglish made it 2-1 when he flitted in and out of the path of several Hibs defenders before edging the ball past goalkeeper McArthur.

Again Hibs equalised, through O'Rourke, but Celtic's Scots-Indian Paul Wilson made it 3-2 and in the final minute Dixie Deans floated a well-timed header past McArthur. It had been a fantastic afternoon's entertainment and a great way to wrap up a world record nine title wins in a row.

Dundee, captained by Tommy Gemmell, had beaten Celtic 1-0 in the League Cup final but their neighbours United couldn't match

them in the Scottish Cup final, going down 3-0 to Celtic. Yet again, however, the domestic Cups were overshadowed by proceedings in the European one, where Celtic had beaten TPS Turku of Finland 9-1 on aggregate and Vejle of Denmark 1-0, taking them into the quarter-final where, for the third time in a decade, they were to meet Basle.

A dazzling opening 20 minutes in Switzerland ended with a Brogan cross being hammered home by Wilson for the first. But a soggy middle period saw Basle take a 2-1 lead before a spectacular shot from Dalglish brought Celtic level. A late penalty gave Basle a 3-2 victory on the night.

At Parkhead, 71,000 saw Celtic take an early lead. Dalglish took a short corner and eased into the box to head Callaghan's cross past Laufenburger. Deans quickly got Celtic's second but two Swiss goals before half-time put Celtic behind in the tie again before Callaghan's volley from a Deans cross brought extra-time. Johnstone and Deans missed good chances before Brogan, in the 98th minute, found Hood on the left wing and his cross was met by Steve Murray, a £50,000 signing from Aberdeen, who head-ed the winner. Fight rather than finesse had seen Celtic through to the semi.

Paul Wilson leaps to head Bobby Lennox's corner into the Airdrie net for Wilson's and Celtic's second goal in the 1975 Scottish Cup final. A Pat McCluskey penalty made the final score 3-1 to Celtic. After the game, Billy McNeill announced his retirement. That made Bobby Lennox the only Lisbon Lion still at Parkhead.

Jock Stein welcomes Pat Stanton to Celtic from Hibs at the beginning of the 1976-77 season. Stanton, Scotland's Player of the Year in 1970, was 31 but the unflappable midfield man did much to bring the double to Parkhead.

Their opponents were to be the Spanish champions Atletico Madrid. Atletico had a Eusebio in their side but he failed to live up to that name, being escorted from the pitch by two policemen at the end of the first leg at Parkhead. As an enduring image of an evening that had utterly horrified the 75,000 Glaswegians present it is highly appropriate.

Atletico, with five Argentinians in their team and managed by Juan Carlos Lorenzo, coach of Racing in 1967, stamped all over the rules and spirit of football.

'It was a non-game,' says David Hay. 'Big Jock said, "Whatever you do, don't get involved." And in a strange way, looking back, we probably were too controlled although maybe in terms of the history of the club it's better that you don't get involved to that extent. We maybe accepted too much until we blew up at the end in the tunnel. There was no flow to the game. We all got kicked that night, even me, and I was normally associated with kicking other people! They were just doing everybody. It became farcical. The goalkeeper would get the ball, just kick it up the park and they wouldn't come out of their box. That was just the way they wanted to play it. They wanted a result at all costs and were prepared to go to those lengths.'

The scoreline, 0-0, reflected the most negative night in Celtic's history. Of the 13 Atletico players who participated, three were sent off – Ayala, Diaz and Quique – and nine were booked. At the end, Atletico's players celebrated as they had played, wildly. Then Jimmy Johnstone was kicked in the back as he made for the dressing-room and that sparked off a brawl that was broken up by 20 policemen. Johnstone, who describes the Atletico

Celtic have just clinched the 1976-77 Championship, their 30th title, after beating Hibs 1-0 at Easter Road. Captain Kenny Dalglish is chaired round the pitch by his team-mates. It was to be Dalglish's last League-winner's medal in Scotland. From left to right: MacDonald, Stanton, Glavin, Burns, Doyle, Dalglish, McGrain, Aitken and Latchford.

players as 'animals', had behaved impeccably despite having been kicked mercilessly throughout. Jock Stein said: 'We will not file an official protest – there is no need to. Everyone who was there saw what happened.'

UEFA let Celtic down

Strong action was expected from UEFA but their only response to the violence in the first game was to give Atletico a risible fine and warn them after the event: 'The committee warn you now that your club will be entirely responsible for any incident whatever at the return match on 24 April on which may depend the future participation by your club in this competition or in future competitions of UEFA.' Atletico had set out to 'kill' the first leg. They had got away with it. There had never been any likelihood that they would approach the return in the same way. Celtic could have withdrawn in protest but they would have been fined heavily by UEFA and instructed to compensate Atletico for lost takings in the return. The bill could have amounted to £100,000 or more.

Before the second leg, Stein told Ian Archer of the *Glasgow Herald*: 'Atletico offended me deeply. I like to think that football and sport are important, that being part of the game is an honourable occupation.

What they did in Glasgow hurt me more than any words can express. That is why I want to beat them here, fairly, on their own ground, in front of their own people.'

Jimmy Johnstone remembers Madrid: 'I was in my bed at about one o'clock in the morning when the phone rang. I was half sleeping and this voice said, "You're dead," and put the phone down. I thought it must be some crank but the following day, the Tuesday, big Jock took me aside and said, "We've had a death threat, they're going to shoot me and you." I said, "I'm going home." He says, "What chance have they got of hitting you when you get out there and you start juking and jiving? I can't move, I'm sitting there in that dug-out."'

There were 1,000 security police backed up by tear gas and water canon inside the Estadio Vicente Calderon that April evening. Celtic were ushered back into their dressing-room after three minutes of their pre-match warm-up as hatred mounted on the terraces. An early header from McNeill went over the bar and Dalglish's shot was tipped round the post by Reina as Celtic defiantly went for a win. The home side were without six players who had been suspended after the first leg but those hackers had been expendable – Lorenzo had kept his better players in reserve for the second game. Two late goals put Atletico into the final.

'As soon as you went out on to the park,' says Johnstone, 'they were nipping you and spitting at you any opportunity they got. That wasn't football. Football is a lovely game, a great game full of lovely people. I would never wish it on anybody and I'd never want to go through it again.' It was little consolation that Celtic had been the moral victors in the semis with Inter in 1972 and Atletico in 1974 and that they would have made better finalists than those two sides, both of whom lost to superior opposition.

Celtic in the early 1970s were still a strong, attractive side, capable of special football. After their win over Ujpest in 1972, the Hungarian newspaper *Magyar Memzet* had commented: 'No football team anywhere in the world would be able to stand its ground against Glasgow Celtic. Celtic are a tough, well disciplined and well balanced side with stamina and go.' Another Hungarian writer in *Nepszabadsac* stated: 'They had superior technique, teamwork, skills and speed... the works in fact. Every player was a defender or an attacker as the situation required.'

There was, however, growing dissatisfaction among the players over pay. Celtic's players had always been on comparatively low basic wages which were supplemented by good winning bonuses. A succession of unexpected winning bonuses had arrived in the mid-1960s along with Stein and those, together with the momentum of European success, kept players happy although after several years some of them began to question how much they were being paid. The new generation of players had never known Celtic to be anything other than successful, pulling in huge crowds and obviously gathering substantial receipts. On international duty, they would discover that the basic wages paid by top English clubs were considerably higher.

Damaging departures

Lou Macari had barely established himself in the Celtic first-team before he decided he wouldn't wait around to see whether Celtic would change their wage structure, moving on to Manchester United in January 1973 for a fee of £200,000. David Hay left for Chelsea in 1974 after a long-term injury had left him suffering financially because he was missing out on bonuses. In a prolonged dispute with the club he had argued for a higher basic wage for the players and, when he returned from the 1974 World Cup, Stein told Hay that he thought it would be better for both parties if the player moved on. Hay went for £250,000. While Celtic received substantial transfer fees such as that one, fractions of those amounts were used to buy new players.

David Hay says: 'Jock was maybe sorry he hadn't had the chance of seeing that group of boys coming through and that was maybe not his fault but the then board's for not paying that bit extra money. I think that's maybe where the mistake lay. We didn't get badly paid but it was all due to bonuses and our

Left-back Andy Lynch scores against Rangers with a 20th minute penalty, the only goal of the 1977 Scottish Cup final. On the left side of the Celtic midfield that day was Alfie Conn, signed for a £65,000 fee from Tottenham Hotspur in March of that year. That made him the first player since World War II to have played for both Celtic and Rangers.

request in 1975 but, through loyalty to Stein and Celtic, signed a new two-year contract.

A sad loss to football

'Big George Connelly could have been our Beckenbauer,' says Jimmy Johnstone. 'I think the environment didn't suit Geordie because he was a quiet big laddie from up the country. I think he thought we were all flymen! He just couldn't mix. But what ability! He was absolutely brilliant. And he didn't think he was good enough. He thought we were all stars and he'd say to me if I did something, "That was brilliant." And you'd say, "Think about yourself, big man." He was very shy. A nice big boy.

'Kenny was home-bred. He was a townie and he had a bit of confidence and cockiness about him. He wasn't shy. His greatest ability was his shadowing of the ball, his holding of it. He took some horrific kicks from boys hitting him from the back and what not. You should have seen his legs sometimes. He got a lot of goals that maybe lesser people who weren't as brave as him wouldn't have got.

'He was always in the right place at the right time and he always knew where he was going, even when he had his back to goal, throwing people. He hadn't tremendous pace, he never took the ball up to anybody and went past them. But he was always in the box, turning, dummying, playing his wee one-twos.'

'Probably the greatest disappointment when I left,' says David Hay, 'was that we never saw our careers through to their peaks together. Louie left, then myself, then Kenny, and George gave it up. I think if we'd have stayed together we'd have sustained a real challenge at the highest level. Deep down none of us really wanted to leave.'

The 1974-75 League season saw Celtic win both Cups, beating Hibs 6-3 in the League Cup final and Airdrie 3-1 in the Scottish Cup final but it was still painful to see the title slip away for the first time in a decade, especially as it went in the direction of Ibrox. Celtic's European Cup challenge ended in the first round at the hands of Olympiakos. Connelly and Hay were badly missed as Celtic lost on a 3-1 aggregate. The season ended with Billy McNeill retiring from football after 832 games for Celtic and Jimmy Johnstone leaving to play for San Jose Earthquakes.

Celtic's 1976-77 European challenge had ended in the first round, when they were beaten on a 4-2 aggregate in the UEFA Cup by Wisla Krakow of Poland. At the end of that season, Kenny Dalglish was transferred to Liverpool. Within a year he had won a European Cup medal, scoring the only goal of the final against Bruges at Wembley.

argument was that the club was doing well so they should maybe give us a pound or two extra.' In the period after Hay's departure, his friend George Connelly found his off-field problems multiplying and he was freed in 1976. Danny McGrain's career was disrupted by a fractured skull in 1972 from which he recovered bravely. During the 1974 World Cup he fell ill and was diagnosed as a diabetic, although he was available for Celtic the following season. Dalglish, the most talented of them all, submitted a transfer

In May 1978, Jock Stein agreed to step down as Celtic manager. Giving up the position he had held with distinction for 13 years was always going to be difficult. Here, the pain is etched on his face as chairman Desmond White introduces new boss Billy McNeill at a press conference. Stein was offered a directorship with responsibility for commercial activities, to be ratified at an AGM later in the year. But before that took place he had decided to accept a lucrative offer to become manager of Leeds United.

In July 1975, Scotland was shocked by the news that Jock Stein had come close to losing his life in a car crash at Lockerbie on the A74. He had been returning from holiday in Minorca with his friend Tony Queen and their wives. Head and chest injuries left him in a critical condition in a Dumfries hospital. It had been a brush with death but within a week Stein was back in good spirits although he was instructed to recuperate away from football during the coming season.

During his absence, Sean Fallon became caretaker-manager and Celtic ended the season trophyless, losing the League Cup final 1-0 to Rangers and going out to the East German side Sachsenring Zwickau on a 2-1 aggregate in the Cup-Winners' Cup quarter-final after beating Valur Reykjavik of Iceland 9-1 on aggregate and Boavista of Portugal 3-1 in the preceding rounds.

Stein was back for the 1976-77 season and immediately guided Celtic to the League Cup final against Aberdeen. They lost that game 2-1 but would be back at Hampden for the Scottish Cup final against Rangers when a 1-0 win gave them the double. Their first Premier League title since reconstruction in 1975 was won with a nine-point lead over Rangers. Dalglish was joint top scorer with midfielder Ronnie Glavin on 26 goals, followed closely by striker Joe Craig, the latter two having been bought from Partick Thistle.

With two world class players, McGrain and Dalglish, in the side and several highly capable others, there appeared to be much for the 55-year-old Stein to look forward to as he entered the autumn of his managerial career but in the close season Kenny Dalglish made up his mind to leave Celtic.

Liverpool paid a British record transfer £440,000 for him and dealt Celtic a massive blow which was compounded in the first League match of the season, against Dundee United, when Pat Stanton was seriously injured. The team also lost Danny McGrain after seven matches to an ankle injury that kept him out for the rest of the season. Celtic were on a downward spiral. After beating Jeunesse d'Esch in the first round of the European Cup they lost on a 4-2 aggregate to Innsbruck of Austria. They lost the League Cup final to Rangers and were knocked out of the Scottish Cup in a fourth round replay at First Division Kilmarnock, an evening on which Roy Aitken was sent off. Worst of all, they ended up fifth in the League.

It would have been too much to ask Jock Stein to rebuild once again from that position and in May 1978 he came to an agreement with the Celtic Board that he would make way for Billy McNeill. Jock Stein had led Celtic to 25 trophies in 13 years. It was the end of the most remarkable managerial reign in British football history.

Under Billy McNeill Celtic once again became the strongest team on the Scottish scene. However, his successor, David Hay, found that circumstances were conspiring against him.

7 Return to Splendour

Billy McNeill returned to Celtic Park in May 1978 primed for action, impatient for success and unwilling to have anything stand in his way. He soon built a team in his image. After his retirement from the game in 1975, he decided to concentrate on business but in April 1977 he accepted an offer to manage Clyde. Within weeks of taking over at Shawfield, he got a telephone call from none other than Jock Stein, the then Celtic boss acting as an intermediary to ask how McNeill would feel about becoming manager of Aberdeen. McNeill accepted that job and in his first season at Pittodrie he took the Dons to the Scottish Cup final and to a runners-up spot in the Premier League.

Twelve months on, Jock Stein again approached McNeill, this time at the Scottish Football Writers' annual dinner in Glasgow, about returning to Parkhead as manager. McNeill had been enjoying life in the North-East but when the opportunity came to return to the only club he had played for it was too good for him to turn down. McNeill's dynamism, combined with his feeling for the club, was just what Celtic needed.

As a player he had been known as 'Caesar' to the support. This nickname had been attached to him in his early playing days at Parkhead after some Celtic players had been to see the film *Ocean's Eleven*, in which 11 wisecracking chums, one of whom was Cesar Romero, get together to plan a heist. The gradual alteration of the actor's name to that of the Roman emperor was appropriate to McNeill, whose qualities as a commanding figure had been well-established as the captain of Jock Stein's great sides.

McNeill resigned from Aberdeen on 29 May, saying: 'I feel really proud of following Jock Stein as boss of Celtic. I am confident I can do a good job. I wouldn't be going if I thought otherwise. Right through my career I have dreamed of the day I might be offered the job as Celtic manager.'

The new manager made a good start with a 2-1 away win at Morton through goals by Ronnie Glavin and centre-half Roddie MacDonald. Three wins, including one over Rangers, followed but then Celtic went through a sticky patch. Danny McGrain, Scotland's Player of the Year in 1977, was still recovering from his ankle injury and Pat Stanton's injury on the first day of the previous season had eventually resulted in his retirement from the game.

McNeill soon began the renewal process. On 18 September he broke the Scottish transfer record by paying Kilmarnock £120,000 for their right-winger Davie Provan. At the end of October, after a demoralising 2-0 defeat at Tynecastle, Celtic's fourth in 11 League games, McNeill's patience ran out.

'We had too many players in the team who are simply not good enough to play for Celtic,' he said. 'We cannot go on disguising the fact.' Asked if there had been any injuries, he responded: 'How could my players get injured the way they played? If anyone is injured then he must have fallen coming out of the bath.'

The following week he signed Murdo MacLeod from Dumbarton for £100,000, a driving midfielder who was to prove the epitome of commitment over the next few years. While the new additions were settling in, Celtic's form continued to waver. Two days before Christmas they lost 1-0 in the second fixture at Cappielow, sending them into sixth place in the Premier League, four points

Billy McNeill leads the celebrations as the final whistle sounds in Celtic's momentous win over Rangers to win the 1978-79 Premier League.

behind leaders Dundee United. Ten days earlier, they had lost a stormy League Cup semi-final to Rangers after extra-time.

Celtic were then given a break – a ten-week one. Due to bad weather, their next League fixture wasn't until 3 March, when, refreshed and ready for the run-in, and with Danny McGrain restored to the right-back position, they defeated Aberdeen 1-0 at Parkhead. By the end of that month they were 10 points behind Dundee United but with six games in hand. Their sole concern was the League, having gone out of the Scottish Cup, at the quarter-final stage, to Aberdeen.

Celtic's late title bid

A month later, after a scrappy 2-1 win over United at Parkhead in front of 37,000, McNeill said: 'I didn't expect us to be challenging for the title. And I still say if we make it to Europe next season we will have done well. Celtic's return to having a great team will be gradual.' Celtic and Rangers were due to meet in a rearranged game at Parkhead on Monday 21 May. By then, a winning run after the United game had taken Celtic to the top of the Premier League, three points clear of Rangers. It was Celtic's final game of the season and a win would take the title to Parkhead. A win or a draw for Rangers would leave the Ibrox side with two games in which to stroll on to the title.

'There was just the usual build-up,' says Murdo MacLeod. 'Big Billy knew how to motivate every player. He didn't go round us individually. He motivated us as a team reminding us of how far we had come and telling us not to throw it away in the last game of the season.'

It was to be an incredible match, one of the most dramatic of all the head-to-heads between these two powerful institutions. After nine minutes Alex MacDonald gave Rangers the lead and shortly after half-time Doyle was sent off for retaliation. Midway through the second half Roy Aitken equalised for the ten-man Celts. With 74 minutes gone, they took the lead through 21-year-old striker George McCluskey but two minutes later Russell equalised.

Rangers' approach had shown they would have been happy with a draw but Celtic still had the initiative. Six minutes from the end, after McCluskey's cross had been parried by

McCloy, Rangers defender Jackson headed the ball past his own goalkeeper. With the seconds ticking away, Murdo MacLeod emphasised Celtic's right to the title with a fierce 20-yarder, a goal fit to win any Championship. 'I remember picking the ball up,' says MacLeod. 'There was a pass on wide left, and a pass on wide right, but I just kept on going forward. I knew I was going to shoot, I knew I wasn't going to pass it. I was saying to myself, "I'm going to hit this ball as hard as I can. If I miss the target it'll go away behind the goals into the Celtic end and it will waste time." But I hit the ball well and it went high and dipped down over McCloy and hit the roof of the net.

'I knew it was late on but not how late it was. The game went by so quickly we had no indication of how long there was to go so we were all geared up to go again although I think then we knew we had won the League. But Rangers only had time to take the centre and the whistle went. So I think I was the last Celtic player to touch the ball that night.'

Celtic had been on top throughout the match, showing tremendous energy and commitment to attack. Billy McNeill was delighted: 'It was simply fantastic. I've never seen a match like it. I asked the team to go out and climb a mountain. When they got to the top they found there was still another hill to scale. They did it marvellously.'

'To score the last goal made it the best night in football ever for me,' says MacLeod. 'Everyone at Celtic Park knew we were going to win it. There was no other team going to stop us that night, whether it was Rangers or whoever, even when we were down to ten men. Later on, I scored in games when we won the Championship but there wasn't the same atmosphere and emotion as there was on that 4-2 night from the fans and players.'

That victory put Celtic back in the European Cup. It was a fresh experience for most of the players at Parkhead and the first round draw took the club to the secluded Communist state of Albania, to play Partizan Tirana. Celtic played poorly and lost the first leg 1-0 but there was a crowd of 51,000 at Parkhead a fortnight later. 'I think a lot of people turned up because they wanted to see what people from Albania looked like,' says MacLeod. Celtic eased to a 4-1 win.

Dundalk of Ireland were next to come to Parkhead and gave Celtic a scare or two. Celtic won 3-2 but those two away goals meant there were some nerve-racking moments in the return. But a 0-0 draw saw Celtic through. Aberdeen had put paid to Celtic's League Cup chances, in the quarter-finals, but the Celts entered the 1980s in pole position in the League. A survivor of the 1960s, Bobby Lennox, had scored the equaliser at Ibrox on 29 December that left the Celts three points clear of Morton and six clear of Rangers at the top.

On the Saturday before welcoming their next opponents in the European Cup to Parkhead Celtic went eight points clear of Morton and St Mirren, and ten ahead of Rangers, with only 12 games remaining.

Aberdeen were also ten points behind and although the Dons had two games in hand the Celts looked to be in an unassailable position. Scottish League business, however, was forgotten as the biggest club game Scotland had seen in years took place at Parkhead on 5 March. Real Madrid were the visitors and their presence saw a crowd of 67,000 come up with £250,000 in gate receipts.

The two sides had played before in friendlies. In 1962, the Real of Alfredo Di Stefano and Ferenc Puskas had obtained a stylish 3-1 win at Parkhead. And a fortnight after Celtic had won the European Cup they had been Di Stefano's chosen opponents in his testimonial match; a match in which Jimmy Johnstone gave what he considers to be his greatest-ever performance as Celtic won 1-0.

Tom McAdam (left) and Roy Aitken (right) leave the pitch after the 4-2 win over Rangers in May 1979. Sweeper McAdam and central midfielder Aitken provided much of the power and drive on which that win, and many others, was based. In 1993, McAdam returned to Parkhead as a coach.

Memories of the great European days, were stirred as the Celtic faithful took their places in the stand and on the terracing on that spring evening. It seemed as though the good times were back, rubber-stamped by the identity of their opponents, European football's most glamorous name.

In the first half a Real side that featured English international Laurie Cunningham and the German Uli Stielike, dominated. But two swashbuckling moves sliced apart the Real defence in the second half for a dramatic Celtic victory. After 52 minutes right-back Alan Sneddon took a MacLeod pass and cut in from the touchline for a low shot that Garcia Ramon couldn't hold. McCluskey came whirling in to deposit the loose ball in the back of the net.

With quarter of an hour remaining, Sneddon was again supplied by MacLeod. This time the defender decided on a high cross to the back post. Winger Johnny Doyle got on the end of it, rising above Sabido and Camacho for a fine header that went spinning into the net.

Before the return, Billy McNeill said: 'There will be no surrender by us. We will certainly tighten up in certain areas, but that's all. There's no point in trying to change our style. We'll be trying to score goals if we can.'

After five minutes of that match, played in front of 110,000 at the Bernabeu Stadium, MacLeod and Doyle carved out a chance that left McCluskey with only Garcia Ramon to beat but the striker sent a poor shot sliding past the post. It was an early alarm call for Real and from then on Celtic were up against it, eventually going down 3-0.

That was the end of European competition for that season but it still looked as though Celtic would be back in the same tournament in 1980-81. Frank McGarvey, rescued from Liverpool reserves by McNeill for another record fee of £250,000, scored the only goal of the Old Firm encounter at the beginning of April but that win was followed by two disastrous defeats, 2-1 at home to Aberdeen and 3-0 at Dundee United. An even worse defeat was to follow, the side going down 5-1 at Dundee, and before the month was out Aberdeen had picked up another win at Parkhead.

The Dons went on to take the title, the first time the Championship had left Glasgow since 1965. 'We maybe got a wee bit complacent,' says MacLeod, 'thinking that we had won it. Our nature as a team was to go and fight for things and I think when things were there for us we seemed to accept it more easily than going out and chasing things.'

George McCluskey shows what it means to score the winning goal in a Scottish Cup final, in this case the 1980 victory over Rangers at Hampden.

The Scottish Cup final was an Old Firm affair. It was a free-flowing game, watched by 70,303; an afternoon to enjoy such things as the cavalier play of Davie Provan on the wing, putting in a performance typical of those that made him the 1980 Scottish Players' Player of the Year. The game remained scoreless until extra-time, when Danny McGrain's long-range potshot was deflected past McCloy by George McCluskey in the 107th minute for the only goal of the game.

The game was destined to be remembered more for the scenes that followed. As the Celtic players ran to their fans at the final whistle, some of their followers got carried away and clambered over the perimeter fence to greet the players. Rangers fans then also climbed over the barriers at their end of the ground. Bottles and stones, fists, boots and iron bars were used in the resulting riot. Eventually, mounted police arrived and sped on to the pitch, with batons raised. Two hundred and ten individuals were arrested.

Certain politicians, including Scottish secretary George Younger, indicated that they placed much of the blame for the riot on Celtic's players running to greet their fans. That wasn't the only blast of hot air to come out of the House of Commons in that or any other year. The real cause of the problem, in addition to the aggressive tendencies of some supporters, was low-key policing at the end of the game: the police had moved outside the ground to head off potential trouble as the fans departed.

That left only a skimpy presence inside Hampden. The long-term result was the Criminal Justice (Scotland) act of 1980. It forbade, among other things, importation of alcohol into football grounds and on supporters' buses. It helped create a better atmosphere at matches.

The New Firm's challenge

After Aberdeen's title win in 1980, the challenge of the 'New Firm' of the Dons and Dundee United intensified. In the semi-finals of both the 1980-81 Scottish Cup and League Cup, United were Celtic's conquerors. In the League, it was champions Aberdeen who took up the early running. Celtic's last match of 1980, two days after Christmas, was at Pittodrie and a 4-1 win for the Dons put them five points clear of Celtic at the top of the Premier League with a game in hand.

The only bright spot in that defeat was a diamond of a volley from Charlie Nicholas. It was further proof of a talent that had lit up the Scottish game like a flare in the night sky since his debut early that season. Charlie wouldn't just score goals; he would do it in style. It was the only way he knew. Even his tap-ins were accompanied by a flourish.

'I joined Celtic Boys' Club when I was 11,' he says. 'My father took me for trials there. My position at that time was inside-right and there were about ten guys out of 40 there who said they were inside-rights. I was at the end of the batch and I panicked and said I was an inside-left, just to get involved. I did five years with Celtic Boys' Club and I got to Under-16 level and I was under a man called Frank Cairney who ran the Boys' Club for many years. Frank was a friend of Jock Stein and he suggested that I should be signed.

'I remember my debut like it was yesterday. I came on against Stirling Albion in the League Cup. We'd lost 1-0 in the first leg and I came on with about 20 minutes to go and we were 2-1 down on aggregate. Tommy Burns scored with a minute to go to put it into extra-time and I scored two in extra-time and I got into the team after that.'

After that setback at Pittodrie Celtic won four League games before facing Rangers at Parkhead. Rangers were a goal ahead at half-time. Then McNeill's practicality combined with Nicholas' flair to create a memorable afternoon. 'Charlie was not pressurising their

The 1980 Scottish Cup final was marred by the actions of some supporters who invaded the field after the game. The pitched battle that followed brought Rangers and Celtic a £20,000 fine apiece.

defenders enough,' said McNeill. 'I pointed out to him that I could still be playing if forwards were to play that way. So he pushed up on their central man and we began to put them under real pressure.' A double from Nicholas and a goal from Roy Aitken gave Celtic a 3-1 win. The win put Celtic eight points clear of Rangers and, more importantly, two ahead of Aberdeen, who had been dropping points with abandon.

In their next eight games Celtic dropped just one point, to Aberdeen, scoring 25 goals and conceding just three. That saw them go to Tannadice for their third-last game of the season, ready to reclaim the title, led by their captain Danny McGrain, now enjoying an Indian summer as Celtic's father figure.

A 3-2 win gave them the title. 'Winning the title was a tremendous experience,' says Charlie Nicholas. 'Danny McGrain had done it many, many times but to see the look on his face was fantastic. That always told the story for me, Danny McGrain's face after winning that Championship.' It was a third trophy in three seasons for Billy McNeill.

Europe had been a disappointment. The Cup-Winners' Cup preliminary round in August brought the Hungarians Diosgyoeri Miskolc to Parkhead. Celtic won 6-0 to make a 2-1 defeat in the second leg meaningless. Politechnica Timisoara of Romania came to Glasgow in the next round and two snappily-taken Nicholas goals gave Celtic a 2-1 win.

An eccentric refereeing performance from Greek referee Nicolas Iangvinus in Romania saw Celtic players, on occasion, being brought down only for the referee to give the opposition a foul. Or the ball would go out for a corner and he would give Politechnica a goal-kick. With Celtic 1-0 behind on the night and losing the tie on away goals, English goalkeeper Peter Latchford was booked for timewasting at a goal-kick. MacDonald and McGarvey were sent off, as was the Romanian goalkeeper. The score remained 1-0 and Celtic were out.

The European Cup draw for the 1981-82 season gave Celtic a tough first round game against the Italian champions Juventus. Five of the side that would win the World Cup for Italy the following summer took the field in front of 60,000 fans at Parkhead. Juve also included Liam Brady, the Irish international. Midway through the second half, a MacLeod shot took a deflection off sweeper Scirea and looped high over Zoff for the only goal of the

game. But goals from Virdis and Bettega in the return gave the Italians a 2-0 win.

Virdis' opening goal had been resulted from a breakaway move after a Celtic attack, with most Celtic players stranded upfield. 'There weren't many places where we played well away from home when we were in Europe,' says MacLeod.

'Maybe we were naïve, thinking we could attack teams but these teams are used to holding the ball and keeping it away from you. They're happy to hit you on the break even when they're at home.'

Danny McGrain, who at his peak was widely regarded as the world's best right-back, shows off the 1982 Premier League trophy. McGrain's knowledge and example was vital in helping along the young players in the early 1980s.

Another side wearing black and white stripes, St Mirren, had won 3-1 at Parkhead on the first day of the season in the League Cup section, a system that was being re-introduced after five years of straight knockout competition. The following Wednesday, defeat at St Johnstone ended Celtic's League Cup challenge. Another unfortunate aspect of that brief League Cup excursion was the form of Charlie Nicholas, who was looking sluggish due to the effects of a mystery virus. He was in and out of the team, and was often on the bench during the first half of the year. On 18 January, in a reserve game at Cappielow, he broke his leg. Celtic would have to do without his unique talents as they went about maintaining their position at the top of the League, where they had been since the first day of the season.

In October, Parkhead had gone into mourning at the death of the popular Johnny Doyle, killed in an accident at his home.

The final Old Firm clash of the season got off to a spectacular start when teenager Danny Crainie, in the side in place of another broken leg victim, McGarvey, scrambled the ball into the Rangers net with just one minute played. A second half goal from Tom McAdam gave Celtic a 2-1 victory that put them eight points clear of the Ibrox side, their closest challengers before that game.

Celtic had gone out of the Cup in the second round at Aberdeen but there would still be the closest thing to a Cup final for Celtic fans on the final day of the season. Fourteen wins in 15 games from Aberdeen, combined with Celtic's 3-0 defeat at Tannadice the previous Saturday, meant the results on the last fixture card of the season would decide the destination of the title.

'Aberdeen had to beat Rangers about 7-0 and we had to lose to St Mirren if Aberdeen were to win the League,' says MacLeod. 'At half-time Aberdeen were 4-0 up and we were 0-0. It was a nervy first-half but we were dominant and in the second-half the goals just came on. We played well and I think the score from Pittodrie made us even more determined. We were saying, "How can a Rangers team lose four goals in a first half?" I won't mention what else we were saying.'

A ten-minute spell midway through the second half settled it. The first goal resulted from a Murdo MacLeod run from the halfway line. He slipped the ball inside to Tommy Burns who rerouted the direction of play, leaving the St Mirren defence floundering and George McCluskey sent a left-foot shot into the corner of the net. A McAdam header and another shot from McCluskey made it 3-0 and Celtic's 33rd League title.

'It was my first season,' says Paul McStay, who had made his debut as a 17 year old three months previously. 'I had played a few games and had been left out of a few games and just at the end I'd managed to get back in for the final game. It was brilliant, my first taste of it and it just makes you want to have more when you see the enjoyment it brings.'

McStay, who showed himself to be the ideal midfield playmaker from his first kick of the ball in the first-team, was to miss only one game in all competitions the following season. Charlie Nicholas, restored to full fitness, made his return.

Cruyff meets Celtic again

Once again, Celtic found they would have to work their passage in Europe from the opening round, the draw pairing them with an Ajax team enjoying a resurgence under the tutelage of the greatest-ever European player, Johan Cruyff. Prices for the game at Parkhead ranged from £2.50 to £10. Beforehand, Cruyff told Ken Gallacher of the *Daily Record*: 'It is not so important for me to win any more. The big thing is to have 60,000 people in the stadium to see Celtic and Ajax and for them all to go back to the next game because they enjoyed themselves. This Ajax team is, I think, like Celtic. They want to go forward constantly. They are not built to be defensive. I know enough about Celtic to realise this promises to be an exciting tie.'

All of the scoring took place in the first half-hour. Olsen ended a fourth minute run with a shot that stole into Pat Bonner's net but after Cruyff had fouled Burns inside the box in the 14th minute Nicholas equalised with the penalty. Lerby made it 2-1 for Ajax but a McGarvey snapshot made it 2-2. 'The first half was the best you could see in European football,' said Cruyff. 'Two teams attacking, two teams scoring goals. What else do the people want to see? In the Celtic team I liked the red-haired man, Burns. The young boy McStay is also good. The fans were so good. They stayed to cheer us and I shall always remember that. It meant we had entertained – that is what I wanted.'

Charlie Nicholas as he will be immortalised in the collective Celtic memory: perfectly balanced and homing in on goal.

'I don't know how we got out with a 2-2 draw,' says Charlie Nicholas. 'They really were a footballing machine. They were superb to watch. It was probably the best game I've ever played in.'

A stunning goal from Nicholas opened the scoring in front of 65,000 in Amsterdam. A magnificent cross-field pass from Paul McStay found left-back Graeme Sinclair on the overlap. He moved the ball on to Nicholas who danced past two defenders, played a one-two with McGarvey and then sent a beautifully-judged chip over goalkeeper Piet Schrijvers. The forward ran towards the 3,000 Celtic fans present. 'That was my favourite goal for Celtic,' he says. 'As soon as I saw it going over the 'keeper and going into the corner I could see, in the background, this supporter running down the sloping terracing doing the "aeroplane". I ran away over to the corner to point at him. I've seen the goal a couple of times on video and I kill myself every time I see this guy.'

Vanenburg equalised for Ajax midway through the second half and when a Frank McGarvey header came off the bar with seven minutes remaining Celtic looked to be heading out of the tournament on the away goals rule. But with two minutes to go, George McCluskey accelerated into the box to prod the ball past Schrijvers for the winner.

Charlie Nicholas remembers that night with relish. 'Billy McNeill's words before we went out in the second leg were, "You are out of this competition. So you might as well go for it." And he was spot on because we were. It was kidology but at the same time it was fact. To win was tremendous. I think Ajax would have won that competition that year if it hadn't been for us. It was such a high to beat a club like Ajax, with Cruyff and all their stars. We'd got Celtic's respectability back.'

The second round draw produced the champions of Spain: Real Sociedad of San Sebastian. In the away leg, Celtic held the Spaniards comfortably until a Satrustegui shot took a deflection off full-back Mark Reid in 74 minutes for the opener. Four minutes later Uralde's shot looked to be covered by Bonner until it took a deflection off Aitken.

'In Sociedad we possibly played our best football in Europe in my time at Celtic,' says MacLeod. 'Against quality opposition we played really well and lost two goals completely against the run of play. It was more likely we would have scored.'

Charlie Nicholas signed off from Celtic duty in May 1983 with two penalties in Celtic's 4-2 win over Rangers.

On the Saturday before the return, 60,408 saw a fantastic Old Firm match end in a 3-2 win for Celtic. But there was to be disappointment for the 55,000 who turned up on the Wednesday. After 25 minutes Uralde was unmarked in the six-yard box for a header that Bonner got a hand to, only for the ball to squirm into the net. Two goals from Murdo MacLeod gave Celtic a win on the night but another pre-Christmas European exit.

'The game was a bogey early on,' says the scorer. 'But our pride made us want to beat them on the night and we scored just before half-time. I had two or three chances, one kicked off the line, one blocked. I could have scored maybe four or five that night. Losing the early goal we were naïve again. It was their first time up the park. They got the corner, had two men in the box and one of them scored. That was us all over although they had to lift their game to defend against us.'

McNeill's angry scenes

During the trip to Hungary in 1980, Billy McNeill had become involved in an argument with football reporter Gerry McNee that had resulted in the latter receiving a black eye. That autumn of 1982, the Celtic manager had a confrontation with referee Andrew Waddell when he stood aggressively head-to-head with the official on the Parkhead touchline during a turbulent game with Aberdeen. A similar lack of composure sometimes appeared to be transmitted to his team's performances during those years, particularly in Europe.

'We had a lot of good players who could make passes,' says Murdo MacLeod. 'We could keep the ball. We could defend reasonably well. We could score goals. We had a good blend in midfield. We had everything. If we had gone into Europe a wee bit more aware of how European teams played we could have done a lot better. It was a lack of experience throughout from everybody. It was the usual Scottish thing of thinking we would beat anybody home or away. That works against us. You've got to believe you'll beat them but you've got to know how you'll beat them, not just because we're Scottish and we'll go out and battle.

'Billy could possibly have made us more aware of the other team. When we played in Scotland we didn't think much about the other team. In Europe you need to be a wee bit more aware of your opposition. I think that's maybe slightly how we got let down.'

Two superb goals, one from Charlie Nicholas, one from Murdo MacLeod, gave Celtic a 2-1 win in the League Cup final against Rangers in December. Celtic had scored 39 goals in 10 games to get there but none were better than the two that graced the final. After 22 minutes, Nicholas intelligently created space for himself on the edge of the box, let the ball run across his body until the time was right to shoot and, using hardly any backlift, sent a first-time shot past Stewart. Nine minutes on, as Celtic thoroughly dominated the game, MacLeod thumped one past Stewart at supersonic speed. MacLeod had been encouraged by McNeill to hover on the edge of the box waiting for scraps and he had done just that.

Celtic chairman Desmond White (centre) welcomes new manager David Hay (right) and his assistant Frank Connor (left) to Celtic Park in the summer of 1983.

That was just one of 46 goals, 14 of them penalties, for Nicholas that season, when his talents blossomed spectacularly. He was almost impossible for defenders to mark, never predictable, never deliberate. Two-footed, light, and elusive, he could use any part of his boot to score and his mastery of the ball was such that he instinctively disguised his intentions, ensuring defenders had lost the plot long before the ball ended up in the net. 'In my first year I was really young and naïve,' he says. 'I don't think I really learned too much but I think when I came back from my broken leg I really did listen to the older guys.'

'The good thing about Charlie,' says MacLeod, 'was that even though he was an individualist he was part of the team, which was pleasing, because a lot of individualists play for themselves. He was the best young player I have seen. He was in a good team and we made chances for him but he always took them. Or he'd make a half-chance himself and take it. A lot of players can show good skills in training games but when it comes to a match they don't try the same things. Charlie would and it would work.'

Nicholas spoiled the Celtic fans with his play that year, giving them more to enthuse about than many players manage in an entire career. He ended up with both the Players' and the Football Writers' Player of the Year awards. 'Davie Provan was a great supplier of goals for me,' he says. 'So was Frank McGarvey. We worked so well together. Even when Frank wasn't there George McCluskey was a good aid to me. George and I were quite similar players but we could play together. We had an understanding.

'Danny McGrain, for me, was a genius. He gave me service in and around the box and I felt comfortable in receiving it. He would give me the ball exactly when and where I wanted it, as did Tommy Burns. You didn't know when he was going to pass it but you knew where he would pass it to you and he was always available to get it back. Tommy never shirked a decision. If we were in trouble he was there. There are very few players like that, who are always prepared to make a mistake to help you. So I was alongside players who educated me.'

Nicholas was missing through injury for the Scottish Cup semi-final and Celtic went down 1-0 to Aberdeen. They had led the League, playing some enthralling stuff, from the beginning of the season, but four days after losing that semi they lost 3-2 at home to Dundee United and then, the following Saturday, at Aberdeen. That handed the initiative to Dundee United and Celtic went into the last day of the season hoping the Tannadice side would lose against Dundee while they were winning at Ibrox. It wasn't to be. Celtic won 4-2 but United won too.

'I knew before the game that I was probably going to be moving,' says Nicholas. 'At half-time it was probably the quietest dressing

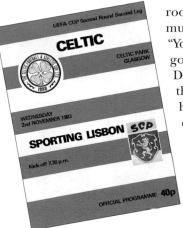

Winger Davie Provan (below) skilfully eludes a desperate challenge in the 1983 UEFA Cup tie against Sporting Lisbon at Parkhead.

Frank McGarvey (below right) seals a famous victory with the fifth and final goal in that match.

room I've been involved in. Billy never said much. He just said to us, in a fairly calm tone, "You have got us in this position. You have got 45 minutes to sort it out. And, by the way, Dundee United are drawing." We came into the main area of the tunnel at Ibrox, we still had a 20-yard walk to the pitch, and all we could hear was "Walk on" and it was just as if a cold shiver went through me. It was incredible that these guys were doing that when we were 2-0 down to Rangers. Before you knew it we were 4-2 up and it could have been more. I remember going to the crowd that day on my own and a mass of photographers running at me and Danny coming to take me away from it. I was crying that day as I walked away from it. It wasn't just the banners, it was the faces of the Celtic supporters.'

Those supporters waited anxiously to see whether Nicholas would leave. 'Billy told me the Board had instructed him to make me an offer. So Billy showed me the offer and I told him it wasn't what I had been anticipating. It wasn't much different from what I was on.

'I told Billy I wanted it resolved and he said, "Well, you've to go and see Desmond White in his business office in West Nile Street." I thought that was particularly strange and I think Billy felt it was strange because Billy always did the deals. I went to see Desmond and he started speaking about things like his time in the RAF and challenges in life and how he had had problems with his arm. He said to me, "I'll understand if the challenges are there and you want to go

somewhere else and you want to move on." I think they were prepared to say, "We can get maybe £600,000 or £700,000 for this guy rather than paying him big money." That's just the way Celtic conducted their business in those days.' Arsenal paid £625,000 for him. His weekly wage there was approximately five times that which Celtic had offered.

McNeill leaves Parkhead

Within weeks, Billy McNeill would also leave, to become manager of Manchester City after a run-in with the board over his terms and conditions. Newspaper reports suggested that four other Premier League bosses, including Ricky McFarlane of St Mirren, were better paid than he was. McNeill later stated that he believed Desmond White had made up his mind that it was time for a parting of the ways. 'I was very sad at the way the thing had happened,' says Tommy Burns. 'I was shocked, because I didn't think he'd be allowed to go away, shocked that they couldn't come to an agreement with somebody who'd been as successful as that for them.

'Big Billy was a good leader for the club. I probably played my best stuff while he was here. He could have an argument with you and then an hour later he'd come and put his arm round you and you'd go away feeling ten-feet tall again. He was a very good motivator. He also had a lot of very, very good players who were young and determined and hungry. He cajoled us and pushed us along

Paul McStay, Scotland's Young Player of the Year in 1983, in command of the situation against Aberdeen. He would go on to become the most-capped player in Celtic's history. By the end of the 1994-95 season, he had made 72 appearances for the Scottish national team.

all the way and I think what we won during that first five years he was here as manager speaks volumes for him.'

Celtic's sixth manager was David Hay, who was 35 years old when he took control on 4 July 1983. Hay had retired from playing with Chelsea at the age of 31, after several eye operations. He had coached Chelsea's youth team, then became assistant manager to Ally MacLeod at Motherwell for two years. In 1991 he became manager at Fir Park, guiding the 'Well to the 1991-92 First Division title. But at the end of that season he had quit, hoping to take up a job in the USA. That never materialised and he then concentrated on running his pub in Paisley.

He had been content with his life outside football.When Celtic asked if he would like to become manager he took a couple of days to consider the offer, as Billy McNeill had done five years previously. 'If it hadn't been the Celtic job I might never have gone back into football,' he says. 'I didn't make any dramatic changes to the structure of the club or the style of play when I came in. There were good players there and Billy had been the same as me, he knew the strength of Celtic. There was only one way and that was an attacking way.'

One of Billy McNeill's last acts as Celtic manager had been to sign a striker, 19-year-old Glasgow University student Brian McClair, from Motherwell for £70,000. He was enormously effective. His tally in 1983-84 stood close comparison with that of Nicholas the previous season, McClair scoring 31 times in open play. He sometimes looked untidy, all arms and legs as he chased everything in sight. But he was hugely productive, capable of running hard at defences, snapping up half-chances or scoring from long-range.

One of his most memorable goals that season came in the League Cup final in March 1984. With Celtic trailing 2-0, he anticipated Tommy Burns' chip over the Rangers defensive wall to volley Celtic's first goal. Mark Reid made it 2-2 with a penalty in the dying seconds but it was Rangers who got the winner in extra-time. Two months later Celtic were back at Hampden for the Scottish Cup final. Black, looking offside, had put Aberdeen ahead midway through the first half and referee Valentine made Roy Aitken the first player to be sent off in a Scottish Cup final since 1929. Celtic equalised through an outstanding goal from Paul McStay in the 85th minute but Mark McGhee got the winner for Aberdeen in extra-time.

Celtic had made an impressive start in the League with five consecutive

The moment that sparked off one of the most controversial nights in the history of European football. Rapid Vienna goalkeeper Ehn has dropped the ball and Tommy Burns is about to score.

Weinhofer lies prone on the Parkhead turf as Rapid captain Krankl (far right) leads the protests over his team-mate's imaginary injury.

This was one of the consequences of the replayed match at Old Trafford for Celtic after two of their supporters attacked Rapid players. They were punished by having to play their next European tie, against Atletico Madrid in 1985, behind closed doors. Yet again Atletico had participated in a freak match at Parkhead.

A miraculous goal from Frank McGarvey wins the centenary Cup final for Celtic. Roy Aitken's superb cross has just been met by the diving McGarvey for a header that curved outwards then bent inwards at the last moment to shave Hamish McAlpine's post as it entered the Dundee United net.

wins but they dropped six points out of ten in October. From then until the end of the season they were second-best to the European Cup-Winners' Cup holders Aberdeen.

In the first round of the UEFA Cup Celtic struggled at home to Aarhus but turned on the style in Denmark for a 5-1 aggregate win. A more glamorous trip presented itself next, a visit to Sporting Lisbon. Two goals from Jordao gave the home side a 2-0 win on a night when Celtic were overrun. The return looked a difficult proposition but a crowd of

Tom McAdam swings with delight on McAlpine's crossbar after Davie Provan's goal in the 1985 Cup final. It was one of many great days in Celtic's history when the fans had played a key role in victory.

almost 40,000 showed the appetite Celtic's fans retained for top class European football.

With 17 minutes gone, one of Frank McGarvey's quick turns on the run shook off a defender like a rag doll and Tommy Burns rose at the back post to get his head to the forward's cross. Two minutes before half-time Celtic were level. Provan's cross was chested down by McAdam and the sweeper, who had begun his career as a striker at Dumbarton, netted with a firmly-struck shot.

Sporting, in green-and-white hoops, suffered another blow on half-time when McClair scored the best goal of the night. He took a Burns pass, made two instantaneous changes of direction that created a huge gap in the Sporting defence and, falling, shot to beat the advancing goalkeeper. Murdo MacLeod made it four and after a 40-yard run Burns picked out McGarvey who slipped the ball past Katziris for the fifth.

'It was as close to the old European nights as I've seen at Celtic Park,' says David Hay. 'It epitomised what Celtic fans imagine a European night to be, flair accompanied by bombardment. They just collapsed even though they were a good team.'

'That was the best we ever played in Europe in a home game in my time at Parkhead,' says Murdo MacLeod. 'We had a lot of good nights at Parkhead but that was a special, special night. There was a lot of hard talking after the first game but it was just a case before the second game of making sure we put them under pressure. The fans were magnificent. It was just a case of being positive and that worked for us because we were at home, it wouldn't work for you away from home if you had 50,000 fans against you.'

'The place was just electric,' says Tommy Burns. 'That was as great a night as I can remember here. I managed to get a goal early on and from then it was just a case of believing that we were just going to run this team into the ground. Everybody seemed to be so pumped up and everybody played to their top form. I think we could have beaten anybody in the world that night because everybody was absolutely flying. We beat them 5-0; it could have been 10-0. They were a decent side but we just produced tidal wave after tidal wave of attack.'

Nottingham Forest were next on the European agenda for a Scotland-England clash that generated huge interest in the preceding weeks. At the City Ground, Celtic were the better side, adjusting to a difficult surface and unlucky not to get at least one away goal. After that 0-0 draw, players and fans came away confident of winning the return in Glasgow. Celtic's mistake was in believing they were involved in a British-style Cup-tie. Forest's style, however, was more European than the Europeans' and the second leg, with Celtic expected to attack from the start, suited them pefectly.

After arriving at Glasgow airport, Forest manager Brian Clough spotted David Hay's pub on the drive through Paisley. He stopped the coach and instructed his players to pile in for a lunchtime session. On leaving, he told the barman that Hay would pay the bill. On the evening of the match Forest were the more relaxed side, content to soak up pressure in front of 67,000 Celtic fans desperate to see a breakthrough goal. The closest Celtic came in the first half was a long, high ball that found Mark Reid all alone inside the Forest penalty area, with only goalkeeper Hans van Breukelen blocking the way to goal. The jam-packed Celtic end craned their heads to watch, ready to celebrate, but the full-back's shot came off the Dutchman's body. Two second half Forest counter-attacks, finished off by Hodge and Walsh, killed the game despite a late headed goal from MacLeod.

Hay feels the pressure

It was just Celtic's third season without a trophy in 20 years and that pedigree put Hay under pressure. But he had quickly earned the respect of the players and they were determined to win something the following season. Hay was an affable man and that was occasionally perceived by those outside the club as weakness. However, his assistant, Frank Connor, was capable of parade ground brusqueness when it was required.

'Davie was a very determined manager,' says Paul McStay. 'All he wanted to do was have success. He's a quiet man. It was wee Frank who did most of the business on the training park. Sometimes you need a partnership so it was a good balance. But Davie would let you know if things weren't right. I was in his office a couple of times.'

As losing Cup-finalists, Celtic were in the following season's European Cup-Winners' Cup. Ghent of Belgium won 1-0 at home and were always dangerous in the return at

Parkhead until a rare headed goal from McStay a minute from the end made it 3-0 to Celtic. Between that game and the next round, Celtic broke the Scottish transfer record to sign Mo Johnston from Watford for £400,000. Johnston had moved south from Partick Thistle a year previously and was to establish himself as the most accomplished Scottish international striker of the 1980s. He was ineligible for Celtic's second round European tie against Rapid Vienna.

Early in the first leg in Vienna, the Rapid midfielder Reinhard Kienast committed two vicious fouls, one on McGarvey, one on the forward Alan McInally, a signing from Ayr United in the close season. Those offences went unpunished by Bulgarian referee Yordan Zhezkov. McGarvey had to go off injured. Shortly after half-time Pacult gave Rapid the lead. Then McStay, having an outstanding game, found McInally who set up McClair for the equaliser. But goals from Lainer and Krankl made it 3-1. McInally was sent off after an over-enthusiastic tackle in the second half, a decision that was hard to swallow after Kienast's earlier behaviour.

In the return, Celtic had the Viennese in a whirl from the kick-off. After 32 minutes,

McStay, again untouchable in the midfield, picked out Provan and the winger's cross was put in the net by McClair. On half-time Celtic went ahead on the night and in the tie, through MacLeod. Tommy Burns became the third man to trouble Vienna when, in the 68th minute, he slid in to force a loose ball into the net after goalkeeper Ehn dropped a McGarvey effort. Ehn and his team-mates raged long and hard about Swedish referee Kjell Johansson's decision to award the goal. Krankl was booked and two minutes later Kienast caught Burns with a punch to the back of the head and was sent off.

Shortly afterwards, Ehn kicked Burns and Celtic were awarded a penalty. The referee, surrounded by Rapid players, went to the Jungle side of the pitch to consult his linesman. Substitute Weinhofer, who had come on for Pacult with a few choice words in his ear from coach Otto Baric, then fell to the ground. He lay prone for nearly ten minutes and play was held up for quarter of an hour before he left the field with his head covered in bandages, like a cartoon caricature of an invalid. Rapid claimed he had been hit on the head by a bottle although TV showed this clearly not to have been the case. Youngster

Scotland's Player of the Year in 1987, Brian McClair, indulging in one of his favourite pastimes, scoring against Rangers. In each of his four seasons at Celtic, from 1983 to 1987, he was the club's top scorer.

Peter Grant failed to make clean contact with the ball at the penalty and sent his kick wide of Ehn's right-hand post.

UEFA's independent observer, Dr Hubert Claessen of West Germany, stated that he had seen a bottle land on the pitch but that it had not touched any players. 'It was almost as if they planned for it,' says David Hay. 'What was lost in all the controversy was how well we played on that night.'

Rapid's underhand tactics

The following day, Rapid telexed UEFA to complain that Celtic had been responsible for the fans' behaviour, citing a precedent from 1972 when a match between Inter Milan and Borussia Moenchengladbach had been replayed. Inter had lost 7-1 but one of their players had been struck by an empty can. Yet by 1984 that case had become discredited. Inter's ex-president had admitted that a party from the Italian club had visited Helsinki to exert 'influence' on the Finnish member of UEFA's disciplinary committee. Mazzola, the Inter captain, also admitted that he had tampered with the evidence.

Nine days later, a UEFA disciplinary committee met to consider Rapid's complaint in the light of Dr Claessen's report. Weinhofer's story was discredited. Kienast was suspended for four games. The coach Baric was suspended from the touchline for three games; he had thrown a bottle back on to the pitch. Celtic were fined £4,000, Rapid £5,000. Rapid appealed, changing their story to Weinhofer having been hit by a coin. The committee that met to consider that story didn't use TV evidence and doubled Rapid's fine but ordered the game to be replayed at a neutral venue! The gate receipts from this third match were to be split between the clubs: more than enough to cover Rapid's fine. It was a ludicrous outcome. How the UEFA officials responsible arrived at their verdict has never been revealed but in the eyes of Celtic's supporters both they and Rapid Vienna remain thoroughly discredited to this day.

The replayed second leg had to take place 100 kilometres from Glasgow. Old Trafford was chosen as the venue. The largest travelling support for a European tie, 40,000, made its way south. With ten Celtic men pressing, Aitken hit the post in the 17th minute. Pacult immediately broke away to score the only goal of the game. Later in the match, a spectator attacked Rapid goalkeeper Feurer and at the end Pacult was kicked by a fan (at the time being held by two policemen) as he left the field. There had been the temptation beforehand to give the tie to Rapid but that could have resulted in another crazy punishment from the unpredictable UEFA. In addition, Celtic believed they were better than Rapid and could beat them again. But on the night the tension was too much for them and they produced a disjointed, fragmented performance.

'I think Pittodrie would have suited us better,' says MacLeod. 'Old Trafford was a ground where players had hardly played – maybe once or twice in testimonials – so we were maybe taking a bit of a chance going down there.' Tommy Burns recalls: 'The Celtic supporters were so psyched up. You could see the venom on their faces when you were driving into Old Trafford. It backfired on us.' David Hay says: 'I maintain that if we had got through that tie, which we should have done, we would have gone all the way.'

'The best opportunity we had in Europe was the Vienna game,' says Paul McStay. 'We were through to the quarter-finals, then the game was replayed. We could have gone even further in that tournament. It really sickened me. Similar incidents have happened since, involving other clubs, and the penalty has not

Murdo MacLeod, one of Billy McNeill's best buys for Celtic. He provided the club with nine years of wholehearted action before leaving for Borussia Dortmund in 1987. MacLeod had been prepared to stay at Parkhead but a verbal offer of a testimonial was withdrawn on the orders of the board.

been as much as the one we had to suffer that time, having to replay the game. Other teams have had to play their next ties 200 miles away or whatever but have still gone through whereas we were penalised and had to replay the game. The feigning of the injury sickened me, it was sad.'

In the League Celtic were always second-best to champions Aberdeen and went out of the League Cup to Dundee United at the quarter-final stage. But the same two teams were to meet in the 100th Scottish Cup final in front of 60,346 people on 18 May 1985. With Celtic trailing 1-0, Hay sent on substitutes Pierce O'Leary and McClair to get more drive in midfield. And with the vast Celtic support stretching their larynxes to the limit as they roared the Bhoys on, two excellent goals won the Cup. With 14 minutes to go, Provan curved a perfectly measured free-kick over the United wall for the equalise. Six minutes from the end McGarvey got the winner.

'The one-off centenary Cup final and who wins it? Celtic,' says Paul McStay. 'Right through the history of the club they've always made the one-offs: the Coronation Cup, the Exhibition Cup, first British team to win the European Cup, the double in the centenary year. Long may it continue.'

In 1985 chairman Desmond White died and was succeeded by Tom Devlin. The following year Devlin also passed away and was replaced by Jack McGinn.

Hay's good record in Cup competitions went AWOL in 1985-86 with Celtic losing to Hibs at Easter Road in the quarter-finals of both the League Cup and the Scottish Cup. Hibs won the League Cup tie 4-3 on penalties after a 4-4 draw and the Scottish Cup tie 4-3. Although entertaining for the fans, those games threw up serious questions about the strength of Celtic's defence. The Cup-Winners' Cup had paired Celtic with Atletico Madrid, Celtic playing well in the away leg to get a 1-1 draw through a Johnston goal. But Atletico's second appearance at Parkhead was another freak game. It was played behind closed doors as a punishment for the misbehaviour of the two fans at Old Trafford. Celtic badly missed their supporters and lost 2-1.

On 14 September, 39,450 fans at the match with Aberdeen at Parkhead observed a respectful silence in honour of the memory of Jock Stein, who had died of a heart attack while managing Scotland in a World Cup tie in Cardiff four days earlier. The passing of

the man who had brought Scottish football in general and Celtic in particular into the modern era was mourned throughout the land.

There had been a series of dramatic endings to the Premier League competition in the years prior to the 1985-86 season but none could match this one. Hearts had gone top of the Premier League before Christmas and remained there for the next five months. As they entered the final day of the League programme on 3 May they were unbeaten in 1986. Celtic were unbeaten in 15 games as they travelled to Love Street, Paisley for their final fixture. However, Celtic were two points behind the Edinburgh side and were trailing them by four goals in terms of goal difference. Both sides faced opponents in the

Celtic goalkeeper Pat Bonner repels the new challenge from Ibrox in the form of Rangers centre-back Terry Butcher. Rangers were revolutionising Scottish football, not in a playing sense but in a financial one, paying hefty fees for players, with wages to match. David Hay, in contrast, had to make do and mend.

lower reaches of the table but Dundee, Hearts' opponents, had an outside chance of a European place if they won the match at Dens Park. But it looked to be expecting too much for Hearts, potential double-winners, to crack after such a long spell unbeaten.

Two goals each from Johnston and McClair and one from McStay saw Celtic take a 5-0 lead with 54 minutes gone. Two of the goals were outstanding. The third was a six-man move begun by McGrain flicking the ball over his shoulder on the edge of his own penalty area. The ball then shuttled speedily from MacLeod back to McGrain to McStay to Aitken to McGrain again to McClair until Johnston slid it into the net at the back post. McStay's goal was brilliantly taken, the ball streaking off the outside of his right boot from 18 yards at lightning speed. But with the half-time score at Dundee 0-0 it looked like an honourable but unsuccessful last-gasp effort. Then two roars filled the sky as news came through that Dundee had scored twice in the final seven minutes of their game.

Murdo MacLeod recalls: 'I did a radio interview with Hugh Keevins [on Radio Clyde] with 15 or 16 games to go. I said it was going to be tight but that we'd take it right up to the last game of the season and we'd win it on the last day even though it could possibly go down to goal difference. And that's the way it worked out. It's better to have things in your own hands but when you're depending on somebody else and it works for you it's great. A lot of people criticise St Mirren, saying they'd lain down to Celtic, but no team in that first half would have lived with us.'

'That team had the capability of doing well,' says David Hay. 'But we needed to strengthen the defence in one or two areas and the money wasn't made available.'

Another European Cup campaign began in September 1986 with a win over Shamrock Rovers of Ireland. In the second round, Mo Johnston got Celtic's goal in a 1-1 home draw with Dynamo Kiev. 'At Parkhead we were man-marking and all that happened was they'd use it to pull us around,' says Murdo MacLeod. 'But that was one of the first times we sat back after the first leg and looked at how they had opened us up. And we learned from it. In Kiev we defended in areas and we were unlucky. We ended up with more of the ball and outplayed them. At 1-1 we had a good chance but missed it and they scored immediately and then got a late goal.'

Kiev had never been beaten at home in Europe but their manager Lobanovsky stated after the game that Celtic's performance had been the best in 21 years of European competition by any foreign team.

In the League Cup final an exceptional goal from Brian McClair had Celtic at 1-1 with the new Rangers until a controversial late penalty was awarded to the Ibrox side by referee David Syme. Rangers won 2-1. In the closing minutes Johnston was sent off, crossing himself in full view of the Rangers support as he left the field. Celtic made an early exit, to Hearts, in the Scottish Cup. The League had appeared to be on its way to Celtic Park but after building up a nine-point lead over Rangers halfway through the season Celtic frittered it away.

Disruption at Parkhead

That second half of Celtic's season was disrupted by a transfer request from Johnston. McClair and MacLeod also became unsettled. McInally, a useful reserve, wanted away. 'If we had strengthened the team around about November with a couple of defenders it may well have been different,' says Hay. 'One of the directors said, "If Davie's going to buy a couple of players the money will have to come out of his own pocket." That epitomised their attitude at that time.'

Billy McNeill had been sacked as manager of Aston Villa at the end of the 1986-87 season. That summer he made a flying visit to Scotland to celebrate the 20th anniversary of the Lisbon Lions' European Cup win, and, with Hay still in position, was approached by Jack McGinn to return to Celtic as manager. There was little chance of him refusing.

'Celtic appointed me when I was probably inexperienced,' says Hay, 'and sacked me when I was more capable of doing the job. Things were done behind my back. The hurt was deep. I felt let down because I had always been an up-front kind of person.

'As manager I felt I did relatively well. People used to say I was laid-back but my approach was to keep things on an even-keel. I was never too demonstrative because I always felt that the traditions of Celtic made that the way to act. It was maybe my undoing because people looked at me and might say I didn't care enough. Nothing could have been further from the truth.'

With Billy McNeill back as manager, Celtic celebrated their centenary year in glorious fashion. The following years, however, brought little happiness to Celtic Park.

8 Celtic Enter a New Age

Celtic began their centenary season wearing a smart new outfit to mark a special period in the club's history. A new design of the traditional hoops had the original club crest, a Celtic cross, replacing the lucky four-leafed clover on the club badge. In the summer of 1987, however, there appeared little chance of the team matching the new strip for style. Key players had left when their contracts came to an end. Both members of the international-class striking partnership of Mo Johnston and Brian McClair had left: Johnston to Nantes for £350,000 and McClair to Manchester United for an £850,000 tribunal fee.

Alan McInally, who had shown promise in several run-outs in the first team the previous season, went to Aston Villa, leaving Celtic bereft of striking power. Murdo MacLeod moved to Germany. Davie Provan retired that summer through illness. A departure that was mourned for sentimental reasons was that of the 37-year-old Danny McGrain on a free transfer to Hamilton Accies.

The handover of power from David Hay to Billy McNeill had been messy and McNeill's sojourn in England had been a far from glorious one. Manchester City and Aston Villa were relegated at the end of the 1986-87 season, during which period he had been manager of both clubs. Initially, he had done well at Maine Road. With no money to work with, he had won City promotion. But after a disagreement over what he saw as interference in his running of the team, he had left City early in the autumn of 1986 for Villa. At the end of the season, with Villa heading for relegation, McNeill was sacked.

Back at Celtic, McNeill had quickly invested in some new players: 30-year-old midfielder Billy Stark from Aberdeen for £75,000, 19-year-old striker Andy Walker from Motherwell for £350,000 and right-back Chris Morris from Sheffield Wednesday for £125,000. He also inherited centre-back Mick McCarthy, a £450,000 signing by Hay the week before he was sacked, and a player McNeill had worked well with at Manchester City. Tommy Craig, who had been appointed Hay's assistant in February after Frank Connor had been sacked by the then manager, remained in place. His coaching expertise would be of great value to McNeill.

Pre-season results were not encouraging; in particular a 5-1 defeat at home to Arsenal. 'We were going back on the plane,' says Charlie Nicholas, 'and a lot of the English guys were saying to me that Celtic were hopeless and that they'd never win anything playing like that. I didn't have an answer.'

Yet McNeill, his appetite sharpened by the lean years in England, was to achieve a year of greatness with that team. It would be one of the most exciting seasons in the club's history. 'Every kick of the ball was good that year,' says Paul McStay. 'It was just amazing. I don't think there was a low point. It was just brilliant because everything went to plan. Everything clicked right from the start and after that there was no stopping us.'

'When Billy came back it was smashing to find he still had the same enthusiasm,' says Tommy Burns. 'He was a great enthusiast. That first season was great.'

The kick-off was at Cappielow on 8 August and Mark McGhee, signed from Hamburg in 1985, scored the first League goal of McNeill's second period as manager when he headed home a McStay free-kick. Stark got the second, then Walker made it 3-0, convert-

Celtic celebrate after a 2-1 win over Dundee United in the 1988 Scottish Cup final had given them the double in their centenary season.

133

After a four-year stay in England, Billy McNeill welcomed with open arms the chance to return to Parkhead in 1987.

ing the rebound after McGhee's fierce shot had hit the bar. Tommy Burns, after an eye-catching run, knocked in the fourth. Wins over Hearts and Motherwell were followed by a defeat at Dunfermline before Rangers arrived at Parkhead on 29 August.

Billy Stark got the only goal of the game in the fifth minute, showing great presence of mind to sweep a low, precisely-angled left-foot drive past Rangers goalkeeper Woods' fingertips. Stark proceeded to show some of the sweet touches that would sugar Celtic's season. It was all too much for Rangers player/manager Graeme Souness who was sent off for a tackle on Stark that had Grant and Aitken in a lather of anger. 'During the first half-hour,' said McNeill afterwards, 'we possibly played the best football I have ever seen in an Old Firm match.'

Rangers had made a big impact in Souness' first season and everyone wanted to see what Celtic's response would be. Now they knew. Andy Walker remembers: 'Experienced players such as Tommy Burns, Roy Aitken, Billy Stark and Mark McGhee helped me. Mark especially gave me a lot of good guidance because he played in the same position as me. In the first eight games we played really well. We wanted to send a message out to our supporters that we were ready to do well and we certainly did that.

'We started off well and I was pleased to get a few goals. It helps you to settle down when the crowd take a liking to you. The big test was playing our first Old Firm game and we played really well that day.'

Three days later, Celtic went out of the League Cup, losing 1-0 at Aberdeen. By coincidence, Celtic had been drawn against Borussia Dortmund, Murdo MacLeod's new club, in the UEFA Cup. A fortnight on from the Rangers match, 41,414 saw Celtic take a 1-0 lead over the first West German side to appear at Parkhead in European competition. McStay sent the ball into Walker's path and he was quick to nick it past De Beer.

Mill equalised midway through the second half but, after Walker and McGhee had both gone close for Celtic, central defender Derek Whyte forced the ball into the net after Dortmund had failed to clear a Paul McStay free-kick. 'I got a good reception at the start of the game,' says Murdo MacLeod, the first ex-Celt to play against the Parkhead club in Europe. 'And the game had just finished when the Jungle started singing "Murdo, Murdo." I waved to them to thank them, then the Celtic end started and then everyone in the stand stood. There were tears in my eyes. I couldn't stay out any longer. It was as big a night for me as anything.'

three players, together with another of Rangers' Englishmen, Roberts, to appear in court on breach of the peace charges.

It was unusual for the law to interfere in an incident that had not noticeably inflamed the crowd. It seemed like a knee-jerk reaction to the bad publicity that the incident, along with TV evidence of Roberts conducting the Rangers crowd in sectarian songs, had received throughout Britain. Celtic had gone 2-0 up in that match but those incidents upset them more than Rangers and the Ibrox side got back to 2-2 right at the death.

A glorious unbeaten run

The following week, the young midfielder Tony Shepherd scored for Celtic and Paul McStay saw a shot rebound from the foot of the post as they lost 2-1 at home to Dundee United. From then until mid-April, however, Celtic went 31 games unbeaten. A 1-0 win at Hibs in late November took them top of the League. They would not be moved from there for the rest of the 1987-88 season. They finished ten points clear of Hearts in the Premier Division and lost only five of 55 games in all competitions.

'We'd score so many goals late on,' says Andy Walker, whose sharp reflexes and speed off the mark saw him finish top scorer that season with 32 goals. 'We went on a ridiculous unbeaten run. I remember we played Hearts and we were 2-0 down with seconds left. Then I got a penalty and Paul McStay scored in the last minute and that stopped Hearts getting away at the top.

'We had a great never-say-die attitude. There were so many last-minute winners and equalisers. Billy McNeill was great to work with. He worked really well with Tommy Craig that year. Tommy was a big influence on all the players and during the pre-season period he was instrumental in laying out the way we played: he stressed the importance of getting the ball back quickly and pressing.'

On the way to the Scottish Cup semi-final, Celtic had beaten Stranraer, Hibs and Partick Thistle without conceding a goal. The semi at Hampden would bring the best two clubs in Scotland together, Celtic and Hearts. A crowd of 65,886 saw Hearts open the scoring on the hour. MacPherson jumped at Bonner and put the goalkeeper off as Whittaker's cross sailed into the net. It looked like a foul

Two of the goals that were vital to Celtic's centenary double. Billy Stark (top) sweeps in the only goal of the match with Rangers in August. Four months later, Andy Walker (far right) watches Frank McAvennie's header loop over replacement goalkeeper Roberts in the Rangers goal.

Mick McCarthy, who had been injured, made his debut in Dortmund. Midway through the first half Celtic, composed in the face of German pressure, nearly scored through Peter Grant. Only a desperate save by De Beer kept his effort out of the net. It was an open, competitive game with both sides creating good scoring chances but two goals from Dortmund in the final 20 minutes put the German side through.

In the second Old Firm clash that season, at Ibrox in mid-October, a scuffle ended in Celtic striker Frank McAvennie, a record £725,000 buy from West Ham that month, being sent off along with Rangers goalkeeper Woods and centre-back Butcher. The procurator fiscal's office in Glasgow ordered those

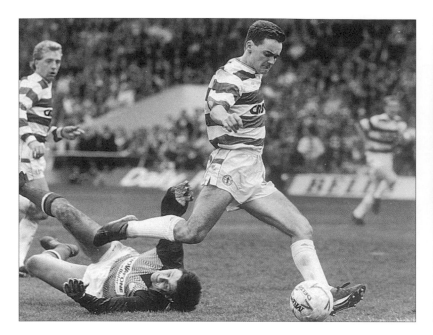

and Bonner remained adamant long after the game that he had been impeded.

Celtic, with McStay ceaselessly inventive in the middle of the park, exerted enormous pressure on the Hearts defence. But as Tommy Burns went to take a corner in front of the Celtic end with three minutes remaining, they were still behind. The ball swung wide, almost to the edge of the penalty area. Hearts goalkeeper Henry Smith looked to have it but, under pressure from Roy Aitken, he dropped the ball and Mark McGhee, with eight Hearts players in attendance, drove it into the net.

With the seconds ticking off, and a replay beckoning, Billy Stark found McAvennie with a throw on the right. The striker sent a high ball to the back post and McGhee used his strength to beat Smith to the ball and nod it down to Walker, who was standing almost on the line. The striker quickly swivelled to shoot high into the net.

The final produced an almost identical situation for Celtic. Before a capacity crowd of 73,000, in a moment loaded with poignancy, Kevin Gallacher, the grandson of Celtic's Patsy, opened the scoring for Dundee United. This time the opposition had scored a goal worthy of the occasion, Gallacher racing past Roy Aitken to score with a powerful 15-yard volley. With 15 minutes remaining, Stark's nifty first-time pass found left-back Anton Rogan on the overlap. He swerved round United right-back Bowman and crossed for McAvennie to head the equaliser.

Celtic stepped up the pace but with seconds remaining extra-time looked likely. A last flurry of action saw Celtic win a corner in front of their vast bank of fans, drawing on their last reserves of energy to roar the team on. Winger Joe Miller, signed from Aberdeen earlier in the season, took the kick. It wasn't a good one, the ball trundling along the ground and away from the main danger area. Substitute Stark made the best of it, getting a shot on target. It came off United defender Narey's shin and into the path of McAvennie who had found space on the edge of the six-yard-box. United goalkeeper Thomson had moved to stop Stark's shot. Frank had a clear view of goal and put the seal on Celtic's most spectacular double. On the sun-baked, overheated terraces the supporters' boisterousness bubbled over into uncontainable delight.

The new life that had been generated in the club by six imaginative signings had provided the fuel for a heartwarming season when Celtic had played with a flair and a passion that was matched by their supporters. 'Throughout the year there were things going on related to the centenary year,' says Andy Walker. 'It was maybe just the wee spur you needed. I've never been to so many supporters' functions in my puff! It conjured up well these images from the past. It was a magical time for the club and having the chance to play a part in it made it extra-special.'

Celtic clinched the Premier League title in 1988 with a 3-0 home win over Dundee at Celtic Park. Andy Walker (above left) takes the ball round Dundee goalkeeper Tom Carson for the second of his two goals in that match. Frank McAvennie (above) celebrates as Walker is grounded. The attendance given of 60,800 was the ground's official capacity but those present on the day estimated that at least a further 10,000 had gained entry.

A lively musical, *The Celtic Story*, a Wildcat Theatre Company production, was seen by 60,000 people during an eight-week run at the Pavilion Theatre. A new £2 million facade was grafted on to the ground. It contained a new gymnasium, a players' lounge, an executive suite and offices as well as The Walfrid, the club's new restaurant. It was, appropriately, named after the Marist brother who played such a big part in Celtic's early history. Celtic, and the Catholic community, had come a long way since the days of the Poor Children's Dinner Table.

A floral arrangement of the club's centenary crest was on display at the Glasgow Garden Festival and an exhibition of Celtic memorabilia was held at the People's Palace on Glasgow Green. On the field, the club played a centenary challenge match in August, against Brazilian side Cruzeiro Belo Horizonte. Celtic won 4-2 in front of 42,000.

An all-round effort

The new faces gave everyone at Celtic many opportunities to smile again. Other individuals who had been at the club for some time had played an equally important role in the success of that year. Pat Bonner's goalkeeping helped Celtic achieve the best defensive record in Britain, conceding just 23 goals in 44 League games. It was also Celtic's best defensive record since World War II.

Tommy Burns was still contributing neat touches. Roy Aitken showed all his qualities of leadership and drive, sometimes in midfield, sometimes in defence. His surges from the middle endeared him to the crowd. He embodied Celtic's traditional drive and will to win that season. Paul McStay embodied its commitment to winning in style. No one had a greater input that year than McStay, Celtic's finest player of modern times.

The child prodigy remembers his first contact with Celtic as a player: 'I was 11 and I was brought in for training once a week, on a Tuesday night to get some coaching. I think I was 12 when I went to Leeds on trial, which was very early. At that time they and a few other clubs were interested but just after that Celtic wanted to sign me. They wanted to sign me as soon as they could and I was quite happy to go along with that. I'd always wanted to be a professional footballer and, if it could be, Celtic would have been my first choice of club to join. It doesn't always work out that way; I was just very lucky that it did for me. That's where it all began.'

Nicknamed 'The Maestro', he is a master of the midfielder's skills. His powers of control are startling. His first touch gives him immediate control over the ball as soon as it arrives; his awareness means he usually shields the ball in the same movement. If he is surrounded by players, a couple of swift shimmies and he's away, the ball still under his command. Once in the clear, he appears blessed with an automatic self-righting mechanism that gives him the required balance to make the best pass available. He also has the footballing equivalent of 20/20 vision.

In that 1987-88 season, he achieved a level of consistency that has rarely been seen at Parkhead. And no matter who had scored for Celtic, McStay always seemed to be celebrating first, as well as longer and harder than anyone else. As a quiet man, that said much about what Celtic's successful celebration of their centenary meant to him.

In the final two matches against Rangers, matches that maintained Celtic's momentum as they rolled on to the title, McStay's talents played a big part in earning two vital wins. At Celtic Park, on 2 January, the Bhoys, in rampant mood, attacked the Rangers defence from the start. A Stark header crept inches over the bar, Joe Miller and Anton Rogan had shots saved by Woods, and Miller had a shot cleared off the line. It was a convincing performance, wholehearted and energetic and laced with subtle touches from Stark and McStay. Rangers came up with nothing sensible by means of a reply but Celtic needed a goal as reward for their initiative. A moment of inspiration from McStay was to provide it.

Walker played the ball to McStay inside the centre circle. On receiving it, the midfielder looked left, appearing ready to pass. Instead, he swivelled swiftly through 180 degrees, losing Trevor Francis simply through his unexpected change of direction. McStay then sized up the options on the right, spotted Morris overlapping and sent a 50-yard pass to him that caught the entire Rangers defence on the turn.

Morris couldn't have been better provided for if someone had rolled the ball gently to him from a couple of feet, and he squared the ball to McAvennie. The striker had also been given yards of space to work in, due to the swiftness of McStay's thinking, and he was

left with an unmissable chance in front of an open goal. A second half header from McAvennie gave Celtic a vital 2-0 win.

In March, Celtic went to Ibrox. With 66 minutes gone, a Celtic attack began with McStay sending a high cross to the back post. An untidy scene resulted as Celtic players tried to get a scoring touch and Rangers desperately tried to clear. Roberts had two attempts at a clumsy header and finally seemed to have eased the pressure on his side by getting the ball out of the penalty box. McStay then stepped in decisively to end all the hesitation, swinging on to the ball 20 yards out for a left-footed volley that went racing into the Rangers net faster than a

A sight that Celtic supporters were to grow familiar with in the 1987-88 season: Paul McStay celebrating.

heat-seeking missile. Celtic sped on to a 2-1 win and the title. The 23-year-old McStay was named Player of the Year by both Scotland's football writers and his fellow players.

After the triumphs of that year, the following season was to produce the mother of all anti-climaxes. Celtic were without Pat Bonner at the beginning of the season through injury. Ian Andrews was bought from Leicester City but had an uncomfortable start to his Celtic career as the Parkhead side crashed to a series of shocking setbacks. The lowest point was a 5-1 defeat in the first Old Firm clash, at Ibrox, when Andrews suffered a severe attack of the jitters.

Alan Rough was brought in to keep Bonner's gloves warm after a 3-1 defeat at Aberdeen on 17 September, a match that turned out to be the final one in Andrews' brief career at Celtic Park. By late September Celtic were third bottom of the Premier League with four points from six games. Although they recovered steadily they never achieved a higher position than third, which was where they ended the 1988-89 season.

The League Cup had seen them knocked out by Dundee United at the quarter-final stage on 31 August. But the European Cup had brought Celtic's season briefly flickering to life. They travelled to Budapest to face Honved and, although they lost 1-0, a forceful performance in the return took them into the second round. In front of 43,000, Stark, Walker, McAvennie and McGhee took advantage of some poor defending by the Hungarians to give Celtic a 4-0 win.

The following round matched them with Werder Bremen of West Germany. In the first leg, played in front of 51,000 at Parkhead, both sides had good chances early on, Karl-Heinz Riedle striking the Celtic post with a header and Joe Miller seeing a shot cleared off the Germans' line. Early in the second half, McAvennie had a shot tipped over the bar by goalkeeper Reck. McAvennie again went close after wriggling away from a German defender but in 57 minutes Wolter broke clear of the Celtic defence to send a high, accurate shot past Bonner. Celtic had their moments in the return but they couldn't breach a German defence well-versed in

the dubious art of gamesmanship. The match ended 0-0 and Celtic were out of the European Cup.

On Boxing Day 1988, Celtic played a second centenary challenge match, against a Red Star Belgrade side that included Dragan Stojkovic and Robert Prosinecki. The match ended 2-2 but the Celtic support went away raving about the style and showmanship displayed by Stojkovic. It was one of the most enjoyable and memorable afternoons in a grim season. Another Parkhead friendly, with Liverpool in April 1989, raised £350,000 for the Hillsborough Disaster fund.

Chasing another Cup

The last resort for Celtic would be the Cup. Wins over Dumbarton, Clydebank and Hearts put them into a semi-final with Hibs, which they would have to handle without McAvennie, by then transferred back to West Ham for £1.25 million. The long-drawn-out nature of that transfer did little for stability at Celtic Park. Goals from Walker, McGhee and McCarthy gave Celtic a 3-1 win over Hibs and a place in the Scottish Cup final.

There were 72,069 at Hampden for a dull final but a goal from Joe Miller brightened the afternoon for the Celtic fans present. Shortly before half-time, he intercepted a Gary Stevens pass-back and redirected it past Rangers goalkeeper Chris Woods for the only goal of the game.

One of the most amazing games in the history of European competition took place at Parkhead the following season. In the first round of the Cup-Winners' Cup Celtic were drawn away to Partizan Belgrade. A goal from midfielder Mike Galloway, signed from Hearts for £500,000 in the summer, gave Celtic hope in a 2-1 defeat.

That close season, McNeill had also spent £600,000 on a replacement for McAvennie, the Polish World Cup striker Dariusz Dziekanowski. He quickly became known as Jacki, after the pronunciation of the first part of his surname, and impressed immediately with his skills. Paul Elliott, an English Under-21 international centre-back, was signed from Italian club Bari for £500,000 but he missed the opening games of the season though injury. He was back in time for the return with Partizan at Parkhead.

Before the move for Dziekanowski,

Dariusz 'Jacki' Dziekanowski exasperated the Celtic fans during his two-and-a-half year stay at Parkhead. He had the all-round talent to be the complete striker but appeared more interested in playing for himself rather than the team.

McNeill seemed to have replaced McAvennie with a man of the same ilk, Mo Johnston. Prior to the Scottish Cup final, Johnston had appeared for a press conference in a Celtic shirt and it was announced that he had signed for a fee of £1.5million.

Johnston had negotiated the transfer himself, saying that he didn't think his agent, Bill McMurdo, would have wanted to be involved in arranging the move.

Nine days later, McMurdo announced that a contractual snag had arisen on Johnston's contract. 'It appears to be insurmountable at the moment, and there's always the distinct possibility it could mean the whole deal will have to be called off.' It was, and in July Rangers stepped in with the requisite cheque and signed the first Catholic to play for them in modern times. FIFA fined Johnston £3,500 for 'unsporting behaviour'.

For Billy McNeill to attempt to sign the player in the first place seemed strange. On reaching the end of his contract, Johnston had given him the runaround before moving to Nantes in 1987. McNeill had publicly criticised the player's behaviour. To go back for the same man, at considerable expense, two years later appeared to be tempting fate.

On the Monday before the return match with Partizan, their coach Momcilo Vukotic resigned, leaving Ivan Golac in charge of the team. There were 49,500 at Parkhead and

they saw Vijacic, poorly marked, put Partizan ahead from a corner after just seven minutes. After 25, Celtic equalised on the night. McStay's free-kick was back-headed by Elliott and Dziekanowski's header flew over Pandurovic in the Partizan goal.

Two minutes after half-time Dziekanowski flipped the ball into the net after Pandurovic had parried Grant's shot. Four minutes later Dordevic made it 2-2. Five minutes later it was 3-2 to Celtic when Jacki kept his head down and his body straight to connect perfectly with Aitken's cut-back. It was a magnificent hat-trick for the Pole. Five minutes later, Djurovski made it 3-3. Walker restored Celtic's lead after Jacki had supplied him with a pass. It was 4-3 to Celtic but at that stage Partizan were going through on away goals. Nine minutes from time Galloway found Jacki; he sent the terraces berserk with his fourth, Celtic's fifth and what looked like the tie-breaker for Celtic.

But with two minutes remaining and Celtic still pressing forward, Scepovic got the goal that put Partizan through on away goals. As Golac and his players danced on the pitch at the end, Celtic supporters stood, numbed into silence. Some had struggled to follow the arithmetical permutations, but by the end everyone knew that Celtic were out of Europe again.

It had been a pulse-quickening Cup tie from beginning to end, one that had seen one of the great individual performances in Parkhead's history, courtesy of Dariusz Dziekanowski. 'I felt we climbed three mountains in 90 minutes – then threw ourselves off them,' said McNeill.

'What an unbelievable game!' says Paul McStay. 'After going ahead at the end we were on the greatest high imaginable. Two minutes later we were down in the depths again. To be involved in a game like that was just amazing. You'd won it but you were out of the tournament. I think everyone there enjoyed it but after a performance like that we should have gone through. We should have just said, "Hold on, there's only two minutes left. We've won the game." It was a brilliant game and we just got caught up in it and said, "Let's go again."'

'That was typical Celtic: just ram, ram ramming it and then losing a goal at the other end,' says Tommy Burns. 'That was always the Achilles heel. We were always of the opinion that we would just go out and play. We had four at the back, three in the midfield and three up front and we would just go out and play anyone, anywhere. There were times when that worked for us but there were other times when we could have improvised a wee bit and changed things here and there and maybe ca'd canny a wee bit. But it was always a question of pushing on and pushing on and we paid a price for that too often.'

Despite the result, the stunning performance by the Pole had given everyone at Parkhead a lift. But that was to be the peak of his career at Celtic. As Billy McNeill would later comment ruefully, Dziekanowski embraced the freedoms of the West a bit too eagerly. His off-field activities began to sap his strength, his play suffered and the following season he would become the most talented reserve in Scotland. His former Legia Warsaw team-mate, full-back Dariusz Wdowczyck joined him in Glasgow in November 1989 on a £400,000 transfer. 'Shuggie', as he became known, gave Celtic steady service until 1994.

Celtic had started the season by going top of the League but a series of slips saw them plummet to a mid-table position and end up fourth. A 1-0 defeat to Aberdeen in the League Cup semi-final saw Roy Aitken sent

The 1991 Scottish Players' Player of the Year, Paul Elliott. The English centre-back was hugely popular with the Celtic fans but his time at the club was overshadowed by a financial dispute with the board.

off. Eight months later, Celtic met the Dons in the Scottish Cup final and a dreadful 0-0 draw saw the first Scottish Cup final to be settled on penalties – 9-8 in Aberdeen's favour. For the first time since 1978, Celtic had failed to qualify for Europe.

McNeill spends again

McNeill again spent heavily in the summer of 1990: £650,000 on Martin Hayes from Arsenal; a record £1million on John Collins from Hibs; and £450,000 on Charlie Nicholas from Aberdeen. Hayes had been languishing in Arsenal's reserves and was soon doing the same at Celtic. Nicholas made sporadic appearances but was not the player he had been. Collins, though, was a good buy, a refined touch player with a good left foot.

It was another barren season. Motherwell won 4-2 in a Scottish Cup semi-final replay and Celtic were never in contention in the League, finishing third. In October, a clever diving header by Elliott had opened the scoring in the League Cup final but Rangers came back to win 2-1 in extra-time after Dziekanowski had shot straight at Woods with only the goalkeeper to beat. McStay had a tremendous game but his supporting players

rarely got their act together and at the final whistle the midfielder, by then Celtic captain, fell to his knees in anguish.

For the first time since the early 1960s, Celtic had gone two seasons without a trophy. Billy McNeill paid for that with his job. His greatest and most memorable triumphs had been achieved largely through his excellent powers of motivation. He had done much to maintain the Celtic tradition, stressing entertainment to be almost as important as results. That handicapped his efforts in the cut-throat European arena, where McNeill's and Celtic's gung-ho approach often cost them ties they should have won.

On 22 May 1991, Billy McNeill left the Parkhead staff for the third time. Chairman Jack McGinn said: 'His first year's success, when we won the League, was phenomenal, and we won the Scottish Cup the next season. I am bound to say I would have expected to go on from that, but the fact is that Celtic have gone two seasons without success. The

supporters expect the board to make a fresh start.' McNeill said: 'I have not produced results over the past two seasons. Every manager knows that if he does not produce, it will be left to someone else to do the job.'

Two months later, Liam Brady became the first manager of Celtic who had never played for the club. He wasn't the first non-Scot or the first Irishman to be the club's manager: Willie Maley had been born in Newry. Brady had made his name at Arsenal as a creative midfielder before playing in Italy with Juventus, Sampdoria, Inter Milan and Ascoli. He returned to Britain in 1987 to join West Ham and, after his retiral as a player, he concentrated on work as a player's agent with fellow Republic of Ireland internationals prominent among his clientele.

When he was being considered for the manager's post at Celtic Park he had his doubts over his suitability for the position. In October 1992 he told Hunter Davies in *The Independent*: 'I doubted if I had the right

Liam Brady began his career as Celtic manager with an exciting 4-3 win over Dundee United at Tannadice in August 1991. From then on, however, his time in charge of the club was filled with almost relentless tension. He had no previous managerial experience and spent approximately £6 million on players with little tangible return. It was unsurprising when he resigned in October 1993.

personality. I am rather reserved, at least in public. I didn't know if I had the knowledge, or the ability to spot players.' As a summary of the reasons why he failed to make an impact at Parkhead it could not be bettered.

Brady frequently complained of having no money to spend. Yet one of his first actions on taking over was to spend £1.1million on Republic of Ireland international Tony Cascarino, a 6ft 2in, 13 stone centre-forward who had been conspicuously unsuccessful at Aston Villa. The striker managed just four goals before being shipped off to Chelsea in February 1992 in exchange for full-back Tom Boyd. Centre-back Gary Gillespie cost £925,000 from Liverpool in August 1991 but he had suffered injury problems in his latter days at Anfield. Unsurprisingly, they were to continue at Parkhead.

Stuart Slater had briefly shown promise as a youngster during his five-year spell beside Brady at West Ham but had not progressed. To spend a club record outlay of £1.5million on him in August 1992 looked like a gamble. It was one that failed to come off.

Tommy Craig, who had been in the running for the manager's job alongside Brady, was gradually eased out of the picture after the arrival of Mick Martin as Brady's assistant. Martin was a nice guy but after he had told his jokes there was little of substance from him to help Celtic through those difficult years. Had Brady been supported by someone with a good in-depth knowledge of the Scottish game he might have been more successful. He did, despite his failings, encourage the team to express themselves. But with his total expenditure close to £6million, Brady should have produced greater success than he did.

Two morale-sapping defeats hit Celtic early in the 1991-92 season. At Airdrie they went out of the League Cup on penalties while in Switzerland they suffered their worst-ever European defeat. A 3-1 aggregate win over Germinal Ekeren of Belgium had taken Celtic to the UEFA Cup second round where they faced Neuchatel Xamax. Brady told his team that he believed the Swiss were weak and that the tie could be won in Switzerland. He fielded three defenders in an attacking formation and by half-time Celtic were trailing 3-0. The end result was 5-1 to the Swiss with Brian O'Neil getting Celtic's goal.

Celtic thought they could undo the damage if they unsettled the Swiss early on in Glasgow. After four minutes, Nicholas missed a penalty. The only goal of the game came from Joe Miller in 52 minutes. Rangers defeated Celtic 1-0 in the Scottish Cup semi-final although the Parkhead side's League position, third, earned them a place in the following season's UEFA Cup.

The summer of 1992 looked likely to bring the departure of Paul McStay. After the final fixture of the season he threw his shirt into the Jungle, seemingly in farewell. McStay was outstanding for Scotland in that summer's European Championship finals in Sweden but decided to remain at Celtic Park after all.

Another fruitless year

In the following season, Aberdeen knocked Celtic out of the League Cup at the semi-final stage; Falkirk put them out of the Scottish Cup in the fourth round. They finished a distant third in the League behind Rangers.

The only bright spot came in Europe. Even then, Celtic's first round UEFA Cup triumph over Cologne had to be viewed in perspective. The German side were, after all, near the foot of the Bundesliga and their 2-0 victory over Celtic on 15 September was their first home win of the season. Despite that, Celtic's performance in the second leg was unexpectedly competent. Goals from McStay, striker Gerry Creaney and Collins gave Celtic a sparkling 3-0 win and the 30,747 present one of the highlights of the early 1990s. The second round draw presented them with stronger German opponents in the shape of Borussia Dortmund. Celtic lost both legs to go out on a 3-1 aggregate.

The beginning of the 1993-94 season saw Celtic struggling again in the League and losing another League Cup semi-final, to Rangers. In the UEFA Cup, Young Boys Berne capitulated on a 1-0 aggregate after extra-time at Parkhead, thanks to an own goal. After a 2-1 defeat at St Johnstone on 6 October that pushed Celtic into ninth place in the Premier League, Brady resigned. His assistant Joe Jordan, who had moved to Parkhead that summer, took charge of the team but he resigned a day later. The board had failed to offer him the manager's job.

That episode put more pressure on Celtic's board. By then, they were veterans of a three-year battle of wills between themselves and Celtic supporters who wished to see radical change at board level. There were

Glasgow. The proposed enterprise would feature a 200-bedroom hotel, an eight-screen cinema complex and some drive-through fast food restaurants. Many other facilities of the type that would normally be associated with American out-of-town sites were also planned for Cambuslang.

The club's press release stated that the first phase of the project, with 32,000 seats in place, would be completed by the end of 1994. Almost two years later, on 25 February 1994, work had still to begin, but on that day David Smith announced that £20 million of underwriting had been obtained for the

While supporters continually agitated in favour of Fergus McCann, the board sat tight on their shares.

Fergus McCann (centre) and Brian Dempsey (second right) meet the press on one of the most historic days in Celtic's existence. It is 4 March 1994 and the family dynasty that had controlled the club for close to a century has just handed power to McCann.

building of the new stadium at Cambuslang. It was the board's last throw of the dice: evidence of that underwriting failed to emerge.

By then, the club was in dire financial trouble. Fergus McCann headed an underwriting group that offered £13.8 million in exchange for new shares. The proposal was put to an emergency general meeting in November 1993 and was turned down by the board. This was after Michael Kelly's claims that the board would step aside if the appropriate funding was offered. After that, 'Sack the Board' became the most popular chant on the terraces. As Rangers strolled to a 3-0 half-time lead in the 1994 Ne'erday game, coins and pie foils were aimed at the directors' box.

Despite a brilliant performance by McStay in the first leg of the second round tie with Sporting Lisbon, Celtic lost the tie on a 2-1 aggregate. By then, the team had a new manager, Lou Macari. After a brief improvement, Celtic's form, with the players affected by the off-field events, dipped again. The 1994 Scottish Cup produced a 1-0 third round defeat at Motherwell. In the League they finished fourth, non-qualifiers for Europe.

The overdraft limit of £5 million had been exceeded and the Bank of Scotland told the board that they were ready to call in the receivers on Thursday 3 March. Chris White and Michael Kelly were then prepared to sell

their shares to Gerald Weisfeld, a recent arrival on the scene whose guarantee to pay off £3 million of the overdraft was acceptable to the bank. Tom Grant and Kevin Kelly, however, were not prepared to sell their shares to him. The terms of the pact prevented that sale of shares going through.

Celtic's new figurehead

On the Thursday, four directors – Grant, Kevin Kelly, McGinn and Farrell – told the bank that they favoured Fergus McCann as the man to take over Celtic from them. As they were a majority, the bank were obliged to favour their proposal over that of Weisfeld. By then, Michael Kelly, Smith and White were ready to cash in their shares. The following day, at the Bank of Scotland in Glasgow's Trongate, Fergus McCann assumed control of Celtic Football Club. Celtic had been eight minutes away from being declared bankrupt.

Later that day, McCann stood on the steps outside Celtic Park and addressed the fans who had stood in the pouring rain waiting for news of their club's fate. 'We have new people, a new plan, a new vision and the strength to go forward. And I can tell you that we have every intention of reaching the objective that you want, which is Celtic at the very top.'

Celtic's ninth manager, Tommy Burns, was appointed in the summer of 1994. He faced an awesome task but there was soon growing evidence that the club was back in business.

9 A Promising Future

The Celtic fans deserved a salute for the way they had helped orchestrate renewal at their club through active demonstrations of anger and organisations such as Celts for Change. They got one. Nine minutes into the 1995 Scottish Cup final, Pierre van Hooijdonk, a mid-season £1.3 million signing from NAC Breda of Holland, got down on one knee and acknowledged the green-and-white masses at Hampden by bringing his outstretched fingertips to the side of his head.

The Dutchman had just scored Celtic's most important goal, up to that point, of the 1990s. An exquisite cross from left-back Tosh McKinlay had floated high into opponents Airdrie's penalty area. Van Hooijdonk timed his jump expertly to direct a header past goalkeeper Martin.

It was a misleadingly bright start to an undistinguished Cup final. Late in the first half, a recurrence of a hamstring injury forced van Hooijdonk to leave the field. He was replaced by Willie Falconer, who almost created another memorable goal early in the second half. He chased the ball to the corner flag and swiftly sent a cross flashing into the penalty area. John Collins anticipated it and found space for a diving header that inched just wide of the post. Late on, Falconer himself had an opportunistic strike saved by Martin. Those brief glimpses of excitement brightened a day of toil.

The afternoon belonged to men like Peter Grant and Albanian defender Rudi Vata, the working men of the Celtic side. Their fighting qualities did much to secure Celtic's 30th Scottish Cup and, even more importantly, their first trophy of any sort for six long, frustrating years.

'I was telling everybody I was okay before it,' says captain Paul McStay. 'But really I was very apprehensive after the period without winning anything. As soon as we scored the goal I just wanted the game to end. The game was 90 minutes long but for me the game lasted as long as my five years as captain and our six years without a trophy. The main thing that day was just winning the trophy. I think everybody felt that.'

It was confirmation of something that was becoming increasingly apparent. Everyone at Parkhead was pulling in the same direction once again.

A year previously that had appeared to be manifestly not the case. Celtic players alleged that they didn't see the then boss Lou Macari too often and that, when they did, he had little to say to them. He criticised his players publicly, in particular in a TV interview after a 1-0 defeat at Partick Thistle in January 1994. It was a heavy-handed tactic and looked like a manoeuvre to clear the way for him to bring in his own players.

Macari's first signing as Celtic manager had hinted at the direction in which he might take the club. Wayne Biggins, a 32-year-old striker bought from Barnsley for £100,000, had spent his entire career in the less exalted regions of the English League – as had Macari. At Swindon, where he made his managerial name, the long-ball game had prevailed, a style of play that made him deeply unpopular with the support at his next club, West Ham United. The London club's supporters, like those at Celtic, were used to something more cultured.

Birmingham and Stoke were the next posts for Macari. During a decade in management in England he had not once been in

Pierre van Hooijdonk (second right) watches as his header flies across the line for the only goal of the 1995 Scottish Cup final.

Tommy Burns' appointment as Celtic manager in July 1994 was hailed by the faithful as an exciting and positive step. He brought with him his assistant at Kilmarnock, Billy Stark. David Hay returned to Parkhead as chief scout. Willie McStay, a former Celtic full-back and Paul's brother, was appointed youth development officer.

charge of a club in the pre-1992 First Division or post-1992 Premier League. Yet the old Celtic board had spent an extensive period courting him to join as manager. The reason why was never fully explained.

At the time of Macari's appointment in October 1993, Fergus McCann had described it as a 'public relations stunt'. As a new era began at Parkhead, there appeared little room for Macari's style of management. In June 1994 he was sacked for an alleged failure to carry out his duties as a manager.

A bright new manager

On 12 July 1994 Tommy Burns was appointed as his successor. After a 16-year career as a Celtic player, he had made an emotional farewell to the fans during a friendly match against Ajax in December 1989. He moved to Kilmarnock where he was appointed player/ assistant manager in 1991 and player/manager in 1992. He led Killie to promotion to the Premier League in his first season as boss and in his second kept them there as well as leading them to a Scottish Cup semi-final. Celtic were found guilty of inducing Burns and his assistant Billy Stark to move and the club was fined a record £100,000.

Celtic had made the best possible choice of new manager. Burns' attitude was positive and realistic. He was ready to work hard. He was a genuine Celtic man. Of all the managers working in Britain he was the individual whose pedigree did most to fulfil the requirements of the club's new executive and, equally importantly, the fans.

'I was very excited at becoming Celtic manager,' says Burns. 'It's a bit like having a dream that you never think is going to become real, the same as becoming a football player here. Then all of a sudden it's reality. Then you get on with the job.

'The job is very much along the lines of what I expected: everybody telling you what to do and who to buy. No matter how many times we tell people that we're trying to start Celtic football club all over again at every level, people are still obsessed with the fact that Rangers have won seven in a row and the idea that we can't let them get to nine.

'Everybody wants to be manager here and make decisions but it's different once you're sitting in the manager's chair. You were looking at a football club that was once great but which no longer had an infrastructure. You've then got to put the whole thing back together again: the boys' club, the youth team, restructure a scouting system that was virtually nonexistent outside of Glasgow. You had maybe one scout in Edinburgh and one in the whole of Ireland and that was it.

John Collins' free-kick (above) sails round the Rangers wall to open the scoring in the 2-0 win at Ibrox in August 1994. McNally, Mowbray and McStay (above right) offer congratulations.

'The support had become detached from the club because of the fact that players had stopped going to meet them and attending their functions. Players in the past had rung them up on the night of their functions and given them excuses why they couldn't make it to Player of the Year nights. All of these things were building up within the support. We had to try and give them their football club back again. The players here are all on a rota now and they've all got to do their bit and go to supporters' functions and try and win our supporters back. The supporters are the most important people of all.

'We've been to Belfast and we've opened up a lot of contacts in the Dublin area. We've got a boys' club going there, the Cherry Orchard Boys' Club, which is affiliated to Celtic Football Club. We've got a boys' club in Belfast. We're spreading our net; we've got a

Phil O'Donnell became Celtic's record signing in September 1994 when he joined the Parkhead club from Motherwell for a fee of £1.75 million. On his debut, against Partick Thistle (right), he scored both goals in Celtic's 2-1 win.

better scouting network all over Ireland now, maybe half-a-dozen bodies as opposed to one. We've got coaching nights going on in Edinburgh and Aberdeen and Dundee so we're doing things that were never done here before which should have been getting done. We've had to work very hard to get it become known that we're doing that type of thing because it had been neglected for so long.

'We started building an atmosphere here where people would enjoy coming in in the morning and enjoy training. We keep a good atmosphere about the place because that is something we've been desperately, desperately short of and I think we've done that. It's a happier place for them to come now.'

'Tommy is the same as he was as a player,' says Paul McStay. 'He's committed and eager and hungry to achieve things here. I think that's what you need: somebody who's played here and knows what it's all about and can talk about the game in a good fashion.'

As Burns started work at the beginning of the definitive transitional season for Celtic, demolition work began on the Parkhead terraces. By December, work was ready to begin on the construction of the new Celtic Park.

It quickly took shape over the following months. Soon, it could be seen for miles around in Glasgow's East End, silhouetted against the sky, the most defiant of responses to those who not long before had been ready to sound the death knell for Celtic Football Club. On 5 August 1995, the new North Stand was opened with a friendly match against Newcastle United. Singer and Celtic fan Rod Stewart cut the green-and-white tape. After 29 minutes, German international and £2.2million club record signing Andreas Thom was tripped inside the penalty area. John Collins took the penalty to score the first goal in front of the new construction.

'At one time I felt that if they had to move down the road and it was the way forward then it had to be done,' says Paul McStay. 'But when you see what's going to be built here it's going to be unbelievable. When it first went up I couldn't believe the height of it. When it's all finished it'll be an amazing platform to play on. I'll be delighted to run out there when it's completed. It's a new era and I'm glad that at the tail end of my career I'm able to join in in it.'

For the 1994-5 season, Celtic had made Hampden Park their temporary home. It was

The success of the share issue in January 1995 enabled Fergus McCann's plans for Celtic's new stadium to continue on schedule. By mid-1995, close to £18 million had been spent on stadium reconstruction.

Apart from the stand, Celtic Park was razed to the ground in the summer of 1994 to make way for the construction of a new all-seater stadium.

The first step in creating the new stadium was the erection of a steel framework that would form the basis of the new 26,000-seater North Stand.

By August 1995 the new North Stand would be ready for its official opening on the fifth day of that month.

Celtic players celebrate the second goal in the 3-1 Scottish Cup semi-final replay victory over Hibs in April 1995.

to prove an up-and-down footballing year. They were unbeaten in their first 11 matches and victories over Ayr United, Dundee and Dundee United took them to the League Cup semi-final against Aberdeen at Ibrox on 26 October. It was a dour match, ridden with fouls, and with the score at 0-0 the game moved into extra-time. Both sides had created so few chances that a penalty shoot-out looked likely. With 99 minutes on the clock, though, 22-year-old centre-back Brian O'Neil made the connection that put Celtic in the final, by glancing a header past Snelders.

From then until Hogmanay, Celtic failed to win a game. That created an unwelcome club record of 11 consecutive League matches without a win. Even that would have been overlooked, however, if Celtic had won the League Cup final, sponsored by Coca-Cola, on 27 November at Ibrox. Their opponents were to be Raith Rovers of the First Division. It would turn out to be an afternoon of misery for Celtic.

After just a few minutes, the electronic scoreboard at 'neutral' Ibrox flashed up the message: 'Congratulations, Raith Rovers, Coca-Cola Cup Winners.' The same scoreboard then produced a reminder that Rangers had won the League six times in succession. Fortunately, most Celtic fans were

absorbed, in those opening minutes, in a match that had already contained more good football than the entire semi with Aberdeen.

In the 19th minute hesitation in the Celtic defence allowed Crawford to wriggle into a scoring position and place a low, powerful shot past goalkeeper Gordon Marshall. After 32 minutes, Celtic equalised. Boyd crossed to the back post where Simon Donnelly knocked the ball down to Andy Walker, back at Celtic after three years at Bolton. The striker sent Raith goalkeeper Thomson the wrong way with a close-range diving header.

From then on it was all Celtic. Donnelly missed the best of many Celtic chances midway through the second half after Nicholas had sent him clear. After much unrewarded pressure, Celtic appeared to have lost their momentum. Extra-time was looking likely. But with just six minutes remaining, Collins found Walker inside the box and when his effort came off a post, Charlie Nicholas was perfectly placed to make it 2-1. It looked sure to be the end for Raith.

Three minutes later, Dalziel headed the equaliser after Marshall had fumbled a 20-yard shot. Extra-time would be played after all. Few chances were created in that period.

Brian McLaughlin in action in the Scottish Cup semi with Hibs. The young player's efforts did much to help bring the Cup to Parkhead. In the quarter-final he was sent tumbling inside the box after running on to a fine McStay pass. John Collins scored with the resulting penalty to put Celtic in the semi.

Simon Donnelly, an elusive forward, was another of the promising youngsters who came through in the mid-1990s.

The game would be decided on penalties. The first five players on each side scored with their kicks, leaving the game to be settled on sudden-death. Rowbotham scored for Raith then Paul McStay stepped up for Celtic only to see his kick saved by Thomson. The League Cup was on its way to Fife.

'We set our stall out regarding how we wanted to play,' says Tommy Burns, 'and the longer the game went everything fell exactly into place. We had them wide in the wide areas, we stretched them by getting balls to the bye-line, we got the crosses in. After the first 15-20 minutes of the game we had played exceptionally well. For 35-40 minutes of the second half we had the ball non-stop. We did everything right except for finishing.

'Then Raith went up the park after we had scored the second. I think the players were thinking to themselves that they had had it snatched away from them. One minute we had done it after five years waiting. The next we had lost a goal. I just don't think we could get ourselves up for the extra-time and I think Raith were possibly the better team then. We looked like a team that had resigned themselves to the fact that we weren't going to get there.

'It was a bitter, bitter disappointment, especially as they had played so very well over the 90 minutes. And yet, ultimately, all people will remember about it is that it was the day we got beaten by Raith Rovers. But you get up the next day and get on with it. You can't think a defeat is the end of the world.

'There were character assassinations done on some of the players here by some people in the media, which was shocking. It took them some time to get over that but the team bounced back three days later in a game against Hibs and gave a great performance, playing with a lot of heart and determination.

There were 4,000 of our supporters at Easter Road that night who were right behind them. It was fantastic and that, to me, epitomised everything Celtic football club is all about. I went up among them before the game, sat down with them and had a blether and they were all telling me not to be downhearted.'

The aftermath of the Raith Rovers defeat saw young players such as Brian McLaughlin and Stuart Gray get extended runs in the first-team. Winger McLaughlin impressed greatly, even drawing comparisons with the great Jimmy Johnstone. Jinky himself is an admirer: 'He definitely has got the touches. I like watching the boy. He's got an ability to go at people and that's exciting. It's what people want. They want that all the time. Going back to the new stadium at Parkhead will give him and everybody else a lift.'

Gray took over at left-back for a spell after an injury to Tosh McKinlay and impressed. 'This year the manager has played myself, Brian, Simon Donnelly, Malky MacKay, Jim Slavin, half a dozen young boys,' he says. 'It's a great boost to us young lads. We know that if we do the business in the reserves we've got a chance. It's up to us to take it. Brian

McLaughlin came into the side at roughly the same time as me. We've been at the club the same amount of time, played in the same youth teams and were brought up together. It was good to have a pal in the team.'

After the League Cup final setback Celtic faced another big date, two months later. On 24 January the club's future success was placed in the hands of the fans. That was the closing date for applications to obtain shares in Celtic, which had been newly created as a public limited company.

Sales of the *Financial Times* did not increase noticeably in the Glasgow area during the preceding weeks. This was one share issue where most buyers were making their purchases on an emotional rather than on a hard-headed businesslike basis. The majority would see no dividend at all before 1998. It was an episode that would provide further confirmation of the special nature of Celtic: the share issue, which had been projected to raise £9.4 million was oversubscribed by £4.4 million. It was the most successful share issue ever for any British football club.

'We are a unique club with unique supporters, a unique tradition and a unique way of playing,' says Burns. 'The supporters make this club special. Even in the bad times they've always stuck by the club. The club had been going steadily downwards for five years and then they have a share issue and it goes through the roof. That shows you the incredible potential we've got here. They've got a great fierce pride in Celtic Football Club and in being a supporter. In this day and age that's really special.'

It was also a major triumph for managing director Fergus McCann. He had just been given a massive vote of confidence by his new shareholders. McCann has provided the club with a strong sense of direction. It is now being guided by a clear thinker and a decision-maker. After many years of woolly thinking, there is a leader on the non-playing side at Celtic Park.

McCann's prudence in financial matters has caused sparks to fly, on occasion, between him and manager Burns. Burns is impatient to build a top-class team and is keen to speculate on buying players of the highest quality. However, an overall balance has to be struck between the cost of building the new stadium, strengthening the first-team pool and erasing the overdraft of £5.3 million.

'Our relationship has been very volatile, up and down,' says Burns. 'I think we can see things from each other's point of view but knowing the way he is and the way I am he'll always be wanting to get his tuppenceworth in and I'll always want to get my tuppenceworth in. Sometimes that's a healthy thing.'

Celtic had brought in the New Year with a 2-0 win over Falkirk on 31 December at Hampden but by then it was clear that the Scottish Cup was their only chance of a trophy. Before that tournament began, the club was boosted by the signing of £1.3 million striker Pierre van Hooijdonk. Wins over lower division opposition in St Mirren and Meadowbank set up a quarter-final with Kilmarnock. The match was played on a Friday night so that it could be shown live on Sky TV. As a taste of Scottish football it wasn't particularly appetising, being notable mainly for a floodlight failure during the first half. When play had resumed, a John Collins penalty was enough to put Celtic into a semi-final with Hibs at Ibrox. As Celtic were using Hampden as their home, the national stadium could not be classified as a neutral venue until they had played their final League match of the 1994-95 season.

A spectacular Cup win

Another Friday evening TV special produced a 0-0 draw. The following Tuesday, though, the third episode in Celtic's TV mini-series gave Sky viewers a performance to rank alongside the best they had seen from Britain's top teams during that season. Celtic's speed of movement and quick thinking in and around the Hibs box was too much for the Edinburgh side to cope with.

On that night the optimism generated by the off-field proceedings was matched by those on the park. Three marvellous goals put them in the final. For the first, McStay's reverse pass left the Hibs defence open-mouthed and Falconer, in superb form, streaked into the penalty area to beat Leighton with a clever, angled shot. John Collins picked up a clearance on the edge of the box to make it two with a tidy chipped shot just before half-time. Phil O'Donnell, with a firm header, made it 3-1.

'If you could get that standard for a good period throughout the season you would be up there challenging,' says Paul McStay. 'That was great stuff, a joy to play in. The second game was unbelievable, everything knitted together.

'The Championship is the ultimate aim. The thing that has been missing has been consistency. To win the Championship you've got to do it week in, week out. The weeks that you're not doing that you've still got to grind out the results even if you're not playing well. That's how you win Championships. What this club needs is to start to pick up bits and bobs on the domestic scene and then look towards the European scene, which is where it's all happening.'

McStay has occasionally been sniped at as being too quiet to be Celtic's captain. But his modest demeanour masks a strong sense of determination. 'What is a captain?' he says. 'Other people's idea of a captain is maybe somebody who just stands and bawls, points, does things like that and maybe doesn't contribute to the game.'

Burns travelled to Amsterdam in February 1995 to look behind the scenes at Ajax, the club that would become that year's European champions. 'I went to see their youth set-up.

They are light years ahead of us. But we can take things from it and learn from it. They have ploughed millions and millions into it.'

Learning from the Dutch

'They bring kids in from all over Holland on different days. They might be losing a day's schooling so they come in, do their training then get their schooling. There's a teacher to hand so once they've had something to eat after training they do their lessons. Then they get bussed home. So they're not missing out on anything. They've got professional running coaches who teach the kids how to run properly when they are ten or 11 years old.

'Ajax never get involved in the frantic market: they educate their young players to play in a particular position. By the time they are 17 or 18 they know exactly what their role is within the team. We've started educating the younger players as to what we're expecting from them during a game rather than waiting until they get older to do it. We've started planting wee seeds such as when to play the ball first time, when to beat somebody and to be aware of their position on the field.

'We're trying to help them stretch themselves and the way to do that is to think about the game. We're also trying to do the same with the first-team players; a lot of players get to a stage in their careers where they think they don't need to learn anything.'

It had always been logical for Celtic to tap the vast reservoir of talent that Scotland holds for them. Burns was ensuring that careful steps are being taken along that route. In the interim, he is prepared to buy players of proven ability to regain Celtic's reputation.

'We're very optimistic for the future,' he said after his first season. 'When you look at that stadium you see that Celtic are becoming a modern-day club. We've got a stadium that's going to be second-to-none and we've got to get the right type of quality players to fill that stadium. Then you can make progress. The supporters are saying that they've waited six years but we've not been here six years, we've been here one year. Fergus McCann only took over a year ago.'

'Celtic is a special club,' says Paul McStay. 'It's got so much history about it, so many achievements to its credit. That's why it's special to me and to all the people involved in it. It gives you so much of a lift in life when

things are going well and depresses you when things aren't going well but you'll always battle to make it better again. You've got to win at Celtic. There's too much at stake not to.'

Even in the most depressing times of the early 1990s, no one who knew the club well believed that Celtic would not regain the strength it had known in its prime. The speed of the recovery, however, has been greater than even the most supreme optimist could have imagined. This is proof once again that Celtic remains one of the world's most extraordinary clubs.

'We've met the challenge of winning something,' said Tommy Burns after the 1995 Scottish Cup final. 'Now we've got to take it a stage further. The potential of this club is frightening. We've got to try and realise that potential.'

Facts and Figures

This section contains all of Celtic's results, team line-ups and goalscorers between 1888 and 1995 in the Scottish Cup, the Scottish League, the Scottish League Cup and in European competitions. There are no statistics for the years from 1939-1946 – no Scottish League or Scottish Cup fixtures took place during those years. Opponents' name in capitals denotes a home fixture.

SCOTTISH CUP 1888-89

			1	2	3	4	5	6	7	8	9	10	11
Sept 1	SHETTLESTON	5-1	Dunning	McKeown	Coleman	Gallagher	Kelly	McLaren	McCallum	J Coleman	Groves	M Dunbar	O'Connor Px5
Sept 22	COWLAIRS	8-0	Dunning	Gallagher	McKeown	Maley	Kelly 1	McLaren	McCallum 2	Coleman	Groves 1	Dunbar 3	T Maley 1
Oct 13	ALBION ROVERS	4-1	Dunning	Jas McLaughlan	McKeown	Gallagher 1	Kelly	McLaren	McCallum	Coleman	Groves 1	Dunbar 1	T Maley 1
Nov 3	St. Bernard's	4-1	Dunning	Gallagher	McKeown	Maley	Kelly	McLaren	McCallum 1	Dunbar	Groves 2	Coleman	T Maley 1
Dec 8	CLYDE	9-2	Dunning	A Collins	McKeown	Gallagher	Kelly	McLaren 2	McCallum	Dunbar	Groves 4	Coleman	T Maley 3
Dec 15	East Stirling	2-1	Dunning	Collins	McKeown	Gallagher	Kelly	T Dunbar	McCallum 2	M Dunbar	Groves	Coleman	T Maley
Jan 12	Dumbarton	4-1 SF	John Kelly	Gallagher	McKeown	Maley	Kelly	McLaren	McCallum	Dunbar 2	Groves 2	Coleman	T Maley
Feb 9	Third Lanark	1-2 F	Kelly	Gallagher	McKeown	Maley	Kelly	McLaren	McCallum 1	Dunbar	Groves	Coleman	T Maley

SCOTTISH CUP 1889-90

			1	2	3	4	5	6	7	8	9	10	11
Sept 7	Queen's Park	0-0	McLaughlan	Reynolds	McKeown	Gallagher	Kelly	McLaren	Madden	Dowds	Groves	Coleman	Dunbar
Sept 14	Queen's Park	1-2	McLaughlin	Reynolds	McKeown	Gallagher	Kelly	W Maley	Madden	Dowds	Groves 1	Coleman	Dunbar

SCOTTISH LEAGUE 1890-91

			1	2	3	4	5	6	7	8	9	10	11
Aug 23	Hearts	5-0	Bell	Reynolds	McKeown	W Maley	Kelly	McLaren	Madden 2	Dowds 1	Groves 2	MDunbar	Crossan
Aug 30	CAMBUSLANG	5-2	Bell	Reynolds	McKeown	P Gallagher	Dowds 3	W Maley	Crossan 2	H Gallagher	Groves	M Dunbar	Madden
Sept 13	Third Lanark	1-2	Bell	Reynolds	McKeown	P Gallagher	W Maley	McLaren	Crossan	Dowds 1	T Maley	Madden	M Dunbar
Oct 25	Abercorn	5-1	Bell	Reynolds	McKeown	P Gallagher 1	Kelly	McLaren	Madden	M Dunbar	Dowds 4	Crossan	Campbell
Jan 24	Vale of Leven	1-3	Bell	Reynolds	McKeown	P Gallagher	Kelly	McLaren	Madden	M Dunbar	Dowds	Campbell 1	McMahon
Feb 7	ST MIRREN	3-2	Bell	Reynolds	McKeown	P Gallagher	Kelly	W Maley	Madden	Boyle 1	Dowds 1	Campbell 1	M Dunbar
Feb 21	Dumbarton (1 goal untraced)	2-2	Bell	Reynolds	McKeown	P Gallagher	Kelly	W Maley	Madden	Boyle	Dowds	M Dunbar 1	McMahon
Feb 28	HEARTS	1-0	Bell	Reynolds	McKeown	P Gallagher	Kelly	W Maley	Madden	Boyle	Dowds	Campbell 1	M Dunbar
Mar 7	Cambuslang	1-3	Bell	P Gallagher	Reynolds	M Dunbar	Kelly	McGhee	Madden 1	Boyle	Dowds	Campbell	McMahon
Mar 14	COWLAIRS	2-0	Bell	Reynolds	McKeown	W Maley	Dolan	P Gallagher	Madden	Boyle	Dowds 2	M Dunbar	Campbell
Mar 21	RANGERS	2-2	Bell	Reynolds	McKeown	W Maley	McGhee	P Gallagher	Madden	Boyle	Dowds 1	McMahon	Campbell 1
Apr 4	ST. Mirren	0-1	Bell	Reynolds	McKeown	McGhee	Dolan	W Maley	Madden	Boyle	Dowds	McMahon	Campbell
Apr 11	DUMBARTON	1-0	Bell	Reynolds	McKeown	P Gallagher	Kelly	W Maley	Madden	McGhee	Dowds	McMahon	Campbell
Apr 25	THIRD LANARK (goal untraced)	1-1	Bell	Reynolds	McKeown	P Gallagher	Kelly	W Maley	Madden	McGhee	Dowds	McMahon	Campbell
Apr 29	Cowlairs (3 goals untraced)	5-0	Dolan	Reynolds	McKeown	McGhee	M Dunbar 2	Kyle	T Dunbar	Cunningham	Dowds	McMahon	Campbell
May 2	Rangers	2-1	Bell	Reynolds	T Dunbar	P Gallagher	Kelly	W Maley	Madden 1	Dowds	Campbell	McMahon	
May 5	VALE OF LEVEN	9-1	Dolan	Reynolds	T Dunbar	P Gallagher	Kelly	W Maley	Campbell 1	McMahon 4	Dowds 1	McGhee 3	Madden
May 12	ABERCORN	2-0	Dolan	T Dunbar	McKeown	P Gallagher	Kelly	W Maley	Madden	McGhee 1	Dowds	McMahon 1	Campbell

* Celtic's first League match was at home to Renton but Renton were expelled from League competition later that season and matches in which they had taken part became void.

SCOTTISH CUP 1890-91

			1	2	3	4	5	6	7	8	9	10	11
Sept 6	RANGERS	1-0	Bell	Reynolds	McKeown	P Gallagher	McCallum	W Maley	Crossan	Dowds	Groves 1	Madden	M Dunbar
Sept 27	CARFIN SHAMROCK	2-2	Bell	McKeown	McCallum	McLaren	W Maley	P Gallagher	M Dunbar	Madden 2	Groves	Dowds	Crossan
Oct 4	Carfin Shamrock	3-1	Bell	Reynolds	McKeown	P Gallagher	Kelly	McLaren	Madden	Dowds	Groves	Crossan	Campbell
Oct 18	Wishaw Thistle (2 untraced)	6-2	Bell	Reynolds	McKeown	P Gallagher	Kelly	McLaren	Madden 2	M Dunbar	Groves	Dowds 1	Campbell 1
Nov 8	Our Boys	3-1	Bell	Reynolds	McKeown	P Gallagher	Kelly	McLaren	Madden	M Dunbar	Coleman	Campbell 1	Crossan 2
Dec 13	Royal Albert*	2-0	Bell	Reynolds	T Dunbar	W Maley	Kelly	McLaren	Madden	M Dunbar	Dowds	Campbell 1	Crossan 1
Dec 20	Dumbarton	0-3 QF	Bell	Reynolds	McKeown	P Gallagher	Kelly	McLaren	Madden	M Dunbar	Dowds	Campbell	Crossan

*Played at Ibrox

SCOTTISH LEAGUE 1891-92

			1	2	3	4	5	6	7	8	9	10	11
Aug 15	Hearts	1-3	Duff	Reynolds	Doyle	Gallagher	J Kelly	Dowds	Madden	McGhee 1	Brady	McMahon	Campbell
Aug 22	RANGERS	3-0	Duff	Reynolds	Doyle	Gallagher	J Kelly	Dowds	Madden 1	Brady	Coleman	Campbell 1	McMahon 1
Aug 29	Clyde	7-2	Duff	Reynolds	Doyle	W Maley	J Kelly	Dowds	McCallum 1	Madden	Brady 1	Campbell	McMahon 5
Sept 5	RENTON	3-0	Duff	Reynolds	Doyle	W Maley	J Kelly	Dowds	McCallum	Brady	Madden	McMahon	Campbell 3
Sept 12	Abercorn	5-2	Duff	Reynolds	Doyle	Dowds	J Kelly	Gallagher	McCallum 2	Brady	Madden 1	McMahon 2	Campbell
Sept 26	DUMBARTON	2-0	Duff	Reynolds	Doyle	W Maley	J Kelly	Dowds	McCallum	Brady	Madden	McMahon 1	Campbell 1
Oct 3	St Mirren	2-1	C Kelly	Reynolds	Doyle	Gallagher	J Kelly	Brady	McCallum 2	Madden	T Maley	Coleman	Campbell
Oct 17	HEARTS	3-1	C Kelly	Reynolds	Doyle	W Maley	J Kelly	Dowds	McCallum	Brady	Madden 1	Campbell	McMahon 2
Oct 24	VALE OF LEVEN	6-1	Duff	Reynolds	Doyle	W Maley	J Kelly	Dowds	McCallum	Brady 1	Madden 4	McMahon 1	Campbell
Dec 26	ST. MIRREN	2-1	Duff	Reynolds	Doyle	T Maley	J Kelly	Dowds	Brady 1	McCallum	Madden	Campbell 1	McMahon
Jan 30	Cambuslang	4-0	Cullen	Reynolds	Doyle	W Maley	J Kelly	Dowds	McCallum	Brady	Coleman 1	Campbell 1	McMahon 1
Feb 27	THIRD LANARK	5-1	Cullen	Doyle	Reynolds	Dowds	J Kelly	W Maley	Campbell 2	McMahon 2	Coleman 1	Brady	McCallum
Mar 19	CLYDE	0-0	Cullen	Doyle	Reynolds	Gallagher	J Kelly	W Maley	McCallum	Brady	Conner	McMahon	Campbell
Apr 2	Vale of Leven	2-2	Cullen	Reynolds	Doyle	Gallagher	J Kelly	W Maley	McCallum 2	Brady	Dowds	McMahon	Campbell
Apr 16	CAMBUSLANG	3-1	Cullen	Reynolds	Doyle	W Maley	J Kelly	Gallgher	Cunningham	McCallum 1	Dowds 1	Campbell 1	McMahon
Apr 18	Leith A	1-2	Cullen	Reynolds	Doyle	Brady	J Kelly	Gallagher	Boyle	McCallum	Dowds	Campbell	McMahon 1
Apr 23	Dumbarton	0-1	Cullen	Reynolds	Doyle	Gallagher	J Kelly	Dowds	Cunningham	Brady	McCallum	Campbell	McMahon
Apr 30	ABERCORN	3-1	Cullen	Reynolds	Doyle	W Maley	J Kelly	Dowds	Cunningham	Brady	McCallum 1	Campbell 1	McMahon
May 5	Renton	4-0	Cullen	Reynolds	Doyle	Gallagher	J Kelly	Dowds	Cunningham	Brady	McCallum 2	Campbell	McMahon 2
May 7	Rangers	1-1	Cullen	Reynolds	Doyle	Gallagher	W Maley	Dowds	Cunningham	Flannagan	McCallum	McMahon	Campbell 1
May 14	LEITH A	2-0	Cullen	Doyle	Reynolds	Gallagher	Dowds	Clifford	Flannagan	Brady	McCallum 1	Foran 1	Campbell
May 24	Third Lanark	3-1	Cullen	Reynolds	Doyle	W Maley	J Kelly	Flannagan	McCallum	Brady	Madden	McMahon 1	Campbell 2

SCOTTISH CUP 1891-92

			1	2	3	4	5	6	7	8	9	10	11
Nov 28	St Mirren	4-2	Kyle	Reynolds	Doyle	W Maley 1	J Kelly	Dowds	Brady	McCallum	Madden 1	McMahon 1	Campbell +og
Dec 19	KILMARNOCK ATH	3-0	Duff	Reynolds	Doyle	W Maley	J Kelly	Dowds 1	Brady 2	McCallum	Madden	McMahon	Campbell
Jan 23	COWLAIRS	4-1 QF	Cullen	Reynolds	Doyle	W Maley	J Kelly	Dowds	McCallum	Brady 2	Madden 1	Campbell	McMahon 1
Feb 6	RANGERS	5-3 SF	Cullen	Reynolds	Doyle	Dowds	J Kelly	W Maley	McCallum 1	Cunningham 1	Brady 2	Campbell	McMahon 1
Apr 9	Queen's Park*	5-1 F	Cullen	Reynolds	Doyle	W Maley	J Kelly	Dowds	McCallum	Brady	Madden	McMahon 2	Campbell 2 +og

*Played at Ibrox

SCOTTISH LEAGUE 1892-93

			1	2	3	4	5	6	7	8	9	10	11
Aug 20	RENTON	4-3	Cullen	Reynolds	Doyle	P. Gallagher	Kelly	Clifford	A Gallagher	Murray	Madden	Foran	Campbell 2+2P
Aug 27	Hearts	1-3	Cullen	T Dunbar	Doyle	W Maley	Kelly	Clifford	Gallagher 1	Coleman	Madden	McMahon	Campbell
Sept 10	ABERCORN	3-2	D McArthur	Reynolds	Doyle	Clifford	Kelly	T Dunbar	Murray	Flannigan 1	Madden 2	McMahon	Campbell
Sept 24	Rangers	2-2	Cullen	Reynolds	Doyle	Maley	Kelly	P Gallagher	Fitzsimmons	Blessington	J Davidson 1	McMahon 1	Campbell

			1	2	3	4	5	6	7	8	9	10	11
Oct 1	CLYDE	3-1	Cullen	Reynolds	Doyle	Maley	Kelly	T Dunbar	Davidson	Blessington	W Lees	McMahon 2	Campbell 1
Oct 15	Dumbarton	3-0	Cullen	Reynolds	Doyle	Maley	Kelly	T Dunbar	Davidson	Blessington 1	Madden	M Dunbar 1	Campbell 1
Oct 22	St Mirren	3-1	Cullen	Reynolds	Doyle	Maley	Kelly	T Dunbar	Davidson	Blessington 1	Madden 1	M Dunbar	Campbell 1
Nov 5	HEARTS	5-0	Cullen	Reynolds	Doyle	Maley	Kelly	T Dunbar	Davidson 1	Blessington	Madden 1	Mulvey 1	Campbell 2
Jan 28	Leith Athletic	1-0	Cullen	Reynolds	T Dunbar	Maley	Kelly	Clifford	Davidson	Blessington	Madden 1	McMahon	Campbell
Feb 11	Abercorn	2-4	Cullen	Reynolds	Doyle	Clifford	Kelly	T Dunbar	Davidson 1	Blessington	Madden	McMahon 1	Campbell
Mar 18	DUMBARTON	5 1	Cullen	Reynolds	T Dunbar	Maley	Kelly 1	McLaughlan	Davidson 2	Blessington 1	McMahon	Mulvey 1	Campbell
Mar 25	Renton	2-0	Cullen	J Curran	Doyle	O'Byrne	McCann	T Dunbar	Davidson	Blessington	Madden	Mulvey 2	E McCann
Apr 22	Third Lanark	6-0	Cullen	T Dunbar	Doyle	Curran	Kelly	Clifford	Davidson	Blessington 1	McMahon 3	Mulvey 1	Campbell 1
Apr 29	RANGERS	3-0	Cullen	T Dunbar	Doyle	Curran	Kelly 1	Gallagher	Madden	Blessington	McMahon 1	Scott	Campbell 1
May 2	ST MIRREN	4-1	Cullen	Reynolds	T Dunbar	Curran	Kelly	McCann	Madden	Blessington	McMahon 1	Davidson	Campbell 2+2P
May 6	Clyde	2-1	Cullen	T Dunbar	Doyle	Curran	Kelly	Gallagher	Madden	Blessington 1	McMahon 1	Davidson	Campbell
May 9	LEITH ATHLETIC	3-1	Cullen	T Dunbar	Doyle	Maley	Kelly	Curran	Madden 1	Blessington	McMahon	Davidson 2	Campbell
May 18	Third Lanark	2-5	Cullen	T Dunbar	Doyle	Curran	Kelly 1	Gallagher	Flannigan	Blessington	Madden	M Dunbar	Campbell 1

SCOTTISH CUP 1892-93

Nov 28	LINTHOUSE	3-1	Cullen	Reynolds	Doyle	Maley	Kelly	T Dunbar	Towie	Blessington	Madden 1	McMahon 2	Campbell
Dec 17	FIFTH KIRKCUDBRIGHT RV	7-0	Cullen	Reynolds	Doyle	Maley	Kelly	T Dunbar	Towie	Blessington	Madden	McMahon	Campbell 7P
Jan 21	THIRD LANARK	5-1	Cullen	Reynolds	Doyle	Maley	Kelly	T Dunbar	Towie 2	Blessington	Madden	McMahon 3	Campbell
Feb 14	ST BERNARD'S	5-0 SF	Cullen	Reynolds	Doyle	Maley	Kelly	T Dunbar	Towie	Blessington 2	Madden 1	McMahon 2	Campbell
Mar 11	Queen's Park	1-2 F	Cullen	Reynolds	Doyle	Maley	Kelly	T Dunbar	Towie	Blessington 1	Madden	McMahon	Campbell

SCOTTISH LEAGUE 1893-94

Aug 12	THIRD LANARK	5-0	Cullen	Reynolds	T. Dunbar	Curran	Kelly	Byrne	Madden 1	Blessington	McMahon 3	Cassidy	Campbell 1
Aug 19	Dundee	4-1	Cullen	Reynolds	T Dunbar	Curran	Kelly	Byrne	Davidson	Blessington	McMahon 2	Cassidy 1	Campbell +OG
Aug 26	DUMBARTON	0-0	Cullen	Reynolds	T Dunbar	Curran	Kelly	Byrne	Madden	Blessington	McMahon	Cassidy	Campbell
Sept 2	Rangers	0-5	Cullen	Reynolds	Doyle	Curran	Kelly	T Dunbar	Davidson	Blessington	Madden	Cassidy	Campbell
Sept 9	Hearts	4-2	Cullen	Reynolds	Doyle	Maley	Kelly	T Dunbar	Madden 1	Blessington	Cassidy	McGinn	Campbell 2 +OG
Sept 23	LEITH ATHLETIC	4-1	Cullen	Reynolds	Doyle	Curran	Kelly	Maley	Madden 1	Blessington	Cassidy 3	McMahon	Campbell
Sept 30	St Mirren	2-1	Cullen	Reynolds	T Dunbar	Maley	Kelly	Byrne	Madden	Blessington 1	Cassidy 1	McMahon	Campbell
Oct 14	ST BERNARD'S	5-2	Cullen	Reynolds	T Dunbar	Maley	Kelly	Byrne	Madden 1	Blessington	Cassidy 1	McMahon 3	Campbell
Nov 4	DUNDEE	3-1	Cullen	Reynolds	Doyle	Maley	Kelly	C. McEleny	Madden 1	Blessington	Cassidy	McMahon	Campbell 2
Nov 11	Renton	3-0	Cullen	Reynolds	Doyle	Maley	Kelly	Byrne	Davidson 1	Blessington 1	Cassidy	McMahon 1	Campbell
Dec 2	RENTON	3-2	Cullen	Reynolds	Doyle	Maley	Kelly	Curran	Madden	Blessington	Cassidy	McMahon 3	Campbell\
Dec 22	Dumbarton	5-4	Cullen	Reynolds	Doyle	Curran	Kelly	Maley	Madden	Blessington 1	Cassidy 1	McMahon 2	Campbell +OG
Dec 28	Third Lanark	3-1	Cullen	Reynolds	Doyle	Curran	T Dunbar	Maley	Madden	Blessington 1	Cassidy	McMahon 1	Divers 1
Jan 20	St Bernard's	2-1	Cullen	Reynolds	Doyle	Maley	Kelly	Curran	Madden 1	Blessington 1	Cassidy	McMahon	Divers
Feb 10	ST MIRREN	5-1	Cullen	Reynolds	Doyle	Curran	Kelly	Maley	Blessington	Divers 2	Cassidy	McMahon 2	Campbell 1
Feb 24	RANGERS	3-2	Cullen	Reynolds	Doyle	Curran	Kelly	McEleny	Madden 1	Blessington 1	Cassidy	McMahon 1	Divers
Mar 10	HEARTS	2-3	Cullen	Reynolds	Doyle 1	Curran	Kelly	Maley	Madden	Blessington	Cassidy	McMahon	Divers 1
Mar 17	Leith Athletic	0-5	Cullen	McDonald	Reynolds	Curran	Kelly	Maley	Madden	Blessington	Cassidy	McGinn	Divers

SCOTTISH CUP 1893-94

Nov 25	HURLFORD	6-0	Cullen	Reynolds	Doyle	McEleny	Kelly	Curran	J Divers	Blessington 2	Cassidy 1	McMahon 1	Campbell 2
Dec 16	ALBION ROVERS	7-0	Cullen	Reynolds	Doyle	Curran	Kelly	Maley	Madden 1	Blessington 1	Cassidy 1	McMahon 4	Divers
Jan 13	ST BERNARD'S	8-1	Cullen	Reynolds	Doyle	Maley	Kelly	Curran	Madden 2	Blessington	Cassidy	McMahon 4	Divers ?x2
Feb 3	Third Lanark	5-3 SF	Cullen	Reynolds	Doyle	Maley	Kelly	Curran	Madden	Blessington 1	Cassidy 1	McMahon 3	Divers
Feb 17	Rangers	1-3 F	Cullen	Reynolds	Doyle	Maley 1	Kelly	Curran	Madden	Blessington	Cassidy	McMahon	Campbell

SCOTTISH LEAGUE 1894-95

Aug 11	Dundee	1-1	Cullen	Reynolds	Doyle	Curran	Kelly	Dowds	Campbell	Madden	Lees 1	Blessington	Cassidy
Aug 18	ST BERNARD'S	5-2	Cullen	T Dunbar	Doyle	Maley	Kelly	McEleny	Davidson	Madden	Lees 2	Blessington 2	Cassidy 1
Aug 25	Third Lanark	1-2	McArthur	T Dunbar	Doyle	Dowds	Maley	McEleny	Madden	Blessington 1	Lees	Cassidy	Divers 2P
Sept 8	St Mirren	3-0	McArthur	T Dunbar	Doyle	McEleny	Maley	Dowds	Campbell	Blessington	Madden	McMahon 2	Cassidy 1
Sept 22	RANGERS	5-3	McArthur	T Dunbar	Doyle	Maley	Kelly	McEleny	Blessington	Madden 1	Cassidy 1	McMahon	Divers 2
Oct 13	Clyde	4-2	McArthur	McDonald	Doyle	McEleny	Kelly	Maley 1	Madden	Blessington	Cassidy	McMahon 2	Divers 1
Oct 20	DUMBARTON	6-0	McArthur	McDonald	Doyle	McEleny	Maley	Powers	Madden 3	Blessington 1	Cassidy 2	McMahon	Davidson
Nov 3	HEARTS	0-2	McArthur	T Dunbar	Doyle	McEleny	Kelly	Maley	Madden	Blessington	Cassidy	McMahon	Campbell
Nov 10	St Bernard's	2-0	McArthur	Reynolds	Doyle	McEleny	Kelly	Maley	Davidson	Blessington	Cassidy 1	McMahon 1	Campbell
Dec 22	ST MIRREN	2-2	McArthur	T Dunbar	Doyle	McEleny	Kelly	Maley	Madden	Blessington 1	McCann	Campbell 1	Divers
Feb 16	Hearts	0-4	McArthur	Reynolds	T Dunbar	James Thom	Kelly	Cassidy	Campbell	Blessington	McCann	McMahon	Divers
Feb 23	Third Lanark	4-4	McArthur	W Arnott	T Dunbar	O'Rourke	Maley	D Thomas	Campbell 2	Blessington	Madden 1	McMahon 1	Divers
Mar 9	Dumbarton	2-0	McArthur	T Dunbar	Doyle	O'Rourke	Maley	McEleny	Jim Devlin	McCann	Madden 1	McMahon 1	Divers
Mar 16	LEITH ATHLETIC	4-0	McArthur	Reynolds	Doyle	McEleny	W Thomson	Maley	Jim Devlin	John Devlin 1	Madden 1	McMahon	WFerguson 2
Mar 23	Rangers	1-1	McArthur	T Dunbar	Doyle	O'Rourke	Kelly	McEleny	Campbell	John Devlin	Jack	McMahon 1	Ferguson
Mar 30	Leith Athletic	6-5	O'Brien	Reynolds	T Dunbar	Maley	Kelly	McEleny	Davidson 2	Madden 1	J. Ferguson 1	Divers 1	W Ferguson 1
Apr 27	CLYDE	2-0	Cullen	Reynolds	Doyle	C McEleny	Kelly	T Dunbar 1	Morrison	R McElhaney	Davidson	Divers 1	Ferguson
May 4	DUNDEE	2-1	McArthur	T Dunbar	Doyle	Trodden	Kelly	C McEleny	Morrison	R McElhaney	Madden 1	Divers 1	Campbell

SCOTTISH CUP 1894-95

Nov 24	QUEEN'S PARK	4-1	McArthur	Reynolds	Doyle	McEleny	Kelly	T Dunbar 1	Madden	Blessington	Cassidy 1	Campbell 2	Divers
Dec 15	Hibernian (Protest Upheld)	0-2	McArthur	T Dunbar	Doyle	McEleny	Kelly	Maley	Madden	Blessington	Cassidy	Campbell	Divers
Dec 29	Hibernian	2-0	McArthur	Reynolds	Doyle 1	McEleny	Kelly	Maley	Madden	Blessington	Divers 1	Campbell	Cassidy
Jan 19	Dundee	0-1	Cullen	T Dunbar	Doyle	McEleny	Kelly	Maley	Madden	Blessington	Divers 1	Campbell	Cassidy

SCOTTISH LEAGUE 1895-96

Aug 10	Dundee	2-1	McArthur	Battles	T Dunbar	O'Rourke	Kelly	King	Morrison	Blessington	Martin 1	McMahon 1	Divers
Aug 17	CLYDE	3-0	McArthur	Battles	Dunbar	O'Rourke	Kelly	King	Morrison	Blessington 1	Martin 1	McMahon 1	Ferguson
Aug 24	Hibernian	2-4	McArthur	Battles 1	Dunbar	Maley	Kelly	King	Morrison	Blessington	Martin	McMahon 1	Divers
Aug 31	ST MIRREN	4-0	McArthur	Meechan	Doyle	O'Rourke	Kelly	McEleny	Morrison	Madden 1	Martin 3	Crossan	Divers
Sept 7	Rangers	4-2	McArthur	Meechan	Battles	O'Rourke	Kelly	Dunbar 2	Madden	Blessington	Martin	Crossan 1	Ferguson 1
Sept 14	HEARTS	0-5	McArthur	Meechan	Battles	O'Rourke	Kelly	Dunbar	Madden	Blessington	Martin	Crossan	Ferguson
Sept 26	St Bernard's	0-3	McArthur	Meechan	Dunbar	McManus	Kelly	McEleny	Madden	Crossan	Martin	McMahon	Ferguson
Sept 28	Dumbarton	3-2	McArthur	Meechan	Doyle	Battles	King	McEleny	Madden	Blessington 1	H McIlvenny	McMahon 1	Divers 1
Oct 5	HIBERNIAN	3-1	McArthur	Meechan	Doyle 1	Maley	Kelly	Battles	Madden	Blessington	Martin 1	McMahon 1	Divers
Oct 12	Clyde	5-1	McArthur	Meechan	Doyle	King	Kelly	Battles	Madden 1	Blessington 1	Martin 2	McMahon 1	Ferguson
Oct 26	DUNDEE	11-0	McArthur	Meechan 1	Doyle 1	Maley	Kelly	Battles 1	Madden	Blessington 2	Martin	McMahon 1	Ferguson 1+4P
Nov 19	Third Lanark	7-0	McArthur	Meechan	Doyle	Maley	Kelly	Battles	Madden	Blessington	Martin 5	McMahon 1	Ferguson 1
Nov 23	Hearts	4-1	McArthur	Meechan	Doyle	Maley	Kelly	Battles	Madden	Blessington 1	Martin 2	McMahon 1	Ferguson
Nov 30	St Mirren	3-1	McArthur	Meechan	Doyle	Maley	Kelly	Battles	Madden	Blessington 2	Martin	McMahon	Ferguson 1
Dec 7	ST BERNARD'S	2-1	McArthur	Meechan	Doyle	King	Kelly	Battles	Madden	Blessington	Martin 1	McMahon 1	Ferguson
Dec 14	RANGERS	6-2	McArthur	Meechan	Doyle	King	Kelly	Battles 1	Morrison 1	Blessington 1	Martin 1	McMahon 2	Ferguson
Dec 21	DUMBARTON	3-0	McArthur	Meechan	Doyle P	King	Kelly	Battles	Madden	Blessington 1	Martin 1	McMahon 1	Ferguson
Jan 29	Third Lanark	2-1	Cullen	Meechan	Doyle	O'Rourke	Maley	Battles	Divers	Blessington 1	Martin	McMahon 1	Ferguson

SCOTTISH CUP 1896

Jan 18	QUEEN'S PARK	2-4	McArthur	Meechan	Doyle P	Maley	Kelly	King	Madden	Blessington	Martin	McMahon 1	Ferguson

SCOTTISH LEAGUE 1896-97

			1	2	3	4	5	6	7	8	9	10	11
Aug 15	Hibernian	1-3	McArthur	Meechan	Doyle	McEleny	Russell	Battles	Madden	Blessington	King	McMahon	Ferguson 1
Aug 17	Clyde	7-2	Cullen	Meechan	Doyle	McEleny	Russell	Battles	Morrison	Blessington	Madden	McMahon	King 7P
Aug 22	ST BERNARD'S	2-0	McArthur	Meechan	Doyle	McEleny	Ressell	Battles	Morrison	Blessington	King 1	McMahon 1	Ferguson
Aug 29	Abercorn	6-0	McArthur	Meechan	Doyle	McEleny	Russell	Battles	Morrison 2	Blessington	King 2	McMahon 2	Ferguson
Sept 5	HEARTS	3-0	McArthur	Meechan	Doyle	McEleny	Russell	Battles	Morrison	King	Hutchinson	McMahon 1	Divers 2
Sept 12	St Bernard's	2-1	McArthur	Meechan	Doyle	McEleny	Russell	Battles	Morrison	Blessington	King	McMahon	Divers 1
Sept 26	ST MIRREN	2-1	Cullen	James Orr	Doyle	Russell	Kelly	Battles	Morrison	Blessington	King	McMahon 2	Divers
Oct 3	Dundee	2-2	Cullen	Meechan	Doyle	McEleny	Russell 1	Battles	Madden	Blessington	King	McMahon 1	Ferguson
Oct 10	RANGERS	1-1	Cullen	Meechan	Doyle	McEleny	Kelly	Battles	Madden	Blessington	King	McMahon 1	Divers
Oct 17	THIRD LANARK	2-0	Cullen	Meechan	Doyle	McEleny 1	Kelly	Battles	Madden	Blessington	Russell 1	McMahon	Divers
Oct 24	Hearts	1-1	McArthur	Dunbar	Doyle	McEleny	Russell	Battles	Blessington 1	King	Hutchinson	McMahon	Divers
Nov 7	ABERCORN	5-0	McArthur	Meechan	Dunbar	Russell	Kelly	Battles	Madden	Blessington	King 2	McMahon 2	Divers 1
Nov 28	HIBERNIAN	1-1	McArthur	Dunbar	Doyle	Russell	Kelly	King	Gilhooly 1	Blessington	Crossan	Maley	Ferguson
Dec 5	Third Lanark	3-0	McArthur	Dunbar	Orr	Russell	Kelly	King	Madden	Blessington 1	McIlvenny	Gilhooly 1	Ferguson 1
Dec 12	CLYDE	4-1	McArthur	Orr	Doyle	Russell	Kelly	King	A. Henderson	Blessington 1	Groves 1	Gilhooly	Ferguson 2
Dec 19	Rangers	0-2	McArthur	Orr	Doyle	Russell	Kelly	King	Morrison	Blessington	Groves	Henderson	Ferguson
Feb 20	DUNDEE	0-1	Cullen	Orr	Dolyle	Russell	Kelly	King	Morrison	Blessington	Madden	Gilhooly	Carlin
Mar 13	St Mirren	0-2	Cullen	Orr	Doyle	Russell	Kelly	Neilsen	Slaven	Blessington	Connachan	King	Henderson

SCOTTISH CUP 1897

Jan 9	Arthurlie	2-4	Cullen	King	Crossan	Farrell	Kelly	Alec King	Morrison	Blessington	McIlvenny 1	Henderson	Ferguson 1

SCOTTISH LEAGUE 1897-98

Sept 4	HIBERNIAN	4-1	McArthur	Welford	Doyle	Reynolds	Russell 1	Willie Orr	Blessington	Campbell	Allan	King 1	Henderson 2
Sept 11	Hearts	0-0	McArthur	Welford	Doyle	Reynolds	Russell	Orr	Blessington	Campbell	Allan	King	Henderson
Sept 20	St Bernard's	2-0	McArthur	J. Orr	Doyle	Goldie	Russell	Orr	Gilhooly 1	Blessington	Campbell	King	Henderson
Sept 25	CLYDE	6-1	McArthur	Welford	Doyle	Goldie	Russell 1	Orr	Gilhooly	Campbell	Allan 2	McMahon 2	King 1
Sept 27	Rangers	4-0	McArthur	Welford	Doyle	Goldie	Russell	Orr	Gilhooly	Campbell 1	Allan 1	McMahon 1	King 1
Oct 2	St Mirren	0-0	McArthur	Welford	Doyle	Goldie	Russell	Orr	Gilhooly	Campbell	Allan	McMahon	King
Oct 9	Third Lanark	1-0	McArthur	Welford	Doyle	Goldie	Russell	Orr	Gilhooly	Campbell	Allan 1	McMahon	King
Oct 23	HEARTS	3-2	McArthur	Welford	Doyle	Goldie	Russell	Orr	Gilhooly	Campbell 2	Allan 1	McMahon	King
Nov 6	Dundee	2-1	Docherty	Welford	Doyle	Goldie	Russell	King	Gilhooly	Campbell	Allan	Blessington	Henderson 2
Nov 27	Hibernian	2-1	McArthur	Welford	W. Orr	Reynolds 1	Russell	King	Gilhooly	Campbell	Allan	McMahon 1	Henderson
Dec 4	THIRD LANARK	4-0	McArthur	Welford	W. Orr	Reynolds	Russell 2	King	Gilhooly	Campbell 1	Allan	McMahon	Peter Somers 1
Dec 11	Partick Thistle	6-3	McArthur	W. Orr	Doyle	Goldie	Russell 1	King	Gilhooly	Campbell 1	Allan 2	McMahon	Somers 2
Dec 18	ST BERNARD'S	5-1	McArthur	Welford	Doyle	Goldie	Russell	King	Gilhooly 2	Campbell	Allan 1	McMahon 2	Lynch
Dec 25	Clyde	9-1	McArthur	Welford	Doyle	Goldie	Russell 2	King	Gilhooly	Campbell 1	Allan 5	McMahon 1	Somers
Jan 15	DUNDEE	2-1	McArthur	Welford	Doyle	Goldie	Russell P	Orr	Allan	Blessington 1	Campbell	McMahon	Henderson
Jan 28	PARTICK THISTLE	3-1	McArthur	Welford	Doyle	Goldie	Russell	Orr	Gilhooly	Campbell 1	Allan 2	McMahon	Henderson
Feb 12	ST MIRREN	3-0	McArthur	Welford	Doyle	Goldie	Russell 1	King	Gilhooly 2	Campbell	Allan	McMahon	Henderson
Apr 11	RANGERS	0-0	McArthur	Welford	Doyle	Orr	Russell	King	Gilhooly	Campbell	Allan	McMahon	Henderson

SCOTTISH CUP 1898

Jan 8	Arthurlie	7-0	McArthur	Welford	Doyle	Goldie 1	Russell	King	Blessington	Campbell 1	Allan 1	McMahon 2	Henderson 2
Jan 21	Third Lanark	2-3	McArthur	Welford	Doyle	Goldie	Russell	Orr	Gilhooly	Blessington	Campbell	King 1	Allan

SCOTTISH LEAGUE 1898-99

Aug 20	THIRD LANARK	2-1	Docherty	Welford	Storrier	Orr	Tom Hynds	King P	Gilhooly	McAuley 1	Campbell	McMahon	Bell
Aug 27	Clyde	0-0	McArthur	Welford	Storrier	Goldie	Hynds	King	Somers	Gilhooly	Campbell	McMahon	Bell
Sept 3	ST MIRREN	4-1	McArthur	Welford	Storrier	Goldie	Hynds 1	King	Bell 1	Gilhooly 1	Campbell	McMahon 1	Fisher
Sept 10	Hibernian	1-2	McArthur	Welford	Storrier	Goldie	Hynds	King	Bell	Gilhooly	Campbell	McMahon 1	Fisher
Sept 19	Hearts	2-2	McArthur	Welford	Storrier	Goldie	Hynds	Orr	Bell 1	Gilhooly	Campbell	McMahon	Fisher 1
Sept 24	RANGERS	0-4	McArthur	Welford	Storrier	Goldie	Hynds	Orr	Bell	King	Campbell	McMahon	Fisher
Sept 27	HIBERNIAN	1-2	McArthur	Davidson	Doyle	Hynds	Dunlevy	Orr	Bell	Campbell	McMahon 1	Somers	Fisher
Oct 1	St Mirren	0-4	McArthur	Davidson	Doyle	Goldie	Hynds	Orr	Moran	Bell	Fisher	McMahon	King
Oct 8	ST BERNARD'S	1-0	McArthur	Storrier	Doyle	Battles	King	Moir	Bell	Gilhooly	Campbell 1	McMahon	Fisher
Oct 29	St Bernard's	3-2	Docherty	Welford	Storrier	Battles	Hynds 1	Orr	Gilhooly	Ross	Campbell 1	McMahon 1	Divers
Nov 5	CLYDE	9-2	McArthur	Storrier	Welford	Goldie	Battles 2	Orr	Bell 1	Divers 1	Campbell	McMahon 3	Fisher 1
Nov 19	Dundee	4-1	McArthur	Welford	Storrier	Goldie	Battles	Orr	Bell 1	Somers 1	Divers 1	McMahon	Fisher 1
Nov 26	PARTICK THISTLE	4-0	McArthur	Storrier	Doyle	Goldie	Battles	King	Bell 1	Somers	Divers 3	McMahon	Gilhooly
Dec 3	Partick Thistle	8-3	Docherty	Welford	Doyle	Goldie	Hynds	Orr 1	Bell	Somers 2	Divers 1	McMahon 3	Fisher
Dec 17	HEARTS	3-2	McArthur	Davidson	Storrier	Orr	Battles	King	Gilhooly 1	Somers 1	Divers	McMahon 1	Bell
Dec 31	Third Lanark	4-2	McArthur	Davidson	Storrier	Goldie	Battles	King	Gilhooly	Somers	Divers 2	McMahon 1	Bell 1
Jan 2	Rangers	1-4	McArthur	Davidson	Storrier	Goldie	Battles	King	Gilhooly	Somers	Divers	McMahon 1	Bell
Jan 7	DUNDEE	4-1	McArthur	Davidson	Welford	Hynds	Breslin	Orr	Bell 3	Campbell	Divers 1	King	Lynch

SCOTTISH CUP 1899

Jan 14	Sixth Galloway RV	8-1	McArthur	Davidson	Storrier	Battles	Hynds	King 1	Hodge 2	Campbell 1	Divers 1	McMahon 3	Bell
Feb 4	ST BERNARD'S	3-0	McArthur	Welford	Storrier	Battles	Marshall	Orr	Hodge 1	Campbell 1	Divers	McMahon 1	Bell
Feb 25	QUEEN'S PARK	2-1	McArthur	Welford	Storrier	Battles	Marshall	Orr	Hodge	Campbell	Divers	McMahon 2	Bell
Mar 11	PORT GLASGOW	4-2 SF	McArthur	Welford	Storrier	King	Marshall	Orr	Hodge	Campbell	Divers 1	McMahon 1	Bell 2
Apr 22	Rangers (N)	2-0 F	McArthur	Welford	Storrier	Battles	Marshall	King	Hodge 1	Campbell	Divers	McMahon 1	Bell

SCOTTISH LEAGUE 1899-1900

Aug 19	CLYDE	3-2	McArthur	Welford	Turnbull	Battles	Marshall 2	Orr	Gilhooly	Campbell	Russell	McMahon 1	Bell
Aug 26	Kilmarnock	2-2	McArthur	Welford	Turnbull	Battles	Marshall 1	King	Hodge	Campbell	Divers 1	McMahon	Bell
Sept 2	THIRD LANARK	5-2	Docherty	Welford	Davidson	Russell	Marshall	Battles	Hodge 1	Gilhooly 2	Campbell 1	King	Bell 1
Sept 9	HIBERNIAN	2-1	Docherty	Welford	Davidson	Russell	Marshall	Battles	Hodge 2	Gilhooly	Campbell	King	Bell
Sept 18	Hibernian	1-1	Docherty	Welford	Davidson	Russell	Marshall	Battles	Hodge	Gilhooly	Divers	Campbell	Bell 1
Sept 23	Clyde	5-0	McArthur	Turnbull	Welford	Russell	Marshall	Battles	Hodge 1	Gilhooly	Campbell 2	King 1	Bell 1
Sept 25	Third Lanark	3-0	McArthur	Turnbull	Welford	Russell	Marshall	Battles	Hodge	Gilhooly 2	Campbell 1	King	Bell
Sept 30	HEARTS	0-2	McArthur	Turnbull	Welford	Russell	Battles	King	Hodge	Gilhooly	Blackwood	Campbell	Bell
Oct 7	Rangers	3-3	McArthur	Turnbull	Welford	Battles	Russell	Orr	Hodge	Gilhooly	Campbell 1	McMahon 1	Bell +OG
Oct 21	St Mirren	2-2	Docherty	Turnbill	Storrier	Battles	Russell	Orr	Hodge	Gilhooly 1	McMahon	King	Bell 1
Oct 28	ST BERNARD'S	5-0	McArthur	Turnbull	Storrier	Battles	Russell	Orr	Hodge 2	Gilhooly 2	Campbell	McMahon 1	Bell
Nov 4	Hearts	2-3	McArthur	Turnbull	Storrier	Battles	Russell	Orr	Hodge	Gilhooly 1	Campbell	McMahon 1	Bell
Nov 25	Dundee	2-1	McArthur	Turnbull	Storrier	Davidson	Russell	King	Hodge	Gilhooly	Divers 1	McMahon	Bell +OG
Dec 2	St Bernard's	1-1	Docherty	Welford	Storrier	King	Russell	Orr	Bell	Gilhooly	Campbell	McMahon 1	Divers
Dec 9	ST MIRREN	3-1	Docherty	Davidson	Storrier	Battles	Russell	King	Bell 2	Gilhooly	Campbell 1	Somers	Divers
Dec 16	KILMARNOCK	3-3	Docherty	Davidson	Storrier	Battles	Hynds	King	Bell	Divers 1	Campbell 1	Somers 1	Hodge
Dec 23	DUNDEE	1-1	McArthur	Davidson	Welford	Hynds	Russell	Orr	Bell	Gilhooly	Campbell	McMahon	Divers 1
Jan 1	RANGERS	3-2	McArthur	Davidson	Turnbull	Russell	Marshall	Orr	Bell 1	Somers	Divers 2	McMahon	Campbell

SCOTTISH CUP 1900

Jan 13	BO'NESS	7-1	McArthur	Davidson	Turnbull	Russell	Marshall	Orr 1	Bell 1	Somers 2	Divers 1	McMahon 2	Campbell
Jan 27	Port Glasgow	5-1	McArthur	Davidson	Battles	Russell	Marshall	Orr	Bell	Campbell 2	Divers	McMahon 1	Gilhooly 2
Feb 17	KILMARNOCK	4-0	McArthur	Davidson	Battles	Hynds	Marshall	Orr	Bell 1	Campbell	Divers 1	McMahon 1	Gilhooly 1
Feb 24	Rangers	2-2 SF	McArthur	Davidson	Battles	Hynds	Marshall	Orr	Bell 1	Campbell P	Divers	McMahon	Gilhooly

			1	2	3	4	5	6	7	8	9	10	11
Mar 10	RANGERS	4-0 SFR	McArthur	Davidson	Battles	Russell	Marshall	Orr	Hodge 1	Campbell	Divers	McMahon 2	Bell 1
Apr 14	Queen's Park	4-3 F	McArthur	Storrier	Battles	Russell	Marshall	Orr	Hodge	Campbell	Divers 2	McMahon 1	Bell 1

SCOTTISH LEAGUE 1900-01

Aug 15	PARTICK THISTLE	3-3	McArthur	Davidson	Storrier	Russell	Hynds	Orr	Hodge	Gilhooly	Campbell 1	McMahon 1	Battles 1
Aug 18	Morton	3-2	McArthur	Davidson	Storrier	Battles	Hynds	Orr	Hodge	Divers 1	Campbell 1	McMahon	Findlay 1
Aug 25	HIBERNIAN	3-1	McArthur	Davidson	Storrier	Battles	Hynds	Orr	Hodge 1	Divers	Campbell	McMahon 2	Findlay
Sept 1	Third Lanark	2-1	McArthur	Davidson	Storrier	Battles	Hynds	Orr	Hodge 1	Gray 1	Campbell	McMahon	Findlay
Sept 8	Queen's Park	2-0	McArthur	Davidson	Storrier	Battles	Russell	Orr	Hodge	McOustra	Campbell	McMahon 2	Findlay
Sept 17	Hearts	2-0	McArthur	Davidson	Storrier	Russell	Loney 1	Hynds	Hodge 1	Divers	Campbell	McMahon	Findlay
Sept 24	THIRD LANARK	5-1	Donnelly	Davidson	Storrier	Russell	Hynds	Orr 1	McOustra 1	Divers 1	Campbell	McMahon	Findlay 2
Sept 30	Hibernian	2-2	McArthur	Davidson	Storrier	Russell	Hynds	Orr	McOustra 1	Divers	Campbell	McMahon	Findlay 1
Oct 6	RANGERS	2-1	McArthur	Davidson	Battles	Russell	Hynds	Orr	McOustra	Divers 1	Campbell 1	McMahon	Findlay
Oct 13	QUEEN'S PARK	2-0	McArthur	Davidson	Battles	Russell	Hynds	Orr	McOustra	Campbell	Divers 1	McMahon 1	Findlay
Oct 27	KILMARNOCK	1-0	McArthur	Davidson	Battles	Russell	McNeill	Orr	Hodge	Campbell 1	Divers	McMahon	McOustra
Nov 3	Kilmarnock	1-2	McArthur	Battles	Storrier	Russell	Hynds	Orr	Hodge 1	Campbell	Divers	McMahon	McOustra
Nov 10	Dundee	1-1	McArthur	Davidson	Battles	Russell	Hynds	Orr	Hodge 1	Campbell	Divers	McMahon	McOustra
Nov 17	HEARTS	1-3	McArthur	Storrier	Battles	Russell	McNeill	Orr	Hodge 1	Campbell	Divers	McMahon	McOustra
Nov 24	MORTON	4-2	McArthur	Davidson	Storrier	Russell	Hynds	Battles	Hodge	Divers	Campbell 2	McMahon 1	McOustra 1
Dec 1	Partick Thistle	6-2	McArthur	Davidson	Storrier	Russell	Hynds	Orr	McOustra	Divers 1	Campbell 2	McMahon 2	Findlay 1
Dec 15	ST MIRREN	3-0	McArthur	Davidson	Battles	Russell	Loney	Orr	McOustra 1	Divers 1	Campbell	McMahon 1	Findlay
Dec 22	DUNDEE	1-2	McArthur	Davidson	Battles	Russell 1	Loney	Orr	Hodge	Divers	Campbell	McMahon	McOustra
Jan 1	Rangers	1-2	Donnelly	Davidson	Storrier	Russell	Loney	Orr	McOustra	Divers	Campbell	McMahon 1	Findlay
Jan 19	St Mirren	4-3	Donnelly	Davidson	Battles	Russell	Loney	Orr	Hodge 1	Gray	Campbell 2	McMahon	Quinn 1

SCOTTISH CUP 1901

Jan 12	RANGERS	1-0	McArthur	Battles	Davidson	Russell	Loney	Orr	McOustra 1	Divers	Campbell	McMahon	Findlay
Feb 9	KILMARNOCK	6-0	Donnelly	Davidson	Battles	Russell	Loney	Orr	McOustra 1	Divers 1	Campbell 2	McMahon 1	Findlay 1
Feb 16	Dundee	1-0	Donnelly	Davidson	Battles	Russell	Loney	Orr	McOustra	Divers	Campbell	McMahon	Findlay 1
Mar 23	ST MIRREN	1-0 SF	McArthur	Davidson	Battles	Russell	Loney	Orr	McOustra	Divers	Campbell 1	McMahon	Quinn
Apr 6	Hearts	3-4 F	McArthur	Davidson	Battles	Russell	Loney	Orr	McOustra 1	Divers	Campbell	McMahon 1	Quinn 1

SCOTTISH LEAGUE 1901-02

Aug 17	DUNDEE	1-1	McFarlane	Davidson	Battles	Loney	Marshall	Orr	Crawford	Divers 1	Campbell	Livingstone	Quinn
Aug 24	Morton	2-1	McFarlane	Davidson	Battles	Russell	Marshall	Hynds	McOustra 1	Livingstone	Campbell 1	Drummond	Quinn
Aug 31	THIRD LANARK	3-2	McFarlane	Davidson	Battles	Moir	Marshall	Hynds	Hodge 1	Livingstone	Campbell P	Drummond	Quinn 1
Sept 7	St Mirren	3-2	McFarlane	Davidson	Battles	Moir	Marshall	Loney	Hodge 2	Livingstone	Campbell 1	Drummond	Quinn
Sept 16	Hibernian	2-1	McArthur	Watson	Davidson	Moir	Loney	Orr	Crawford 1	Livingstone	Campbell	McMahon 1	McOustra
Sept 21	MORTON	2-1	McFarlane	Watson	Battles	Moir	Loney	Orr	Crawford	Livingstone	Campbell 1	McMahon 1	Divers
Sept 23	Third Lanark	2-0	McFarlane	Watson	Davidson	Moir	Marshall	Orr	Hodge 1	Livingstone	McOustra	McMahon	Crawford 1
Sept 28	Kilmarnock	1-0	McFarlane	Watson	Battles	Moir	Marshall	Orr	Crawford	Livingstone 1	Quinn	McMahon	Findlay
Oct 5	Rangers	2-2	McFarlane	Watson	Battles	Moir	Marshall	Orr	Crawford	Livingstone	Campbell	McMahon	Quinn 1 +OG
Oct 19	QUEEN'S PARK	1-0	McFarlane	Watson	Davidson	Moir	Marshall	Orr	McOustra	Livingstone	Quinn	McMahon	Findlay 1
Nov 2	Hearts	2-2	McFarlane	Battles	Davidson	Russell	Marshall	Orr	McOustra	Livingstone	Campbell 1	McDermott	Drummond 1
Nov 9	ST MIRREN	3-1	McFarlane	Watson	Battles	Loney	Marshall	Orr	Hodge	Livingstone 3	Campbell	McMahon	McOustra
Nov 16	Dundee	3-2	McFarlane	Watson	Davidson	Loney	Marshall	Orr	Hodge	Livingstone	Campbell 2	McMahon 1	Quinn
Nov 30	HEARTS	1-2	McFarlane	Watson	Davidson	Russell	Marshall	Loney	McDermott	Livingstone	Mair	McMahon 1	Quinn
Dec 7	Queen's Park	2-3	McFarlane	Watson	Battles	Loney	Marshall	Orr	McOustra	Livingstone	Campbell 1	McMahon 1	Quinn
Dec 14	HIBERNIAN	2-2	McFarlane	Davidson	Battles	Loney	Marshall	Orr	Hodge 1	Livingstone	Campbell P	McMahon	Quinn
Dec 28	KILMARNOCK	4-2	McFarlane	Watson	Battles	Loney	Marshall	Orr	Hodge 1	McOustra 3	Campbell	McMahon	Quinn
Jan 1	RANGERS	2-4	McFarlane	Watson	Battles	Loney	Marshall 1	Orr	Hodge	Livingstone	Campbell	McMahon 1	McOustra

SCOTTISH CUP 1902

Jan 11	THORNLIEBANK	3-0	McFarlane	Davidson	Battles	Loney	Marshall	McOustra	Walls	Livingstone 2	Campbell P	McDermott	Quinn
Jan 25	Arbroath	3-2	McFarlane	Watson	Battles	Loney	Marshall	Orr 1	McOustra	Livingstone	Campbell 1	McMahon 1	Quinn
Feb 15	Hearts	1-1	McFarlane	Watson	Battles	Loney	Russell	Orr	Hodge	McDermott	Livingstone	McMahon	Quinn 1
Feb 22	HEARTS	2-1	McFarlane	Davidson	Battles	Loney	Russell	Orr	Livingstone	McDermott	Campbell	McMahon 2	Quinn
Mar 22	St Mirren	3-2 SF	McFarlane	Watson	Battles	Loney	Marshall	Orr	Livingstone 1	McDermott 1	Campbell 1	McMahon	Quinn
Apr 28	HIBERNIAN	0-1 F	McFarlane	Watson	Battles	Loney	Marshall	Orr	McCafferty	McDermott	McMahon	Livingstone	Quinn

SCOTTISH LEAGUE 1902-03

Aug 16	Hibernian	1-1	McPherson	Watson	Battles	Moir	Loney	Orr	Crawford	Campbell 1	Quinn	McDermott	Hamilton
Aug 23	ST MIRREN	2-2	McPherson	Watson	Battles	Moir	Loney	Orr	Crawford 1	Campbell 1	Quinn	McMahon	Hamilton
Aug 30	Third Lanark	2-1	McPherson	Watson	MacLeod	Moir	Marshall 1	Orr	Quinn	Somers	Campbell	McDermott 1	Hamilton
Sept 6	QUEEN'S PARK	1-1	McPherson	Battles	MacLeod	Moir	Marshall	Orr	Quinn	Somers	Campbell P	McDermott	Hamilton
Sept 15	Hearts	2-1	McPherson	Watson	MacLeod	Moir	Loney	Orr	Quinn 1	Somers	Campbell 1	McDermott	Hamilton
Sept 20	Kilmarnock	3-1	McPherson	Watson	MacLeod	Moir	Loney	Orr	Quinn	Somers	Campbell 3	McDermott	Hamilton
Sept 27	THIRD LANARK	1-0	McPherson	Watson	MacLeod	Moir	Loney	Orr	Crawford	Somers	Campbell 1	McDermott	Hamilton
Sept 29	HEARTS	2-2	McPherson	Watson	MacLeod	Moir	Marshall	Orr	Crawford	Somers 1	Campbell 1	McMenemy	Hamilton
Oct 4	Queen's Park	1-2	McPherson	Battles	MacLeod	Moir	Loney	Orr	Quinn	Somers	Campbell 1	McDermott	Hamilton
Oct 18	RANGERS	1-1	McPherson	Watson	MacLeod	Moir	Loney	Orr	McCafferty	McDermott	Quinn	Campbell P	Hamilton
Nov 1	KILMARNOCK	3-1	McPherson	Watson	MacLeod	Moir	Loney	Orr	Walls	Somers 1	Campbell 1	Quinn	Hamilton
Nov 15	PARTICK THISTLE	4-1	McPherson	Watson	MacLeod	Moir	Loney	Orr	Murray 1	McDermott	Quinn 1	Somers 1	Hamilton
Nov 22	PORT GLASGOW ATHLETIC	3-0	McPerhson	Watson	MacLeod	Moir	Loney 1	Orr	Murray	McMenemy 1	Quinn	Campbell	Hamilton 1
Nov 29	DUNDEE	2-2	McPherson	Watson	MacLeod	Battles	Loney 1	Orr	Murray	McMenemy	Quinn	Somers	Hamilton 1
Dec 6	Partick Thistle	0-0	McPherson	Battles	MacLeod	Watson	Loney	Orr	Murray	Somers	Quinn	McMahon	Hamilton
Dec 13	St Mirren	1-3	McPherson	Watson	MacLeod	Moir	Loney	Orr	Murray 1	Somers	Battles	McMahon	Quinn
Dec 20	MORTON	1-1	McPherson	H Watson	MacLeod	Moir	Loney	Watson	Murray	McDermott 1	Campbell	McMahon	Quinn
Jan 1	Rangers	3-3	McPherson	Watson	MacLeod	Moir	Loney	Orr	Murray	Somers	Campbell 1	McMahon 2	Quinn
Jan 2	HIBERNIAN	0-4	McPherson	Watson	MacLeod	Moir	Loney	Orr	Murray	Somers	Campbell	McMahon	Hamilton
Mar 7	Port Glasgow Athletic	1-1	McPherson	Battles	MacLeod	Moir	P Watson	Orr	Walls	McMenemy 1	Loney	Murray	Quinn
Mar 14	Morton	2-0	McPherson	Battles	MacLeod	Loney	P Watson	Marshall	Walls	Murray	Clark 1	Somers	Hamilton 1
Mar 21	Dundee	0-2	McPherson	Battles	MacLeod	Moir	Marshall	Loney	Walls	Murray	Clark	Somers	Quinn

SCOTTISH CUP 1903

Jan 24	ST MIRREN	0-0	McPherson	Watson	MacLeod	Moir	Loney	Orr	Murray	Somers	Campbell	McMahon	Quinn
Jan 31	St Mirren	1-1	McPherson	Watson	Battles	Loney	Marshall	Orr	Murray	McDermott	Campbell	McMahon	Quinn
Feb 14	ST MIRREN	4-0	McPherson	Watson 1	Battles	Moir	Marshall	Orr	Murray 1	McDermott	Campbell 1	McMahon 1	Quinn
Feb 21	PORT GLASGOW ATHLETIC	2-0	McPherson	Watson	Battles	Moir	Marshall	Orr	Murray	McDermott 1	Campbell 1	McMahon	Quinn
Feb 28	RANGERS	0-3	McPherson	Watson	Battles	Moir	Loney	Orr	Murray	McDermott	Campbell	McMahon	Quinn

SCOTTISH LEAGUE 1903-04

Aug 15	PARTICK THISTLE	2-1	McPherson	Battles	Strang	Moir	Young	Hay	Muir	Somers	Bennett 1	McMenemy 1	Quinn
Aug 22	St Mirren	1-0	McPherson	Watson	Battles	Moir	Young	Hay	Muir	Grassam	Bennett	Somers 1	Quinn
Aug 29	THIRD LANARK	1-3	McPherson	Watson	Battles	Moir	Young	Hay	Muir	Grassam	Bennett 1	Somers	Quinn
Sept 5	Hibernian	2-0	McPherson	Watson	Battles	Moir	Young	Hay	Muir	Graham	Bennett 1	Somers 1	Quinn
Sept 26	HIBERNIAN	1-0	Adams	Watson	Battles	Moir	Young	Hay	Muir	McMenemy	Gilligan 1	Bennett	Quinn
Sept 28	Third Lanark	1-3	Adams	Watson	McLeod	Moir	Young	Hay	Muir	Graham	Bennett	McMenemy	Quinn 1

			1	2	3	4	5	6	7	8	9	10	11
Oct 3	QUEEN'S PARK	3-0	Adams	Watson	Battles	Orr 2 (1P)	Loney	Hay	Muir	McMenemy 1	Gilligan	Bennett	Hamilton
Oct 10	DUNDEE	4-2	Adams	Watson	Battles	Orr 2 (1P)	Loney	Hay	Muir	McMenemy	Gilligan 2	Bennett	Quinn
Oct 17	Rangers	0-0	Adams	Watson	Battles	Orr	Loney	Hay	Bennett	McMenemy	Gilligan	Somers	Quinn
Oct 24	HEARTS	4-0	Adams	Watson	Battles	Orr	Loney	Hay	Bennett 1	McMenemy 1	Gilligan 2	Somers	Quinn
Oct 31	Queen's Park	0-1	Adams	Watson	Battles	Orr	Loney	Hay	Bennett	McMenemy	Gilligan	Somers	Quinn
Nov 14	Kilmarnock	6-1	Adams	Watson	Battles	Orr	Loney	Hay	Bennett	McMenemy	Gilligan 2	Somers 2	Quinn +OG
Dec 5	Morton	1-0	Adams	Watson	Battles	Orr	Young	Hay	Bennett	McMenemy	Gilligan 1	Somers	Quinn
Dec 12	AIRDRIE	3-0	Adams	Watson	Battles	Orr 1	Young	Hay	Muir 1	McMenemy	Quinn	Somers	Hamilton 1
Dec 19	Partick Thistle	4-0	Adams	Watson	Battles	Orr	Loney	Hay	Muir	McMenemy	Bennett 2	Somers	Hamilton 2
Dec 26	PORT GLASGOW ATHLETIC	4-1	Adams	Watson	Battles	Orr	Loney	Hay 1	Muir	McMenemy	Gilligan 3	Somers	Hamilton
Jan 1	RANGERS	2-2	Adams	Watson	Battles	Orr	Loney	Hay	Muir	McMenemy 1	Bennett 1	Somers	Hamilton
Jan 9	Airdrie	3-4	Adams	Watson	MacLeod	Young	Loney	Hay P	Muir	McMenemy 1	Gilligan	Somers	Hamilton 1
Jan 16	MOTHERWELL	6-0	Adams	Battles	MacLeod	Orr	Young	Hay	Muir	McMenemy 3	Gilligan 1	Somers 1	Hamilton 1
Jan 23	MORTON	5-1	Adams	Battles	MacLeod	Orr	Young	Hay	Muir 3	McMenemy	Bennett 2	Somers	Hamilton
Jan 30	Dundee	1-2	Adams	Battles	MacLeod	Orr	Young	Hay	Muir	McMenemy	Bennett 1	Somers	Hamilton
Feb 6	Port Glasgow Athletic	3-2	McPherson	Battles	MacLeod	Orr	Young	Loney	Muir	Graham	Gilligan	McMenemy	Quinn 3
Mar 12	ST MIRREN	3-1	Adams	MacLeod	Battles	Young	Loney	Hay	Muir	Somers	Gilligan 1	Quinn 1	Hamilton 1
Mar 26	Motherwell	2-1	Adams	MacLeod	Battles	Young	Loney	Orr	Muir	McMenemy	Bennett 2	Quinn	Hamilton
Apr 2	Hearts	1-2	Adams	MacLeod	Orr	Young	Loney	Hay	Muir	McMenemy 1	Somers	Quinn	Hamilton
Apr 23	KILMARNOCK	6-1	Adams	MacLeod	Strang	Orr	Young	Hay	Graham	McMenemy 1	Quinn 5	Somers	Hamilton

SCOTTISH CUP 1904

Feb 13	St Bernard's	4-0	Adams	Battles	MacLeod	Orr 2	Loney	Hay	Muir	McMenemy 2	Bennett	Somers	Hamilton
Feb 20	DUNDEE	1-1	Adams	Battles	MacLeod	Orr	Loney	Hay	Muir	McMenemy	Bennett	Somers	Hamilton 1
Feb 27	Dundee	0-0	Adams	MacLeod	Orr	Young	Loney	Hay	Bennett	McMenemy	Gilligan	Somers	Quinn
Mar 5	DUNDEE	5-0	Adams	MacLeod	Orr	Young	Loney	Hay	Muir 2	McMenemy 1	Bennett 1	Quinn 1	Hamilton
Mar 19	THIRD LANARK	2-1 SF	Adams	MacLeod	Orr	Young	Loney	Hay	Muir 1	McMenemy	Bennett	Quinn 1	Hamilton
Apr 16	Rangers	3-2 F	Adams	MacLeod	Orr	Young	Loney	Hay	Muir	McMenemy	Quinn 3	Somers	Hamilton

SCOTTISH LEAGUE 1904-05

Aug 20	Partick Thistle	5-0	Adams	MacLeod	Orr	Young 1	Loney	Hay 1	McLean 1	McMenemy 1	Bennett 1	Somers	Hamilton
Aug 27	Port Glasgow Athletic	4-1	Adams	MacLeod	Orr	Black	Loney	Hay	McLean 1	McMenemy	Quinn 3	Somers	Hamilton
Sept 3	HEARTS	1-1	Adams	MacLeod	Orr	Black	Loney	Hay	McLean	McMenemy	Quinn	Somers 1	Hamilton
Sept 17	St Mirren	3-2	Adams	MacLeod	Orr	Young	Loney	Hay 1	McLean	McMenemy	Quinn 2	Somers	McNair
Sept 19	Hearts	0-2	Adams	MacLeod	Orr	Young	Loney	Hay	McLean	McMenemy	Quinn	Somers	McNair
Sept 26	THIRD LANARK	2-1	Adams	MacLeod	Orr	Young	Loney	Hay	Bennett	McMenemy 2	Quinn	Somers	Hamilton
Oct 1	Queen's Park	3-2	Adams	MacLeod	Orr	Young	Loney	Hay	Bennett 1	McMenemy	Quinn 1	Somers	Hamilton +OG
Oct 15	RANGERS	2-2	Adams	MacLeod	Orr	Young	Loney	Hay	Bennett 1	McMenemy 1	Quinn	Somers	Hamilton
Oct 22	Third Lanark	2-1	Adams	MacLeod	Orr	Young	Loney	Hay	Bennett	McMenemy	Quinn 2	Somers	Hamilton
Oct 29	QUEEN'S PARK	1-1	Adams	MacLeod	Orr	Young	Loney	Hay	Bennett	McMenemy	Quinn 1	Somers	Hamilton
Nov 5	Kilmarnock	3-0	Adams	MacLeod	Hay	Young	Loney	Black	Bennett	Somers	McIlvenny	Quinn 1	Hamilton 1
Nov 12	Hibernian	2-2	Adams	MacLeod	Orr	Black	Loney	Hay	McLean	Somers	McIlvenny	Quinn 1	Hamilton +OG
Nov 19	DUNDEE	3-0	Adams	MacLeod	Hay	Young	Loney 1	Black	McLean	McMenemy	Bennett 2	Somers	Hamilton
Nov 26	Airdrie	3-1	Adams	MacLeod	Hay	Young	Loney	Black	McLean	McMenemy 2	Bennett 1	Quinn	Hamilton
Dec 3	MOTHERWELL	4-2	Adams	MacLeod	Orr	Black	Loney	Hay	McLean 1	Somers 1	Bennett 1	Quinn 1	Hamilton
Dec 10	Morton	1-0	Adams	MacLeod	Hay	Young	Loney	Black	McLean	Somers	Bennett	Quinn 1	Hamilton
Dec 17	PARTICK THISTLE	2-2	Adams	MacLeod	Hay P	Young	Loney	Black	McLean	Somers 1	Bennett	Quinn	Hamilton
Dec 24	ST MIRREN	1-0	Adams	MacLeod	Orr	Young	Loney	Hay	Bennett	Somers 1	McIlvenny	Quinn	Hamilton
Dec 31	KILMARNOCK	3-1	Adams	MacLeod	Orr P	Young	Loney 1	Hay	McLean	Somers	Bennett	McIlvenny 1	Hamilton
Jan 3	AIRDRIE	2-3	Adams	MacLeod	Hay	Young	Loney 1	McNair	McLean	Somers 1	Bennett	McIlvenny	Hamilton
Jan 7	PORT GLASGOW ATHLETIC	3-0	Adams	H Watson	Orr	Young	Loney	Hay	McLean	Somers	Bennett	McIlvenny	Hamilton 2 +OG
Jan 14	Dundee	1-2	Adams	MacLeod	Orr	Young	Loney	Hay	McLean 1	Somers	Bennett	Quinn	Hamilton
Jan 21	HIBERNIAN	2-0	Adams	MacLeod	Orr	Young	Loney	Hay	Bennett	Somers 2	Quinn	McIlvenny	Hamilton
Feb 4	MORTON	5-2	Adams	MacLeod	Orr	Black	Loney 2	Hay	Bennett 1	McMenemy 1	Quinn 1	Somers	Hamilton
Feb 25	Rangers	4-1	Adams	MacLeod	Orr	McNair	Loney	Hay	Bennett	McMenemy	Quinn 2	Somers	Hamilton 2
Mar 4	Motherwell	6-2	Adams	MacLeod	Orr	McNair 1	Loney 1	Hay	Bennett	McMenemy	Quinn 3	Somers 1	Hamilton

*May 6: Play off for Scottish league Championship (Hampden) Celtic 2 Rangers 1

SCOTTISH CUP 1905

Jan 28	Dumfries	2-1	Adams	MacLeod	Orr	Young	Loney	Hay	Bennett 1	Somers	Quinn 1	McIlvenny	Hamilton
Feb 11	LOCHGELLY UNITED	3-0	Adams	MacLeod	Orr	Black	Loney	Hay	Bennett	McMenemy	Quinn	Somers 1	Hamilton
Feb 25	PARTICK THISTLE	3-0	Adams	MacLeod	Orr P	McNair	Loney	Hay	Bennett 1	McMenemy 1	Quinn	Somers	Hamilton
Mar 25	RANGERS	0-2 SF	Adams	MacLeod	Orr	Young	Loney	Hay	Bennett	McMenemy	Quinn	Somers	Hamilton

SCOTTISH LEAGUE 1905-06

Aug 19	MOTHERWELL	3-1	Adams	Campbell	MacLeod	Young	Loney	Hay	Bennett 1	McMenemy	Quinn 2	Somers	McNair
Aug 26	Kilmarnock	4-2	Adams	MacLeod	Orr	Young	Loney	Hay 1	Bennett	McMenemy 1	Quinn	Somers 1	Hamilton 1
Sept 2	HIBERNIAN	1-0	Adams	MacLeod	Orr	McNair	Loney	Hay	Bennett 1	McMenemy	Quinn	Somers	Hamilton
Sept 11	Hearts	1-1	Adams	MacLeod	Orr	Young	Loney	Hay	Bennett	McMenemy 1	Quinn	Somers	Hamilton
Sept 16	Falkirk	5-0	Adams	Campbell	MacLeod	Young	Loney 1	Hay	A McNair	McMenemy	Bennett 2	Quinn 2	Hamilton
Sept 25	Third Lanark	1-0	Adams	MacLeod	Orr	Young	Loney	Hay	McNair 1	McMenemy	Bennett	Quinn	Hamilton
Sept 30	AIRDRIE	2-1	Adams	MacLeod	Orr P	Young	Loney	Hay	McNair	McMenemy 1	Bennett	Quinn	Hamilton
Oct 14	QUEEN'S PARK	5-1	Adams	Campbell	Orr	Young 1	Loney	Hay	Bennett	McMenemy	Quinn 3	McNair	Hamilton 1
Oct 21	Rangers	2-3	Adams	Campbell	Orr P	Young	Loney	Hay	Bennett	McMenemy	Quinn	Somers 1	Hamilton
Oct 28	DUNDEE	3-1	Adams	Campbell	Orr P	Young 1	Loney	Hay	Bennett	McMenemy	Quinn	McNair 1	Hamilton
Nov 4	Partick Thistle	3-0	Adams	Campbell	Orr	Wilson	Loney	Hay	Bennett	McNair 1	Quinn	Somers 1	Hamilton +OG
Nov 11	PORT GLASGOW ATHLETIC	0-1	Adams	Campbell	Orr	Wilson	Loney	Hay	Bennett	McNair	Quinn	Somers	Hamilton
Nov 18	Morton	4-0	Adams	Campbell	Orr	McNair	Loney	Hay	McMenemy	Somers	Bennett 2	Quinn 1	Hamilton 1
Nov 25	ST MIRREN	2-1	Adams	Campbell	Orr	McNair	Loney	Hay	McMenemy	Somers 1	Bennett	Quinn	Hamilton +OG
Dec 2	Port Glasgow Athletic	1-0	Adams	MacLeod	Orr	McNair	Loney 1	Hay	Bennett	McMenemy	Quinn	Somers	Hamilton
Dec 9	ABERDEEN	1-0	Adams	MacLeod	Orr	Young	Loney	Hay	Bennett	McMenemy 1	Quinn	Somers	Hamilton
Dec 16	Motherwell	4-0	Adams	MacLeod	Orr	McNair	Loney	Hay	Bennett	McMenemy 1	Quinn 2	Wilson	Hamilton 1
Dec 23	MORTON	4-0	Adams	Campbell	Orr P	McNair	Loney	Hay	Bennett 1	McMenemy 1	Quinn 1	Wilson	Hamilton
Dec 30	Hibernian	1-0	Adams	MacLeod	Orr	Young	Loney	Hay	Bennett	McMenemy	Quinn 1	Somers	Hamilton
Jan 1	RANGERS	1-0	Adams	MacLeod	Orr	McNair	Loney	Hay	Bennett	McMenemy	Quinn	Somers	Hamilton 1
Jan 2	KILMARNOCK	2-0	Adams	MacLeod	Orr	McNair	Loney	Hay	Bennett 1	McMenemy	Quinn	Somers	Hamilton 1
Jan 6	FALKIRK	7-0	Adams	Campbell	MacLeod	Young	McNair	Hay P	Bennett 3	McMenemy 2	Quinn	Somers	J Bauchop 1
Jan 13	Airdrie	5-2	Adams	MacLeod	Orr P	McNair	Loney	Hay	Bennett	McMenemy	Quinn 3	Somers	Hamilton 1
Jan 20	PARTICK THISTLE	4-1	Adams	MacLeod	Orr	Young	Loney	Hay	McNair 1	McMenemy 1	Bennett 2	Somers	Hamilton
Feb 3	Dundee	0-1	Adams	MacLeod	Orr	Young	Loney	Hay	McNair	McMenemy	Bennett	Somers	Hamilton
Feb 17	St Mirren	3-1	Adams	MacLeod	McNair	Young	Loney	Hay P	Shaw	McMenemy 1	Quinn	Somers	Bauchop 1
Mar 3	Aberdeen	0-1	Adams	Hay	Orr	Young	Loney	Wilson	Bauchop	McMenemy	Bennett	Somers	Hamilton
Mar 10	Queen's Park	6-0	Adams	MacLeod	McNair	Young	Loney	Hay	Bennett 1	McMenemy	Quinn 4	Somers	Hamilton 1
Apr 21	HEARTS	1-0	Adams	Watson	MacLeod	Young	McNair	Hay	Garry	McMenemy	Bennett	Quinn 1	Hamilton
May 7	THIRD LANARK	0-1	Adams	MacLeod	Orr	Young	Loney	Hay	Garry	McMenemy	Quinn	Somers	Bauchop

SCOTTISH CUP 1906

Jan 27	Dundee	2-1	Adams	MacLeod	Orr	McNair	Loney	Hay	Bennett	McMenemy	Quinn	Somers 1	Hamilton +OG
Feb 10	BO'NESS	3-0	Adams	MacLeod	Orr	Young	Loney 1	Hay	Bennett	McMenemy 1	Quinn 1	Somers	Hamilton
Feb 24	HEARTS	1-2	Adams	MacLeod	Orr	McNair	Loney	Hay	Bennett	McMenemy 1	Quinn	Somers	Hamilton

SCOTTISH LEAGUE 1906-07

			1	2	3	4	5	6	7	8	9	10	11
Aug 18	Motherwell	6-0	Sinclair	Craig	McNair	Young	Loney 1	Hay 1	Bennett	McMenemy	Quinn 3	Somers 1	Hamilton
Aug 25	KILMARNOCK	5-0	Sinclair	McNair	Orr P	Young	Loney	Hay	Templeton 1	McMenemy	Quinn 2	Somers	Hamilton 1
Sept 1	Morton	2-0	Sinclair	McNair	Orr	Young	Loney	Hay	Templeton	McMenemy	Quinn 1	Somers 1	Hamilton
Sept 15	HEARTS	3-0	Sinclair	MacLeod	McNair	Young	Loney	Hay	Templeton	McMenemy	Quinn 1	Somers	Hamilton 2
Sept 24	THIRD LANARK	2-0	Sinclair	MacLeod	Bauchop	Young	McNair	Hay	Templeton	McMenemy 1	Quinn 1	Somers	Hamilton
Sept 29	Airdrie	2-0	Sinclair	MacLeod	Orr	Young	McNair	Hay	Templeton	McMenemy	Quinn 2	Somers	Hamilton
Oct 13	ABERDEEN	2-1	Adams	MacLeod	McNair	Young	Wilson	Hay	Bennett 1	McMenemy	Quinn	Somers 1	Templeton
Oct 20	Dundee	0-0	Adams	MacLeod	McNair	Young	Wilson	Hay	Templeton	McMenemy	Bennett	Somers	Hamilton
Oct 27	RANGERS	2-1	Adams	MacLeod	McNair	Young	Wilson	McMeneny	Templeton 1	Somers 1	Bennett	Quinn	Hamilton
Nov 3	Hamilton Academicals	5-2	Adams	MacLeod	Craig	Young P	Wilson	McNair	Bennett	Somers 1	Quinn 3	Garry	Templeton
Nov 10	HIBERNIAN	2-1	Adams	Craig	Orr	Young	Wilson	McNair	Templeton 1	McMenemy 1	Bennett	Somers	Hamilton
Nov 17	Falkirk	3-2	Adams	MacLeod	Craig	Young	Wilson	McNair	Templeton	McMenemy	Bennett 3	Quinn	Hamilton
Nov 24	CLYDE	3-3	Adams	MacLeod	Craig	Young 2(1P)	Wilson	McNair	Bennett	McMenemy	Quinn 1	Somers	Hamilton
Dec 1	PARTICK THISTLE	4-1	Adams	MacLeod	Orr	Young	McNair	Mitchell	Bennett	McMenemy 2	Quinn 1	Somers 1	Templeton
Dec 8	St Mirren	3-0	Adams	MacLeod	Orr	Young	McNair	Mitchell	Bennett	McMenemy	Quinn 3	Somers	Templeton
Dec 15	Queen's Park	4-0	Adams	MacLeod	Orr	Young	McNair	Mitchell	Bennett	McMenemy 1	Quinn 1	Somers	Templeton 2
Dec 22	PORT GLASGOW ATHLETIC	4-0	Adams	MacLeod	Mitchell	Young	McNair	Hay	Bennett 1	McMenemy 1	Quinn 2	Somers	Bauchop
Dec 29	Kilmarnock	2-2	Adams	MacLeod	Hay	Young	McNair	Mitchell	Bennett	McMenemy	Quinn 1	Somers	Hamilton 1
Dec 31	AIRDRIE	2-1	Adams	Hay	Orr P	Young	McNair	Mitchell	Bennett	McMenemy	Quinn 1	Somers	Templeton
Jan 1	Rangers	1-2	Adams	MacLeod	Orr	Young	McNair	Hay	Bennett	McMenemy	Quinn	Somers 1	Templeton
Jan 2	HAMILTON ACADEMICALS	2-0	Adams	MacLeod	Hay	Young P	Loney	Mitchell	Templeton	Somers	Bennett	McNair	Hamilton 1
Jan 5	FALKIRK	3-2	Adams	MacLeod	Hay	Young	McNair 1	Mitchell	Bennett	McMenemy	Quinn 2	Somers	Hamilton
Jan 12	Clyde	2-0	Adams	MacLeod	Hay	Young	McNair	Mitchell	Bennett	McMenemy	Bauchop 1	Somers 1	Hamilton
Jan 19	MORTON	2-1	Adams	MacLeod	Orr	Young	Loney	Hay	Bennett	McMenemy 1	McNair 1	Somers	Templeton
Mar 2	Aberdeen	2-2	Adams	Craig	Orr P	Hay	Wilson	Mitchell	Templeton	McMenemy	Bennett	Somers 1	Hamilton
Mar 16	Third Lanark	1-2	Adams	MacLeod	Orr	Young	Wilson	Hay	Templeton	McMenemy	Quinn 1	Garry	Hamilton
Mar 23	DUNDEE	0-0	Adams	MacLeod	Orr	Young	McNair	Hay	Templeton	McMenemy	Bennett	Quinn	Hamilton
Apr 1	QUEEN'S PARK	2-1	Adams	MacLeod	Orr	Young	McNair	Hay	Bennett	McMenemy	Quinn 1	Bauchop	Hamilton 1
Apr 24	Partick Thistle	2-0	Adams	MacLeod	Orr	Young	McNair	Hay	Bennett 1	McMenemy	Quinn 1	Templeton	Hamilton
Apr 27	ST MIRREN	1-1	Adams	MacLeod	Weir	Young	Loney	Hay	Bennett	McMenemy	Quinn 1	Somers	Bauchop
May 4	Port Glasgow Athletic	1-1	Adams	MacLeod	Orr P	Young	Loney	Hay	Bennett	McMenemy	Quinn	Somers	Bauchop
May 8	Hibernian	1-0	Adams	Craig	Weir	Morrison	Loney	Mitchell	Templeton	McMenemy	Garry	Bauchop	Hamilton +OG
May 11	Hearts	3-3	Adams	Craig	Orr	Young 1	McNair	Loney	Garry 1	Somers	Quinn	Bauchop 1	Templeton
May 15	MOTHERWELL	1-1	Adams	Craig	Hay	Young	Loney	Mitchell	Bennett	McMenemy	Bauchop 1	Templeton	Hamilton

SCOTTISH CUP 1907

Feb 2	CLYDE	2-1	Adams	MacLeod	Orr	Young	McNair	Hay	Templeton	McMenemy	Bennett 1	Somers	Hamilton 1
Feb 9	Morton	0-0	Adams	MacLeod	Orr	Young	McNair	Hay	Templeton	McMenemy	Bennett	Somers	Hamilton
Feb 16	MORTON	1-1	Adams	MacLeod	Orr	Young	McNair	Hay	Templeton	McMenemy 1	Bennett	Somers	Hamilton
Feb 23	MORTON	2-1	Adams	MacLeod	Orr	Young	McNair	Hay 1	Templeton	McMenemy 1	Bennett	Somers	Hamilton
Mar 9	Rangers	3-0	Adams	MacLeod	Orr	Young	McNair	Hay 1	Bennett	McMenemy	Quinn	Somers 1	Hamilton 1
Mar 30	HIBERNIAN	0-0 SF	Adams	MacLeod	Orr	Young	McNair	Hay	Templeton	McMenemy	Quinn	Bennett	Hamilton
Apr 6	Hibernian	0-0 SFR	Adams	MacLeod	Orr	Young	McNair	Hay	Bennett	McMenemy	Quinn	Somers	Hamilton
Apr 13	HIBERNIAN	3-0 SFR	Adams	MacLeod	Orr	Young	McNair	Hay	Bennett	McMenemy 1	Quinn 1	Somers 1	Templeton
Apr 20	Hearts	3-0 F	Adams	MacLeod	Orr P	Young	McNair	Hay	Bennett	McMenemy	Quinn	Somers 2	Templeton

SCOTTISH LEAGUE 1907-08

Aug 15	HAMILTON ACADEMICALS	3-0	Adams	MacLeod	Weir	Young	McNair	Loney	Bennett	McMenemy	Quinn	Somers 1	Hamilton 2
Aug 17	MOTHERWELL	3-0	Adams	MacLeod	Weir	Young	McNair	Loney	Bennett 1	McMenemy	Quinn 2	Somers	Hamilton
Aug 24	Morton	3-2	Adams	MacLeod	Weir	Young	McNair	Loney	Bennett	McMenemy	Kivlichan 2	Somers	Hamilton 1
Aug 31	DUNDEE	3-2	Adams	MacLeod	Hay	Young	Loney	McNair	Bennett	McMenemy	Quinn 1	Somers 2	Templeton
Sept 7	FALKIRK	3-2	Adams	MacLeod	Weir	Young	Loney	Hay	Bennett 1	McMenemy 1	Quinn 1	Somers	Templeton
Sept 14	Kilmarnock	0-0	Adams	MacLeod	Weir	Loney	McNair	Hay	Bennett	McMenemy	Kivlichan	Somers	Templeton
Sept 21	AIRDRIE	1-1	Adams	MacLeod	Weir	Hay	Loney	Mitchell	Bennett	McMenemy	Quinn 1	Somers	Templeton
Sept 23	Aberdeen	1-2	Adams	Orr	Weir	Mitchell	Loney	Hay	Bennett	McMenemy	Quinn 1	Somers	Hamilton
Sept 30	Third Lanark	3-1	Adams	McNair	Weir	Hay 2P	Loney	Mitchell	Bennett	McMenemy 1	Quinn	Somers	Hamilton
Oct 5	Hibernian	2-1	Adams	McNair	Weir	Young	Loney	Hay	Bennett	McMenemy	Quinn 1	Somers	Hamilton 1
Nov 2	PORT GLASGOW ATHLETIC	5-0	Adams	Craig	Hay	Young 1	Loney	Mitchell	Bennett	McMenemy	McLean 3	Quinn 1	Semple
Nov 9	Clyde	2-0	Adams	MacLeod	Hay	Young	Loney 1	Mitchell	Bennett	McMenemy	McLean	Quinn 1	Semple
Nov 16	QUEEN'S PARK	4-1	Adams	MacLeod	Weir	Young	McNair	Hay	Bennett	McMenemy	Kivlichan 1	Somers 2	Quinn 1
Nov 23	Hearts	0-1	Adams	MacLeod	McNair	Young	Loney	Hay	Bennett	McMenemy	Kivlichan	Somers	Quinn
Dec 7	ST MIRREN	4-0	Adams	MacLeod	Weir	Young	McNair 1	Hay	Bennett	McMenemy	McLean 2	Somers	Quinn 1
Dec 14	Hamilton Academicals	4-2	Adams	MacLeod	Weir	Young	McNair	Hay 1	Bennett	McLean 1	Quinn 2	Kivlichan	Semple
Dec 21	KILMARNOCK	4-1	Adams	MacLeod	Weir	Young	McNair	Hay	Bennett 1	McLean	Quinn 1	Somers 1	Hamilton 1
Dec 28	Airdrie	0-0	Adams	MacLeod	Weir	Young	McNair	Mitchell	Bennett	McMenemy	Quinn	Somers	Hamilton
Jan 1	RANGERS	2-1	Adams	MacLeod	Weir	Young	McNair	Mitchell	Bennett	McMenemy 1	Quinn	Somers	Hamilton 1
Jan 2	ABERDEEN	3-0	Adams	MacLeod	McNair	Young	Loney	Mitchell	Bennett	McMenemy	Quinn 1	Somers	Semple 1 +OG
Jan 11	CLYDE	5-1	Adams	MacLeod	Weir	Young	Loney	Mitchell	Bennett	McMenemy	McLean 2	Somers 1	Hamilton 2
Jan 18	Motherwell	2-2	Adams	MacLeod	Weir	Young	McNair 1	Mitchell	Bennett	McMenemy	McLean	Somers 1	Hamilton
Feb 1	PARTICK THISTLE	4-1	Adams	MacLeod	Weir	Young	McNair	Mitchell	Bennett	McMenemy 1	McLean 2	Somers 1	Hamilton
Feb 15	Port Glasgow Athletic	3-0	Adams	McNair	Weir	Young	Loney	Mitchell	Bennett	McMenemy 2	Kivlichan 1	Somers	Hamilton
Feb 29	THIRD LANARK	1-1	Adams	MacLeod	Weir	Young	Loney	Mitchell	Semple	Kivlichan	Quinn	Somers	Hamilton +OG
Mar 17	HIBERNIAN	4-0	Adams	MacLeod	Weir	Young	Loney 1	Mitchell	Kivlichan	McMenemy 1	Quinn	Somers 1	Hamilton 1
Mar 14	Partick Thistle	3-0	Adams	MacLeod	Weir	Young	Loney	Hay	Bennett P	McMenemy	Kivlichan 1	Somers 1	Hamilton
Mar 28	Dundee	0-2	Adams	MacLeod	Weir	Young	Loney	Hay	Bennett	McMenemy	Quinn	Somers	Hamilton
Apr 4	MORTON	2-0	Adams	Hay	Weir	Young	Loney 1	Mitchell	Bennett	McMenemy	Kivlichan	McLean 1	Hamilton
Apr 11	Queen's Park	2-0	Adams	Hay	Weir	Young	Loney	Mitchell	Bennett	McMenemy 1	Quinn 1	Somers	Hamilton
Apr 20	HEARTS	6-0	Adams	MacLeod	Weir	Young	Loney 1	Hay	Bennett	McMenemy 1	Quinn 3	Somers	Hamilton 1
Apr 25	Rangers	1-0	Adams	McNair	Weir	Young	Loney	Hay	Bennett 1	McMenemy	Quinn	Somers	Hamilton
Apr 27	Falkirk	1-1	Adams	MacLeod	Weir	Young	Loney	Hay	Mitchell	McMenemy	Bennett	Somers	Semple 1
Apr 30	St Mirren	2-2	Adams	MacLeod	Weir	Kivlichan	Loney	Hay	McLean	Sanderson	Bennett 2	Somers	Semple

SCOTTISH CUP 1908

Jan 25	PEEBLES ROVERS	4-0	Adams	MacLeod	Weir	Loney	McNair	Mitchell	Kivlichan 2	McMenemy	Bennett	Somers 1	Hamilton 1
Feb 8	Rangers	2-1	Adams	McNair	Weir	Young	Loney	Mitchell	Bennett	McMenemy	Kivlichan 2	Somers	Hamilton
Feb 22	Raith Rovers	3-0	Adams	McNair	Weir	Young	Loney	Mitchell	Bennett	McMenemy 2	Kivlichan 1	Somers	Hamilton
Mar 21	Aberdeen	1-0 SF	Adams	McNair	Weir	Young	Loney	Hay	Bennett	McMenemy 1	Quinn	Somers	Hamilton
Apr 18	St Mirren	5-1 F	Adams	McNair	Weir	Young	Loney	Hay	Bennett 2	McMenemy	Quinn 1	Somers 1	Hamilton 1

SCOTTISH LEAGUE 1908-09

Aug 15	Morton	5-0	Adams	MacLeod	Weir	Young	Loney	Hay	Munro	McMenemy 1	Quinn 4	McLean	Hamilton
Aug 22	KILMARNOCK	5-1	Adams	MacLeod	Weir	Young	Loney	Hay	Munro 2	McMenemy 1	Quinn 2 (1P)	Somers	Hamilton
Aug 29	Dundee	1-2	Adams	MacLeod	Weir	Young	Loney	Hay	Munro	McMenemy	Quinn	Somers 1	Hamilton
Sept 5	ST MIRREN	0-1	Adams	MacLeod	Weir	Young	Loney	Hay	Moran	McMenemy	Quinn	Somers	Hamilton
Sept 28	THIRD LANARK	1-0	Adams	McNair	Weir	Young	Loney	Hay	Kivlichan	McMenemy	McLean	Somers	Hamilton 1
Oct 10	DUNDEE	2-0	Adams	McNair	Hay	Young	Dodds	Mitchell	Kivlichan	McMenemy	Quinn	Somers	Hamilton 2
Oct 31	Clyde	2-0	Adams	McNair	Weir	Young	Loney	Hay	Munro	McMenemy 1	McLean 1	Somers	Quinn
Nov 7	PARTICK THISTLE	3-0	Adams	McNair	Weir	Young	Loney	Hay	Munro	McMenemy 3	McLean	Sanderson	Quinn
Nov 14	PORT GLASGOW ATHLETIC	2-1	Adams	McNair	Weir	Young	Loney	Hay	Munro	McMenemy	Quinn 1	Somers	Hamilton 1

			1	2	3	4	5	6	7	8	9	10	11
Nov 21	Airdrie	2-1	Adams	McNair	Weir	Young	Loney	Hay	Munro	McMenemy	Quinn 2	Somers	Hamilton
Nov 28	QUEEN'S PARK	4-0	Adams	McNair	Weir	Young	Loney	Hay	Munro	McMenemy 3	Quinn	Somers 1	Hamilton
Dec 5	Motherwell	2-1	Adams	McNair	Weir	Young	Loney 1	Hay	Kivlichan	McMenemy 1	Quinn	McLean	Hamilton
Dec 12	HIBERNIAN	2-0	Adams	McNair	Weir	Young	Loney 1	Hay	Munro	McMenemy	Quinn 1	Kivlichan	Hamilton
Dec 19	Aberdeen	2-0	Adams	McNair	Weir	Young	Loney	Hay	Moran	McMenemy	Quinn	Somers	Hamilton
Dec 26	CLYDE	0-1	Adams	McNair	Weir	Young	Loney	Hay	Kivlichan	McMenemy	Quinn	Somers	Hamilton
Jan 1	Rangers	3-1	Adams	McNair	Weir	Dodds	Loney	Hay	Munro 1	McMenemy 1	Quinn	Somers	Hamilton 1
Jan 2	Kilmarnock	1-3	Young	McNair	Weir	Dodds	Loney 1	Hay	Munro	McMenemy	Quinn	Somers	Hamilton
Jan 9	HEARTS	1-1	Oliver	McNair	Weir	Young	Loney	Hay	Munro	McMenemy	McLean	Quinn 1	Hamilton
Jan 30	FALKIRK	2-0	Adams	McNair	Weir	Young	Loney	Hay	Kivlichan	McMenemy	Quinn 1	Somers	Hamilton 1
Feb 13	Port Glasgow Athletic	4-1	Adams	McNair	Weir	Young	Loney	Hay	Munro	Kivlichan 2	Quinn 1	Somers	Hamilton 1
Feb 24	ABERDEEN	2-0	Adams	Craig	Hay	Young	Loney	Dodds	Kivlichan	McMenemy	Quinn 1	Somers 1	Hamilton
Mar 6	Falkirk	1-1	Adams	Hay	Weir	Young	Loney	Dodds P	Munro	McMenemy	Quinn	Kivlichan	Semple
Mar 13	RANGERS	2-3	Adams	Dodds	Hay	Young	Loney	Mitchell	Munro 1	McMenemy	Quinn 1	Kivlichan	Hamilton
Mar 29	PARTICK THISTLE	1-0	Oliver	McNair	Weir	Young	Dodds	Hay	Munro	McMenemy	Kivlichan 1	Somers	Hamilton
Apr 3	St Mirren	1-0	Adams	Craig	Weir	Young	Dodds	Mitchell	Munro	Kivlichan	McLean 1	Johnstone	Hamilton
Apr 12	Third Lanark	1-1	Adams	McNair	Weir	Young	Dodds	Hay	Kivlichan	McMenemy	McLean	Somers 1	Hamilton
Apr 19	Hearts	2-1	Adams	McNair	Weir	Mitchell	Dodds	Hay	Kivlichan	McMenemy 2	Quinn	Somers	Hamilton
Apr 21	HAMILTON ACADEMICALS	1-1	Adams	Craig	Weir	Young	McNair	Hay	Kivlichan	McMenemy	Quinn 1	Somers	Hamilton
Apr 22	MORTON	5-1	Adams	McNair	Weir	Young	Dodds	Hay	Munro 2	Somers	McLean 1	Quinn	Atkinson 2
Apr 24	AIRDRIE	0-0	Adams	McNair	Weir	Young	Dodds	Hay	Kivlichan	McMenemy	McLean	Quinn	Hamilton
Apr 26	MOTHERWELL	4-0	Adams	McNair	Weir	Young	Dodds	Mitchell	McLean 1	McMenemy	Quinn 3	Somers	Hamilton
Apr 28	Queen's Park (at Cathkin)	5-0	Adams	McNair	Weir	Young	Dodds	Hay	McLean 2	McMenemy	Quinn 3	Somers	Hamilton
Apr 29	Hibernian	0-1	Adams	McNair	Weir	Young	Dodds	Hay	McLean	McMenemy	Quinn	Somers	Hamilton
Apr 30	Hamilton Academicals	2-1	Adams	McNair	Weir	Young	Dodds	Hay	McLean	McMenemy 1	Quinn	Somers	Hamilton 1

*both games v. Partick at home. 'Jags' homeless.

SCOTTISH CUP 1909

Jan 23	Leith Athletic	4-2	Adams	McNair	Weir	Young	Loney	Hay 1	Kivlichan	McMenemy	Quinn 3	Somers	Hamilton
Feb 6	PORT GLASGOW ATHLETIC	4-0	Adams	McNair	Weir	Young	Loney	Hay 2	Munro	Kivlichan	Quinn 1	Somers	Hamilton 1
Feb 20	AIRDRIE	3-1	Adams	McNair	Weir	Young	Loney	Hay	Kivlichan	McMenemy 2	Quinn	Somers	Hamilton 1
Mar 20	CLYDE	0-0 SF	Adams	McNair	Hay	Young	Loney	Dodds	Munro	McMenemy	Quinn	Somers	Hamilton
Mar 27	CLYDE	2-0 SFR	Adams	McNair	Weir	Young	Dodds	Hay	Munro	McMenemy	Quinn 1	Somers	Hamilton + OG
Apr 10	Rangers	2-2 F	Adams	McNair	Weir	Young	Dodds	Hay	Munro	McMenemy	Quinn 1	Somers	Hamilton + OG
Apr 17	Rangers	1-1 FR	Adams	McNair	Weir	Young	Dodds	Hay	Kivlichan	McMenemy	Quinn 1	Somers	Hamilton

('Riot' final - cup withheld)

SCOTTISH LEAGUE 1909-10

Aug 17	HAMILTON ACADEMICALS	3-1	Adams	McNair	Weir	Young	Dodds	Hay 1	Munro	McMenemy 1	Quinn 1	Somers	Hamilton
Aug 21	FALKIRK	2-0	Adams	McNair	Weir	Young	Dodds	Hay	Kivlichan 1	McMenemy 1	Quinn	Somers	Hamilton
Aug 28	Hibernian	0-1	Adams	McNair	Weir	Young	Dodds	Hay	Kivlichan	McMenemy	Quinn	Somers	Hamilton
Sept 4	MOTHERWELL	2-2	Adams	McNair	Weir	Young	Loney	Dodds	Kivlichan	McMenemy 1	Quinn	Johnstone 1	Hamilton
Sept 11	Morton	1-2	Adams	McIntosh	Weir	Young	Loney	Hay	McLean	McMenemy	Quinn 1	Somers	Hamilton
Sept 18	Hamilton AC	5-1	Adams	Hay	Weir	Young	Loney	Mitchell	Kivlichan	McMenemy 3	McLean 1	Johnstone 1	Hamilton
Sept 20	Hearts	2-1	Adams	McNair	Weir	Young	Loney	Hay	Kivlichan 1	McMenemy	McLean 1	Johnstone	Hamilton
Sept 27	Third Lanark	1-0	Adams	McNair	Weir	Young	Loney	Hay	Kivlichan	McMenemy 1	McLean	Quinn	Hamilton
Oct 2	DUNDEE	1-0	Adams	McNair	Weir	Young	Loney	Hay	Kivlichan	McMenemy	Quinn P	Johnstone	Hamilton
Oct 16	Port Glasgow Athletic	3-2	Adams	McNair	Weir P	Young	McIntosh	Hay	Munro	McMenemy	Quinn 1	Johnstone 1	Hamilton
Oct 23	QUEEN'S PARK	6-0	Adams	McNair	Weir	Young	Loney	Hay	Kivlichan 1	McMenemy	Quinn 2	Johnstone 2	Hamilton 1
Oct 30	Rangers	0-0	Adams	McNair	Weir	Young	Loney	Hay	Munro	McMenemy	Quinn	Johnstone	Hamilton
Nov 6	HEARTS	1-0	Adams	McNair	Weir	Young	Loney	Hay	Kivlichan	McMenemy	Quinn	Johnstone	Hamilton 1
Nov 13	Partick Thistle	3-1	Adams	McNair	Hay	Young	Loney 1	Mitchell	Kivlichan	McMenemy	Quinn 2	Johnstone	Hamilton
Nov 20	AIRDRIE	3-1	Adams	McNair	Hay	Young	Loney	Mitchell	Kivlichan	McMenemy	Quinn 1	Johnstone 2	Hamilton
Nov 27	Aberdeen	1-0	Adams	McNair	Hay	Young	Loney	Mitchell	John Young	McMenemy	Lachie McLean	Johnstone 1	Hamilton
Dec 4	KILMARNOCK	2-1	Adams	McNair	Hay	Young	Loney 1	Mitchell	Robertson	McMenemy	Quinn 1	Johnstone	Hamilton
Dec 11	ST MIRREN	1-1	Adams	McNair	Hay	Young	Loney	Mitchell	Robertson	McMenemy 1	Quinn	Johnstone	Hamilton
Dec 18	Motherwell	3-1	Adams	McNair	McIntosh	Young	Loney	Hay 1	Kivlichan	McMenemy 1	Quinn 1	Johnstone	Hamilton
Dec 25	Kilmarnock	1-0	Adams	McIntosh	Weir	Young	Loney	Hay	Kivlichan	McMenemy	Quinn 1	Johnstone	Robertson
Jan 1	RANGERS	1-1	Adams	McNair	Weir	Young	Loney	Hay	Kivlichan	McMenemy	Quinn	Johnstone	Hamilton 1
Jan 3	Clyde	1-0	Adams	McIntosh	Weir	Young	Loney	Mitchell	Kivlichan	Somers	Quinn 1	Johnstone	Hamilton
Jan 8	Airdrie	2-0	Adams	McIntosh	Weir	Young	Loney	Mitchell	Kivlichan 2	Somers	Quinn	Johnstone	Hamilton
Jan 15	PORT GLASGOW ATHLETIC	4-0	Adams	McIntosh	Weir	Young	Loney 1	Mitchell	Kivlichan	McMenemy	Quinn 2	Johnstone	Hamilton 1
Jan 29	St Mirren	1-2	Adams	McNair	Weir	Young	Loney	Mitchell	Kivlichan	McMenemy	Quinn 1	Johnstone	Hamilton
Mar 16	THIRD LANARK	2-0	Duncan	McNair	Weir	Young	Loney	Hay	Kivlichan	Johnstone 1	Quinn P	L McLean	Hamilton
Mar 19	Queen's Park	1-0	Duncan	McNair	McIntosh	Young	Dodds	Mitchell	Munro	Johnstone	Kivlichan 1	L McLean	Hamilton
Mar 26	Partick Thistle	3-1	Duncan	McNair	Hay	Young	Dodds	Mitchell	Munro	McMenemy	Quinn 3	Johnstone	Hamilton
Mar 29	CLYDE	2-1	Duncan	McNair	Hay	Young	Dodds	Mitchell	Kivlichan	McMenemy	Quinn 2P	Johnstone	Hamilton
Apr 6	MORTON	3-0	Duncan	McNair	Hay	Young	Loney	Dodds	Kivlichan	Johnstone 1	Quinn 1	McMenemy 1	Hamilton
Apr 9	ABERDEEN	2-0	Duncan	McNair	Hay	Young	Loney	Dodds	Kivlichan	Johnstone 1	Quinn 1	McMenemy	Hamilton
Apr 23	Falkirk	0-2	Duncan	McNair	Hay	Young	Loney	Dodds	Kivlichan	McMenemy	Quinn	Johnstone	Hamilton
Apr 25	HIBERNIAN	0-0	Duncan	McNair	Hay	Young	Dodds	Mitchell	Munro	McMenemy	Allan	Johnstone	Hamilton
Apr 30	Dundee	0-0	Duncan	McNair	Hay	Young	Dodds	Mitchell	Munro	John Young	Allan	Johnstone	Hamilton

SCOTTISH CUP 1910

Jan 22	Dumbarton	2-1	Adams	McIntosh	Weir	Young	Loney 1	Mitchell	Kivlichan	McMenemy 1	Quinn	Johnstone	Hamilton
Feb 12	THIRD LANARK	3-1	Adams	McNair	Weir	Young	Loney	Hay	Kivlichan	McMenemy	Quinn 3	Johnstone	Robertson
Feb 19	ABERDEEN	2-1	Adams	McNair	McIntosh	Dodds	Loney	Hay	Munro	McMenemy 1	Quinn 1	Johnstone	Kivlichan
Mar 12	Clyde	1-3 SF	L R Roose	McNair	Weir	McIntosh	Loney	Hay	Munro	Kivlichan 1	Quinn	Johnstone	Hamilton

SCOTTISH LEAGUE 1910-11

Aug 17	AIRDRIE	3-0	Adams	McAteer	McNair	Dodds	Loney 1	Hay	Kivlichan	McMenemy	Quinn 2	McCann	Hamilton
Aug 20	Falkirk	1-2	Adams	McAteer	McNair	Young	Loney	Hay	Kivlichan	McMenemy	Quinn P	McCann	Hamilton
Aug 27	MORTON	0-1	Adams	McNair	Dodds	Young	Loney	Hay	Munro	McMenemy	Quinn	Johnstone	Kivlichan
Sept 3	Kilmarnock	0-1	Adams	McAteer	McNair	Young	Loney	Hay	Munro	McMenemy	Quinn	Johnstone	Kivlichan
Sept 17	DUNDEE	2-1	Adams	McNair	Hay	Young	Loney	Mitchell	Kivlichan	McMenemy 1	Quinn 1	Johnstone	Hamilton
Sept 19	Hibernian	4-0	Adams	McNair	Hay	Young	Loney	Mitchell	Kivlichan	McMenemy 1	Quinn 2	Johnstone 1	Hamilton
Setp 26	Partick Thistle	1-1	Adams	McNair	Hay	Young	Loney	Mitchell	Kivlichan	McMenemy 1	Quinn	Johnstone	McAtee
Oct 1	Queen's Park	1-0	Adams	McNair	Hay	Young	Dodds	Mitchell	Kivlichan 1	McMenemy	Quinn	Johnstone	McAtee
Oct 3	Raith Rovers	1-2	Adams	McNair	Hay	Young	McAteer 1	Mitchell	Munro	McMenemy	Quinn	Johnstone	McCann
Oct 15	HEARTS	0-0	Adams	McNair	Hay	Young	Loney	Dodds	McAtee	McMenemy	Kivlichan	Quinn	Hamilton
Oct 22	Hamilton Academicals	1-0	Adams	McNair	Hay	Young	Loney	Dodds	Kivlichan	McMenemy	Quinn 1	Johnstone	Hamilton
Oct 29	RANGERS	0-1	Adams	McNair	Hay	Young	Loney	Dodds	Munro	McMenemy	Kivlichan	Johnstone	Hamilton
Nov 5	ST MIRREN	5-0	Adams	McNair	Hay	Young	Loney 1	Dodds	Munro	McMenemy 1	Kilvichan 2	Johnstone 1	Hamilton
Nov 12	Airdrie	0-0	Adams	McNair	Hay	Young	Loney	Dodds	Kivlichan	Johnstone	Quinn	McCann	Hamilton
Nov 19	THIRD LANARK	0-0	Adams	McNair	Hay	Young	Loney	Dodds	Blair	McMenemy	Quinn	Johnstone	Kivlichan
Nov 26	Dundee	0-1	Adams	McNair	Hay	Young	Loney	Dodds	Kivlichan	McMenemy	Quinn	Hastie	McAtee
Dec 3	MOTHERWELL	3-0	Adams	McNair	Hay	Young	Loney	Dodds	Kivlichan 1	McMenemy 1	Quinn 1	Hastie	Hamilton
Dec 10	Clyde	2-0	Adams	McNair	Hay	Young	Loney 1	Dodds	Kivlichan	McMenemy 1	Quinn	Hastie	Hamilton
Dec 17	KILMARNOCK	2-0	Adams	McNair	Hay	Young	McAteer	Dodds	McAtee	McMenemy 1	Quinn 1	Hastie	Hamilton
Dec 24	Morton	1-1	Adams	McNair	Hay	Young	Loney	Dodds	McAtee	McMenemy	Quinn 1	Hastie	Hamilton
Dec 31	RAITH ROVERS	5-0	Adams	McNair	Hay	Young	McAteer 1	Mitchell	Kivlichan	McMenemy 2	Quinn 1	Hastie 1	Hamilton

			1	2	3	4	5	6	7	8	9	10	11
Jan 2	Rangers	1-1	Adams	McNair	Hay	Young	McAteer 1	Dodds	Kivlichan	McMenemy	Quinn	Hastie	Johnstone
Jan 3	CLYDE	2-0	Adams	McNair	Hay	Young	McAteer	Dodds	McAtee 1	McMenemy	Quinn 1	Hastie	Johnstone
Jan 7	PARTICK THISTLE	2-0	Adams	McNair	Hay	Young	Loney	Dodds	McAtee 1	McMenemy	Quinn 1	Hastie	Johnstone
Jan 14	Aberdeen	0-1	Adams	McNair	Hay	Young	Loney	Dodds	Kivlichan	McMenemy	Quinn	Hastie	Johnstone
Jan 21	FALKIRK	0-0	Adams	McNair	Hay	Young	Loney	Dodds	McAtee	McMenemy	Quinn	Hastie	Hamilton
Feb 4	Motherwell	1-2	Adams	McNair	Hay	Mitchell	McAteer	Dodds	McAtee	McMenemy	McCann	Hastie 1	Johnstone
Feb 18	QUEEN'S PARK	2-0	Adams	McNair	Hay	Young	Loney	Mitchell	McAtee 1	McMenemy	Kivlichan	Hastie 1	Hamilton
Mar 18	St Mirren	1-1	Adams	McNair	Geechrin	O'Neill	McAteer	Mitchell	Kivlichan	John Young	McAtee 1	Hastie	Hamilton
Mar 25	HIBERNIAN	2-0	Adams	McNair	Dodds	Young	McAteer	Hay	Kivlichan 1	McMenemy	McAtee 1	Hastie	Hamilton
Apr 1	Hearts	1-1	Adams	McNair	Dodds	Young	McAteer	Mitchell	Kivlichan	McCann 1	McAtee	Hastie	Hamilton
Apr 17	Third Lanark	1-1	Adams	McNair	Hay	Young	McAteer	Dodds	McAtee	McMenemy 1	Quinn	McCann	Hamilton
Apr 26	HAMILTON ACADEMICALS	3-0	Adams	McNair	McGregor	Young	Dodds	Mitchell	McAtee 1	McMenemy	Quinn 1	Johnstone 1	Hamilton
Apr 29	ABERDEEN	0-0	Adams	McNair	McGregor	Young	Dodds	Hay	McAtee	Johnstone	Quinn	Kivlichan	Hamilton

SCOTTISH CUP 1911

Jan 28	St Mirren	2-0	Adams	McNair	Hay	Young	McAteer	Dodds	Kivlichan	McMenemy 1	Quinn	Hastie 1	Hamilton
Feb 11	GALSTON	1-0	Adams	McNair	Hay	Young	Loney	Dodds	McAtee	McMenemy	Quinn 1	Hastie	Hamilton
Feb 25	CLYDE	1-0	Adams	McNair	Hay	Young	Loney	Dodds	Kivlichan	McMenemy 1	Quinn	Johnstone	Hamilton
Mar 11	ABERDEEN	1-0 SF	Adams	McNair	Hay	Young	McAteer	Dodds	Kivlichan	McMenemy	Quinn 1	Johnstone	Hamilton
Apr 8	Hamilton Academicals	0-0 F	Adams	McNair	Dodds	Young	McAteer	Hay	Kivlichan	McMenemy	Quinn	Hastie	Hamilton
Apr 15	Hamilton Academicals	2-0 FR	Adams	McNair	Hay	Young	McAteer 1	Dodds	McAtee	McMenemy	Quinn 1	Kivlichan	Hamilton

SCOTTISH LEAGUE 1911-12

Aug 15	AIRDRIE	3-0	Adams	McNair	Dodds P	Young	McAteer	Mitchell	McAtee	McMenemy	Brown 1	Donaldson	Hamilton 1
Aug 19	FALKIRK	3-1	Adams	McNair	McGregor	Young	Loney	Dodds	McAtee	McMenemy 1	Brown 1	Donaldson	Hamilton 1
Aug 26	Morton	1-1	Adams	McNair	Dodds	Young	Loney	Mitchell	McAtee	McMenemy 1	Brown	Donaldson	Hamilton
Sept 2	CLYDE	3-2	Adams	McNair	Dodds	Young	McAteer	Loney	Brown	McMenemy 1	Quinn 2	Travers	Hamilton
Sept 16	Dundee	1-3	Adams	McNair	Dodds	Young	McAteer	Johnstone	McAtee	McMenemy 1	Nichol	Donaldson	Brown
Sept 23	Kilmarnock	2-0	Adams	McNair	Dodds	Young	McAteer	Johnstone	McAtee	McMenemy 1	Nichol 1	Brown	Hamilton
Sept 25	PARTICK THISTLE	3-0	Adams	McNair	McGregor	Young	Dodds	Johnstone	McAtee	McMenemy 1	Nichol 2	Donaldson	Brown
Sept 30	Hearts	1-2	Adams	McNair	Dodds	Young	McAteer 1	Johnstone	McAtee	McMenemy	Nichol	Donaldson	Brown
Oct 2	Raith Rovers	2-1	Adams	McNair	Dodds	Young	McAteer	Johnstone	McAtee	McMenemy 1	Nichol 1	Travers	Hamilton
Oct 7	Hamilton Academicals	0-1	Adams	McNair	Dodds	Young	McAteer	Johnstone	McAtee	McMenemy	Brown	Travers	Hamilton
Oct 14	ABERDEEN	1-0	Adams	McNair	McCormack	Young	Dodds	Johnstone	Brown	McMenemy	Nichol	Donaldson 1	Hamilton
Oct 21	Rangers	1-3	Adams	McNair	Dodds	Young	Loney	Johnstone	McAtee 1	Travers	Nichol	Donaldson	Hamilton
Oct 28	HIBERNIAN	3-1	Adams	McNair	Dodds	Young	Loney	Johnstone	McAtee P	Travers	Black	Donaldson 1	Brown 1
Nov 4	Falkirk	1-1	Adams	McNair	Dodds	Young	Loney	Johnstone	McAtee	Travers	Nichol	Donaldson	Brown 1
Nov 11	HAMILTON ACADEMICALS	2-1	Adams	McNair	Dodds	Young	Loney	Johnstone	McAtee	Travers	Nichol 1	Donaldson 1	Brown
Nov 18	Hibernian	1-1	Adams	McNair	Dodds	Young	Loney	Johnstone	McAtee	Travers	Nichol	Donaldson 1	Brown
Nov 25	Motherwell	2-3	Adams	McNair	Dodds	Young	Loney	Johnstone	McAtee	Travers 1	Black 1	Donaldson	Brown
Dec 2	ST MIRREN	3-1	Adams	McNair	Dodds	Young	Loney 1	Johnstone 1	McAtee	Gallacher	Quinn	Donaldson 1	Brown
Dec 9	Queen's Park	4-1	Mulrooney	McNair	Dodds 1	Young	Loney	Johnstone	McAtee	Gallacher 1	Quinn 2	Donaldson	Brown
Dec 16	Third Lanark	0-1	Mulrooney	McNair	Dodds	Young	Loney	Johnstone	McAtee	Gallacher	Quinn	Donaldson	Brown
Dec 23	MORTON	1-1	Mulrooney	McNair	Dodds	Young	Loney	Johnstone 1	McAtee	Gallacher	Quinn	McMenemy	Hamilton
Dec 30	Airdrie	0-0	Mulrooney	McNair	Dodds	Young	McAteer	Mitchell	McAtee	McMenemy	Black	Donaldson	Brown
Jan 1	RANGERS	3-0	Mulrooney	McNair	Dodds	Young	Loney	Johnstone	McAtee	McMenemy	Quinn 3	Travers	Brown
Jan 2	Clyde	1-1	Mulrooney	McGregor	Dodds	Young	Loney	Mitchell	McAtee	McMenemy	Quinn	Travers	Brown
Jan 6	HEARTS	1-1	Mulrooney	McNair	Dodds	Young	Loney	Johnstone	McAtee	McMenemy	Quinn	Travers 1	Brown
Jan 13	MOTHERWELL	2-0	Mulrooney	McNair	Dodds	Young	McAteer	Johnstone	McAtee 1	McMenemy	Quinn 1	Travers	Hamilton
Jan 20	St Mirren	1-1	Mulrooney	McNair	Dodds	Young	McAteer	Johnstone	McAtee	McMenemy	Nichol 1	Travers	Hamilton
Feb 3	THIRD LANARK	3-1	Mulrooney	McNair	McGregor	Young	Loney	Johnstone	McAtee P	Gallacher 1	Quinn	Travers	Clark 1
Feb 17	QUEEN'S PARK	2-1	Mulrooney	McGregor	Dodds	Young	McAteer	Mitchell	McAtee P	Gallacher	Black	Travers 1	Clark
Mar 2	DUNDEE	2-0	Mulrooney	McGregor	Dodds	Young	Loney	Johnstone	McAtee	Gallacher	Nichol 1	Travers	Brown 1
Mar 16	Partick Thistle	1-1	Mulrooney	McGregor	Dodds	Young	Loney	Johnstone	McAtee	McMenemy	Nichol 1	Travers	Brown
Mar 23	Aberdeen	1-1	Mulrooney	McGregor	Dodds	Young	Loney	Johnstone	McAtee	Gallacher	Nichol	McMenemy 1	Brown
Apr 13	KILMARNOCK	2-0	Mulrooney	McNair	Dodds	Young	Loney	Johnstone	McAtee	Gallacher	Nichol 1	Gibson 1	Brown
Apr 20	RAITH ROVERS	1-1	Mulrooney	McNair	Dodds	Young	Loney	Johnstone	McAtee 1	McMenemy	Nichol	Gibson	Brown

SCOTTISH CUP 1912

Jan 27	DUNFERMLINE	1-0	Mulrooney	McNair	Dodds	Young	Loney	Johnstone	McAtee	McMenemy	Quinn	Travers	Brown 1
Feb 10	EAST STIRLINGSHIRE	3-0	Mulrooney	McNair	Dodds	Young	Loney	Johnstone	McAtee	McMenemy	Quinn 2	Travers 1	Brown
Feb 24	Aberdeen	2-2	Mulrooney	McNair	Dodds	Young	Loney	Johnstone	McAtee 1	McMenemy	Quinn 1	Travers	Brown
Mar 9	ABERDEEN	2-0	Mulrooney	McNair	Dodds	Young	Loney	Johnstone	McAtee	McMenemy	Quinn	Travers 2	Brown
Mar 30	Hearts	3-0 SF	Mulrooney	McNair	Dodds	Young	Loney	Johnstone	McAtee	Gallacher	Quinn	McMenemy 2	Brown 1
Apr 6	Clyde	2-0 F	Mulrooney	McNair	Dodds	Young	Loney	Johnstone	McAtee	Gallacher 1	Quinn	McMenemy 1	Brown

SCOTTISH LEAGUE 1912-13

Aug 17	Falkirk	0-0	Mulrooney	McGregor	Dodds	Young	Loney	Johnstone	McAtee	Gallacher	Quinn	McMemeny	Brown
Aug 24	HIBERNIAN	1-1	Mulrooney	McGregor	Dodds	Young	Loney	Mitchell	McAtee	Gallacher	Johnstone	McMenemy 1	Brown
Aug 31	Kilmarnock	2-0	Mulrooney	McGregor	Dodds	Young	Loney	Mitchell	McAtee	Gallacher	Johnstone 1	McMemeny	Gray 1
Sept 7	ABERDEEN	2-0	Mulrooney	McNair	Dodds	Young	Loney	Mitchell	McAtee	Gallacher	Johnstone 1	McMemeny 1	Gray
Sept 14	Airdrie	4-1	Mulrooney	McNair	Dodds	Young	Loney	Mitchell	McAtee	Gallacher 1	Johnstone 1	McMemeny 1	Gray 1
Sept 21	Dundee	1-3	Mulrooney	McNair	Dodds	Young	Loney	Mitchell	McAtee	Gallacher	Johnstone	McMemeny 1	Gray
Sept 30	Partick Thistle	3-2	Boyle	McNair	Dodds	Young	Loney	Mitchell	McAtee 1	Gallacher	Brown 1	Johnstone	Gray 1
Oct 5	MORTON	1-0	Boyle	McNair	Dodds	Young	Loney	Mitchell	McAtee	Gallacher	Quinn 1	Johnstone	Gray
Oct 19	Raith Rovers	1-2	Boyle	McNair	McGregor	Young	Dodds P	Mitchell	McAtee	Johnstone	Quinn	Brown	Gray
Oct 25	RANGERS	3-2	Mulrooney	McNair	McGregor	Young	Dodds	Mitchell	McAtee	Gallacher 1	Quinn 1	Johnstone	Brown 1
Nov 2	Third Lanark	1-0	Mulrooney	McNair	Dodds	Johnstone	Young	Mitchell	McAtee	Gallacher 1	Quinn	Browning	Brown
Nov 9	HEARTS	1-0	Mulrooney	McNair	Dodds	Young	Loney	Mitchell	McAtee	Gallacher	Quinn	McMenemy 1	Brown
Nov 16	Queen's Park	1-0	Mulrooney	McNair	Dodds	Young	Loney	Mitchell	McAtee 1	Gallacher	Quinn	McMenemy	Brown
Nov 23	MOTHERWELL	1-2	Mulrooney	McNair	Dodds	Jarvis	Loney	Mitchell	McAtee	Gallacher	Quinn 1	McMenemy	Brown
Nov 30	Clyde	1-1	Mulrooney	McNair	Dodds	Young	Loney	Mitchell	McAtee	Gallacher	Quinn	McMemeny	Browning 1
Dec 7	HAMILTON ACADEMICALS	2-1	Mulrooney	McNair	Dodds	Young	Loney	Mitchell	McAtee 1	Gallacher	Quinn	McMenemy 1	Browning
Dec 14	Morton	2-1	Mulrooney	McNair	Dodds	Young	Loney P	Mitchell	McAtee	Gallacher	Quinn	McMenemy	Browning 1
Dec 21	DUNDEE	2-0	Mulrooney	McNair	Dodds	Young	Johnstone	Mitchell	McAtee	Gallacher 1	Quinn 1	McMenemy	Browning
Dec 28	St Mirren	3-1	Mulrooney	McNair	Dodds	Young	Johnstone	Mitchell	McAtee 1	Gallacher	Quinn 1	McMenemy	Browning 1
Jan 1	Rangers	1-0	Mulrooney	McNair	Dodds	Young	Loney	Johnstone	McAtee	Gallacher	Quinn 1	McMenemy	Browning
Jan 2	CLYDE	3-0	Mulrooney	McNair	Dodds	Young P	Johnstone	Mitchell	McAtee	Gallacher	Quinn 1	McMenemy 1	Browning
Jan 4	PARTICK THISTLE	1-0	Mulrooney	McNair	Dodds	Young	Johnstone	Mitchell	McAtee	Galagher 1	Quinn	McMenemy	Browning
Jan 11	QUEEN'S PARK	1-0	Mulrooney	McNair	Dodds	Young	Johnstone	Mitchell	McAtee	Gallacher 1	Quinn	Browning	Brown
Jan 18	Hibernian	0-1	Mulrooney	McNair	Dodds	Young	Johnstone	Mitchell	McAtee	Gallacher	Quinn	McMenemy	Browning
Jan 25	AIRDRIE	1-1	Mulrooney	McNair	Dodds	Young	Johnstone	Mitchell	Gray 1	Gallacher	Quinn	Browning	Brown
Feb 1	THIRD LANARK	2-0	Mulrooney	McNair	Dodds	Young	Loney	Johnstone	Browning	Gallacher 2	Brown	McMenemy	Gray
Feb 15	Aberdeen	0-3	Mulrooney	McNair	Dodds	Young	Loney	Johnstone	McAtee	Gallacher	Brown	McMenemy	Browning
Mar 15	Motherwell	0-1	Boyle	McNair	Dodds	Young	Loney	Johnstone	McAtee	Gallacher	Quinn	Cassidy	Browning
Mar 22	FALKIRK	1-2	Boyle	McNair	Dodds	Young	Loney	Johnstone	McAtee	Gallacher	Quinn	McMenemy	Browning 1
Mar 24	RAITH ROVERS	4-1	Boyle	McNair	Dodds	Jarvis	Young	Johnstone	McAtee	Gallacher 1	Quinn 3	Browning	Gray
Mar 29	KILMARNOCK	4-1	Boyle	McNair	Dodds	Jarvis	Young	Johnstone	McAtee	Gallacher 1	Quinn 1	Browning 2	Gray
Apr 5	ST MIRREN	2-1	Boyle	McGregor	Dodds	Johnstone	Young	Mitchell	McAtee	Gallacher	Jarvis	Browining 1	Gray 1
Apr 21	Hearts	0-0	Mulrooney	McNair	Dodds	Young	Loney	Johnstone	McAtee	Gallacher	Jarvis	Browning	Cassidy
Apr 26	Hamilton Academicals	1-0	Mulrooney	McNair	Dodds	Young	Loney	Johnstone	McAtee	Gallacher	Jarvis	Browning	Cassidy

SCOTTISH CUP 1913

			1	2	3	4	5	6	7	8	9	10	11
Feb 8	ARBROATH	4-0	Mulrooney	McNair	Dodds	Young	Loney	Mitchell	Johnstone 2	Gallacher 1	Quinn	McMenemy	Brown 1
Feb 22	PEEBLES ROVERS	3-0	Mulrooney	McNair	Dodds	Young	Loney	Johnstone	McAtee	Gallacher	Quinn 1	McMenemy 2	Gray
Mar 8	HEARTS	0-1	Mulrooney	McNair	Dodds	Young	Loney	Mitchell	McAtee	Gallacher	Quinn	McMenemy	Johnstone

SCOTTISH LEAGUE 1913-14

Aug 16	AYR UNITED	5-1	Shaw	McNair	Dodds	Young	Loney	McMaster	McAtee 2	Gallacher 1	Connolly 2	Browning	Hill
Aug 23	Motherwell	1-1	Shaw	McNair	Dodds	Young	Johnstone	McMaster	McAtee	Gallacher	Connolly 1	Browning	Hill
Aug 30	FALKIRK	4-0	Shaw	McNair	Dodds	Young	Johnstone	McMaster	McAtee 1	Gallacher	Connolly 1	McMenemy 1	Browning 1
Sept 6	Hibernian	2-1	Shaw	McNair	Dodds	Johnstone	Loney	McMaster	McAtee	Gallacher	Connolly	McMenemy 2	Browning
Sept 13	ST MIRREN	0-2	Shaw	McNair	Dodds	Young	Johnstone	McMaster	McAtee	Gallacher	Connolly	McMenemy	Browning
Sept 15	Hearts	0-2	Shaw	McNair	Dodds	Young	Johnstone	McMaster	McAtee	Gallacher	Connolly	McMenemy	Browning
Sept 20	Morton	4-0	Shaw	McNair	Dodds	Young	Johnstone	McMaster	McAtee	Gallacher 2	Quinn 2	McMenemy	Browning
Sept 29	CLYDE	2-0	Shaw	McNair	McGregor	Young	Dodds	McMaster	McAtee	Gallacher 1	Connolly	McMenemy 1	Browning
Oct 4	ABERDEEN	2-1	Shaw	McNair	Dodds	Young	Johnstone	McMaster	McAtee 1	Gallacher	Connolly	McMenemy	Browning 1
Oct 11	Aberdeen	1-0	Shaw	McNair	McGregor	Young 1	Johnstone	McMaster	McAtee	Gallacher	Dodds	Cassidy	Browning
Oct 18	DUNDEE	1-0	Shaw	McNair	Dodds	Young	Johnstone	McMaster	McAtee 1	Gallacher	Whitehead	McColl	Browning
Oct 25	Rangers	2-0	Shaw	McNair	Dodds	Young	Johnstone	McMaster	McAtee 1	Gallacher	Whitehead 1	McColl	Browning
Nov 1	KILMARNOCK	4-0	Shaw	McNair	Dodds	Young	Johnstone	McMaster	McAtee	Gallacher 2	Whitehead	McColl 2	Browning
Nov 8	Queen's Park	2-0	Shaw	McNair	Dodds P	Young	Johnstone	McMaster	McAtee 1	Gallacher	Whitehead	McColl	Browning
Nov 15	Dumbarton	4-0	Shaw	McNair	Dodds	Young	Johnstone	McMaster	McAtee	Gallacher 2	Whitehead 1	McColl	Browning +OG
Nov 22	HAMILTON ACADEMICALS	1-0	Shaw	McNair	Dodds	Young	Johnstone	McMaster	McAtee	Gallacher 1	Whitehead	Crone	Browning
Nov 29	Airdrie	1-0	Shaw	McNair	McGregor	Young	Johnstone	Dodds	McAtee	Gallacher 1	Whitehead	McColl	Browning
Dec 6	THIRD LANARK	3-0	Shaw	McNair	McGregor	Young	Johnstone	Dodds	McAtee	Gallacher 1	Owers 1	Crone 1	Browning
Dec 13	Raith Rovers	2-1	Shaw	McNair	McGregor	Young	Johnstone	Dodds	McAtee	Gallacher	Owers 1	Crone	Browning 1
Dec 20	MOTHERWELL	0-0	Shaw	McNair	McGregor	Young	Johnstone	Dodds	Connolly	Gallacher	Owers	Crone	Browning
Dec 27	Ayr United	6-0	Shaw	McNair	Dodds	Young	Johnstone	McMaster	McAtee	Gallacher	Owers 4	McMenemy	Browning 2
Jan 1	RANGERS	4-0	Shaw	McNair	Dodds	Young 1	Johnstone	McMaster	McAtee	Gallacher	Owers	McMenemy 1	Browning 2
Jan 3	Partick Thistle	0-0	Shaw	McNair	Dodds	Young	Johnstone	McMaster	McAtee	Gallacher	Owers	McMenemy	Browning
Jan 5	Clyde	1-0	Shaw	McGregor	Dodds	Davidson	Johnstone	McMaster	McAtee	Galagher	Owers 1	Crone	Browning
Jan 10	DUMBARTON	4-0	Shaw	McGregor	Dodds	Davidson	Johnstone	McMaster	McAtee	Gallacher 3	Owers 1	McColl	Browning
Jan 17	Dundee	1-0	Shaw	McGregor	Dodds	McMaster	Johnstone	Davidson	McMenemy	Gallacher	Owers	McColl	Browning 1
Jan 24	AIRDRIE	1-0	Shaw	McGregor	Dodds	Young	Johnstone	McMaster 1	McAtee	Gallacher	Owers	McMenemy	Browning
Jan 31	St Mirren	3-0	Shaw	McGregor	Dodds P	Young	Johnstone 1	McMaster	McAtee	McMenemy	Owers 1	McColl	Browning
Feb 14	MORTON	3-0	Shaw	McNair	McGregor	Young	Johnstone	Davidson	McAtee	Gallacher 1	McColl 1	Crone	Browning 1
Feb 28	Falkirk	0-1	Shaw	McGregor	McMaster	Young	Johnstone	Davidson	McGregor	Gallacher	McColl	Crone	McAtee
Mar 24	HEARTS	0-0	Shaw	McNair	Dodds	Young	Johnstone	McMaster	McAtee	Gallacher	McColl	McMenemy	Browning
Apr 1	Third Lanark	3-1	Shaw	McNair	Dodds	Young	Johnstone	McMaster	McAtee	Gallacher 2	Owers	McMenemy 1	Browning
Apr 8	Kilmarnock	1-0	Shaw	McNair	Dodds	Young	Johnstone	McMaster	McAtee	Gallacher 1	Owers	McMenemy	Browning
Apr 13	QUEEN'S PARK	5-0	Shaw	McNair	Dodds	Young	Johnstone	McMaster	McAtee 1	Gallacher 1	McColl 2	McMenemy 1	Browning
Apr 18	HIBERNIAN	3-0	Shaw	McNair	Dodds	Young	Johnstone	McMaster	McAtee	Gallacher	McColl 1	McMenemy 2	Browning
Apr 24	Hamilton Academicals	2-1	Shaw	McNair	Dodds	Young	Johnstone	McMaster	McAtee	Gallacher	McColl 1	Crone 1	Browning
Apr 25	PARTICK THISTLE	1-1	Shaw	McNair	Dodds	Young	Johnstone	McMaster	McAtee	Gallacher	McColl	McMenemy 1	Browning
Apr 29	RAITH ROVERS	2-1	Shaw	McNair	Dodds	Young	Johnstone	McMaster	McAtee	Gallacher 2	McColl	McMenemy	Browning

SCOTTISH CUP 1914

Feb 7	Clyde	0-0	Shaw	McGregor	Dodds	Young	Johnstone	McMaster	McAtee	Gallacher	Owers	McMenemy	Browning
Feb 10	CLYDE	2-0	Shaw	McGregor	Dodds	Young	Johnstone	McMaster	McAtee	Gallacher 2	Quinn	McColl	Browning
Feb 21	Forfar Athletic	5-0	Shaw	McGregor	Dodds P	Young	Johnstone	Davidson	McAtee	Gallacher	McColl 3	McMenemy 1	Browning
Mar? 7	Motherwell	3-1	Shaw	McNair	Dodds	Young	Johnstone	McMaster	McAtee 1	Gallacher 1	McColl 1	McMenemy	Browning
Mar 28	Third Lanark	2-0 SF	Shaw	McNair	Dodds	Young	Johnstone	McMaster	McAtee 1	Gallacher	Owers 1	McMenemy	Browning
Apr 11	Hibernian	0-0 F	Shaw	McNair	Dodds	Young	Johnstone	McMaster	McAtee	Gallacher	Owers	McMenemy	Browning
Apr 16	Hibernian	4-1 FR	Shaw	McNair	Dodds	Young	Johnstone	McMaster	McAtee	Gallacher	McColl 2	McMenemy	Browning 2

SCOTTISH LEAGUE 1914-15

Aug 15	Hearts	0-2	Shaw	McNair	Dodds	Young	Johnstone	McMaster	McAtee	Gallacher	McColl	McMenemy	Browning
Aug 22	MOTHERWELL	1-0	Shaw	McNair	Dodds	Young	Johnstone	McMaster	McAtee	Gallacher	McColl 1	McMenemy	Browning
Aug 29	St Mirren	3-3	Shaw	McGregor	Dodds	Young	Johnstone	McMaster	McAtee	Gallacher 1	McColl 1	Browning 1	Gray
Sept 5	MORTON	6-2	Shaw	McGregor	Dodds	Young	McMenemy	McMaster	McAtee 4	Gallacher	McColl	Crone 2	Browning
Sept 19	Hibernian	1-1	Shaw	McNair	McGregor	Young	Dodds	Jarvis	McAtee	Gallacher	McColl 1	McMenemy	Browning
Sept 26	Dundee	3-1	Shaw	McNair	McGregor	Young	Dodds	McMaster	McAtee	Gallacher 1	McColl 2	McMenemy	Browning
Sept 28*	Clyde (H)	3-0	Shaw	McNair	McGregor	Young	Dodds	McMaster	McAtee	Gallacher	McColl 1	McMenemy 1	Browning 1
Oct 3	DUNDEE	6-0	Shaw	McNair	McGregor	Young	Dodds	McMaster	McAtee	Gallacher	McColl 1	McMenemy 2	Browning 3
Oct 5	Raith Rovers	2-2	Shaw	McNair	McGregor	Young	Dodds	Johnstone	McAtee	Gallacher	McColl 1	McMenemy	Browning + OG
Oct 10	Ayr United	0-1	Shaw	McNair	McGregor	Young	Dodds	Johnstone	McAtee	Gallacher	McColl	McMenemy	Browning
Oct 17	FALKIRK	1-0	Shaw	McNair	Dodds	Young	Johnstone	McMaster	McAtee	Gallacher 1	Quinn	McMenemy	Browning
Oct 24	Hamilton Academicals	1-0	Shaw	McNair	Dodds	Young	Johnstone	McMaster	McAtee	Gallacher	Quinn 1	McMenemy	Browning
Oct 31	RANGERS	2-1	Shaw	McNair	Dodds	Young	Johnstone	McMaster	McAtee	Gallacher 1	Quinn	McMenemy 1	Browning
Nov 7	Kilmarnock	3-1	Shaw	McNair	Dodds	Young	Johnstone	McMaster	McAtee 1	Crone	McColl	McMenemy 2	Browning
Nov 14	THIRD LANARK	1-0	Shaw	McNair	McGregor	Young	Johnstone	McMaster	McAtee	Crone	McColl 1	McMenemy	Browning
Nov 21	AYR UNITED	4-0	Shaw	McNair	McGregor	Young	Johnstone	McMaster	McAtee	Gallacher 3	McColl	McMenemy	Browning 1
Nov 28	Dumbarton	4-1	Shaw	McNair	Dodds	Young	Johnstone	McMaster	McAtee 1	Gallacher 1	McColl 2	McMenemy 1	Browning
Dec 5	Aberdeen	1-0	Shaw	McNair	Dodds	Young	Johnstone	McMaster	McAtee	McGregor	McColl	McMenemy 1	Browning
Dec 12	QUEEN'S PARK	5-1	Shaw	McNair	Dodds	Young	Johnstone	McMaster	McAtee	Crone 3	Quinn 2	McColl	Browning
Dec 19	Airdrie	1-0	Shaw	McNair	Dodds	Young	Johnstone	McMaster	McAtee	Gallacher	McColl 1	McMenemy	Browning
Dec 26	HAMILTON ACADEMICALS	3-1	Shaw	McNair	Dodds	Young	Johnstone	McMaster	McAtee	Gallacher 2	Quinn 1	McMenemy	Browning
Jan 1	Rangers	1-2	Shaw	McNair	Dodds	Young	Johnstone	McMaster	McAtee	Gallacher	McColl	McMenemy	Browning 1
Jan 2	CLYDE	2-0	Shaw	McNair	McGregor	Young	Johnstone	Dodds	McAtee	Gallacher	McColl	McMenemy	Browning 2
Jan 4	KILMARNOCK	2-0	Shaw	McNair	McGregor	Young	Johnstone 1	Dodds	McAtee	Crone	McColl 1	McMenemy	Browning
Jan 9	PARTICK THISTLE	6-1	Shaw	McNair	Dodds P	Young	Johnstone	McMaster	McAtee	Gallacher 3	McColl 1	McMenemy	Browning 1
Jan 16	Falkirk	1-0	Shaw	McGregor	Dodds	Young	Johnstone	McMaster	McAtee	Gallacher	McColl	McMenemy	Browning 1
Jan 30	HEARTS	1-1	Shaw	McNair	Dodds	Young	Johnstone	McMaster	McAtee 1	Gallacher	Quinn	McMenemy	Browning
Feb 6	ST MIRREN	2-1	Shaw	McNair	Dodds	Young	Johnstone	McMaster	McAtee	Gallacher	McColl 2	McMenemy	Browning
Feb 13	Morton	2-0	Shaw	McNair	McGregor	Young	Johnstone	Dodds	McAtee	Gallacher 1	McColl 1	McMenemy	Browning
Feb 20	DUMBARTON	1-0	Shaw	McNair	Dodds	Young	Johnstone	McMaster	McAtee	Gallacher	McColl 1	McMenemy	Browning
Feb 27	Partick Thistle	2-0	Shaw	McNair	Dodds P	Young	Johnstone	McMaster	McAtee	Gallacher	McColl 1	McMenemy	Browning
Mar 6	HIBERNIAN	5-1	Shaw	McNair	Dodds P	Young	Johnstone	McMaster	McAtee 1	Gallacher	McColl 1	McMenemy 2	Browning +OG
Mar 27	RAITH ROVERS	3-1	Shaw	McNair	McGregor	Young	Dodds	McMaster	McAtee	McMenemy	McColl 3	Johnstone	Browning
Apr 3	AIRDRIE	3-0	Shaw	McNair	Dodds	Young	Johnstone	McMaster	McAtee	Gallacher	McColl 1	McMenemy 1	Browning 1
Apr 5	Queen's Park	3-0	Shaw	McNair	Dodds	Young	Johnstone	McMaster	McAtee	Gallacher 1	McColl 1	McMenemy 1	Browning
Apr 10	ABERDEEN	1-0	Shaw	McNair	Dodds	Young	Johnstone	McMaster	McAtee	Gallacher	McColl	McMenemy 1	Browning
Apr 17	Third Lanark	4-0	Shaw	McNair	Dodds	Young	Johnstone	McMaster	McAtee	Gallacher	McColl 1	McMenemy 1	Browning 2
Apr 24	Motherwell	1-1	Shaw	McNair	Dodds	Young	Johnstone	McMaster	McAtee	Gallacher	McColl	McMenemy	Browning 1

SCOTTISH LEAGUE 1915-16

Aug 21	MOTHERWELL	3-1	Shaw	McGregor	Dodds 1	Young	Johnstone	McMaster	McAtee	Gallacher 1	McColl 1	Cassidy	Browning
Aug 28	Airdrie	5-0	Shaw	McGregor	Dodds	Young	Johnstone	McMaster	McAtee	Gallacher	McColl 4	McMenemy	Browning 1
Sept 4	FALKIRK	2-1	Shaw	McGregor	Dodds	Young	Johnstone	McMaster	McAtee	Gallacher 2	McColl	McMenemy	Browning
Sept 11	Morton	1-0	Shaw	McGregor	Dodds	Young 1	Johnstone	McMaster	McAtee	Gallacher	McColl	McMenemy	Browning

			1	2	3	4	5	6	7	8	9	10	11
Sept 18	Dundee	2-0	Shaw	McGregor	Dodds	Young	Johnstone	McMaster	McAtee	Gallacher 1	McColl	McMenemy	Browning 1
Sept 27	CLYDE	5-0	Shaw	McNair	Dodds	Young	Johnstone	McMaster	McAtee 1	Gallacher	McColl 2	McMenemy 1	Browning 1
Oct 2	Hibernian	4-0	Shaw	McNair	Dodds	Young	Johnstone	McMaster 1	McAtee 1	Gallacher 1	McColl 1	Cassidy	Browning
Oct 16	Hamilton Academicals	3-2	Shaw	McNair	Dodds	Young 1	Johnstone	McMaster	McCabe	Gallacher 1	McColl 1	Browning	McMenemy
Oct 23	ST MIRREN	0-2	Shaw	McNair	Dodds	Young	Johnstone	McMaster	Cassidy	Gallacher	McColl	Browning	McCabe
Oct 30	Rangers	0-3	Shaw	McNair	Dodds	Young	Johnstone	McMaster	McAtee	Gallacher	McColl	McMenemy	Browning
Nov 6	ABERDEEN	3-1	Shaw	McNair	Dodds	Young	Johnstone	McMaster	Crone	Gallacher 1	McColl 2	McMenemy	Browning
Nov 13	Hearts	0-2	Shaw	McNair	McGregor	McMaster	Johnstone	Dodds	McAtee	Gallacher	McColl	McMenemy	Browning
Nov 20	KILMARNOCK	2-0	Shaw	McNair	McGregor	Dodds	Johnstone	McMaster	McAtee	Gallacher	McColl 1	McMenemy	Browning +OG
Nov 27	RAITH ROVERS	2-0	Shaw	McNair	McGregor	Dodds	Johnstone	McMaster	McAtee	Gallacher 1	McColl 1	McMenemy	Browning
Dec 4	QUEEN'S PARK	6-2	Shaw	McNair	McGregor	Young	Dodds 1	McMaster	McAtee	Johnstone 1	McColl 3	McMenemy	Browning 1
Dec 11	Ayr United	4-0	Shaw	McNair	McGregor	Young	Johnstone	Dodds	McAtee	Gallacher 2	McColl	McMenemy 1	Browning 1
Dec 18	Partick Thistle	4-0	Shaw	McNair	Dodds	Young	Johnstone	McMaster	McAtee 1	Gallacher	McColl	McMenemy 2	Browning 1
Dec 25	AIRDRIE	6-0	Shaw	McNair	Dodds	Young	Johnstone	McMaster	McAtee	Gallacher 3	McColl 1	McMenemy 1	Browning 1
Jan 1	RANGERS	2-2	Shaw	McNair	Dodds	Young	Johnstone	McMaster	McAtee 1	Gallacher	McColl 1	McMenemy	Browning
Jan 3	Clyde	3-1	Shaw	McNair	Dodds	Young	Johnstone	McMaster	McAtee	Gallacher	McColl 2	Crone 1	Browning
Jan 8	Dumbarton	2-1	Shaw	McNair	Dodds	Young	Johnstone 1	McMaster	McAtee	Gallacher	McColl	Crone	Browning 1
Jan 15	HIBERNIAN	3-1	Shaw	McNair	McGregor	Young	Dodds	McMaster	McAtee	Gallacher 1	McColl 2	Johnstone	Browning
Jan 22	Third Lanark	4-0	Shaw	McNair	Dodds P	Young	Johnstone	McMaster	McAtee 2	Gallacher	McColl 1	McMenemy	Browning
Jan 29	AYR UNITED	3-1	Shaw	McNair	Dodds	Young	Johnstone	McMaster	McAtee 1	Gallacher 1	McColl 1	McMenemy	Browning
Feb 5	Aberdeen	4-0	Shaw	McNair	Dodds	Young	Johnstone	McMaster	McAtee	Gallacher 2	McColl 1	McMenemy 1	Browning
Feb 12	DUMBARTON	6-0	Shaw	McNair	Dodds	Young	Johnstone	McMaster 2	McAtee 3 (1P)	Gallacher 1	McColl	McMenemy	Browning
Feb 19	Queen's Park	1-0	Shaw	McNair	Dodds	Young	Johnstone	McMaster	McAtee	Gallacher 1	McColl	McMenemy	Browning
Feb 26	DUNDEE	3-0	Shaw	McNair	Dodds 1	Young	Johnstone	McMaster	McAtee	Gallacher	McColl 2	McMenemy	Browning
Mar 4	Kilmarnock	3-0	Shaw	McNair	Dodds	Young	Johnstone	McMaster	McAtee	Gallacher 1	McColl 2	McMenemy	Browning
Mar 11	HAMILTON ACADEMICALS	5-1	Shaw	McNair	Dodds	Young	Johnstone	McMaster	McAtee	Gallacher	McColl 4	McMenemy 1	Browning
Mar 18	St Mirren	5-0	Shaw	McNair	Dodds	Young	Johnstone	McMaster	McAtee 1	Gallacher 1	McColl 2	McMenemy	Browning 1
Apr 1	MORTON	0-0	Shaw	McGregor	Dodds	Young	Johnstone	McMaster	McAtee	Gallacher	McColl	McMenemy	Browning
Apr 8	Falkirk	2-0	Shaw	McNair	Dodds	Young	Johnstone	McMaster	Crone 1	Gallacher	O'Kane 1	McMenemy	Browning
Apr 15	RAITH ROVERS	6-0	Shaw	McNair	McGregor	Young	Dodds 1	McMaster	McAtee	Gallacher 3	O'Kane 2	McMenemy	Browning
	Motherwell	3-1	Shaw	McNair	McGregor	Young	Dodds P	McMaster	McAtee	Gallacher	Cassidy	McMenemy 1	Browning 1
Apr 22	HEARTS	0-0	Shaw	McNair	Dodds	Young	Johnstone	McMaster	McAtee	Gallacher	O'Kane	McMenemy	Browning
Apr 24	THIRD LANARK	4-1	Shaw	McGregor	Dodds	Young	Johnstone	McMaster	McAtee	Gallacher 1	O'Kane 3	McMenemy	Browning
Apr 29	PARTICK THISTLE	5-0	Shaw	McNair	Dodds	Young	Johnstone	McMaster	McAtee	Gallacher 3	O'Kane 2	McMenemy	Browning

SCOTTISH LEAGUE 1916-17

Aug 21	St Mirren	5-1	Shaw	McNair	McStay	Young	Johnstone	Dodds	McAtee	Gallacher 4	O'Kane 1	McMenemy	Browning
Aug 28	HIBERNIAN	3-1	Shaw	McNair	McStay	Dodds	Johnstone	McMaster	McAtee	Gallacher	O'Kane 1	McMenemy	Browning 2
Sept 2	Ayr United	1-0	Shaw	McNair	McStay	Young	Wilson	Dodds	McAtee	Gallacher	O'Kane 1	McMenemy	Browning
Sept 9	AIRDRIE	3-1	Shaw	McNair	McStay	Young	Wilson	Dodds	McAtee	Gallacher 1	O'Kane 2	McMenemy	Browning
Sept 16	Motherwell	4-0	Shaw	McNair	McStay	Young	Wilson	Dodds	McAtee 2	Gallacher 2	O'Kane	McMenemy	Browning
Sept 30	HEARTS	1-0	Shaw	McNair	McStay	Young	Wilson	Dodds	McAtee	Gallacher	O'Kane	McMenemy	Browning 1
Oct 14	Falkirk	1-1	Shaw	McNair	McGregor	McStay	Wilson	Dodds	Connolly	Gallacher 1	O'Kane	McMenemy	Browning
Oct 21	MORTON	0-0	Shaw	McNair	McStay	Dodds	Wilson	Hamill (A)	McColl	Gallacher	O'Kane	McMenemy	Browning
Oct 28	RANGERS	0-0	Shaw	McNair	Dodds	Wilson	Hamill	McMaster	McColl	Gallacher	O'Kane	McMenemy	Browning
Nov 4	Dundee	2-1	Shaw	McNair	Dodds	Wilson	Hamill	McStay	O'Kane	Gallacher 1	McColl	McMenemy	Browning 1
Nov 11	Queen's Park	3-1	Shaw	McNair	Dodds 1	Wilson	Hamill	McStay	Ribchester	Gallacher 1	Connolly	McColl 1	Browning
Nov 18	PARTICK THISTLE	0-0	Shaw	McNair	Dodds	Wilson	Hamill	McStay	Ribchester	Gallacher	O'Kane	McColl	Browning
Nov 25	ABERDEEN	1-0	Shaw	McNair	Dodds	Wilson	Hamill	McStay	McAtee	Gallacher	McColl	McMenemy 1	Browning
Dec 2	Raith Rovers	4-1	Shaw	McNair	Dodds	Wilson	McStay	Brown	McAtee	McMenemy	McColl 3	Cassidy	Browning 1
Dec 9	AYR UNITED	5-0	Shaw	McNair	Dodds	Wilson	Hamill	McStay	McAtee	Gallacher 3	McColl	McMenemy 1	Browning 1
Dec 16	Hamilton Academicals	4-0	Shaw	McNair	Dodds P	Wilson	McStay	Brown	McAtee	Gallacher	McColl 1	McMenemy	Browning 2
Dec 23	Partick Thistle	2-0	Shaw	McNair	Dodds	Wilson	McStay	Brown	McAtee	McMenemy	McColl 1	Cassidy	Browning 1
Dec 30	FALKIRK	2-0	Shaw	McNair	Dodds	Wilson	McStay	McMaster	McAtee	Connolly	McColl 1	McMenemy	Browning 1
Jan 1	Rangers	0-0	Shaw	McNair	Dodds	Wilson	McStay	McMaster	McAtee	Connolly	McColl	McMenemy	Browning
Jan 2	CLYDE	0-0	Shaw	McNair	Dodds	Wilson	McStay	Brown	McAtee	O'Kane	McColl	McMenemy	Browning
Jan 6	MOTHERWELL	1-0	Shaw	McNair	Dodds P	Wilson	McStay	Brown	McAtee	O'Kane	McColl	McMenemy	Browning
Jan 13	Hearts	1-0	Shaw	McNair	Dodds	Wilson	McStay	Brown	McAtee	O'Kane	McColl 1	McMenemy	Browning
Jan 20	DUMBARTON	1-1	Shaw	McNair	Dodds	Wilson	McStay	Brown	McAtee	Adam McLean	McColl 1	McMenemy	Browning
Jan 27	Third Lanark	0-0	Shaw	McNair	Dodds	Wilson	McStay	Brown	McAtee	McMenemy	McColl	Cassidy	Browning
Feb 3	RAITH ROVERS	5-0	Shaw	McNair	Dodds	Wilson	McStay	Brown	McAtee 1	Gallacher 2	McColl 2	McMemeny	Browning
Feb 10	Morton	1-0	Shaw	McNair	Dodds	Wilson	McStay	Brown	McAtee	Gallacher	McColl 1	McMenemy	McLean
Feb 17	DUNDEE	2-0	Shaw	McNair	Dodds	Wilson	McStay	Brown	McAtee	Gallacher	McColl 2	McMenemy	McLean
Feb 24	Kilmarnock	2-2	Shaw	McNair	Dodds	Wilson	McStay	Brown	McAtee	Gallacher 1	McColl	McMenemy 1	McLean
Mar 3	QUEEN'S PARK	3-2	Shaw	McNair	Dodds	Wilson	McStay	Brown	McAtee	Gallacher	McColl 1	McMenemy 1	Browning 1
Mar 10	HAMILTON ACADEMICALS	6-1	Shaw	McNair	Dodds	Wilson	McStay	Brown	McAtee	Gallacher 1	McColl 4	McMenemy 1	Browning
Mar 17	Airdrie	2-1	Shaw	McNair	Dodds	Wilson	McStay	Brown	McAtee 1	Gallacher 1	McColl	McMenemy	Browning
Mar 24	Aberdeen	0-0	Shaw	McNair	Dodds	Wilson	McStay	Brown	McAtee	O'Kane	McColl	McLean	Browning
Mar 31	ST MIRREN	3-0	Shaw	McNair	Dodds P	Wilson	McStay	Brown	McAtee	Gallacher 1	McColl 1	McMenemy	Browning
Apr 7	Dumbarton	3-1	Shaw	McNair	Dodds P	Wilson	McStay	Brown	McAtee	Gallacher	McColl 1	McMenemy	Browning 1
Apr 9	THIRD LANARK	2-0	Shaw	McNair	Dodds	Wilson	McStay	Brown	McAtee	Gallacher 1	McColl 1	McMenemy	Browning
Apr 14	Hibernian	1-0	Shaw	McNair	Dodds	Wilson	McStay	Brown	McAtee	Gallacher 1	McColl	McMenemy	Browning
Apr 21	KILMARNOCK	0-2	Shaw	McNair	Dodds	Wilson	McStay	Brown	McAtee	Gallacher	McColl	McMenemy	Browning
Apr 28	Clyde	5-0	Shaw	Fullerton	Dodds 1	Wilson	McStay	Brown	McAtee	Gallacher 1	McColl 2	Browning	McLean 1

SCOTTISH LEAGUE 1917-18

Aug 18	AYR UNITED	4-0	Shaw	McNair	Livingstone	Wilson	Dodds	Brown	McAtee	Gallacher	McColl 2	McMenemy	Browning 2
Aug 25	Falkirk	3-1	Shaw	McNair	Dodds	Wilson	McMaster	Brown	McAtee 1	Gallacher 1	McColl	McMenemy 1	Browning
Sept 1	CLYDE	3-2	Shaw	McNair	Dodds	Wilson	McMaster	Brown	McLean	McMenemy	McColl 3	Brodie	Browning
Sept 15	PARTICK THISTLE (at GP)	2-1	Shaw	McNair	McGregor	Wilson	Dodds	Brown	McAtee	Gallacher	McColl 2	McMenemy	Browning
Sept 24	Third Lanark	2-0	Shaw	Dodds	Livingstone	Wilson	Cringan	Brown	McAtee	Gallacher	McColl 1	Browning 1	McLean
Sept 29	Hearts	1-0	Shaw	McNair	Livingstone	McMaster	Cringan	Brown	McAtee	Gallacher	McColl	Browning	McLean 1
Oct 13	KILMARNOCK	2-3	Shaw	McNair	Livingstone	McMaster	Cringan	Brown	McAtee	Gallacher 1	McColl	Browning	McLean 1
Oct 20	Rangers	2-1	Shaw	McNair	McGregor	McMaster	Cringan	Brown	McAtee 1	Gallacher	McColl 1	Jackson	Browning
Oct 27	QUEEN'S PARK	3-0	Shaw	McNair	McGregor	McMaster	Cringan	Brown	McAtee 1	Gallacher	McColl	Jackson 1	Browning 1
Nov 3	Airdrie	0-2	Shaw	McNair	Dodds	McMaster	Cringan	Brown	McAtee	Gallacher	McColl	Jackson	Browning
Nov 10	HAMILTON ACADEMICALS	1-0	Shaw	McNair	Dodds	McMaster	Cringan	Brown	McAtee	Gallacher	McLean 1	McMenemy	Browning
Nov 17	Dumbarton	2-0	Shaw	McNair	McGregor	Dodds	Cringan	Brown	McAtee	Gallacher 1	McLean	McMenemy	Browning 1
Nov 24	HIBERNIAN	2-0	Shaw	McNair	McGregor	Dodds 1	Cringan	Brown	McAtee	Gallacher	McLean 1	McMenemy	Browning
Dec 1	Morton	1-1	Shaw	McNair	McGregor	Dodds	Cringan	Brown	McAtee	Gallacher	McLean 1	McCormack	Browning
Dec 8	CLYDEBANK	3-0	Shaw	McNair	McGregor	Dodds	Cringan	Brown	Jackson	Gallacher	McLean 1	McCormack 1	Browning +OG
Dec 15	Motherwell	4-3	Shaw	Wilson	Dodds	McInally	Cringan	Brown	McAtee 1	Gallacher 1	McLean	Jackson 1	Browning 1
Dec 22	DUMBARTON	3-0	Shaw	McNair	Livingstone	Dodds	Cringan	Brown	Wilson	Gallacher 2	McLean	McMenemy 1	Browning
Dec 29	Ayr United	2-1	Shaw	McNair	Dodds	Jackson	Cringan	Brown	McAtee	Gallacher	McLean 2	McMenemy	Browning
Jan 1	RANGERS	0-0	Shaw	McNair	Dodds	Jackson	Cringan	Brown	McAtee	Gallacher	Bauchop	McMenemy	Browning
Jan 2	Clyde	4-1	Shaw	McNair	Dodds	Wilson	Cringan 1	Jackson	McAtee	Gallacher P	McLean	McMenemy 1	Browning 1
Jan 5	St Mirren	0-0	Shaw	Wilson	Dodds	Stewart	Cringan	Jackson	McAtee	Gallacher	McLean	McMenemy	Browning
Jan 12	FALKIRK	0-0	Shaw	McNair	Dodds	Wilson	Cringan	Brown	McAtee	Gallacher	McLean	McMenemy	Jackson
Jan 23	AIRDRIE	3-3	Shaw	McNair	Dodds	Jackson	Cringan	Brown 1	McAtee	Gallacher 1	McLean 1	McMenemy	B rowning
Feb 2	Queen's Park	2-0	Shaw	McNair	Dodds	Jackson	Cringan	Brown	Kelly (A)	Gallacher 1	McLean	McMenemy 1	Browning
Feb 9	HEARTS	3-0	Shaw	McNair	Dodds	Jackson	Cringan	Brown	ORT	Gallacher 1	McLean 1	McMenemy 1	Browning

			1	2	3	4	5	6	7	8	9	10	11
Feb 16	Hamilton Academicals	2-1	Shaw	McNair	Dodds	Jackson	Cringan	Brown	McAtee	Gallacher	McLean 2	McMenemy	Browning
Feb 23	MORTON	2-0	Shaw	McNair	McGregor	Dodds	Cringan	Brown	McAtee	Gallacher 2	McLean	McMenemy	Jackson
Mar 2	Clydebank	2-1	Shaw	McNair	Dodds	Jackson	Cringan	Brown	McAtee	Gallacher P	McColl	McMenemy	Browning 1
Mar 9	Partick Thistle	0-0	Shaw	McNair	Dodds	Wilson	Cringan	Brown	McAtee	Gallacher	McColl	McMenemy	Browning
Mar 16	ST MIRREN	1-0	Shaw	McNair	McGregor	Jackson	Cringan	Brown	McAtee	Gallacher	McColl 1	McMenemy	OLT
Mar 23	THIRD LANARK	1-3	Shaw	McNair	McGregor	Jackson	Cringan	Brown	McAtee	Gallacher 1	McColl	McMenemy	Browning
Mar 30	Kilmarnock	3-1	Shaw	McNair	Livingstone	Jackson	Cringan	Brown	McLean 1	Gallacher 1	Cassidy	McMenemy	Browning 1
Apr 6	Hibernian	2-0	Shaw	McNair	Dodds	Jackson	Cringan	Brown	McAtee 1	Gallacher 1	McLean	McMenemy	Browning
Apr 13	MOTHERWELL	1-1	Shaw	McNair	Dodds	Jackson	Cringan	Brown	McAtee	Gallacher 1	McLean	McMenemy	Browning

SCOTTISH LEAGUE 1918-19

Aug 17	Hibernian	3-0	Shaw	McNair	Livingstone	McEvoy	Jackson	W Brown	Burns	Gallacher	McLean 1	McColl 1	Browning +OG
Aug 24	MORTON	1-1	Shaw	McNair	Livingstone	McEvoy	Jackson	W Brown	Burns	Gallacher	McLean 1	McColl	Browning
Aug 31	Clyde	3-0	Shaw	McNair	Livingstone	Barber (A)	Cringan	W Brown	Burns	Gallacher 2P	McLean 1	Jackson	Browning
Sept 7	AYR UNITED	1-0	Shaw	McNair	McGregor	Barber	Cringan 1	W Brown	Burns	Gallacher	McColl	Jackson	Browning
Sept 14	Queen's Park	3-0	Shaw	McNair	Livingstone	McEvoy	Cringan	W Brown	Burns	Gallacher 2	McLean	McColl 1	Browning
Sept 28	Falkirk	2-1	Shaw	McNair	McGregor	Jackson	Cringan	W Brown	Burns	Gallacher	McLean	McColl 1	Brodie 1
Sept 30	THIRD LANARK	3-1	Shaw	McGinnigle (A)	Livingstone	Jackson	Cringan	W Brown	'Burns	Gallacher	McLean	McColl	Kelly
Oct 12	Kilmarnock	1-1	Syme	McNair	McGregor	McEvoy	Price	Hugh Brown	Burns	Gallacher	McLean	W Brown 1	McColl
Oct 19	RANGERS	0-3	Syme	McNair	McGregor	McEvoy	Cringan	H Brown	Burns	Gallacher	Elliot (A)	W Brown	McLean
Oct 26	Dumbarton	5-0	Shaw	McNair	Livingstone	McEvoy	Cringan 1	H Brown	Burns 3	Gallacher	McLean 1	Mitchell	Corcoran
Nov 2	ST MIRREN	1-0	Shaw	McNair	Livingstone	McEvoy	Cringan	H Brown	McLean 1	Gallacher	McColl	Mitchell	Browning
Nov 9	HEARTS	1-1	Shaw	McNair	Livingstone	McEvoy	Cringan	H Brown	McLean	Gallacher 1	McColl	Mitchell	Browning
Nov 23	Partick Thistle	1-0	Shaw	McNair	Livingstone	McEvoy	Cringan	H Brown	Corcoran	Gallacher 1	McColl	Barber	McLean
Dec 7	Motherwell	1-3	Shaw	McNair	Livingstone	McEvoy	Cringan	H Brown	Corcoran	Barber	McColl 1	McLean	Browning
Dec 14	DUMBARTON	2-0	Shaw	McNair	McStay	Price	Cringan	H Brown	Burns	Mitchell	McColl 1	McMenemy 1	McLean
Dec 21	Hamilton Academicals	2-1	Shaw	McNair	McStay	Price	Cringan	H Brown	Burns	Mitchell	McColl	McMenemy 1	McLean 1
Dec 28	HIBERNIAN	2-0	Shaw	McNair	Dodds	McStay	Cringan	H Brown	McLean	Gallacher	McColl 1	McMenemy	Browning 1
Jan 1	Rangers	1-1	Shaw	McNair	Taylor (A)	McStay	Cringan	Dodds	Cassidy	Gallacher	McColl	McMenemy 1	McLean
Jan 2	CLYDE	2-0	Shaw	McNair	Dodds	McStay	Cringan	H Brown	Burns 1	Shea (A)	McColl	McMenemy	Gallacher 1
Jan 4	Third Lanark	3-2	Shaw	McNair	Dodds	McStay	Cringan	H Brown	Duncan (A)	McMenemy 1	McColl 1	Cassidy	McLean 1
Jan 11	CLYDEBANK	3-1	Shaw	McNair	Taylor	McStay	Cringan	Dodds P	Duncan	McMenemy	McColl 1	Cassidy 1	McLean
Jan 18	St Mirren	4-0	Shaw	McNair	Dodds	McStay	Cringan	H Brown 1	McAtee 1	Gallacher 1	McColl	McMenemy	McLean 1
Jan 25	MOTHERWELL	0-0	Shaw	McNair	Dodds	McStay	Cringan	H Brown	McAtee	Gallacher	McColl	McMenemy	McLean
Feb 1	KILMARNOCK	2-1	Shaw	McNair	Dodds	McStay	Cringan	H Brown	McAtee	Gallacher	McColl	McMenemy	McLean 1 +OG
Feb 8	Airdrie	2-1	Shaw	McNair	Dodds P	McStay	Cringan	H Brown 1	McAtee	Gallacher	McColl	McMenemy	McLean
Feb 15	HAMILTON ACADEMICALS	4-1	Shaw	McNair	Taylor	McStay 1	Cringan	H Brown	McAtee	Gallacher	McColl 3	McMenemy	McLean
Feb 22	PARTICK THISTLE	2-1	Shaw	McGregor	Taylor	Price	McStay	H Brown	Cassidy	Gallacher 1	McColl	McMenemy	McLean 1
Mar 8	Morton	0-0	Shaw	McNair	McStay	Price	Cringan	H Brown	McAtee	Gallacher	Cassidy	McMenemy	McLean
Mar 15	QUEEN'S PARK	2-0	Shaw	Livingstone	McGregor	H Brown	McStay	Price	McAtee	Gallacher	McColl	Cassidy 2	McLean
Apr 12	Clydebank	2-0	Shaw	McNair	Taylor	McStay	Cringan	H Brown	McAtee	Gallacher	McColl 2	McMenemy	McLean
Apr 19	FALKIRK	4-0	Shaw	McNair	Dodds	McStay	Cringan	H Brown	McAtee	Gallacher 3	McColl 1	McMenemy	McLean
Apr 21	AIRDRIE	3-0	Shaw	McNair	Dodds	McStay	Cringan	H Brown	McAtee	Gallacher 2	McColl	McMenemy 1	McLean
Apr 28	Hearts	3-2	Shaw	McNair	Dodds	McStay	Cringan	H Brown	McAtee 1	Gallacher	McColl 2	McMenemy	McLean
May 10	Ayr United	2-0	Shaw	McNair	Dodds	McStay	Cringan	H Brown	McAtee 1	Gallacher	McColl	McMenemy	McLean 1

LEAGUE 1919-20

Aug 16	CLYDEBANK	3-1	Shaw	McNair	Livingstone	McStay	Cringan	H Brown	Watson	Gallacher	McInally 3	McMenemy	McLean
Aug 18	DUMBARTON	3-1	Shaw	McNair	McStay	Gilchrist	Cringan	Brown	Watson	Gallacher	McInally 3	McMenemy	McLean
Aug 23	Hamilton Academicals	2-1	Shaw	McNair	McStay	Gilchrist	Cringan	Brown	Watson	Gallacher	McInally 1	McMenemy 1	McLean
Aug 27	Kilmarnock	1-0	Shaw	McNair	McStay	Gilchrist	Cringan	Brown	Watson	Gallacher	McInally	McMenemy	McLean 1
Aug 30	RAITH ROVERS	3-0	Shaw	McNair	McStay	Gilchrist	Cringan	Brown	McAtee	Gallacher 1	McInally 2	McMenemy	McLean
Sept 13	Hearts	1-0	Shaw	McNair	McStay	Gilchrist	Cringan	Brown	McAtee	Gallacher 1	McInally	McMenemy	McLean
Sept 27	CLYDE	3-1	Shaw	McNair	Dodds	Gilchrist	Cringan	McStay	McAtee	McMenemy	McInally 3	Cassidy	McLean
Sept 29	Third Lanark	4-1	Shaw	McNair	McStay	Gilchrist	Cringan	Cassidy	Watson	McMenemy	McInally 2	McLean 2	McAtee
Oct 11	HIBERNIAN	7-3	Shaw	McNair	McStay	Gilchrist 1	Cringan	Brown	Watson 1	Gallacher 3	McInally 2	McMenemy	McLean
Oct 18	Rangers	0-3	Shaw	McNair	McStay	Gilchrist	Cringan	Cassidy	McAtee	Gallacher	McInally	McMenemy	McLean
Oct 25	QUEEN'S PARK	3-1	Lawrie	McNair	McStay P	Gilchrist	Cringan 1	Brown	Watson 1	McMenemy	McColl	Cassidy	McLean
Nov 1	Morton	2-1	Lawrie	McNair	McStay P	Gilchrist	Cringan	Brown	Watson	Gallacher	McColl	McMenemy	McLean 1
Nov 8	FALKIRK	1-1	Lawrie	McNair	McStay	Gilchrist	Cringan	Brown	Watson	Gallacher	McInally 1	McMenemy	Pratt
Nov 15	Ayr United	1-1	Shaw	McNair	Livingstone	Gilchrist	McStay P	McMaster	McAtee	McMenemy	McColl	Cassidy	McLean
Nov 22	PARTICK THISTLE	0-0	Shaw	McNair	McStay	Gilchrist	Cringan	McMaster	Watson	Gallacher	McColl	Cassidy	McLean
Nov 29	Aberdeen	1-0	Shaw	McNair	Livingstone	Gilchrist	Cringan	McMaster	Watson	Gallacher	McInally	McLean	McColl +OG
Dec 6	MOTHERWELL	5-0	Shaw	McNair	McStay	Gilchrist	Cringan	McMaster	Watson 1	Gallacher 2	McInally	McMenemy 2	McLean
Dec 13	Airdrie	0-0	Shaw	McNair	McStay	Gilchrist	Cringan	McMaster	Watson	Gallacher	McInally	McMenemy	McLean
Dec 20	Dumbarton	0-0	Shaw	McNair	Livingstone	Gilchrist	Cringan	McStay	McAtee	Gallacher	Cassidy	McMenmy	McLean
Dec 27	THIRD LANARK	2-1	Shaw	McNair	Dodds	Gilchrist	Cringan	McMaster	McInally	McMenemy	McColl	Cassidy	McLean 2
Jan 1	RANGERS	1-1	Shaw	McNair	McStay	Gilchrist	Cringan 1	McMaster	McAtee	McMenemy	McInally	Cassidy	McLean
Jan 3	Raith Rovers	3-0	Shaw	Livingstone	McStay	Gilchrist	Cringan	McMaster	McAtee 1	McMenemy	McInally 1	Cassidy 1	McLean
Jan 5	Clyde	2-0	Shaw	McStay	Livingstone	Gilchrist	Cringan	McMaster	McAtee 1	McMenemy	McInally 1	Cassidy	McLean
Jan 10	MORTON	1-1	Shaw	McStay	Livingstone	Gilchrist	Cringan	McMaster	McAtee	McMenemy	McInally	Cassidy	McLean 1
Jan 17	Kilmarnock	3-2	Shaw	McNair	McStay	Gilchrist	Cringan	McMaster	McAtee 1	McMenemy	Craig 2	Cassidy	McLean
Jan 24	Clydebank	0-2	Shaw	McNair	McStay	Gilchrist	CringaN	McMaster	McAtee	McMenemy	McColl	Craig	Mclean
Jan 31	Dundee	1-2	Shaw	McNair	McStay	Gilchrist	Cringan	McMaster	McAtee	McMenemy	McLean	Cassidy 1	McColl
Feb 14	ALBION ROVBRS	3-0	Shaw	McNair	Dodds	McStay	Cringan	McMaster	McAtee	McMenemy	McInally 1	Cassidy	McLean 2
Feb 28	HAMILTON ACADEMICALS	2-0	Shaw	Livingstone	Dodds	Gilchrist	McStay P	McMaster	McAtee	Gallacher	McInally	Cassidy 1	McLean
Mar 13	Queen's Park	2-1	Shaw	McStay	Dodds	Gilchrist	Cringan	McMaster	McAtee	McKay 1	McInally	Cassidy 1	McLean
Mar 27	Falkirk	2-1	Shaw	McNair	Dodds	McStay	Cringan	McMaster	McAtee	Gallacher	McInally	Cassidy 1	McLean 1
Apr 3	St Mirren	2-0	Shaw	McNair	Dodds	McStay	Cringan	McMaster	McAtee	Gallacher 1	McInally 1	Cassidy	McLean
Apr 5	Partick Thistle	2-1	Shaw	McNair	Dodds	McStay	Cringan	McMaster	McAtee 1	Gallacher	McInally 1	Cassidy	McLean
Apr 10	ABERDEEN	5-0	Shaw	Livingstone	Dodds	McStay	Cringan	McMaster	McAtee	Gallacher 2	McInally 1	Cassidy 1	McLean 1
Apr 14	Albion Rovers	5-0	Shaw	McNair	Dodds	McStay 1	Cringan	McMaster	McAtee	Gallacher 1	McInally 2	Cassidy	McLean 1
Apr 17	Motherwell	0-0	Shaw	McNair	Dodds	McStay	Cringan	McMaster	McFarlane	Gallacher	McInally	Cassidy	McLean
Apr 19	Hibernian	2-1	Shaw	McNair	Dodds	McStay	Cringan	McMaster	McFarlane	McKay	McInally 2	Cassidy	McLean
Apr 22	ST MIRREN	2-2	Shaw	Livingstone	McStay P	McMaster	Cringan	Dodds	McFarlane	McMenemy	McInally 1	Cassidy	McLean
Apr 24	AYR UNITED	4-0	Shaw	McNair	Livingstone	Gilchrist	Cringan	McStay	Watson 1	McKay 2	Craig 1	Cassidy	McLean
Apr 26	DUNDEE	1-1	Shaw	McNair	Livingstone	Gilchrist	Cringan	McStay P	McMaster	McKay	Craig	Cassidy	McLean
Apr 28	AIRDRIE	1-0	Shaw	McNair	Livingstone	McStay	Cringan	McMaster	Watson	McKay 1	McInally	Craig	McLean
May 1	HEARTS	3-0	Shaw	McNair	Livingstone	McStay	Cringan 1	McMaster	Gilchrist	McKay 1	McInally 1	Cassidy	McLean

SCOTTISH CUP 1920

Feb 7	Dundee	3-1	Shaw	McNair	Dodds	McStay	Cringan 1	McMaster	McAtee	McMenemy	McInally 1	Cassidy	McLean 1
Feb 21	PARTICK THISTLE	2-0	Shaw	McNair	Dodds	McStay 1	Cringan	McMaster	McAtee	McMenemy	McInally 1	Cassidy	McLean
Mar 6	Rangers	0-1	Shaw	McNair	Dodds	McStay	Cringan	McMaster	McAtee	McMenemy	Gallacher	Cassidy	McLean

LEAGUE 1920-21

Aug 18	Hamilton Academicals	1-1	Shaw	McNair	McStay	Gilchrist	Cringan	McMaster	McAtee	Gallacher	McInally 1	Cassidy	McLean
Aug 21	Albion Rovers	1-0	Shaw	McNair	McStay	Gilchrist	Cringan	McMaster 1	Watson	McKay	McInally	Cassidy	McLean
Aug 28	Aberdeen	2-1	Shaw	McNair	McStay P	Gilchrist	Cringan	McMaster	McAtee	McLean	McInally	Cassidy	Pratt + OG

			1	2	3	4	5	6	7	8	9	10	11
Sept 1	MORTON	1-1	Shaw	McNair	McStay	Gilchrist	Cringan	McMaster	McAtee	Gallacher	McInally 1	Cassidy	McLean
Sept 7	MOTHERWELL	1-0	Shaw	McNair	McStay	Gilchrist	Pratt	McMaster	McAtee	Gallacher	McInally 1	Cassidy	McLean
Sept 11	HAMILTON ACADEMICALS	2-1	Shaw	McNair	McStay	Gilchrist	Pratt	McMaster	McAtee	Gallacher	McInally 1	Cassidy 1	Miller
Sept 20	Hibernian	3-0	Shaw	McNair	McStay	Gilchrist	Cringan	McMaster	McAtee	Gallacher	McInally 1	Cassidy 1	McLean 1
Sept 25	AYR UNITED	3-1	Shaw	McNair	McStay	Gilchrist	Cringan	McMaster	McAtee 1	Gallacher	McInally 1	Cassidy 1	McLean
Sept 27	THIRD LANARK	3-0	Shaw	McNair	McStay	Gilchrist 1	Cringan	Pratt	McAtee	Gallacher	McInally 1	Cassidy	McLean 1
Oct 9	QUEEN'S PARK	5-1	Shaw	McNair	McStay	Gilchrist	Cringan	Pratt	McAtee	Gallacher 1	McInally	Cassidy 3	McLean +OG
Oct 12	FALKIRK	4-1	Shaw	McNair	McStay	Gilchrist	Cringan	Pratt	McAtee	Gallacher	McInally 2	Cassidy 1	McLean 1
Oct 16	Dundee	2-1	Shaw	McNair	McStay	Gilchrist	Cringan	Pratt	McAtee 1	Gallacher	McInally 1	Cassidy	McLean
Oct 23	RANGERS	1-2	Shaw	McNair	McStay	Gilchrist	Cringan	Pratt	McAtee	Gallacher	McInally	Cassidy 1	McLean
Oct 26	ALBION ROVERS	0-2	Shaw	McNair	McStay	Gilchrist	Cringan	Pratt	McFarlane	Gallacher	Craig	Cassidy	McLean
Oct 30	Hearts	1-0	Shaw	McNair	Livingstone	Gilchrist	Cringan	McStay	McAtee	Gallacher	McLean	Cassidy 1	Pratt
Nov 6	Dumbarton	3-1	Shaw	McNair	Livingstone	Gilchrist	Cringan 1	McStay	McAtee	Gallacher	McLean 1	Cassidy 1	Pratt
Nov 13	KILMARNOCK	2-0	Shaw	McNair	McStay	Price	Cringan	McMaster	McAtee	Gallacher 1	McInally	Cassidy 1	McLean
Nov 20	Clyde	1-2	Shaw	McNair	McStay	Price	Cringan	McMaster	McAtee	Gallacher	McInally 1	Cassidy	McLean
Nov 27	RAITH ROVERS	5-0	Shaw	McNair	McStay	McMaster	Cringan 1	Pratt	McAtee 1	Gallacher 1	Longmuir 2	Cassidy	McLean
Dec 4	Falkirk	3-1	Shaw	McNair	McStay	McMaster	Cringan	Cassidy	McAtee	Gallacher	McInally 2	McFarlane	McLean 1
Dec 11	PARTICK THISTLE	1-0	Shaw	McNair	McStay	Murphy	Cringan	McMaster	McAtee	Gallacher 1	McInally	Cassidy	McLean
Dec 18	AIRDRIE	2-1	Shaw	McNair	McStay	Murphy	Cringan	McMaster	McAtee	Gallacher 1	McInally 1	Cassidy	McLean
Dec 25	St Mirren	2-0	Shaw	McNair	McStay	Murphy	Cringan	McMaster	McAtee	Gallacher	McInally 1	Cassidy 1	McFarlane
Jan 1	Rangers	2-0	Shaw	McNair	McStay	Gilchrist	Cringan	McMaster	McAtee	Gallacher	McInally	Cassidy 2	McLean
Jan 3	CLYDE	1-0	Shaw	McNair	McStay	Gilchrist	Cringan	McMaster	McAtee	Gallacher	McInally	Cassidy 1	McLean
Jan 8	Clydebank	2-0	Shaw	Glasgow	Livingstone	Gilchrist	Cringan	Murphy	McAtee 1	Gallacher	McInally 1	Cassidy	McLean
Jan 15	Morton	1-1	Shaw	Murphy	Livingstone	Gilchrist	Cringan	McMaster	McAtee	Gallacher	McInally 1	Cassidy	McLean
Jan 22	Motherwell	1-1	Shaw	McNair	McStay	Gilchrist	Murphy	McMaster	McAtee	Gallacher	McInally	Cassidy	McLean +OG
Jan 29	ABERDEEN	3-1	Shaw	Livingstone	McStay P	McFarlane	Murphy	McMaster	McAtee	Gallacher	McInally 1	Cassidy	McLean 1
Feb 12	ST MIRREN	6-0	Shaw	Livingstone	Glasgow	Gilchrist	Murphy	McMaster	McAtee	Gallacher 2	McInally 3	McFarlane	McLean 1
Feb 23	Third Lanark	2-1	Shaw	Livingstone	McStay	Gilchrist	Murphy	McMaster	McLean 1	Gallacher	McInally 1	Cassidy	McFarlane
Feb 26	Queen's Park	2-0	Shaw	Murphy	Livingstone	Gilchrist	Pratt	McMaster 1	Watson	Gallacher 1	McInally	McLean	McFarlane
Mar 9	DUNDEE	2-0	Shaw	Livingstone	McStay	Murphy	Pratt	McMaster	McAtee	Gallacher	McInally 2	Cassidy	McLean
Mar 12	Ayr United	1-3	Shaw	Livingstone	Murphy	McFarlane	Pratt	McMaster	Watson	Gallacher	McInally	McKay	McLean 1
Mar 19	HEARTS	3-2	Shaw	Murphy	McStay 2P	Gilchrist	Pratt	McMaster	McLean	Gallacher	Longmuir	Cassidy 1	McFarlane
Mar 26	Kilmarnock	2-3	Shaw	Murphy	McStay	Gilchrist	Pratt	McMaster	McLean	Gallacher	McInally 1	Cassidy 1	McFarlane
Mar 28	Partick Thistle	1-0	Shaw	Livingstone	McStay	Gilchrist	Pratt	McMaster	McLean	Gallacher 1	McInally	Cassidy	McFarlane
Apr 2	DUMBARTON	1-1	Shaw	Livingstone	McStay P	Gilchrist	Murphy	McMaster	McLean	Gallacher	McInally	Cassidy	McFarlane
Apr 9	Raith Rovers	0-2	Shaw	Livingstone	McStay	Gilchrist	Pratt	McMaster	McLean	McKay	McInally	Cassidy	McFarlane
Apr 20	CLYDEBANK	1-1	Shaw	McNair	McStay	Gilchrist	Pratt	McMaster	Gallacher	McKay P	McInally	Cassidy	McLean
Apr 23	HIBERNIAN	3-0	Shaw	McNair	McStay	Gilchrist	Murphy	McMaster	McLean	Gallacher	McInally 2	Cassidy	Miller 1
Apr 30	Airdrie	3-2	Shaw	McNair	Murphy	Gilchrist	McStay	McMaster	McLean 1	Gallacher 1	McInally 1	Cassidy	Miller

SCOTTISH CUP 1921

Feb 5	Vale of Leven	3-0	Shaw	Livingstone	McStay	Gilchrist	Murphy	McMaster	McAtee	Gallacher	McInally	Cassidy 2	McLean 1
Feb 19	East Fife	3-1	Shaw	Livingstone	McStay	Gilchrist	Murphy	McMaster	McLean	Gallacher 1	McInally 2	Cassidy	McFarlane
Mar 5	HEARTS	1-2	Shaw	Livingstone	McStay	Gilchrist	Murphy	McMaster	McAtee	Gallacher 1	McInally	Cassidy	McLean

SCOTTISH LEAGUE 1921-22

Aug 15	RAITH ROVERS	4-0	Shaw	McStay	Dodds	Gilchrist	Cringan	McMaster	McAtee 1	Gallacher	Longmuir 2	Cassidy 1	McLean
Aug 20	HIBERNIAN	3-1	Shaw	McStay	Dodds	Gilchrist	Cringan	McMaster	McAtee	Gallacher	Longmuir 2	Cassidy 1	McLean
Aug 24	Airdrie	2-0	Shaw	McNair	Dodds	Gilchrist	McStay	McFarlane	McAtee	Gallacher 1	Longmuir	Cassidy	McLean 1
Aug 27	Raith Rovers	1-1	Shaw	McNair	Dodds	Gilchrist	Cringan	McMaster	McAtee	Gallacher	Longmuir	Cassidy	McLean 1
Sept 6	DUMBARTON	4-0	Collins	McNair	Dodds	Gilchrist	Cringan	McMaster	McAtee	Gallacher 1	McInally 2	Cassidy 1	McLean
Sept 10	Aberdeen	1-1	Shaw	McNair	Dodds	Gilchrist	Cringan	McMaster	McAtee	Gallacher	McInally 1	Cassidy	McLean
Sept 19	Hibernian	1-2	Shaw	McNair	Dodds	Gilchrist	Cringan	McMaster	McAtee	Gallacher 1	McInally	Cassidy	Pratt
Sept 24	Dumbarton	5-0	Shaw	McNair	McStay	Gilchrist	Cringan	Murphy	McMaster	Gallacher 1	McInally 2	Cassidy	McLean 2
Sept 26	MORTON	1-0	Shaw	McNair	McStay	Gilchrist	Cringan	Murphy	McLean 1	Gallacher	Longmuir	Cassidy	McFarlane
Oct 4	ST MIRREN	2-0	Shaw	McNair	McStay	Gilchrist	Cringan	Murphy	McAtee	Gallacher 1	McInally	Cassidy 1	Longmuir
Oct 8	Dundee	0-0	Shaw	McNair	Mcstay	Gilchrist	Cringan	Murphy	McAtee	Gallacher	McInally	Cassidy	Longmuir
Oct 15	ALBION ROVERS	3-1	Shaw	McNair	McStay	Gilchrist 1	Cringan	Murphy	McAtee	Gallacher 1	McInally 1	Cassidy	Miller
Oct 22	Rangers	1-1	Shaw	McNair	McStay	Gilchrist	Cringan	Murphy	McAtee	Gallacher	McInally 1	Cassidy	Longmuir
Oct 29	AYR UNITED	2-1	Shaw	McNair	McStay P	Gilchrist	Cringan	Murphy	McAtee	Gallacher	McInally 1	Cassidy	Miller
Nov 5	HEARTS	3-0	Shaw	McNair	McStay	Gilchrist	Cringan	McMaster	McAtee	Gallacher	McInally	Cassidy 1	Dodds 2
Nov 12	Kilmarnock	3-4	Shaw	McNair	McStay	Gilchrist	Cringan	McMaster	McAtee	Gallacher	McInally 3	Cassidy	McLean
Nov 19	QUEEN'S PARK	3-1	Collins	McNair	McStay 1	Gilchrist	Cringan	McMaster	McAtee	McLean	McInally 1	Cassidy 1	Dodds
Nov 26	Motherwell	1-1	Shaw	McNair	McStay	Gilchrist	Cringan	Murphy	McAtee	Cassidy 1	McInally	Craig	McMaster
Dec 3	AIRDRIE	1-0	Shaw	McNair	Murphy	Gilchrist	Cringan	McMaster	McAtee	Gallacher	McInally	Cassidy 1	McLean
Dec 10	Ayr United	0-0	Shaw	McNair	Dodds	Gilchrist	Cringan	McMaster	McAtee	Gallacher	Craig	Cassidy	McLean
Dec 17	CLYDEBANK	6-0	Shaw	McNair	Dodds P	Gilchrist	Cringan	McMaster	McAtee	Gallacher 1	McLean 1	Cassidy 2	McFarlane 1
Dec 24	FALKIRK	0-0	Shaw	McNair	Dodds	Gilchrist	McStay	Cringan	McAtee	Gallacher	McLean	Cassidy	McFarlane
Dec 31	Hamilton Academicals	3-1	Shaw	McStay P	Dodds	Gilchrist	Cringan	McMaster	McAtee 1	Gallacher 1	McInally	Cassidy	McLean
Jan 2	RANGERS	0-0	Shaw	McNair	Dodds	Gilchrist	Cringan	McMaster	McAtee	Gallacher	McInally	Cassidy	McLean
Jan 3	Clyde	1-1	Shaw	McNair	Dodds	Gilchrist	Cringan	McMaster	Connolly	Gallacher 1	McInally	Cassidy	McLean
Jan 7	THIRD LANARK	2-0	Shaw	McNair	McStay	Gilchrist	Cringan	McMaster	Connolly	Gallacher 1	McInally 1	Cassidy	McLean
Jan 14	Clydebank	2-0	Shaw	McNair	Dodds	Gilchrist	Cringan	Murphy	McAtee	Gallacher 1	McInally	McFarlane 1	McLean
Jan 21	ABERDEEN	2-0	Shaw	McNair	Dodds	Gilchrist	Cringan	McStay	McAtee	Gallacher	McInally 1	McFarlane 1	McLean
Feb 4	Partick Thistle	0-0	Shaw	McNair	Dodds	Gilchrist	Cringan	McStay	McAtee	Gallacher	McInally	McFarlane	McLean
Feb 14	St Mirren	2-0	Shaw	McNair	Dodds	Gilchrist	Cringan	McMaster	McAtee	Gallacher	McInally 2	Cassidy	McLean
Feb 18	CLYDE	1-0	Shaw	McNair	McStay	Gilchrist	Cringan	McMaster	McAtee	Gallacher	McInally	Cassidy 1	McLean
Mar 1	HAMILTON ACADEMICALS	4-0	Shaw	McNair	Dodds P	Gilchrist	Cringan	McMaster	McAtee	Gallacher	McInally 1	McFarlane	McLean 2
Mar 4	Third Lanark	0-0	Shaw	McNair	Dodds	Gilchrist	McStay	McMaster	McAtee	Cassidy	Hilley	McFarlane	McLean
Mar 11	KILMARNOCK	1-0	Shaw	McNair	Dodds	Gilchrist	McStay	McMaster	McAtee	Gallacher	McFarlane	Cassidy 1	McLean
Mar 15	MOTHERWELL	2-0	Shaw	McNair	Dodds	Gilchrist	Cringan	McStay	McAtee	Gallacher 2	Glancy	Cassidy	McLean
Mar 18	FALKIRK	1-1	Shaw	McNair	Dodds	Gilchrist	Cringan	McStay	McAtee	Gallacher	McLean	Cassidy 1	McFarlane
Mar 25	Hearts	2-1	Shaw	McNair	Dodds	Gilchrist	Cringan	McStay	McAtee 1	Gallacher	Cassidy 1	McFarlane	McLean
Apr 1	Queen's Park	3-1	Shaw	McNair	Dodds	Gilchrist 1	Cringan	McStay	McAtee	Gallacher	Cassidy 2	McFarlane	McLean
Apr 8	DUNDEE	4-0	Shaw	McNair	Dodds	Murphy	McStay	McMaster	McAtee 1	Gallacher 1	Cassidy 2	McFarlane	McLean
Apr 15	Albion Rovers	2-0	Shaw	McNair	Dodds	Gilchrist	McStay	McMaster	McAtee	Gallacher 1	Cassidy	McFarlane 1	McLean
Apr 17	PARTICK THISTLE	3-0	Shaw	McNair	Dodds	Gilchrist	Cringan	McStay 1	McAtee	Gallacher 2	Cassidy	McFarlane	McLean
Apr 29	Morton	1-1	Shaw	McNair	Dodds	Gilchrist	Cringan	McMaster	McAtee 1	Gallacher	Cassidy	McFarlane	McLean

SCOTTISH CUP 1922

Jan 28	MONTROSE	4-0	Shaw	McNair	Dodds	Gilchrist	Cringan	McMaster	McAtee	Gallacher	McInally 1	McFarlane 2	McLean 1
Feb 11	Third Lanark	1-0	Shaw	McNair	Dodds	Gilchrist	Cringan	McStay	McAtee	Gallacher	McInally	Cassidy	McLean 1
Feb 25	HAMILTON ACADEMICALS	1-3	Shaw	McNair	Dodds P	Gilchrist	Cringan	McMaster	McAtee	Gallacher	McInally	Cassidy	McLean

SCOTTISH LEAGUE 1922-23

Aug 19	Alloa Athletic	3-2	Shaw	McNair	Hilley	Gilchrist	Cringan	McStay P	McAtee	Gallacher 1	Cassidy 1	McFarlane	McLean
Aug 26	HAMILTON ACADEMICALS	2-1	Shaw	McNair	Hilley	Gilchrist	Cringan	McStay	McAtee	Gallacher	Crilly	Cassidy 1	McLean 1
Sept 9	RAITH ROVERS	3-0	Shaw	McStay	Hilley	Gilchrist 1	Cringan	McFarlane	McAtee	Gallacher	Crilly	Cassidy 1	McLean 1
Sept 18	Hibernian	0-1	Shaw	McStay	Hilley	Gilchrist	Cringan	McFarlane	McAtee	Gallacher	Crilly	Cassidy	McLean
Sept 23	Dundee	1-0	Shaw	McStay	Hilley	Gilchrist	Cringan	McFarlane	McAtee	Gallacher	Cassidy	JB Murphy 1	McLean
Sept 25	Aberdeen	1-3	Shaw	McNair	Hilley	Gilchrist	Cringan	McMaster	McAtee	Gallacher	Cassidy 1	JB Murphy	McFarlane
Oct 7	PARTICK THISTLE	4-3	Shaw	McNair	Hilley	Gilchrist	Cringan	McFarlane 1	Connolly	Gallacher 2 (1P)	Cassidy 1	Cairney	JB Murphy

			1	2	3	4	5	6	7	8	9	10	11
Oct 14	MOTHERWELL	1-0	Hughes	McNair	Hilley	Gilchrist	Cringan	McStay	Connolly	Gallacher	Cassidy 1	McFarlane	JB Murphy
Oct 21	Morton	1-0	Hughes	McStay	Hilley	Gilchrist	Cringan	McFarlane	McAtee	Gallacher	Cassidy 1	JB Murphy	Connolly
Oct 28	RANGERS	1-3	Hughes	McNair	Hilley	Gilchrist	Cringen	McStay	McAtee	Gallacher 1	Cassidy	McFarlane	Connolly
Nov 4	Clyde	1-0	Hughes	Cringan	JB Murphy	Gilchrist	W McStay	J McStay	McAtee	Gallacher	McFarlane 1	Thomson	Connolly
Nov 11	AYR UNITED	1-4	Hughes	Cringan	J B Murphy	Gilchrist	W McStay P	J McStay	Connolly	Gallacher	McLean	Thomson	McFarlane
Nov 18	Airdrie	0-1	Shaw	McNair	W McStay	Gilchrist	Cringan	J McStay	Connolly	Gallacher	Cassidy	Thomson	McFarlane
Nov 25	THIRD LANARK	3-0	Shaw	McNair	W McStay	Gilchrist	Cringan	J McStay	Connolly	Gallacher	Cassidy 3	McFarlane	McLean
Dec 2	Albion Rovers	3-2	Shaw	McNair	W McStay	Gilchrist	Cringan	J McStay	Connolly	Gallacher 1	Cassidy 1	McFarlane	McLean +OG
Dec 9	FALKIRK	1-1	Shaw	McNair	W McStay 1	Gilchrist	Cringan	J McStay	McAtee	Gallacher	Cassidy	McFarlane	McLean
Dec 16	Hearts	3-0	Shaw	McNair	W McStay	Gilchrist	Cringan	J McStay	McAtee	Gallacher 1	McLean 1	McFarlane 1	Connolly
Dec 23	KILMARNOCK	1-2	Shaw	McNair	W McStay	Gilchrist	Cringan	J McStay	McAtee	Gallacher	McLean 1	McFarlane	Connolly
Dec 30	Raith Rovers	3-0	Shaw	JB Murphy	W McStay	Gilchrist 1	Cringan	J McStay	McAtee	J F Murphy	Cassidy 2	McFarlane	McLean
Jan 1	Rangers	0-2	Shaw	JB Murphy	W McStay	Gilchrist	Cringan	McMaster	McAtee	Gallacher	Cassidy	McFarlane	McLean
Jan 2	CLYDE	0-0	Shaw	JB Murphy	W McStay	Gilchrist	Cringan	McMaster	Connolly	Cairney	Cassidy	McFarlane	McLean
Jan 6	ABERDEEN	1-2	Shaw	JB Murphy	W McStay	Gilchrist	Cringan	McMaster	Connolly	Cairney	Cassidy 1	McFarlane	McLean
Jan 20	Third Lanark	0-1	Shaw	W McStay	Hilley	Gilchrist	Cringan	J McStay	McAtee	McGrory	Cassidy	McFarlane	McLean
Jan 31	HIBERNIAN	0-0	Shaw	McNair	Hilley	W McStay	Cringan	J McStay	McAtee	McGrory	Cassidy	McFarlane	McLean
Feb 3	Kilmarnock	3-4	Shaw	W McStay	Hilley	J McStay	Cringan	McFarlane	McAtee 1	McGrory 1	McLean	Cassidy 1	Connolly
Feb 14	ALBION ROVERS	1-1	Shaw	W McStay	Hilley	J McStay	Cringan	McFarlane	McAtee	Gallacher	Cassidy P	McLean	Connolly
Feb 17	Falkirk	0-0	Shaw	Hilley	Grainger	J McStay	Cringan	McFarlane	Gallacher	McLean	Cassidy	Thomson	Connolly
Feb 27	ST MIRREN	1-0	Shaw	Hilley	W McStay	Grainger	Cringan	McFarlane	McAtee	Gallacher	Cassidy 1	McLean	Connolly
Mar 3	ALLOA ATHLETIC	1-0	Shaw	McNair	Hilley	J McStay	W McStay	Grainger	McAtee	Thomson	McLean	J F Murphy 1	Connolly
Mar 14	Hamilton Academicals	1-1	Shaw	Hilley	W McStay	J McStay	Cringan	Grainger	McAtee	McFarlane	Cassidy 1	McLean	Connolly
Mar 17	DUNDEE	2-1	Shaw	McNair	Hilley	J McStay	W McStay 2(1P)	McFarlane	McAtee	Gallacher	Cassidy	McLean	Connolly
Mar 24	MORTON	3-1	Shaw	McNair	Hilley	J McStay	W McStay	McFarlane	McAtee	Gallacher	Cassidy 3	McLean	Connolly
Apr 2	Partick Thistle	2-0	Shaw	Hilley	W McStay	J McStay	Cringan	McFarlane	McAtee	Gallacher 2	Cassidy	McLean	Connolly
Apr 7	HEARTS	2-1	Shaw	McNair	Hilley	J McStay	Cringan	McFarlane	Thomson 1	Gallacher	Cassidy 1	McLean	Connolly
Apr 10	St Mirren	0-1	Shaw	McNair	Hilley	J McStay	Cringan	McFarlane	Thomson	Gallacher	Cassidy	McLean	Connolly
Apr 21	Motherwell	0-0	Shaw	McNair	W McStay	J McStay	Cringan	McFarlane	McAtee	Gallacher	Cassidy	McLean	Connolly
Apr 26	Ayr United	1-0	Shaw	McNair	W McStay	J McStay	Cringan	McFarlane	McAtee	Gallacher	Cassidy 1	McLean	Thomson
Apr 28	AIRDRIE	1-1	Shaw	McNair	W McStay P	J McStay	Cringan	McFarlane	McAtee	Gallacher	Cassidy	McLean	Thomson

SCOTTISH CUP 1923

Jan 13	Lochgelly Utd	3-2	Shaw	McNair	W McStay	Gilchrist	Cringan	J McStay	McAtee	Cairney	Cassidy 3	McFarlane	McLean
Jan 27	HURLFORD	4-0	Shaw	Hilley	W McStay	J McStay	Cringan	J F Murphy	McAtee	McGrory	Cassidy 4	McFarlane	McLean
Feb 10	EAST FIFE	2-1	Shaw	W McStay	Hilley	J McStay	Cringan	McFarlane	McAtee	Gallacher	Cassidy 2	McLean	Connolly
Feb 24	RAITH ROVERS	1-0	Shaw	McNair	W McStay	J McStay	Cringan	McFarlane	McAtee	Gallacher	Cassidy	McLean 1	Connolly
Mar 10	Motherwell	2-0 SF	Shaw	McNair	W McStay	J McStay	Cringan	McFarlane	McAtee 1	Gallacher	Cassidy 1	McLean	Connolly
Mar 31	Hibernian	1-0 F	Shaw	McNair	W McStay	J McStay	Cringan	McFarlane	McAtee	Gallacher	Cassidy 1	McLean	Connolly

SCOTTISH LEAGUE 1923-24

Aug 18	FALKIRK	2-1	Shaw	McNair	Hilley	Grainger	Cringan	McFarlane	McAtee	Gallacher	Cassidy 2	McLean	Connolly
Aug 25	Clydebank	0-0	Shaw	W McStay	Hilley	J McStay	Cringan	Grainger	Connolly	Gallacher	Cassidy	McFarlane	McLean
Sept 1	PARTICK THISTLE	1-2	Shaw	McNair	Hilley	Grainger	Cringan	McFarlane	Connolly	Gallacher	Cassidy 1	McLaughlin	McLean
Sept 8	Queen's Park	2-0	Shaw	W McStay	Hilley	J McStay	Cringan	McFarlane	McAtee	Gallacher	Cassidy 1	McLean 1	Connolly
Sept 17	Hibernian	0-0	Shaw	W McStay	Hilley	J McStay	Cringan	McFarlane	McAtee	Gallacher	McLean	Thomson	Connolly
Sept 22	Ayr United	2-4	Shaw	W McStay	Hilley	J McStay	Cringan	McFarlane	McAtee 1	Gallacher 1	Cassidy	McLean	Connolly
Sept 24	MORTON	3-0	Shaw	McNair	Hilley	J McStay	W McStay P	McFarlane	McAtee 1	Gallacher	Cassidy 1	Thomson	McLean
Sept 29	Aberdeen	2-0	Shaw	McNair	Hilley	J McStay	W McStay	McFarlane	McAtee	Gallacher	Cassidy	Thomson	McLean 2
Oct 6	CLYDE	4-0	Shaw	McNair	Hilley	J McStay	W McStay	Grainger	Connolly	Gallacher	Cassidy 3	Thomson	McLean 1
Oct 13	Hearts	0-0	Shaw	McNair	Hilley	J McStay	W McStay	McFarlane	McAtee	Gallacher	Cassidy	Thomson	McLean
Oct 20	RAITH ROVERS	0-0	Shaw	McNair	Hilley	J McStay	W McStay	Grainger	McAtee	Gallacher	Cassidy	Thomson	McLean
Oct 27	Rangers	0-0	Shaw	McNair	Hilley	J McStay	W McStay	McFarlane	McAtee	Gallacher	Cassidy	Thomson	McLean
Nov 3	AIRDRIE	2-2	Shaw	McNair	Hilley	J McStay	W McStay P	McFarlane	Connolly	Gallacher	Cassidy 1	Thomson	McLean
Nov 10	Hamilton Academicals	5-2	Shaw	McNair	Hilley	J McStay	W McStay	McFarlane	McAtee	Gallacher 1	Cassidy 1	Thomson 1	McLean 2
Nov 17	DUNDEE	0-0	Shaw	McNair	Hilley	J McStay	W McStay	McFarlane	McAtee	Gallacher	Cassidy	Thomson	McLean
Nov 24	St Mirren	1-0	Shaw	McNair	Hilley	J McStay	W McStay	McFarlane	McAtee	Gallacher	Cassidy 1	Thomson	McLean
Dec 1	THIRD LANARK	3-1	Shaw	McNair	Hilley	J McStay	W McStay	McFarlane	McAtee	Gallacher 1	Cassidy 1	Thomson	McLean 1
Dec 8	Kilmarnock	1-1	Shaw	McNair	Hilley	J McStay	W McStay	McFarlane	McAtee	Gallacher	Cassidy	Thomson 1	McLean
Dec 15	MOTHERWELL	2-1	Shaw	McNair	Hilley	J McStay	W McStay	McFarlane 1	McAtee	Gallacher	Cassidy 1	Thomson	McLean
Dec 22	Dundee	1-2	Shaw	McNair	Hilley	J McStay	W McStay	McFarlane	McAtee	Gallacher	Cassidy 1	Thomson	McLean
Jan 1	RANGERS	2-2	Shaw	McNair	Hilley	J McStay	W McStay P	McFarlane	Connolly	Gallacher	Cassidy	Thomson 1	McLean
Jan 2	Clyde	0-0	Shaw	Grainger	Hilley	J McStay	W McStay	McFarlane	Connoly	Gallacher	Cassidy	Thomson	McLean
Jan 5	HAMILTON ACADEMICALS	1-0	Shaw	McNair	Hilley	J McStay	W McStay	McFarlane	McAtee	Gallacher	Cassidy 1	Thomson	McLean
Jan 12	Third Lanark	3-1	Shaw	Grainger	Hilley	J McStay	W McStay	McFarlane	McAtee	Gallacher	Cassidy 2	Thomson	McLean 1
Jan 19	ABERDEEN	4-0	Shaw	McNair	Hilley	J McStay	W McStay	McFarlane	McAtee	Gallacher 1	Cassidy 2	Thomson	McLean 1
Feb 2	Morton	0-1	Shaw	McNair	Hilley	J McStay	McGhee	McFarlane	McAtee	Gallacher	Cassidy	Thomson	McLean
Feb 13	Motherwell	1-0	Shaw	McNair	Hilley	Wilson	J McStay	McFarlane	McAtee	Gallacher	Cassidy	Thomson	McLean +OG
Feb 16	QUEEN'S PARK	1-0	Shaw	McNair	Hilley	Wilson	J McStay	McFarlane	McAtee	Gallacher	McLean 1	Thomson	Connolly
Feb 26	HEARTS	4-1	Shaw	McNair	Hilley	Wilson	J McStay	McFarlane 1	McAtee	Gallacher	Cassidy 3	Thomson	McLean
Mar 1	Partick Thistle	1-1	Shaw	McNair	Hilley	J McStay	W McStay	Wilson	McAtee	Thomson	Cassidy 1	McFarlane	Connolly
Mar 4	CLYDEBANK	1-2	Shaw	Grainger	W McStay 1	Wilson	J McStay	McFarlane	McAtee	Gilgun	Cassidy	Thomson	Connolly
Mar 8	KILMARNOCK	2-1	Shaw	McNair	W McStay	Wilson	J McStay	McFarlane	Connolly 1	Gallacher	Cassidy 1	Thomson	McLean
Mar 15	Falkirk	1-3	Shaw	McNair	W McStay	Wilson	J McStay	McFarlane	McAtee	McLean	Gilgun	Thomson	Connolly 1
Mar 22	Raith Rovers	0-1	Shaw	McNair	W McStay	Wilson	J McStay	McFarlane	McAtee	Gallacher	McLean	Thomson	Connolly
Mar 29	Airdrie	0-2	Shaw	McNair	W McStay	Wilson	J McStay	McFarlane	McAtee	Gallacher	McLean	Thomson	Connolly
Apr 5	AYR UNITED	3-0	Shaw	McNair	Hilley	J McStay	W McStay	McFarlane	McAtee	Gallacher 1	Cassidy 1	Thomson	Connolly 1
Apr 12	ST MIRREN	0-1	Shaw	W McStay	Hilley	Wilson	J McStay	McFarlane	McAtee	Gallacher	Cassidy	Thomson	Connolly
Apr 26	HIBERNIAN	1-1	Shaw	W McStay	Hilley	Wilson	J McStay	McFarlane	Thomson	Gallacher	Cassidy	Gilgun 1	Connolly

SCOTTISH CUP 1924

Jan 24	Kilmarnock	0-2	Shaw	McNair	Hilley	J McStay	W McStay	McFarlane	McAtee	Gallacher	Cassidy	Thomson	McLean

LEAGUE 1924-25

Aug 16	Dundee	0-0	Shaw	Grainger	Hilley	J McStay	W McStay	McFarlane	Connolly	Gallacher	McGrory	Thomson	McLean
Aug 19	Partick Thistle	2-2	Shaw	McNair	Hilley	J McStay	W McStay P	McFarlane	Connolly	Gallacher	McGrory	Thomson 1	McLean
Aug 23	AIRDRIE	1-1	Shaw	McNair	Hilley	J McStay	W McStay	McFarlane	Connolly	Gallacher 1	McGrory	Thomson	McLean
Aug 30	Falkirk	2-1	Shaw	W McStay	Hilley	Wilson	J McStay	McFarlane	Connolly	Gallacher 1	McGrory 1	Thomson	McLean
Sept 6	Aberdeen	4-0	Shaw	W McStay	Hilley	Wilson	J McStay	McFarlane	Connolly	Gallacher	McGrory	Thomson 1	McLean 3
Sept 13	ST MIRREN	5-0	Shaw	W McStay P	Hilley	Wilson	J McStay	McFarlane	Connolly	Gallacher 1	McGrory 1	Thomson 1	McLean 1
Sept 15	Hibernian	3-2	Shaw	W McStay	Hiley	Wilson	J McStay	McFarlane	Connolly	Gallacher	McGrory 2	Thomson	McLean 1
Sept 27	MOTHERWELL	4-0	Shaw	W McStay	Hilley	Wilson	J McStay	McFarlane	Connolly	Gallacher 1	McGrory 3	Thomson	McLean
Sept 29	COWDENBEATH	3-1	Shaw	W McStay P	Hilley	Wilson	J McStay	McFarlane	Leitch	Gallacher	McLean 2	Thomson	Connolly
Oct 11	HEARTS	1-0	Shaw	McNair	Hilley	Wilson P	J McStay	McFarlane	Connolly	Gallacher	McGrory	Thomson	McLean
Oct 18	St Johnstone	0-0	Shevlin	W McStay	Hilley	Wilson	J McStay	McFarlane	Connolly	Gallacher	McGrory	Thomson	McLean
Oct 25	RANGERS	0-1	Shevlin	W McStay	Hilley	Wilson	J McStay	McFarlane	Connolly	Gallacher	McGrory	Thomson	Corrigan
Nov 1	Morton	0-1	Shevlin	W McStay	Hilley	Wilson	J McStay	McFarlane	Connolly	Gallacher	McGrory	Thomson	Blair
Nov 8	KILMARNOCK	6-0	Shevlin	W McStay	Hilley	Wilson 1	J McStay	McFarlane	Healey	Gallacher	Fleming 4	Thomson	Connolly 1
Nov 15	Queen's Park	1-3	Shevlin	W McStay 1	Hilley	Wilson	J McStay	McFarlane	Healey	Gallacher	Fleming	Thomson	Connolly
Nov 22	Third Lanark	1-1	Shevlin	McNair	Hilley	Wilson	W McStay	J McStay	Connolly	Gallacher	Fleming 1	McFarlane	Thomson
Nov 29	PARTICK THISTLE	1-2	Shevlin	McNair	Hilley	J McStay	W McStay	McFarlane	Leitch	Gallacher	Fleming	Thomson 1	Connolly

			1	2	3	4	5	6	7	8	9	10	11
Dec 6	AYR UNITED	2-0	Shevlin	W McStay	Hilley	J McStay	Wilson	McFarlane	Connolly	Gallacher 1	Fleming	Thomson 1	McLean
Dec 13	Hearts	1-3	Shevlin	W McStay	Hilley	Wilson	J McStay	McFarlane	Connolly	Gallacher 1	Fleming	Thomson	McLean
Dec 20	HAMILTON ACADEMICALS	0-2	Shevlin	W McStay	Hilley	Wilson	J McStay	McFarlane	Connolly	Blair	Fleming	Thomson	McLean
Dec 27	Raith Rovers	2-2	Shevlin	McNair	Hilley	J McStay	W McStay	McFarlane	Connolly 1	Wilson	Fleming 1	Thomson	McLean
Jan 1	Rangers	1-4	Shevlin	W McStay	Hilley	Wilson	J McStay	McFarlane	Connolly	Corrigan	Fleming 1	Thomson	McLean
Jan 3	Airdrie	1-3	Shevlin	W McStay	Hilley	Wilson	J McStay	McFarlane	Connolly	Corrigan	Fleming	Thomson 1	McLean
Jan 5	THIRD LANARK	7-0	Shevlin	W McStay P	Hilley	J McStay 1	McGrogan	McFarlane	Connolly 2	Wilson	Fleming	Thomson 1	McLean 2
Jan 10	ABERDEEN	3-1	Shevlin	W McStay	Hilley	J McStay	McGrogan	McFarlane	Connolly	Wilson	Fleming 2	Thomson	Gallacher 2
Jan 17	Motherwell	0-1	Shaw	W McStay	Hilley	J McStay	McGrogan	McFarlane	Connolly	Gallacher	Fleming	Thomson	McGrory
Jan 31	HIBERNIAN	1-1	Shevlin	W McStay	Hilley	Wilson	J McStay	McFarlane	Connolly	Gallacher	McGrory	Thomson	McLean 1
Feb 11	Ayr United	2-1	Shevlin	McNair	Hilley	Fleming	McGrogan	McFarlane 1	Connolly	Wilson	McGrory	Thomson 1	Gallacher
Feb 14	ST JOHNSTONE	2-1	Shevlin	McNair	Hilley	Wilson	McGrogan	McFarlane	Connolly 1	Gallacher	Fleming	Thomson 1	McGrory
Feb 24	Hamilton Academicals	4-0	Shevlin	W McStay	Hilley	Wilson	J McStay	McFarlane	Connolly	Gallacher	McGrory 3	Thomson 1	McLean
Feb 28	DUNDEE	4-0	Shevlin	McNair	Hilley	Wilson	J McStay	McFarlane	Connolly	Fleming	McGrory 2	Thomson	McLean 2
Mar 14	Cowdenbeath	0-3	Shevlin	McNair	Hilley	Wilson	J McStay	Corrigan	Connolly	Fleming	McGrory	Thomson	Gordon
Mar 24	MORTON	2-1	Shevlin	W McStay	Hilley	Wilson 1	J McStay	McFarlane	Connolly	Fleming	McGrory	Thomson 1	McLean
Mar 28	RAITH ROVERS	2-0	Shevlin	W McStay	Hilley	Wilson	J McStay	McFarlane	Connolly	Gallacher	McGrory 1	Thomson 1	McLean
Apr 1	FALKIRK	6-1	Shevlin	W McStay	Hilley	Wilson	J McStay	McFarlane	Connolly	Gallacher	McGrory 4	Thomson 1	McLean 1
Apr 15	Kilmarnock	1-2	Shevlin	McNair	W McStay	Wilson	J McStay	McFarlane	Connolly	Fleming 1	McGrory	Thomson	McLean
Apr 18	QUEEN'S PARK	1-1	Shevlin	McNair	Hilley	J McStay	W McStay	McFarlane	Connolly 1	Wilson	McGrory	Thomson	McLean
Apr 25	St Mirren	1-2	Shevlin	W McStay	Hilley	Wilson P	J McStay	McFarlane	Connolly	Gallacher	McGrory	Thomson	McLean

SCOTTISH CUP 1925

Jan 24	Third Lanark	5-1	Shevlin	W McStay	Hilley	Wilson	J McStay	McFarlane	Connolly	Gallacher 1	McGrory 4	Thomson	McLean
Feb 7	ALLOA	2-1	Shevlin	W McStay	Hilley	Wilson	J McStay	McFarlane	Connolly	Gallacher	McGrory 2	Thomson	McLean
Feb 21	SOLWAY STAR	2-0	Shevlin	W McStay	Hilley	J McStay	McGrogan	McFarlane	Connolly	Gallacher	McGrory 1	Thomson 1	McLean
Mar 7	St Mirren	0-0	Shevlin	W McStay	Hilley	Wilson	J McStay	McFarlane	Connolly	Gallacher	McGrory	Thomson	McLean
Mar 10	ST MIRREN	1-1	Shevlin	W McStay	Hilley	Wilson	J McStay	McFarlane	Connolly	Gallacher	McGrory	Thomson	McLean +OG
Mar 16	St Mirren	1-0	Shevlin	W McStay	Hilley	Wilson	J McStay	McFarlane	Connolly	Gallacher	McGrory 1	Thomson	McLean
Mar 21	Rangers	5-0 SF	Shevlin	W McStay	Hilley	Wilson	J McStay	McFarlane	Connolly	Gallacher	McGrory 2	Thomson 1	McLean 2
Apr 11	Dundee	2-1 F	Shevlin	W McStay	Hilley	Wilson	J McStay	McFarlane	Connolly	Gallacher 1	McGrory 1	Thomson	McLean

SCOTTISH LEAGUE 1925-26

Aug 15	HIBERNIAN	5-0	Shevlin	W McStay	Hilley	Wilson	J McStay	McFarlane	Connolly 1	Thomson	McGrory 3	McInally	McLean 1
Aug 22	Clydebank	2-1	Shevlin	W McStay	Hilley	Wilson	J McStay	McFarlane	Connolly	Thomson 1	McGrory 1	McInally	McLean
Aug 29	HAMILTON ACADEMICALS	2-0	Shevlin	W McStay	Hilley	Wilson	J McStay 1	McFarlane	Connolly	Thomson	McGrory	McInally 1	McLean
Sept.12	COWDENBEATH	6-1	Shevlin	W McStay	Hilley	Wilson	J McStay	McFarlane	Connolly	Thomson 1	McGrory 2	McInally 1	McLean 2
Sept 19	Dundee United	0-1	Shevlin	W McStay	Hilley	Wilson	J McStay	McFarlane	Connolly	Thomson	McGrory	McInally	McLean
Sept 26	FALKIRK	3-1	Shevlin	W McStay	Hilley	Wilson	J McStay	McFarlane	Connolly	Thomson	McGrory 1	McInally 1	McLean
Oct 3	Airdrie	1-5	Shevlin	W McStay	Hilley	Wilson	J McStay	McFarlane	Gallacher	Thomson	McGrory 1	McInally	McLean
Oct 13	QUEEN'S PARK	4-1	Shaw	W McStay	Hilley	Wilson	J McStay	Gilfeather	Connolly 1	Thomson 1	McGrory 1	McInally 1	McLean
Oct 17	Rangers	0-1	Shevlin	W McStay	Hilley	Wilson	J McStay	McFarlane	Connolly	Thomson	McGrory	McInally	McLean
Oct 24	Morton	5-0	Shaw	W McStay	Hilley	Wilson	J McStay	McFarlane	Connolly	Thomson 1	McGrory 2	McInally 1	McLean 1
Oct 31	DUNDEE	0-0	Shevlin	Callaghan	Hilley	J McStay	McColgan	McFarlane	Connolly	Wilson	McInally	Thomson	McGrory
Nov 7	Aberdeen	4-2	Shevlin	W McStay	Hilley	Wilson	J McStay	McFarlane	Connolly	Thomson 2	McGrory 1	McInally 1	McLean
Nov 14	Raith Rovers	2-1	Shevlin	W McStay	Hilley	Wilson	J McStay	McFarlane	Connolly	Thomson	McGrory 2	McInally	McLean
Nov 25	HEARTS	3-0	Shevlin	W McStay	Hilley	Wilson	J McStay	McFarlane	Connolly	Thomson 1	McGrory 1	McInally 1	McLean
Nov 28	St Johnstone	3-0	Shevlin	W McStay	Hilley	Wilson	J McStay	McFarlane	Connolly	Thomson 1	McGrory 1	McInally	McLean 1
Dec 5	CLYDEBANK	1-1	Shevlin	W McStay	Hilley	Wilson	J McStay	McFarlane	Connolly	Thomson	McGrory 1	McInally	McLean
Dec 12	St Mirren	2-0	Shevlin	W McStay	Hilley	Wilson	J McStay	McFarlane	Connolly	Thomson 1	McGrory 1	McInally	McLean
Dec 19	AIRDRIE	3-2	Shevlin	W McStay	Hilley	Wilson	J McStay	McFarlane	Connolly	Thomson 2	McGrory 1	McInally	McLean
Dec 26	Cowdenbeath	1-1	Shevlin	W McStay	Hilley	Wilson	J McStay	McFarlane	Connolly	Thomson	McGrory	McInally	McLean 1
Jan 1	RANGERS	2-2	Shevlin	W McStay	Hilley	Wilson	J McStay	McFarlane	Connolly	Thomson	McGrory 1	McInally 1	McLean
Jan 2	Queen's Park	4-1	Shevlin	W McStay	Hilley	Wilson	J McStay	McFarlane	Leitch	Thomson 1	McGrory 2	McInally	McLean 1
Jan 4	PARTICK THISTLE	3-0	Shevlin	W McStay	Hilley	Wilson	J McStay	McFarlane	Connolly	Thomson	McGrory 3	McInally	McLean
Jan 9	RAITH ROVERS	1-0	Shevlin	W McStay P	Hilley	Wilson	J McStay	McFarlane	Connolly	Thomson	McColgan	McInally	McLean
Jan 16	Hibernian	4-4	Shevlin	W McStay	Hilley	Wilson	J McStay	McFarlane 1	Connolly	Thomson	McGrory	McInally 2	McLean 1
Jan 30	MOTHERWELL	3-1	Shevlin	Callaghan	Hilley	Wilson	J McStay	McFarlane	Connolly	Thomson 1	McGrory 1	McInally	McLean 1
Feb 10	Kilmarnock	1-2	Shevlin	W McStay P	Hilley	Wilson	J McStay	McFarlane	Connolly	Thomson	McGrory	McInally	McLean
Feb 13	Falkirk	1-1	Shevlin	W McStay	Hilley	Wilson	J McStay	McFarlane	Connolly	Thomson	McGrory	McInally	McLean 1
Mar 3	Hearts	2-1	Shevlin	W McStay	Hilley	Wilson	J McStay	McFarlane	Connolly 1	Thomson	McGrory	McInally 1	McLean
Mar 9	ST MIRREN	6-1	Shevlin	W McStay	Hilley	Wilson	J McStay	McFarlane	Connolly	Thomson	McGrory 3	McInally 1	McLean 2
Mar 17	Dundee	2-1	Shevlin	W McStay	Hilley	Wilson	J McStay	McFarlane	Connolly	Thomson	McGrory 1	McInally	Malloy 1
Mar 24	ST JOHNSTONE	4-1	Shevlin	W McStay	Callaghan	Wilson	J McStay	McFarlane	Connolly	Thomson 1	McGrory 1	McInally 1	Malloy +OG
Mar 27	Motherwell	1-2	Shevlin	W McStay	Hilley	Wilson	J McStay	McFarlane	Connolly	Thomson	McGrory	McInally 1	Malloy
Mar 30	ABERDEEN	4-1	Shevlin	W McStay	Hilley	Wilson	J McStay	McFarlane	Connolly	Thomson 1	McGrory 1	McInally 2	Malloy
Apr 3	KILMARNOCK	0-0	Shevlin	W McStay	Hilley	Wilson	J McStay	McFarlane	Connolly	Thomson	McGrory	McInally	McLean
Apr 5	Partick Thistle	0-0	Shevlin	Callaghan	Hilley	Wilson	W McStay	J McStay	Connolly	Thomson	McGrory	Leitch	McLean
Apr 14	MORTON	3-1	Shevlin	Callaghan	Hilley	Wilson	W McStay	J McStay	Connolly 1	Thomson	McGrory 1	McInally 1	Malloy
Apr 17	Hamilton Academicals	3-1	Shevlin	Callaghan	Hilley	Wilson	J McStay	Gilfeather	Connolly 1	Leitch 1	McGrory 1	McInally	McLean
Apr 24	DUNDEE UNITED	6-2	Shevlin	W McStay	Hilley	Wilson	J McStay	McFarlane 1	Connolly	Thomson	McGrory 2	McInally	McLean 3

SCOTTISH CUP 1926

Jan 23	Kilmarnock	5-0	Shevlin	W McStay	Hilley	Wilson	J McStay	McFarlane	Connolly	Thomson 2	McGrory 1	McInally 1	McLean 1
Feb 6	HAMILTON ACADEMICALS	4-0	Shevlin	W McStay	Hilley	Wilson	J McStay	McFarlane	Connolly	Thomson 1	McGrory 1	McInally 1	McLean 1
Feb 20	Hearts	4-0	Shevlin	W McStay	Hilley	Wilson	J McStay	McFarlane	Connolly 1	Thomson	McGrory 1	McInally 2	McLean
Mar 6	DUMBARTON	6-1	Shevlin	W McStay P	Hilley	Wilson	J McStay	McFarlane	Connolly	Thomson 1	McGrory 2	McInally	McLean 2
Mar 20	Aberdeen	2-1 SF	Shevlin	W McStay	Hilley	Wilson	J McStay	McFarlane	Connolly	Thomson	McGrory 1	McInally 1	Malloy
Apr 10	St Mirren	0-2 F	Shevlin	W McStay	Hilley	Wilson	J McStay	McFarlane	Connolly	Thomson	McGrory	McInally	Leitch

SCOTTISH LEAGUE 1926-27

Aug 14	Kilmarnock	3-2	Shevlin	W McStay	Hilley	Wilson	J McStay	McFarlane	Connolly	Thomson	McGrory 1	McInally 1	McLean 1
Aug 21	COWDENBEATH	2-0	Shevlin	W McStay	Hilley	Wilson	J McStay	McFarlane	Connolly	Thomson 1	McGrory 1	McInally	McLean
Aug 28	Queen's Park	6-1	Shevlin	W McStay P	Hilley	Wilson	J McStay	Doyle	Connolly 1	Thomson	McGrory 4	McInally	McLean
Sept 4	MORTON	3-0	Shevlin	W McStay	Hilley	Wilson 1	J McStay	McFarlane	Connolly	Thomson 1	McGrory	Doyle 1	Malloy
Sept 11	Clyde	2-2	Shevlin	Callaghan	Hilley	Wilson	J McStay	McFarlane	Connolly	Thomson	McGrory 1	Doyle 1	Malloy
Sept 18	HAMILTON ACADEMICALS	2-2	Shevlin	W McStay	Hilley	Wilson	J McStay	McFarlane	Connolly 2	Thomson	McGrory	Doyle	McLean
Sept 25	Hibernian	2-3	Shevlin	W McStay	Hilley	Wilson	Donoghue	McFarlane	Connolly	Thomson	McGrory 1	Blair	McLean 1
Oct 2	DUNDEE	0-0	Shevlin	W McStay	Hilley	Wilson	Donoghue	McFarlane	Connolly	Thomson	McGrory	McInally	McLean
Oct 16	St Mirren	1-3	Shevlin	W McStay	Hilley	Wilson	J McStay	McFarlane	Connolly	Thomson	McGrory 1	McInally	McLean
Oct 23	ABERDEEN	6-2	Shevlin	W McStay	Hilley	Wilson	J McStay	McFarlane	Connolly	Thomson	McGrory 5	McInally	McLean 1
Nov 6	Airdrie	2-2	Shevlin	W McStay	Hilley	Wilson	J McStay	McFarlane	Connolly 1	Thomson	McGrory 1	McInally	McLean
Nov 13	HEARTS	1-0	Shevlin	W McStay	Hilley	Wilson	J McStay	McFarlane	Connolly	Thomson	McGrory	McInally	McLean.1
Nov 20	Dunfermline Ath	6-0	Shevlin	W McStay	Hilley	Wilson	Donoghue	McFarlane	Connolly	Thomson	McGrory 4	McInally	McLean 2
Nov 27	DUNDEE UNITED	7-2	Shevlin	W McStay	Hilley	Wilson	Donoghue	McFarlane	Connolly	Thomson1	McGrory 5	McInally	McLean 1
Dec 4	Motherwell	1-0	Shevlin	W McStay	Hilley	Wilson	Donohue	McFarlane	Connolly	Thomson	McGrory 1	McInally	McLean
Dec 11	ST JOHNSTONE	4-0	Shevlin	W McStay	Hilley	Wilson	Donoghue	McFarlane	Connolly 1	Thomson 1	McGrory 2	McInally	McLean
Dec 18	Partick Thistle	3-0	Shevlin	W McStay	Hilley	Wilson	Donoghue	McFarlane	Connolly	Thomson	McGrory 1	McInally	McLean 2
Dec 25	KILMARNOCK	4-0	Shevlin	W McStay 1	Hilley	Wilson	Donoghue	McFarlane	Connolly	Thomson	McGrory 1	McInally 2	McLean
Jan 1	Rangers	1-2	Shevlin	W McStay	Hilley	Wilson	Donoghue	McFarlane	Connolly	Thomson 1	McGrory	McInally	McLean
Jan 3	QUEEN'S PARK	2-3	Shevlin	W McStay	Hilley	Wilson	J McStay	McFarlane	Connolly	Thomson 1	McGrory	McInally	McLean 1

			1	2	3	4	5	6	7	8	9	10	11
Jan 8	Morton	6-2	Shevlin	W McStay	Hilley	Wilson	Donoghue	McFarlane	Connolly	Thomson 1	McGrory 1	McInally 3	McLean 1
Jan 15	CLYDE	7-0	Shevlin	W McStay	Hilley	J McStay	Donoghue	McFarlane	Connolly	Thomson	McGrory 5	McInally	McLean 2
Feb 2	HIBERNIAN	2-3	Shevlin	W McStay	Hilley	Wilson	Donoghue	McFarlane	Connolly	Thomson 1	McGrory	McInally	McLean 1
Feb 12	Dundee	2-1	J Thomson	W McStay	Hilley	Wilson	Donoghue	Doyle	Connolly	Thomson 1	McGrory 1	McInally	McLean
Feb 16	Hamilton Academicals	3-3	Thomson	W McStay	Hilley	Wilson	J McStay	McFarlane	Connolly	Thomson	McGrory 3	McInally	McLean
Feb 23	FALKIRK	3-1	Thomson	W McStay	Hilley	Donoghue	J McStay	McFarlane	Connolly	Thomson 1	McGrory 2	Doyle	McLean
Feb 26	St Mirren	6-2	Thomson	Donoghue	Hilley	Doyle	J McStay	McFarlane	Connolly	Thomson	McGrory 4	McInally 1	McLean 1
Mar 9	Aberdeen	0-0	Thomson	W McStay	Hilley	Wilson	J McStay	McFarlane	Connolly	Thomson	McGrory	McInally	McLean
Mar 12	Cowdenbeath	1-2	Thomson	W McStay	Hilley	Wilson	J McStay	McFarlane	Connolly	Thomson	McGrory	McInally 1	McLean
Mar 16	AIRDRIE	2-1	Thomson	W McStay	Hilley	Wilson	J McStay	McFarlane	Connolly	Thomson	McGrory 1	McInally	McLean +OG
Mar 30	Hearts	0-3	Thomson	W McStay	Hilley	Wilson	J McStay	McFarlane	Connolly	Thomson	McGrory	McInally	McLean
Apr 2	DUNFERMLINE	2-1	Thomson	Callaghan	Hilley	Wilson	J McStay	McFarlane	McArdle	Thomson 1	McGrory 1	Doyle	Connolly
Apr 6	Falkirk	1-4	Thomson	W McStay	Hilley	Wilson	J McStay	McFarlane	Connolly	Thomson 1	McGrory	McMenemy	McCallum
Apr 9	Dundee United	3-3	Thomson	Callaghan	Hilley	Wilson	J McStay	McFarlane	Connolly 1	McMenemy 1	McNally	McInally 1	McCallum
Apri18	RANGERS	0-1	Thomson	W McStay	Hilley	Wilson	J McStay	McFarlane	Connolly	Thomson	McInally	McMenemy	McLean
Apr 20	MOTHERWELL	3-2	Thomson	W McStay	Hilley	Wilson	J McStay	McFarlane	Connolly 1	Thomson	Donoghue 1	McInally	McLean
Apr 23	St Johnstone	0-1	Thomson	W McStay	Callaghan	Wilson	J McStay	Turnbull	Connolly	Thomson	McInally	McMenemy	McCallum
Apr 30	PARTICK THISTLE	2-1	Thomson	Callaghan	Hilley	Donoghue	J McStay	Turnbull	Connolly	Thomson	McNally	McInally	McLean 2

SCOTTISH CUP 1927

Jan 22	Queen of the South	0-0	Shevlin	W McStay	Hilley	J McStay	Donoghue	McFarlane	Connolly	Thomson	McGrory	McInally	McLean
Jan 26	QUEEN OF THE SOUTH	4-1	Shevlin	W McStay	Hilley	Wilson	Donoghue	McFarlane	Connolly	Thomson 1	McGrory 2	McInally	McLean 1
Feb 5	Brechin City	6-3	Shevlin	W McStay	Hilley	Wilson	Donoghue	Doyle	Connolly	Thomson	McGrory 4	McInally 1	McLean 1
Feb 19	Dundee	4-2	Thomson	W McStay P	Hilley	Wilson	J McStay	McFarlane	Connolly 1	Thomson	McGrory 1	McInally	McLean 1
Mar 5	Bo'ness	5-2	Thomson	W McStay	Hilley	Wilson	J McStay	McFarlane	Connolly	Thomson 1	McGrory 2	McInally 1	McLean 1
Mar 26	Falkirk	1-0 SF	Thomson	W McStay	Hilley	Wilson	J McStay	McFarlane	Connolly	Thomson	McGrory	McInally	McLean 1
Apr 16	East Fife	3-1 F	Thomson	W McStay	Hilley	Wilson	J McStay	McFarlane	Connolly 1	Thomson	McInally	McMenemy	McLean 1 +OG

SCOTTISH LEAGUE 1927-28

Aug 13	HIBERNIAN	3-0	Thomson	W McStay	Hilley	Wilson	J McStay	McFarlane	Connolly	Thomson 1	McGrory 1	McInally	McLean 1
Aug 16	KILMARNOCK	6-1	Thomson	W McStay	Hilley	Wilson	J McStay	McFarlane	Connolly 1	Thomson	McGrory 1	McInally 2	McLean 1 +OG
Aug 20	Hamilton Academicals	0-0	Thomson	W McStay	Hilley	Wilson	J McStay	McFarlane	Connolly	Thomson	McGrory	McInally	McLean
Aug 27	FALKIRK	3-0	Thomson	W McStay	McGonagle	Wilson	J McStay	McFarlane	Connolly	Thomson 1	McGrory 1	McInally 1	McLean
Sept 3	Raith Rovers	3-0	Thomson	W McStay	McGonagle	Wilson	J McStay	McFarlane	Connolly	Thomson	McGrory 2	McInally 1	McLean
Sept 10	QUEEN'S PARK	3-0	Thomson	W McStay	McGonagle	Wilson	J McStay	Doyle	Connolly	Thomson 1	McGrory 1	McMenemy 1	McLean
Sept 17	Dunfermline	1-1	Thomson	W McStay	McGonagle	Wilson	J McStay	Doyle	Connolly	Thomson	McGrory	McInally	McLean 1
Sept 24	CLYDE	3-0	Thomson	W McStay	McGonagle	Wilson	J McStay	McFarlane	Connolly	Thomson 1	McGrory 2	McInally	McLean
Oct 1	Dundee	4-1	Thomson	W McStay	McGonagle	Wilson P	J McStay	McFarlane	Connolly	Thomson 1	McGrory 2	McInally	McLean
Oct 15	Rangers	0-1	Thomson	W McStay	McGonagle	Wilson	J McStay	McFarlane	Connolly	Thomson	McGrory	McInally	McLean
Oct 22	Aberdeen	1-3	Thomson	W McStay	McGonagle	Wilson 1	J McStay	McFarlane	Connolly	Thomson	McGrory	McMenemy	McLean
Oct 29	ST MIRREN	6-0	Thomson	J McStay	McGonagle	Wilson	Donoghue	McFarlane	Connolly 2	Thomson	McGrory 4	McMenemy	McLean
Nov 5	AIRDRIE	3-2	Thomson	W McStay	McGonagle	Wilson	J McStay	McFarlane	Connolly	Thomson	McInally 3	McMemeny	McLean
Nov 12	Hearts	2-2	Thomson	W McStay	McGonagle	Wilson	J McStay	McFarlane	Connolly	Thomson	McGrory 2	McInally	McLean
Nov 19	COWDENBEATH	1-1	Thomson	W McStay	McGonagle	Wilson	J McStay	McFarlane	Connolly	Thomson	McGrory 1	McInally	McLean
Nov 26	Bo'ness	1-0	Thomson	J McStay	McGonagle	Wilson	Donoghue	McFarlane	Connolly	Thomson 1	McGrory	McInally	McLean
Dec 3	MOTHERWELL	1-2	Thomson	W McStay	McGonagle	Wilson	J McStay	McFarlane	Connolly	Thomson	McGrory	McInally 1	McLean
Dec 10	St Johnstone	5-3	Thomson	W McStay	McGonagle	Wilson 1	J McStay	McFarlane	Connolly	Thomson 1	McGrory 3	McMenemy	McLean
Dec 17	PARTICK THISTLE	0-0	Thomson	W McStay	McGonagle	Wilson	J McStay	McFarlane	Connolly	Thomson	McGrory	McMenemy	McLean
Dec 24	Hibernian	2-2	Thomson	J McStay	W McStay	Wilson	Donoghue	McFarlane	Connolly	McMenemy	McGrory 1	Thomson 1	McLean
Jan 2	RANGERS	1-0	Thomson	W McStay	McGonagle	Wilson	J McStay	McFarlane	Connolly	Thomson	McGrory 1	McInally	McLean
Jan 3	Queen's Park	3-1	Thomson	W McStay	McGonagle	Wilson	J McStay	McFarlane	Connolly	Thomson	McGrory 3	McInally	McLean
Jan 7	Falkirk	3-1	Thomson	W McStay	McGonagle	Wilson	J McStay	McFarlane	Connolly	Thomson	McGrory 3	Doyle	McLean
Jan 14	DUNFERMLINE	9-0	Thomson	W McStay	McGonagle	Wilson	J McStay	Doyle	Connolly	Thomson	McGrory 8	McInally	McLean
Jan 28	Kilmarnock	2-2	Thomson	W McStay	McGonagle	Wilson	J Mcstay	McFarlane	Connolly	Thomson	McGrory 1	McInally 1	McLean
Feb 11	Clyde	1-0	Thomson	W McStay	McGonagle	Wilson	J McStay	McFarlane	Connolly	Thomson	McGrory	McInally 1	McLean
Feb 14	DUNDEE	3-1	Thomson	W McStay	McGonagle	Wilson	J McStay	McFarlane	Connolly	Thomson 1	McGrory 1	Doyle	McInally 1
Feb 21	St Mirren	2-0	Thomson	W McStay	McGonagle	Wilson	J McStay	McFarlane	Connolly	Thomson	McGrory	McInally 1	McLean 1
Feb 25	ABERDEEN	1-1	Thomson	Geddes	Sinclair	Wilson	J McStay	McFarlane	Connolly	Thomson	McInally 1	Doyle	McLean
Mar 6	HAMILTON ACADEMICALS	4-0	Thomson	W McStay	McGonagle	Wilson	J McStay	McFarlane	Connolly 1	Thomson	McGrory 3	Doyle	McLean
Mar 17	HEARTS	2-1	Thomson	W McStay	McGonagle	Wilson	J McStay	McFarlane	Connolly	Thomson	McGrory 2	Doyle	McLean
Mar 28	Cowdenbeath	2-0	Thomson	W McStay	McGonagle	Wilson	J McStay	McFarlane	Connolly	Thomson	McGrory 1	Doyle	McLean 1
Mar 31	BO'NESS	4-1	Thomson	W McStay	McGonagle	Donoghue	J McStay	McFarlane	Connolly	Thomson	McGrory 2	Wilson 1	McLean 1
Apr 7	Motherwell	1-3	Thomson	W McStay	McGonagle	Wilson	J McStay	McFarlane	Connolly	Thomson	McGrory	McInally	McLean 1
Apr 10	Airdrie	1-3	Thomson	W McStay	Donoghue	Wilson	J McStay	McFarlane	Connolly	Thomson 1	McGrory	McInally	McCallum
Apr 18	ST JOHNSTONE	3-0	Thomson	W McStay	Donoghue	Wilson	J McStay	McFarlane	Connolly	McMenemy	McGrory	McInally 2	McLean 1
Apr 21	Partick Thistle	3-3	Thomson	W McStay P	Donoghue	Wilson	J McStay	McFarlane	Connolly	Thomson	McGrory 2	McInally	McLean
Apr 23	RAITH ROVERS	0-3	Thomson	Geddes	Sinclair	Wilson	J McStay	McFarlane	Connolly	McMenemy	McGrory	McInally	McLean

SCOTTISH CUP 1928

Jan 21	BATHGATE	3-1	Thomson	W McStay	McGonagle	Wilson	J McStay	Doyle	Connolly	Thomson	McGrory	McInally 1	McLean 2
Feb 4	Keith	6-1	Thomson	W McStay	McGonagle	Wilson	J McStay	McFarlane	Connolly	Thomson	McGrory 3	McInally 3	McLean
Feb 18	ALLOA	2-0	Thomson	W McStay	McGonagle	Wilson	J McStay	McFarlane	Connolly 1	Thomson	McGrory 1	McInally	McLean
Mar 3	Motherwell	2-0	Thomson	W McStay	McGonagle	Wilson	J McStay	McFarlane	Connolly	Thomson	McGrory 1	Doyle 1	McLean
Mar 24	Queen's Park	2-1 SF	Thomson	W McStay	McGonagle	Wilson	J McStay	McFarlane	Connolly	Thomson	McGrory 1	Doyle	McLean 1
Apr 14	Rangers	0-4 F	Thomson	W McStay	Donoghue	Wilson	J McStay	McFarlane	Connolly	Thomson	McGrory	McInally	McLean

SCOTTISH LEAGUE 1928-29

Aug 11	Dundee	1-0	Thomson	W McStay	McGonagle	Wilson	J McStay	McFarlane	Gray	Thomson	McGrory 1	Joe Riley	McCallum
Aug 18	AIRDRIE	4-1	Thomson	W McStay	McGonagle	Wilson	J McStay	McFarlane	Gray	McMenemy	McGrory 3	Thomson	McCallum 1
Aug 25	Ayr United	2-0	Thomson	W McStay	McGonagle	Wilson	J McStay	McFarlane	Gray 2 (1P)	McMenemy	McGrory	Thomson	McCallum
Sept 8	KILMARNOCK	3-0	Thomson	W McStay	McGonagle	Wilson	J McStay	McFarlane	Connolly 1	Thomson	McGrory 1	Gray P	McWilliams
Sept 15	Cowdenbeath	1-0	Thomson	W McStay	McGonagle	Donoghue	J McStay	McFarlane	Connolly	Thomson	McGrory 1	Gray	McCallum
Sept 22	ST MIRREN	0-3	Thomson	W McStay	McGonagle	Donoghue	J McStay	McFarlane	Connolly	Thomson	McGrory	Gray	McCallum
Sept 29	Hamilton Academicals	1-1	Nicol	W McStay	McGonagle	Wilson	J McStay	McFarlane	Connolly	Thomson	McNally 1	Gray	McCallum
Oct 13	Motherwell	3-3	Thomson	W McStay	McGonagle	Wilson	J McStay	McFarlane	Connolly 1	Thomson	McGrory	Gray 2 (1P)	McCallum
Oct 20	RANGERS	1-2	Thomson	W McStay	McGonagle	Wilson	J McStay	McFarlane	Connolly	Thomson	McGrory 1	Gray	McCallum
Oct 27	Queen's Park	4-4	Thomson	W McStay	McGonagle	Wilson	J McStay	McFarlane	Connolly	Thomson	McGrory 2	Riley 2	McCallum
Nov 3	RAITH ROVERS	3-1	Thomson	W McStay	McGonagle	Wilson	J McStay	McFarlane	Connolly	Thomson 1	McGrory 2	Riley	McCallum
Nov 10	Aberdeen	2-2	Thomson	W McStay	McGonagle	Wilson	J McStay	McFarlane	Connolly 1	Thomson	Gray	Riley	McCallum +OG
Nov 17	CLYDE	4-0	Thomson	W McStay	McGonagle	Wilson	J McStay	McFarlane	Connolly	Gray 2	McInally 1	Thomson	McWilliams+OG
Nov 24	Third Lanark	2-0	Thomson	W McStay	McGonagle	Wilson	J McStay	McFarlane	Connolly 1	Gray	McGrory	Thomson 1	McWilliams
Dec 1	ST JOHNSTONE	0-0	Thomson	W McStay	McGonagle	Wilson	J McStay	McFarlane	Connolly	Gray	McNally	Thomson	McWilliams
Dec 8	Falkirk	0-3	Thomson	W McStay	McGonagle	Wilson	J McStay	McFarlane	Connolly	Gray	McNally	Thomson	McCallum
Dec 15	HEARTS	1-0	Thomson	W McStay	McGonagle	Wilson	J McStay	McFarlane	Connolly 1	Thomson	Gray	Riley	McCallum
Dec 22	Airdrie	1-0	Thomson	W McStay	McGonagle	Wilson	J McStay	McFarlane	Connolly	Thomson	McNally	Riley	McCallum
Dec 29	DUNDEE	2-1	Thomson	W McStay	McGonagle	Wilson	J McStay	McFarlane	Connolly	Riley	Gray 1	Thomson 1	Crozier
Jan 1	Rangers	0-3	Thomson	W McStay	McGonagle	Wilson	J McStay	McFarlane	Connolly	Riley	Gray	Thomson	Crozier
Jan 5	AYR UNITED	3-0	Thomson	W McStay	McGonagle	Wilson	J McStay	McFarlane	Connolly 1	Thomson	Gray 2	Riley	McCallum
Jan 12	Partick Thistle	0-3	Thomson	W McStay	McGonagle	Wilson	J McStay	McFarlane	Connolly	Thomson	Gray	Riley	McCallum
Jan 26	Hearts	1-2	Thomson	W McStay	McGonagle	Wilson	J McStay	Donoghue	Connolly	Thomson	Gray	Scarff 1	McCallum
Feb 9	St Mirren	1-0	Thomson	W McStay	McGonagle	Wilson	J McStay	Donoghue	Connolly	Thomson	McGrory	Scarff 1	McCallum

			1	2	3	4	5	6	7	8	9	10	11
Feb 12	COWDENBEATH	1-0	Thomson	W McStay	McGonagle	Wilson	J McStay	McFarlane	Connolly	Thomson	McGrory 1	Scarff	McCallum
Feb 19	HAMILTON ACADEMICALS	3-0	Thomson	W McStay	McGonagle	Wilson	J McStay	Donoghue	Connolly	Thomson	McGrory 3	Scarff	McCallum
Feb 23	Hibernian	1-2	Thomson	W McStay	McGonagle	Wilson	J McStay	Donoghue	Connolly	Thomson	McGrory 1	Scarff	McCallum
Mar 9	Raith Rovers	4-1	Thomson	W McStay	McGonagle	Wilson	J McStay	Donoghue	Connolly	Prentice 1	Gray	Scarff 3	McWilliams
Mar 16	ABERDEEN	2-2	Thomson	Geatons	McGonagle	Wilson	J McStay	Donoghue	Connolly 1	Thomson	McGrory 1	Scarff	Gray
Mar 19	MOTHERWELL	2-0	Thomson	Geatons	McGonagle	Wilson	J McStay	Donoghue	Connolly 1	Thomson	Gray	Scarff 1	Hughes
Mar 26	Clyde	1-0	Thomson	W McStay	McGonagle	Wilson	J McStay	Donoghue	Connolly	Thomson 1	McGrory	Scarff	Hughes
Mar 30*	THIRD LANARK	3-1	Thomson	W McStay	McGonagle P	Wilson	J McStay	Donoghue	Connolly	Thomson	McGrory 1	Scarff	Hughes +OG
Apr 1**	PARTICK THISTLE	1-0	Thomson	W McStay	McGonagle	Wilson	J McStay	Donoghue	Connolly	Thomson	Gray 1	Scarff	Hughes
Apr 6	St Johnstone	1-1	Thomson	W McStay	McGonagle	Wilson	J McStay	Prentice	Connolly	Thomson	Gray 1	Scarff	McWilliams
Apr 13***	HIBERNIAN	1-4	Thomson	W McStay	McGonagle	Wilson	J McStay	Prentice	Connolly	Thomson	McGrory 1	Scarff	Hughes
Apr 17****	QUEEN'S PARK	1-2	Thomson	W McStay	McGonagle	Wilson	J McStay	Prentice	Connolly	Thomson	McGrory 1	Scarff	Hughes
Apr 20*	FALKIRK	3-0	Thomson	W McStay	McGonagle	Wilson	J McStay	Donoghue	Connolly	Thomson	Gray	Scarff 2	Hughes 1
Apr 27	Kilmarnock	3-2	Thomson	W McStay	McGonagle	Wilson	J McStay	Donoghue	Connolly 1	Thomson	McGrory 1	Scarff	Hughes 1

* Shawfield ** Firhiill *** Easter Rd **** Hampden. Home games switched because of ground reconstruction at Celtic Park.

SCOTTISH CUP 1929

Jan 19	ARTHURLIE	5-1	Thomson	W McStay	McGonagle	Wilson	J McStay 1	Donoghue	Connolly 1	Thomson	McGrory 3	Scarff	Gray
Feb 2	E. STIRLING	3-0	Thomson	W McStay	McGonagle	Wilson	J McStay 1	McFarlane	Connolly	Thomson	McGrory 2	Scarff	Gray
Feb 16	ARBROATH	4-1	Thomson	W McStay	McGonagle	Wilson	J McStay	McFarlane	Connolly	Thomson	McGrory 4	Scarff	McCallum
Mar 6	MOTHERWELL	0-0	Thomson	W McStay	McGonagle	Wilson	J McStay	Donoghue	Connolly	Thomson	McGrory	Scarff	Gray
Mar 13	Motherwell	2-1	Thomson	W McStay	McGonagle	Wilson	J McStay	Donoghue	Connolly 1	Thomson	McGrory 1	Scarff	Gray
Mar 23	Kilmarnock	0-1 SF	Thomson	W McStay	McGonagle	Wilson	J McStay	Donoghue	Connolly	Thomson	McGrory	Scarff	Gray

SCOTTISH LEAGUE 1929-30

Aug 10	HEARTS	2-1	Thomson	Geatons	McGonagle	Wilson	J McStay	Donoghue	Connolly	Thomson	McGrory 2	Scarff	Kavanagh
Aug 17	Morton	2-1	Thomson	Geatons	McGonagle	Wilson	McStay	Donoghue	Connolly	Thomson	McNally	Scarff 2	Kavanagh
Aug 24	ABERDEEN	3-4	Thomson	Geatons	McGonagle	Wilson	McStay	Donoghue	Connolly	Thomson	McGrory 1	Scarff 1	Kavanagh 1
Aug 31	Hamilton Academicals	3-2	Thomson	Geatons	McGonagle	Wilson	McStay	Donoghue	Connolly	Thomson	McGrory 3	Scarff	Kavanagh
Sept 14	Airdrie	1-0	Thomson	McCallum	McGonagle	Geatons	McStay	Robertson	Connolly	Thomson	McGrory 1	Scarff	Kavanagh
Sept 21	DUNDEE	1-1	Thomson	McCallum	McGonagle	Wilson	McStay	Robertson	Connolly	Thomson	McNally 1	Scarff	Kavanagh
Sept 28	Ayr United	3-1	Thomson	Geatons	McGonagle	Wilson	McStay	Robertson	Connolly	Thomson	McGrory 3(1P)	Scarff	Kavanagh
Oct 5	FALKIRK	7-0	Thomson	McCallum	McGonagle	Wilson	McStay	Robertson	Connolly 2	Thomson 1	McGrory 3	Scarff 1	Kavanagh
Oct 19	QUEEN'S PARK	2-1	Thomson	McCallum	McGonagle	Wilson	McStay	Robertson	Connolly	Thomson 1	McGrory	Scarff 1	Napier
Oct 23	Dundee United	2-2	Thomson	McCallum	McGonagle	Wilson	McStay	Robertson	Connolly	Scarff 1	McGrory	Napier 1	Kavanagh
Oct 26	Rangers	0-1	Thomson	McCallum	McGonagle	Wilson	Gallacher	Robertson	Connolly	Thomson	McNally	Scarff	Kavanagh
Nov 2	HIBERNIAN	4-0	Kelly	McCallum	Prentice	Wilson	Gallacher	Robertson	Connolly 1	Thomson	McNally 1	Napier 1	Kavanagh 1
Nov 9	Motherwell	1-2	Thomson	McCallum	McGonagle	Wilson	McStay	Robertson	Connolly	Thomson	McGrory	Napier 1	Kavanagh
Nov 16	COWDENBEATH	2-1	Thomson	McCallum	Hughes	Wilson P	McStay	Robertson	B. Thomson	Scarff	McGrory	Napier 1	Kavanagh
Nov 23	St Johnstone	6-1	Thomson	McCallum	Hughes	Wilson	McStay	Robertson 1	R. Thomson 1	A. Thomson	McGrory 3	Napier 1	Connolly
Nov 30	Partick Thistle	2-3	Thomson	Geatons	McGonagle	Wilson	McStay	Prentice	R. Thomson	A. Thomson	McGrory 1	Napier	Connolly 1
Dec 7	ST MIRREN	3-0	Thomson	Geatons	McGonagle	Wilson	McStay 1	Hughes	R. Thomson	A. Thomson	McGrory 1	Napier 1	Connolly
Dec 14	Kilmarnock	1-1	Thomson	Geatons	McGonagle	Wilson	McStay	Robertson	R. Thomson	A. Thomson	McGrory 1	Napier	Connolly
Dec 21	Hearts	3-1	Thomson	Geatons	McGonagle	Wilson	McStay	Robertson	R. Thomson 1	A. Thomson	McGrory 1	Napier	Connolly 1
Dec 28	MORTON	0-1	Thomson	Geatons	McGonagle	Wilson	McStay	Robertson	R. Thomson	A. Thomson	McNally	Napier	Connolly
Jan 1	RANGERS	1-2	Thomson	Geatons	McGonagle	Wilson	McStay	Robertson	R .Thomson	A. Thomson	McGrory	Napier 1	Connolly
Jan 2	Queen's Park	1-2	Thomson	McCallum	McGonagle	Wilson	McStay	Robertson	Connolly	A. Thomson	Napier 1	Scarff	Kavanagh
Jan 4	Aberdeen	1-3	Thomson	Hughes	McGonagle	Wilson	McStay	Robertson	Connolly	A. Thomson	Scarff	Napier 1	Kavanagh
Jan 25	Clyde	3-2	Thomson	Geatons	McGonagle	Wilson P	McStay	Robertson	R Thomson 1	A. Thomson	McGrory 1	Napier	Connolly
Feb 5	AIRDRIE	1-2	Thomson	Barrie	McGonagle	Wilson	McStay	Robertson	R Thomson	A. Thomson	McGrory	Napier 1	Hughes
Feb 8	Dundee	2-2	Kelly	Wilson	McGonagle	Geatons	McStay	Robertson	Connolly	A. Thomson	McGrory 1	Scarff	Napier 1
Feb 18	AYR UNITED	4-0	Kelly	Cook	McGonagle	Wilson	McStay	Robertson	R. Thomson	A. Thomson	Scarff 4	Napier	Hughes
Feb 22	Falkirk	1-0	Kelly	Cook	McGonagle	Wilson	Geatons	Robertson	R Thomson	A. Thomson	Scarff 1	Napier	Connolly
Mar 1	DUNDEE UNITED	7-0	Kelly	Cook	McGonagle	Wilson	Geatons	Robertson	R Thomson	A. Thomson 1	Scarff 4	Napier 1	Hughes 1
Mar 8	Hibernian	2-0	Kelly	Cook	McGonagle	Wilson	Geatons	Robertson	R Thomson	Scarff 1	McGrory 1	Napier	Hughes
Mar 15	MOTHERWELL	0-4	Kelly	Cook	McGonagle	Wilson	Geatons	Robertson	R Thomson	A. Thomson	Scarff	Napier	Hughes
Mar 22	Cowdenbeath	2-1	Kelly	Cook	McGonagle	Wilson	McStay	Geatons	R Thomson	A. Thomson	Scarff 1	Napier 1	Hughes
Mar 29	ST JOHNSTONE	6-2	Thomson	Cook	McGonagle	Wilson	McStay	Geatons	R Thomson	A. Thomson 1	McGrory 3	Scarff 1	Napier 1
Apr 5	PARTICK THISTLE	2-0	Thomson	Hughes	McGonagle	Wilson	McStay	Geatons	R Thomson	A. Thomson	McGrory 2	Napier	Kavanagh
Apr 12	St Mirren	0-0	Kelly	Cook	McGonagle	Geatons	McStay	Robertson	R Thomson	A. Thomson	McGrory	Napier	Kavanagh
Apr 15	HAMILTON ACADEMICALS	3-0	Thomson	Cook	McGonagle	Wilson	McStay	Geatons	R Thomson	A. Thomson	McGrory 2	Scarff	Napier 1
Apr 19	Kilmarnock	4-0	Thomson	Cook	McGonagle	Wilson P	McStay	Robertson	Connolly	A. Thomson	McGrory 2	Scarff	Napier 1
Apr 21	CLYDE	0-2	Thomson	Cook	McGonagle	Wilson	McStay	Robertson	Connolly	A. Thomson	McGrory	Scarff	Napier

SCOTTISH CUP 1930

Jan 18	Inverness Caledonian	6-0	Thomson	Geatons	McGonagle	Wilson P	McStay	Robertson	R. Thomson	A. Thomson	McGrory 2	Napier 1	Connolly 1 +OG
Feb 1	ARBROATH	5-0	Thomson	Geatons	McGonagle	Wilson	McStay	Robertson	R. Thomson 1	A.Thomson 1	McGrory 2	Scarff 1	Connolly
Feb 15	ST MIRREN	1-3	Kelly	Geatons	McGonagle	Wilson	McStay	Robertson	Connolly	A. Thomson 1	McGrory	Scarff	Napier

SCOTTISH LEAGUE 1930-31

Aug 9	KILMARNOCK	3-1	Thomson	Cook	McGonagle	Wilson	McStay	Robertson	McCallum 2	A. Thomson	Scarff	Napier 1	Tierney
Aug 16	Falkirk	2-3	Thomson	Cook	McGonagle	Wilson	McStay	Robertson	McCallum	A. Thomson	Scarff 2	Napier	Tierney
Aug 23	HIBERNIAN	6-0	Thomson	Cook	McGonagle	Wilson	McStay 1	Robertson	R. Thomson 1	Smith 1	Scarff 3	Napier	Tierney
Aug 30	East Fife	6-2	Thomson	Cook	McGonagle	Wilson	McStay	Robertson	R. Thomson	A. Thomson 1	Scarff 2	Napier 3(2P)	Tierney
Sept 6	ABERDEEN	1-0	Thomson	Morrison	McGonagle	Wilson	McStay	Robertson	R .Thomson	A. Thomson	Scarff	Napier P	Tierney
Sept 13	Hamilton Academicals	0-0	Thomson	Morrison	McGonagle	Wilson	McStay	Whitelaw	R .Thomson	A. Thomson	Scarff	Napier	Tierney
Sept 20	RANGERS	2-0	Thomson	Morrison	McGonagle	Wilson	McStay	Geatons	R. Thomson 1	A. Thomson 1	McGrory	Scarff	Napier
Sept 27	Queen's Park	3-3	Thomson	Morrison	McGonagle	Wilson	McStay	Geatons	R. Thomson	Scarff	McGrory	Napier	Tierney
Oct 4	MORTON	4-1	Thomson	Morrison	McGonagle	Wilson	McStay	Geatons	R. Thomson 1	A. Thomson	McGrory 3	Scarff	Napier
Oct 18	ST MIRREN	3-1	Thomson	Cook	McGonagle	Robertson	Geatons	Whitelaw	R.Thomson	A. Thomson	McGrory 2	Scarff 1	Napier
Oct 25	Motherwell	3-3	Robertson	Cook	McGonagle	Geatons	McStay	Whitelaw	R.Thomson	A. Thomson 1	McGrory 1	Scarff 1	Napier
Nov 1	PARTICK THISTLE	5-1	Thomson	Cook	McGonagle	Wilson	McStay	Geatons	R. Thomson	A. Thomson	McGrory 2	Scarff 2	Napier 1
Nov 8	HEARTS	2-1	Thomson	Cook	McGonagle	Wilson	McStay	Geatons	R. Thomson	A. Thomson	McGrory	Scarff 1	Napier 1
Nov 15	Cowdenbeath	1-1	Thomson	Cook	McGonagle	Wilson 1	McStay	Geatons	R. Thomson	A. Thomson	McGrory	Scarff	Napier
Nov 22	Ayr United	6-2	Thomson	Cook	Hughes	Wilson	McStay	Geatons	R Thomson	A. Thomson	McGrory 2	Scarff 2	Napier 2
Dec 6	Airdrie	2-1	Thomson	Cook	McGonagle	Wilson	McStay	Geatons	R. Thomson	A. Thomson 1	McGrory 1	Scarff	Napier
Dec 13	LEITH ATHLETIC	4-0	Thomson	Cook	McGonagle	Wilson	McStay	Geatons 1	R. Thomson	A.Thomson	McGrory 1	Scarff	Napier 2P
Dec 20	Kilmarnock	3-0	Thomson	Cook	McGonagle	Wilson	McStay	Geatons	R. Thomson	A. Thomson	McGrory 3	Scarff	Napier
Dec 27	FALKIRK	3-0	Thomson	Cook	McGonagle	Wilson	McStay	Geatons	R. Thomson	A. Thomson 1	McGrory 1	Scarff	Napier P
Jan 1	Rangers	0-1	Thomson	Cook	McGonagle	Wilson	McStay	Geatons	R. Thomson	A. Thomson	McGrory	Scarff	Napier
Jan 3	Hibernian	0-0	Thomson	Cook	McGonagle	Wilson	McStay	Geatons	R. Thomson	A. Thomson	McGrory	Scarff	Napier
Jan 10	EAST FIFE	9-1	Thomson	Cook	McGonagle	Wilson	McStay	Geatons	R. Thomson 1	A. Thomson	McGrory 5	Scarff 3	Napier
Jan 24	Aberdeen	1-1	Thomson	Cook	McGonagle	Wilson	McStay	Geatons	R. Thomson	A. Thomson	Cowan 1	Scarff	Napier
Feb 7	Morton	1-0	Thomson	Cook	McGonagle	Wilson	McStay	Geatons	R. Thomson	A. Thomson 1	Scarff	Napier	Hughes
Feb 18	CLYDE	0-1	Thomson	Cook	McGonagle	Wilson	McStay	Geatons	R Thomson	A Thomson	McGrory	Scarff	Napier
Feb 21	St Mirren	3-1	Robertson	Cook	McGonagle	Geatons	McStay	Whitelaw	R Thomson 2	A Thomson	McGrory	Napier 1	Kavanagh
Feb 24	HAMILTON ACADEMICALS	2-1	Thomson	Cook	McGonagle	Geatons	McStay	Whitelaw	R Thomson 1	A Thomson	McGrory 1	Scarff	Kavanagh
Mar 4	MOTHERWELL	4-1	Thomson	Cook	McGonagle	Geatons	McStay	Scarff	R Thomson	A Thomson	McGrory 4	Napier	Kavanagh
Mar 7	Partick Thistle	0-1	Thomson	Cook	McGonagle	Geatons	McStay	Scarff	R Thomson	A Thomson	McGrory	Napier	Kavanagh
Mar 18	Hearts	1-1	Thomson	Cook	McGonagle	Geatons	McStay	Scarff	R Thomson	A Thomson	McGrory	Napier	Hughes 1
Mar 21	COWDENBEATH	6-0	Thomson	Cook	McGonagle	Geatons	McStay 1	Scarff	R Thomson	A Thomson	McGrory 4	Napier P	Hughes

			1	2	3	4	5	6	7	8	9	10	11
Mar 24	DUNDEE	2-2	Thomson	Cook	McGonagle	Geatons	McStay	Whitelaw	R Thomson 1	A Thomson	Scarff	Napier	Hughes 1
Apr 4	AYR UNITED	4-1	Thomson	Cook	McGonagle	Wilson	McStay	Geatons	R Thomson	A Thomson	McGrory 1	Scarff 1	Napier +2OG
Apr 6	Clyde	2-0	Thomson	Cook	McGonagle	Wilson	McStay	Geatons	R Thomson 1	A Thomson	McGrory	Scarff	Napier P
Apr 18	AIRDRIE	3-1	Thomson	Cook	McGonagle	Geatons	McStay	Whitelaw	R Thomson	A Thomson	McGrory 1	Scarff 1	Napier P
Apr 22	Dundee	0-0	Thomson	Cook	McGonagle	Whitelaw	McStay	Scarff	R Thomson	A Thomson	McGrory	Napier	Hughes
Apr 25	Leith Athletic	3-0	Thomson	Cook	McGonagle	Whitelaw	McStay	Scarff	A Thomson	Smith	McGrory 3	Napier	Hughes
Apr 28	QUEEN'S PARK	1-1	Thomson	Cook	McGonagle	Whitelaw	McStay	Scarff	A Thomson	Smith	McGrory 1	Napier	Hughes

SCOTTISH CUP 1931

Jan 17	East Fife	2-1	Thomson	Cook	McGonagle	Wilson	McStay	Geatons	R Thomson	A Thomson	McGrory	Scarff 1	Napier 1
Feb 4	Dundee United	3-2	Thomson	Cook	McGonagle	Wilson	McStay	Geatons	R Thomson	A Thomson	Hughes	Scarff 2	Napier 1
Feb 14	Morton	4-1	Thomson	Cook	McGonagle	Wilson	McStay	Geatons	R Thomson	A Thomson	McGrory 3	Scarff	Napier 1
Feb 28	ABERDEEN	4-0	Thomson	Cook	McGonagle	Geatons	McStay	Scarff	R Thomson 3	A Thomson	McGrory 1	Napier	Kavanagh
Mar 14	Kilmarnock	3-0 SF	Thomson	Cook	McGonagle	Geatons	McStay	Scarff	R Thomson	A Thomson	McGrory 1	Napier 1	Hughes 1
Apr 11	Motherwell	2-2 F	Thomson	Cook	McGonagle	Wilson	McStay	Geatons	R Thomson	A Thomson	McGrory 1	Scarff	Napier +OG
Apr 15	Motherwell	4-2 FR	Thomson	Cook	McGonagle	Wilson	McStay	Geatons	R Thomson 2	A Thomson	McGrory 2	Scarff	Napier

SCOTTISH LEAGUE 1931-32

Aug 8	Leith Athletic	3-0	Thomson	Cook	McGonagle	Wilson	McStay	Scarff	R Thomson 1	A Thomson	McGrory 2	Napier	Whitney
Aug 15	DUNDEE UNITED	3-2	Thomson	Cook	McGonagle	Wilson	McStay	Scarff	R Thomson	A Thomson 1	McGrory 2	Napier	Whitney
Aug 19	HEARTS	3-0	Thomson	Cook	McGonagle	Wilson	McStay	Geatons	R Thomson	A Thomson	Scarff 2	Napier 1	Whitney
Aug 22	Aberdeen	1-1	Thomson	Cook	McGonagle	Wilson	McStay	Geatons	R Thomson	A Thomson	Scarff	Napier	Whitney 1
Aug 26	COWDENBEATH	7-0	Thomson	Cook	McGonagle	Wilson	McStay	Scarff	R Thomson	A Thomson 1	McGrory 4	Napier 1	Solis 1
Aug 29	HAMILTON ACADEMICALS	6-1	Thomson	Cook	McGonagle	Wilson	McStay	Geatons	R Thomson	A Thomson	McGrory 3	Scarff 3	Solis
Sept 2	Third Lanark	3-3	Thomson	Morrison	McGonagle	Wilson	McStay	Geatons	R Thomson	A Thomson	McGrory 2	Scarff 1	Solis
Sept 5	Rangers	0-0	Thomson	Cook	McGonagle	Wilson	McStay	Geatons	R Thomson	A Thomson	McGrory	Scarff	Napier
Sept 12	QUEEN'S PARK	2-2	Falconer	Cook	McGonagle	Wilson	McStay	Geatons	R Thomson	A Thomson	McGrory	Napier P	Solis 1
Sept 19	Morton	3-3	Falconer	Whitelaw	McGonagle	Wilson	McStay	Geatons	R Thomson	A Thomson	Hughes 1	Napier 1+P	Solis
Sept 26	FALKIRK	4-1	Falconer	Cook	McGonagle	Wilson	McStay	Geatons	R Thomson	A Thomson	McGrory 1	Scarff	Napier 2 +OG
Oct 3	Kilmarnock	3-2	Falconer	Cook	McGonagle	Wilson	Geatons	Whitelaw	R Thomson	A Thomson	McGrory 2	Napier 1	Hughes
Oct 10	CLYDE	1-1	Coen	Cook	McGonagle	Morrison	McStay	Hughes 1	R Thomson	A Thomson	McGrory	Scarff	Kavanagh
Oct 17	Dundee	0-2	Coen	Cook	McGonagle	Morrison	McStay	Hughes	R Thomson	A Thomson	McGrory	Scarff	Napier
Oct 24	AYR UNITED	4-2	Coen	Cook	McGonagle	Wilson	McStay	Scarff	R Thomson	A Thomson	McGrory 1	Napier 1	McGhee 2
Oct 31	Motherwell	2-2	Kennaway	Cook	McGonagle	Geatons	McStay	Whitelaw	McGhee	A Thomson	Scarff	Napier 2	Hughes
Nov 14	PARTICK THISTLE	1-2	Falconer	Cook	McGonagle	Geatons	McStay	Scarff	R Thomson	A Thomson 1	McGrory	Napier	McGhee
Nov 21	Hearts	1-2	Kennaway	Cook	McGonagle	Geatons	McStay	Whitelaw	R Thomson	A Thomson	McGrory 1	Scarff	Napier
Nov 28	Cowdenbeath	2-1	Kennaway	Cook	Morrison	Wilson	McStay	Geatons	R Thomson 2	Scarff	McGrory	Napier	Kavanagh
Dec 5	THIRD LANARK	5-0	Kennaway	Morrison	McGonagle	Wilson	McStay	Geatons	R Thomson	A Thomson	McGrory 3	Scarff	Napier 2
Dec 12	AIRDRIE	6-1	Kennaway	Morrison	McGonagle	Wilson	McStay	Scarff	R Thomson	A Thomson	McGrory 2	Napier 3	Solis 1
Dec 19	LEITH ATHLETIC	6-0	Kennaway	Morrison	McGonagle	Wilson	McStay	Scarff	R Thomson 1	A Thomson	McGrory 4	Napier 1	Solis
Dec 26	Dundee United	0-1	Kennaway	Cook	McGonagle	Wilson	McStay	Whitelaw	R Thomson	A Thomson	McGrory	Napier	Hughes
Jan 1	RANGERS	1-2	Kennaway	Cook	McGonagle	Wilson	McStay	Morrison	R Thomson	A Thomson	McGrory 1	Napier	Hughes
Jan 2	Queen's Park	3-0	Falconer	Cook	McGonagle	Wilson	McStay	Whitelaw	R Thomson	Smith	Hughes	Napier 2(1P)	Solis +OG
Jan 9	ABERDEEN	2-0	Falconer	Cook	McGonagle	Wilson 1	NcStay	Whitelaw	R Thomson	Smith	Hughes 1	Napier	Solis
Jan 23	Hamilton Academicals	0-1	Kennaway	Cook	McGonagle	Wilson	McStay	Geatons	R Thomson	A Thomson	Hughes	Napier	O'Donnell
Feb 6	Falkirk	0-2	Kennaway	Cook	Morrison	Wilson	McStay	Geatons	McGhee	A Thomson	Hughes	Smith	Kavanagh
Feb 20	Clyde	1-2	Kennaway	Cook	McGonagle	Wilson	McStay	Geatons	McCallum	A Thomson	Napier P	Smith	McWilliams
Feb 27	DUNDEE	0-2	Kennaway	Cook	McGonagle	Wilson	McStay	Geatons	McGhee	A Thomson	Napier	Smith	Kavanagh
Mar 5	Ayr United	3-2	Kennaway	Cook	McGonagle	Wilson	McStay	Geatons	O'Donnell 2	A Thomson 1	Napier	Smith	Kavanagh
Mar 12	MOTHERWELL	2-4	Kennaway	Cook	McGonagle	Morrison	McStay	Geatons	Napier	A Thomson 1	O'Donnell 1	Smith	Kavanagh
Mar 19	St Mirren	2-1	Kennaway	Cook	McGonagle	Wilson	McStay	Geatons	Napier	A Thomson 1	O'Donnell 1	Smith	Kavanagh 1
Mar 28	ST MIRREN	1-0	Kennaway	Cook	McGonagle	Wilson	McStay	Geatons	R Thomson	Napier	O'Donnell	A Thomson 1	Kavanagh
Apr 2	MORTON	6-3	Kennaway	Cook	McGonagle	Wilson	McStay	Geatons	R Thomson	A Thomson 2	O'Donnell 4	Napier	Kavanagh
Apr 9	Airdrie	1-1	Kennaway	Cook	McGonagle	Wilson	McStay	Geatons	McGonagle	A Thomson	O'Donnell 1	Smith	Kavanagh
Apr 23	KILMARNOCK	4-1	Kennaway	Cook	McGonagle	Wilson	McStay	Geatons	McGrory	A Thomson 1	O'Donnell	Napier P	Kavanagh 2
Apr 30	Partick Thistle	2-0	Kennaway	Cook	McGonagle	Wilson	McStay	Geatons	O'Donnell	A Thomson	McGrory	Napier	McDonald 2

SCOTTISH CUP 1932

Jan 16	FALKIRK	3-2	Falconer	Cook	McGonagle	Wilson	McStay	Geatons	R Thomson	A Thomson	Hughes	Napier 2(1P)	Whitelaw +OG\
Jan 30	St Johnstone	4-2	Kennaway	Cook	McGonagle	Wilson	McStay	Geatons	McGhee	A Thomson 1	Napier 3	Smith	Kavanagh
Feb 13	Motherwell	0-2	Kennaway	Cook	McGonagle	Wilson	McStay	Geatons	A Thomson	Smith	McGrory	Napier	Kavanagh

SCOTTISH LEAGUE 1932-33

Aug 13	ABERDEEN	3-0	Kennaway	Cook	McGonagle	Wilson	McStay	Geatons	R Thomson	A Thomson	McGrory 1	Napier P	Cameron 1
Aug 16	THIRD LANARK	4-2	Kennaway	Cook	McGonagle	Wilson	McDonald	Geatons	R Thomson	A Thomson	McGrory 2	Napier 1	Cameron 1
Aug 20	Hamilton Academicals	1-1	Kennaway	Cook	McGonagle	Wilson	McDonald	Geatons	R Thomson	A Thomson	McGrory 1	Napier	Cameron
Aug 24	PARTICK THISTLE	1-2	Kennaway	Cook	McGonagle	Wilson	McDonald	Geatons	R Thomson	A Thomson	McGrory	Napier 1	Cameron
Aug 27	MORTON	7-1	Kennaway	Cook	McGonagle	Wilson	McStay	Geatons	R Thomson 1	A Thomson 1	McGrory 2	O'Donnell	Napier 3
Aug 30	AYR UNITED	4-1	Kennaway	Cook	McGonagle	Wilson	McStay	Geatons	R Thomson	A Thomson	McGrory 1	Napier 2(1P)	McGillivray 1
Sept 3	Falkirk	1-1	Kennaway	Cook	McGonagle	Wilson	McStay	Geatons	R Thomson	A Thomson	McGrory	Napier	McGillivray 1
Sept 10	RANGERS	1-1	Kennaway	Cook	McGonagle	Wilson	McStay	Geatons	McGillivray	A Thomson	McGrory 1	Napier	O'Donnell
Sept 14	East Stirling	3-1	Kennaway	Cook	McGonagle	Geatons	McStay	Hughes	R Thomson	A Thomson	McGrory	Napier 3(1P)	McDonald
Sept 17	Queen's Park	1-4	Kennaway	Hogg	Morrison	Greatons	McStay	Hughes	R Thomson	A Thomson	O'Donnell 1	Connor	Napier
Sept 24	KILMARNOCK	0-0	Kennaway	Cook	Morrison	Wilson	McStay	Geatons	McGillivray	A Thomson	McGrory	Napier	Hugh O'Donnell
Oct 1	Hearts	1-1	Kennaway	Cook	Hogg	Wilson	McStay	Geatons	Napier 1	A Thomson	F. O'Donnell	Smith	H O'Donnell
Oct 8	ST JOHNSTONE	5-0	Kennaway	Cook	Hogg	Wilson	McStay	Geatons	Napier 1+P	A Thomson	F. O'Donnell 1	Smith	H O'Donnell 2
Oct 15	Clyde	2-0	Kennaway	Cook	Hogg	Wilson	McStay	Geatons 1	Napier	A Thomson	F. O'Donnell 1	Smith	H O'Donnell
Oct 22	MOTHERWELL	4-1	Kennaway	Cook	Hogg	Wilson	McStay	Geatons	Napier	A Thomson 1	Crum 2	Smith 1	H O'Donnell
Oct 29	St Mirren	1-3	Kennaway	Cook	McGonagle	Wilson	McStay	Geatons	Napier P	A Thomson	Crum	Smith	H O'Donnell
Nov 5	Partick Thistle	0-3	Kennaway	Cook	McGonagle	Wilson	McStay	Geatons	Napier	A Thomson	Crum	Smith	H O'Donnell
Nov 12	EAST STIRLING	3-0	Kennaway	Cook	McGonagle	Wilson	McStay	Geatons	F O'Donnell	A Thomson 3	McGrory	Napier	H O'Donnell
Nov 19	COWDENBEATH	3-0	Kennaway	Cook	McGonagle	Wilson	McStay	Geatons	R Thomson	A Thomson	McGrory 1	Napier 2P	H O'Donnell
Nov 26	Third Lanark	4-0	Wallace	Cook	McGonagle	Wilson	McStay	Geatons	R Thomson	A Thomson	McGrory 2	Napier 2	H O'Donnell
Dec 3	Airdrie	3-0	Kennaway	Cook	McGonagle	Wilson	McStay	Geatons	R Thomson 2	A Thomson	McGrory	Napier P	H O'Donnell
Dec 10	DUNDEE	3-2	Kennaway	Hogg	McGonagle	Wilson	McStay	Geatons 1	R Thomson	A Thomson	McGrory 1	Napier	H O'Donnell+OG
Dec 17	Ayr United	1-0	Wallace	Cook	McGonagle	Wilson	McStay	Geatons	R Thomson	A Thomson	McGrory 1	Napier	H O'Donnell
Dec 24	Aberdeen	0-1	Wallace	Cook	McGonagle	Wilson	McStay	Geatons	R Thomson	A Thomson	McGrory	Napier	H O'Donnell
Dec 26	QUEEN'S PARK	2-0	Wallace	Cook	McGonagle	Wilson	McStay	Geatons	R Thomson	A Thomson	F O'Donnell 1	Napier	H O'Donnell 1
Dec 31	HAMILTON ACADEMICALS	0-3	Wallace	Hogg	McGonagle	Wilson	McStay	Geatons	R Thomson	Smith	F O'Donnell	Napier	H O'Donnell
Jan 2	Rangers	0-0	Kennaway	Hogg	McGonagle	Wilson	McStay	Geatons	R Thomson	A Thomson	F O'Donnell	Napier	H O'Donnell
Jan 7	Morton	1-0	Kennaway	Hogg	McGonagle	Wilson	McStay	Geatons	R Thomson	A Thomson	McGrory 1	Napier	H O'Donnell
Jan 14	FALKIRK	0-1	Kennaway	Hogg	Morrison	Wilson	McStay	Geatons	R Thomson	A Thomson	McGrory	Napier	McDonald
Jan 28	Kilmarnock	2-2	Kennaway	Hogg	McGonagle P	Wilson	McStay	Geatons	R Thomson	A Thomson	F O'Donnell	Smith	H O'Donnell 1
Feb 11	HEARTS	3-2	Wallace	Hogg	McGonagle	Wilson	McStay	Hughes	R Thomson 1	A Thomson	McGrory 2	Napier	H O'Donnell
Feb 25	St Johnstone	0-1	Wallace	Hogg	McGonagle	Wilson	McStay	Hughes	R Thomson	A Thomson	McGrory	Napier	H O'Donnell
Mar 11	Motherwell	2-4	Wallace	Hogg	McGonagle	Wilson	McDonald	Hughes	R Thomson	Napier	McGrory 1	F O'Donnell 1	H O'Donnell
Mar 25	Cowdenbeath	5-1	Kennaway	Hogg	McGonagle	Wilson	McStay	Geatons	R Thomson 2	A Thomson	McGrory 3	Napier	H O'Donnell
Apr 3	ST MIRREN	0-0	Kennaway	Hogg	McGonagle	Wilson	McStay	Geatons	R Thomson	A Thomson	McGrory	Napier	H O'Donnell
Apr 10	CLYDE	2-1	Kennaway	Hogg	McGonagle	Wilson	McStay	Geatons	R Thomson	A Thomson	McGrory 2	Napier	H O'Donnell
Apr 18	AIRDRIE	2-1	Wallace	Hogg	McGonagle	Wilson	McStay	Geatons	R Thomson	A Thomson 1	Paterson 1	F O'Donnell	H O'Donnell
Apr 22	Dundee	0-3	Wallace	Hogg	McGonagle	Wilson	McStay	Hughes	R Thomson	A Thomson	Paterson	Smith	H O'Donnell

SCOTTISH CUP 1933

			1	2	3	4	5	6	7	8	9	10	11
Jan 21	Dunfermline	7-1	Kennaway	Hogg	McGonagle	Wilson	McStay	Geatons	R Thomson 1	A Thomson	McGrory 3	Napier	H O'Donnell 3
Feb 4	FALKIRK	2-0	Kennaway	Hogg	McGonagle	Wilson	McStay	Hughes	R Thomson	A Thomson	McGrory 2	Napier	H O'Donnell
Feb 18	PARTICK THISTLE	2-1	Wallace	Hogg	McGonagle	Wilson	McStay	Hughes	R Thomson 1	A Thomson	McGrory 1	Napier	H O'Donnell
Mar 4	Albion Rovers	1-1	Wallace	Hogg	McGonagle	Wilson	McStay	Hughes	R Thomson	A Thomson	McGrory	Napier 1	H O'Donnell
Mar 8	ALBION ROVERS	3-1	Wallace	Hogg	McGonagle	Wilson	McStay	Hughes	R Thomson	A Thomson 1	McGrory	Napier 1+P	H O'Donnell
Mar 18	Hearts	0-0 SF	Kennaway	Hogg	McGonagle	Wilson	McStay	Geatons	R Thomson	A Thomson	McGrory	Napier	H O'Donnell
Mar 22	Hearts	2-1 SFR	Kennaway	Hogg	McGonagle	Wilson	McStay	Geatons	R Thomson	A Thomson 1	McGrory 1	Napier	H O'Donnell
Apr 15	Motherwell	1-0 F	Kennaway	Hogg	McGonagle	Wilson	McStay	Geatons	R Thomson	A Thomson	McGrory 1	Napier	H O'Donnell

SCOTTISH LEAGUE 1933-34

Aug 12	Queen of the South	2-3	Kennaway	Hogg	McGonagle P	Wilson	McStay	Napier	R Thomson	A Thomson	McGrory 1	Buchan	H O'Donnell
Aug 19	FALKIRK	2-2	Kennaway	Hogg	McGonagle P	McDonald	McStay	Hughes	R Thomson	A Thomson	McGrory 1	F O'Donnell	Napier
Aug 23	Partick Thistle	3-0	Kennaway	Hogg	McGonagle	McDonald	McStay	Hughes	Crum 1	A Thomson	McGrory 1	F O'Donnell 1	H O'Donnell
Aug 26	Kilmarnock	3-4	Kennaway	Hogg	McGonagle 1	McDonald	McStay	Hughes	Crum 1	A Thomson	McGrory	F O'Donnell	Connor 1
Sept 2	HEARTS	0-0	Kennaway	Hogg	McGonagle	Wilson	McStay	Hughes	Crum	Buchan	McGrory	Napier	Connor
Sept 9	Rangers	2-2	Kennaway	Hogg	McGonagle	Wilson	McStay	Hughes	Crum	Buchan	McGrory 2	Napier	Connor
Sept 19	COWDENBEATH	7-0	Kennaway	Hogg	McGonagle	Wilson	McStay	Hughes	Crum	A Thomson	McGrory 3	Napier 2+P	HO'Donnell 1
Sept 23	St Johnstone	1-1	Kennaway	Hogg	McGonagle	Wilson	McStay	Hughes	Crum	Buchan 1	Dunn	F O'Donnell	H O'Donnell
Sept 30	QUEEN'S PARK	3-1	Wallace	Hogg	McGonagle	Dawson	McStay 1	Hughes	Crum	Buchan	Dunn	A Thomson 1	H O'Donnell 1
Oct 7	Aberdeen	0-3	Wallace	Hogg	McGonagle	Wilson	McStay	Hughes	Crum	Buchan	Dunn	F O'Donnell	H O'Donnell
Oct 21	Motherwell	1-1	Kennaway	Hogg	McGonagle	Wilson	McStay	Hughes	Dunn	A Thomson	Crum 1	F O'Donnell	H O'Donnell
Oct 28	HIBERNIAN	2-1	Kennaway	Hogg	McGonagle	Wilson	McStay	Hughes	Dunn	A Thomson	Crum 2	F O'Donnell	McGrory
Nov 4	PARTICK THISTLE	2-0	Kenneway	Hogg	Morrison	Wilson	McStay	Hughes	Napier	A Thomson	Crum	F O'Donnell 1	McGrory 1
Nov 11	Cowdenbeath	1-0	Kennaway	Hogg	McGonagle	Wilson	McStay	Hughes	Napier	A Thomson	Crum	F O'Donnell 1	McGrory
Nov 18	Ayr United	1-3	Kennaway	Hogg	McGonagle	Wilson	McStay	Geatons	Crum	Napier	McGrory	F O'Donnell 1	Hughes
Nov 25	THIRD LANARK	3-1	Kennaway	Hogg	McGonagle	Wilson	McStay	Geatons	Crum	A Thomson	McGrory 1	F O'Donnell 2(1P)	Hughes
Dec 2	AIRDRIE	4-0	Kenneway	Hogg	McGonagle	Wilson	McStay	Geatons	Crum 1	A Thomson 1	McGrory 1	F O'Donnell	Hughes 1
Dec 9	Dundee	2-3	Kenneway	Hogg	McGonagle	Wilson	McDonald	Geatons	Crum 1	A Thomson	McGrory	F O'Donnell 1	Hughes
Dec 23	QUEEN OF THE SOUTH	0-1	Kennaway	Hogg	McGonagle	Wilson	McStay	Geatons	Crum	F O'Donnell	McGrory	Napier	Hughes
Dec 25	Queen's Park	3-2	Kennaway	Hogg	McGonagle	Wilson	McStay	Hughes	Napier 1	A Thomson	McGrory 1	F O'Donnell 1	Geatons
Dec 30	Falkirk	0-2	Kennaway	Hogg	McGonagle	Wilson	McDonald	Hughes	Napier	Smith	McGrory	F O'Donnell	Geatons
Jan 1	RANGERS	2-2	Kennaway	Hogg	McGonagle 1	Wilson	McStay	Hughes	Napier	A Thomson	McGrory 1	F O'Donnell	McDonald
Jan 6	KILMARNOCK	4-1	Kennaway	Hogg	McGonagle	Dawson	McStay	Hughes	Napier 1	A Thomson	McGrory 2	F O'Donnell	McDonald 1
Jan 13	Hearts	1-2	Kennaway	Hogg	McGonagle P	Dawson	McStay	Hughes	Napier	A Thomson	McGrory	F O'Donnell	McDonald
Jan 27	ST JOHNSTONE	0-0	Kennaway	Hogg	McGonagle	Wilson	McStay	Hughes	Napier	A Thomson	McGrory	F O'Donnell	McDonald
Feb 24	ABERDEEN	2-2	Wallace	Hogg	McGonagle	Dawson	McStay	Geatons	Crum 1	A Thomson	Dunn 1	F O'Donnell	H O'Donnell
Mar 10	MOTHERWELL	3-0	Kennaway	Hogg	McGonagle	Geatons	McStay	Hughes	Crum	Smith	McGrory	F O'Donnell 1	H O'Donnell 2
Mar 17	Hibernian	2-1	Kennaway	Hogg	McGonagle	Geatons	McStay	Hughes	Crum	Smith	McGrory 1	F O'Donnell	H O'Donnell 1
Mar 24	AYR UNITED	0-3	Kennaway	Hogg	McGonagle	Geatons	McStay	Hughes	Crum	Buchan	McGrory	F O'Donnell	H O'Donnell
Mar 31	Third Lanark	1-1	Kennaway	Hogg	McGonagle	Geatons	McStay	Hughes	Crum	Smith	McGrory 1	F O'Donnell	H O'Donnell
Apr 2	CLYDE	2-1	Kennaway	Hogg	McGonagle	Wilson	McDonald	Hughes	Crum	F O'Donnell 1+P	McGrory	Divers	H O'Donnell
Apr 7	Airdrie	4-2	Kennaway	Hogg	McGonagle	Wilson	McDonald	Hughes	Crum	Divers	F O'Donnell 1+P	H O'Donnell	Murphy 2
Apr 11	ST MIRREN	3-0	Kennaway	Hogg	Morrison	Wilson	McDonald	Hughes	Crum	Divers	F O'Donnell 3	H O'Donnell	Murphy
Apr 14	Hamilton Academicals	1-1	Kennaway	Hogg	Morrison	Wilson	McStay	Hughes	Crum	A Thomson	F O'Donnell P	Divers	H O'Donnell
Apr 18	Clyde	1-1	Kennaway	Hogg	McGonagle	Wilson	McStay	Hughes	Crum	A Thomson	F O'Donnell 1	Divers	H O'Donnell
Apr 21	DUNDEE	3-2	Kennaway	Hogg	McGonagle	Wilson	McStay	Hughes	Crum	A Thomson	F O'Donnell 1	Divers 2	H O'Donnell
Apr 23	HAMILTON ACADEMICALS	5-1	Wallace	Hogg	McGonagle	Geatons 1	McStay	Hughes	Crum 2	A Thomson	F O'Donnell 2	Divers	H O'Donnell
Apr 28	St Mirren	2-1	Wallace	Hogg	McGonagle	Morrison	McStay	Geatons 1	Crum	Divers	F O'Donnell 1	McDonald	H O'Donnell

SCOTTISH CUP 1934

Jan 20	Dalbeattie Star	6-0	Kennaway	Hogg	McGonagle	Dawson	McStay	Hughes	Napier	A Thomson	Crum 4	F O'Donnell 2	McDonald
Feb 3	Ayr United	3-2	Kennaway	Hogg	McGonagle P	Dawson	McStay	Hughes	Napier	A Thomson	McGrory	F O'Donnell 1	H O'Donnell 1
Feb 17	FALKIRK	3-1	Kennaway	Hogg	McGonagle	Geatons	McStay	Hughes	Crum	A Thomson	McGrory 1	F O'Donnell 2	H O'Donnell
Mar 3	St Mirren	0-2	Kennaway	Hogg	McGonagle	Wilson	McStay	Geatons	Crum	A Thomson	McGrory	F O'Donnell	H O'Donnell

SCOTTISH LEAGUE 1934-35

Aug 11	KILMARNOCK	4-1	Kennaway	Hogg	McGonagle	Geatons	McDonald	Hughes	Napier	F O'Donnell	McGrory 2	McInally 1	H O'Donnell 1
Aug 18	Hearts	0-0	Kennaway	Hogg	McGonagle	Dawson	Geatons	Paterson	Delaney	McDonald	McGrory	F O'Donnell	H O'Donnell
Aug 22	Motherwell	0-1	Kennaway	Hogg	McGonagle	Morrison	Geatons	Paterson	Delaney	McDonald	McGrory	F O'Donnell	Napier
Aug 25	ST JOHNSTONE	0-0	Kennaway	Hogg	McGonagle	Morrison	Geatons	Paterson	Delaney	McDonald	F O'Donnell	McInally	Napier
Sept 1	Queen's Park	0-1	Kennaway	Hogg	Morrison	Geatons	McDonald	Hughes	Delaney	Buchan	McGrory	F O'Donnell	McInally
Sept 8	RANGERS	1-1	Kennaway	Hogg	McGonagle	Morrison	Geatons	Hughes 1	Delaney	McInally	McGrory	McDonald	Napier
Sept 11	HIBERNIAN	4-0	Kennaway	Hogg	Morrison P	Napier	Geatons	Hughes	Delaney 1	Buchan	McGrory 1	McDonald 1	Murphy
Sept 15	Hamilton Academicals	2-4	Kennaway	Hogg	Morrison	Napier	Geatons	Hughes	Delaney 1	Buchan	McGrory 1	McDonald	Murphy
Sept 22	ABERDEEN	4-1	Kennaway	Hogg	McGonagle	Napier	Geatons	Hughes	Delaney	McInally 1	F O'Donnell 2	McDonald	Murphy 1
Sept 29	Albion Rovers	1-2	Kennaway	Hogg	McGonagle	Dawson	Geatons	Hughes	Delaney	McInally	F O'Donnell	Napier	Murphy 1
Oct 1	Dundee	0-0	Kennaway	Hogg	McGonagle	Napier	Geatons	Paterson	Delaney	Buchan	Dunn	McDonald	Murphy
Oct 6	QUEEN OF THE SOUTH	1-2	Kennaway	Hogg	McGonagle	Napier	Geatons	Paterson	Delaney 1	Buchan	Dunn	McDonald	Murphy
Oct 13	Clyde	3-0	Kennaway	Hogg	McGonagle	Geatons	McDonald	Paterson	Delaney 1	Buchan 1	McGrory 1	F O'Donnell	H O'Donnell
Oct 20	Partick Thistle	3-1	Kennaway	Hogg	Morrison	Geatons	McDonald	Paterson	Delaney	Buchan	F O'Donnell 2	Napier	H O'Donnell 1
Oct 27	DUNFERMLINE	3-0	Kennaway	Hogg	McGonagle	Geatons	McDonald	Paterson	Delaney	Buchan 1	F O'Donnell 2	Napier	H O'Donnell
Nov 3	AYR UNITED	7-0	Kennaway	Hogg	McGonagle	Geatons	McDonald	Paterson P	Delaney 2	Buchan 1	F O'Donnell 2	Napier	H O'Donnell 1
Nov 10	Falkirk	2-1	Kennaway	Hogg	McGonagle	Geatons	McDonald	Paterson	Delaney	Buchan	F O'Donnell 1	Napier 1	H O'Donnell
Nov 17	Airdrie	2-0	Kennaway	Hogg	McGonagle	Geatons	McDonald	Paterson P	Delaney	Buchan	F O'Donnell 1	Napier	H O'Donnell
Nov 24	DUNDEE	4-0	Kennaway	Hogg	McGonagle	Geatons	McDonald	Paterson	McGrory	Buchan 4	F O'Donnell	Napier	H O'Donnell
Dec 1	St Mirren	4-2	Kennaway	Hogg	McGonagle	Geatons	McDonald	Paterson 2P	McGrory	Buchan 1	F O'Donnell 1	Napier	H O'Donnell
Dec 8	MOTHERWELL	3-2	Kennaway	Hogg	McGonagle	Geatons	McDonald	Paterson	McGrory 1	Buchan	F O'Donnell	Napier	H O'Donnell 2
Dec 15	Hibernian	2-3	Kennaway	Hogg	McGonagle	Geatons	Mcdonald	Paterson	McGrory 1	Buchan	F O'Donnell 1	Napier	H O'Donnell
Dec 22	Kilmarnock	3-2	Kennaway	Morrison	McGonagle	Geatons	McDonald	Paterson P	McGrory	Buchan	F O'Donnell 1	Napier 1	H O'Donnell
Dec 25	QUEEN'S PARK	4-1	Kennaway	Morrison	McGonagle	Dawson	McDonald	Paterson	Delaney 2	Crum 1	McGrory 1	Napier	H O'Donnell
Dec 29	HFARTS	4-2	Kennaway	Hogg	McGonagle	Dawson	McDonald	Paterson	Delaney	Crum 1	McGrory 3	Napier	H O'Donnell
Jan 1	Rangers	1-2	Kennaway	Hogg	McGonagle	Dawson	McDonald	Paterson P	Delaney	Crum	McGrory	Napier	H O'Donnell
Jan 5	St Johnstone	1-0	Kennaway	Hogg	McGonagle	Dawson	McDonald	Paterson	Crum	Buchan	McGrory 1	F O'Donnell	H O'Donnell
Jan 12	HAMILTON ACADEMICALS	3-1	Kennaway	Hogg	Morrison	Dawson	Geatons	Paterson	Delaney 2	Buchan	McGrory 1	Crum	H O'Donnell
Jan 19	Aberdeen	0-2	Kennaway	Hogg	Morrison	Dawson	Geatons	Paterson	Delaney	Buchan	McGrory	Crum	H O'Donnell
Feb 2	ALBION ROVERS	5-1	Kennaway	Hogg	McGonagle	Geatons	McDonald	Paterson	Delaney 3	Buchan	Dunn 1	Crum	H O'Donnell 1
Feb 16	Queen of the South	4-3	Kennaway	Hogg	McGonagle	Morrison	McDonald	Paterson P	Delaney	Buchan 1	McGrory 1	F O'Donnell 1	H O'Donnell
Feb 23	PARTICK THISTLE	3-1	Kennaway	Hogg	Morrison	Napier	McDonald	Paterson	Delaney	Buchan 1	McGrory 1	Crum	H O'Donnell 1
Mar 2	CLYDE	0-2	Kennaway	Hogg	McGonagle	Napier	McDonald	Paterson	Delaney	Buchan	McGrory	Crum	H O'Donnell
Mar 16	Dunfermline	3-1	Kennaway	Hogg	McGonagle	Napier	Geatons	Paterson	Crum	Buchan 1	McGrory 1	Willie Fagan	H O'Donnell
Mar 23	Ayr United	0-1	Kennaway	Hogg	McGonagle	Napier	Geatons	Paterson	Delaney	Buchan	McGrory	F O'Donnell	H O'Donnell
Apr 13	AIRDRIE	2-0	Kennaway	Hogg	McGonagle	Paterson	Geatons	Hughes	Delaney	Buchan 1	McGrory	F O'Donnell	H O'Donnell 1
Apr 17	FALKIRK	7-3	Kennaway	Hogg	McGonagle	Paterson	Geatons	Hughes	Delaney 2	Buchan 1	McGrory 2	F O'Donnell 1	H O'Donnell 1
Apr 27	ST MIRREN	2-1	Kennaway	Hogg	McGonagle	Paterson	Geatons	Hughes	Delaney	Buchan	McGrory	McInaly 1	H O'Donnell

SCOTTISH CUP 1935

Jan 26	MONTROSE	4-1	Kennaway	Hogg	Morrison	Geatons	McDonald	Paterson P	Crum	Buchan 1	McGrory	F O'Donnell 2	H O'Donnell
Feb 9	PARTICK THISTLE	1-1	Kennaway	Hogg	McGonagle	Geatons	McDonald	Paterson	Delaney	Buchan	McGrory	Crum	H O'Donnell 1
Feb 13	Partick Thistle	3-1	Kennaway	Hogg	Morrison	Dawson	McDonald	Paterson	Delaney	Buchan	McGrory 1	Napier	H O'Donnell 2
Mar 9	Aberdeen	1-3	Kennaway	Hogg	Morrison	Geatons	McDonald	Paterson	Delaney	Buchan	McGrory 1	Napier	H O'Donnell

SCOTTISH LEAGUE 1935-36

			1	2	3	4	5	6	7	8	9	10	11
Aug 10	Aberdeen	1-3	Kennaway	Hogg	McGonagle	Geatons	Lyon	Paterson	Delaney	Buchan	McGrory 1	McDonald	Crum
Aug 17	HAMILTON ACADEMICALS	1-0	Kennaway	Hogg	McGonagle	Geatons	Lyon	Paterson	Delaney	Buchan	McGrory 1	McDonald	Crum
Aug 24	St Johnstone	3-2	Kennaway	Hogg	McGonagle	Geatons	Lyon	Paterson	Delaney 1	Buchan	McGrory 2	McDonald	Crum
Aug 28	THIRD LANARK	6-0	Kennaway	Hogg	McGonagle	Geatons	Lyon	Paterson	Delaney	Buchan 2	McGrory 3	McDonald	Crum 1
Aug 31	QUEEN'S PARK	3-0	Kennaway	Hogg	Morrison	Geatons	Lyon	Paterson	Delaney 2	Buchan	McGrory 1	McDonald	Crum
Sept 7	Queen of the South	3-1	Kennaway	Hogg	McGonagle	Geatons 1	Lyon	Paterson	Delaney 1	Buchan	McGrory 1	McDonald	Crum
Sept 14	ALBION ROVERS	4-0	Kennaway	Hogg	McGonagle	Geatons	Lyon	Paterson	Delaney 1	Buchan	McGrory 3	McDonald	Crum
Sept 16	DUNFERMLINE	5-3	Kennaway	Hogg	McGonagle	Geatons	Lyon	Paterson	Delaney 1	Buchan 1	McGrory 3	McDonald	Crum
Sept 21	Rangers	2-1	Kennaway	Hogg	McGonagle	Geatons	Lyon	Paterson	Delaney	Buchan	Crum 1	McDonald	Murphy 1
Sept 28	HEARTS	2-1	Kennaway	Hogg	McGonagle	Geatons	Lyon	Paterson	Delaney 1	Buchan	Crum 1	McDonald	Murphy
Oct 5	Kilmarnock	1-1	Kennaway	Hogg	Morrison	Geatons	Lyon	Paterson	Miller	Buchan	Crum	McInally 1	Fitzsimmons
Oct 19	AIRDRIE	4-0	Foley	Hogg	Morrison	Geatons	Lyon	Paterson	Delaney 1	Buchan 1	McGrory 2	Crum	Murphy
Oct 26	Motherwell	2-1	Kennaway	Hogg	Morrison	Geatons	Lyon	Paterson	Delaney	Buchan	McGrory 1	Crum	Murphy 1
Nov 2	DUNDEE	4-2	Kennaway	Hogg	Morrison	Geatons	Lyon	Paterson	Delaney 2	Buchan	McGrory 1	Crum 1	Murphy
Nov 9	Hibernian	5-0	Kennaway	Hogg	Morrison	Geatons	Lyon	Paterson	Delaney 1	Buchan 1	McGrory 2	Crum	Murphy 1
Nov 16	ARBROATH	5-0	Kennaway	Hogg	Morrison	Geatons	Lyon P	Paterson	Delaney 1	Buchan	McGrory 2	Crum	Murphy 1
Nov 23	Ayr United	2-0	Kennaway	Hogg	Morrison	Geatons	Lyon	Paterson	Delaney 1	Buchan	McGrory 1	Crum	Murphy
Nov 30	PARTICK THISTLE	1-1	Kennaway	Hogg	McGonagle	Geatons	Lyon	Paterson	Fitzsimmons	Buchan	McGrory	Crum	Murphy 1
Dec 7	Third Lanark	3-1	Kennaway	Hogg	McGonagle	Geatons	Lyon	Paterson	Crum	Buchan	McGrory 1	Divers	Murphy 1 +OG
Dec 14	Dunfermline	0-1	Kennaway	Hogg	Morrison	Geatons	Lyon	Paterson	Mills	Buchan	Crum	Divers	Murphy
Dec 21	ABERDEEN	5-3	Kennaway	Hogg	McGonagle	Morrison	Lyon	Paterson	Fagan	Buchan 1	McGrory 3	Crum	Murphy 1
Dec 28	Hamilton Academicals	2-0	Foley	Hogg	McGonagle	Morrison	Lyon	Paterson	Fagan	Buchan 1	Hughes 1	Crum	Murphy
Jan 1	RANGERS	3-4	Foley	Hogg	McGonagle	Morrison	Lyon	Paterson	Delaney	Buchan	McGrory	Crum	Murphy
Jan 4	ST JOHNSTONE	2-0	Foley	Hogg	Morison	Paterson	Lyon P	Hughes	Delaney	Buchan	McGrory	Crum	Murphy 1
Jan 11	Queen of the South	5-0	Foley	Hogg	Morrison	Geatons	Lyon	Paterson	Fagan	Buchan	McGrory 3	Crum 1	Murphy 1
Jan 18	Albion Rovers	3-0	Kennaway	Hogg	Morrison	Geatons	Lyon	Paterson	Fagan 1	Buchan	McGrory 1	Crum	Murphy 1
Feb 1	Hearts	0-1	Kennaway	Hogg	Morrison	Geatons	Lyon	Paterson	Delaney	Buchan	McGrory	Crum	Murphy
Feb 15	KILMARNOCK	4-0	Kennaway	Hogg	Morrison	Geatons	Lyon 1	Paterson	Delaney 1	Buchan 1	McGrory 1	Crum	Murphy
Feb 22	Queen's Park	3-2	Kennaway	Hogg	Morrison	Geatons	Lyon	Hughes	Delaney	Buchan	McGrory 2	Crum	Murphy 1
Feb 29	Clyde	4-0	Kennaway	Hogg	Morrison	Geatons	Lyon	Hughes 1	Delaney	Buchan P	McGrory 1	Crum 1	Murphy
Mar 7	Airdrie	3-2	Kennaway	Hogg	Morrison	Geatons	Lyon	Paterson	Delaney	Buchan	McGrory 2	Crum 1	Murphy
Mar 14	MOTHERWELL	5-0	Kennaway	Hogg	Morrison	Geatons	Lyon	Paterson	Delaney 1	Buchan 1	McGrory 3	Crum	Murphy
Mar 21	Dundee	2-0	Kennaway	Hogg	Morrison	Geatons	Lyon	Paterson	Delaney 1	Buchan	McGrory 1	Crum	Murphy
Mar 28	HIBERNIAN	4-1	Kennaway	Hogg	Morrison	Geatons	Lyon P	Paterson	Delaney	Buchan	McGrory 1	Crum 1	Murphy 1
Apr 11	Arbroath	2-0	Kennaway	Hogg	Morrison	Geatons	Lyon	Paterson	Delaney 1	Buchan	McGrory 1	Crum	Murphy
Apr 13	CLYDE	2-1	Kennaway	Hogg	Morrison	Geatons	Lyon	Paterson	Delaney 1	Buchan	McGrory 1	Crum	Murphy
Apr 18	AYR UNITED	6-0	Kennaway	Hogg	Morrison	Geatons	Lyon 1	Paterson	Delaney	Buchan 1	McGrory 3	Crum	Murphy 1
Apr 25	Partick Thistle	3-1	Kennaway	Hogg	Morrison	Geatons	Lyon P	Paterson	Delaney	Buchan	Fagan 2	Crum	Murphy

SCOTTISH CUP 1936

Jan 25	Berwick	w/o											
Feb 8	ST JOHNSTONE	1-2	Kennaway	Hogg	Morrison	Geatons	Lyon	Paterson	Delaney	Buchan 1	McGrory	Crum	Murphy

SCOTTISH LEAGUE 1936-37

Aug 8	ST JOHNSTONE	3-2	Kennaway	Hogg	Morrison	Geatons	Lyon	Paterson	Delaney	Buchan 1	McGrory	Crum	Murphy 2
Aug 15	Clyde	1-1	Kennaway	Hogg	Paterson	Geatons	Lyon	McDonald	Delaney	Buchan	Fagan 1	Crum	Murphy
Aug 19	St Johnstone	1-2	Kennaway	Hogg	Hughes	Geatons	Lyon	Paterson	Delaney	Buchan 1	Crum	Fagan	Murphy
Aug 22	QUEEN OF THE SOUTH	5-0	Kennaway	Hogg	John Boyle	Dawson	Lyon	Paterson	Delaney 1	Buchan 1	Fagan 2	Crum 1	Murphy
Aug 29	Albion Rovers	3-1	Foley	Hogg	Boyle	Geatons	Lyon	Paterson P	Delaney	Buchan	Fagan 1	Crum 1	Murphy
Sept 5	KILMARNOCK	2-4	Kennaway	Hogg	Boyle	Geatons	Lyon	Paterson	Delaney	Buchan	Fagan 2	Crum	Murphy
Sept 9	CLYDE	3-1	Kennaway	Hogg	Boyle	Geatons	Lyon	Paterson P	Delaney 1	Buchan 1	Crum	Fagan	Murphy
Sept 12	Hamilton Academicals	2-1	Kennaway	Hogg	Boyle	Geatons	Lyon	Paterson	Delaney	Buchan	Crum 2	Divers	Murphy
Sept 19	RANGERS	1-1	Kennaway	Hogg	Morrison	Geatons	Miller	Paterson	Delaney 1	Buchan	Crum	McDonald	Murphy
Sept 26	Hearts	1-0	Kennaway	Hogg	Morrison	Geatons	Lyon	Paterson	Delaney 1	Buchan	Crum	McDonald	Murphy
Oct 3	ABERDEEN	3-2	Kennaway	Hogg	Morrison	Geatons	Lyon	Paterson	Delaney 2	Buchan 1	McGrory	Crum	Murphy
Oct 10	Queen's Park	2-0	Kennaway	Hogg	Morrison	Geatons	Lyon	Paterson	Delaney 1	Buchan	McGrory 1	Crum	McDonald
Oct 17	Dundee	0-0	Kennaway	Hogg	Morrison	Geatons	Lyon	Paterson	Delaney	Buchan	McGrory	Crum	McDonald
Oct 24	HIBERNIAN	5-1	Kennaway	Hogg	Morrison	Geatons	Lyon	Paterson P	Delaney 1	Buchan 1	McGrory	Crum 2	McDonald
Oct 31	Arbroath	3-2	Kennaway	Boyle	Morrison	Geatons	Lyon	Paterson	Delaney 1	Buchan 1	McGrory 1	Crum	Murphy
Nov 7	ST MIRREN	3-0	Kennaway	Hogg	Morrison	Geatons	Lyon	Paterson	Delaney	Buchan 2	McGrory	Crum	Murphy 1
Nov 14	Partick Thistle	1-1	Kennaway	Hogg	Morrison	Geatons	Lyon	Paterson	Delaney	Buchan	McGrory 1	Crum	Murphy
Nov 21	THIRD LANARK	6-3	Kennaway	Hogg	Morrison	Geatons	Lyon 1	Paterson	Delaney	Buchan 1	McGrory 3	Crum 1	Murphy
Nov 28	DUNFERMLINE	3-1	Kennaway	Hogg	Morrison	Geatons	Lyon	Paterson	Delaney	Buchan	McGrory 2	Crum	Murphy 1
Dec 5	Falkirk	3-0	Kennaway	Hogg	Morrison	Geatons	Lyon	Paterson	McInally 1	Carruth 1	McGrory 1	Crum	Murphy
Dec 12	MOTHERWELL	3-2	Kennaway	Hogg	Morrison	Geatons	Lyon	Paterson	Delaney 2	Carruth	McGrory	Crum 1	Murphy
Dec 19	Queen of the South	0-1	Kennaway	Hogg	Morrison	Geatons	Lyon	Paterson	Delaney	Buchan	McGrory	Crum	Murphy
Dec 26	ALBION ROVERS	4-0	Kennaway	Hogg	Morrison	Geatons	Lyon	Paterson	Delaney 2	Buchan	McGrory 1	Crum	Murphy 1
Jan 1	Rangers	0-1	Kennaway	Hogg	Morrison	Geatons	Lyon	Paterson	Delaney	Buchan	McGrory	Crum	Murphy
Jan 2	QUEEN'S PARK	4-0	Kennaway	Hogg	Morrison	Geatons	Lyon	Paterson	Delaney	McDonald	McGrory 2+P	Crum	Murphy +OG
Jan 9	Kilmarnock	3-3	Kennaway	Hogg	Morrison	Geatons	Lyon	Miller	Delaney	Buchan	Carruth 2	Crum	McGrory +OG
Jan 16	HAMILTON ACADEMICALS	3-3	Kennaway	Hogg	Morrison	Duffy	Lyon	Geatons	Delaney 1	Buchan	Carruth 1	Crum	McDonald 1
Jan 23	Aberdeen	0-1	Kennaway	Hogg	Morrison	Geatons	Lyon	Paterson	Crum	Buchan	Carruth	McDonald	McGrory
Feb 6	HEARTS	3-2	Kennaway	Hogg	Morrison	Dawson	Miller	Paterson	Delaney	Buchan 1	McGrory 2	Crum	Murphy
Feb 20	DUNDEE	1-2	Kennaway	Hogg	Morrison	Geatons	Lyon	Paterson	Delaney	Buchan	McGrory 1	Crum	Murphy
Mar 6	Hibernian	2-2	Kennaway	Hogg	Morrison	Geatons	Lyon	Paterson	Delaney	Buchan	McGrory 1	Crum 1	Murphy
Mar 20	St Mirren	2-1	Kennaway	Hogg	Morrison	Geatons	Lyon	Paterson	McDonald	Buvchan	McGrory 1	Crum	Murphy 1
Mar 27	PARTICK THISTLE	1-1	Kennaway	Boyle	Hogg	Geatons	Lyon	Paterson	Delaney	Buchan	McGrory	Divers 1	Murphy
Mar 29	FALKIRK	1-0	Kennaway	Boyle	Morrison	Dawson	Geatons P	Paterson	Delaney	McDonald	Crum	Divers	Fitzsimmons
Apr 6	Third Lanark	2-4	Tom Doyle	Hogg	Morrison	Dawson	Lyon	Paterson	McDonald	Buchan 2	McGrory	Crum	Fitzsimmons
Apr 10	Dunfermline Athletic	4-3	Doyle	Hogg	Morrison	Geatons	Lyon	Paterson	Dawson 1	Crum 2	Carruth	Divers 1	Murphy
Apr 16	ARBROATH	5-1	Doyle	Boyle	Morrison	Geatons	Lyon	Paterson	Dawson 2	Divers 1	Carruth 2	Crum	Murphy
Apr 30	Motherwell	0-8	Kennaway	Hogg	Morrison	Geatons	Lyon	Paterson	Delaney	Buchan	McGrory	Crum	Murphy

SCOTTISH CUP 1937

Jan 30	Stenhousemuir	1-1	Kennaway	Hogg	Morrison	Geatons	Lyon	Paterson	Carruth	Buchan	McGrory 1	Crum	Murphy
Feb 3	STENHOUSEMUIR	2-0	Kennaway	Hogg	Morrison	Geatons	Lyon	Paterson	Delaney	Buchan	McGrory 2	Crum	Murphy
Feb 13	Albion Rovers	5-2	Kennaway	Hogg	Morrison	Geatons	Lyon	Paterson	Delaney 1	Buchan 2	McGrory 2	Crum	Murphy
Feb 27	East Fife	3-0	Kennaway	Hogg	Morrison	Geatons	Lyon	Paterson	Delaney	Buchan 1	McGrory 2	Crum	Murphy
Mar 17	MOTHERWELL	4-4	Kennaway	Hogg	Morrison	Geatons	Lyon P	Paterson	Delaney	Buchan 1	McGrory	Crum 2	Murphy
Mar 24	Motherwell	2-1	Kennaway	Hogg	Morrison	Geatons	Lyon	Paterson	Delaney	Buchan 1	McGrory 1	Crum	Murphy
Apr 3	Clyde	2-0 SF	Kennaway	Hogg	Morrison	Geatons	Lyon	Paterson	Delaney	Buchan	McGrory 1	Crum	Murphy +OG
Apr 24	Aberdeen	2-1 F	Kennaway	Hogg	Morrison	Geatons	Lyon	Paterson	Delaney	Buchan 1	McGrory	Crum 1	Murphy

SCOTTISH LEAGUE 1937-38

Aug 14	Queen of the South	2-2	Kennaway	Hogg	Morrison	Geatons	Lyon	Paterson	Delaney	Buchan 1	McGrory 1	Crum	Murphy
Aug 18	Hamilton Academicals	2-1	Kennaway	Hogg	Morrison	Geatons	Lyon	Paterson	Delaney	Buchan	McGrory 1	Crum	Murphy 1
Aug 21	MORTON	4-0	Kennaway	Hogg	Morrison	Geatons	Lyon	Paterson	Delaney	Buchan 2	McGrory	Crum 2	Murphy
Aug 25	QUEEN OF THE SOUTH	2-2	Kennaway	Hogg	Morrison	Geatons	Lyon	Paterson	Delaney	Buchan 1+P	McGrory	Crum	Murphy
Aug 28	Kilmarnock	1-2	Kennaway	Hogg	Boyle	Geatons	Lyon	Paterson	Delaney	Buchan 1	McGrory	Crum	Murphy

			1	2	3	4	5	6	7	8	9	10	11
Sept 4	HAMILTON ACADEMICALS	4-2	Kennaway	Hogg	Morrison	McDonald	Lyon	Paterson	Delaney	Buchan P	Carruth 3	Crum	Murphy
Sept 7	Rangers	1-3	Kennaway	Hogg	Morrison	Geatons	Lyon	Paterson	Delaney	Buchan	Carruth	Crum	Murphy 1
Sept 15	Morton	3-2	Kennaway	Hogg	Paterson	Duffy	Lyon	McDonald	Delaney	Buchan 2	McGrory	Crum	Murphy 1
Sept 18	HEARTS	2-1	Kennaway	Hogg	Lyon	McDonald	Miller	Paterson	Delaney 1	Buchan	Crum 1	Divers	Murphy
Sept 25	Aberdeen	1-1	Kennaway	Hogg	Lyon	McDonald	Miller	Paterson	Delaney	Buchan	McGrory 1	Crum	Murphy
Oct 2	CLYDE	3-1	Doyle	Hogg	Lyon	McDonald	Miller	Paterson	Delaney	Buchan 1	McGrory 1	Crum 1	Murphy
Oct 9	Arbroath	0-2	Doyle	Hogg	Morrison	McDonald	Lyon	Paterson	Delaney	Buchan	McGrory	Crum	Murphy
Oct 16	QUEEN'S PARK	4-3	Kennaway	Hogg	Morrison	Geatons	Miller	Paterson	Crum 1	McDonald 1	McGrory 1	Buchan	Murphy +OG
Oct 23	ST JOHNSTONE	6-0	Kennaway	Hogg	Morrison	Geatons	Miller	Paterson	Crum 1	McDonald	Carruth 3	Buchan 1	Murphy 1
Nov 6	PARTICK THISTLE	6-0	Kennaway	Hogg	Morrison	Geatons 1	Lyon	Paterson	Delaney	Buchan 1	Carruth 2	Crum 2	Murphy
Nov 13	Third Lanark	1-1	Kennaway	Hogg	Morrison	McDonald	Lyon	Paterson	Delaney	Buchan P	Carruth	Crum	Murphy
Nov 20	Ayr United	1-1	Kennaway	Hogg	Morrison	Lynch	Lyon	Paterson	Delaney	McDonald	Carruth 1	Crum	Murphy
Nov 27	FALKIRK	2-0	Kennaway	Hogg	Morrison	Lynch	Lyon	Paterson	Delaney 1	McDonald	Carruth 1	Crum	Murphy
Dec 4	Motherwell	2-1	Kennaway	Hogg	Morrison	Lynch	Lyon	Paterson	Delaney	McDonald	Carruth 1	Crum	Murphy 1
Dec 18	Hibernian	3-0	Kennaway	Hogg	Morrison	Lynch	Lyon	Paterson	Crum	McDonald 1	Carruth 1	Divers 1	Murphy
Dec 25	Kilmarnock	8-0	Kennaway	Hogg	Morrison	Lynch	Lyon	Paterson	Delaney 1	McDonald 1	Crum 2	Divers 2	Murphy 2
Jan 1	RANGERS	3-0	Kennaway	Hogg	Morrison	Lynch	Lyon	Paterson	Carruth	McDonald P	Crum	Divers 2	Murphy
Jan 3	Queen's Park	3-0	Kennaway	Hogg	Morrison	Lynch	Lyon	Geatons	Carruth	McDonald	Crum 1	Divers 1	Murphy 1
Jan 8	Hearts	4-2	Kennaway	Hogg	Morrison	Lynch	Lyon	Paterson	Carruth	McDonald	Crum 2	Divers 2	Murphy
Jan 15	ABERDEEN	5-2	Kennaway	Hogg	Morrison	Lynch	Lyon	Paterson	Carruth 1	McDonald 2	Crum 2	Divers	Murphy
Jan 29	Clyde	6-1	Kennaway	Hogg	Morrison	Geatons	Lyon	Paterson	Lynch 1	McDonald 1	Crum 1	Divers 2	Murphy 1
Feb 5	ARBROATH	4-0	Kennaway	Hogg	Morrison	Geatons	Lyon	Paterson	Lynch	McDonald	Crum 3	Divers 1	Murphy
Feb 19	St Johnstone	2-1	Kennaway	Hogg	Morrison	Geatons	Lyon	Paterson	Lynch	McDonald	Crum	Divers 2	Murphy
Feb 26	ST MIRREN	5-1	Kennaway	Hogg	Morrison	Lynch	Lyon	Paterson	Delaney	McDonald 2+P	Crum 1	Divers 1	Murphy
Mar 12	Partick Thistle	6-1	Kennaway	Hogg	Morrison	Geatons 1	Lyon	Paterson	Delaney 2	McDonald	Crum 1	Divers 1	Murphy 1
Mar 19	THIRD LANARK	1-1	Kennaway	Hogg	Lyon	Lynch	Geatons	Paterson	Delaney	McDonald	Crum 1	Divers	Murphy
Mar 26	AYR UNITED	1-1	Kennaway	Hogg	Davitt	Geatons	Lyon	Paterson	Delaney	McDonald 1	Crum	Divers	Fitzsimmons
Apr 2	Falkirk	0-3	Kennaway	Hogg	Morrison	Geatons	Lyon	Paterson	Carruth	McDonald	Crum	Divers	Murphy
Apr 9	MOTHERWELL	4-1	kennaway	Hogg	Morrison	Geatons	Lyon	Paterson	Carruth 2	McDonald P	Crum	Divers 1	Murphy
Apr 16	Dundee	3-2	Kennaway	Hogg	Morrison	Geatons	Lyon	Paterson	Delaney	Carruth 1	Crum	Divers 2	Murphy
Apr 18	DUNDEE	3-0	Kennaway	Hogg	Morrison	Geatons	Lyon 2P	Paterson	Delaney	Carruth	Crum	Divers 1	Murphy
Apr 23	St Mirren	1-3	Kennaway	Hogg	Morrison	Geatons	Lyon	Paterson	Delaney 1	Carruth	Crum 2	Divers	Murphy
Apr 30	HIBERNIAN	3-0	Kennaway	Hogg	Morrison	Geatons	Lyon P	Paterson	Delaney 1	Carruth	Crum	Divers 1	Murphy

SCOTTISH CUP 1938

Jan 22	Third Lanark	2-1	Kennaway	Hogg	Morrison	Lynch	Lyon	Paterson	Carruth	McDonald	Crum 2	Divers	Murphy
Feb 12	NITHSDALE WANDERERS	5-0	Kennaway	Hogg	Morrison	Geatons	Lyon	Paterson	Lynch	McDonald	Carruth 2	Divers	Murphy 3
Mar 5	KILMARNOCK	1-2	Kennaway	Hogg	Morrison	Lynch	Lyon	Paterson	Delaney	McDonald P	Crum	Divers	Murphy

SCOTTISH LEAGUE 1938-39

Aug 13	KILMARNOCK	9-1	Kennaway	Hogg	Morrison	Geatons 1	Lyon P	Paterson	Delaney 2	McDonald 1	Crum P	Divers 2	Murphy 1
Aug 20	Hamilton Academicals	1-0	Kennaway	Hogg	Morrison	Geatons	Miller	Paterson	Delaney 1	McDonald	Crum	Divers	Murphy
Aug 24	Kilmarnock	0-0	Kennaway	Hogg	Morrison	Geatons	Lyon	Paterson	Delaney	McDonald	Crum	Divers	Murphy
Aug 27	ABERDEEN	1-2	Kennaway	Hogg	Morrison	Geatons	Lyon	Paterson	Delaney 1	McDonald	Crum	Divers	Murphy
Sept 3	Hearts	5-1	Kennaway	Hogg	Morrison	Lynch	Lyon	Paterson	Delaney	McDonald 2	Crum 1	Divers 1	Murphy 1
Sept 10	RANGERS	6-2	Kennaway	Hogg	Morrison	Geatons	Lyon 1+P	Paterson	Delaney 1	McDonald 3	Crum	Divers	Murphy
Sept 14	HAMILTON ACADEMICALS	1-2	Kennaway	Hogg	Morrison	Geatons	Lyon	Paterson	Delaney 1	McDonald	Crum	Divers	Murphy
Sept 17	Clyde	4-1	Kennaway	Hogg	Morrison	Geatons	Lyon	Paterson	Lynch 1	McDonald 1	Crum 1	Divers 1	Murphy
Sept 24	RAITH ROVERS	6-1	Kennaway	Hogg	Morrison	Geatons	Lyon	Paterson	Lynch	McDonald 2	Crum 3	Divers	Murphy 1
Oct 1	Albion Rovers	8-1	Kennaway	Hogg	Paterson	Lynch	Lyon	Geatons 1	Delaney 2	McDonald	Crum 5	Divers	Murphy
Oct 12	QUEEN OF THE SOUTH	5-1	Kennaway	Hogg	Morrison	Geatons	Lyon P	Paterson	Delaney 2	McDonald	Crum	Divers 2	Murphy
Oct 22	Partick Thistle	0-0	Kennaway	Hogg	Morrison	Geatons	Lyon	Paterson	Delaney	McDonald	Crum	Divers	Birrell
Oct 29	THIRD LANARK	6-1	Kennaway	Hogg	Morrison	Geatons	Lyon	Paterson	Delaney	McDonald 2	Crum 1	Divers 1	Birrell 1 +OG
Nov 5	AYR UNITED	3-3	Kennaway	Hogg	Morrison	Geatons	Lyon	Paterson	Delaney 1	McDonald 1	Crum	Divers	Murphy 1
Nov 12	Falkirk	1-1	Kennaway	Hogg	Morrison	Geatons	Lyon	Paterson	Delaney	McDonald	Crum	Divers	Murphy +OG
Nov 19	MOTHERWELL	1-3	Kennaway	Hogg	Morrison	Lynch	Lyon	Paterson	Carruth	McDonald 1	Crum	Divers	Murphy
Nov 26	Arbroath	2-0	Kennaway	Hogg	Morrison	Geatons 1	Lyon	Paterson	Delaney	Watters	Crum 1	Divers	Murphy
Dec 3	HIBERNIAN	5-4	Kennaway	Hogg	Morrison	Geatons	Lyon	Paterson	Delaney 1	Watters 2	Crum	Divers	Murphy 2
Dec 10	St Johnstone	1-1	Kennaway	Hogg	Morrison	Geatons	Lyon	Paterson	Delaney	Divers	Crum	Watters	Murphy 1
Dec 17	ST MIRREN	3-2	Kennaway	Hogg	Morrison	Geatons	Lyon	Paterson	Delaney	Watters	Crum	Divers 2	Murphy P
Dec 24	Aberdeen	1-3	Kennaway	Hogg	Morrison	Geatons	Lyon	Paterson	Delaney 1	Watters	Crum	Divers	Murphy
Dec 31	HEARTS	2-2	Kennaway	Hogg	Morrison	Geatons	Lyon	Paterson	Delaney	Watters 2	Crum	Divers	Murphy
Jan 1	Rangers	1-2	Kennaway	Hogg	Morrison	Lynch	Lyon	Geatons	Delaney	Carruth 1	Watters	Murphy	Birrell
Jan 3	QUEEN'S PARK	0-1	Doherty	Hogg	Morrison	Duffy	O'Neill	Geatons	Delaney	Anderson	Carruth	Watters	Murphy
Jan 7	Raith Rovers	0-4	Kennaway	Hogg	Morrison	Geatons	Lyon	Duffy	Lynch	McDonald	Watters	Murphy	Burrell
Jan 25	ALBION ROVERS	4-1	Kennaway	Hogg	Morrison	Lynch	Lyon	Geatons	Delaney	McDonald	Crum	Divers 4	Murphy
Jan 28	Queen of the South	1-1	Kennaway	Hogg	Morrison	Lynch	Lyon	Geatons	Delaney	McDonald	Crum	Divers 1	Murphy
Feb 11	CLYDE	3-1	Kennaway	Hogg	Morrison	Lynch	Lyon	Paterson	Anderson 1	McDonald 1	Crum	Divers	Birrell 1
Feb 25	PARTICK THISTLE	3-1	Doherty	Hogg	Morrison	Lynch	O'Neill	Paterson	Anderson	McDonald	Carruth 3	Divers	Murphy
Mar 8	Third Lanark	2-0	Kennaway	Hogg	Morrison	Lynch	Lyon 1	McDonald	Anderson	Divers	Carruth 1	Murphy	Birrell
Mar 11	Ayr United	4-1	Kenneway	Hogg	Morrison	Lynch	Lyon	McDonald	Delaney 1	Anderson	Carruth 1	Divers 1	Murphy 1
Mar 18	FALKIRK	1-2	Kennaway	Hogg	Morrison	Lynch	Lyon	Geatons	Anderson	McDonald	Carruth	Divers	Murphy 1
Apr 1	ARBROATH	2-0	Kennaway	Hogg	Morrison	Geatons	O'Neill	Paterson	Delaney	McDonald 1	Carruth	Divers 1	Murphy
Apr 5	Motherwell	3-2	Kennaway	Hogg	Paterson	Geatons	Lyon	McDonald	Crum	Anderson 1	Carruth	Divers	Murphy 2
Apr 8	Hibernian	0-1	Kennaway	Hogg	Paterson	Geatons	Lyon	McDonald	Crum	Anderson	Carruth	Divers	Murphy
Apr 10	Queen's Park	2-1	Kennaway	Hogg	Geatons	Lynch	O'Neill	McDonald	Crum	Anderson 1	Carruth	Divers	Murphy +OG
Apr 22	ST JOHNSTONE	1-1	Kennaway	Hogg	Morrison	McDonald	Lyon	Paterson	Crum 1	Anderson	Carruth	Divers	Murphy
Apr 29	St Mirren	1-2	Kennaway	Hogg	Morrison	Lynch	Lyon	Paterson	Anderson	McDonald	Carruth	Divers 1	Murphy

SCOTTISH CUP 1939

Jan 21	Burntisland Shipyard	8-3	Kennaway	Hogg	Morrison	Lynch	Lyon	Geatons	Delaney 1	McDonald 2	Crum 3	Watters 1	Murphy P
Feb 4	Montrose	7-1	Kennaway	Hogg	Morrison	Lynch	Lyon	Paterson	Delaney 1	McDonald 1	Crum 3	Divers 2	Murphy
Feb 18	Hearts	2-2	Kennaway	Hogg	Morrison	Lynch	Lyon	Paterson	Delaney 1	McDonald 1	Crum	Divers	Murphy
Feb 22	HEARTS	2-1	Kennaway	Hogg	Morrison	Lynch	Lyon	Paterson	Delaney	McDonald	Crum	Divers 2	Murphy
Mar 4	Motherwell	1-3	Kennaway	Hogg	Morrison	Lynch	Lyon	Paterson	Delaney 1	McDonald	Crum	Divers	Murphy

SCOTTISH LEAGUE 1946-47

Aug 10	MORTON	1-2	Miller	Hogg	Milne	W Gallacher	Corbett	McAulay	Sirrell	Kiernan	Rae 1	Bogan	Shields
Aug 14	Clyde	2-2	Miller	Hogg	Milne	W Gallacher	Corbett	McAulay	Sirrell	Kiernan	Cantwell 2	Bogan	Shields
Aug 17	Aberdeen	2-6	Miller	Hogg	Milne	W Gallacher	Corbett	McAulay	Sirrell	Kiernan 2	Cantwell	Bogan	Shields
Aug 21	HEARTS	2-3	Miller	Hogg	Milne	W Gallacher	Corbett	McAuley	Sirrell	Kiernan 1	Cantwell	Bogan	Evans 1
Aug 28	Hamilton Academicals	2-2	Miller	Hogg	Milne	Sirrell	Corbett	McAuley	Hazlett	Kiernan P	Cantwell 1	Bogan	Evans
Aug 31	St Mirren	1-0	Miller	Lamb	Milne	W Gallacher	Corbett	McAuley	Cantwell 1	Kiernan	Rae	Bogan	Evans
Sept 4	THIRD LANARK	1-4	Miller	McDonald	Milne	W Gallacher	Corbett	McAuley	Rae	Kiernan	Cantwell	Bogan	Evans
Sept 7	RANGERS	2-3	Miller	McDonald	Milne	McMillan	Corbett	McAuley	Bogan 1	Kiernan 1	Cantwell	W Gallacher	Hazlett
Sept 14	Queen of the South	1-3	Miller	McDonald	Milne	Lynch	Corbett	Baillie	Bogan	Kiernan 1	Cantwell	W Gallacher	Hazlett
Nov 2	Falkirk	4-1	Miller	Hogg	McDonald	Lynch	McMillan	Milne	Evans 1	Kiernan	Rae 2	McAloon	Hazlett
Nov 9	Hibernian	4-1	Miller	Hogg	McDonald	Lynch	Corbett	Milne	Evans 1	Kiernan 1	Rae	McAloon 2	Hazlett
Nov 16	Partick Thistle	1-4	Miller	Hogg	McDonald	Lynch	Corbett	Milne	Evans	Kiernan	Rae	McAloon 1	Hazlett
Nov 23	Motherwell	2-1	Miller	Hogg	McDonald	Lynch	McMillan	Milne	Jordan	Kiernan	Rae 1	McAloon 1	Hazlett
Nov 30	KILMARNOCK	4-2	Miller	Hogg	McDonald	Lynch	McMillan	Milne	Jordan	Kiernan 1+P	Rae 1	McAloon 1	Hazlett

			1	2	3	4	5	6	7	8	9	10	11
Dec 7	Morton	1-2	Miller	Hogg	McDonald	Lynch	McMillan	Milne	Jordan 1	Kiernan	Rae	McAloon	Hazlett
Dec 14	CLYDE	3-3	Miller	Hogg	Mallan	Lynch	McMillan	Milne	Evans	Kiernan	Airlie 2	McAloon	Hazlett
Dec 21	Hearts	1-2	Miller	Hogg	Mallan	Lynch	McMillan	Milne	Evans	Kiernan	Airlie 1	McAloon	Hazlett
Dec 25	QUEEN'S PARK	1-0	Miller	Hogg	Mallan	Lynch	McMillan	Milne	Evans	Kiernan	Rae 1	Airlie	Hazlett
Dec 28	HAMILTON ACADEMICALS	2-1	Miller	Hogg	Mallan	Lynch	McMillan	Milne	Evans	McAloon 2	Airlie	W Gallacher	Hazlett
Jan 1	Rangers	1-1	Miller	Hogg	Mallan	Lynch	McMillan	Milne	Evans	McAloon	Airlie	W Gallacher	Hazlet 1
Jan 2	ABERDEEN	1-5	Miller	Hogg	Mallan	Lynch	McMillan	Milne	Evans	McAloon	Airlie	W Gallacher	Hazlett
Jan 4	QUEEN OF THE SOUTH	2-0	Miller	Hogg	Mallan	W Gallacher	McMillan	Milne	Docherty	McAloon 1	Rae P	Evans	O'Sullivan
Jan11	Queen's Park	3-1	Miller	Hogg	Mallan	W Gallacher	Corbett	Milne	Docherty	McAloon 1	Rae 2	Evans	O'Sullivan
Jan 18	Third Lanark	0-0	Miller	Hogg	Mallan	W Gallacher	Corbett	Milne	Docherty	McAloon	Rae	Evans	O'Sullivan
Feb 22	ST MIRREN	2-1	Miller	Hogg	Mallan	Lynch	Corbett	McAuley	Hazlett 1	Kiernan 1	Rae	Evans	O'Sullivan
Mar 22	PARTICK THISTLE	2-0	Miller	Hogg	Mallan	R Quinn	Corbett	Milne	F Quinn	McAloon 1	Kiernan 1	Evans	Hazlett
Mar 29	Kilmarnock	2-1	Miller	Hogg	Mallan	R Quinn	Crobett	Milne	F Quinn	McAloon 1	Kiernan 1	Evans	Hazlett
Apr 12	Hibernian	0-2	Ugolini	Hogg	Mallan	McPhail	Corbett	Milne	F Quinn	McAloon	Kiernan	Evans	Cannon
Apr 26	FALKIRK	0-0	Miller	Hogg	Mallan	McPhail	Corbett	Milne	F Quinn	McAloon	Bogan	Evans	Cannon
May 13	MOTHERWELL	3-2	Miller	Hogg	Milne	McPhail	Corbett	McAuley	F Quinn	McAloon 1	Rae P	Sirrell 1	Cannon

LEAGUE CUP 1946

Sept 21	Hibernian	2-4	Miller	Hogg	Milne	Lynch	Corbett	McAuley	Bogan 1	Kiernan	Rae	W Gallacher 1	Hazlett
Sept 28	THIRD LANARK	0-0	Miller	Hogg	Milne	Lynch	McMillan	McAuley	Bogan	Kiernan	Rae	Sirrell	Paton
Oct 5	Hamilton Academicals	2-2	Miller	Hogg	Milne	Lynch	McMillan	McAuley	Bogan	Kiernan 2	Cantwell	McAloon	Paton
Oct 12	HIBERNIAN	1-1	Miller	Hogg	McDonald	Lynch	McMillan	McAuley	Bogan	Kiernan	Rae	McAloon 1	Paton
Oct 19	Third Lanark	3-2	Ugolini	Hogg	McDonald	Lynch	McMillan	McAuley	Bogan 1	Kiernan 1+P	Rae	McAloon	Paton
Oct 26	HAMILTON ACADEMICALS	3-1	Miller	Hogg	McDonald	Lynch	McMillan	Milne	Bogan	Kiernan 2	Rae 1	McAloon	Hazlett

SCOTTISH CUP 1947

Jan 25	Dundee	1-2	Miller	Hogg	Mallan	Lynch	Corbett	Milne	Docherty	Kiernan	Rae	McAloon 1	Evans

SCOTTISH LEAGUE 1947-48

Aug 13	Airdrie	2-3	Miller	Hogg	Mallan	McPhail	Corbett	McAuley 1	Hazlett	Evans	Kiernan P	Sirrell	Paton
Aug 27	QUEEN'S PARK	4-0	Miller	Boden	Mallan	McPhail 1	Corbett	McAuley	Bogan	R Quinn	Rae 1	Evans 1	Paton 1
Sept 20	Rangers	0-2	Miller	Ferguson	Milne	R Quinn	Corbett	McAuley	Bogan	McAloon	J Gallacher	Evans	Kapler
Sept 27	MOTHERWELL	0-1	Miller	Ferguson	Milne	R Quinn	Corbett	McAuley	Bogan	Sirrell	J Gallacher	Evans	Paton
Oct 4	Aberdeen	0-2	Ugolini	Ferguson	Mallan	R Quinn	Corbett	McAuley	Hazlett	Bogan	Rae	Evans	Paton
Oct 11	MORTON	3-2	Miller	Hogg	Milne	Boden	Corbett	McAuley	Hazlett	Bogan 1	McLaughlin 1	Evans	Paton 1
Oct 18	Clyde	0-2	Miller	Mallan	Milne	McPhail	Corbett	McAuley	Paton	Bogan	McLaughlin	Evans	Kapler
Oct 25	QUEEN OF THE SOUTH	4-3	Miller	Mallan	Milne	McPhail	Corbett	McAuley	Bogan	T McDonald 1	Evans	Sirrell 1	Paton 2
Nov 8	FALKIRK	0-3	Miller	Mallan	Milne	McPhail	Corbett	McAuley	Bogan	W Gallacher	Evans	Sirrell	Paton
Nov 15	Partick Thistle	5-3	Ugolini	Mallan	Milne	McPhail	Corbett P	McAuley	Bogan 1	T McDonald 2	Walsh 1	Evans	Paton
Nov 22	St Mirren	2-1	Ugolini	Mallan	Milne	McPhail	Corbett	McAuley 1	Bogan	T McDonald	Walsh 1	Evans	Paton
Dec 6	DUNDEE	1-1	Miller	Mallan	Milne	McPhail	Corbett	McAuley	Bogan	T McDonald 1	Walsh	Evans	Paton
Dec 13	Hibernian	1-1	Miller	Mallan	Milne	McPhail	Corbett	McAuley	Bogan	T McDonald	Walsh	Evans	Paton 1
Dec 20	AIRDRIE	0-0	Miller	Mallan	Milne	McPhail	Corbett	McAuley	Bogan	T McDonald	Walsh	Evans	Paton
Dec 25	HEARTS	4-2	Miller	Mallan	Milne	McPhail	Corbett	McAuley	Bogan 1	T McDonald 2	Walsh 1	Evans	Paton
Dec 27	Queen's Park	2-3	Miller	Mallan	Milne	McPhail	Corbett	McAuley	Bogan	T McDonald 1	Walsh	Evans	Paton 1
Jan 2	RANGERS	0-4	Miller	Mallan	Milne	McPhail	Corbett	McAuley	Bogan	T McDonald	Walsh	Evans	Paton
Jan 3	Hearts	0-1	Miller	Mallan	Milne	McPhail	Corbett	McAuley	Mitchell	W Gallacher	Rae	Evans	Paton
Jan 10	ABERDEEN	1-0	Miller	Ferguson	Milne	McPhail	Corbett 1	McAuley	Paton	T McDonald	Gormley	W Gallacher	Kapler
Jan 17	Morton	0-4	Miller	Hogg	Ferguson	McMillan	Corbett	McAuley	Paton	W Gallacher	Walsh	McPhail	Kapler
Jan 24	PARTICK THISTLE	1-2	Miller	Hogg	Milne	McMillan	Corbett	McAuley	Paton	McPhail 1	Rae	Evans	Kapler
Jan 31	CLYDE	0-0	Miller	Mallan	Milne	McMillan	Corbett	McAuley	Bogan	McPhail	Evans	T McDonald	Paton
Feb 14	Queen of the South	0-2	Miller	Mallan	Milne	McMillan	Corbett	McAuley	Bogan	McPhail	Evans	W Gallacher	Paton
Feb 28	Falkirk	1-0	Miller	Mallan	Milne	W Gallacher	Corbett P	McAuley	Bogan	McPhail	Weir	T McDonald	Paton
Mar 13	ST MIRREN	0-0	Miller	Mallan	Milne	W Gallacher	Corbett	Baillie	Bogan	McPhail	Weir	Evans	Paton
Mar 20	Motherwell	3-0	Miller	Mallan	Milne	W Gallacher	Corbett	Baillie	Bogan	McPhail 2	Weir 1	Evans	Paton
Mar 29	Third Lanark	1-5	Miller	Mallan	Milne	W Gallacher	Corbett	Baillie	Paton	T McDonald	Walsh	Evans 1	Kapler
Apr 3	HIBERNIAN	2-4	Miller	Fraser	McAuley	W Gallacher	Mallan	Baillie	Bogan	McPhail	Lavery 1	Evans 1	Paton
Apr 10	THIRD LANARK	1-3	Miller	Mallan	McAuley	W Gallacher	Corbett	Baillie	Bogan 1	McPhail	Weir	Evans	Kapler
Apr 17	Dundee	3-2	Miller	Hogg	Mallan	Evans	Corbett	McAuley	Weir 3	McPhail	Lavery	W Gallacher	Paton

LEAGUE CUP 1947

Aug 9	Rangers	0-2	Miller	Hogg	Mallan	McPhail	Corbett	McAuley	F Quinn	McAloon	Kiernan	Sirrell	Paton
Aug 13	DUNDEE	1-1	Miller	Hogg	Mallan	McPhail	Corbett	McAuley	Kiernan	Sirrell	J Gallacher	Evans	Paton1
Aug 23	THIRD LANARK	3-1	Miller	Boden	Mallan	McPhail	Corbett	McAuley	Bogan	R Quinn 1	J Gallacher 2	Evans	Paton
Sept 1	RANGERS	2-0	Miller	Hogg	Mallan	McPhail	Corbett	McAuley	Bogan	R Quinn	J Gallacher 1	Evans	Paton 1
Sept 8	Dundee	1-4	Miller	Hogg	P McDonald	McPhail	Corbett	McAuley	Bogan 1	R Quinn	Rae	Evans	Paton
Sept 13	Third Lanark	2-3	Miller	Boden	Milne	McPhail	Corbett	McAuley P	McDonald	Sirrell	J Gallacher	Evans	Kapler

SCOTTISH CUP 1948

Feb 7	COWDENBEATH	3-0	Miller	Mallan	Milne	McMillan	Corbett	McAuley	Bogan	McPhail 2	Evans	W Gallacher 1	Paton
Feb 21	MOTHERWELL	1-0	Miller	Mallan	Milne	McMillan	Corbett	McAuley	Bogan	McPhail	Weir	T McDonald	Paton 1
Mar 6	MONTROSE	4-0	Miller	Mallan	Milne	W Gallacher	Corbett	McAuley	Bogan	McPhail 2	Weir 1	Evans	Paton 1
Mar 27	Morton (N)	0-1	Miller	Mallan	Milne	W Gallacher	Corbett	McAuley	Bogan	McPhail	Weir	Evans	Paton

SCOTTISH LEAGUE 1948-49

Aug 11	MORTON	0-0	Miller	Milne	Mallan	Evans	Boden	McAuley	Weir	McPhail	Lavery	Tully	Paton
Aug 18	Aberdeen	0-1	Miller	Milne	Mallan	Evans	Boden	McAuley	Weir	McPhail	Lavery	Tully	Paton
Aug 21	RANGERS	0-1	Miller	Milne	Mallan	Evans	Boden	McAuley	T Docherty	McPhail	Weir	Tully	Paton
Aug 28	Hearts	2-1	Miller	Mallan	Milne	Evans	Boden	McAuley	Weir	McPhail 2(1P)	J Gallacher	Tully	Paton
Sept 1	QUEEN OF THE SOUTH	2-2	Miller	Milne	Mallan	Evans	McMillan	McAuley	Weir	McPhail	J Gallacher 2	Tully	Paton
Sept 4	Albion Rovers	3-3	Miller	Milne	Mallan	Evans	McMillan	McAuley	Weir 2	Bogan	J Gallacher	Tully 1	Paton
Oct 23	DUNDEE	0-1	Miller	Milne	Mallan	Docherty	Boden	Baillie	Weir	McPhail	J Gallacher	Tully	Paton
Oct 30	Hibernian	2-1	Miller	Milne	McGuire	Evans	Boden	Baillie	Weir	Tully	J Gallacher	Johnston 2	Paton
Nov 6	Clyde	4-0	Bonnar	McGuire	Milne	Docherty	Boden	Baillie	Sirrell	Tully	J Gallacher 2	Johnston	Paton 2
Nov 13	EAST FIFE	0-1	Bonnar	McGuire	Milne	Evans	Boden	Baillie	Sirrell	Tully	J Gallacher	Johnston	Paton
Nov 20	Third Lanark	2-3	Miller	McGuire	Milne	Evans	Boden	Baillie	Weir	Tully	J Gallacher 1	Johnston	Paton 1
Nov 27	FALKIRK	4-4	Miller	McGuire	Milne	Evans	Docherty	McAuley	Weir	Tully	J Gallacher 3	Johnston	Paton
Dec 4	Partick Thistle	2-1	Miller	McGuire	Milne	Evans	Boden	McAuley	Weir 1	Johnston	J Gallacher	Tully	Paton
Dec 11	St Mirren	1-1	Miller	Milne	Mallan	Evans	Boden	McAuley	Weir	Johnston	J Gallacher	Tully 1	Paton
Dec 18	MOTHERWELL	3-2	Miller	Milne	Mallon	Evans	Boden	McAuley P	Weir	Johnston 1	J Gallacher	Tully	Paton 1
Dec 25	ABERDEEN	3-0	Miller	Milne	Mallan	Evans	Boden	McAuley	Weir	Johnston 1	McPhail 1	Tully	Paton 1
Jan 1	Rangers	0-4	Miller	Milne	Mallan	Evans	Boden	McAuley	Weir	Johnston	J Gallacher	Tully	Paton
Jan 3	HEARTS	2-0	Miller	Boden	Mallan	Evans	McPhail	McAuley	Weir	Johnston	J Gallacher 1	Tully 1	Paton
Jan 8	Morton	0-0	Miller	Boden	Mallan	Evans	McPhail	McAuley	Weir	W Gallacher	Johnston	Tully	Paton
Jan 15	ALBION ROVERS	3-0	Miller	Boden	Mallan	Docherty	McPhail	McAuley	Weir	Johnston	J Gallacher 2	Tully 1	Paton
Jan 29	Queen of the South	0-1	Miller	Boden	Mallan	Evans	McPhail	McAuley	Sirrell	Johnston	J Gallacher	Tully	Paton
Feb 12	HIBERNIAN	1-2	Miller	McGuire	Milne	McPhail P	Boden	McAuley	Weir	Evans	Johnston	W Gallacher	Tully
Feb 26	East Fife	2-3	Bonnar	Mallan	Milne	McPhail	Boden	Baillie	Weir	Docherty 1	Johnston 1	Tully	Paton
Mar 12	Falkirk	1-1	Bonnar	Mallan	Milne	McPhail	Boden	McAuley	Weir	Docherty 1	Johnston	Tully	Paton
Mar 19	PARTICK THISTLE	3 0	Bonnar	Mallan	Milne	McPhail	Boden	McAuley	Weir 2	Evans	Johnston	Tully	J Gallacher 1
Mar 26	ST MIRREN	2-1	Bonnar	Mallan	Milne	McPhail	Boden	McAuley	Weir 1	Evans	J Gallacher	Johnston	Tully
Apr 2	Motherwell	1-0	Bonnar	McGuire	Milne	Evans	Boden	McAuley	Weir	McPhail	J Gallacher 1	Johnston	Tully

			1	2	3	4	5	6	7	8	9	10	11
Apr 11	Dundee	2-3	Bonnar	Mallan	Milne	McPhail	Boden	McAuley	Weir	Docherty	Johnston 2	W Gallacher	Tully
Apr 16	THIRD LANARK	1-2	Bonnar	Mallan	McGuire	Evans	Boden	McAuley	Weir	D Weir	Johnston	Docherty	Tully 1
Apr 18	CLYDE	2-1	Miller	McGuire	Baillie	Evans	Boden	McAuley	Johnston 1	J Docherty	Weir 1	Tully	Paton

LEAGUE CUP 1948

Sept 11	HIBERNIAN	1-0	Miller	Milne	Mallan	Evans	Boden	McAuley	Weir 1	W Gallacher	J Gallacher	Tully	Paton
Sept 18	Clyde	2-0	Miller	Milne	Mallan	Evans	Boden	McAuley	Weir	W Gallacher 1	J Gallacher 1	Tully	Paton
Sept 25	RANGERS	3-1	Miller	Milne	Mallan	Evans	Boden	McAuley	Weir 1	W Gallacher 1	J Gallacher 1	Tully	Paton
Oct 2	Hibernian	2-4	Miller	Milne	Mallan	Evans	Boden	McAuley	Weir	W Gallacher	J Gallacher 2	Tully	Paton
Oct 9	CLYDE	3-6	Miller	Milne	Mallan	Evans	McGrory	McAuley	Weir	W Gallacher	J Gallacher 2	Sirrell	Paton 1
Oct 16	Rangers	1-2	Miller	Milne	Mallan	Evans	Boden	McAuley	Weir	McPhail P	J Gallacher	Tully	Paton

SCOTTISH CUP 1949

Jan 22	Dundee United	3-4	Miller	Boden	Mallan	Evans	McPhail	McAuley	Weir	Johnston	J Gallacher 2	Tully 1	Paton

SCOTTISH LEAGUE 1949-50

Sept 10	Queen of the South	2-0	Miller	McGuire	Baillie	Evans	Boden	McAuley	Collins	McPhail	Haughney 1	Taylor 1	Tully
Sept 17	HEARTS	3-2	Miller	McGuire	Milne	Evans	Boden	McAuley	Weir	Collins 1	Haughney	Taylor 1	Tully
Sept 24	Rangers	0-4	Miller	McGuire	Milne	Evans	Boden	Baillie	Collins	McPhail	Haughney	Taylor	Rennett
Oct 1	RAITH ROVERS	2-2	Miller	Boden	Mallan	Cairney	McGrory	Baillie	Collins	Johnston	Haughney 1	Taylor 1	Rennett
Oct 8	Motherwell	2-1	Miller	Boden	Milne	Evans	McGrory	McAuley	Collins 1	McPhail 1	Haughney	Taylor	Tully
Oct 15	ABERDEEN	4-2	Miller	Boden	Milne	Evans	McGrory	McAuley	Collins 1	McPhail 2	Haughney	Taylor	Tully
Oct 22	Dundee	0-3	Miller	Mallan	Milne	Evans	Boden	McAuley	Collins	McPhail	Haughney	Taylor	Tully
Oct 29	HIBERNIAN	2-2	Miller	Mallan	Milne	Evans 1	McGrory	McAuley	Collins	McPhail	Haughney 1	Tully	Rennett
Nov 5	CLYDE	4-1	Miller	Boden	Mallan	Evans	McGrory	McAuley	Collins	McPhail	Haughney 1	Tully	Rennett 3
Nov 12	Stirling Albion	1-2	Miller	Boden	Milne	Evans	McGrory	McAuley	Collins	McPhail 1	Haughney	Tully	Rennett
Nov 19	THIRD LANARK	2-1	Miller	Boden	Milne	Evans	McGrory	Baillie	Collins	McPhail 1	Haughney 1	Tully	Rennett
Nov 26	Falkirk	1-1	Miller	Boden	Milne	Evans	McGrory	Baillie	Collins	Haughney 1	Weir	Tully	Rennett
Dec 3	PARTICK THISTLE	1-0	Miller	Boden	Milne	Evans	McGrory	Baillie	Haughney	McPhail	Weir	Tully	Rennett 1
Dec 10	ST MIRREN	0-0	Miller	Boden	Milne	Evans	McGrory	Baillie	Weir	McPhail	Haughney	Tully	Rennett
Dec 17	East Fife	1-5	Miller	Boden	Milne	Evans	McGrory	Baillie	Collins	McPhail	J Gallacher 1	Tully	Haughney
Dec 24	Queen of the South	3-0	Miller	Boden	Milne	Evans	McGrory	Baillie	Collins 1	McPhail	Haughney 2	Tully	Rennett
Dec 31	Hearts	2-4	Miller	Boden	Milne	Evans	McGrory	Baillie	Weir	Collins 2	Haughney	Tully	Rennett
Jan 2	RANGERS	1-1	Bonnar	Boden	Mallan	Evans	McGrory	Baillie	Collins	Haughney	Weir 1	Taylor	Tully
Jan 3	Raith Rovers	1-1	Bonnar	McGuire	Mallan	Evans	McGrory	Baillie	Taylor	Haughney 1	Weir	Peacock	Tully
Jan 7	MOTHERWELL	3-1	Bonnar	Boden	Mallan	Evans	McGrory	Baillie	Collins	Taylor 1	Weir	McAuley 1	Tully +OG
Jan 14	Aberdeen	0-4	Bonnar	Boden	Mallan	Evans	McGrory	Baillie	Collins	Taylor	Weir	McAuley	Tully
Jan 21	DUNDEE	2-0	Bonnar	Boden	McAuley	Evans	McGrory	Baillie	Collins	McPhail	Weir	Taylor	Tully
Feb 4	Hibernian	1-4	Bonnar	Boden	McAuley	Evans 1	McGrory	Baillie	Collins P	McPhail	Weir	Tully 1	Taylor
Feb 18	STIRLING ALBION	2-1	Bonnar	Boden	McAuley	Toner	McGrory	Baillie	Collins	McPhail	Weir 2	Haughney	Tully
Mar 4	FALKIRK	4-3	Bonnar	Boden	McAuley	Evans	Toner	Baillie	Weir 1	Haughney	McPhail 2+P	Tully	Rennett
Mar 11	Third Lanark	0-1	Bonnar	Boden	McAuley	Evans	McGrory	Baillie	Collins	Taylor	McPhail	Docherty	Rennett
Mar 18	St Mirren	1-0	Bonnar	Boden	McAuley	Evans	McGrory	Baillie	Collins	Fernie	McPhail	Peacock	Haughney 1
Mar 25	EAST FIFE	4-1	Bonnar	Boden	McAuley	Evans	McGrory	Baillie	Collins	Fernie	McPhail 3+P	Peacock	Tully
Apr 10	Partick Thistle	0-1	Bonnar	Boden	Milne	Evans	McGrory	Baillie	Collins	Fernie	McPhail	Peacock	Haughney
Apr 15	Clyde	2-2	Bonnar	Fallon	Milne	Mallan	McGrory	Baillie	Collins	Fernie 1	McPhail	Tully 1	Rennett

LEAGUE CUP 1949

Aug 13	RANGERS	3-2	Miller	McGuire	Baillie	Evans	Boden	McAuley	Collins	McPhail 1+P	Johnston	Tully	Haughney 1
Aug 17	Aberdeen	5-4	Miller	McGuire	Baillie	Evans	Boden	McAuley	Collins 1	McPhail 1	Johnston	Tully	Haughney 3
Aug 20	St Mirren	0-1	Miller	McGuire	Baillie	Evans	Boden	Milne	Collins	McPhail	Johnston	Tully	Haughney
Aug 27	Rangers	0-2	Miller	Mallan	Baillie	Evans	Boden	McAuley	Collins	McPhail	Johnston	Tully	Haughney
Aug 31	ABERDEEN	1-3	Miller	Mallan	Baillie	Evans	Boden	McAuley	Collins	McPhail	Haughney 1	Peacock	Tully
Sept 3	ST MIRREN	4-1	Miller	McGuire	Baillie	Evans	McGrory	McAuley 1	Collins	McPhail 1	Haughney 1	Taylor	Tully 1

SCOTTISH CUP 1950

Jan 28	Brechin	3-0	Bonnar	Boden	McAuley	Evans	McGrory	Baillie	Collins	McPhail 1	Weir 2	Taylor	Tully
Feb 15	Third Lanark	1-1	Bonnar	Boden	McAuley	Evans	McGrory	Baillie	Collins	McPhail	Weir 1	Taylor	Tully
Feb 20	THIRD LANARK	4-1	Bonnar	Boden	McAuley	Evans	McGrory	Baillie	Collins	McPhail 3	Weir	Haughney	Tully 1
Feb 25	ABERDEEN	0-1	Bonnar	Boden	McAuley	Evans	McGrory	Baillie	Collins	McPhail	Weir	Tully	Rennett

SCOTTISH LEAGUE 1950-51

Sept 9	MORTON	3-4	Bonnar	Haughney	Milne	Evans	McGrory	Baillie	Collins	Fernie	McPhail 2+P	Peacock	Tully
Sept 23	RANGERS	3-2	Bonnar	Fallon	Milne	Evans	Mallon	Baillie	Collins	D Weir 1	McPhail P	Peacock 1	Tully
Sept 30	Raith Rovers	2-1	Bonnar	Fallon	Milne	Evans	Mallan	Millsopp	J Weir 1	D Weir	McPhail	Peacock 1	Tully
Oct 7	RAITH ROVERS	2-3	Bonnar	Fallon	Milne	Evans	Mallon	Millsopp	Collins	D Weir	McPhail	Peacock 2	Tully
Oct 14	Aberdeen	1-2	Bonnar	Fallon	Milne	Evans	Mallan	Baillie	Collins	D Weir	McPhail 1	Peacock	Tully
Oct 21	DUNDEE	0-0	Bonnar	Fallan	Milne	Evans	Mallan	Baillie	Millsopp	Fernie	J Weir	Peacock	Tully
Oct 28	Morton	2-0	Bonnar	Fallon	Milne	Evans	Mallan	Baillie	J Weir	Collins 1	McPhail 1	Peacock	Tully
Nov 4	Clyde	3-1	Bonnar	Fallon	Milne	Evans	Mallan	Baillie	J Weir 1	Collins 1	McPhail 1	Peacock	Tully
Nov 11	FALKIRK	3-0	Bonnar	Fallon	Milne	Evans	Mallan	Baillie	J Weir	Collins P	McPhail 1	Peacock 1	Tully
Nov 18	Airdrie	4-2	Bonnar	Fallon	Milne	Evans	Mallan	Baillie	J Weir	Collins 1+P	McPhail 1	Peacock	Tully 1
Nov 25	THIRD LANARK	1-1	Bonnar	Fallon	Milne	Evans	Mallan	Baillie	J Weir	Collins	McPhail 1	Peacock	Tully
Dec 2	Partick Thistle	1-0	Bonnar	Fallon	Milne	Evans	Mallan	Baillie	J Weir 1	Collins	McPhail	Peacock	Tully
Dec 9	St Mirren	0-0	Bonnar	Fallon	Milne	Evans	Mallan	Baillie	J Weir	Collins	McPhail	Peacock	Tully
Dec 16	EAST FIFE	6-2	Bonnar	Fallon	Milne	Evans	Mallan	Baillie	J Weir	Collins 3	McPhail 3	Peacock	Tully
Dec 30	HEARTS	2-2	Bonnar	Fallon	Milne	Evans	Mallan	Baillie	J Weir	Collins	McAlinden 2	Peacock	Tully
Jan 1	Rangers	0-1	Bonnar	Fallon	Milne	Evans	Mallan	Baillie	J Weir	Collins	McPhail	Peacock	Tully
Jan 6	Motherwell	1-2	Bonnar	Fallon	Rollo	Evans	Mallan	Baillie	J Weir 1	Boden	McAlinden	Peacock	Tully
Jan 13	ABERDEEN	3-4	Bonnar	Fallon	Rollo	Evans	Mallan	Baillie	J Weir	Collins P	McAlinden	Peacock	Tully 2
Jan 20	Dundee	1-3	Bonnar	Fallon	Rollo	Evans	McGrory	Baillie	J Weir 1	Collins	Haughney	Peacock	McDowall
Feb 3	HIBERNIAN	0-1	Hunter	Fallon	Rollo	Evans	Boden	Baillie	Collins	Fernie	J Weir	Peacock	Tully
Feb 17	Falkirk	2-0	Hunter	Fallon	Rollo	Evans	Boden	Baillie	J Weir	Collins 1	Haughney 1	Peacock	Fernie
Mar 3	Third Lanark	0-2	Hunter	Fallon	Rollo	Evans	Boden	Baillie	J Weir	Collins	Haughney	Peacock	Tully
Mar 17	ST MIRREN	2-1	Hunter	Fallon	Rollo	Evans	Boden	Baillie	J Weir 1	Collins P	McPhail	Peacock	Tully
Mar 24	East Fife	0-3	Hunter	Fallon	Rollo	Evans	Boden	Baillie	J Weir	Collins	Fernie	Peacock	Tully
Apr 7	Hearts	1-1	Hunter	Fallon	Rollo	Evans	Boden	Baillie	Collins 1	Fernie	McAlinden	Peacock	Tully
Apr 11	AIRDRIE	0-1	Hunter	Fallon	Rollo	Millsopp	Boden	Baillie	Collins	Fernie	Haughney	Peacock	Tully
Apr 16	PARTICK THISTLE	0-3	Hunter	Fallon	Rollo	Millsopp	McGrory	Baillie	J Weir	Collins	McAlinden	Peacock	Tully
Apr 25	MOTHERWELL	3-1	Hunter	Fallon	Rollo	Evans	Boden	Baillie	J Weir 1	Collins 1+P	McPhail	Peacock	Tully
Apr 28	CLYDE	1-0	Hunter	Mallan	Rollo	Evans	Boden	Baillie	J Weir	Collins 1	McPhail	Peacock	Tully
Apr 30	Hibernian	1-3	Hunter	Haughney	Rollo	Evans	Boden	Baillie	J Weir 1	Collins	Walsh	Peacock	Millsopp

LEAGUE CUP 1950

Aug 12	EAST FIFE	2-0	Bonnar	Haughney	Milne	Evans	McGrory	Baillie	Collins	Fernie	McPhail 1	Peacock 1	Tully
Aug 16	Third Lanark	2-1	Bonnar	Haughney	Milne	Evans	McGrory	Baillie	Collins 1	Fernie 1	McPhail	Peacock	Tully
Aug 19	RAITH ROVERS	2-1	Bonnar	Haughney	Milne	Evans	McGrory	Baillie	Collins	Fernie	McPhail 2	Peacock	Tully
Aug 26	East Fife	1-1	Bonnar	Haughney	Milne	Evans	McGrory	Baillie	Collins	Fernie	McPhail 1	Peacock	Tully
Aug 30	THIRD LANARK	3-1	Bonnar	Haughney	Milne	Evans	McGrory	Baillie	Collins 1	Fernie	McPhail 2P	Peacock	Tully
Sept 2	Raith Rovers	2-2	Bonnar	Haughney	Milne	Evans	McGrory	Baillie	Collins 1	Fernie	McPhail	Peacock 1	Tully
Sept 16	MOTHERWELL	1-4	Bonnar	Haughney	Milne	Evans	McGrory	Baillie	Collins	Fernie	McPhail 1	Peacock	J Weir
Sept 20	Motherwell	1-0	Bonnar	Fallon	Milne	Boden	Mallan	Baillie	Collins	Evans	McPhail 1	Peacock	Tully

SCOTTISH CUP 1951

Date	Opponent	Score	1	2	3	4	5	6	7	8	9	10	11
Jan 27	East Fife	2-2	Bonnar	Fallon	Rollo	Evans	McGrory	Baillie	Collins 1	Millsopp	J Weir 1	Peacock	Tully
Jan 31	EAST FIFE	4-2	Hunter	Fallon	Rollo	Evans	McGrory	Baillie	J Weir	Collins 1	McPhail 2	Peacock 1	Tully
Feb 10	DUNS	4-0	Hunter	Fallon	Rollo	Evans	Boden	Baillie	J Weir 2	Collins	D Weir 1	Peacock 1	Haughney
Feb 24	Hearts	2-1	Hunter	Fallon	Rollo	Evans	Boden	Baillie	J Weir 1	Collins	McPhail 1	Peacock	Tully
Mar 10	ABERDEEN	3-0	Hunter	Fallon	Rollo	Evans	Boden	Baillie	J Weir	Collins	McPhail 2	Peacock	Tully 1
Mar 31	Raith Rovers	3-2 SF	Hunter	Fallon	Rollo	Evans	Boden	Baillie	J Weir 1	Collins	McPhail 1	Peacock	Tully 1
Apr 21	Motherwell	1-0 F	Hunter	Fallon	Rollo	Evans	Boden	Baillie	J Weir	Collins	McPhail 1	Peacock	Tully

SCOTTISH LEAGUE 1951-52

Date	Opponent	Score	1	2	3	4	5	6	7	8	9	10	11
Sept 8	Motherwell	2-2	Bonnar	Fallon	Rollo	Evans	Boden	Baillie	Collins	Walsh	McPhail	Peacock 1	Tully 1
Sept 22	Rangers	1-1	Devanney	Fallon	Rollo	Evans	Boden	Baillie	Collins 1	Walsh	McPhail	Peacock	Tully
Sept 29	HEARTS	1-3	Bonnar	Fallon	Rollo	Evans	Boden	Baillie	Collins	D Weir	Walsh	Peacock 1	Tully
Oct 10	Morton	1-0	Bonnar	Fallon	Rollo	Evans	Boden	Baillie	Millsopp 1	Collins	J Weir	Peacock	Tully
Oct 20	Dundee	1-2	Bell	Fallon	Rollo	Evans	Mallan	Baillie	Collins	Boden	McPhail	Peacock	Millsopp +OG
Oct 27	HIBERNIAN	1-1	Bell	Fallon	Rollo	Evans	Mallan	Baillie	Collins	Walsh	McPhail 1	Peacock	Tully
Nov 3	THIRD LANARK	2-2	Bell	Fallon	Rollo	Evans	Mallan	Baillie	Collins	Walsh 1	McAlinden	McPhail	Tully +OG
Nov 10	Stirling Albion	1-2	Bell	Fallon	Rollo	Evans	Boden	Baillie	Collins	Walsh	McAlinden 1	McPhail	Tully
Nov 17	AIRDRIE	3-1	Bell	Fallon	Rollo	Evans	Boden	Baillie	Collins	Walsh 1	McPhail 1	Peacock 1	Tully
Nov 24	Queen of the South	0-4	Bell	Fallon	Rollo	Evans	Boden	Baillie	Collins	Walsh	McPhail	Peacock	McAlinden
Dec 1	PARTICK THISTLE	2-1	Bell	Fallon	Rollo	Evans	Boden	Baillie	Collins 1	Walsh 1	Heron	Peacock	Lafferty
Dec 8	ST MIRREN	2-1	Bell	Fallon	Rollo	Evans	Stein	Baillie	Collins	Walsh	Lafferty 2	peacock	McPhail
Dec 15	East Fife	1-3	Bell	Fallon	Rollo	Evans	Stein	Baillie	Collins	Walsh 1	Lafferty	Peacock	Fernie
Dec 22	MOTHERWELL	2-2	Bell	Fallon	Jack	Evans	Stein	Baillie	Collins	Walsh	Lafferty 1	Peacock 1	Tully
Dec 29	Aberdeen	1-3	Bell	Fallon	Jack	Evans	Stein	Baillie	Collins 2P	Walsh 1	J Weir	Peacock	Tully +OG
Jan 1	RANGERS	1-4	Bell	Fallon	Jack	Evans	Stein	Baillie	Collins	Walsh	J Weir	Peacock	Tully 1
Jan 2	Hearts	1-2	Bonnar	Fallon	Rollo	Evans	Stein	Baillie	Collins P	Walsh	Lafferty	Peacock	Tully
Jan 12	Raith Rovers	0-1	Bonnar	Fallon	Rollo	Evans	Stein	Baillie	Collins	Peacock	Lafferty	Morrison	Tully
Jan 19	DUNDEE	1-1	Bonnar	Fallon	Rollo	Evans	Stein	Baillie	Collins	Walsh 1	McPhail	Tully	Peacock
Feb 2	Hibernian	1-3	Bonnar	Fallon	Rollo	Evans	Stein	Baillie	Collins	Walsh 1	McPhail	Tully	Peacock
Feb 16	STIRLING ALBION	3-1	Bonnar	Fallon	Baillie	Evans	Stein	Millsopp	Collins 1+P	Walsh	McPhail 1	Peacock	Tully
Feb 23	RAITH ROVERS	0-1	Bonnar	Fallon	Baillie	Evans	Stein	Millsopp	Collins	Walsh	McPhail	Peacock	Haughney
Feb 27	Airdrie	1-2	Bonnar	Fallon	Baillie	Evans	Stein	Millsopp	J Weir	Collins 1	McAlinden	McPhail	Peacock
Mar 1	QUEEN OF THE SOUTH	6-1	Bonnar	Fallon	Baillie	Evans	Stein	Millsopp	J Weir 2	Collins 1	McPhail 1	Peacock 1	Tully 1
Mar 5	MORTON	2-2	Bonnar	Fallon	Baillie	Fernie	Stein	Millsopp	J Weir	Collins	McPhail 1	Peacock 1	Tully
Mar 8	Partick Thistle	4-2	Bonnar	Fallon	Baillie	Fernie	Stein	Millsopp 1	J Weir	Collins 1	McPhail 2	Peacock	Tully
Mar 15	St Mirren	1-3	Bonnar	Fallon	Baillie	Evans	Stein	Millsopp	J Weir	Collins	McPhail 1	Peacock	Tully
Mar 22	EAST FIFE	2-1	Bonnar	Fallon	Baillie	Fernie	Stein	Millsopp	J Weir	Collins	McPhail 1	Boden	Tully 1
Mar 29	ABERDEEN	2-0	Bonnar	Fallon	Baillie	Fernie	Boden	Millsopp	J Weir 1	Collins	McPhail 1	Walsh	Tully
Apr 12	Third Lanark	3-3	Bonnar	Fallon	Baillie	Fernie	Boden	Millsopp	J Weir	Collins 1+P	McPhail 1	Walsh	Tully

LEAGUE CUP 1951

Date	Opponent	Score	1	2	3	4	5	6	7	8	9	10	11
Aug 11	THIRD LANARK	1-1	Bonnar	Haughney	Rollo	Evans	Mallan	Baillie	Collins	Walsh	Fallon 1	Peacock	Tully
Aug 15	Airdrie	1-1	Bonnar	Haughney	Rollo	Evans	Mallan	Baillie	Collins	Walsh	Fallon	Peacock 1	Tully
Aug 18	MORTON	2-0	Bonnar	Fallon	Rollo	Evans 1	Mallan	Baillie	Collins	Walsh	Heron 1	Peacock	Tully
Aug 25	Third Lanark	1-0	Bonnar	Fallon	Rollo	Evans	Mallan	Baillie	Collins	Walsh 1	Heron	Peacock	Tully
Aug 29	AIRDRIE	2-0	Bonnar	Fallon	Rollo	Evans	Mallan	Baillie	Collins	Walsh 1	Heron 1	Peacock	Tully
Sept 1	Morton	0-2	Bonnar	Fallon	Rollo	Evans	Mallan	Baillie	Collins	Walsh	Heron	Peacock	Tully
Sept 15	FORFAR ATHLETIC	4-1	Devanney	Fallon	Rollo	Evans	Mallan	Baillie 1	Collins 1	Walsh 1	McPhail	Peacock 1	Tully
Sept 19	Forfar Athletic	1-1	Devanney	Fallon	Rollo	Evans	Mallan	Baillie	Millsopp	Walsh	McPhail	Peacock 1	Tully
Oct 13	Rangers	0-3	Bonnar	Fallon	Rollo	Evans	Boden	Baillie	J Weir	Collins	McPhail	Peacock	Tully

SCOTTISH CUP 1952

Date	Opponent	Score	1	2	3	4	5	6	7	8	9	10	11
Jan 30	THIRD LANARK	0-0	Bonnar	Fallon	Rollo	Evans	Stein	Baillie	Collins	Walsh	McPhail	Peacock	Tully
Feb 4	Third Lanark	1-2	Bonnar	Fallon	Rollo 1	Evans	Stein	Baillie	Collins	Walsh	McPhail	Peacock	Tully

SCOTTISH LEAGUE 1952-53

Date	Opponent	Score	1	2	3	4	5	6	7	8	9	10	11
Sept 6	FALKIRK	5-3	Bonnar	Boden	Fallon	Evans	Stein	Baillie	Weir	Fernie 1	McPhail 3	Tully 1	Millsopp
Sept 13	Raith Rovers	1-1	Bonnar	Boden	Fallon	Evans	Stein	Baillie	Walsh	Fernie	McPhail	Tully 1	Peacock
Sept 20	RANGERS	2-1	Bonnar	Boden	Meechan	Evans	Stein	Baillie	Rollo 1	Walsh 1	Fallon	Tully	Peacock
Sept 27	Aberdeen	2-2	Bonnar	Boden	Meechan	Evans	Stein	Baillie	Rollo	Walsh	Fallon 1	Tully	Peacock 1
Oct 4	MOTHERWELL	3-0	Bonnar	Boden	Meechan	Evand	Stein	Baillie	Hepbutn	Walsh P	Fallon 1	Fernie	Peacock 1
Oct 11	Clyde	2-1	Bonnar	Boden	Meechan	Evans	Stein	Baillie	Hepburn	Walsh	Fallon	Tully	Peacock 2
Oct 18	QUEEN OF THE SOUTH	1-1	Bonnar	Boden	Meechan	Evans	Stein	Baillie	Hepburn	Walsh	Fallon	Tully	Peacock 1
Oct 25	Hearts	0-1	Hunter	Haughney	Meechan	Evans	Stein	Baillie	Fernie	Walsh	Fallon	Tully	Peacock
Nov 1	St Mirren	2-1	Hunter	Boden	Fallon	Evans	Stein	Baillie	Duncan 1	Fernie 1	McPhail	Tully	Peacock
Nov 8	THIRD LANARK	5-4	Hunter	Boden	Fallon	Evans	Stein	Baillie	Walsh 1	Fernie	Lafferty 1	Tully 1	Peacock 1 +OG
Nov 15	Partick Thistle	0-3	Hunter	Boden	Meechan	Evans	Stein	Baillie	Walsh	Fernie	McPhail	Tully	Peacock
Nov 22	Airdrie	0-0	Hunter	Boden	Fallon	Evans	Stein	Baillie	Hepburn	Fernie	McPhail	Walsh	Peacock
Dec 6	Hibernian	1-1	Hunter	Boden	Fallon	Evans	Stein	Rollo	McPhail	Fernie	McIlroy 1	Walsh	Peacock
Dec 13	DUNDEE	5-0	Hunter	Boden	Fallon	Evans	Stein	Peacock	Collins	Fernie 3	McIlroy 1	Walsh	Tully 1
Dec 20	Falkirk	3-2	Hunter	Boden	Fallon	Evans	Stein	Jack	Collins 1	Fernie	McIlroy 1	Tully	Peacock 1
Dec 27	RAITH ROVERS	0-1	Hunter	Mallan	Meechan	Evans	Stein	Peacock	Collins	Fernie	McIlroy	Tully	Duncan
Jan 1	Rangers	0-1	Hunter	Haughney	Meechan	Evans	Stein	Rollo	Collins	Fernie	McIlroy	Peacock	Tully
Jan 10	Motherwell	2-4	Bonnar	Haughney	Meechan	Evans	Stein	Rollo	Collins	Fernie 1	McIlroy	Tully	Peacock 1
Jan 17	CLYDE	2-4	Hunter	Haughney	Meechan	Evans	Stein	Jack	Hepburn	Fernie	McGrory 1	Collins	Tully 1
Jan 31	Queen of the South	1-2	Bonnar	Meechan	Fallon	Evans	Stein	Jack	Collins	Fernie	McGrory	Peacock	Tully 1
Feb 14	HEARTS	1-1	Bonnar	Boden	Meechan	Evans	Stein	Fernie	Walsh	McPhail P	McGrory	Tully	Peacock
Feb 28	Third Lanark	3-1	Hunter	Haughney	Meechan	Evans	Stein	McPhail	Collins	Walsh 1	McGrory 2	Fernie	Tully
Mar 7	PARTICK THISTLE	3-1	Hunter	Haughney	Meechan	Evans	McIlroy	McPhail	Collins	Fernie	McGrory	Walsh 2	Tully 1
Mar 18	AIRDRIE	0-1	Hunter	Haughney	Meechan	Evans	Stein	McPhail	Collins	Fernie	McGrory	Walsh	Tully
Mar 21	East Fife	1-4	Hunter	Haughney	Meechan	Evans	Stein	McPhail	Walsh	Fernie	McGrory	Duffy	Tully +OG
Mar 28	HIBERNIAN	1-3	Hunter	Haughney	Fallon	Evans	Stein	McPhail	Collins P	Walsh	McGrory	Fernie	Tully
Apr 4	Dundee	0-4	Bonnar	Haughney	Fallon	Evans	McIlroy	Stein	Walsh	Duffy	McPhail	Fernie	Tully
Apr 11	ST MIRREN	3-2	Bonnar	Haughney	Meechan	Evans	Stein	Conroy	Collins 1	Fernie 1	Fallon 1	McPhail	Tully
Apr 15	ABERDEEN	1-3	Bonnar	Haughney	Meechan	Evans	Stein	McGrory	Collins	Walsh	Fallon	McPhail 1	Peacock
Apr 18	EAST FIFE	1-1	Bonnar	Haughney	Fallon	Evans	Jack	McGrory	Hepburn	Collins	Walsh 1	Peacock	Tully

LEAGUE CUP 1952

Date	Opponent	Score	1	2	3	4	5	6	7	8	9	10	11
Aug 9	St Mirren	1-0	Bonnar	Boden	Fallon	Evans	Stein	Baillie	J Weir	McPhail	McDonald 1	Tully	Peacock
Aug 13	PARTICK THISTLE	2-5	Bonnar	Boden	Fallon	Evans	Stein	Baillie	J Weir	McPhail	McDonald 1	Tully 1	Peacock
Aug 16	HIBERNIAN	1-0	Bonnar	Boden	Fallon	Evans	Stein	Baillie	Millsopp	Fernie	McPhail 1	Tully	Haughney
Aug 23	ST MIRREN	3-1	Bonnar	Boden	Fallon	Evans	Stein	Baillie	Millsopp	Fernie 1	McPhail 1	Tully	Peacock 1
Aug 27	Partick Thistle	1-0	Bonnar	Boden	Fallon	Evans	Stein	Baillie	Walsh	Fernie	Whyte	Tully	Peacock 1
Aug 30	Hibernian	0-3	Bonnar	Meechan	Fallon	Boden	Stein	Baillie	Millsopp	Fernie	Walsh	Tully	Peacock

SCOTTISH CUP 1953

Date	Opponent	Score	1	2	3	4	5	6	7	8	9	10	11
Jan 24	Eyemouth	4-0	Bonnar	Meechan	Rollo	Evans	Stein	Jack	Collins	Fernie	McGrory 4	Peacock	Tully
Feb 7	Stirling Albion	1-1	Bonnar	Boden	Fallon	Evans	Stein	Jack	Collins	Fernie	McGrory 1	McPhail	Tully
Feb 11	STIRLING ALBION	3-0	Bonnar	Boden	Meechan	Evans	Stein	Fernie	Collins	McPhail	McGrory 2	Peacock 1	Tully

			1	2	3	4	5	6	7	8	9	10	11
Feb 21	Falkirk	3-2	Bonnar	Haughney	Meechan	Evans	Stein	McPhail	Collins	Walsh	McGrory 1	Fernie 1	Tully 1
Mar 14	Rangers	0-2	Hunter	Haughney	Meechan	Evans	Stein	McPhail	Collins	Fernie	McGrory	Walsh	Tully

SCOTTISH LEAGUE 1953-54

Sept 5	Hamilton Academicals	0-2	Bell	Haughney	Meechan	Evans	Stein	Baillie	Collins	Walsh	McPhail	Peacock	Fernie
Sept 12	CLYDE	1-0	Bell	Haughney	Fallon	Evans	Stein	McPhail	Collins 1	Fernie	Walsh	Peacock	Duncan
Sept 19	Rangers	1-1	Bell	Haughney	Fallon	Evans	Stein	Peacock	Collins	Walsh	McPhail	Tully	Duncan 1
Sept 26	ABERDEEN	3-0	Bell	Haughney	Fallon	Evans	Stein	Peacock	Collins 3P	Walsh	Duncan	Tully	Mochan
Oct 10	RAITH ROVERS	3-0	Hunter	Haughney	Fallon	Evans	Stein	Peacock	Collins 1	Fernie 2	McPhail	Walsh	Duncan
Oct 17	Queen of the South	1-2	Hunter	Haughney	Rollo	Evans	McIlroy	Peacock	Higgins	Collins P	McPhail	Walsh	Duncan
Oct 24	HEARTS	2-0	Hunter	Haughney	Fallon	Evans	Stein	Peacock	Collins	Fernie	McPhail 1	Walsh 1	Mochan
Oct 31	Dundee	1-1	Bonnar	Haughney	Meechan	Evans	Stein	Peacock	Collins	Fernie	McPhail 1	Walsh	Tully
Nov 7	HIBERNIAN	2-2	Bonnar	Haughney	Meechan	Evans	Stein 1	Peacock	Collins 1	Fernie	McPhail	Walsh	Tully
Nov 14	East Fife	1-4	Bonnar	Haughney	Meechan	Evans	Stein	Peacock	Collins	Fernie 1	McPhail	Walsh	Duncan
Nov 21	AIRDRIE	4-1	Bonnar	Haughney	Meechan	Evans	Stein	Peacock	Collins	Fernie	McPhail 1	Walsh	Mochan 3
Nov 28	PARTICK THISTLE	2-1	Bonnar	Haughney	Meechan	Evans	Stein	Peacock	Collins	Fernie 2	McPhail	Walsh	Mochan
Dec 5	Stirling Albion	1-2	Bonnar	Haughney	Meechan	Evans	Stein	Peacock 1	Collins	Fernie	Hemple	Walsh	Mochan
Dec 12	ST MIRREN	4-0	Bonnar	Haughney	Meechan	Evans	Stein	Peacock	Collins	Fernie	Hemple 1	Walsh 2	Mochan 1
Dec 26	Clyde	7-1	Bonnar	Haughney	Meechan	Evans	Stein	Peacock	Higgins 2	Fernie	Hemple 1	Collins 2	Mochan 2
Jan 1	RANGERS	1-0	Bonnar	Haughney	Meechan	Evans	Stein	Peacock	Higgins	Fernie	McPhail	Collins	Mochan 1
Jan 2	Aberdeen	0-2	Bonnar	Haughney	Meechan	Evans	Stein	Peacock	Collins	Fernie	Hemple	Walsh	Mochan
Jan 9	FALKIRK	1-0	Bonnar	Haughney	Meechan	Evans	Stein	Peacock	Higgins 1	Fernie	McPhail	Collins	Mochan
Jan 16	Raith Rovers	0-2	Bonnar	Haughney	Meechan	Evans	Stein	Peacock	Higgins	Fernie	McPhail	Collins	Mochan
Jan 23	QUEEN OF THE SOUTH	3-1	Bonnar	Haughney	Meechan	Evans	Stein	Peacock	Higgins	Fernie	McPhail 1	Collins	Mochan 2
Feb 6	Hearts	2-3	Hunter	Haughney 2P	Meechan	Evans	Stein	Peacock	Collins	Fernie	Walsh	Tully	Mochan
Feb 20	DUNDEE	5-1	Bell	Haughney	Meechan	Evans	Stein	Peacock	Higgins 1	Fernie 1	Walsh 1	Tully	Mochan 2
Mar 6	EAST FIFE	4-1	Bell	Haughney	Meechan	Evans	Stein	Peacock	Higgins 2	Fernie 1	Walsh 1	Tully	Mochan
Mar 17	Airdrie	6-0	Bonnar	Boden	Meechan	Evans	McIlroy	Peacock	Higgins 1	Fernie P	Fallon 1	Collins	Mochan 3
Mar 20	Partick Thistle	3-1	Bonnar	Haughney	Meechan	Evans	Stein	Peacock	Higgins	Fernie 1	Fallon 2	Walsh	Mochan
Mar 29	STIRLING ALBION	4-0	Bonnar	Boden	Meechan	Evans	Stein	Peacock	Higgins	Fernie 1	Fallon 1	Collins	Mochan 2
Apr 7	St Mirren	3-1	Bonnar	Haughney P	Meechan	Evans	Stein	Peacock	Collins 1	Fernie	Fallon	Tully 1	Mochan
Apr 14	Falkirk	3-0	Bonnar	Haughney	Meechan	Evans	Stein	Peacock	Higgins	Fernie	Fallon 1	Tully	Mochan 2
Apr 17	Hibernian	3-0	Bonnar	Haughney	Meechan	Evans	Stein	Peacock	Higgins 1	Fernie	Fallon	Tully	Mochan 2
Apr 26	HAMILTON ACADEMICALS	1-0	Bonnar	Ryan	Meechan	Haughney 1	McIlroy	Peacock	Higgins	Collins	Fallon	Tully	Mochan

LEAGUE CUP 1953

Aug 8	ABERDEEN	0-1	Bonnar	Haughney	Rollo	Evans	Stein	McPhail	Tully	Walsh	Mochan	Peacock	Fernie
Aug 12	East Fife	1-1	Bonnar	Haughney	Rollo	Evans	Stein	McPhail	Collins	Walsh	Mochan	Peacock 1	Fernie
Aug 15	Airdrie	1-2	Bonnar	Haughney	Rollo	Evans	Stein	McPhail	Collins	Walsh 1	Mochan	Peacock	Fernie
Aug 22	Aberdeen	2-5	Hunter	Haughney	Rollo	Evans	Stein	McPhail	Walsh 1	Fernie	Whyte	Peacock	Mochan 1
Aug 26	EAST FIFE	0-1	Bonnar	Haughney	Meechan	Evans	Stein	McPhail	Collins	Fernie	Mochan	Peacock	McMillan
Aug 29	AIRDRIE	2-0	Bonnar	Haughney	Meechan	Evans	McIlroy	Baillie	Collins	Walsh 1	McPhail 1	Peacock	McMillan

SCOTTISH CUP 1954

Feb 17	Falkirk	2-1	Bell	Haughney	Meechan	Evans	Stein	Peacock	Higgins 1	Fernie 1	Walsh	Tully	Mochan
Feb 27	Stirling Albion	4-3	Bell	Haughney P	Meechan	Evans	Stein	Peacock	Higgins 1	Fernie	Walsh	Tully	Mochan 1 +OG
Mar 6	Hamilton Academicals	2-1	Bell	Haughney P	Meechan	Evans	Stein	Peacock	Higgins	Fernie 1	McPhail	Tully	Mochan
Mar 27	Motherwell	2-2 SF	Bonnar	Haughney	Meechan	Evans	Stein	Peacock	Higgins	Fernie	Fallon 1	Tully	Mochan 1
Apr 5	Motherwell	3-1 SFR	Bonnar	Haughney	Meechan	Evans	Stein	Peacock	Higgins	Fernie 1	Fallon	Tully	Mochan 1 +OG
Apr 24	Aberdeen	2-1 F	Bonnar	Haughney	Meechan	Evans	Stein	Peacock	Higgins	Fernie	Fallon 1	Tully	Mochan +OG

SCOTTISH LEAGUE 1954-55

Sept 11	Clyde	2-2	Bonnar	Haughney	Meechan	Evans	Stein	Peacock	Higgins	Boden	Fallon	Fernie 1	Walsh 1
Sept 18	RANGERS	2-0	Bonnar	Haughney	Fallon	Evans	Stein	Peacock	Higgins 1	Boden	Walsh 1	Fernie	Mochan
Sept 25	Raith Rovers	3-1	Bell	Haughney 2P	Fallon	Evans	Stein	Peacock	Higgins	Boden	Walsh	Fernie	Mochan 1
Oct 2	KILMARNOCK	6-3	Bonnar	Haughney	Fallon	Evans	Stein	Conroy	Higgins 2	Boden	Walsh 1	Fernie 2	Mochan 1
Oct 9	Aberdeen	2-0	Bonnar	Haughney P	Fallon	Evans	Stein	Peacock	Higgins	Tully	Walsh	Fernie	Mochan 1
Oct 16	QUEEN OF THE SOUTH	1-1	McMahon	Haughney P	Fallon	Evans	Stein	Peacock	Higgins 1	Tully	Walsh	Smith	Mochan
Oct 30	FALKIRK	3-1	Bonnar	Haughney	Fallon	Evans	Stein	Peacock	Higgins 1	Tully	Walsh 1	Fernie	Mochan
Nov 6	St Mirren	1-1	Bonnar	Haughney	Fallon	Evans	Stein	Peacock	Higgins	Tully	Walsh 1	Fernie	Collins
Nov 13	STIRLING ALBION	7-0	Bonnar	Haughney	Fallon	Evans	Stein	Peacock	Higgins 2	Tully 1	Walsh 3	Fernie 1	Collins
Nov 27	Partick Thistle	2-4	Bonnar	Haughney	Fallon	Evans	Stein	Peacock	Higgins	Tully	Walsh 1	Fernie	Collins 1
Nov 27	Motherwell	2-2	Bonnar	Haughney	Fallon	Evans	Boden	Peacock	Higgins 1	Smith	Walsh 1	Fernie	Collins
Dec 4	EAST FIFE	2-2	Bonnar	Haughney	Fallon	Evans	Stein	Peacock	Higgins	Tully	Walsh 1	Fernie	Mochan 1
Dec 11	Hibernian	5-0	Bell	Haughney	Meechan	Evans	Stein	Peacock	Higgins 1	Tully	Walsh 2	Fernie 2	Collins
Dec 18	DUNDEE	4-1	Bell	Haughney P	Meechan	Evans	Stein	Peacock	Rowan 1	Tully	Walsh	Fernie 1	Collins +OG
Dec 25	CLYDE	2-2	Bell	Haughney	Meechan	Evans	Stein	Peacock	Boden 1	Tully	Walsh	Fernie	Collins 1
Jan 1	Rangers	1-4	Bell	Haughney	Meechan	Evans	Stein	Peacock	Boden	Tully	Walsh	Fernie 1	Collins
Jan 3	RAITH ROVERS	4-1	Bell	Haughney	Meechan	Evans 1	Stein	Peacock	Collins 1	Tully 1	Walsh 1	Fernie	Mochan
Jan 8	Kilmarnock	2-1	Bell	Haughney	Meechan	Evans	Stein	Peacock	Boden	Tully 1	Walsh	Fernie	Mochan +OG
Jan 22	Queen of the South	2-0	Bonnar	Haughney	Meechan	Evans	Stein	Peacock	Collins	Walsh	Fallon	Fernie 2	Mochan
Jan 29	HEARTS	2-0	Bonnar	Haughney	Meechan	Evans	Stein	Peacock	Higgins	Walsh 2	Fallon	Fernie	Collins
Feb 12	Falkirk	1-1	Bonnar	Haughney	Meechan	Evans	Stein	Peacock	Collins	Walsh	Fallon	Fernie 1	Mochan
Feb 26	ST MIRREN	5-2	Bonnar	Haughney P	Meechan	Evans	Stein	Peacock	Walsh 1	Smith 1	Fallon	Fernie 1	Collins 1
Mar 9	Stirling Albion	3-2	Bonnar	Haughney P	Meechan	Evans	Stein 1	Peacock	Walsh	Tully	Fallon	Boden 1	Collins
Mar 12	PARTICK THISTLE	0-0	Bonnar	Haughney	Meechan	Evans	Stein	Peacock	Walsh	Tully	Fallon	Fernie	Collins
Mar 19	MOTHERWELL	1-0	Bonnar	Haughney	Meechan	Evans	Stein	Peacock	Collins	Walsh	Fallon	Mochan 1	Tully
Mar 30	East Fife	4-3	Bonnar	Haughney	Meechan	Evans	Stein	Peacock	Collins	Walsh 2	Mochan 2	McPhail	Tully
Apr 2	HIBERNIAN	1-2	Bonnar	Haughney	Meechan	Evans	Stein	Peacock	Collins	Reid	McPhail	Mochan	Tully 1
Apr 9	Dundee	1-0	Bonnar	Haughney	Meechan	Conroy	Evans	Peacock	Walsh	Reid 1	McPhail	Mochan	Tully
Apr 16	ABERDEEN	2-1	Bonner	Haughney	Meechan	Evans	Stein	Peacock	Collins	Reid	McPhail 1	Mochan	Tully 1
Apr 30	Hearts	3-0	Bonnar	Haughney	Fallon	Evans	Stein	Peacock	Collins 1	Fernie	Walsh	Tully	Mochan 2

LEAGUE CUP 1954

Aug 14	FALKIRK	3-0	Bonnar	Haughney	Meechan	Ecans	Stein	Peacock	Higgins 1	Fernie	Fallon 2	Tully	Mochan
Aug 18	Dundee	1-3	Bonnar	Haughney	Meechan	Evans	Stein	Peacock	Higgins	Fernie	Fallon	Tully	Mochan 1
Aug 21	HEARTS	1-2	Bonnar	Haughney	Meechan	Evans	Stein	Peacock	Higgins 1	Fernie	Fallon	Tully	Mochan
Aug 28	Falkirk	2-2	Bonnar	Haughney P	Meechan	Evans	Stein	Peacock	Higgins	Fernie	Fallon 1	Tully	Mochan
Sept 1	DUNDEE	0-1	Bonnar	Haughney	Jack	Evans	Stein	Peacock	Collins	Walsh	Fallon	Tully	Mochan
Sept 4	Hearts	2-3	Bonnar	Haughney	Baillie	Evans	Stein	Peacock	Collins 1	Fernie	Fallon	Tully 1	Duncan

SCOTTISH CUP 1955

Feb 5	Alloa Athletic	4-2	Bonnar	Haughney P	Meechan	Evans	Stein	Peacock 1	Collins	Walsh 2	Fallon	Fernie	Mochan
Feb 19	Kilmarnock	1-1	Bonnar	Haughney	Meechan	Evans	Stein	Peacock	Smith 1	Walsh	Fallon	Fernie	Collins
Feb 23	KILMARNOCK	1-0	Bonnar	Haughney	Meechan	Evans	Stein	Peacock	Smith	Walsh 1	Fallon	Fernie	Collins
Mar 5	HAMILTON ACADEMICALS	2-1	Bonnar	Haughney	Meechan	Evans	Stein	Peacock	Tully	Smith	Fallon	Fernie 1	Collins 1
Mar 26	Airdrie	2-2 SF	Bonnar	Haughney	Meechan	Evans	Stein	Peacock	Collins	Fernie 1	Walsh 1	Mochan	Tully
Apr 4	Airdrie	2-0 SFR	Bonnar	Haughney	Meechan	Evans	Stein	Peacock	Collins	Fernie	McPhail 2	Walsh	Tully
Apr 23	Clyde	1-1 F	Bonnar	Haughney	Meechan	Evans	Stein	Peacock	Collins	Fernie	McPhail	Walsh 1	Tully
Apr 27	Clyde	0-1 FR	Bonnar	Haughney	Meechan	Evans	Stein	Peacock	Walsh	Fernie	Fallon	McPhail	Tully

SCOTTISH LEAGUE 1955-56

			1	2	3	4	5	6	7	8	9	10	11
Sept 10	Falkirk	1-3	Beattie	Haughney	Meecham	Evans	Jack	Peacock	Craig	Boden	McPhail	Smith	Mochan 1
Sept 17	STIRLING ALBION	3-0	Beattie	Haughney	Fallon	Fernie	Evans	Peacock	Smith	Collins	McPhail 1	Tully 2	Mochan
Sept 24	Rangers	0-0	Beattie	Boden	Fallon	Fernie	Evans	Peacock	Docherty	Collins	Haughney	Smith	Mochan
Oct 1	RAITH ROVERS	2-0	Beattie	Boden	Fallon	Reid	Evans	Peacock	Collins	McVittie 1	Sharkey 1	Fernie	Tully
Oct 8	Hearts	1-2	Beattie	Boden	Fallon	Whyte	Jack	Mochan	Higgins	Fernie 1	Sharkey	Rowan	Tully
Oct 15	MOTHERWELL	2-2	Beattie	Boden	Mochan	Whyte	Evans	Peacock	Collins	McVittie 1	Sharkey	Fernie 1	Tully
Oct 22	Clyde	3-1	Beattie	Boden	Mochan	Fernie P	Evans	Peacock	Higgins 1	Collins	Walsh 1	Smith	Tully
Oct 29	DUNFERMLINE ATHLETIC	4-2	Beattie	Boden	Mochan	Fernie	Evans	Peacock	Higgins	Collins	Walsh 3	Smith	Tully 1
Nov 5	EAST FIFE	0-0	Beattie	Boden	Mochan	Fernie	Evans	Peacock	Collins	McVittie	Walsh	Smith	Tully
Nov 12	Dundee	2-1	Beattie	Boden	Meechan	Whyte	Evans	Peacock	Collins	Fernie	Walsh	Smith	Mochan 2
Nov 19	ST MIRREN	3-0	Beatie	Meechan	Fallon	Whyte	Evans	Peacock	Collins	Fernie 1	Sharkey 1	Walsh	Mochan 1
Nov 26	Airdrie	2-1	Beattie	Boden	Meechan	Whyte	Evans	Peacock	Collins	Fernie	Sharkey 1	Walsh	Mochan 1
Dec 3	Stirling Albion	3-0	Beattie	Boden	Meechan	Whyte	Evans	Peacock	Collins	Fernie 1	Sharkey	Walsh 1	Mochan 1
Dec 10	KILMARNOCK	0-2	Beattie	Haughney	Meechan	Conroy	Evans	Peacock	Higgins	Fernie	Sharkey	Collins	Mochan
Dec 17	PARTICK THISTLE	5-1	Beattie	Haughney P	Goldie	Evans	Stein	Peacock	Higgins	Fernie	Sharkey 1	Collins	Mochan 3
Dec 24	Hibernian	3-2	Beattie	Haughney	Goldie	Evans	Stein	Peacock	Walsh	Fernie	Sharkey 1	Collins	Mochan 2
Dec 31	Queen of the South	3-1	Beattie	Haughney	Fallon	Whyte	Evans	Peacock	Walsh	Fernie	Sharkey 1	Collins 1	Mochan 1
Jan 2	RANGERS	0-1	Beattie	Haughney	Fallon	Evans	Stein	Peacock	McVittie	Fernie	Sharkey	Collins	Mochan
Jan 7	Aberdeen	0-1	Beattie	Haughney	Fallon	Evans	Stein	Peacock	Smith	Fernie	Sharkey	Collins	Mochan
Jan 21	Raith Rovers	1-1	Beattie	Haughney	Fallon	Boden	Evans	Peacock	Walsh	Fernie	Sharkey 1	Collins	Mochan
Jan 28	HEARTS	1-1	Beattie	Haughney	Goldie	Evans	Stein	Peacock	Collins	Fernie	Sharkey	Walsh 1	Mochan
Feb 11	Motherwell	2-2	Beattie	Haughney	Fallon	Goldie	Evans	Peacock	Collins	Fernie	McAlindon	Tully 1	Smith 1
Feb 25	CLYDE	4-1	Beattie	Haughney P	Fallon	Boden	Evans	Peacock	Collins 1	Smith	Walsh 1	Tully	Mochan 1
Mar 7	Dunfermline Athletic	1-1	Beattie	Haughney	Fallon	Boden	Evans	Peacock	Collins 1	Fernie	Walsh	Tully	Mochan
Mar 10	East Fife	0-3	Beattie	Haughney	Fallon	Boden	Evans	Peacock	Craig	Fernie	Mochan	Tully	Collins
Mar 17	DUNDEE	1-0	Beattie	Haughney	Fallon	Evans	Stein	Peacock	Collins 1	Fernie	Sharkey	Smith	Tully
Mar 28	St Mirren	2-0	Beattie	Haughney	Goldie	Boden	Evans	Peacock 1	Craig	Collins	Mochan 1	Fernie	Tully
Mar 31	AIRDRIE	3-1	Beattie	Haughney	Meechan	Goldie	Evans	Peacock	McAlindon 1	Collins	Mochan 2	Fernie	Tully
Apr 10	ABERDEEN	1-1	Beattie	Haughney	Fallon	Goldie	Evans	Peacock	McAlindon 1	Craig	Mochan	Fernie	Tully
Apr 13	Kilmarnock	0-0	Beattie	Haughney	Fallon	Smith	Jack	Peacock	McAlindon	Sharkey	Mochan	Fernie	Tully
Apr 23	Partick Thistle	0-2	Beattie	Haughney	Kennedy	Goldie	Evans	Peacock	Craig	Smith	Mochan	Fernie	Tully
Apr 25	HIBERNIAN	0-3	Bonnar	Haughney	Fallon	Goldie	Evans	Peacock	Craig	Fernie	Sharkey	Walsh	Mochan
Apr 28	QUEEN OF THE SOUTH	1-3	Bonnar	Haughney	Fallon	Goldie	Evans	Peacock	Higgins	Fernie	Sharkey	Walsh 1	Mochan
Apr 30	FALKIRK	1-0	Bonnar	Haughney	Fallon	Boden	Jack	Peacock	Higgins	Fernie 1	Sharkey	Walsh	Mochan

LEAGUE CUP 1955

			1	2	3	4	5	6	7	8	9	10	11
Aug 13	QUEEN OF THE SOUTH	4-2	Bonnar	Haughney	Fallon	Evans	Stein	McPhail	Collins 1	Fernie 1	Walsh 1	Tully	Mochan 1
Aug 17	Queen of the South	2-0	Bonnar	Haughney	Fallon	Conroy	Evans	McPhail	Collins	Fernie	McAlindon	Walsh 1	Mochan +OG
Aug 20	FALKIRK	5-1	Bonnar	Haughney	Fallon	Evans	Stein	Peacock	Collins 2	Fernie 1	Walsh	Tully 1	Mochan 1
Aug 27	Rangers	4-1	Bonnar	Haughney	Fallon	Evans	Stein	Peacock	Collins	Fernie	Mochan 1	Smith 2	McPhail 1
Aug 31	RANGERS	0-4	Bonnar	Haughney	Fallon	Evans	Stein	Peacock	Collins	McVittie	Mochan	Smith	McPhail
Sept 3	Falkirk	1-1	Beattie	Haughney	Meechan	Smith	Evans	Peacock	Collins	Fernie	Docherty	Tully	Mochan 1

SCOTTISH CUP 1956

			1	2	3	4	5	6	7	8	9	10	11
Feb 4	Morton	2-0	Beattie	Haughney	Goldie	Evans	Boden	Peacock	Collins 1	Fernie	Sharkey	Tully 1	Mochan
Feb 18	Ayr United	3-0	Beattie	Haughney	Fallon	Boden	Evans	Peacock	Collins 2	Smith	McAlindon	Tully	Mochan 1
Mar 3	AIRDRIE	2-1	Beattie	Haughney	Fallon	Boden	Evans	Peacock	Collins 1	Fernie	Walsh	Tully 1	Mochan
Mar 24	Clyde	2-1 SF	Beattie	Haughney P	Fallon	Boden	Evans	Peacock	Collins	Walsh	Sharkey 1	Fernie	Tully
Apr 21	Hearts	1-3 F	Beattie	Meechan	Fallon	Smith	Evans	Peacock	Craig	Haughney 1	Mochan	Fernie	Tully

SCOTTISH LEAGUE 1956-57

			1	2	3	4	5	6	7	8	9	10	11
Sept 8	QUEEN'S PARK	2-0	Beattie	Haughney	Fallon	Evans	Jack	Peacock	Mochan 1	Collins 1	McPhail	Fernie	Tully
Sept 22	RANGERS	0-2	Beattie	Haughney	Fallon	Evans	Jack	Peacock	Higgins	Collins	McPhail	Fernie	Mochan
Sept 29	Motherwell	0-1	Beattie	Haughney	Fallon	Evans	Jack	Peacock	Mochan	Collins	McPhail	Fernie	Tully
Oct 13	Falkirk	1-0	Beattie	Haughney	Fallon	Evans	Jack	Peacock	Craig	Walsh	McPhail	Collins 1	Fernie
Oct 20	RAITH ROVERS	1-1	Beattie	Haughney	Fallon	Evans	Jack	Peacock	Craig	Smith	McPhail 1	Tully	Walsh
Nov 3	Dundee	1-2	Beattie	Haughney	Fallon	Smith	Jack	Peacock	Tully	Collins	McPhail	Fernie	Mochan 1
Nov 10	EAST FIFE	4-0	Beattie	Haughney P	Kennedy	Smith	Jack	Peacock	Higgins 1	Ryan 1	Mochan 1	Fernie	Tully
Nov 17	Ayr United	3-1	Beattie	Haughney P	Fallon	Smith	Jack	Peacock	Tully 1	Ryan	McPhail 1	Fernie	Mochan
Nov 24	PARTICK THISTLE	1-1	Beattie	Haughney	Fallon	Evans	Jack	Peacock	Tully	Ryan	McPhail	Fernie	Mochan 1
Dec 1	HEARTS	1-1	Beattie	Haughney	Fallon	Evans	Jack	Peacock	Higgins	Ryan	McPhail 1	Fernie	Mochan
Dec 8	St Mirren	2-0	Beattie	Haughney	Meechan	Evans	Jack	Peacock	Higgins 1	Ryan	Mochan 1	Sharkey	Fernie
Dec 15	DUNFERMLINE ATHLETIC	3-1	Beattie	Haughney	Meechan	Evans	Jack	Peacock	Higgins 1	Ryan	Mochan 1	Fernie 1	Tully
Dec 22	Airdrie	7-3	Beattie	Haughney	Meechan	Evans	Jack	Peacock	Higgins 4	Ryan 1	Mochan 1	Fernie 1	Tully
Dec 29	Hibernian	3-3	Beattie	Haughney	Meechan	Evans	Jack	Peacock	Smith 1	Ryan 1	Mochan 1	Fernie	Tully
Jan 1	Rangers	0-2	Beattie	Haughney	Meechan	Evans	Jack	Peacock	Smith	Ryan	Mochan	Fernie	Tully
Jan 2	KILMARNOCK	1-1	Beattie	Haughney	Kennedy	Evans	Jack	Peacock	Smith	Ryan	Mochan 1	Fernie	Tully
Jan 5	Queen's Park	0-2	Beattie	Haughney	Meechan	Evans	Jack	Peacock	Smith	Ryan	Mochan	Fernie	Tully
Jan 12	MOTHERWELL	2-1	Beattie	Haughney	Kennedy	Evans	Jack	Peacock	Higgins	Ryan	Sharkey	Fernie	Mochan
Jan 19	Queen of the South	3-4	Beattie	Haughney	Kennedy	Evans	Jack	Peacock	Higgins 1	Tully	Sharkey	Fernie	Mochan 1 +OG
Jan 26	FALKIRK	4-0	Beattie	Haughney	Fallon	Evans	Jack	Peacock	Higgins	Fernie	McPhail 1	Mochan 1	Collins 1 +OG
Feb 9	Raith Rovers	1-3	Beattie	Haughney	Fallon	Evans	Jack	Peacock	Higgins	Fernie 1	McPhail	Mochan	Collins
Feb 23	ABERDEEN	2-1	Beattie	Haughney	Fallon	Evans	Jack	Peacock 1	Higgins 1	Fernie	McPhail	Mochan	Collins
Mar 6	DUNDEE	1-1	Beattie	Haughney P	Fallon	Evans	Jack	Peacock	Higgins	Fernie	McPhail	Mochan	Collins
Mar 9	East Fife	0-2	Beattie	Haughney	Fallon	Evans	Jack	Peacock	McAlindon	Fernie	Byrne	Mochan	Collins
Mar 16	AYR UNITED	4-0	Beattie	Haughney P	Fallon	Evans	Jack	Peacock	Higgins	Collins 1	Byrne 2	Mochan	Tully
Mar 30	Hearts	1-3	Beattie	Haughney	Meechan	Evans	Jack	Peacock	Higgins	Fernie	Byrne	Collins 1	Mochan
Apr 10	Partick Thistle	1-3	Beattie	Haughney	Fallon	Evans	Jack	Mochan	Collins	Fernie	Higgins	Byrne 1	Tully
Apr 13	Dunfermline Athletic	1-0	Beattie	Haughney	Fallon	Evans	Jack	Peacock	Fernie	Collins	McAlindon 1	Smith	Tully
Apr 17	ST MIRREN	2-3	Beattie	Haughney P	Fallon	Evans	Jack	Peacock	Higgins	Fernie 1	Mochan	Collins	Tully
Apr 20	AIRDRIE	3-0	Beattie	Haughney P	Fallon	Evans	Jack	Peacock	Collins 1	Fernie	McAlindon 1	Smith	Mochan
Apr 22	Aberdeen	1-0	McCreadie	Haughney	Fallon	Evans	Jack	Mochan	Higgins	Fernie	Ryan	Collins	Tully +OG
Apr 26	Kilmarnock	0-0	Bonnar	Haughney	Fallon	Evans	Jack	Mochan	Higgins	Fernie	Ryan	Collins	Tully
Apr 27	HIBERNIAN	2-1	Bonnar	Haughney P	Fallon	Evans	Jack	Peacock	Higgins	Fernie 1	Ryan	Collins	Mochan
Apr 29	QUEEN OF THE SOUTH	0-0	Bonner	Haughney	Goldie	Evans	Meechan	Peacock	Higgins	Fernie	Byrne	Collins	Mochan

LEAGUE CUP 1956

			1	2	3	4	5	6	7	8	9	10	11
Aug 11	Aberdeen	2-1	Beattie	Haughney	Fallon	Evans	Jack	Peacock	Higgins 1	Collins	McPhail	Fernie 1	Tully
Aug 15	RANGERS	2-1	Beattie	Haughney	Fallon	Evans	Jack	Peacock	Higgins	Collins 1	McPhail	Fernie	Tully 1
Aug 18	EAST FIFE	2-1	Beattie	Haughney	Kennedy	Evans	Jack	Peacock	Higgins	Collins	McPhail 1	Fernie 1	Tully
Aug 25	ABERDEEN	3-2	Beattie	Haughney	Fallon	Evans	Jack	Peacock	Smith	Collins 1	McPhail	Fernie 1	Tully 1
Aug 29	Rangers	0-0	Beattie	Haughney	Fallon	Evans	Jack	Peacock	Tully	Collins	McPhail	Fernie	Mochan
Sept 1	East Fife	1-0	Beattie	Haughney	Fallon	Evans	Jack	Peacock	Smith	Collins	McPhail 1	Fernie	Mochan
Sept 12	DUNFERMLINE ATHLETIC	6-0	Beattie	Haughney	Fallon	Evans	Jack	Peacock	Mochan 2	Collins 1	McPhail 2	Fernie	Tully +OG
Sept 15	Dunfermline Athletic	0-3	Beattie	Haughney	Fallon	Evans	Jack	Peacock	Mochan	Collins	Walsh	Fernie	Smith
Oct 6	Clyde	2-0 SF	Beattie	Haughney	Fallon	Evans	Jack	Peacock	Smith	Collins	McPhail 2	Fernie	Mochan
Oct 27	Partick Thistle	0-0 F	Beattie	Haughney	Fallon	Evans	Jack	Peacock	Walsh	Collins	McPhail	Tully	Fernie
Oct 31	Partick Thistle	3-0 FR	Beattie	Haughney	Fallon	Evans	Jack	Peacock	Tully	Collins 1	McPhail 2	Fernie	Mochan

SCOTTISH CUP 1957

Feb 2	Forres Mechanics	5-0	Beattie	Haughney	Fallon	Evans	Jack	Peacock	Higgins 1	Fernie	McPhail 3	Mochan 1	Collins
Feb 16	RANGERS	4-4	Beattie	Haughney	Fallon	Evans	Jack	Peacock	Higgins 1	Fernie 1	McPhail 1	Mochan	Collins 1
Feb 20	Rangers	2-0	Beattie	Haughney	Fallon	Evans	Jack	Peacock	Higgins 1	Fernie	McPhail	Mochan 1	Collins
Mar 2	ST MIRREN	2-1	Beattie	Haughney	Fallon	Evans	Jack	Peacock 1	Higgins 1	Fernie	McPhail	Mochan	Collins
Mar 23	Kilmarnock	1-1 SF	Beattie	Haughney	Fallon	Evans	Jack	Peacock	Higgins 1	Fernie	Byrne	Mochan	Collins
Mar 27	Kilmarnock	1-3 SFR	Beattie	Haughney	Fallon	Evans	Jack	Peacock	Higgins	Fernie	Byrne	Mochan	Collins 1

SCOTTISH LEAGUE 1957-58

Sept 7	Falkirk	1-0	Beattie	Donnelly	Fallon	Fernie 1	Evans	Peacock	Tully	Collins	Conway	Wilson	Auld
Sept 21	Rangers	3-2	Beattie	Donnelly	Fallon	Fernie	Evans	Peacock	Sharkey	Collins 1	McPhail 1	Wilson 1	Tully
Oct 12	RAITH ROVERS	1-1	Beattie	Donnelly	Fallon	Fernie	Evans	Peacock	Tully	Collins	Mochan 1	Wilson	Smith
Oct 26	Third Lanark	2-0	Beattie	Goldie	Fallon	Fernie	Evans	Peacock	Tully	Collins 2	McPhail	Wilson	Mochan
Nov 2	KILMARNOCK	4-0	Beattie	Goldie	Fallon	Fernie	Evans	Peacock	Tully	Collins	McPhail 1	Wilson 1	Mochan 2
Nov 9	East Fife	3-0	Beattie	Donnelly	Fallon	Fernie	Evans	Peacock	Tully	Collins	McPhail 2	Wilson	Mochan 1
Nov 16	ST MIRREN	2-2	Beattie	Donnelly	Fallon	Fernie	Evans	Peacock	Tully	Divers 1	McPhail	Wilson 1	Mochan
Nov 23	Hibernian	1-0	Beattie	Donnelly	Fallon	Fernie	Evans	Peacock	Tully	Collins	McPhail	Wilson 1	Mochan
Nov 30	Airdrie	5-2	Beattie	Donnelly	Fallon	Fernie	Evans	Peacock 1	Tully	Collins 1+P)	McPhail	Wilson 2	Mochan
Dec 7	DUNDEE	0-0	Beattie	Donnelly	Fallon	Fernie	Evans	Peacock	Jackson	Colins	McPhail	Wilson	Mochan
Dec 14	Clyde	6-3	Beattie	Donnelly	Fallon	Fernie	Evans	Peacock	Smith 2	Collins	McPhail 2	Wilson 1	Mochan +OG
Dec 21	PARTICK THISTLE	2-3	Beattie	Donnelly	Fallon	Fernie	Jack	Peacock	Smith	Collins	McPhail	Wilson	Mochan 2
Dec 25	QUEEN OF THE SOUTH	1-2	Beattie	Donnelly	Fallon	Jack	Evans	Peacock	Smith	Collins	Conway 1	Wilson	Mochan
Dec 28	HEARTS	0-2	Beattie	Fallon	Kennedy	Smith	Evans	Peacock	Conway	Collins	Ryan	Wilson	Mochan
Jan 1	RANGERS	0-1	Beattie	Fallon	Kennedy	Smith	Evans	Peacock	McVittie	Colrain	Ryan	Wilson	Mochan
Jan 2	Queen's Park	3-0	Beattie	Fallon	Kennedy	Smith	Evans	Peacock	McVittie 1	Colrain	Ryan	Wilson 2	Mochan
Jan 4	FALKIRK	2-2	Beattie	Fallon	Kennedy	Smith	Evans	Peacock	Ryan	Colrain 1	Byrne 1	Wilson	Mochan
Jan 11	Motherwell	3-1	Beattie	Donnelly	Fallon	Smith	Evans	Peacock	Collins 1	Ryan	Byrne	Wilson	Mochan 1 +OG
Jan 18	ABERDEEN	1-1	Beattie	Donnelly	Fallon	Smith	Evans	Peacock	Collins 1	Ryan	Byrne	Wilson	Auld
Jan 25	Raith Rovers	2-1	Beattie	Donnelly	Fallon	Fernie	Evans	Peacock	Collins 1	Smith	Byrne 1	Wilson	Mochan
Feb 22	Kilmarnock	1-1	Beattie	Donnelly	Fallon	Fernie	Evans	Peacock	Collins	Smith	McPhail	Wilson 1	Byrne
Mar 5	EAST FIFE	4-0	Beattie	Donnelly	Fallon	Fernie	Evans	Peacock	Collins 1	Smith	Byrne 3	Wilson	Mochan
Mar 8	St Mirren	1-1	Beattie	Donnelly	Fallon	Fernie	Evans	Peacock	Collins P	Smith	Byrne	Wilson	Tully
Mar 14	Hearts	3-5	Beattie	Donnelly	Fallon	Fernie	Evans	Peacock	Collins P	Smith 1	McPhail	Wilson	Byrne 1
Mar 19	HIBERNIAN	4-0	Beattie	Meechan	Fallon	Fernie	Evans	Peacock	McVittie	Collins	McPhail 1	Wilson 3	Byrne
Mar 22	AIRDRIE	4-2	Beattie	Meechan	Fallon	Fernie	Evans	Peacock	McVittie	Collins 2+P	McPhail	Wilson	Byrne 1
Mar 29	Dundee	3-5	Beattie	Meechan	Mochan	Fernie	Evans	Peacock	Collins P	McVittie 1	McPhail	Wilson 1	Byrne
Apr 5	Aberdeen	1-0	Beattie	Meechan	Mochan	Smith	Evans	Peacock	Collins	McVittie	Byrne 1	Wilson	Fernie
Apr 7	QUEEN'S PARK	5-1	Beattie	Meechan	Mochan	Smith 1	Evans	Conroy	McVittie 1	Collins	Byrne 1	Wilson 2	Fernie
Apr 9	CLYDE	6-2	Beattie	Meechan	Mochan	Smith	Evans	Conroy	McVittie 1	Collins 2	McPhail 1	Wilson 1	Fernie 1
Apr 12	Partick Thistle	1-0	Beattie	Meechan	Mochan	Smith	Evans	Peacock	McVittie	Collins 1	McPhail	Wilson	Fernie
Apr 16	Queen of the South	3-4	Beattie	Meechan	Mochan	Smith	Jack	Conroy	McVittie	Collins	McPhail 1	Wilson 2	Fernie
Apr 21	MOTHERWELL	2-2	Beattie	Meechan	Mochan	Smith	Evans	Peacock	Collins	Colrain	McPhail	Wilson 2	Fernie
Apr 30	THIRD LANARK	4-1	Haffey	Meechan	Mochan	Smith	Evans	Peacock 1	Collins P	Fernie	McPhail	Wilson 2	McVittie

LEAGUE CUP 1957

Aug 10	AIRDRIE	3-2	Beattie	Meechan	Fallon	Fernie	Evans	Peacock 1	Tully	Collins	McPhail 1	Smith	Mochan 1
Aug 14	East Fife	4-1	Beattie	Meechan	Fallon	Wilson	Evans	Peacock	Tully	Collins 1	McPhail 2	Sharkey	Mochan 1
Aug 17	Hibernian	1-3	Beattie	Meechan	Fallon	Fernie	Evans	Peacock	Tully	Collins 1	McPhail	Sharkey	Mochan
Aug 24	Airdrie	2-1	Beattie	Donnelly	Fallon	Fernie 1	Evans	Peacock	Tully	Collins	McPhail	Smith 1	Auld
Aug 28	EAST FIFE	6-1	Beattie	Donnelly	Fallon	Fernie	Evans	Peacock	Tully	Collins 1	McPhail 2	Wilson 2	Auld 1
Aug 31	HIBERNIAN	2-0	Beattie	Donnelly	Fallon	Fernie	Evans	Peacock	Tully	Collins	McPhail 1	Wilson 1	Auld
Sept 11	THIRD LANARK	6-1	Beattie	Donnelly	Fallon	Fernie	Evans	Peacock	Tully	Collins 2	McPhail 2	Wilson 1	Auld 1
Sept 14	Third Lanark	3-0	Beattie	Donnelly	Fallon	Fernie	Evans	Peacock	Tully	Collins 1	McPhail 1	Wilson 1	Auld
Sept 28	Clyde	4-2 SF	Beattie	Donnelly	Fallon	Fernie 1	Evans	Peacock	Smith	Collins 1	McPhail 1	Wilson 1	Auld
Oct 19	Rangers	7-1 F	Beattie	Donnelly	Fallon	Fernie P	Evans	Peacock	Tully	Collins	McPhail 3	Wilson 1	Mochan 2

SCOTTISH CUP 1958

Feb 1	Airdrie	4-3	Beattie	Donnelly	Fallon	Fernie 1	Evans	Peacock	Collins 1	Smith	Byrne 2	Wilson	Mochan
Feb 15	STIRLING ALBION	7-2	Beattie	Donnelly	Fallon	Fernie	Evans	Peacock	Collins	Smith 2	Byrne 2	Wilson 2	Mochan 1
Mar 1	CLYDE	0-2	Beattie	Donnelly	Fallon	Smith	Evans	Peacock	Collins	Fernie	Byrne	Wilson	Mochan

SCOTTISH LEAGUE 1958-59

Aug 20	Clyde	1-2	Beattie	MacKay	Mochan	Fernie	Evans	Peacock	Tully	Collins	Byrne	Wilson	Auld 1
Sept 6	RANGERS	2-2	Beattie	MacKay	Mochan	Fernie	McNeill	Peacock	Smith 1	Tully	Conway	Collins 1	Auld
Sept 13	Kilmarnock	4-1	Beattie	MacKay	Mochan	Fernie	McNeill	Peacock	Tully	Smith 1	Colrain 1	Wilson	Auld 2 (1P)
Sept 20	RAITH ROVERS	3-1	Beattie	MacKay	Mochan	Smith 1	Jack	Peacock	Tully	Fernie 2	Colrain	Wilson	Auld
Sept 27	Aberdeen	1-3	Beattie	MacKay	Mochan	Smith	McNeill	Peacock 1	Tully	Fernie	Colrain	Wilson	Auld
Oct 4	QUEEN OF THE SOUTH	3-1	Beattie	Donnelly	Mochan	Crerand	McNeill	Smith	Colrain	Fernie	Conway 1	Divers 1	Auld 1
Oct 11	FALKIRK	3-4	Beattie	Donnelly	Mochan	Crerand	McNeill	Smith	Colrain	Fernie 1	Conway	Divers 2	Auld
Oct 18	Airdrie	4-1	Beattie	MacKay	Mochan	Fernie 1	McNeill	Smith 1	Higgins	Jackson	Byrne 1	Divers 1	Auld
Oct 25	THIRD LANARK	3-1	Beattie	MacKay	Mochan 1	Fernie	McNeill	Smith	Higgins	Jackson	Byrne	Wilson	Auld 2P
Nov 1	Dundee	1-1	Beattie	MacKay	Mochan	Fernie	McNeill	Peacock	Higgins 1	Jackson	Conway	Wilson	Auld
Nov 8	Dunfermline Athletic	0-1	Beattie	MacKay	Mochan	Fernie	McNeill	Peacock	Higgins	Jackson	Conway	McVittie	Auld
Nov 15	ST MIRREN	3-3	Beattie	MacKay	Mochan	Fernie	McNeill	Peacock	Higgins	Jackson	Conway	McVittie	Auld 2(1P) +OG
Nov 22	Partick Thistle	0-2	Beattie	MacKay	Mochan	Fernie	McNeill	Peacock	McVittie	Jackson	Conway	Colrain	Auld
Nov 29	Hibernian	2-3	Beattie	MacKay	Mochan	Crerand	McNeill	Peacock	Higgins 1	McVittie	Conway	Colrain 1	Auld
Dec 13	STIRLING ALBION	7-3	Beattie	MacKay	Mochan	Smith	Evans	Peacock	McVittie 1	Jackson 1	Colrain 3	Divers 2	Auld
Dec 20	Hearts	1-1	Beattie	MacKay	Mochan	Smith	Evans	Peacock	Higgins 1	Jackson	Colrain	Divers	McVittie
Dec 27	CLYDE	3-1	Beattie	MacKay	Mochan	Smith	Evans	Peacock	McVittie 1	Jackson	Colrain 2	Divers	Auld
Jan 1	Rangers	1-2	Beattie	MacKay	Mochan	Smith	Evans	Peacock 1	McVittie	Jackson	Colrain	Divers	Auld
Jan 2	MOTHERWELL	3-3	Beattie	MacKay	Kennedy	Smith	Evans	Peacock	Higgins	Jackson	Colrain 2	Divers 1	Auld
Jan 21	KILMARNOCK	2-0	Haffey	MacKay	Mochan	Smith	Evans	Peacock 1	Higgins	Jackson	Colrain	Divers	Auld +OG
Jan 24	Queen of the South	2-2	Haffey	MacKay	Mochan	McNeill	Evans	Smith	Slater	Jackson	Colrain 1	Divers	Auld 1
Feb 7	Falkirk	2-3	Haffey	MacKay	Mochan	Smith	Evans	Peacock	Slater	Wilson	Colrain 1	Divers 1	Auld
Feb 21	Third Lanark	1-1	Haffey	MacKay	Mochan	Smith	Evans	Peacock	Wilson 1	Jackson	Colrain	Divers	McVittie
Mar 4	DUNDEE	1-1	Haffey	MacKay	Mochan P	Smith	Evans	Crerand	Higgins	Jackson	Lochhead	Wilson	Divers
Mar 7	DUNFERMLINE ATHLETIC	3-1	Haffey	MacKay	Mochan P	Smith	Evans	McNeill	Colrain	Jackson 2	Lochhead	Wilson	Divers
Mar 10	AIRDRIE	1-2	Haffey	MacKay	Mochan	Smith	Evans	Peacock	McVittie	Chalmers	Colrain 1	Wilson	Auld
Mar 18	St Mirren	0-1	Haffey	MacKay	Mochan	Smith	Evans	Peacock	McVittie	Jackson	Byrne	Wilson	Divers
Mar 21	PARTICK THISTLE	2-0	Haffey	MacKay	Mochan	Smith	Evans	Peacock	Slater 1	Colrain 1	Lochhead	Wilson	Divers
Mar 25	ABERDEEN	4-0	Haffey	MacKay	Mochan P	McNeill	Evans	Peacock	McVittie	Colrain 1	Lochhead 2	Divers	Auld
Mar 28	HIBERNIAN	3-0	Beattie	MacKay	Mochan	Smith	Evans	Peacock	McVittie	Colrain	Lochhead 1	Wilson 2	Divers
Apr 6	Raith Rovers	1-3	Haffey	MacKay	Mochan P	Smith	Evans	Peacock	McVittie	Colrain	Conway	Divers	Auld
Apr 8	Motherwell	0-2	Haffey	Kurila	Mochan	Smith	McNeill	Peacock	McVittie	Colrain	Conway	Divers	Auld
Apr 11	Stirling Albion	1-0	Haffey	Donnelly	Mochan	Smith	McNeill	Peacock	Slater	McVittie 1	Lochhead	Colrain	Auld
Apr 18	HEARTS	2-1	Haffey	Donnelly	Mochan	MacKay	Evans	Peacock	Smith 1	McVittie	Byrne	Colrain	Auld 1

LEAGUE CUP 1958

Aug 9	Clyde	4-1	Beattie	MacKay	Mochan	Fernie	Evans	Peacock	Tully 1	Collins 1	Conway	Wilson 1	Auld 1
Aug 13	AIRDRIE	3-3	Beattie	MacKay	Kennedy	Fernie	Evans	Peacock	Tully	Collins 1	Conway 1	Wilson	Auld 1
Aug 16	St MIRREN	3-0	Beattie	MacKay	Mochan	Fernie	Evans	Peacock	Tully 1	Collins 1	Conway 1	Wilson	Auld
Aug 23	CLYDE	2-0	Haffey	MacKay	Mochan	Fernie	McNeill	Peacock	Tully	Collins	Conway	Wilson 1	Auld 1

			1	2	3	4	5	6	7	8	9	10	11
Aug 27	Airdrie	2-1	Haffey	MacKay	Mochan	Fernie	McNeill	Peacock 1	Tully	Collins	Conway 1	Wilson	Auld
Aug 30	St Mirren	3-6	Haffey	MacKay	Mochan	Fernie	McNeill	Peacock	Tully	Collins 2P	Conway	Wilson	Auld 1
Sept 10	COWDENBEATH	2-0	Beattie	MacKay	Mochan	Fernie	McNeill	Peacock	Smith	Tully	Jackson	Collins 1	Auld 1
Sept 17	Cowdenbeath	8-1	Beattie	MacKay	Mochan	Smith	McNeill	Peacock	Tully	Fernie	Colrain 2	Wilson 4	Auld 1 +OG
Oct 1	Partick Thistle	1-2	Beattie	Donnelly	Mochan	Smith	McNeill	Peacock	Tully	Fernie	Conway 1	Divers	Auld

SCOTTISH CUP 1959

Jan 31	ALBION ROVERS	4-0	Haffey	MacKay	Mochan	Smith	Evans	Peacock	Tully	Jackson 1	Colrain	Wilson 2	Auld +OG
Feb 18	CLYDE	1-1	Haffey	MacKay	Mochan	Smith	Evans	Peacock	McVittie 1	Paton	Colrain	Divers	Conway
Feb 23	Clyde	4-3 ??	Haffey	MacKay	Mochan	Smith	Evans	Peacock	McVittie 1	Colrain	Lochhead	Wilson 2	Auld 1
Feb 28	RANGERS	2-1	Haffey	MacKay	Mochan	Smith	Evans	Peacock	McVittie 1	Jackson	Lochhead	Wilson	Divers 1
Mar 16	Stirling Albion	3-1	Haffey	MacKay	Mochan	Smith	Evans	Peacock	McVittie	Jackson	Lochhead 1	Wilson 1	Divers 1
Apr 4	St Mirren	0-4 SF	Haffey	MacKay	Mochan	Smith	Evans	Peacock	McVittie	Jackson	Lochhead	Wilson	Divers

SCOTTISH LEAGUE 1959-60

Aug 19	KILMARNOCK	2-0	Haffey	McNeill	Mochan	MacKay	Evans	Peacock	Carroll	O'Hara	Conway 1	Divers 1	Mackle
Sept 5	Rangers	1-3	Haffey	McNeill	Kennedy	MacKay	Evans	Peacock	Mcvittie	Jackson 1	Conway	Divers	Auld
Sept 12	HEARTS	3-4	Haffey	McNeill	Donnelly	MacKay	Evans	Peacock	Auld 1	Jackson	Conway 1	Divers 1	Mackle
Sept 19	Raith Rovers	3-0	Haffey	McNeill	Mochan	Smith	Evans	Peacock	Chalmers 2	Jackson 1	Conway	Divers	Auld
Sept 26	CLYDE	1-1	Fallon	Curran	Mochan	Smith	Evans	Peacock	Chalmers	Jackson	Conway	Divers	Mackle 1
Oct 3	Arbroath	5-0	Fallon	Curran	Mochan	Smith	McNeill	Clark	Chalmers 2	Jackson 2	Conway 1	Divers	Auld
Oct 10	ABERDEEN	1-1	Fallon	Curran	Mochan	Smith	Evans	Clark	Chalmers	Jackson	Conway 1	Peacock	Auld
Oct 17	Third Lanark	2-4	Fallon	MacKay	Mochan	Smith	Evans	Peacock	Slater	Jackson 1	Conway	Divers 1	Auld
Oct 24	MOTHERWELL	5-1	Fallon	MacKay	Mochan	Smith	Evans	Peacock	Chalmers	Jackson 1	Colrain 1	Divers 2	Auld
Oct 31	Hibernian	3-3	Fallon	MacKay	Mochan	Smith	Evans	Peacock 1	Chalmers	Jackson 1	Colrain 1	Divers	Auld
Nov 7	AYR UNITED	2-3	Fallon	MacKay	Donnelly	Smith	Evans	Peacock	Chalmers	Jackson	Colrain	Divers 1	Auld 1
Nov 14	DUNFERMLINE ATHLETIC	4-2	Fallon	MacKay	Mochan	Smith	Evans	Peacock	Chalmers	Jackson1	Colrain	Divers 3	Auld
Nov 21	Stirling Albion	2-2	Fallon	Donnelly	Mochan	MacKay	Evans	Peacock	Chalmers	Jackson	Colrain 1	Divers	Auld 1
Nov 28	Partick Thistle	1-3	Fallon	Donnelly	Mochan	MacKay	Evans	Peacock	Chalmers	O'Hara	Colrain	Divers 1	Auld
Dec 5	DUNDEE	2-3	Fallon	Donnelly	Mochan P	Crerand	Evans	Peacock	Chalmers 1	Smith	Lochhead	Divers	Auld
Dec 12	AIRDRIE	0-0	Haffey	MacKay	Kennedy	McNeill	Evans	Peacock	Auld	Smith	Colrain	Mochan	Byrne
Dec 19	St Mirren	3-0	Haffey	MacKay	Kennedy	McNeill	Evans	Peacock	Auld	O'Hara 1	Colrain 1	Mochan 1	Byrne
Dec 26	Kilmarnock	1-2	Haffey	MacKay	Kennedy	McNeill	Evans	Peacock	Auld	O'Hara	Colrain	Mochan 1	Byrne
Jan 1	RANGERS	0-1	Haffey	MacKay	Kennedy	McNeill	Evans	Peacock	Auld	Smith	Carroll	Mochan	Byrne
Jan 2	Hearts	1-3	Haffey	MacKay	Kennedy	McNeill	Evans	Peacock 1	Carrol	Smith	Byrne	Mochan	Auld
Jan 7	RAITH ROVERS	1-0	Haffey	MacKay	Kennedy	McNeill	Evans	Peacock	Carroll	Smith	Byrne	Mochan 1	Auld
Jan 16	Clyde	3-3	Haffey	MacKay	Kennedy	Crerand	Kurila	Peacock	Carrol	O'Hara	Byrne 2	Mochan P	Divers
Jan 23	ARBROATH	4-0	Haffey	MacKay	Kennedy	Crerand	Evans	Peacock	Carrol 1	O'Hara	Byrne 1	Mochan	Divers
Feb 6	Aberdeen	2-3	Haffey	MacKay	Kennedy	Crerand	Evans	Peacock	Carrol	O'Hara	Byrne	Mochan 2P	Divers
Mar 7	HIBERNIAN	1-0	Haffey	MacKay	Kennedy	McNeill	Evans	Peacock	Auld	Smith	Conway 1	Chalmers	Byrne
Mar 16	Ayr United	1-1	Haffey	MacKay	Kennedy	Crerand 1	Evans	Peacock	Smith	Colrain	Conway	Divers	Byrne
Mar 19	Dunfermline Athletic	2-3	Haffey	MacKay	Kennedy	McNeill	Evans	Peacock	Conway 1	Smith	Mochan	Divers	Byrne 1
Mar 21	Motherwell	2-1	Haffey	MacKay	Kennedy	Crerand	McNeill	Peacock	Smith	Colrain	Mochan 2	Divers	Byrne
Mar 26	STIRLING ALBION	1-1	Haffey	MacKay	Kennedy	McNeill	Evans	Peacock	Smith	Colrain	Mochan 1	Divers	Conway
Mar 28	THIRD LANARK	4-0	Haffey	MacKay	Kennedy	Crerand	McNeill	Peacock	Smith	Colrain 1	Mochan P	Chalmers 2	Byrne
Apr 12	PARTICK THISTLE	2-4	Haffey	MacKay	Kennedy	McNeill	Evans	Peacock	Chalmers 2	Colrain	Mochan	Divers	Gallacher
Apr 16	Dundee	0-2	Haffey	MacKay	Kennedy	McNeill	Evans	Peacock	Carroll	Chalmers	Mochan	Colrain	Gallacher
Apr 18	Airdrie	5-2	Fallon	MacKay	Kennedy	Crerand	Evans	Peacock	Carroll	Chalmers 3	Mochan 1	Divers	Gallacher +OG
Apr 30	ST MIRREN	3-3	Fallon	MacKay	Kennedy	McNeill	Evans	Peacock	Carroll	Chalmers 2	Mochan 1	Gallagher	Divers

LEAGUE CUP 1959

Aug 8	Raith Rovers	1-2	Haffey	McNeill	Mochan	MacKay	Evans	Peacock	Smith	McVittie	Byrne	Colrain	Mackle 1
Aug 12	PARTICK THISTLE	1-2	Haffey	McNeill	Mochan P	MacKay	Evans	Smith	Carroll	Colrain	Byrne	Divers	Mackle
Aug 15	Airdrie	2-4	Haffey	McNeill	Mochan	MacKay	Evans	Smith	Carroll 1	McVittie	Colrain	Divers	Byrn +OG
Aug 22	RAITH ROVERS	1-0	Haffey	McNeill	Kennedy	MacKay	Evans	Peacock	McVittie	O'Hara	Conway	Gallacher	Auld
Aug 26	Partick Thistle	2-0	Haffey	McNeill	Kennedy	MacKay	Evans	Peacock	McVittie	Jackson 2	Conway	O'Hara	Auld
Aug 29	AIRDRIE	2-2	Haffey	McNeill	Kennedy	MacKay	Evans	Peacock	Mcvittie	Jackson	Lochhead	Divers 2	Auld P

SCOTTISH CUP 1960

Feb 13	St Mirren	1-1	Haffey	HacKay	Kennedy	McNeill	Evans	Peacock	Smith	Colrain	Mochan	Divers	Byrne 1
Feb 24	ST MIRREN	4-4	Haffey	MacKay	Kennedy	McNeill	Evans	Peacock	Smith	Colrain	Mochan 2	Divers 2	Byrne
Feb 29	ST MIRREN	5-2	Haffey	MacKay	Kennedy	McNeill	Evans	Peacock	Smith	Colrain	Mochan 4+P	Divers	Byrne
Mar 5	Elgin City	2-1	Haffey	MacKay	Kennedy	McNeill	Evans	Peacock	Smith 1	Colrain	Mochan	Divers 1	Byrne
Mar 12	PARTICK THISTLE	2-0	Haffey	MacKay	Kennedy	McNeill	Evans	Peacock	Smith 1	Colrain 1	Mochan	Divers	Auld
Apr 2	Rangers	1-1 SF	Haffey	MacKay	Kennedy	McNeill	Evans	Peacock	Chalmers 1	Colrain	Mochan	Divers	Byrne
Apr 6	Rangers	1-4 SF	Haffey	MacKay	Kennedy	McNeill	Evans	Peacock	Chalmers	Colrain	Mochan 1	Jackson	Divers

SCOTTISH LEAGUE 1960-61

Aug 24	Kilmarnock	2-2	Fallon	MacKay	Kennedy	Crerand	McNeill	Peacock	Carroll 1	Chalmers	Hughes	Divers	Mochan 1
Sept 10	RANGERS	1-5	Fallon	MacKay	Kennedy	Crerand	Kurila	Peacock	Conway	Chalmers 1	Carroll	Divers	Hughes
Sept 17	Third Lanark	0-2	Fallon	MacKay	Kennedy	Crerand	McNeill	Peacock	Carroll	Chalmers	Hughes	Divers	Auld
Sept 24	ABERDEEN	0-0	Fallon	MacKay	Kennedy	Crerand	McNeill	Peacock	Conway	Gallacher	Carroll	Divers	Auld
Oct 1	Airdrie	0-2	Goldie	MacKay	Kennedy	Crerand	McNeill	Peacock	Carroll	Divers	Mochan	Chalmers	Byrne
Oct 8	ST MIRREN	4-2	Haffey	MacKay	Kennedy	Crerand	McNeill	Clark	Chalmers	Fernie	Carroll 1	Divers 1	Auld 2
Oct 15	Hibernian	6-0	Haffey	MacKay	Kennedy	Crerand	McNeill	Peacock	Chalmers 2	Fernie 1	Carroll 1	Divers 1	Auld 1
Oct 22	Clyde	3-0	Haffey	Donnelly	Kennedy	Crerand	McNeill	Peacock 1	Chalmers	Fernie	Carroll 1	Divers	Auld 1
Oct 29	AYR UNITED	2-0	Haffey	MacKay	Kennedy	Crerand	McNeill	Peacock	Chalmers	Fernie	Carroll 1	Divers 1	Auld
Nov 5	Raith Rovers	2-2	Haffey	MacKay	Kennedy	Jackson	McNeill	Peacock	Chalmers 1	Fernie 1	Carroll	Divers	Auld
Nov 12	PARTICK THISTLE	0-1	Haffey	MacKay	Kennedy	Kurila	McNeill	Peacock	Chalmers	Fernie	Carroll	Divers	Auld
Nov 19	Dunfermline Athletic	2-2	Haffey	MacKay	Kennedy	Crerand	McNeill	Peacock	Chalmers 1	Fernie	Carroll 1	Divers	Auld
Nov 26	St Johnstone	1-2	Haffey	MacKay	Kennedy	Crerand	McNeill	Peacock	Chalmers 1	Fernie	Carroll	Divers	Auld
Dec 10	DUNDEE UNITED	1-1	Haffey	MacKay	Kennedy	Crerand	McNeill	Peacock	Conway	Chalmers	Hughes 1	Divers	Auld
Dec 17	Hearts	1-2	Haffey	MacKay	Kennedy	Crerand 1	McNeill	Peacock	Chalmers	Fernie	Hughes	Divers	Auld
Dec 24	MOTHERWELL	1-0	Haffey	MacKay	Kennedy	Crerand	McNeill	Peacock	Carroll	Chalmers	Kelly	Divers 1	Byrne
Dec 26	DUNDEE	2-1	Haffey	MacKay	Kennedy	Crerand	McNeill	Peacock	Carroll	Chalmers	Conway 1	Kelly	Byrne 1
Dec 31	KILMARNOCK	3-2	Haffey	MacKay	Kennedy	Crerand	McNeill	Peacock	Chalmers 2	Divers	Conway	Gallacher 1	Byrne
Jan 2	Rangers	1-2	Haffey	MacKay	Kennedy	Crerand	McNeill	Peacock	Chalmers	Divers 1	Conway	Fernie	Byrne
Jan 7	THIRD LANARK	2-3	Haffey	MacKay	Kennedy	Crerand	McNeill	Peacock	Gallacher	Divers 1	Conway	Chalmers 1	Fernie
Jan 14	Aberdeen	3-1	Haffey	MacKay	Kennedy	Crerand	McNeill	Peacock	Gallacher 1	Divers 1	Hughes	Chalmers 1	Auld
Jan 21	AIRDRIE	4-0	Haffey	MacKay	Kennedy	Crerand 1	McNeill	Clark	Gallacher	Divers 1	Hughes	Chalmers 2	Auld
Feb 4	St Mirren	1-2	Haffey	MacKay	Kennedy	Crerand	McNeill	Peacock 1	Gallacher	Divers	Hughes	Fernie	Auld
Feb 18	HIBERNIAN	2-0	Haffey	MacKay	Kennedy	Crerand	McNamee	Peacock	Gallacher	Fernie	Hughes	Chalmers 2	Byrne
Feb 27	CLYDE	6-1	Haffey	MacKay	Kennedy	Crerand	McNeill	Peacock 1	Gallacher 1	Fernie	Hughes 2	Chalmers 1	Byrne 1
Mar 4	Ayr United	3-1	Haffey	MacKay	Kennedy	Crerand	McNeill 1	Peacock 1	Gallacher	Fernie 1	Hughes	Chalmers	Byrne
Mar 18	Partick Thistle	2-1	Haffey	MacKay	Kennedy	Crerand	McNeill	Clark	Gallacher	Fernie	Hughes	Chalmers 1	Byrne 1
Mar 20	RAITH ROVERS	1-1	Haffey	MacKay	Kennedy	Crerand	McNeill	Clark	Gallacher	Fernie	Hughes	Chalmers 1	Byrne
Mar 25	DUNFERMLINE ATHLETIC	2-1	Haffey	MacKay	Kennedy	Crerand	McNeill	Clark	Gallacher	Fernie	Hughes	Chalmes	Byrne
Apr 5	ST JOHNSTONE	1-1	Haffey	MacKay	Kennedy	Crerand	McNeill	Clark	Gallacher	Fernie 1	Hughes	Chalmers	Byrne
Apr 8	Dundee	1-0	Haffey	MacKay	Kennedy	Crerand	McNeill	Clark	Gallacher	Fernie	Hughes	Chalmers1	Byrne
Apr 10	Dundee United	1-1	Haffey	MacKay	Kennedy	Crerand	McNeill	Clark	Gallacher	Fernie	Hughes 1	Chalmers	Byrne
Apr 29	Motherwell	2-2	Haffey	MacKay	O'Neill	Crerand	McNeill	Clark	Chalmers 1	Carroll	Hughes	Fernie 1	Byrne
May 2	HEARTS	1-3	Haffey	Curran	O'Neill	Kelly	Kurila	Clark	Carroll	Divers 1	Hughes	Chalmers	Byrne

LEAGUE CUP 1960

			1	2	3	4	5	6	7	8	9	10	11
Aug 13	THIRD LANARK	2-0	Haffey	MacKay	Kennedy	Crerand	McNeill	Peacock	Carroll	Chalmers	Hughes 1	Mochan 1	Divers
Aug 17	Partick Thistle	1-1	Haffey	MacKay	Kennedy	Crerand	McNeill	Peacock	Carroll 1	Chalmers	Hughes	Divers	Mochan
Aug 20	Rangers	3-2	Haffey	MacKay	Kennedy	Crerand	McNeill	Peacock	Carroll 1	Chalmers	Hughes 1	Divers 1	Mochan
Aug 27	Third Lanark	3-1	Fallon	MacKay	Kennedy	Crerand	McNeill	Peacock	Conway	Chalmers	Hughes 2	Divers 1	Mochan
Aug 31	PARTICK THISTLE	1-2	Fallon	MacKay	Kennedy	Crerand	Kurila	Peacock	Carroll	Chalmers	Hughes 1	Divers	Mochan
Sept 3	Rangers	1-2	Fallon	MacKay	Kennedy	Crerand	Kurila	Peacock	Carroll	Chalmers 1	Hughes	Divers	Mochan

SCOTTISH CUP 1961

Jan 28	Falkirk	3-1	Haffey	MacKay	Kennedy	Crerand	McNeill	Peacock 2	Gallacher	Divers	Hughes	Fernie	Auld
Feb 11	MONTROSE	6-0	Haffey	MacKay	Kennedy	Crerand	McNeill	Peacock	Gallacher	Divers	Hughes 2	Chalmers 2	Byrne 1
Feb 25	Raith Rovers	4-1	Haffey	MacKay	Kennedy	Crerand	McNeill	Peacock	Gallacher	Fernie 1	Hughes 1	Chalmers 1	Byrne
Mar 11	HIBERNIAN	1-1	Haffey	MacKay	Kennedy	Crerand	McNeill	Peacock	Gallacher	Fernie	Hughes	Chalmers 1	Byrne
Mar 16	Hibernian	1-0	Haffey	MacKay	Kennedy	Crerand	McNeill	Clark 1	Gallacher	Fernie	Hughes	Chalmers	Byrne
Apr 1	Airdrie (N)	4-0	Haffey	MacKay	Kennedy	Crerand	McNeill	Clark	Gallacher	Fernie 1	Hughes 2	Chalmers 1	Byrne
Apr 22	Dunfermline Athletic (N)	0-0 F	Haffey	MacKay	Kennedy	Crerand	McNeill	Clark	Gallacher	Fernie	Hughes	Chalmers	Byrne
Apr 26	Dunfermline Athletic (N)	0-2 F	Haffey	MacKay	O'Neill	Crerand	McNeill	Clark	Gallacher	Chalmers	Hughes	Fernie	Byrne

SCOTTISH LEAGUE 1961-62

Aug 23	Kilmarnock	2-3	Connor	Donnelly	Kennedy	Jackson	McNeill	Clark	Carroll	Fernie	Hughes	Divers 1	Chalmers 1
Sept 9	THIRD LANARK	1-0	Connor	MacKay	Kennedy	Crerand	McNeill	Price	Chalmers	Jackson	Hughes	Divers 1	Fernie
Sept 16	Rangers	2-2	Haffey	MacKay	Kennedy	Crerand	McNeill	Price	Chalmers	Jackson	Hughes	Divers 1	Fernie 1
Sept 23	DUNDEE UNITED	3-1	Haffey	MacKay	Kennedy	Crerand	McNeill	Price	Chalmers 1	Jackson 1	Hughes 1	Divers	Carroll
Sept 30	Falkirk	1-3	Haffey	MacKay	Kennedy	Crerand	McNeill	Price	Chalmers	Jackson	Hughes 1	Divers	Carroll
Oct 14	STIRLING ALBION	5-0	Haffey	MacKay	Kennedy	Crerand	McNeill	Price	Chalmers	Jackson	Hughes 3	Divers 1	Carrol 1
Oct 18	St Johnstone	3-0	Haffey	MacKay	Kennedy	Crerand	McNeill	Price	Chalmers	Jackson 1	Hughes	Divers 1	Carroll 1
Oct 21	Hearts	1-2	Haffey	MacKay	Kennedy	Crerand	McNeill	Price	Chalmers	Jackson	Hughes 1	Divers	Carroll
Oct 28	DUNFERMLINE ATHLETIC	2-1	Haffey	MacKay	Kennedy	Crerand	McNamee	Price	Chalmers	Jackson	Hughes	Divers	Carroll 1
Nov 4	Dundee	1-2	Haffey	MacKay	Kennedy	Crerand	McNamee	Clark	Chalmers	Jackson	Hughes	Divers	Carroll 1
Nov 15	ST MIRREN	7-1	Haffey	MacKay	Kennedy	Crerand	McNamee	Price	Chalmers 2	Jackson 2	Hughes 1	Divers	Carroll 2
Nov 18	AIRDRIE	3-0	Haffey	MacKay	Kennedy	Crerand	McNamee	Price	Chalmers	Jackson 2	Hughes 1	Divers	Carroll
Nov 25	Aberdeen	0-0	Haffey	MacKay	Kennedy	Crerand	McNeill	Price	Chalmers	Jackson	Hughes	Divers	Carroll
Dec 2	PARTICK THISTLE	5-1	Haffey	MacKay	Kennedy	Crerand	McNeill	Price	Chalmers 2	Jackson 1	Hughes 1	Divers 1	Carroll
Dec 16	HIBERNIAN	4-3	Haffey	MacKay	Kennedy	Crerand	McNeill	Price	Chalmers	Jackson	Hughes 1	Divers 3	Carroll
Dec 23	Raith Rovers	4-0	Haffey	MacKay	Kennedy	Crerand	McNeill	Price	Chalmers 1	Jackson	Hughes	Divers 2	Carroll 1
Jan 6	KILMARNOCK	2-2	Haffey	MacKay	Kennedy	Crerand	McNeill	Price	Chalmers 1	Jackson	Hughes	Divers	Carroll 1
Jan 10	Third Lanark	1-1	Haffey	MacKay	Kennedy	Crerand	McNeill	Price	Chalmers 1	Jackson	Hughes	Divers	Carroll
Jan 13	Dundee United	5-4	Haffey	MacKay	Kennedy	Crerand 1	McNeill	Price	Chalmers	Jackson 2	Hughes 2	Divers	Carroll
Jan 20	FALKIRK	3-0	Haffey	MacKay	Kennedy	Crerand 1	McNeill	Price	Chalmers	Jackson 1	Hughes	Divers 1	Carroll
Jan 22	MOTHERWELL	1-1	Haffey	MacKay	Kennedy	Crerand	McNeill	Price	Chalmers	Jackson 1	Hughes	Divers	Carroll
Feb 3	ST JOHNSTONE	3-1	Haffey	MacKay	Kennedy	Crerand	McNeill	Price	Carroll	Jackson	Hughes 1	Divers 2	Byrne
Feb 10	Stirling Albion	0-1	Haffey	MacKay	Kennedy	Clark	McNamee	Price	Carroll	Jackson	Hughes	Divers	Byrne
Feb 21	HEARTS	2-2	Haffey	MacKay	Kennedy	Crerand	McNeill	Price	Brogan	Chalmers	Hughes 1	Divers 1	Carroll
Feb 24	Dunfermline Athletic	3-0	Haffey	MacKay	Kennedy	Crerand	McNeill	Clark	Chalmers	Jackson	Hughes 2	Divers 1	Brogan
Mar 3	Dundee	2-1	Haffey	MacKay	Kennedy	Crerand	McNeill 1	Price	Brogan 1	Lennox	Hughes	Divers	Carroll
Mar 17	Airdrie	0-1	Haffey	MacKay	Kennedy	Crerand	McNeill	Clark	Carroll	Chalmers	Hughes	Divers	Byrne
Mar 24	ABERDEEN	2-0	Haffey	MacKay	O'Neill	Crerand	McNeill	Clark	Brogan 2	Chalmers	Hughes	Divers	Byrne
Mar 26	St Mirren	5-0	Haffey	MacKay	O'Neill	Crerand	McNeill	Clark	Brogan	Chalmers 2	Carroll 1	Divers 2	Byrne
Apr 4	Partick Thistle	2-1	Haffey	Donnelly	Kennedy	Crerand	McNeill	Clark	Brogan 1	Chalmers	Hughes 1	Divers	Byrne
Apr 7	Hibernian	1-1	Haffey	MacKay	Kennedy	Crerand	McNeill	Clark	Brogan	Chalmers	Hughes	Divers 1	Byrne
Apr 9	RANGERS	1-1	Haffey	Donnelly	Kennedy	MacKay	McNeill	Clark	Chalmers	Carroll	Hughes	Divers	Brogan
Apr 21	RAITH ROVERS	0-1	Haffey	MacKay	Kennedy	Crerand	McNeill	Clark	Brogan	Chalmers	Carroll	Divers	Byrne
Apr 23	Motherwell	4-0	Haffey	MacKay	Kennedy	Crerand	McNeill	Clark	Chalmers 1	Gallacher	Carroll 2	Divers	Brogan

LEAGUE CUP 1961

Aug 12	Partick Thistle	3-2	Connor	MacKay	Kennedy	Kurila	McNeill	Clark	Carroll	Jackson 2	Hughes 1	Divers	Chalmers
Aug 16	ST JOHNSTONE	0-1	Connor	MacKay	Kennedy	Kurila	McNeill	Clark	Carroll	Jackson	Hughes	Divers	Chalmers
Aug 19	Hibernian	2-2	Connor	Donnelly	Kennedy	Price	McNeill	Clark	Carroll	Fernie	Hughes 1	Divers	Chalmers 1
Aug 26	PARTICK THISTLE	3-2	Connor	MacKay	Kennedy	Jackson	McNeill	Clark	Carroll 1	Fernie	Hughes 2	Divers	Chalmers
Aug 30	St Johnstone	0-2	Connor	MacKay	Kennedy	Jackson	McNeill	Clark	Carroll	Fernie	Hughes	Divers	Chalmers
Sept 2	HIBERNIAN	2-1	Connor	MacKay	Kennedy	Crerand	McNeill	Price	Chalmers	Jackson	Hughes	Divers 2	Fernie

SCOTTISH CUP 1961-62

Dec 13	COWDENBEATH	5-1	Haffey	MacKay	Kennedy	Crerand	McNeill	Price	Chalmers 2	Jackson 1	Hughes 1	Divers 1	Carroll
Jan 27	Morton	3-1	Haffey	MacKay	Kennedy	Crerand	McNeill	Price	Chalmers	Jackson 1	Hughes	Divers 1	Carroll 1
Feb 17	Hearts	4-3	Haffey	MacKay	Kennedy	Crerand 1	McNeill	Price	Chalmers 1	Jackson	Hughes	Divers 2	Carroll
Mar 10	THIRD LANARK	4-4	Haffey	MacKay	Kennedy	Crerand	McNeill	Clark	Brogan 1	Chalmers 2	Hughes 1	Divers	Carroll
Mar 14	Third Lanark (N)	4-0	Haffey	MacKay	Kennedy	Crerand	McNeill	Clark	Brogan	Chalmers 1	Hughes 2	Divers	Byrne 1
Mar 31	St Mirren (N)	1-3	Haffey	MacKay	Kennedy	Crerand	McNeill	Clark	Brogan	Chalmers	Hughes	Divers	Byrne 1

SCOTTISH LEAGUE 1962-63

Aug 22	Falkirk	3-1	Haffey	MacKay	Kennedy	Crerand	McNeill	McNamee	Chalmers	Divers	Hughes 1	Jackson 1	Byrne1
Sept 8	RANGERS	0-1	Haffey	MacKay	Kennedy	Crerand	McNeill	Price	Lennox	Gallacher	Hughes	Murdoch	Byrne
Sept 15	Clyde	3-1	Haffey	MacKay	Kennedy	Crerand	McNeill	Price	Chalmers 1	Gallacher	Carroll	Divers 2	Byrne
Sept 22	ABERDEEN	1-2	Haffey	MacKay	Kennedy	Crerand	McNeill	Price	Chalmers	Divers	Hughes 1	Murdoch	Carroll
Sept 29	Raith Rovers	2-0	Haffey	MacKay	Kennedy	Crerand	McNeill 1	O'Neill	Chalmers	Murdoch 1	Hughes	Gallacher	Byrne
Oct 6	KILMARNOCK	1-1	Haffey	MacKay	Kennedy	Crerand	McNeill	O'Neill	Chalmers	Jackson	Carroll 1	Murdoch	Byrne
Oct 13	Motherwell	2-0	Haffey	MacKay	Kennedy	Crerand	McNeill	O'Neill	Chalmers	Lennox	Carroll 1	Gallacher 1	Brogan
Oct 20	DUNDEE UNITED	1-0	Haffey	MacKay	O'Neill	Clark	McNamee	Price	Chalmers 1	Divers	Carroll	Gallacher	Brogan
Oct 27	Airdrie	6-1	Haffey	MacKay	O'Neill	Crerand	McNamee	Price	Chalmers	Craig 2	Divers 3	Gallacher 1	Byrne
Nov 3	St Mirren	7-0	Haffey	MacKay 1	O'Neill	Crerand	McNamee	Price 1	Chalmers 3	Craig	Divers 1	Gallacher 1	Byrne
Nov 10	QUEEN OF THE SOUTH	0-1	Haffey	O'Neill	Kennedy	Crerand	McNeill	Price	Carroll	Craig	Divers	Gallacher	Jeffrey
Nov 17	Dundee	0-0	Haffey	Young	Kennedy	Crerand	McNeill	O'Neill	Murdoch	Craig	Divers	Gallacher	Byrne
Nov 24	PARTICK THISTLE	0-2	Haffey	Young	Kennedy	Crerand	McNeill	O'Neill	Chalmers	Murdoch	Divers	Gallacher	Jeffrey
Dec 1	Hibernian	1-1	Haffey	MacKay	Kennedy	Crerand	McNeill	Price	Chalmers	Craig	Divers	Murdoch 1	Jeffrey
Dec 8	HEARTS	2-2	Haffey	MacKay	Kennedy	Crerand	McNeill	Price 1	Chalmers	Divers	Hughes 1	Murdoch	Brogan
Dec 15	Third Lanark	0-2	Haffey	MacKay	Kennedy	McNeill	McNamee	Price	Chalmers	Craig	Divers	Gallacher	Brogan
Dec 26	DUNFERMLINE ATHLETIC	2-1	Haffey	MacKay	Kennedy	Crerand	McNeill	Price	Chalmers	Gallacher	Hughes 1	Divers	Brogan
Dec 29	FALKIRK	2-1	Haffey	MacKay	Kennedy	Crerand	McNeill	Price	Chalmers	Murdoch	Hughes	Gallacher 2	Brogan
Jan 1	Rangers	0-4	Haffey	MacKay	Kennedy	Crerand	McNeill	Price	Chalmers	Murdoch	Hughes	Gallacher	Brogan
Jan 5	Aberdeen	5-1	Haffey	Young	Gemmell	McNamee	McNeill	Price	Gallacher	Craig 2	Hughes 3	Divers	Chalmers
Mar 2	AIRDRIE	3-1	Haffey	Young	Kennedy	McNamee	McNeill	Price	Murdoch	Craig	Hughes	Divers 2	Brogan
Mar 9	ST MIRREN	1-1	Haffey	MacKay	Kennedy	McNamee	McNeill	Price	Murdoch	Craig	Hughes	Divers	Brogan
Mar 16	Queen of the South	5-2	Haffey	MacKay	Gemmell	McNamee 1	McNeill	Price	Murdoch	Craig 3	Byrne	Divers	Brogan 1
Mar 19	RAITH ROVERS	4-1	Haffey	MacKay	Kennedy	McNamee 1	McNeill	Price	Gallacher	Craig	Chalmers 1	Divers	Brogan 2
Mar 23	DUNDEE	4-1	Haffey	MacKay	Kennedy	McNamee	McNeill	Price	Murdoch	Craig 1	Hughes 1	Divers	Brogan 1
Mar 27	Kilmarnock	0-6	Madden	Young	Kennedy	MacKay	Cushley	Price	Johnstone	Craig	Chalmers	Gallacher	Brogan
Apr 2	Partick Thistle	5-1	Haffey	MacKay 1	O'Neill	McNamee	McNeill	Price	Chalmers	Craig 2	Divers 1	Murdoch 1	Brogan
Apr 6	HIBERNIAN	2-0	Haffey	MacKay	O'Neill	McNamee	McCarron	Price 1	Chalmers	Craig	Divers	Lennox	Jeffrey
Apr 20	THIRD LANARK	2-1	Haffey	MacKay	O'Neill	McNamee	McNeill	Price	Chalmers	Murdoch	Divers	Craig 2	Brogan
Apr 27	Dunfermline Athletic	1-1	Haffey	MacKay	O'Neill	McNamee	McNeill	Price	Chalmers	Murdoch	Hughes	Divers 1	Brogan

			1	2	3	4	5	6	7	8	9	10	11
Apr 29	Hearts	3-4	Haffey	MacKay	Kennedy	McNamee	Cushley	Price	Johnstone 1	Lennox	Divers 1	Chalmers 1	Brogan
May 6	CLYDE	2-0	Haffey	MacKay 1	Kennedy	McNamee	McNeill	Clark	Johnstone	Murdoch	Hughes 1	Divers	Chalmers
May 11	Dundee United	0-3	Haffey	MacKay	Kennedy	McNamee	McNeill	Price	Johnstone	Murdoch	Hughes	Divers	Chalmers
May 13	MOTHERWELL	6-0	Haffey	MacKay	Kennedy	McNamee	McNeill	Price	Brogan	Craig 1	Divers 1	Chalmers 3	Hughes

LEAGUE CUP 1962

Aug 11	HEARTS	3-1	Haffey	MacKay	Kennedy	Crerand	McNeill	Price	Lennox	Gallacher 1	Hughes 1	Murdoch 1	Byrne
Aug 15	Dundee	0-1	Haffey	MacKay	Kennedy	Crerand	McNeill	Price	Lennox	Gallacher	Hughes	Murdoch	Byrne
Aug 18	DUNDEE UNITED	4-0	Haffey	MacKay	Kennedy	Crerand 1	McNeill	Price	Chalmers	Gallacher 1	Hughes 2	Murdoch	Byrne
Aug 25	Hearts	2-3	Haffey	MacKay	Kennedy	Crerand	McNeill	Price	Lennox	Gallacher	Hughes 1	Murdoch 1	Byrne
Aug 29	DUNDEE	3-0	Haffey	MacKay	Kennedy	Crerand	McNeill	Price	Lennox	Gallacher 1	Hughes 2	Murdoch	Byrne
Sept 1	Dundee United	0-0	Haffey	MacKay	Kennedy	Crerand	McNeill	Price	Lennox	Gallacher	Hughes	Murdoch	Byrne

SCOTTISH CUP 1963

Jan 28	Falkirk	2-0	Haffey	Young	Gemmell	McNamee	McNeill	Price	Gallacher 1	Craig	Hughes 1	Divers	Chalmers
Mar 6	HEARTS	3-1	Haffey	MacKay	Kennedy	McNamee 1	McNeill	Price	Murdoch 1	Craig	Hughes 1	Divers	Brogan
Mar 13	GALA FAIRYDEAN	6-0	Haffey	MacKay	Kennedy	McNamee	McNeill	Price	Gallacher	Murdoch 3	Hughes 2	Divers 1	Brogan
Mar 30	St Mirren	1-0	Haffey	MacKay	Kennedy	McNamee	McNeill	Price	Chalmers	Murdoch	Hughes	Divers	Brogan 1
Apr 13	Raith Rovers (N)	5-2	Haffey	MacKay 2	O'Neill	McNamee	McNeill	Price	Chalmers 1	Murdoch	Divers 1	Gallacher	Brogan 1
May 4	Rangers (N)	1-1 F	Haffey	MacKay	Kennedy	McNamee	McNeill	Price	Johnstone	Murdoch 1	Hughes	Divers	Brogan
May 15	Rangers (N)	0-3 F	Haffey	MacKay	Kennedy	McNamee	McNeill	Price	Craig	Murdoch	Divers	Chalmers	Hughes

FAIRS CITIES' CUP 1962-63

Sept 26	Valencia	2-4	Fallon	MacKay	Kennedy	Crerand	McNeill	O'Neill	Chalmers	Jackson	Carroll 2	Gallacher	Byrne
Oct 24	VALENCIA	2-2	Haffey	MacKay	O'Neill	Crerand 1	McNamee	Clark	Chalmers	Craig	Divers	Gallacher	Byrne

SCOTTISH LEAGUE 1963-64

Aug 21	QUEEN OF THE SOUTH	4-0	Haffey	MacKay	Gemmell	Clark	McNeill	Price	F Brogan	Turner	Divers	Chalmers 2	Jeffrey 1
Sept 7	Rangers	1-2	Haffey	MacKay	Gemmell	Clark	McNeill	O'Neill	Lennox	Turner	Divers	Chalmers 1	F Brogan
Sept 14	THIRD LANARK	4-4	Haffey	MacKay	Gemmell	Clark	McNeill	O'Neill	Lennox 1	Turner 1	Divers 1	Chalmers	F Brogan 1
Sept 21	Falkirk	0-1	Haffey	MacKay	Gemmell	J Brogan	McNeill	Clark	Lennox	Chalmers	Hughes	Divers	F Brogan
Sept 28	St Mirren	1-2	Haffey	MacKay	Gemmell	McNamee	McNeill	J Brogan	Lennox	Turner	Divers	Chalmers 1	F Brogan
Oct 5	DUNFERMLINE ATHLETIC	2-2	Fallon	Young	Gemmell	MacKay	Cushley	Kennedy	Johnstone	Murdoch 1	Chalmers	Turner	F Brogan 1
Oct 12	ABERDEEN	3-0	Haffey	Young	Gemmell	MacKay 1	Cushley	Kennedy	Johnstone	Murdoch	Chalmers 2	Divers	Hughes
Oct 19	Dundee United	3-0	Haffey	Young	Gemmell	Clark	McNeill	Kennedy	Johnstone	Murodch 1	Chalmers	Divers	Hughes 1
Oct 26	AIRDRIE	9-0	Haffey	Young	Gemmell	Clark	McNeill	Kennedy	Gallacher 1	Murdoch 1	Chalmers 1	Divers 3	Hughes 3
Nov 2	East Stirlingshire	5-1	Haffey	Young	Gemmell	Clark	McNeill	Kennedy	Gallacher	Murdoch	Chalmers 3	Divers 1	Hughes 1
Nov 9	PARTICK THISTLE	5-3	Haffey	Young	Gemmell	Clark	Cushley	Kennedy	Johnstone 1	Murdoch	Chalmers 3	Divers	Hughes 1
Nov 16	Hibernian	1-1	Fallon	Young	Gemmell	Clark	McNeill	Kennedy	Johnstone	Murodch 1	Chalmers	Divers	Hughes
Nov 23	KILMARNOCK	5-0	Fallon	Young	Gemmell	Clark	McNeill	Kennedy	Johnstone 1	Murdoch	Chalmers	Divers 1	Hughes 3
Nov 30	Dundee	1-1	Fallon	Young	Gemmell	Clark	McNeill	Kennedy	Gallacher	Murdoch 1	Chalmers	Divers	Hughes
Dec 7	ST JOHNSTONE	3-1	Fallon	Young	Gemmell	Clark	McNeill	Kennedy	Johnstone	Murdoch 3	Chalmers	Divers	Lennox
Dec 14	Hearts	1-1	Fallon	Young	Gemmell	Clark	Cushley	Kennedy	Johnstone	Murdoch	Chalmers	Divers 1	Lennox
Dec 21	MOTHERWELL	2-1	Fallon	Young	Gemmell	Clark 1	McNeill	Kennedy	Johnstone	Murdoch	Chalmers	Divers 1	Hughes
Dec 28	Queen of the South	2-0	Fallon	Young	Gemmell	Clark	McNeill	Kennedy	Johnstone 1	Murdoch	Chalmers 1	Divers	Hughes
Jan 1	RANGERS	0-1	Fallon	Young	Gemmell	Clark	McNeill	Kennedy	Johnstone	Murdoch	Chalmers	Divers	Hughes
Jan 2	Third Lanark	1-1	Fallon	Young	Gemmell	J Brogan	Cushley	Kennedy	Johnstone	Divers 1	Chalmers	Gallacher	Hughes
Jan 4	FALKIRK	7-0	Fallon	Young	Gemmell	Clark	McNeill	Kennedy	Johnstone 1	Murdoch	Chalmers 3	Divers 2	Hughes 1
Jan 18	ST MIRREN	3-0	Fallon	Young	Gemmell	Clark	McNeill	Kennedy	Johnstone 1	Murdoch	Chalmers 1	Divers 1	Hughes
Feb 1	Dunfermline Athletic	0-1	Fallon	Young	Gemmell	Clark	McNeill	Kennedy	Johnstone	Murdoch	Chalmers	Gallacher	Hughes
Feb 8	Aberdeen	3-0	Fallon	Young	Gemmell	Clark	McNeill	Kennedy	Johnstone	Murdoch	Chalmers	Divers 1	F Brogan 1
Feb 19	DUNDEE UNITED	1-0	Fallon	Young	Gemmell	Henderson	McNeill	Kennedy	Johnstone	Turner	Chalmers 1	Divers	F Brogan
Feb 22	Airdrie	2-0	Fallon	Young	Gemmell	Henderson	McNeill	Kennedy	Gallacher	Turner	Chalmers	Divers	F Brogan 2
Feb 29	EAST STIRLINGSHIRE	5-2	Fallon	Young	Gemmell	Clark	McNamee	Kennedy	Johnstone	Murdoch 2	Chalmers 3	Divers	Hughes
Mar 11	Partick Thistle	2-2	Fallon	Young	Gemmell	MacKay	McNeill	Kennedy	Johnstone	Murdoch 1	Chalmers	Divers 1	Hughes
Mar 14	HIBERNIAN	5-0	Fallon	Young	Gemmell	MacKay	McNeill	Kennedy	Johnstone	Murdoch 2	Chalmers 2	Divers 1	Hughes
Mar 21	Kilmarnock	0-4	Fallon	Young	Gemmell	Clark	McNeill	Kennedy	Johnstone	Murdoch	Chalmers	Divers	Hughes
Mar 28	Motherwell	4-0	Fallon	Young	O'Neill	Clark	McNeill	Kennedy	Johnstone 1	Murdoch 1	Chalmers 2	Gallacher	Hughes
Apr 1	DUNDEE	2-1	Fallon	Young	O'Neill	Clark	McNeill	Kennedy	Johnstone	Murdoch	Chalmers 1	Gallacher 1	Hughes
Apr 4	St Johnstone	1-1	Fallon	Young	O'Neill	Clark	McNeill	Kennedy	Johnstone	Murdoch 1	Chalmers	Gallacher	Divers
Apr 18	HEARTS	1-1	Fallon	Young	Gemmell	Clark	McNeill	Kennedy	Johnstone	Murdoch	Chalmers 1	Gallacher	Hughes

LEAGUE CUP 1963

Aug 10	RANGERS	0-3	Haffey	MacKay	Gemmell	McNamee	McNeill	Price	Johnstone	Turner	Hughes	Chalmers	Murdoch
Aug 14	Kilmarnock	0-0	Haffey	MacKay	Gemmell	Clark	McNeill	Price	Johnstone	Turner	Hughes	Chalmers	Murdoch
Aug 17	QUEEN OF THE SOUTH	1-1	Haffey	MacKay	Gemmell	McNamee	McNeill	Clark	Chalmers	Murdoch	Hughes	Turner	F Brogan 1
Aug 24	Rangers	0-3	Haffey	MacKay	Gemmell	Clark	McNeill	Price	Gallacher	Turner	Divers	Chalmers	Jeffrey
Aug 28	KILMARNOCK	2-0	Haffey	MacKay	Gemmell	Clark	McNeill	Price	Gallacher 1	Turner	Divers 1	Chalmers	Jeffrey
Aug 31	Queen of the South	3-2	Haffey	MacKay	Gemmell	Clark	McNeill	Price	Gallacher 1	Turner	Divers	Chalmers 2	Jeffrey

SCOTTISH CUP 1964

Jan 11	EYEMOUTH UNITED	3-0	Fallon	Young	Gemmell	Clark	McNeill	Kennedy	Johnstone	Turner	Chalmers 2	Gallacher 1	Hughes
Jan 25	Morton	3-1	Fallon	Young	Gemmell	Clark	McNeill	Kennedy	Johnstone 1	Murdoch	Chalmers	Gallacher 1	Hughes 1
Feb 15	AIRDRIE	4-1	Fallon	Young	Gemmell	Clark	McNeill	Kennedy	Johnstone 1	Murdoch 1	Chalmesr 1	Divers	Hughes 1
Mar 7	Rangers	0-2	Fallon	Young	Gemmell	Murdoch	McNeill	Kennedy	F Brogan	Johnstone	Chalmers	Divers	Hughes

EUROPEAN CUP-WINNERS' CUP 1963-64

Sept 17	Basle	5-1	Haffey	MacKay	Gemmell	McNamee	McNeill	Clark	Lennox 1	Chalmers	Hughes 3	Divers 1	F Brogan
Oct 9	BASLE	5-0	Haffey	Young	Gemmell	MacKay	McNeill	Kennedy	Johnstone 1	Mudoch 1	Chalmers 1	Divers 2	Hughes
Dec 4	DINAMO ZAGREB	3-0	Fallon	Young	Gemmell	Clark	McNeill	Kennedy	Johnstone	Murdoch	Chalmers 2	Divers	Hughes 1
Dec 11	Dinamo Zagreb	1-2	Fallon	Young	Gemmell	Clark	McNeill	Kennedy	Johnstone	Murdoch 1	Chalmers	Divers	Hughes
Feb 26	SLOVAN BRATISLAVA	1-0	Fallon	Young	Gemmell	Clark	McNeill	Kennedy	Johnstone	Murdoch 1	Chalmers	Divers	Hughes
Mar 4	Slovan Bratislava	1-0	Fallon	Young	Gemmell	Clark	McNeill	Kennedy	Johnstone	Murdoch	Chalmers	Divers	Hughes 1
Apr 15	M.T.K. (h)	3-0 SF	Fallon	Young	Gemmell	Clark	McNeill	Kennedy	Johnstone 1	Murdoch	Chalmers 2	Gallacher	Hughes
Apr 29	M.T.K. (a)	0-4 SF	Fallon	Young	Gemmell	Clark	McNeill	Kennedy	Johnstone	Murdoch	Chalmers	Gallacher	Hughes

SCOTTISH LEAGUE 1964-65

Aug 19	Motherwell	3-1	Fallon	Young	Gemmell	Clark	McNeill	Kennedy	Johnstone	Murdoch 1	Chalmers 1	Divers	Lennox 1
Sept 5	RANGERS	3-1	Fallon	Young	Gemmell	Brogan	Cushley	Kennedy	Johnstone	Divers	Chalmers 2	Gallacher	Hughes 1
Sept 12	Clyde	1-1	Fallon	Young	Gemmell	Clark	Cushley	Kennedy	Johnstone	Murdoch	Chalmers 1	Gallacher	Lennox
Sept 19	DUNDEE UNITED	1-1	Fallon	Young	Gemmell	Clark	Kennedy	Brogan	Johnstone	Murdoch	Chalmers 1	Gallacher	Hughes
Sept 26	Hearts	2-4	Fallon	MacKay	Gemmell	Clark	Young	Kennedy	Curley	Murdoch 1	Chalmers	Johnstone	Lennox 1
Oct 10	Aberdeen	3-1	Fallon	Young	Gemmell	Clark	Cushley	Kennedy	Johnstone	Murdoch 1	Chalmers 1	Divers	Hughes 1
Oct 12	MORTON	1-0	Fallon	Young	Gemmell	Clark	Cushley	Kennedy	Johnstone	Murdoch	Chalmers	Divers 1	Hughes
Oct 17	ST MIRREN	4-1	Fallon	Young	Gemmell	clark	Cushley	Kennedy	Hughes 1	Murdoch 1	Chalmers	Divers 2	Haverty
Oct 28	Kilmarnock	2-5	Fallon	Young	Gemmell 1	Brogan	Cushley	Kennedy	Johnstone	Murdoch	Chalmers	Gallacher 1	Lennox
Oct 31	AIRDRIE	2-1	Fallon	Young	Gemmell	Clark	Cushley	Kennedy	Johnstone	Murdoch	Chalmers 2	Gallacher	Lennox
Nov 7	St Johnstone	0-3	Fallon	Young	Gemmell	Murdoch	Cushley	Kennedy	Hughes	Johnstone	Chalmers	Divers	Lennox
Nov 14	DUNDEE	0-2	Fallon	Young	Gemmell	Clark	Cushley	Kennedy	Johnstone	Murdoch	Chalmers	Maxwell	Hughes
Nov 21	FALKIRK	3-0	Simpson	Young	Gemmell	Murdoch	McNeill	Kennedy	Johnstone	Gallacher	Chalmers	Maxwell 1	Hughes 2
Nov 28	Third Lanark	3-0	Simpson	Young	Gemmell	Murdoch 1	McNeill	Kennedy	Johnstone	Gallacher	Hughes 1	Maxwell	Lennox
Dec 12	Partick Thistle	4-2	Simpson	Young	Gemmell	Clark	McNeill	O'Neill	Johnstone	Murdoch	Hughes 2	Maxwell 1	Gallacher 1

			1	2	3	4	5	6	7	8	9	10	11
Dec 19	DUNFERMLINE ATHLETIC	1-2	Simpson	Young	Gemmell	Clark	McNeill	Kennedy	Johnstone	Murdoch	Hughes	Maxwell	Gallacher 1
Dec 26	MOTHERWELL	2-0	Simpson	Young	O'Neill	Clark	McNeill	Kennedy	Johnstone	Murdoch	Hughes 2	Divers	Lennox
Jan 1	Rangers	0-1	Simpson	Young	Gemmell	Clark	McNeill	Kennedy	Johnstone	Murdoch	Hughes	Divers	Gallacher
Jan 2	CLYDE	1-1	Simpson	Young	Gemmell	Clark	McNeill	Kennedy	Lennox	Maxwell	Hughes 1	Divers	Gallacher
Jan 9	Dundee United	1-3	Simpson	Young	Gemmell	Clark	McNeill	Brogan	Johnstone	Murdoch	Hughes 1	Divers	Gallacher
Jan 16	HEARTS	1-2	Fallon	Young	Gemmell 1	Brogan	McNeill	Kennedy	Johnstone	Murdoch	Hughes	Gallacher	Auld
Jan 23	Morton	3-3	Fallon	Young	Gemmell 1	Brogan	McNeill	Clark	Johnstone	Murdoch	Hughes 1	Lennox 1	Auld
Jan 30	ABERDEEN	8-0	Fallon	Young	Gemmell	Clark	McNeill	Brogan	Chalmers	Murdoch 1	Hughes 5	Lennox 1	Auld 1
Feb 13	St Mirren	5-2	Fallon	Young	Gemmell	Clark	McNeill	Brogan 1	Chalmers 1	Murdoch 1	Hughes 1	Lennox 1	Auld
Feb 27	KILMARNOCK	2-0	Fallon	Young	Gemmell	Clark	McNeill	Brogan	Chalmers 1	Murdoch	Hughes 1	Lennox	Auld
Mar 10	Airdrie	6-0	Fallon	Young	Gemmell	Clark	McNeill	Brogan	Chalmers	Murdoch	Hughes 1	Lennox	Auld 5
Mar 13	ST JOHNSTONE	0-1	Fallon	Young	Gemmell	Clark	McNeill	Brogan	Chalmers	Murdoch	Hughes	Lennox	Auld
Mar 20	Dundee	3-3	Fallon	Young	Kennedy	Murdoch	McNeill	Clark	Johnstone 1	Chalmers	Hughes	Lennox 2	Auld
Mar 22	HIBERNIAN	2-4	Fallon	Young	Kennedy	Brogan	McNeill	Clark	Chalmers	Murdoch	Hughes	Maxwell	Lennox 2
Apr 3	THIRD LANARK	1-0	Fallon	Young	Gemmell	Murdoch	McNeill	Clark	Chalmers	Gallacher	Hughes	Lennox	Auld
Apr 7	Hibernian	4-0	Fallon	Young	Gemmell	Murdoch 1	McNeill	Clark	Chalmers	Gallacher	Hughes	Lennox 1	Auld 2
Apr 14	Falkirk	2-6	Fallon	Young	Gemmell	Murdoch	Cushley	O'Neill	Johnstone	Gallacher	Hughes	Lennox 1	Auld 1
Apr 17	PARTICK THISTLE	1-2	Fallon	Young	Kennedy	Murdoch	McNeill	Clark	Johnstone	Lennox	Chalmers 1	Auld	Hughes
Apr 28	Dunfermline Athletic	1-5	Fallon	Gemmell	O'Neill	Clark	McNeill	Brogan	Johnstone	Murdoch	Hughes 1	Maxwell	Lennox

LEAGUE CUP 1964

Aug 8	PARTICK THISTLE	0-0	Fallon	Young	Gemmell	Clark	McNeill	Kennedy	Johnstone	Murdoch	Chalmers	Gallacher	Lennox
Aug 12	Hearts	3-0	Fallon	Young	Gemmell	Clark	McNeill	Brogan	Johnstone	Murdoch 2	Chalmers 1	Gallacher	Lennox
Aug 15	KILMARNOCK	4-1	Fallon	Young	Gemmell	Clark	McNeill	Brogan	Johnstone 1	Murdoch	Chalmers 1	Gallacher 2	Lennox
Aug 22	Partick Thistle	5-1	Fallon	Young	Gemmell	Clark	McNeill	Kennedy	Johnstone 1	Murdoch	Chalmers 3	Gallacher 1	Lennox
Aug 26	HEARTS	6-1	Fallon	Young	Gemmell	Clark	McNeill	Kennedy 1	Johnstone	Murdoch 3	Chalmers	Gallacher 2	Lennox
Aug 29	Kilmarnock	0-2	Fallon	Young	Gemmell	Clark	McNeill	Kennedy	Johnstone	Murdoch	Chalmers	Gallacher	Hughes
Sept 9	East Fife	0-2	Fallon	Young	Gemmell	Brogan	Cushley	Kennedy	Johnstone	Divers	Chalmers	Gallacher	Hughes
Sept 16	EAST FIFE	6-0	Fallon	Young	Gemmell	Clark	Cushley	Kennedy 1	Johnstone	Murdoch	Chalmers 5	Gallacher	Hughes
Sept 29	Morton (N)	2-0	Fallon	Young	Gemmell	Clark	Cushley	Kennedy	Johnstone	Murdoch	Chalmers	Gallacher 1	Lennox 1
Oct 24	Rangers (N)	1-2 F	Fallon	Young	Gemmell	Clark	Cushley	Kennedy	Johnstone 1	Murdoch	Chalmers	Divers	Hughes

SCOTTISH CUP 1965

Feb 6	St Mirren	3-0	Fallon	Young	Gemmell	Clark	McNeill	Brogan	Chalmers 1	Murdoch	Hughes	Lennox 2	Auld
Feb 20	Queen's Park	1-0	Fallon	Young	Gemmell	Clark	McNeill	Brogan	Chalmers	Murdoch	Hughes	Lennox 1	Auld
Mar 6	KILMARNOCK	3-2	Fallon	Young	Gemmell	Clark	McNeill	Brogan	Chalmers	Murdoch	Hughes 1	Lennox 1	Auld 1
Mar 27	Motherwell (N)	2-2	Fallon	Young	Gemmell	Murdoch	McNeill	Clark	Johnstone	Gallacher	Hughes	Lennox 1	Auld 1
Mar 31	Motherwell (N)	3-0	Fallon	Young	Gemmell	Murdoch	McNeill	Clark	Chalmers 1	Gallacher	Hughes 1	Lennox 1	Auld
Apr 24	Dunfermline Athletic (N)	3-2 F	Fallon	Young	Gemmell	Murdoch	McNeill 1	Clark	Chalmers	Gallacher	Hughes	Lennox	Auld 2

FAIRS CITIES' CUP 1964-65

Sept 23	Leixoes	1-1	Fallon	Young	Gemmell	Clark	Cushley	Kennedy	Johnstone	Murdoch 1	Chalmers	Gallacher	Lennox
Oct 7	LEIXOES	3-0	Fallon	Young	Gemmell	Clark	Cushley	Kennedy	Johnstone	Murdoch 1	Chalmers 2	Gallacher	Lennox
Nov 18	Barcelona	1-3	Simpson	Young	Gemmell	Clark	Cushley	Kennedy	Johnstone	Murdoch	Chalmers	McNeill	Hughes 1
Dec 2	BARCELONA	0-0	Simpson	Young	Gemmell	Murdoch	McNeill	O'Neill	Johnstone	Chalmers	Hughes	Gallacher	Lennox

SCOTTISH LEAGUE 1965-66

Aug 25	Dundee United	4-0	Fallon	Young 1	Gemmell 1	Murdoch	McNeill	Clark	Chalmers	Divers 1	McBride 1	Lennox	Gallacher
Sept 11	CLYDE	2-1	Fallon	Young 1	Gemmell 1	Murdoch	McNeill	Clark	Chalmers	Divers	McBride	Lennox	Hughes
Sept 18	Rangers	1-2	Fallon	Young	Gemmell	Murdoch	McNeill	Clark	Johnstone	Divers	Hughes 1	Lennox	Auld
Sept 25	ABERDEEN	7-1	Simpson	Young	Gemmell	Murdoch	McNeill	Clark	Johnstone 2	Auld 1	McBride 1	Lennox 2	Hughes 1
Oct 9	HEARTS	5-2	Simpson	Young	Gemmell	Murdoch	McNeill	Clark	Johnstone	Gallacher 1	McBride 2	Lennox 2	Hughes
Oct 16	Falkirk	4-3	Fallon	Young	Gemmell	Murdoch 1	McNeill	Clark	Johnstone 1	Gallacher	McBride	Lennox 2	Hughes
Oct 27	Dundee	2-1	Simpson	Young	Gemmell	Murdoch	McNeill	Clark	Johnstone	Gallacher	McBride 1	Lennox 1	Hughes
Oct 30	STIRLING ALBION	6-1	Simpson	Young	Gemmell	Murdoch 1	McNeill	Clark	Johnstone	Gallacher	McBride 2	Lennox	Hughes 3
Nov 6	PARTICK THISTLE	1-1	Simpson	Young	Gemmell	Murdoch	McNeill	Clark	Johnstone	Gallacher	McBride 1	Lennox	Hughes
Nov 13	St Johnstone	4-1	Simpson	Craig	Gemmell	Murdoch	McNeill	Clark	Johnstone 1	Gallacher	McBride 1	Lennox	Hughes 2
Nov 20	HAMILTON ACADEMICALS	5-0	Simpson	Craig	Gemmell 1	Murdoch 1	McNeill	Clark	Johnstone 1	Gallacher	McBride 1	Lennox	Auld 1
Nov 27	KILMARNOCK	2-1	Simpson	Craig	Gemmell	Murdoch	Cushley	Clark	Johnstone	McBride 1	Chalmers	Lennox	Hughes 1
Dec 10	HIBERNIAN	2-0	Simpson	Young	Gemmell	Murdoch	Cushley	Clark	Johnstone	Gallacher	McBride 1	Lennox	Hughes 1
Dec 17	Dunfermline Athletic	2-0	Simpson	Craig	Gemmell	Murdoch	Cushley	Clark	Johnstone	Gallacher	McBride	Chalmers 2	Hughes
Dec 25	MORTON	8-1	Simpson	Craig	Gemmell	Murdoch 1	Cushley	Clark	Johnstone	Gallacher	McBride 3	Chalmers 2	Hughes 2
Jan 1	Clyde	3-1	Simpson	Craig	Gemmell	Murdoch	Cushley	Clark	Johnstone	Lennox 1	McBride 2	Chalmers	Auld
Jan 3	RANGERS	5-1	Simpson	Craig	Gemmell	Murdoch 1	Cushley	Clark	Johnstone	Gallacher 1	McBride	Chalmers 3	Hughes
Jan 8	DUNDEE UNITED	1-0	Simpson	Craig	Gemmell	Murdoch	Cushley	Clark	Johnstone	Gallacher 1	McBride	Chalmers	Hughes
Jan 15	Aberdeen	1-3	Simpson	Craig	Gemmell	Murdoch	Cushley	Clark	Johnstone	Gallacher	McBride 1	Chalmers	Hughes
Jan 22	MOTHERWELL	1-0	Simpson	Craig	Gemmell	Murdoch	Cushley	Clark	Johnstone	Lennox	McBride 1	Chalmers	Hughes
Jan 29	Hearts	2-3	Simpson	McNeill	Gemmell	Murdoch	Cushley	Clark	Johnstone	Gallacher	McBride 1	Lennox	Hughes 1
Feb 12	FALKIRK	6-0	Simpson	Craig	Gemmell	Murdoch	McNeill	Clark	Johnstone	McBride 3	Chalmers	Auld 2	Hughes 1
Feb 26	Stirling Albion	0-1	Simpson	Young	Gemmell	Murdoch	McNeill	Clark	Johnstone	McBride	Chalmers	Auld	Hughes
Feb 28	DUNDEE	5-0	Simpson	McNeill	Gemmell 1	Murdoch	Cushley	Clark	Johnstone	McBride 3	Chalmers 1	Auld	Hughes
Mar 12	ST JOHNSTONE	3-2	Simpson	McNeill	Gemmell	Murdoch	Cushley	Clark	Johnstone	Auld	Chalmers 2	McBride 1	Hughes
Mar 19	Hamilton Academicals	7-1	Simpson	Craig	Gemmell	Brogan	McNeill	Clark	Johnstone 2	McBride 2	Chalmers 1	Lennox 1	Auld 1
Mar 21	Partick Thistle	2-2	Simpson	Young	Gemmell	Brogan	McNeill	Clark	Johnstone	McBride	Chalmers	Lennox 1	Auld 1
Mar 29	Kilmarnock	2-0	Simpson	Young	Gemmell	Murdoch	McNeill	Clark	Johnstone	McBride	Chalmers	Lennox 2	Auld
Apr 5	St Mirren	3-0	Simpson	Young	Gemmell	Murdoch	McNeill	Clark	Johnstone	McBride 2	Chalmers 1	Lennox	Auld
Apr 9	ST MIRREN	5-0	Simpson	Young	Gemmell	Cattanach	McNeill	Clark	Johnstone	McBride	Chalmers 2	Gallacher 1	Auld 2
Apr 16	Hibernian	0-0	Simpson	Young	Gemmell	Murdoch	McNeill	Clark	Johnstone	Lennox	McBride	Auld	Hughes
Apr 30	Morton	2-0	Simpson	Craig	Gemmell	Murdoch	McNeill	Clark	Johnstone 1	Gallacher	Chalmers	Lennox 1	Auld
May 4	DUNFERMLINE ATHLETIC	2-1	Simpson	Craig	Gemmell	Murdoch	McNeill	Clark	Johnstone 1	Gallacher	Chalmers	Lennox 1	Auld
May 7	Motherwell	1-0	Simpson	Craig	Gemmell	Murdoch	McNeill	Clark	Johnstone	Gallacher	Chalmers	Lennox 1	Auld

LEAGUE CUP 1965

Aug 14	Dundee United	1-2	Fallon	Young	Gemmell	Murdoch	McNeill	Clark	Johnstone	Gallacher	Chalmers	Lennox	Auld 1
Aug 18	MOTHERWELL	1-0	Fallon	Young	Gemmell	Murdoch	McNeill	Clark	Johnstone	Divers 1	Chalmers	Lennox	Auld
Aug 21	DUNDEE	0-2	Fallon	Young	Gemmell	Murdoch	McNeill	Clark	Johnstone	Divers	McBride	Lennox	Auld
Aug 28	DUNDEE UNITED	3-0	Fallon	Young 1	Gemmell	Murdoch	McNeill	Clark	Chalmers 1	Divers	McBride 1	Lennox	Hughes
Sept 1	Motherwell	3-2	Fallon	Young	Gemmell	Murdoch	McNeill	Clark	Chalmers	Divers	Hughes 1	Lennox 2	Gallacher
Sept 4	Dundee	3-1	Fallon	Young	Gemmell	Murdoch	McNeill	Clark	Chalmers	Divers 1	McBride 1	Lennox	Hughes 1
Sept 15	Raith Rovers	8-1 QF	Fallon	Young	Gemmell	Murdoch	McNeill	Clark	Johnstone 1	Gallacher	McBride 3	Lennox 1	Hughes 3
Sept 22	RAITH ROVERS	4-0 QF	Kennedy	Young	Gemmell	Murdoch 1	Cushley	Clark	Johnstone	Lennox	Chalmers 1	Auld 2	Hughes
Oct 4	Hibernian (N)	2-2 SF	Simpson	Young	Gemmell	Murdoch	McNeill	Clark	Johnstone	Gallacher	McBride 1	Lennox 1	Hughes
Oct 18	Hibernian (N)	4-0 SFR	Simpson	Young	Gemmell	Murdoch 1	McNeill	Clark	Johnstone	Gallacher	McBride 1	Lennox 1	Hughes 1
Oct 23	Rangers (N)	2-1 F	Simpson	Young	Gemmell	Murdoch	McNeill	Clark	Johnstone	Gallacher	McBride	Lennox	Hughes 2P

SCOTTISH CUP 1966

Feb 5	STRANRAER	4-0	Simpson	Craig	Gemmell	Murdoch 1	McNeill	Clark	Johnstone	Gallacher 1	McBride 1	Lennox 1	Hughes
Feb 23	Dundee	2-0	Simpson	Craig	Gemmell	Murdoch	McNeill	Clark	Johnstone	McBride 1	Chalmers 1	Auld	Hughes
Mar 5	Hearts	3-3	Simpson	McNeill	Gemmell	Murdoch	Cushley	Clark	Johnstone	McBride 1	Chalmers 1	Auld 1	Hughes
Mar 9	HEARTS	3-1	Simpson	Craig	Gemmell	Murdoch 1	McNeill	Clark	Johnstone 1	McBride	Chalmers 1	Gallacher	Hughes
Mar 26	Dunfermline Athletic (N)	2-0 SF	Simpson	Young	Gemmell	Murdoch	McNeill	Clark	Johnstone	McBride	Chalmers 1	Lennox	Auld 1
Apr 23	Rangers (N)	0-0 F	Simpson	Young	Gemmell	Murdoch	McNeill	Clark	Johnstone	McBride	Chalmers	Gallacher	Hughes
Apr 27	Rangers (N)	0-1 FR	Simpson	Craig	Gemmell	Murdoch	McNeill	Clark	Johnstone	McBride	Chalmers	Auld	Hughes

EUROPEAN CUP-WINNERS' CUP 1965-66

			1	2	3	4	5	6	7	8	9	10	11	SUBS
Sept 29	Go Ahead	6-0	Simpson	Young	Gemmell	Murdoch	McNeill	Clark	Johnstone 2	Gallacher	Chalmers	Lennox 3	Hughes 1	
Oct 7	GO AHEAD	1-0	Simpson	Craig	Gemmell	Murdoch	McNeill	Clark	Johnstone	Chalmers	McBride 1	Lennox	Hughes	
Nov 3	Aarhus	1-0	Simpson	Young	Gemmell	Murdoch	McNeill	Clark	Johnstone	Gallacher	McBride 1	Lennox	Hughes	
Nov 17	AARHUS	2-0	Simpson	Craig	Gemmell	Murdoch	McNeill 1	Clark	Johnstone 1	Gallacher	McBride	Lennox	Hughes	
Jan 12	DINAMO KIEV	3-0	Simpson	Craig	Gemmell 1	Murdoch 2	Cushley	Clark	Johnstone	Gallacher	McBride	Chalmers	Hughes	
Jan 26	Dinamo Kiev	1-1	Simpson	Craig	Gemmell 1	McNeill	Cushley	Clark	Johnstone	Murdoch	McBride	Chalmers	Hughes	
Apr 14	LIVERPOOL	1-0	Simpson	Young	Gemmell	Murdoch	McNeill	Clark	Johnstone	McBride	Chalmers	Lennox 1	Auld	
Apr 19	Liverpool	0-2	Simpson	Young	Gemmell	Murdoch	McNeill	Clark	Lennox	McBride	Chalmers	Auld	Hughes	

SCOTTISH LEAGUE 1966-67

Sept 10	Clyde	3-0	Simpson	Gemmell	O'Neill	Murdoch	McNeill	Clark	Chalmers 1	Lennox	McBride 1	Auld	Hughes 1	
Sept 17	RANGERS	2-0	Simpson	Gemmell	O'Neill	Murdoch	McNeill	Clark	Johnstone	Lennox	McBride 1	Auld 1	Hughes	
Sept 24	Dundee	2-1	Simpson	Gemmell	O'Neill	Murdoch	McNeill	Clark	Johnstone	Lennox 1	McBride	Auld	Hughes	(Chalmers 1)
Oct 1	ST JOHNSTONE	6-1	Simpson	Gemmell	O'Neill	Murdoch	McNeill	Clark	Johnstone 2	Lennox 2	McBride 2	Auld	Hughes	
Oct 8	Hibernian	5-3	Simpson	Gemmell	O'Neill	Murdoch	McNeill	Clark	Johnstone	McBride 4	Chalmers 1	Auld	Hughes	
Oct 15	AIRDRIE	3-0	Simpson	Young	Gemmell	Clark	McNeill	O'Neill	Chalmers	Lennox 2	McBride 1	Gallacher	Hughes	
Oct 24	AYR UNITED	5-1	Simpson	Gemmell 1	O'Neill	Murdoch	McNeill	Clark	Johnstone 2	Lennox 1	Chalmers	Auld	Hughes 1	
Nov 2	STIRLING ALBION	7-3	Simpson	Gemmell	O'Neill	Murdoch	McNeill	Clark	Johnstone 1	Gallacher	McBride 3	Chalmers 2	Auld 1	(Craig)
Nov 5	ST MIRREN	1-1	Simpson	Craig	O'Neill	Murdoch	Gemmell	Clark	Johnstone	McBride	Chalmers	Auld	Lennox	
Nov 12	Falkirk	3-0	Simpson	Gemmell	O'Neill	Murdoch	McNeill	Clark	Chalmers	Gallacher	McBride 2	Lennox	Auld 1	
Nov 19	Dunfermline Athletic	5-4	simpson	Gemmell	O'Neill	Murdoch 1	McNeill	Clark	Johnstone 1	McBride 2	Chalmers	Lennox	Auld 1	
Nov 26	HEARTS	3-0	Simpson	Gemmell	O'Neill	Murdoch	McNeill	Clark	Johnstone	Chalmers	McBride 2	Lennox	Auld	
Dec 3	Kilmarnock	0-0	Simpson	Gemmell	O'Neill	Murdoch	McNeill	Clark	Johnstone	Chalmers	McBride	Lennox	Auld	
Dec 10	MOTHERWELL	4-2	Simpson	Gemmell	O'Neill	Murdoch 1	McNeill	Clark	Johnstone	Wallace	Chalmers 3	Lennox	Auld	
Dec 17	PARTICK THISTLE	6-2	Simpson	Gemmell	O'Neill	Murdoch 1	McNeill	Clark	Chalmers 2	Wallace 2	McBride 1	Lennox	Auld	
Dec 24	Aberdeen	1-1	Simpson	Gemmell	O'Neill	Murdoch	McNeill	Clark	Chalmers	Auld	McBride	Wallace	Lennox	
Dec 31	Dundee United	2-3	Simpson	Gemmell	O'Neill	Murdoch	McNeill	Clark	Chalmers	Lennox 1	Wallace 1	Auld	Hughes	
Jan 7	DUNDEE	5-1	Simpson	Craig	Gemmell	Murdoch 1	McNeill	Clark	Johnstone 1	Wallace 2	Chalmers	Gallacher 1	Lennox	
Jan 11	CLYDE	5-1	Simpson	Craig	Gemmell 1	Murdoch	McNeill	Clark	Johnstone	Wallace	Chalmers 2	Gallacher 1	Lennox 1	
Jan 14	St Johnstone	4-0	Simpson	Craig	Gemmell	Murdoch	McNeill	Clark	Johnstone 2	Wallace	Chalmers 1	Auld	Lennox 1	
Jan 21	HIBERNIAN	2-0	Simpson	Craig	Gemmell	Murdoch	McNeill	Clark	Johnstone	Wallace 1	Chalmers 1	Auld	Hughes	
Feb 4	Airdrie	3-0	Simpson	Craig	Gemmell	Murdoch	McNeill	Clark	Johnstone 1	Wallace	Chalmers 1	Auld 1	Hughes	
Feb 11	Ayr United	5-0	Simpson	Craig	Gemmell	Murdoch	McNeill	Clark	Johnstone 1	Wallace	Chalmers 3	Gallacher	Hughes 1	
Feb 25	Stirling Albion	1-1	Simpson	Craig	Gemmell	Murdoch	McNeill	Clark	Johnstone	Wallace	Chalmers	Auld	Hughes 1	
Mar 4	St Mirren	5-0	Simpson	Craig	Gemmell 1	Murdoch	McNeill	Clark	Hughes 1	Gallacher	Wallace 2	Lennox 1	Auld	
Mar 18	DUNFERMLINE ATHLETIC	3-2	Simpson	Gemmell 1	O'Neill	Murdoch	McNeill	Clark	Hughes	Gallacher	Chalmers 1	Wallace 1	Lennox	
Mar 20	FALKIRK	5-0	Simpson	Craig	Gemmell 1	Murdoch	McNeill	Clark	Johnstone	Wallace	Chalmers 2	Auld 1	Hughes 1	
Mar 25	Hearts	3-0	Simpson	Craig	Gemmell 1	Murdoch	McNeill	Clark	Johnstone	Wallace 1	Chalmers	Auld 1	Hughes	(Lennox)
Mar 27	Partick Thistle	4-1	Simpson	Craig	Gemmell	Wallace	McNeill	Clark	Johnstone	Gallacher	Chalmers 2	Lennox 1	Hughes	
Apr 8	Motherwell	2-0	Simpson	Craig	Gemmell 1	Wallace 1	McNeill	Clark	Hughes	Lennox	Chalmers	Gallacher	Auld	(Brogan)
Apr 19	ABERDEEN	0-0	Simpson	Craig	Gemmell	Murdoch	McNeill	Clark	Johnstone	Wallace	Chalmers	Auld	Lennox	
May 3	DUNDEE UNITED	2-3	Simpson	Craig	Gemmell 1	Murdoch	McNeill	Clark	Johnstone	Gallacher	Wallace 1	Lennox	Hughes	
May 6	Rangers	2-2	Simpson	Craig	Gemmell	Murdoch	McNeill	Clark	Johnstone 2	Wallace	Chalmers	Auld	Lennox	
May 15	KILMARNOCK	2-0	Fallon	Craig	Gemmell	Murdoch	Cushley	Cark	Johnstone	McNeill	Wallace 1	Auld	Lennox 1	

LEAGUE CUP 1966

Aug 13	Hearts	2-0	Simpson	Gemmell	O'Neill	Murdoch	McNeill	Clark	Johnstone	McBride 2	Chalmers	Lennox	Auld	
Aug 17	CLYDE	6-0	Simpson	Gemmell	O'Neill	Murdoch	McNeill	Clark	Johnstone	McBride 3	Chalmers 1	Lennox 2	Auld	
Aug 20	ST MIRREN	8-2	Simpson	Gemmell	O'Neill	Murdoch	McNeill	Clark	Johnstone	McBride 4	Chalmers 1	Lennox 2	Auld 1	
Aug 27	HEARTS	3-0	Simpson	Gemmell	O'Neill	Murdoch	McNeill	Clark	Johnstone	McBride 2	Chalmers 1	Hughes	Auld	
Aug 31	Clyde	3-1	Simpson	Gemmell 1	O'Neill	Murdoch	McNeill	Clark	Johnstone	McBride 2	Chalmers	Lennox	Auld	
Sept 3	St Mirren	1-0	Simpson	Craig	Gemmell	Murdoch 1	McNeill	Clark	Johnstone	McBride	Chalmers	Lennox	Gallacher	(O'Neill)
Sept 14	DUNFERMLINE ATHLETIC	6-3	Simpson	Gemmell	O'Neill	Murdoch	McNeill 1	Clark	Johnstone 1	McBride 1	Chalmers	Auld 2	Hughes 1	
Sept 21	Dunfermline Athletic	3-1	Simpson	Gemmell	O'Neill	Murdoch	McNeill 1	Clark	Johnstone	Chalmers 2	McBride	Auld	Hughes	
Oct 17	Airdrie (N)	2-0 SF	Simpson	Gemmell	O'Neill	Murdoch	McNeill	Clark	Johnstone	McBride 1	Chalmers	Auld	Lennox	
Oct 29	Rangers (N)	1-0 F	Simpson	Gemmell	O'Neill	Murdoch	McNeill	Clark	Johnstone	Lennox 1	McBride	Auld	Hughes	(Chalmers)

SCOTTISH CUP 1967

Jan 28	ARBROATH	4-0	Simpson	Craig	Gemmell	Murdoch	McNeill	Clark	Gallacher	Wallace	Chalmers	Auld	Hughes	
Feb 18	ELGIN CITY	7-0	Simpson	Cattanach	Gemmell	Murdoch	McNeill	Clark	Johnstone	Lennox 3	Chalmers 1	Gallacher	Hughes 1	(Wallace 2)
Mar 11	QUEEN'S PARK	5-3	Simpson	Cattanach	Gemmell 1	Murdoch 1	McNeill	Clark	Johnstone	Wallace 1	Chalmers 1	Auld	Lennox 1	
Apr 1	Clyde (N)	0-0 SF	Simpson	Craig	Gemmell	Wallace	McNeill	Clark	Johnstone	Auld	Chalmers	Lennox	Hughes	
Apr 5	Clyde (N)	2-0 SRF	Simpson	Craig	Gemmell	Wallace	McNeill	Clark	Johnstone	Lennox 1	Chalmers	Gallacher	Auld 1	(Hughes)
Apr 29	Aberdeen (N)	2-0 F	Simpson	Craig	Gemmell	Murdoch	McNeill	Clark	Johnstone	Wallace 2	Chalmers	Auld	Lennox	

EUROPEAN CUP 1966-67

Sept 28	ZURICH	2-0	Simpson	Gemmell 1	O'Neill	Murdoch	McNeill	Clark	Johnstone	McBride 1	Chalmers	Auld	Hughes	
Oct 5	Zurich	3-0	Simpson	Gemmell 2	O'Neill	Murdoch	McNeill	Clark	Johnstone	Lennox	Chalmers 1	Auld	Hughes	
Nov 30	Nantes	3-1	Simpson	Gemmell	O'Neill	Murdoch	McNeill	Clark	Johnstone	Chalmers 1	McBride 1	Lennox 1	Auld	
Dec 7	NANTES	3-1	Simpson	Gemmell	O'Neill	Murdoch	McNeill	Clark	Johnstone1	Gallacher	Chalmers1	Auld	Lennox1	
Mar 1	Vojvodina	0-1	Simpson	Craig	Gemmell	Murdoch	McNeill	Clark	Johnstone	Lennox	Chalmers	Auld	Hughes	
Mar 8	VOJVODINA	2-0	Simpson	Craig	Gemmell	Murdoch	McNeill 1	Clark	Johnstone	Lennox	Chalmers 1	Gallacher	Hughes	
Apr 12	DUKLA	3-1 SF	Simpson	Craig	Gemmell	Murdoch	McNeill	Clark	Johnstone 1	Wallace 2	Chalmers	Auld	Hughes	
Apr 25	Dukla	0-0 SF	Simpson	Craig	Gemmell	Murdoch	McNeill	Clark	Johnstone	Wallace	Chalmers	Auld	Lennox	
May 25	InterMilan	2-1 F	Simpson	Craig	Gemmell 1	Murdoch	McNeill	Clark	Johnstone	Wallace	Chalmers 1	Auld	Lennox	

SCOTTISH LEAGUE 1967-68

Sept 9	CLYDE	3-0	Simpson	Shevlane	Gemmell	Murdoch	McNeill	Clark	Chalmers	McMahon 1	Wallace	Auld 1	Lennox 1	(Hughes)
Sept 16	Rangers	0-1	Simpson	Cattanach	Gemmell	Murdoch	McNeill	Clark	Johnstone	Wallace	Chalmers	Auld	Lennox	
Sept 23	ST JOHNSTONE	1-1	Simpson	Craig	Gemmell	Murdoch 1	McNeill	Clark	Johnstone	McMahon	Wallace	Auld	Lennox	(Cattanach)
Sept 30	Stirling Albion	4-0	Simpson	Craig	Gemmell	Murdoch	McNeill	Clark	Chalmers	Lennox 1	Wallace 1	Auld 2	Hughes	(O'Neill)
Oct 7	HIBERNIAN	4-0	Simpson	Craig	Gemmell	Murdoch 2	McNeill	Clark	Johnstone 1	Lennox	Wallace 1	Auld	Hughes	
Oct 14	Partick Thistle	5-1	Simpson	Craig	Gemmell	Murdoch	McNeill 1	Clark	Johnstone	Lennox 4	Wallace	Auld	Hughes	(Brogan)
Oct 24	MOTHERWELL	4-2	Simpson	Craig	Gemmell	Murdoch	McNeill 1	Clark	Chalmers 1	Lennox 1	Wallace 1	Auld	Hughes	
Nov 11	Airdrie	2-0	Simpson	Gemmell	O'Neill	Brogan 1	McNeill	Clark	Hughes	Wallace	Chalmers	Murdoch 1	Auld	(McBride)
Nov 15	KILMARNOCK	3-0	Simpson	Gemmell	O'Neill	Murdoch	McNeill	Brogan	Johnstone	Chalmers 1	Wallace	Auld 1	Hughes 1	
Nov 18	FALKIRK	3-0	Simpson	Gemmell	O'Neill	Murdoch	McNeill	Brogan	Johnstone	Chalmers 2	McBride	Auld	Hughes 1	(Wallace)
Nov 25	Raith Rovers	2-0	Simpson	Gemmell 1	O'Neill	Murdoch	McNeill	Brogan	Johnstone	Wallace 1	Chalmers	Auld	Hughes	(McBride)
Dec 2	DUNDEE UNITED	1-1	Simpson	Shevlane	Gemmell	Murdoch 1	McNeill	Clark	Johnstone	Chalmers	Wallace	Auld	Hughes	(McBride)
Dec 9	HEARTS	3-1	Simpson	Craig	Gemmell	Murdoch	McNeill	Clark	Johnstone	Wallace	Chalmers 1	Lennox 1	Hughes	
Dec 16	Dundee	5-4	Simpson	Craig	Gemmell	Murdoch	McNeill 1	Clark	Johnstone 1	Wallace 2	Hughes	Lennox 1	Auld	
Dec 23	Morton	4-0	Simpson	Craig	Gemmell	Murdoch	McNeill	Clark	Johnstone	Lennox	McBride 3	Auld	Hughes 1	
Dec 30	DUNFERMLINE ATHLETIC	3-2	Simpson	Craig	Gemmell	Murdoch	McNeill 1	Clark	Johnstone	Chalmers 2	McBride	Auld	Hughes	
Jan 1	Clyde	3-2	Simpson	Cattanach	Gemmell	Murdoch	McNeill	Brogan	Lennox	Chalmers 2	McBride 1	Auld	Hughes	
Jan 2	RANGERS	2-2	Fallon	Cattanach	Gemmell	Brogan	McNeill	Clark	Johnstone	Murdoch 1	Hughes	Lennox	Auld 1	(Quinn)
Jan 20	Hibernian	2-0	Simpson	Cattanach	Gemmell	Murdoch	McNeill	Clark	Johnstone	Wallace	Chalmers	Lennox 1	Hughes	(Auld)
Feb 3	PARTICK THISTLE	4-1	Simpson	Craig	Gemmell 1	Murdoch	McNeill 1	Clark	Johnstone	Wallace	Hughes	Auld	Lennox 2	
Feb 10	Motherwell	1-0	Simpson	Craig	Gemmell	Murdoch	McNeill	Clark	Johnstone	Wallace	Hughes 1	Auld	Lennox	(Chalmers)
Feb 14	STIRLING ALBION	2-0	Simpson	Craig	Gemmell 1	Murdoch	McNeill	Clark	Johnstone	Wallace 1	Hughes	Gallacher	Lennox	(Chalmers)
Mar 2	Kilmarnock	6-0	Simpson	Gemmell	O'Neill	Murdoch	McNeill	Brogan	Johnstone	Lennox 1	Wallace 4	Gallacher	Hughes	(Quinn 1)

			1	2	3	4	5	6	7	8	9	10	11	SUBS
Mar 6	ABERDEEN	4-1	Simpson	Gemmell	O'Neill	Murdoch	McNeill 1	Brogan	Johnstone	Lennox 3	Wallace	Gallacher	Hughes	(Hay)
Mar 13	AIRDRIE	4-0	Simpson	Craig	Gemmell	Murdoch	McNeill	Brogan	Johnstone	Gallacher	Wallace 3	Lennox 1	Hughes	(Chalmers)
Mar 16	Falkirk	3-0	Simpson	Craig	Gemmell 1	Murdoch	McNeill	Brogan	Johnstone	Lennox 1	Wallace 1	Gallacher	Hughes	
Mar 23	RAITH ROVERS	5-0	Simpson	Craig	Gemmell	Murdoch	McNeill	Brogan	Johnstone	Lennox 1	Wallace 3	Gallacher	Hughes 1	(Chalmers)
Mar 26	St Johnstone	6-1	Simpson	Craig	Gemmell	Murdoch	McNeill	Brogan	Johnstone 1	Lennox 4	Wallace 1	Gallacher	Hughes	
Mar 30	Dundee United	5-0	Simpson	Craig	Gemmell	Murdoch	McNeill	Brogan	Johnstone 1	Lennox 2	Wallace 1	Gallacher	Hughes	(Cattanach 1)
Apr 6	Hearts	2-0	Simpson	Craig	Gemmell	Murdoch	McNeill	Brogan	Johnstone 1	Lennox 1	Wallace	Gallacher	Hughes	
Apr 10	Aberdeen	1-0	Simpson	Craig	Gemmell	Murdoch	McNeill	Brogan	Johnstone	Lennox 1	Wallace	Gallacher	Hughes	
Apr 13	DUNDEE	5-2	Simpson	Craig	Gemmell	Murdoch	McNeill	Brogan	Johnstone	Lennox 2	Wallace	Gallacher	Hughes 2	
Apr 20	MORTON	2-1	Simpson	Craig	Gemmell	Murdoch	McNeill	Brogan	Johnstone	Lennox 1	Wallace 1	Gallacher	Hughes	
Apr 30	Dunfermline Athletic	2-1	Simpson	Craig	Gemmell	Murdoch	McNeill	Brogan	Johnstone	Lennox 2	Wallace	Gallacher	Hughes	(Connelly)

LEAGUE CUP 1967

Aug 12	DUNDEE UNITED	1-0	Simpson	Craig	Gemmell	Murdoch	McNeill	Clark	Johnstone 1	Wallace	Chalmers	Auld	Lennox	
Aug 16	Rangers	1-1	Simpson	Craig	Gemmell 1	Murdoch	McNeill	Clark	Johnstone	Wallace	Chalmers	Auld	Lennox	
Aug 19	ABERDEEN	3-1	Simpson	Craig	Gemmell 1	Murdoch	McNeill	Clark	Johnstone	Wallace	Chalmers	Auld 1	Lennox 1	
Aug 26	Dundee United	1-0	Simpson	Craig	Gemmell	Murdoch	McNeill	Clark	Johnstone	Gallacher	Wallace	Auld	Lennox 1	
Aug 30	RANGERS	3-1	Simpson	Craig	Gemmell	Murdoch 1	McNeill	Clark	Johnstone	Wallace 1	Chalmers	Auld	Lennox 1	
Sept 2	Aberdeen	5-1	Simpson	Craig 1	Gemmell 1	Clark	McNeill	O'Neill	Johnstone 1	Wallace	Murdoch	McMahon 1	Lennox	(Auld) 1
Sept 13	AYR UNITED	6-2	Simpson	Gemmell	O'Neill	Murdoch 1	McNeill	Clark	Johnstone 2	McMahon 1	Wallace	Lennox 2	Hughes	(Cattanach)
Sept 27	Ayr United	2-0	Fallon	Shevlane	O'Neill	Cattanach	McNeill	Brogan 1	Wallace 1	Gallacher	McBride	Auld	Hughes	(Macari)
Oct 11	Morton (N)	7-1 SF	Simpson	Craig 2	Gemmell	Murdoch	McNeill	Clark	Johnstone 1	Lennox 1	Wallace 1	Auld	Hughes 2	
Oct 28	Dundee (N)	5-3 F	Simpson	Craig	Gemmell	Murdoch	McNeill	Clark	Chalmers 2	Lennox 1	Wallace 1	Auld	Hughes 1	(O'Neill)

SCOTTISH CUP 1968

Jan 27	DUNFERMLINE ATHLETIC	0-2	Simpson	Cattanach	Gemmell	Murdoch	McNeill	Brogan	Johnstone	Wallace	McBride	Auld	Hughes	(Chalmers)

EUROPEAN CUP 1967-68

Sept 20	DINAMO KIEV	1-2	Simpson	Craig	Gemmell	Murdoch	McNeill	Clark	Johnstone	Wallace	Chalmers	Auld	Lennox 1	
Oct 4	Dinamo Kiev	1-1	Simpson	Craig	Gemmell	Murdoch	McNeill	Clark	Johnstone	Lennox 1	Wallace	Auld	Hughes	

INTER-CONTINENTAL CHAMPIONSHIP 1967

Oct 18	RACING CLUB	1-0	Simpson	Craig	Gemmell	Murdoch	McNeill 1	Clark	Johnstone	Lennox	Wallace	Auld	Hughes	
Nov 1	Racing Club	1-2	Fallon	Craig	Gemmell 1	Murdoch	McNeill	Clark	Johnstone	Chalmers	Wallace	O'Neill	Lennox	
Nov 4	Racing Club (N)	0-1	Fallon	Craig	Gemmell	Murdoch	McNeill	Clark	Johnstone	Lennox	Wallace	Auld	Hughes	

SCOTTISH LEAGUE 1968-69

Sept 7	Clyde	3-0	Simpson	Craig	Gemmell 1	Brogan 1	McNeill	Clark	Johnstone	Lennox 1	McBride	Connelly	Hughes	(Chalmers)
Sept 14	RANGERS	2-4	Simpson	Gemmell	O'Neill	Brogan	McNeill	Clark	Johnstone	Connelly	Wallace 2	Lennox	Hughes	(Chalmers)
Sept 21	Dunfermline Athletic	1-1	Simpson	Craig	Gemmell	Murdoch	McNeill	Brogan	Johnstone 1	Wallace	Chalmers	Lennox	Hughes	
Sept 28	ABERDEEN	2-1	Simpson	Craig	Gemmell	Murdoch	McNeill	Brogan	Johnstone	Lennox	Wallace	Connelly 1	Hughes	
Oct 5	DUNDEE UNITED	2-0	Simpson	Craig	Gemmell 1	Murdoch 1	McNeill	Brogan	Johnstone	Wallace	Chalmers	McBride	Hughes	(Connelly)
Oct 12	Hearts	1-0	Simpson	Craig	Gemmell	Clark	McNeill	Brogan	Connelly	Wallace	McBride	Chalmers 1	Lennox	
Oct 19	ST JOHNSTONE	2-1	Simpson	Craig	Gemmell	Clark	McNeill 1	Brogan	Johnstone	Connelly	Chalmers	Lennox 1	Hughes	
Oct 26	Morton	1-1	Simpson	Craig	Gemmell	Murdoch	McNeill	Brogan	Johnstone	McBride 1	Wallace	Lennox	Hughes	
Nov 2	DUNDEE	3-1	Simpson	Craig	Gemmell	Murdoch	McNeill	Brogan	Johnstone 1	Wallace	Chalmers 2	Lennox	Hughes	
Nov 9	Arbroath	5-0	Fallon	Craig	Gemmell	Murdoch	McNeill 1	Brogan	Johnstone	Wallace 1	Chalmers 3	Lennox	Hughes	(Auld)
Nov 16	RAITH ROVERS	2-0	Fallon	Craig	Gemmell	Murdoch 2	McNeill	Brogan	Johnstone	Lennox	Wallace	Auld	Hughes	
Nov 23	Partick Thistle	4-0	Fallon	Craig	Gemmell	Murdoch	McNeill	Brogan	Johnstone	Lennox 1	Chalmers	Callaghan 1	Hughes 2	(Wallace)
Nov 30	Hibernian	5-2	Fallon	Craig	Gemmell 1	Murdoch	McNeill 1	Brogan	Johnstone	Callaghan	Wallace	Lennox 1	Hughes 2	(Chalmers)
Dec 7	ST MIRREN	5-0	Fallon	Craig	Gemmell 1	Murdoch	McNeill	Brogan	Johnstone 1	Lennox	Chalmers 2	Callaghan	Hughes 1	(Wallace)
Dec 14	Falkirk	0-0	Fallon	Craig	Gemmell	Murdoch	McNeill	Brogan	Johnstone	Lennox	Wallace	Callaghan	Hughes	
Dec 21	KILMARNOCK	1-1	Fallon	Craig	Gemmell	Murdoch	McNeill	Brogan	Johnstone	Callaghan	Chalmers 1	Auld	Hughes	
Dec 28	Airdrie	0-0	Fallon	Craig	Gemmell	Murdoch	McNeill	Brogan	Johnstone	Wallace	Hughes	Chalmers	Lennox	
Jan 1	CLYDE	5-0	Fallon	Craig	Gemmell 1	Murdoch	McNeill	Brogan	Johnstone	Lennox 1	Wallace 1	Callaghan 2	Hughes	(Auld)
Jan 2	Rangers	0-1	Fallon	Craig	Gemmell	Brogan	McNeill	Clark	Johnstone	Murdoch	Wallace	Lennox	Hughes	(Chalmers)
Jan 4	DUNFERMLINE ATHLETIC	3-1	Fallon	Craig	Gemmell	Murdoch	McNeill	Brogan	Hughes	Wallace 2	Chalmers	Callaghan	Lennox 1	(Johnstone)
Jan 11	Aberdeen	3-1	Simpson	Craig	Gemmell	Murdoch	McNeill	Brogan	Johnstone	Callaghan	Wallace 2	Lennox	Hughes 1	
Jan 18	Dundee United	3-1	Simpson	Craig	Gemmell	Murdoch	McNeill	Brogan	Johnstone	Callaghan	Wallace	Lennox 1	Hughes 1	(McMahon 1)
Feb 1	HEARTS	5-0	Simpson	Craig	Gemmell	Murdoch 1	McNeill	Brogan 1	Johnstone 1	Lennox 1	Wallace 1	Chalmers	Auld	
Mar 5	ARBROATH	7-1	Fallon	Craig	Gemmell	Murdoch	McNeill	Brogan	Johnstone 1	Wallace 3	Chalmers 2	Callaghan	Hughes 1	(Auld)
Mar 8	Raith Rovers	3-1	Fallon	Craig	Gemmell	Murdoch	McNeill	Brogan	Johnstone	Lennox	Wallace 2	Callaghan	Hughes	(Auld 1)
Mar 15	PARTICK THISTLE	1-0	Fallon	Craig	Gemmell	Murdoch	McNeill	Brogan	Johnstone	Chalmers	Wallace	Auld	Hughes 1	
Mar 24	HIBERNIAN	1-1	Fallon	Craig	O'Neill	Murdoch	McNeill	Brogan	Johnstone	Lennox	Wallace 1	Auld	Hughes	
Mar 29	St Mirren	3-0	Fallon	Craig 1	Gemmell	Murdoch	McNeill	Brogan	Johnstone	Hood 1	Wallace	Lennox	Hughes 1	(Callaghan)
Apr 1	St Johnstone	3-2	Fallon	Craig	Gemmell 1	Murdoch	McNeill	Brogan	Johnstone	Hood 1	Wallace 1	Lennox	Hughes	(Clark)
Apr 9	FALKIRK	5-2	Fallon	Craig	O'Neill	Murdoch	McNeill	Clark	Johnstone	Hood 1	Wallace 2	Auld	Lennox 2	(Callaghan)
Apr 19	AIRDRIE	2-2	Fallon	Craig	Gemmell 1	Murdoch	McNeill	Brogan	Johnstone	Hood	Wallace	Auld	Lennox 1	
Apr 21	Kilmarnock	2-2	Fallon	Craig	Gemmell 1	Murdoch	McNeill	Clark	Johnstone	Callaghan	Wallace	Chalmers	Hood	(Lennox)
Apr 28	MORTON	2-4	Fallon	Cattanach	Gemmell	Murdoch	McNeill	Clark	Connelly	Chalmers	Wallace 1	Hood 1	Auld	(Callaghan)
Apr 30	Dundee	2-1	Fallon	Craig	O'Neill	Murdoch	McNeill	Clark	Chalmers	Wallace	Hood 1	Auld	Macari 1	

LEAGUE CUP 1968

Aug 10	Rangers	2-0	Simpson	Gemmell	O'Neill	Murdoch	McNeill	Brogan	Connelly	Johnstone	Wallace 2	Lennox	Hughes	(Clark)
Aug 14	MORTON	4-1	Simpson	Gemmell 1	O'Neill	Murdoch 1	McNeill	Brogan	Johnstone	Connelly	Wallace 1	Lennox	Hughes 1	(Macari)
Aug 17	PARTICK THISTLE	4-0	Simpson	Gemmell	O'Neill	Murdoch	McNeill	Brogan	Johnstone	Connelly	Wallace 4	Lennox	Hughes	(Auld)
Aug 24	RANGERS	1-0	Simpson	Gemmell	O'Neill	Murdoch	McNeill	Brogan	Johnstone	Connelly	Wallace 1	Lennox	Hughes	
Aug 28	Morton	3-0	Fallon	Gemmell	O'Neill	Murdoch	McNeill	Brogan	Johnstone	Lennox 1	Wallace 1	Connelly	Hughes 1	
Aug 31	Partick Thistle	6-1	Fallon	Craig	O'Neill	Murdoch	McNeill	Brogan	Mohnstone	Lennox 5	Wallace	Connelly	Hughes	
Sept 11	HAMILTON ACADEMICALS	10-0	Simpson	Craig	Gemmell	Brogan	McNeill	Clark	Macari	Lennox 5	McBride	Chalmers 5	Hughes	(Johnstone)
Sept 25	Hamilton Academicals	4-2	Wraith	Craig	Gorman	Connelly	Hay	Clark 1	McMahon 1	McBride 2	Quinn	Gallacher	Macari	(Dalglish)
Oct 9	Clyde (N)	1-0 SF	Simpson	Craig	Gemmell	Murdoch	McNeill	Brogan	Lennox	Wallace	Chalmers	McBride	Hughes	(Connelly 1)
Apr 5	Hibernian (N)	6-2 F	Fallon	Craig 1	Gemmell	Murdoch	McNeill	Brogan	Johnstone	Wallace 1	Chalmers	Auld 1	Lennox 3	(Clark)

SCOTTISH CUP 1969

Jan 25	Partick Thistle	3-3	Simpson	Craig	Gemmell	Murdoch 1	McNeill	Brogan	Johnstone	Callaghan	Wallace 1	Lennox	Hughes 1	
Jan 29	PARTICK THISTLE	8-1	Simpson	Craig	Gemmell 1	Murdoch	McNeil 1	Brogan	Johnstone 1	Callaghan 2	Wallace 1	Lennox 1	Hughes 1	(Chalmers)
Feb 12	Clyde	0-0	Simpson	Craig	Gemmell	Murdoch	McNeill	Brogan	Johnstone	Lennox	Wallace	Callaghan	Chalmers	(Auld)
Feb 24	CLYDE	3-0	Fallon	Gemmell	O'Neill	Murdoch 1	McNeill	Hay	Johnstone	Lennox	Wallace	Chalmers 1	Hughes 1	(Callaghan)
Mar 1	ST JOHNSTONE	3-2	Fallon	Craig	Gemmell	Murdoch	McNeill	Clark	Johnstone	Lennox 1	Wallace	Chalmers 1	Hughes 1	
Mar 22	Morton (N)	4-1 SF	Fallon	Craig	Gemmell	Murdoch	McNeill 1	Brogan	Johnstone 1	Wallace 1	Chalmers 1	Auld	Hughes	(Callaghan)
Apr 26	Rangers (N)	4-0 F	Fallon	Craig	Gemmell	Murdoch	McNeill 1	Brogan	Connelly 1	Chalmers 1	Wallace	Lennox 1	Auld	(Clark)

EUROPEAN CUP 1968-69

Sept 18	St Etienne	0-2	Simpson	Craig	O'Neill	Brogan	McNeill	Clark	Connelly	Johnstone	Wallace	Lennox	Hughes	
Oct 2	ST ETIENNE	4-0	Simpson	Craig 1	Gemmell 1	Murdoch	McNeill	Brogan	Johnstone	Wallace	Chalmers 1	McBride 1	Hughes	
Nov 13	RED STAR BELGRADE	5-1	Fallon	Craig	Gemmell	Murdoch 1	McNeill	Brogan	Johnstone 2	Wallace 1	Chalmers	Lennox 1	Hughes	
Nov 27	Red Star Belgrade	1-1	Fallon	Craig	Gemmell	Brogan	McNeill	Clark	Connelly	Lennox	Chalmers	Murdoch	Hughes	(Wallace 1)
Feb 19	Milan	0-0	Fallon	Craig	Gemmell	Clark	McNeill	Brogan	Johnstone	Murdoch	Wallace	Lennox	Hughes	(Auld)
Mar 12	MILAN	0-1	Fallon	Craig	Gemmell	Clark	McNeill	Brogan	Johnstone	Wallace	Chalmers	Murdoch	Hughes	(Auld)

SCOTTISH LEAGUE 1969-70

			1	2	3	4	5	6	7	8	9	10	11	SUBS
Aug 30	ST JOHNSTONE	2-2	Fallon	Craig	Gemmell	Brogan	McNeill	Clark	Johnstone	Connelly	Wallace	Hood 1	Chalmers 1	(Macari)
Sept 3	Kilmarnock	4-2	Fallon	Craig	Gemmell	Murdoch	McNeill	Clark	Johnstone	Hood	Wallace 2	Chalmers	Lennox 2	
Sept 6	Dunfermline Athletic	1-2	Fallon	Craig	Gemmell	Murdoch	McNeill	Clark	Johnstone	Hood	Wallace	Chalmers	Lennox	(Callaghan)
Sept 13	HIBERNIAN	1-2	Fallon	Hay	Gemmell	Murdoch	McNeill	Clark	Johnstone 1	Hood	Wallace	Chalmers	Lennox	(Callaghan)
Sept 20	Rangers	1-0	Fallon	Craig	Gemmell	Brogan	McNeill	Clark	Johnstone	Hood 1	Wallace	Hay	Lennox	
Sept 27	CLYDE	2-1	Fallon	Hay	Gemmell	Brogan	McNeill	Clark	Johnstone	Hood	Wallace	Lennox 2	Hughes	(Craig)
Oct 4	RAITH ROVERS	7-1	Simpson	Hay	Gemmell	Dalglish	McNeill	Clark	Johnstone 2	Lennox 2	Wallace 1	Callaghan 1	Hughes 1	(Hood)
Oct 11	Airdrie	2-0	Simpson	Craig	Gemmell	Brogan	Connelly	Callaghan	Johnstone	Hood	Wallace 1	Chalmers 1	Lennox	(Hughes)
Oct 29	Aberdeen	3-2	Fallon	Craig	Hay	Murdoch 1	McNeill	Clark	Johnstone 1	Callaghan	Hughes	Hood	Auld	(Brogan 1)
Nov 1	Ayr United	4-2	Fallon	Craig	Hay	Murdoch 2	McNeill	Brogan	Johnstone 2	Callaghan	Hughes	Macari	Auld	
Nov 8	HEARTS	0-2	Fallon	Craig	Gemmell	Murdoch	McNeill	Brogan	Johnstone	Dalglish	Hughes	Macari	Callaghan	
Nov 15	Motherwell	2-1	Fallon	Craig	Gemmell	Murdoch	McNeill	Clark	Johnstone	Hood 1	Wallace	Auld	Hughes 1	(Hay)
Nov 29	Morton	3-0	Fallon	Hay	Gemmell	Murdoch	McNeill	Brogan	Johnstone	Hood 1	Wallace 1	Macari 1	Hughes	(Auld)
Dec 1	ST MIRREN	2-0	Williams	Hay	Gemmell	Murdoch	McNeill	Brogan	Hughes	Hood	Wallace	Macari 2	Auld	
Dec 6	DUNDEE	1-0	Fallon	Hay	Gemmell 1	Murdoch	McNeill	Brogan	Johnstone	Hood	Walace	Macari	Auld	
Dec 13	St Johnstone	4-1	Fallon	Hay	Gemmell 1	Murdoch	McNeill	Brogan	Johnstone	Hood 1	Wallace 2	Auld	Hughes	
Dec 17	DUNDEE UNITED	7-2	Fallon	Hay	Gemmell 1	Murdoch 1	McNeill	Brogan	Johnstone	Hood 1	Wallace 2	Auld 1	Hughes 1	(Craig)
Dec 20	KILMARNOCK	3-1	Fallon	Hay	Gemmell 1	Murdoch	McNeill	Brogan	Johnstone	Hood	Wallace	Auld	Hughes 2	(Craig)
Dec 27	PARTICK THISTLE	8-1	Williams	Craig	Hay	Murdoch	McNeill 1	Brogan	Johnstone	Hood	Wallace 2	Auld 2	Hughes 3	(Lennox)
Jan 1	Clyde	2-0	Williams	Craig	Hay	Murdoch	McNeill	Brogan	Macari 1	Hood	Wallace	Auld	Hughes 1	
Jan 3	RANGERS	0-0	Williams	Hay	Gemmell	Murdoch	McNeill	Brogan	Johnstone	Hood	Wallace	Auld	Hughes	
Jan 17	Hibernian	2-1	Williams	Hay	Gemmell	Murdoch	McNeill 1	Brogan	Johnstone	Hood	Wallace	Auld	Hughes 1	(Craig)
Jan 31	DUNFERMLINE ATHLETIC	3-1	Williams	Craig	Gemmell	Murdoch	McNeill	Brogan	Macari 1	Hay	Wallace 1	Lennox 1	Hughes	
Feb 16	Partick Thistle	5-1	Williams	Craig	Gemmell 2	Brogan	McNeill	Hay	Johnstone 1	Hood 1	Wallace	Lennox	Hughes	(Macari 1)
Feb 25	Raith Rovers	2-0	Williams	Craig	Gemmell 1	Hay	McNeill 1	Brogan	Johnstone	Macari	Wallace	Hood	Lennox	(Auld)
Feb 28	AIRDRIE	4-2	Williams	Craig	Gemmell	Hay	McNeill	Brogan	Johnstone 2	Lennox 1	Wallace 1	Callaghan	Macari	(Hood)
Mar 7	Dundee United	2-0	Williams	Hay	Gemmell	Murdoch	McNeill 2	Brogan	Johnstone	Hood	Wallace	Callaghan	Lennox	(Auld)
Mar 10	MORTON	4-0	Williams	Hay	Gemmell	Callaghan	McNeill	Brogan	Johnstone	Macari	Wallace	Auld 1	Lennox 1	(Murdoch)
Mar 21	AYR UNITED	3-0	Williams	Hay	Gemmell	Connelly	McNeill	Brogan	Macari	Wallace 2	Hood	Callaghan	Lennox 1	(Murdoch)
Mar 25	ABERDEEN	1-2	Williams	Craig	Gemmell	Murdoch	McNeill	Brogan	Johnstone	Connelly	Wallace	Lennox	Auld	
Mar 28	Hearts	0-0	Williams	Hay	Gemmell	Murdoch	Connelly	Brogan	Callaghan	Wallace	Quinn	Macari	Lennox	
Apr 4	MOTHERWELL	6-1	Williams	Hay	Craig	Murdoch 1	McNeill	Brogan	Johnstone 1	Connelly	Wallace 1	Lennox 3	Hughes	(Macari)
Apr 6	Dundee	2-1	Fallon	Craig	Gemmell	Murdoch	McNeill	Hay	Callaghan	Lennox 1	Hood	Auld 1	Hughes	(Wallace)
Apr 18	St Mirren	3-2	Williams	Craig	Gemmell	Murdoch	Connelly	Brogan	Hood 1	Davidson 1	Hughes	Callaghan 1	Lennox	(Cattanach)

LEAGUE CUP 1969

Aug 9	AIRDRIE	6-1	Fallon	Hay	Gemmell 1	Murdoch	McNeill	Clark	Connelly 1	Hood 1	Wallace 1	Lennox	Hughes 2	(Auld)
Aug 13	Rangers	1-2	Fallon	Hay	Gemmell	Murdoch	McNeill	Clark	Connelly	Hood 1	Wallace	Lennox	Hughes	(Auld)
Aug 16	RAITH ROVERS	5-0	Fallon	Craig	Gemmell	Brogan	McNeill 1	Clark	Connelly	Hood 1	Wallace 2	Lennox	Hughes 1	(Chalmers)
Aug 20	RANGERS	1-0	Fallon	Craig	Gemmell 1	Murdoch	McNeill	Clark	Johnstone	Hood	Wallace	Lennox	Hughes	(Brogan)
Aug 23	Airdrie	3-0	Fallon	Craig	Gemmell	Murdoch	McNeill 1	Clark	Johnstone	Hood	Wallace 1	Lennox 1	Hughes	(Chalmers)
Aug 27	Raith Rovers	5-2	Fallon	Craig	Gemmell	Brogan 1	McNeill	Clark	Connelly	Hood 2	Wallace	Chalmers 2	Auld	(Johnstone)
Sept 10	Aberdeen	0-0	Fallon	Hay	Gemmell	Murdoch	McNeill	Clark	Hood	Chalmers	Wallace	Callaghan	Lennox	(Brogan)
Sept 24	ABERDEEN	2-1	Fallon	Hay	Gemmell	Brogan	McNeill	Clark	Wallace	Chalmers	Johnstone	Hood	Lennox 1	
Oct 8	Ayr United (N)	3-3 SF	Fallon	Hay	Gemmell 1	Dalglish	McNeill	Clark	Hood	Lennox	Wallace	Callaghan	Hughes 1	(Auld 1)
Oct 13	Ayr United (N)	2-1 SFR	Simpson	Craig	Gemmell	Dalglish	McNeill	Brogan	Johnstone	Hood 1	Chalmers 1	Callaghan	Hughes	(Wallace)
Oct 25	St Johnstone (N)	1-0 F	Fallon	Craig	Hay	Murdoch	McNeill	Brogan	Callaghan	Hood	Hughes	Chalmers	Auld 1	(Johnstone)

SCOTTISH CUP 1970

Jan 24	DUNFERMLINE ATHLETIC	2-1	Williams	Hay	Gemmell	Murdoch	McNeill	Brogan	Johnstone	Hood 1	Wallace	Auld	Hughes 1	(Craig)
Feb 7	DUNDEE UNITED	4-0	Williams	Hay	Gemmell	Murdoch	McNeill	Brogan	Macari 1	Wallace 1	Hood	Lennox	Hughes 2	(Craig)
Feb 21	RANGERS	3-1	Williams	Craig	Gemmell	Murdoch	McNeill	Brogan	Johnstone 1	Lennox 1	Wallace	Hay 1	Hughes	(Hood)
Mar 14	Dundee (N)	2-1 SF	Williams	Hay	Gemmell	Murdoch	McNeill	Brogan	Johnstone	Macari 1	Wallace	Callaghan	Lennox 1	
Apr 11	Aberdeen (N)	1-3 F	Williams	Hay	Gemmell	Murdoch	McNeill	Brogan	Johnstone	Wallace	Connelly	Lennox 1	Hughes	(Auld)

EUROPEAN CUP 1969-70

Sept 17	Basle	0-0	Fallon	Hay	Gemmell	Brogan	McNeill	Clark	Johnstone	Wallace	Chalmers	Lennox	Hughes	(Hood)
Oct 1	BASLE	2-0	Fallon	Hay	Gemmell 1	Clark	McNeill	Callaghan	Johnstone	Wallace	Chalmers	Hood 1	Lennox	
Nov 12	BENFICA	3-0	Fallon	Craig	Gemmell 1	Murdoch	McNeill	Clark	Johnstone	Hood 1	Wallace 1	Auld	Hughes	
Nov 26	Benfica	0-3	Fallon	Craig	Gemmell	Murdoch	McNeill	Brogan	Johnstone	Callaghan	Wallace	Auld	Hughes	(Hood/Connelly)
Mar 4	FIORENTINA	3-0	Williams	Hay	Gemmell	Murdoch	McNeill	Brogan	Johnstone	Lennox	Wallace 1	Auld 1	Hughes	(Hood)
Mar 18	Fiorentina	0-1	Williams	Hay	Gemmell	Connelly	McNeill	Brogan	Johnstone	Murdoch	Wallace	Auld	Lennox	(Callaghan)
Apr 1	Leeds United	1-0 SF	Williams	Hay	Gemmell	Murdoch	McNeill	Brogan	Johnstone	Connelly 1	Wallace	Lennox	Auld	(Hughes)
Apr 15	LEEDS UNITED	2-1	Williams	Hay	Gemmell	Murdoch 1	McNeill	Brogan	Johnstone	Connelly	Hughes 1	Auld	Lennox	
May 6	Feyenoord (N)	1-2 F	Williams	Hay	Gemmell 1	Murdoch	McNeill	Brogan	Johnstone	Wallace	Hughes	Auld	Lennox	(Connelly)

SCOTTISH LEAGUE 1970-71

Aug 29	MORTON	2-0	Williams	McGrain	Gemmell	Murdoch	McNeill	Brogan	Johnstone	Hay	Hood	Lennox 2	Macari	(Connelly)
Sept 5	Clyde	5-0	Williams	McGrain	Hay 1	Murdoch	McNeill	Brogan	Hughes	Connelly	Hood	Lennox	Macari 2	(Davidson 1)
Sept 12	RANGERS	2-0	Williams	McGrain	Hay	Murdoch 1	McNeill	Brogan	Johnstone	Connelly	Hood	Lennox	Hughes1	
Sept 19	Hibernian	0-2	Williams	McGrain	Hay	Murdoch	McNeill	Brogan	Johnstone	Connelly	Hood	Lennox	Hughes	
Sept 26	DUNDEE	3-0	Williams	McGrain	Hay	Murdoch	Connelly	Brogan	Johnstone 2	Callaghan	Hood	Macari 1	Wilson	(Lennox)
Oct 3	Dunfermline Athletic	2-0	Williams	McGrain	Hay	Murdoch	McNeill	Connelly	Davidson	Johnstone	Wallace 1	Macari 1	Lennox	(Hood)
Oct 10	ST JOHNSTONE	1-0	Williams	Hay	McGrain	Connelly	McNeill	Callaghan	Johnstone	Wallace 1	Hood	Lennox	Macari	(Quinn)
Oct 17	Airdrie	3-1	Williams	Craig	Hay	Murdoch	McNeill	Cattanach	Johnstone	Connelly	Wallace	Hood 2	Lennox 1	(Dalglish)
Oct 28	HEARTS	3-2	Williams	Craig	Hay	Murdoch	McNeill	Cattanach	Johnstone	Hood 1	Wallace 2	Connelly	Lennox	
Oct 31	Motherwell	5-0	Williams	Craig	Hay	Murdoch	McNeill	Cattanach	Johnstone 1	Hood 3	Wallace	Connelly 1	Lennox	(Macari)
Nov 7	COWDENBEATH	3-0	Williams	Craig	Brogan	Murdoch	McNeill	Cattanach	Johnstone	Hood	Wallace 1	Connelly 2	Hughes	
Nov 14	KILMARNOCK	3-0	Williams	Craig	Gemmell	Murdoch 1	McNeill	Brogan	Johnstone 1	Lennox	Wallace 1	Connelly	Hughes	(Hood)
Nov 21	Falkirk	0-0	Williams	Craig	Gemmell	Murdoch	McNeill	Brogan	Johnstone	Connelly	Hughes	Hay	Lennox	(Wallace)
Nov 28	ST MIRREN	3-0	Fallon	Craig	Gemmell 1	Murdoch	McNeill	Brogan	Davidson 2	Hood	Wallace	Hay	Hughes	(Connelly)
Dec 5	Dundee United	2-1	Fallon	Craig	Gemmell	Murdoch	McNeill	Brogan	Johnstone	Connelly	Macari	Davidson 1	Hughes	
Dec 12	ABERDEEN	0-1	Fallon	Craig	Gemmell	Murdoch	McNeill	Brogan	Johnstone	Connelly	Macari	Hay	Hughes	(Hood)
Dec 19	Ayr United	2-1	Williams	Craig	Gemmell	Murdoch	McNeill	Hay	Johnstone	Lennox	Hood 1	Callaghan	Hughes 1	(Macari)
Dec 26	Morton	3-0	Williams	Craig	Gemmell	Murdoch	Connelly	Hay	Chalmers 1	Hood	Wallace 1	Callaghan	Lennox 1	
Jan 2	Rangers	1-1	Williams	Craig	Gemmell	Brogan	Connelly	Hay	Johnstone 1	Hood	Wallace	Callaghan	Lennox	
Jan 9	HIBERNIAN	2-1	Williams	Craig	Gemmell	Murdoch	McNeill	Brogan	Johnstone	Wallace	Hood 1	Callaghan 1	Lennox	
Jan 16	Dundee	8-1	Williams	Craig	Gemmell	Murdoch	McNeill	Brogan	Johnstone 2	Wallace 2	Hood 2	Callaghan 1	Auld	
Jan 30	DUNFERMLINE ATHLETIC	1-0	Williams	Craig	Gemmell	Murdoch	McNeill	Brogan	Johnstone	Wallace 1	Hood	Callaghan	Auld	(Hay)
Feb 6	St Johnstone	2-3	Williams	Craig	Gemmell	Brogan	McNeill	Hay	Johnstone	Wallace 1	Hood 1	Callaghan	Hughes	(Chalmers)
Feb 20	AIRDRIE	4-1	Williams	Hay	Gemmell	Connelly	McNeill	Brogan	Johnstone	Hood 1	Wallace 2	Callaghan	Lennox	(Macari 1)
Feb 27	Hearts	1-1	Williams	Hay	Gemmell	Connelly	McNeill	Brogan	Johnstone	Hood 1	Wallace	Callaghan	Lennox	
Mar 13	Cowdenbeath	5-1	Williams	Craig	Hay	Callaghan	McNeill 1	Brogan	Chalmers	Hood 2	Wallace	Davidson	Hughes 1	(Lennox 1)
Mar 20	Kilmarnock	4-1	Williams	Hay	Gemmell	Callaghan	McNeill	Brogan	Johnstone	Hood 2	Wallace	Davidson 1	Hughes 1	(Auld)
Mar 27	FALKIRK	4-0	Williams	Hay	Gemmell	Callaghan	McNeill	Brogan	Johnstone	Hood 2	Wallace 1	Davidson	Hughes 1	(Murdoch)
Apr 10	DUNDEE UNITED	1-1	Williams	Hay	Gemmell	Dalglish	McNeill	Brogan	Johnstone	Hood	Wallace 1	Callaghan	Auld	
Aug 12	MOTHERWELL	3-0	Williams	Craig	Brogan	Connelly	McNeill	Hay	Johnstone 1	Lennox	Wallace 1	Callaghan	Hood 1	(Murdoch)
Aug 17	Aberdeen	1-1	Williams	Craig	Brogan	Connelly	McNeill	Hay	Johnstone	Lennox	Wallace	Callaghan	Hood 1	(Quinn)
Aug 27	St Mirren	2-2	Williams	Craig	Brogan	Connelly	McNeill	Hay	Johnstone	Lennox 1	Wallace	Callaghan	Hood 1	
Aug 29	AYR UNITED	2-0	Williams	Craig	Brogan	Connelly	McNeill	Hay	Johnstone	Lennox 1	Wallace 1	Callaghan	Macari	(Dalglish)
May 1	CLYDE	6-1	Williams	Craig	Gemmell	Murdoch	McNeill	Clark	Johnstone	Wallace 2	Chalmers 1	Auld	Lennox 3	

LEAGUE CUP 1970

			1	2	3	4	5	6	7	8	9	10	11	SUBS
Aug 8	Hearts	2-1	Fallon	Craig	Gemmell	Connelly	McNeill	Brogan	Johnstone 1	Lennox	Hood	Hay	Hughes 1	
Aug 12	CLYDE	5-3	Williams	Craig	Gemmell	Hay	McNeill	Brogan	Johnstone 2	Hood	Connelly	Lennox 3	Hughes	(Wallace)
Aug 15	DUNDEE UNITED	2-2	Fallon	Craig	Gemmell	Hay	McNeill	Brogan	Callaghan 1	Hood	Connelly	Lennox 1	Hughes	(Wallace)
Aug 19	Clyde	2-0	Williams	Hay	Gemmell 2	Murdoch	McNeill	Brogan	Callaghan	Connelly	Wallace	Hood	Lennox	(Macari)
Aug 22	HEARTS	4-2	Williams	Hay	Gemmell	Murdoch	McNeill	Brogan	Johnstone	Hood	Connelly 1	Lennox	Hughes 2	(Macari 1)
Aug 26	Dundee United	2-2	Williams	Hay 1	Gemmell	Murdoch	Connelly	Brogan	Callaghan	Johnstone	Hood	Macari 1	Hughes	(McGrain)
Sept 9	Dundee	2-2	Williams	McGrain	Hay	Murdoch	McNeill	Brogan	Johnstone	Connelly	Hood	Macari	Hughes	
Sept 23	DUNDEE	5-1	Williams	McGrain	Hay	Murdoch	McNeill	Brogan	Johnsone	Connelly	Hood 1	Macari 2	Hughes 1	(Wilson 1)
Oct 7	Dumbarton (N)	0-0 SF	Williams	Craig	McGrain	Murdoch	McNeill	Hay	Johnstone	Connelly	Hood	Macari	Lennox	(Wallace)
Oct 12	Dumbarton (N)	4-3 SFR	Williams	Quinn	McGrain	Murdoch	McNeill	Hay	Johnstone	Connelly	Wallace 1	Lennox 2	Wilson	(Macari 1)
Oct 24	Rangers (N)	0-1 F	Williams	Craig	Quinn	Murdoch	McNeill	Hay	Johnstone	Connelly	Wallace	Hood	Macari	(Lennox)

SCOTTISH CUP 1971

			1	2	3	4	5	6	7	8	9	10	11	SUBS
Jan 23	QUEEN OF THE SOUTH	5-1	Williams	Craig	Gemmell	Murdoch	McNeill 1	Hay	Johnstone	Wallace 1	Hood 2	Callaghan 1	Auld	(Brogan)
Feb 13	DUNFERMLINE ATHLETIC	1-1	Williams	Hay	Gemmell	Connelly	McNeill	Brogan	Johnstone	Wallace 1	Hood	Callaghan	Auld	(Lennox)
Feb 17	Dunfermline Athletic	1-0	Williams	Hay	Gemmell	Connelly	McNeill	Brogan	Johnstone	Wallace	Hood 1	Callaghan	Lennox	
Mar 6	RAITH ROVERS	7-1	Williams	Hay	Gemmell 1	Callaghan 1	McNeill	Brogan	Johnstone	Hood	Wallace 1	Davidson 1	Lennox 3	(Connelly)
Apr 3	Airdrie (N)	3-3 SF	Williams	Hay	Gemmell	Callaghan	McNeill	Brogan	Johnstone 1	Hood 2	Wallace	Davidson	Hughes	(Lennox)
Apr 7	Airdrie (N)	2-0 SFR	Williams	Hay	Gemmell	Callaghan	McNeill	Brogan	Johnstone 1	Hood 1	Wallace	Dalglish	Auld	
May 8	Rangers (N)	1-1 F	Williams	Craig	Brogan	Connelly	McNeill	Hay	Johnstone	Lennox 1	Wallace	Callaghan	Hood	
May 12	Rangers (N)	2-1 FR	Williams	Craig	Brogan	Connelly	McNeill	Hay	Johnstone	Macari 1	Hood 1	Callaghan	Lennox	(Wallace)

EUROPEAN CUP 1970-71

			1	2	3	4	5	6	7	8	9	10	11	SUBS
Sept 16	KOKKOLA	9-0	Williams	McGrain	Brogan	Murdoch	McNeill 1	Hay	Johnstone 1	Connelly	Hood 3	Lennox	Hughes 1	(Davidson 1, Wilson 2)
Sept 30	Kokkola	5-0	Fallon	Craig	Brogan	Murdoch	Connelly	Cattanach	Davidson 1	Wallace 2	Chalmers	Callaghan 1	Lennox	(McGrain)
Oct 21	Waterford	7-0	Williams	Craig	Quinn	Murdoch 2	McNeill	Hay	Connelly	Macari 2	Wallace 3	Hood	Lennox	(Chalmers, Davidson)
Nov 4	WATERFORD	3-2	Williams	Craig	Gemmell	Murdoch	McNeill	Hay	Johnstone 2	Lennox	Wallace	Connelly	Hughes 1	(Hood, Brogan)
Mar 10	Ajax	0-3	Williams	Hay	Gemmell	Connelly	McNeill	Brogan	Johnstone	Craig	Wallace	Callaghan	Lennox	
Mar 24	AJAX	1-0	Williams	Hay	Gemmell	Callaghan	McNeill	Brogan	Johnstone 1	Hood	Wallace	Auld	Hughes	(Lennox, Davidson)

SCOTTISH LEAGUE 1971-72

			1	2	3	4	5	6	7	8	9	10	11	SUBS
Sept 4	CLYDE	9-1	Williams	Hay	Gemmell	Murdoch 1	McNeill 1	Connelly	Johnstone	Lennox 3	Dalglish 1	Callaghan 1	Macari 2	(Wallace)
Sept 11	Rangers	3-2	Williams	Brogan	Hay	Murdoch	McNeill	Connelly	Johnstone 1	Lennox	Dalglish 1	Callaghan	Macari 1	
Sept 18	MORTON	3-1	Williams	Hay	Brogan	Murdoch	McNeill	Connelly	Hood 1	Lennox 1	Dalglish	Callaghan	Macari	(Wallace)
Sept 25	Airdrie	5-0	Williams	Craig	Brogan	Hay	McNeill	Connelly	Wallace	Lennox 1	Dalglish 1	Callaghan	Macari 3	(Hughes)
Oct 2	ST JOHNSTONE	0-1	Williams	Craig	Brogan	Hay	McNeill	Connelly	Johnstone	Dalglish	Wallace	Callaghan	Macari	(Lennox)
Oct 9	Hibernian	1-0	Williams	Hay	Gemmell	Murdoch	McNeill	Connelly	Johnstone	Lennox	Hood	Macari 1	Callaghan	
Oct 16	DUNDEE	3-1	Williams	Hay	Gemmell	Murdoch	McNeill	Connelly	Johnstone	Hood	Dalglish 3	Callaghan	Macari	
Oct 27	Dunfermline Athletic	2-1	Connaghan	Craig	Hay	Murdoch	McNeill 1	Connelly	Dalglish	Macari	Hood	Lennox 1	Callaghan	(Brogan)
Oct 30	Ayr United	1-0	Connaghan	Craig	Brogan	Hay	McNeill	Connelly	Dalglish 1	Macari	Davidson	Lennox	Hood	
Nov 6	ABERDEEN	1-1	Connaghan	Craig	Brogan	Hay	McNeill	Connelly	Johnstone	Hood 1	Dalglish	Macari	Callaghan	
Nov 13	Dundee United	5-1	Connaghan	Craig	Brogan	Hay	McNeill	Connelly	Johnstone	Hood 2	Dalglish 1	Macari 1	Callaghan	(Lennox 1)
Nov 20	FALKIRK	2-0	Connaghan	Craig	Quinn	Callaghan	McNeill 1	Hay	Johnstone	Macari	Dalglish 1	Lennox	Hood	
Nov 27	Partick Thistle	5-1	Connaghan	Hay	Quinn	Callaghan	McNeill	Connelly	Johnstone 1	Dalglish 1	Deans 1	Macari	Hood 1	
Dec 4	KILMARNOCK	5-1	Connaghan	Hay	Quinn	Callaghan	McNeill	Connelly	Johnstone 2	Dalglish 2	Deans 1	Macari	Hood	(Wilson)
Dec 11	EAST FIFE	2-1	Connaghan	Hay	Quinn	Callaghan	McNeill	Brogan	Johnstone	Dalglish	Deans 2	Hood	Wilson	
Dec 18	Motherwell	5-1	Connaghan	Hay	Quinn	Dalglish 2	McNeill	Connelly	Johnstone 1	Lennox 1	Deans 1	Callaghan	Hood	
Dec 25	HEARTS	3-2	Connaghan	Hay	Quinn	Dalglish	McNeill	Connelly	Johnstone 1	Lennox	Deans 1	Callaghan	Hood 1	
Jan 1	Clyde	7-0	Connaghan	Hay	Brogan	Dalglish 1	McNeill	Connelly	Davidson 1	Lennox	Deans 2	Callaghan	Hood 2	(McGrain)
Jan 3	RANGERS	2-1	Connaghan	Hay	Brogan 1	Dalglish	McNeill	Connelly	Johnstone 1	Lennox	Deans	Callaghan	Hood	
Jan 8	Morton	1-1	Connaghan	Hay	Brogan	Dalglish	McNeill	Connelly	Johnstone	Lennox	Deans	Callaghan	Hood 1	
Jan 15	AIRDRIE	2-0	Connaghan	Hay	Brogan	Callaghan	McNeill	Connelly	Johnstone	Dalglish 1	Deans	Lennox 1	Hood	
Jan 22	St Johnstone	3-0	Williams	Craig	Brogan	Hay	McNeill	Connelly	Johnstone	Dalglish 1	Deans 2	Lennox	Hood	(Callaghan)
Jan 29	HIBERNIAN	2-1	Williams	Craig	Brogan	Hay	McNeill	Connelly	Johnstone	Dalglish	Deans 1	Lennox	Hood 1	
Feb 19	DUNFERMLINE ATHLETIC	1-0	Williams	Hay	Brogan	Murdoch	McNeill	Connelly	Dalglish	Macari 1	Deans	Lennox	Hood	
Mar 4	AYR UNITED	2-0	Williams	Hay	Brogan	Murdoch	McNeill	Connelly	Hood	Dalglish	Deans 2	Callaghan	Lennox	(McCluskey)
Mar 11	Aberdeen	1-1	Williams	McGrain	Brogan	Murdoch	McNeill	Connelly	Hood	Hay	Dalglish	Macari	Lennox 1	(Callaghan)
Mar 25	Falkirk	1-0	Williams	McGrain	Quinn	Hay	McNeill	Connelly	Davidson 1	Dalglish	Deans	Callaghan	Wilson	(Macari)
Apr 1	PARTICK THISTLE	3-1	Williams	Craig	Quinn	Murdoch	McNeill	Connelly	Johnstone 1	Davidson 2	Deans	Callaghan	Lennox	
Apr 8	Kilmarnock	3-1	Williams	Craig	McCluskey	Murdoch	McNeill	Connelly	Johnstone	Davidson 1	Deans 1	Callaghan	Lennox	(Wilson 1)
Apr 15	East Fife	3-0	Williams	Craig	Quinn	Murdoch	McNeill	Connelly	Hood 1	Dalglish	Deans 2	Callaghan	Macari	(McCluskey)
Apr 22	MOTHERWELL	5-2	Williams	Craig	McCluskey	Murdoch 2	McNeill	Connelly	Johnstone	Dalglish	Deans 2	Callaghan	Lennox 1	
Apr 25	DUNDEE UNITED	3-0	Williams	Craig	Brogan	Murdoch	McNeill	Connelly	Johnstone 1	Dalglish	Deans 1	Callaghan	Lennox 1	
Apr 29	Hearts	1-4	Williams	Craig	Brogan	Murdoch 1	McNeill	Connelly	Hood	Hay	Deans	Macari	Dalglish	
May 1	Dundee	1-1	Williams	Craig	Brogan	Dalglish	McNeill	Connelly	Johnstone	Deans	Macari 1	Callaghan	Lennox	

LEAGUE CUP 1971

			1	2	3	4	5	6	7	8	9	10	11	SUBS
Aug 14	Rangers *	2-0	Williams	Craig	Hay	Murdoch	McNeill	Connelly	Johnstone 1	Lennox	Dalglish 1	Callaghan	Hughes	
Aug 18	Morton	1-0	Williams	McGrain	Hay	Murdoch	McNeill	Connelly	Johnstone	Lennox 1	Dalglish	Callaghan	Hughes	
Aug 21	Ayr United	3-0	Williams	McGrain	Hay 1	Murdoch	McNeill	Connelly	Johnstone	Lennox	Dalglish 1	Callaghan	Hughes 1	
Aug 25	MORTON	0-1	Williams	McGrain	Hay	Murdoch	McNeill	Connelly	Johnstone	Lennox	Dalglish	Callaghan	Hughes	
Aug 28	Rangers	3-0	Williams	Brogan	Hay	Murdoch	McNeill	Connelly	Johnstone	Lennox 1	Dalglish 1	Callaghan 1	Macari	(Hood)
Aug 30	AYR UNITED	4-1	Williams	McGrain	Gemmell	Hay 1	McNeill	Connelly	Johnstone	Lennox 1	Dalglish 1	Callaghan	Macari 1	(Hood)
Sept 8	Clydebank	5-0	Williams	Craig	Gemmell	Hay	Brogan	Connelly	Hood 1	Lennox	Wallace 1	Callaghan 1	Macari 2	(Dalglish)
Sept 22	CLYDEBANK	6-2	Williams	Craig	Brogan	Hay	McNeill	Connelly	Hood 3	McLaughlin	Macari 2	Callaghan	Lennox	(Hughes)
Oct 6	St Mirren	3-0 SF	Williams	Craig	Gemmell	Hay 1	McNeill	Connelly	Johnstone	Lennox 1	Hood 1	Callaghan	Macari (Wallace)	
Oct 23	Partick Thistle	1-4 F	Williams	Hay	Gemmell	Murdoch	Connelly	Brogan	Johnstone	Dalglish 1	Hood	Callaghan	Macari (Craig)	

*This was officially Celtic's home tie, though played at Ibrox because of the reconstruction of Celtic Park.

EUROPEAN CUP 1971-72

			1	2	3	4	5	6	7	8	9	10	11	SUBS
Sept 15	B1903 Copenhagen	1-2	Marshall	Craig	Gemmell	Murdoch	McNeill	Connelly	Johnstone	Lennox	Dalglish	Callaghan	Macari 1	(Wallace)
Sept 29	B1903 COPENHAGEN	3-0	Williams	Craig	Brogan	Hay	McNeill	Connelly	Johnstone	Lennox	Wallace 2	Callaghan 1	Macari	(Hughes)
Oct 20	SLIEMA WAND	5-0	Williams	Hay	Gemmell 1	Murdoch	Connelly	Brogan 1	Johnstone	Dalglish	Hood 2	Callaghan	Macari 1	(Lennox, Davidson)
Nov 3	Sliema Wand	2-1	Williams	Craig	Gemmell	Dalglish	McNeill	Connelly	Callaghan	Hood 1	Macari	Davidson	Lennox 1	(Hancock)
Mar 8	Ujpest Dozsa	2-1	Williams	McGrain	Brogan	Murdoch	McNeill	Connelly	Hood	Hay	Dalglish	Macari 1	Lennox	
Mar 22	UJPEST DOZSA	1-1	Williams	McGrain	Brogan	Murdoch	McNeill	Connelly	Hood	Hay	Dalglish	Macari 1	Lennox	(Johnstone)
Apr 5	Inter Milan	0-0 SF	Williams	Craig	Brogan	Murdoch	McNeill	Connelly	Johnstone	Dalglish	Macari	Callaghan	Lennox	(McCluskey)
Apr 19	INTER MILAN	0-0 SF	Williams	Craig	McCluskey	Murdoch	McNeill	Connelly	Johnstone	Dalglish	Macari	Callaghan	Lennox	(Deans)

(aet - lost on pens)

SCOTTISH CUP 1972

			1	2	3	4	5	6	7	8	9	10	11	SUBS
Feb 5	ALBION ROVERS	5-0	Williams	Hay	Brogan	Murdoch 1	McNeill	Connelly	Dalglish	Macari 1	Deans 1	Callaghan 2	Wilson	(McCluskey)
Feb 26	DUNDEE	4-0	Williams	Hay	Brogan	Murdoch	McNeill	Connelly	Hood	Dalglish 1	Deans 1	Callaghan	Lennox 2	
Mar 18	HEARTS	1-1	Williams	McGrain	Brogan	Murdoch	McNeill	Callaghan	Hood	Hay	Deans 1	Macari	Lennox	
Mar 27	Hearts	1-0	Williams	Craig	Hay	Murdoch	McNeill	Connelly	Hood	Macari 1	Dalglish	Callaghan	Lennox	(Quinn)
Apr 12	Kilmarnock	3-1 SF	Williams	Craig	McCluskey	Murdoch	McNeill	Connelly	Johnstone	Macari 1	Deans 2	Callaghan	Lennox	
May 6	Hibernian	6-1 F	Williams	Craig	Brogan	Murdoch	McNeill 1	Connelly	Johnstone	Deans 3	Macari 2	Dalglish	Callaghan	

SCOTTISH LEAGUE 1972-73

			1	2	3	4	5	6	7	8	9	10	11	SUBS
Sept 2	KILMARNOCK*	6-2	Connaghan	McGrain	Brogan	Murdoch 1	McNeill	Connelly	Hood 3	Dalglish	Deans 2	Callaghan	Wilson	(Lennox)
Sept 9	Morton	2-0	Williams	McGrain	McCluskey	Murdoch 2	McNeill	Connelly	Hood	Dalglish	Deans	Callaghan	Lennox	(Macari)
Sept 16	RANGERS*	3-1	Williams	McGrain	McCluskey	Murdoch	McNeill	Connelly	Johnstone 1	Deans	Dalglish 1	Macari 1	Callaghan	(Hood)
Sept 23	Dundee	0-2	Williams	McGrain	Quinn	Murdoch	McNeill	Connelly	Johnstone	McCluskey	Dalglish	Macari	Callaghan	(Deans)
Sept 30	AYR UNITED	1-0	Williams	McGrain	McCluskey	Murdoch	McNeill	Callaghan	Johnstone	Dalglish	Deans 1	Macari	Hood	
Oct 7	AIRDRIE	1-1	Connaghan	McGrain	McCluskey	Murdoch	McNeill	Connelly	Hood	Dalglish	Macari	Callaghan	Lennox 1	(Davidson)
Oct 14	Partick Thistle	4-0	Williams	Hay 1	Brogan	Murdoch	McNeill	Connelly	Dalglish 1	Macari	Deans 1	Callaghan	Lennox 1	(Hood)
Oct 21	EAST FIFE	3-0	Williams	Hay	McGrain	Murdoch	McNeill	Connelly	Dalglish	Macari 1	Deans 1	Callaghan	Lennox	(Hood 1)
Oct 28	Aberdeen	3-2	Williams	McGrain	McCluskey	Hay	McNeill	Connelly	Dalglish 1	Macari 1	Deans 1	Callaghan	Lennox	
Nov 4	DUNDEE UNITED	3-1	Williams	Hay	Brogan	Connelly	McNeill	McCluskey	Johnstone 1	Dalglish 1	Deans	Macari 1	Callaghan	(Hood)
Nov 11	Motherwell	5-0	Williams	McGrain	Brogan	McCluskey	Connelly	Hay	Johnstone	Deans	Dalglish 2	Hood 2	Callaghan	
Nov 18	HEARTS	4-2	Williams	McGrain	Quinn	McCluskey	Hay	Brogan	Johnstone 1	Deans 1	Dalglish 1	Hood 1	Callaghan	(Lennox)
Nov 25	Falkirk	3-2	Connaghan	McGrain	Brogan	McCluskey	Connelly	Hay	Hood	Deans 1	Dalglish 2	Lennox	Callaghan	(Quinn)
Dec 2	Dumbarton	6-1	Connaghan	McGrain	Brogan	McCluskey 3	Connelly	Hay	Hood 1	Deans	Dalglish	Murdoch	Macari	(Johnstone 1)
Dec 16	Arbroath	2-1	Williams	McGrain	Brogan	McCluskey	McNeill	Hay	Johnstone	Connelly	Dalglish	Murdoch	Hood 2	(Lennox)
Dec 23	HIBERNIAN	1-1	Williams	Hay	Brogan	McCluskey	McNeill	Connelly	Johnstone	Deans	Dalglish 1	Hood	Callaghan	(Lennox)
Jan 6	Rangers	1-2	Williams	Hay	Brogan	McCluskey	McNeill	Connelly	Johnstone	Deans 1	Dalglish	Callaghan	Macari	(Hood)
Jan 13	DUNDEE	2-1	Williams	McGrain	Brogan	Murdoch	McNeill	Connelly	Johnstone 1	Deans	Dalglish 1	Callaghan	Hood	(Lennox)
Jan 20	Ayr United	3-1	Williams	McGrain	Brogan	Murdoch	McNeill	Connelly	Johnstone	Deans 1	Dalglish 2	Callaghan	Hood	(Lennox)
Jan 27	Airdrie	1-2	Hunter	McGrain	Brogan	Murdoch	McNeill	Connelly	Johnstone	Deans 1	Dalglish	Callaghan	Hood	(Lennox)
Feb 7	Kilmarnock	4-0	Hunter	McGrain	Quinn	Murdoch	McNeill	Connelly	Johnstone 1	Deans	Dalglish 2	Callaghan 1	Lennox	(Hood)
Feb 10	PARTICK THISTLE	1-1	Hunter	McGrain	Quinn	Murdoch 1	McNeill	Connelly	Johnstone	Deans	Dalglish	Callaghan	Lennox	(Lynch)
Feb 17	East Fife	2-2	Hunter	McGrain	Quinn	Murdoch	McNeill	Connelly	Johnstone	Deans 2	Dalglish	Hood	Callaghan	
Feb 28	ST JOHNSTONE	4-0	Hunter	McGrain	Quinn	Murdoch	McNeill	Connelly	Johnstone	Dalglish 1	Deans	Hay 1	Lennox 2	(McLaughlin)
Mar 3	ABERDEEN	2-0	Hunter	McGrain	Quinn	Murdoch	McNeill	Connelly	Johnstone	Dalglish 1	Deans	Hood	Lennox 1	(McCluskey)
Mar 6	MORTON	1-0	Hunter	McGrain	Quinn	Hay	McNeill	Connelly	Dalglish	Wilson 1	Deans	Hood	Lennox	
Mar 10	Dundee United	2-2	Hunter	McGrain	Quinn	Hay	McNeill	Connelly	Johnstone	Dalglish	Deans	Hood	Lennox 2	(Wilson)
Mar 24	Hearts	2-0	Hunter	McGrain	Brogan	Murdoch	McNeill	Connelly	Hood	Davidson	Deans 1	Hay	Lennox 1	(Wilson)
Mar 31	FALKIRK	4-0	Hunter	McGrain	Brogan	Murdoch	McNeill	Connelly	Hood 1	Lennox 2	Deans 1	Hay	Callaghan	(McLaughlin)
Apr 3	MOTHERWELL	2-0	Hunter	McGrain	Brogan	Hay	McNeill	Connelly	Hood	Dalglish	Deans	Lennox	Callaghan	(McCluskey)
Apr 14	St Johnstone	3-1	Hunter	McGrain	Brogan	Murdoch	McNeill	Connelly	Johnstone 1	Hood	Dalglish 2	Hay	Callaghan	
Apr 18	DUMBARTON	5-0	Hunter	McGrain	Brogan	Murdoch	McNeill	Connelly	Johnstone	Deans 3	Dalglish 1	Hay	Callaghan 1	(Hood)
Apr 21	ARBROATH	4-0	Hunter	McGrain	Brogan	Murdoch	McNeill	Connelly	Hood 1	Deans 1	Dalglish 1	Hay 1	Callaghan	
Apr 28	Hibernian	3-0	Hunter	McGrain	Brogan	Murdoch	McNeill	Connelly	Johnstone	Deans 2	Dalglish 1	Hay	Callaghan	

LEAGUE CUP 1972

			1	2	3	4	5	6	7	8	9	10	11	SUBS
Aug 12	Stirling Albion	3-0	Connaghan	Brogan	Quinn	Murdoch	McNeill	Connelly	Johnstone	Dalglish 1	Macari 2	Callaghan	Wilson	(Davidson)
Aug 16	EAST FIFE	1-1	Connaghan	McGrain	Quinn	Murdoch	McNeill	Connelly	Johnstone	Dalglish 1	Macari	Callaghan	Davidson	(Wilson)
Aug 19	Arbroath	5-0	Connaghan	McGrain	Quinn	Murdoch 1	McNeill	Connelly	Hood	Dalglish 2	Deans 2	Macari	Callaghan	(McLaughlin)
Aug 23	East Fife	3-2	Connaghan	McGrain	Quinn	Hay	McNeill	Connelly	Hood	Dalglish 2	Deans	Callaghan	Lennox 1	(McCluskey)
Aug 26	STIRLING ALBION	3-0	Connaghan	McGrain	Quinn	Murdoch	McNeill	Connelly	Hood	Deans 1	Dalglish 1	Hay	Lennox	
Aug 28	ARBROATH*	3-3	Connaghan	McGrain	Quinn	Hay	McNeill	Connelly	McLaughlin	Deans	Dalglish 1	Hood 1	Lennox	(McCluskey)
Sept 20	Stranraer	2-1	Connaghan	McGrain	McCluskey	Murdoch	McNeill	Connelly	McLaughlin	Davidson 1	Deans	Lennox 1	Hood	
Oct 4	STRANRAER	5-2	Williams	McCluskey	Quinn	Murdoch 1	McNeill	Callaghan	Johnstone	Davidson 1	Deans 1	Lennox 2	Wilson	(McLaughlin)
Oct 11	Dundee	0-1	Williams	Hay	Brogan	Murdoch	McNeill	Connelly	Dalglish	Macari	Deans	Callaghan	Lennox	
Nov 1	DUNDEE (aet)	3-2	Williams	Hay	McGrain	McCluskey	Connelly	Callaghan	Johnstone	Dalglish	Deans	Macari 2	Lennox 1	(Hood)
Nov 20	Dundee (N)	4-1	Williams	McGrain	Brogan	McCluskey	Connelly	Hay	Johnstone	Deans 2	Dalglish 1	Hood 1	Callaghan	
Nov 27	Aberdeen (N)	3-2 SF	Williams	McGrain	Brogan	McCluskey	Connelly	Hay	Johnstone 1	Deans	Dalglish	Hood 1	Callaghan 1	
Dec 9	Hibernian	1-2 F	Williams	McGrain	Brogan	McCluskey	McNeill	Hay	Johnstone	Connelly	Dalglish 1	Hood	Macari	(Callaghan)

EUROPEAN CUP 1972-73

			1	2	3	4	5	6	7	8	9	10	11	SUBS
Sept 13	ROSENBORG*	2-1	Williams	McGrain	Callaghan	Murdoch	McNeill	Connelly	Hood	Dalglish	Deans 1	Macari 1	Wilson	(Lennox)
Sept 27	Rosenborg	3-1	Williams	McGrain	McCluskey	Murdoch	McNeill	Connelly	Johnstone	Hood 1	Dalglish 1	Macari 1	Callaghan	
Oct 25	UJPEST DOSZA	2-1	Williams	Hay	McGrain	Connelly	McNeill	Callaghan	Johnstone	Dalglish 2	Deans	Macari	Hood	(Lennox, McCluskey)
Nov 8	Ujpest Dosza	0-3	Williams	McGrain	Brogan	Hay	McNeill	McCluskey	Johnstone	Connelly	Dalglish	Callaghan	Lennox	(Hood, Deans)

SCOTTISH CUP 1973

			1	2	3	4	5	6	7	8	9	10	11	SUBS
Feb 3	EAST FIFE	4-1	Hunter	McGrain	Quinn	Murdoch	McNeill	Connelly	Johnstone	Deans 2	Dalglish 2	Callaghan	Lennox	(Hood)
Feb 24	Motherwell	4-0	Hunter	McGrain	Quinn	Murdoch	McNeill	Connelly	Johnstone	Dalglish 1	Deans 2	Hay	Lennox 1	(Hood)
Mar 17	ABERDEEN	0-0	Hunter	McGrain	Brogan	Murdoch	McNeill	Connelly	Johnstone	Dalglish	Deans	Hay	Lennox	
Mar 21	Aberdeen	1-0	Hunter	McGrain	Brogan	Murdoch	McNeill 1	Connelly	Johnstone	Hood	Deans	Hay	Lennox	(Davidson)
Apr 7	Dundee (N)	0-0 SF	Hunter	McGrain	Brogan	Murdoch	McNeill	Connelly	Dalglish	Lennox	Deans	Hay	Callaghan	(Johnstone)
Apr 11	Dundee (N) (aet)	3-0 SFR	Hunter	McGrain	Brogan	Murdoch	McNeill	Connelly	Johnstone	Dalglish	Deans	Hay	Callaghan	(Hood)
May 5	Rangers (N)	2-3 F	Hunter	McGrain	Brogan	Murdoch	McNeill	Connelly 1	Johnstone	Deans	Dalglish 1	Hay	Callaghan	(Lennox)

(* Hampden)

SCOTTISH LEAGUE 1973-74

			1	2	3	4	5	6	7	8	9	10	11	SUBS
Sept 1	Dunfermline Athletic	3-2	Hunter	McGrain	Brogan	Murray	McNeill	Connelly	McLaughlin	Hood 1	Dalglish	Hay	Lenox	(Wilson 1)
Sept 8	CLYDE	5-0	Hunter	McGrain 1	Brogan	Murray	McNeill	Connelly	McLaughlin	Hood	Dalglish 1	Hay	Lennox 3	(Johnstone, Wilson)
Sept 15	Rangers	1-0	Hunter	McGrain	Brogan	Murray	McNeill	Connelly	Johnstone 1	Hood	Dalglish	Hay	Wilson	(Callaghan)
Sept 29	St Johnstone	1-2	Hunter	McGrain	Brogan	Murray	McNeill	Connelly	Johnstone	Dalglish	Deans 1	Hay	Hood	(Callaghan)
Oct 6	MOTHERWELL	2-0	Hunter	McGrain	Brogan	Murray	McNeill	Connelly	Johnstone	Dalglish	Deans 1	Callaghan	Wilson 1	
Oct 13	Dundee	1-0	Hunter	McGrain	Brogan	Murray	McNeill	Connelly	Hood	Deans	Dalglish	Hay	Callaghan 1	(Wilson)
Oct 20	HIBERNIAN	1-1	Hunter	McGrain	Brogan	Murray	McNeill	Connelly	Hood	Dalglish	Lennox	Hay	Callaghan	(Deans, McCluskey 1)
Oct 27	Hearts	3-1	Hunter	McGrain	Brogan	McCluskey	MacDonald	Connelly 1	Johnstone	Murray	Deans	Hay	Dalglish 2	
Nov 3	EAST FIFE	4-2	Hunter	McGrain	Brogan	McCluskey	McNeill	Connelly	Johnstone	Murray	Deans 2	Hood 1	Dalglish 1	(Callaghan, Lynch)
Nov 10	Ayr United	1-0	Hunter	McGrain	Brogan	McCluskey	McNeill	Connelly	Lennox	Murray	Deans	Callaghan	Dalglish 1	
Nov 17	PARTICK THISTLE	7-0	Hunter	McGrain	Quinn	McCluskey	McNeill	Murray	Lennox 1	Hood	Deans 6	Callaghan	Dalglish	(McNamara, Wilson)
Nov 24	Dumbarton	2-0	Hunter	McGrain	Brogan	McCluskey	McNeill	Murray	Lennox 1	Hood	Wilson	Callaghan	Dalglish 1	(Johnstone)
Dec 1	Arbroath	2-1	Hunter	McGrain	Brogan	Mccluskey	McNeill	Murray	Johnstone	Hood	Wilson 1	Callaghan	Dalglish 1	
Dec 8	DUNDEE UNITED	3-3	Hunter	McGrain	Brogan	McCluskey	McNeill	Murray	Hood 1	Hay	Wilson	Callaghan 1	Dalglish 1	(Lennox)
Dec 22	FALKIRK	6-0	Hunter	McGrain	Brogan	McCluskey	McNeill	Hay	Hood	Murray	Deans 4	Dalglish 1	Lennox 1	
Dec 29	DUNFERMLINE ATHLETIC	6-0	Hunter	McGrain	Brogan	McCluskey	McNeill	Hay	Hood 2	Murray	Deans 2	Dalglish 2	Lennox	(Ritchie, Wilson)
Jan 1	Clyde	2-0	Hunter	McGrain	Brogan	McCluskey	McNeill	Hay	Hood	Murray	Deans	Dalglish 1	Lennox 1	(Connelly, Wilson)
Jan 5	RANGERS	1-0	Hunter	McGrain	Brogan	McCluskey	McNeill	Hay	Hood	Murray	Deans	Dalglish	Lennox 1	
Jan 19	ST JOHNSTONE	3-0	Hunter	McGrain	Brogan	McCluskey	McNeill	Hay	Hood	Murray 1	Davidson	Dalglish	Lennox 1	(Lynch)
Feb 2	Motherwell	2-3	Hunter	McGrain	Brogan	McCluskey	McNeill	Hay	Hood	Murray 1	Deans	Dalglish	Lennox 1	
Feb 10	DUNDEE	1-2	Hunter	McGrain	Brogan	Connelly	McNeill	Hay 1	Hood	Murray	Deans	Dalglish	Lennox	(Callaghan)
Feb 23	Hibernian	4-2	Hunter	McGrain	Brogan	Connelly	McNeill	Hay	Hood	Murray	Deans 2	Dalglish 1	Wilson 1	
Mar 2	HEARTS	1-0	Hunter	McGrain	Brogan	Connelly	MacDonald	Hay	Hood	Murray	Deans	Dalglish	Wilson	(McCluskey, Bone)
Mar 16	AYR UNITED	4-0	Connaghan	Hay	Brogan	Murray	McNeill	Connelly	Johnstone 2	Bone	Deans 2	Callaghan	Dalglish	(Hood, Wilson)
Mar 23	Partick Thistle	0-2	Connaghan	Hay	Brogan	Murray	McNeill	McCluskey	Johnstone	Bone	Deans	Callaghan	Dalglish	(Wilson, Hood)
Mar 30	DUMBARTON	3-3	Hunter	McGrain	Brogan	Murray	McNeill	McCluskey	Johnstone	Hood	Deans 1	Callaghan	Wilson 1	(Dalglish 1)
Apr 6	ARBROATH	1-0	Connaghan	McGrain	Hay	Murray	McNeill	McCluskey	Johnstone	Hood	Deans	Callaghan	Dalglish 1	(Wilson)
Apr 13	Dundee United	2-0	Connaghan	McGrain	Brogan	Murray 1	McNeill	McCluskey	Hood	Bone	Dalglish	Hay 1	Wilson	(Callaghan)
Apr 17	East Fife	6-1	Connaghan	McGrain	Quinn	Murray	McNeill	McCluskey	Hood 2	Dalglish 1	Deans 1	Callaghan	Lennox 1	(Wilson)
Apr 20	ABERDEEN	2-0	Connaghan	McGrain	Brogan	Hay	McNeill	McCluskey	Johnstone	Murray	Deans 1	Hood	Dalglish	(Lennox 1, Callaghan)
Apr 27	Falkirk	1-1	Connaghan	Hay	Brogan	Murray	McNeill	McCluskey	Hood	Dalglish 2	Deans	Callaghan	Lennox	(McGrain)
Apr 29	Aberdeen	0-0	Hunter	McGrain	Quinn	McCluskey	Welsh	Brogan	Dalglish	Hay	Deans	Davidson	Callaghan	(Hood)
Apr 30	MORTON	1-1	Hunter	McNamara	McCluskey	Hood	McNeill	Welsh	Johnstone	Wilson	Deans	Lennox	Lynch	(McLaughlin 1)
May 6	Morton	0-0	Connaghan	Hay	Brogan	McCluskey	Welsh	Callaghan	Johnstone	Murray	Davidson	Hood	Lennox	(Dalglish, Deans)

LEAGUE CUP 1973

			1	2	3	4	5	6	7	8	9	10	11	SUBS
Aug 8	ARBROATH	2-1	Hunter	McGrain	Brogan	Murray	McNeill	Connelly	McLaughlin	Hood	Lennox 1	Hay	Lynch 1	(Deans)
Aug 15	Falkirk	2-0	Hunter	McGrain	Brogan	Murray	McNeill	Connelly	Johnstone	McLaughlin	Deans	Hay 1	Lennox 1	(Hood, Callaghan)
Aug 18	Rangers	2-1	Hunter	McGrain	Brogan	Murray	McNeill	Connelly	Johnstone	McLaughlin	Dalglish	Hay	Lennox 1	(Hood 1, Callaghan)
Aug 22	FALKIRK	2-1	Hunter	McGrain	Brogan	Murray	McNeill	Connelly	Johnstone	McLaughlin	Hood	Hay	Lennox 1	(Callaghan, Lynch)
Aug 25	RANGERS	1-3	Hunter	McGrain	Brogan	Murray	McNeill	Connelly	Johnstone	McLaughlin	Dalglish	Hay	Lennox 1	(Hood)
Aug 29	Arbroath	3-1	Hunter	McGrain	Brogan	Murdoch	MacDonald	Connelly	McLaughlin	Hood	Dalglish 1	Callaghan	Lennox 1	(Wilson 1)
Sept 12	Motherwell	2-1	Hunter	McGrain	Brogan	Murray 1	McNeill	Connelly	Johnstone	Hood 1	Dalglish	Hay	Lennox	(Wilson, Callaghan)
Oct 6	MOTHERWELL (aet)	0-1	Hunter	McGrain	Brogan	Murray	McNeill	Connelly	Johnstone	Dalglish	Deans	Callaghan	Wilson	(Hood, McCluskey)
Oct 29	MOTHERWELL	3-2	Hunter	McGrain	Brogan	McCluskey	MacDonald	Connelly	Johnstone 1	Murray 1	Deans 1	Callaghan	Dalglish	(Wilson)
Oct 31	ABERDEEN	3-2	Hunter	McGrain	Brogan	McCluskey 1	McNeill	Connelly	Hood	Murray	Deans	Hay	Dalglish 2	
Nov 21	Aberdeen	0-0	Hunter	McGrain	Brogan	McCluskey	McNeill	Murray	Lennox	Hood	Deans	Callaghan	Dalglish	(Johnstone)
Dec 5	Rangers (N)	3-1 SF	Hunter	McGrain	Brogan	McCluskey	McNeill	Murray	Hood 3	Hay	Wilson	Callaghan	Dalglish	
Dec 15	Dundee (N)	0-1 F	Hunter	McGrain	Brogan	McCluskey	McNeill	Murray	Hood	Hay	Wilson	Callaghan	Dalglish	(Johnston, Connelly)

EUROPEAN CUP 1973-74

			1	2	3	4	5	6	7	8	9	10	11	SUBS
Sept 19	TPS Turku	6-1	Hunter	McGrain	Brogan	Murray	McNeill	Connelly 1	Johnstone 1	Hay	Hood 1	Callaghan 2	Wilson	(Davidson, Deans)
Oct 3	TPS Turku	3-0	Hunter	McCluskey	Brogan	Murray	McNeill	Connelly	Johnstone 2	Dalglish	Deans 1	Davidson	Wilson	(McNamara)
Oct 24	VEJLE	0-0	Hunter	McGrain	Hay	Murray	Connelly	McCluskey	Johnstone	Hood	Dalglish	Callaghan	Lennox	(Wilson)
Nov 6	Vejle	1-0	Hunter	McGrain	Brogan	McCluskey	McNeill	Connelly	Lennox 1	Murray	Deans	Hay	Dalglish	
Feb 27	Basle	2-3	Williams	McGrain	Brogan	Connelly	McNeill	Hay	Hood	Murray	Deans	Dalglish 1	Wilson 1	(Callaghan)
Mar 20	BASLE (aet))	4-2	Connaghan	Hay	Brogan	Murray 1	McNeill	Connelly	Johnstone	Hood	Deans 1	Callaghan 1	Dalglish 1	(McCluskey)
Apr 10	ATLETICO MADRID	0-0	Connaghan	Hay	Brogan	Murray	McNeill	McCluskey	Johnstone	Hood	Deans	Callaghan	Dalglish	(Wilson)
Apr 24	Atletico Madrid	0-2	Connaghan	McGrain	Brogan	Hay	McNeill	McCluskey	Johnstone	Murray	Dalglish	Hood	Lennox	

SCOTTISH CUP 1974

			1	2	3	4	5	6	7	8	9	10	11	SUBS
Jan 27	CLYDEBANK	6-1	Hunter	McGrain	Brogan	McCluskey	McNeill	Hay	Hood	Callaghan	Deans 3	Dalglish	Lennox	(Wilson, Davidson 1)
Feb 17	STIRLING ALBION	6-1	Hunter	McGrain	Brogan	Connelly	McNeill	Hay	Hood 2	Murray 2	Deans	Dalglish 1	Wilson 1	(Davidson, McCluskey)
Mar 10	MOTHERWELL	2-2	Connaghan	Hay	Brogan	Connelly	MacDonald	McCluskey	Hood 2	Murray	Deans	Dalglish	Wilson	
Mar 13	Motherwell	1-0	Connaghan	Hay	Brogan	Connelly	McNeill	McCluskey	Hood	Murray	Deans 1	Bone	Dalglish	(Callaghan)
Apr 3	Dundee (N)	1-0 SF	Connaghan	Hay	Brogan	Murray	McNeill	McCluskey	Johnstone 1	Hood	Deans	Callaghan	Dalglish	
May 4	Dundee United (N)	3-0 F	Connaghan	McGrain	Brogan	Murray 1	McNeill	McCluskey	Johnstone	Hood 1	Deans 1	Hay	Dalglish	(Callaghan)

SCOTTISH LEAGUE 1974-75

Aug 31	KILMARNOCK	5-0	Connaghan	McGrain	McCluskey	Connelly	McNeill	Callaghan	Johnstone 1	Murray 1	Dalglish 1	Davidson 1	Wilson 1	
Sept 7	Clyde	4-2	Connaghan	McGrain	Brogan	Connelly	McNeill	McCluskey 1	Johnstone	Murray	Dalglish 1	Davidson 1	Wilson	(Lennox 1)
Sept 14	RANGERS	1-2	Connaghan	McGrain	Brogan	McCluskey	McNeill	Callaghan	Johnstone	Murray	Dalglish 1	Davidson	Wilson	(Hood)
Sept 21	Motherwell	2-1	Connaghan	McGrain	McCluskey	Murray	McNeill	Callaghan	Johnstone	Hood	Dalglish	Lennox 2	Wilson	
Sept 28	AYR UNITED	5-3	Connaghan	McGrain	Brogan	Murray	McNeill	McCluskey	Hood 1	Dalglish 1	Deans 1	Callaghan	Wilson 2	(Johnstone, Lennox)
Oct 5	Dumbarton	3-1	Hunter	McGrain	Brogan	Murray	McNeill	MacDonald	Johnstone 1	Dalglish 1	Deans	Hood	Wilson	(McCluskey)
Oct 12	ARBROATH	1-0	Hunter	McGrain	Brogan	Murray 1	MacDonald	McCluskey	Johnstone	Hood	Deans	Callaghan	Wilson	
Oct 19	HIBERNIAN	5-0	Hunter	McGrain	Brogan	Murray 1	McNeill	McCluskey	Johnstone 1	Dalglish	Deans 3	Hood	Wilson	(MacDonald)
Nov 2	ABERDEEN	1-0	Hunter	MacDonald	Brogan	Murray	McNeill	McCluskey	Johnstone	Hood	Deans	Dalglish	Wilson 1	(Lennox)
Nov 6	Partick Thistle	2-1	Hunter	MacDonald	Brogan	Murray	McNeill	McCluskey	Hood	Dalglish	Deans	Callaghan	Wilson	
Nov 9	Dundee United	0-0	Hunter	MacDonald	Brogan	Murray	McNeill	McCluskey	Hood	Dalglish	Deans	Davidson	Wilson	(Bone)
Nov 16	AIRDRIE	6-0	Hunter	McGrain	Brogan	Murray 2	McNeill 1	McCluskey	Dalglish	Glavin 1	Deans	Lennox 1	Wilson 1	(MacDonald)
Nov 23	Hearts	1-1	Hunter	McGrain	Brogan	Murray	McNeill	McCluskey	Dalglish	Glavin	Deans	Lennox	Wilson 1	(Callaghan, Johnstone)
Nov 30	Morton	1-0	Connaghan	McGrain	Brogan	Murray 1	McNeill	McCluskey	Dalglish	Glavin	Bone	Lennox	Wilson	
Dec 7	DUNFERMLINE ATHLETIC	2-1	Hunter	McGrain	Brogan	Murray	McNeill	McCluskey	Dalglish	Glavin	Bone 1	Lennox	Wilson	(Welsh)
Dec 14	Dundee	6-0	Hunter	McGrain	Brogan	Murray	McNeill	Connelly	Johnstone 2	Glavin	Dalglish 3	Callaghan	Wilson	(Hood, MacDonald)
Dec 21	ST JOHNSTONE	3-1	Hunter	McGrain	Brogan 1	Murray 1	McNeill	Connelly	Johnstone	Hood	Dalglish 1	Callaghan	Wilson	(Lennox)
Dec 28	Kilmarnock	1-0	Hunter	McGrain	Brogan	Murray	McNeill	Connelly	Hood	Glavin	Dalglish 1	Callaghan	Wilson	
Jan 1	CLYDE	5-1	Hunter	McGrain	McCluskey	Glavin 1	McNeill	Connelly	Johnstone	Dalglish 1	Deans 1	Callaghan 2	Wilson	(Hood)
Jan 4	Rangers	0-3	Hunter	McGrain	Brogan	Murray	McNeill	McCluskey	Hood	Glavin	Dalglish	Callaghan	Wilson	(Johnstone)
Jan 11	MOTHERWELL	2-3	Hunter	McGrain	McCluskey	Murray	McNeill	MacDonald	Hood 2	Glavin	Deans	Dalglish	Wilson	
Jan 18	Ayr United	5-1	Hunter	McGrain	Brogan	Murray 1	McNeill	Connelly	Hood 1	Dalglish	Deans 2	Callaghan	Wilson	(Glavin)
Feb 8	Arbroath	2-2	Hunter	McGrain	Brogan	Murray	McNeill	Connelly	Hood 1	Dalglish 1	Deans	Callaghan	Wilson	(Glavin, Lynch)
Feb 11	DUMBARTON	2-2	Hunter	McGrain	Brogan	Murray	McNeill	Connelly	Hood 1	Glavin	Dalglish	Callaghan	Wilson 1	(Johnstone)
Feb 22	Hibernian	1-2	Latchford	McGrain	McCluskey	Murray	MacDonald	Connelly	Hood	McNamara	Deans	Dalglish	Wilson 1	
Mar 1	PARTICK THISTLE	3-2	Latchford	McGrain	McCluskey 1	Murray	McNeill	Connelly	Hood 1	Glavin	Deans	Dalglish 1	Wilson	
Mar 12	Aberdeen	2-3	Latchford	McGrain	McCluskey	Glavin	McNeill	Connelly	Hood	Wilson	Dalglish	Callaghan	Lynch 2	
Mar 15	DUNDEE UNITED	0-1	Latchford	McGrain	McCluskey	MacDonald	McNeill	Callaghan	Johnstone	Glavin	Dalglish	Hood	Lynch	(Wilson)
Mar 22	Airdrie	0-1	Latchford	McCluskey	Brogan	Glavin	Welsh	Connelly	Johnstone	Dalglish	Deans	Callaghan	Lennox	(Hood, Wilson)
Mar 29	HEARTS	4-1	Latchford	McGrain	McCluskey	Connelly	McNeill	Callaghan	Johnstone	Glavin 1	Dalglish 2	Hood	Wilson 1	(Lynch)
Apr 5	MORTON	1-1	Latchford	McGrain	McCluskey	Glavin	MacDonald	Connelly	Hood	Dalglish	Deans	Lennox	Wilson	(Callaghan, McLaughlin)
Apr 12	Dunfermline Athletic	3-1	Latchford	McGrain	McCluskey	MacDonald	McNeill	Lynch	Wilson 2	Murray	Dalglish	Glavin	Lennox 1	
Apr 19	DUNDEE	1-2	Latchford	McGrain	McCluskey	MacDonald	McNeill	Lynch	Wilson	Murray	Dalglish	Glavin 1	Lennox	(Burns)
Apr 26	St Johnstone	1-2	Latchford	McGrain	Lynch	Murray	McNeill	MacDonald	Johnstone	Glavin 1	Deans	Callaghan	Dalglish	(Hood, Lennox)

LEAGUE CUP 1974

Aug 10	MOTHERWELL	2-1	Connaghan	McCluskey	Brogan	Murray	McNeill	Callaghan	Johnstone	Hood	Dalglish 1	Wilson	Lennox	(Bone)
Aug 14	Ayr United	2-3	Hunter	McGrain	McCluskey	Murray 1	McNeill	Connelly 1	Johnstone	Hood	Wilson	Callaghan	Lennox	(McNamara, Dalglish)
Aug 17	DUNDEE UNITED	1-0	Connaghan	McCluskey	Brogan	McNamara 1	McNeill	Connelly	Johnstone	Murray	Deans	Callaghan	Wilson	(Hood)
Aug 21	AYR UNITED	5-2	Connaghan	McGrain	McCluskey	Connelly	McNeill	Callaghan	Johnstone 2	Murray	Wilson 2	Dalglish	Lennox 1	(Hood, McNamara)
Aug 24	Dundee United	1-0	Connaghan	McGrain	McCluskey	Connelly	McNeill	Callaghan	Johnstone	Murray	Wilson 1	Dalglish	Lennox	
Aug 28	Motherwell	2-2	Connaghan	McNamara	Brogan	McCluskey	MacDonald	Connelly	Hood	Dalglish 2	Bone	Davidson	Wilson	
Sept 11	HAMILTON ACADEMICALS	2-0	Connaghan	McGrain	Brogan	McCluskey	McNeill	Callaghan	Johnstone	Murray	Hood 2	Davidson	Wilson	(Lennox)
Sept 25	Hamilton Academicals	4-2	Hunter	McGrain	Brogan	McNamara 1	McNeill	McCluskey	Dalglish	Bone	Deans 1	Callaghan 1	Wilson	(Lennox 1)
Oct 9	Airdrie (N)	1-0 SF	Hunter	McGrain	Brogan	McNamara	McNeill	McCluskey	Hood	Murray 1	Deans	Dalglish	Wilson	(Lennox)
Oct 26	Hibernian (N)	6-3 F	Hunter	McGrain	Brogan	Murray 1	McNeill	McCluskey	Johnstone 1	Hood	Deans 3	Dalglish	Wilson 1	

EUROPEAN CUP 1974-75

Sept 18	OLYMPIAKOS	1-1	Connaghan	McGrain	Brogan	Murray	McNeill	McCluskey	Johnstone	Hood	Dalglish	Callaghan	Wilson 1	(Lennox)
Oct 2	Olympiakos	0-2	Connaghan	McGrain	Brogan	Murray	McNeill	McCluskey	Johnstone	Dalglish	Deans	Callaghan	Wilson	(Lennox, Hood)

SCOTTISH CUP 1975

Jan 25	Hibernian	2-0	Hunter	McGrain	Brogan	Murray 1	McNeill	Connelly	Hood	Dalglish	Deans 1	Callaghan	Wilson	(Glavin)
Feb 15	CLYDEBANK	4-1	Barclay	McGrain	McCluskey	Murray	MacDonald 1	Connelly	Hood	McNamara 1	Deans	Dalglish 2	Wilson	
Mar 8	Dumbarton	2-1	Latchford	McGrain	McCluskey	MacDonald	McNeill	Callaghan	Hood	Glavin 1	Lynch	Dalglish	Wilson 1	
Apr 2	Dundee (N)	1-0 SF	Latchford	McGrain	McCluskey	Connelly	McNeill	Callaghan	Hood	Glavin 1	Dalglish	Lennox	Wilson	
May 3	Airdrie (N)	3-1 F	Latchford	McGrain	Lynch	Murray	McNeill	McCluskey 1	Hood	Glavin	Dalglish	Lennox	Wilson 2	

SCOTTISH LEAGUE 1975-76

Aug 30	Rangers	1-2	Latchford	McGrain	Lynch	P McCluskey	MacDonald	Edvaldsson	McNamara	Wilson	Dalglish 1	Callaghan	Lennox	(Connelly, Ritchie)
Sept 6	DUNDEE	4-0	Latchford	McGrain	Lynch	P McCluskey	Edvaldsson	McNamara 1	Glavin	Wilson	Dalglish	Callaghan	Lennox 3	(Connelly)
Sept 13	Motherwell	1-1	Latchford	McGrain	Lynch	Connelly	MacDonald	Edvaldsson	Wilson	McNamara	Dalglish 1	Callaghan	Lennox	(Hood)
Sept 20	St Johnstone	2-1	Lachford	McGrain	Lynch	P McCluskey 2	MacDonald	Edvaldsson	Wilson	Dalglish	Deans	Callaghan	Lennox	(Hood)
Sept 27	DUNDEE UNITED	2-1	Latchford	McGrain	Lynch	P McCluskey	MacDonald 1	Edvaldsson	Wilson	Glavin	Dalglish 1	Callaghan	Lennox	(Hood)
Oct 4	HEARTS	3-1	Latchford	McGrain	Lynch	P McCluskey	MacDonald	Edvaldsson	Wilson 1	Dalglish	Deans 1	Callaghan	Hood 1	(Lennox)
Oct 11	Aberdeen	2-1	Latchford	McGrain	Lynch	P McCluskey	MacDonald	Edvaldsson	Wilson	Dalglish 1	Deans 1	Callaghan	Hood	(Lennox, Ritchie)
Nov 1	RANGERS	1-1	Latchford	McGrain	Lynch	P McCluskey	MacDonald	Edvaldsson	G McCluskey	Dalglish	Deans	Callaghan	Wilson 1	(Hood)

			1	2	3	4	5	6	7	8	9	10	11	SUBS
Nov 8	Dundee	0-1	Latchford	McGrain	Lynch	P McCluskey	MacDonald	Edvaldsson	Hood	Dalglish	Deans	McNamara	Lennox	(G McCluskey)
Nov 12	Ayr United	7-2	Latchford	McGrain	Lynch	P McCluskey	MacDonald 1	Edvaldsson 3	Wilson	Dalgihsh 1	Deans 2	McNamara	Callaghan	
Nov 15	MOTHERWELL	0-2	Latchford	McGrain	Lynch	P McCluskey	MacDonald	Edvaldsson	Wilson	Dalglish	Deans	McNamara	Callaghan	(Lennox)
Nov 22	ST JOHNSTONE	3-2	Latchford	McGrain	Lynch	P McCluskey	MacDonald	Edvaldsson	G McCluskey	Dalglish 1	Deans	Callaghan	Lennox 2	
Nov 29	Dundee United	3-1	Latchford	McGrain	Lynch 1	P McCluskey	MacDonald	Edvaldsson	Wilson	Dalglish	Deans 1	Callaghan	Lennox 1	
Dec 6	Hearts	1-0	Latchford	McGrain	Lynch	P McCluskey	MacDonald	Edbaldsson	Hood	Dalglish	Deans 1	Callaghan	Lennox	(Wilson)
Dec 10	HIBERNIAN	1-1	Latchford	McGrain	Lynch	P McCluskey	MacDonald	Edbaldsson	Hood	Dalglish	Deans 1	Callaghan	Lennox	(McNamara)
Dec 13	ABERDEEN	0-2	Latchford	McGrain	Lynch	P McCluskey	MacDonadl	Edvaldsson	Wilson	Dalglish	Deans	Callaghan	Lennox	(Hood)
Dec 20	Hibernian	3-1	Latchford	McGrain	Lynch	Edvaldsson 1	MacDonald	P McCluskey	McNamara 1	Dalglish	Deans 1	Callaghan	Lennox	
Dec 27	AYR UNITED	3-1	Latchford	McGrain	Lynch	Edvaldsson 2	MacDonald	P McCluskey	McNamara	Dalglish 1	Deans	Callaghan	Lennox	
Jan 1	Rangers	0-1	Latchford	McGrain	Lynch	Edvaldsson	MacDonald	P McCluskey	McNamara	Dalglish	Deans	Callaghan	Lennox	
Jan 3	DUNDEE	3-3	Latchford	McGrain	Lynch	Edvaldsson	MacDonald	P McCluskey	McNamara	Dalglish 2	Deans 1	Callaghan	Wilson	
Jan 10	Motherwell	3-1	Latchford	McGrain	P McCluskey	Edvaldsson	MacDonald	Lynch	Glavin	Murray	Deans 2	Dalglish 1	Lennox	
Jan 17	St Johnstone	4-3	Latchford	McGrain	P McCluskey	Edvaldsson 1	MacDonald 1	Lynch	Glavin	Murray	Deans 1	Dalglish 1	Lennox	
Jan 31	DUNDEE UNITED	2-1	Hunter	McGrain	Lynch	Ritchie	Edvaldsson	P McCluskey	Wilson 1	Dalglish 1	Deans	McNamara	Callaghan	(Hood)
Feb 7	HEARTS	2-0	Latchford	McGrain	Lynch	P McCluskey	Edvaldsson	Casey	Ritchie	Glavin	Deans	Dalglish 2	Wilson	
Feb 21	Aberdeen	1-0	Latchford	McGrain	Lynch	P McCluskey	Aitken	Edvaldsson	Ritchie	Dalglish	Deans	Glavin	Wilson	(Lennox 1)
Feb 28	HIBERNIAN	4-0	Latchford	McGrain	Lynch	P McCluskey	Aitken	Edvaldsson	Wilson 1	Dalglish 1	Deans 1	Glavin	Lennox 1	
Mar 20	Dundee	1-0	Latchford	McGrain	Lynch	P McCluskey	Aitken	Edvaldsson	Doyle	Dalglish 1	MacDonald	McNamara	Hood	(Wilson)
Mar 27	MOTHERWELL	4-0	Latchford	McGrain	Lynch	P McCluskey	Aitken	Edvaldsson	Deans 1	McNamara	MacDonald	Dalglish 2	Lennox 1	(Wilson)
Apr 3	ST JOHNSTONE	1-0	Latchford	McGrain	Lynch	P McCluskey	Aitken	Edvaldsson	McNamara	Deans	MacDonald	Dalglish 1	Lennox	(Wilson)
Apr 10	Dundee United	2-3	Latchford	McGrain	Lynch	P McCluskey	Aitken	Edvaldsson	Hood	Dalglish 2	Deans	Glavin	Lennox	
Apr 17	ABERDEEN	1-1	Latchford	McGrain	Edvaldsson	Glavin	Aitken	Callaghan	Doyle	Dalglish 1	Deans	Burns	Lennox	(Wilson, Ritchie)
Apr 21	Hibernian	0-2	Latchford	McGrain	Lynch	P McCluskey	Aitken	Edvaldsson	Wilson	Dalglish	Deans	Glavin	Lennox	
Apr 24	AYR UNITED	1-2	Larchford	McGrain	Lynch	P McCluskey	Aitken	Edvaldsson	Doyle	McNamara	Deans 1	Dalglish	Burns	
Apr 26	RANGERS	0-0	Latchford	McGrain	Lynch	P McCluskey	Aitken	Edvaldsson	Doyle	Dalglish	MacDonald	Burns	Lennox	(McNamara)
May 1	Ayr United	5-3	Latchford	McGrain	Lynch	P McCluskey 1	Aitken	MacDonald	Doyle	Dalglish 2	Ritchie 1	Burns	Lennox 1	(Hannah)
May 3	Hearts	0-1	Latchford	P McCluskey	Callaghan	McNamara	Aitken	MacDonald	Lennox	Ritchie	Deans	Edvaldsson	Burns	(Wilson, Hannah)

LEAGUE CUP 1975

			1	2	3	4	5	6	7	8	9	10	11	SUBS
Aug 9	ABERDEEN	1-0	Latchford	McGrain	Lynch	P McCluskey	MacDonald	Edvaldsson	Hood	Dalglish 1	Wilson	Glavin	Lennox	(McNamara)
Aug 13	Hearts	0-2	Latchford	McGrain	Lynch	P McCluskey	MacDonald	Edvaldsson	Hood	Dalglish	Wilson	Glavin	Lennox	(McNamara)
Aug 16	DUMBARTON	3-1	Latchford	McGrain	Lynch	P McCluskey	MacDonald	Edvaldsson 1	McNamara	Dalglish	Wilson 1	Glavin	Lennox 1	(Hood)
Aug 20	HEARTS	3-1	Latchford	McGrain	Lynch 1	P McCluskey	MacDonald	Edvaldsson 1	Glavin 1	Wilson	Dalglish	McNamara	Hood	
Aug 23	Dumbarton	8-0	Latchford	McGrain 1	Lynch	P McCluskey	MacDonald	Edvaldsson	Glavin	Wilson 2	Dalglish 2	McNamara	Hood 2	(Callaghan 1)
Aug 27	Aberdeen	2-0	Latchford	McGrain	Lynch	P McCluskey	MacDonald	Edvaldsson	McNamara	Wilson	Dalglish	Callaghan	Lennox 1	(Connelly, Ritchie 1)
Sept 10	Stenhousemuir	2-0	Latchford	McGrain	Lynch	McNamara	Edvaldsson	Connelly	Wilson	Dalglish 1	Deans	Glavin	Lennox 1	
Sept 24	STENHOUSEMUIR	1-0	Latchford	Aitken	Lynch 1	Edvaldsson	MacDonald	P McCluskey	Dalglish	McNamara	Deans	Glavin	Lennox	(Hood, Casey)
Oct 7	Partick Thistle (N)	1-0 SF	Latchford	McGrain	Lynch	P McCluskey	MacDonald	Edvaldsson 1	Wilson	Dalglish	Deans	Callaghan	Hood	
Oct 25	Rangers (N)	0-1 F	Latchford	McGrain	Lynch	P McCluskey	MacDonald	Edvaldsson	Hood	Dalglish	Wilson	Callaghan	Lennox	(McNamara, Gavin)

SCOTTISH CUP 1976

			1	2	3	4	5	6	7	8	9	10	11	SUBS
Jan 24	Motherwell	2-3	Latchford	McGrain	Lynch 1	P McCluskey	MacDonald	Edvaldsson	McNamara	Glavin	Deans	Dalglish 1	Lennox	

EUROPEAN CUP-WINNERS' CUP 1975-76

			1	2	3	4	5	6	7	8	9	10	11	SUBS
Sept 16	Valur	2-0	Latchford	McGrain	Lynch	P McCluskey	MacDonald 1	Edvaldsson	Hood	McNamara	Dalglish	Callaghan	Wilson 1	
Oct 1	VALUR	7-0	Latchford	McGrain	Lynch	P McCluskey 1	MacDonald	Edvaldsson 1	Wilson	Dalglish 1	Deans 1	Callaghan 1	Hood 2	(Casey, G McCluskey)
Oct 22	Boavista	0-0	Latchford	McGrain	Lynch	P McCluskey	MacDonald	Edvaldsson	Callaghan	McNamara	Wilson	Hood	Lennox	
Nov 5	BOAVISTA	3-1	Latchford	McGrain	Lynch	P McCluskey	MacDonald	Edvaldsson 1	G McCluskey	Dalglish 1	Deans 1	McNamara	Callaghan	(Lennox)
Mar 3	SACHSENRING ZWICKAU	1-1	Latchford	McGrain	Lynch	P McCluskey	Aitken	Edvaldsson	Wilson	Dalglish	Deans	Hood	Lennox	
Mar 17	Sachsenring Zwickau	0-1	Latchford	McGrain	Callaghan	MacDonald	Aitken	P McCluskey	Wilson	Dalglish	Edvaldsson	Glavin	Hood	(McNamara, Casey)

SCOTTISH LEAGUE 1976-77

			1	2	3	4	5	6	7	8	9	10	11	SUBS
Sept 4	RANGERS	2-2	Latchford	McGrain	Lynch	Stanton	MacDonald	P McCluskey	Doyle	Glavin	Wilson 2	Burns	Dalglish	
Sept 11	Dundee United	0-1	Latchford	McGrain	Lynch	Stanton	MacDonald	P McCluskey	Doyle	Glavin	Wilson	Burns	Dalglish	
Sept 18	HEARTS	2-2	Latchford	McGrain	Lynch	Glavin 1	Aitken	Stanton	Doyle	Dalglish	Craig	Burns	Wilson	(G McCluskey 1)
Sept 25	Kilmarnock	4-0	Latchford	McGrain	Lynch	Stanton	MAcDonald 1	Aitken	Dalglish 1	Glavin	Craig 1	Burns	Doyle 1	(Wilson, Callaghan)
Oct 2	HIBERNIAN	1-1	Latchford	McGrain	Lynch	Stanton	MacDonald	Aitken	Dalglish 1	Glavin	Craig	Burns	Doyle	(Wilson)
Oct 16	Ayr United	2-0	Latchford	McGrain	Lynch	Stanton	MacDonald	Aitken	Doyle	Glavin 1	Craig 1	Dalglish	Wilson	
Oct 20	DUNDEE UNITED	5-1	Latchford	McGrain	Lynch	Stanton	MacDonald	Aitken	Doyle	Glavin 3	Craig 1	Dalglish	Wilson	(Burns, Lennox 1)
Oct 23	Aberdeen	1-2	Latchford	McGrain	Lynch	Stanton	MacDonald	Aitken	Doyle	Glavin	Craig	Dalglish 1	Wilson	
Oct 30	MOTHERWELL	2-0	Latchford	McGrain	Lynch	Stanton	MacDonald	Aitken	Doyle	Glavin	Craig	Dalglish 2	Wilson	
Nov 20	Hearts	4-3	Latchford	McGrain	Lynch	Stanton	MacDonald 1	Aitken	Doyle	Glavin 1	Craig	Dalglish 1	Lennox 1	
Nov 24	Rangers	1-0	Latchford	McGrain	Lynch	Stanton	MacDonald	Aitken	Doyle	Glavin	Craig 1	Dalglish	Lennox	(Wilson)
Nov 27	KILMARNOCK	2-1	Latchford	McGrain	Lynch	Stanton	MacDonald	Aitken	Doyle	Glavin	Craig 1	Dalglish	Wilson 1	
Dec 18	AYR UNITED	3-0	Latchford	McGrain	Lynch	Stanton	MacDonald	Aitken	Doyle 1	Glavin	Craig	Dalglish 1	Wilson 1	(Edvaldsson, Gibson)
Dec 26	ABERDEEN	2-2	Latchford	McGrain	Burns	Stanton	MacDonald	Aitken	Doyle	Glavin	Craig 2	Dalglish	Wilson	
Jan 8	Dundee United	2-1	Latchford	McGrain	Lynch	Stanton	MacDonald	Aitken	Doyle 1	Glavin	Craig	Dalglish 1	Wilson	
Jan 11	RANGERS	1-0	Latchford	McGrain	Lynch	Stanton	MacDonald	Aitken	Doyle	Glavin	Craig	Dalglish	Wilson	
Jan 22	Kilmarnock	3-1	Latchford	McGrain	Lynch	Stanton	MacDonald	Aitken	Doyle	Glavin 2	Craig	Dalglish	Wilson 1	(P McCluskey, Gibson)
Feb 5	HIBERNIAN	4-2	Latchford	McGrain	Lynch	Stanton	MacDonald	Aitken	Doyle	Glavin 2	Craig 1	Dalglish	Wilson	(Edvaldsson 1)
Feb 7	HEARTS	5-1	Latchford	McGrain	Lynch 1	Stanton	Edvaldsson 1	Aitken	Doyle	Glavin 1	Craig 1	Dalglish	Wilson	
Feb 12	PARTICK THISTLE	2-0	Latchford	McGrain	Lynch	Stanton	Edvaldsson	Aitken	Doyle	Glavin 1	Craig	Dalglish 1	Wilson	(P McCluskey)
Feb 19	Ayr United	4-2	Latchford	McGrain	Lynch 1	Stanton	Edvaldsson	Aitken	Doyle	Glavin	Craig 1	Dalglish 2	Wilson	(Burns)
Feb 22	Partick Thistle	4-2	Latchford	McGrain	Lynch	Stanton	Edvaldsson	Aitken 1	Doyle	Glavin 1	Craig 1	Dalglish	Wilson	(P McCluskey, Burns)
Mar 5	Aberdeen	0-2	Latchford	McGrain	Lynch	Stanton	Edvaldsson	P McCluskey	Doyle	Glavin	Craig	Aitken	Dalglish	(Conn)
Mar 9	PARTICK THISTLE	2-1	Latchford	McGrain	Burns	Stanton	Edvaldsson	Aitken	Doyle 1	Glavin	Craig	Dalglish	Conn 1	
Mar 16	MOTHERWELL	2-2	Latchford	McGrain	Lynch	Stanton	Edvaldsson 1	Aitken	Doyle	Glavin 1	Craig	Dalglish	Conn	
Mar 19	Rangers	2-2	Latchford	McGrain	Burns	Stanton	Edvaldsson	Aitken 2	Doyle	Glavin	Craig	Dalglish	Conn	
Mar 26	DUNDEE UNITED	2-0	Baines	McGrain	Burns	Stanton	Edvaldsson	Aitken	Doyle	Glavin 1	Craig 1	Dalglish	Conn	
Mar 30	Hibernian	1-1	Baines	McGrain	Burns	Stanton	Edvaldsson	P McCluskey	Gibson	Glavin 1	Craig	Dalglish	Conn	
Apr 2	Hearts	3-0	Baines	McGrain	Lynch	Stanton	MacDonald	Aitken 1	Doyle	Glavin 1	Craig 1	Dalglish	Conn	(Edvaldsson)
Apr 9	KILMARNOCK	1-0	Baines	McGrain	Lynch	Stanton	MacDonald	Aitken	Doyle	Glavin	Craig	Edvaldsson	Conn	(Burns, Wilson)
Apr 13	Motherwell	0-3	Baines	McGrain	Lynch	Stanton	Edvaldsson	Aitken	Conn	Glavin	Craig	Dalglish	Burns	
Apr 16	Hibernian	1-0	Latchford	McGrain	Lynch	Stanton	MacDonald	Aitken	Doyle	Glavin	Craig 1	Dalglish	Conn	(Burns)
Apr 20	ABERDEEN	4-1	Latchford	McGrain	Lynch	Stanton	MacDonald	Aitken	Doyle	Glavin 1	Craig 1	Dalglish 1	Conn 1	
Apr 23	Partick Thistle	1-1	Latchford	McGrain	Lynch	Stanton	MacDonald	Aitken 1	Doyle	Glavin	Craig	Dalglish	Conn	(Burns, Wilson)
Apr 30	AYR UNITED	2-0	Latchford	McGrain	Lynch	Stanton	MacDonald	Aitken	Doyle	Dalglish 1	Craig	Burns	Conn	(Edvaldsson 1)
May 10	Motherwell	2-2	Latchford	McGrain	Burns 1	Stanton	MacDonald	Aitken	Dalglish 1	Edvaldsson	Craig	Conn	Wilson	

LEAGUE CUP 1976

			1	2	3	4	5	6	7	8	9	10	11	SUBS
Aug 14	Dundee United	1-0	Latchford	McGrain	Lynch	P McCluskey	MacDonald	Edvaldsson	Doyle	Glavin	G McCluskey	Burns	Dalglish 1	(Wilson)
Aug 18	DUMBARTON	3-0	Latchford	McGrain	Lynch	P McCluskey	MacDonald	Edvaldsson	Doyle 1	Glavin	G McCluskey	Dalglish 2	Wilson	(Lennox, Hannah)
Aug 21	Arbroath	5-0	Lachford	McGrain 1	Lynch	P McCluskey	MacDonald	Edvaldsson 1	Doyle	Glavin 1	Dalglish 1	Burns	Wilson 1	(G McCluskey, Lennox)
Aug 25	Dumbarton	3-3	Latchford	McGrain	Lynch	P McCluskey	MacDonald 1	Edvaldsson	Doyle 4	Glavin	Dalglish	Burns	Wilson 1	
Aug 28	ARBROATH	2-1	Latchford	McGrain	Lynch	Edvaldsson	MacDonald	Aitken	Doyle 1	Glavin	Dalglish	Burns	Wilson 1	(P McCluskey)
Sept 1	DUNDEE UNITED	1-1	Latchford	McGrain	Callaghan	Glavin	MacDonald 1	Aitken	Henderson	Dalglish	Wilson	Burns	Lennox	(P McCluskey)
Sept 22	Albion Rovers	1-0	Connaghan	McGrain	Lynch	Aitken	MacDonald	P McCluskey	Doyle	Glavin	G McCluskey	Callaghan 1	Lennox	(Dalglish)
Oct 6	ALBION ROVERS	5-0	Connaghan	McGrain	Lynch	Edvaldsson	MacDonald	Callaghan	Doyle 2	Glavin	Wilson	Dalglish 3	Lennox	
Oct 25	Hearts (N)	2-1 SF	Latchford	McGrain	Lynch	Edvaldsson	MacDonald	Aitken	Doyle	Glavin	Dalglish 2	Callaghan	Wilson	
Nov 6	Aberdeen (N)	1-2 F	Latchford	McGrain	Lynch	Edvaldsson	MacDonald	Aitken	Doyle	Glavin	Dalglish 1	Burns	Wilson	(Lennox)

SCOTTISH CUP 1977

			1	2	3	4	5	6	7	8	9	10	11	SUBS
Jan 29	Airdrie	1-1	Latchford	McGrain	Lynch	Stanton	MacDonald	Aitken	Doyle 1	Glavin	Craig	Dalglish	Wilson	(Burns)
Feb 2	AIRDRIE	5-0	Latchford	McGrain	Lynch	Stanton	MacDonald	Aitken	Doyle	Glavin 1	Craig 4	Dalglish	Wilson	(Burns, McLaughlin)
Feb 27	AYR UNITED	1-1	Latchford	McGrain	Lynch	Stanton	MacDonald	Aitken	Doyle	Glavin 1	Criag	Dalglish	Wilson	(Edvaldsson)
Mar 2	Ayr United	3-1	Latchford	McGrain	Lynch	Stanton	Edvaldsson	P McCluskey	Doyle 1	Glavin 1	Craig	Aitken 1	Dalglish	
Mar 13	QUEEN OF THE SOUTH	5-1	Latchford	McGrain	Burns	Stanton	Edvaldsson	Aitken	Doyle	Glavin 3	Craig 1	Dalglish 1	Wilson	(Gibson, Casey)
Apr 6	Dundee (N)	2-0 SF	Baines	McGrain	Lynch	Stanton	MacDonald	Aitken	Doyle	Glavin	Craig 2	Dalglish	Conn	
May 7	Rangers (N)	1-0 F	Latchford	McGrain	Lynch 1	Stanton	MacDonald	Aitken	Dalglish	Edvaldsson	Craig	Conn	Wilson	

UEFA CUP 1976-77

Sept 15	WISLA KRAKOW	2-2	Latchford	McGrain	Lynch	Glavin	MacDonald 1	Edvaldsson	Doyle	Dalglish 1	Wilson	Burns	Lennox	
Sept 29	Wisla Krakow	0-2	Latchford	McGrain	Lynch	Edvaldsson	MacDonald	P McCluskey	Doyle	Glavin	Dalglish	Aitken	Wilson	

SCOTTISH LEAGUE 1977-78

Aug 13	DUNDEE UNITED	0-0	Latchford	McGrain	Lynch	Stanton	MacDonald	Aitken	Glavin	Edvaldsson	Craig	Burns	Conn	(Doyle, Lennox)
Aug 20	Ayr United	1-2	Latchford	McGrain	Kay	Aitken	MacDonald	Burns	Glavin	Edvaldsson	Craig 1	Lennox	Wilson	(Doyle, Casey)
Aug 27	MOTHERWELL	0-1	Latchford	McGrain	Kay	Casey	MacDonald	Aitken	Glavin	Edvaldsson	Craig	Burns	Doyle	
Sept 10	Rangers	2-3	Latchford	McGrain	Lynch	Edvaldsson 2	MacDonald	Casey	Doyle	Dowie	Glavin	Burns	Wilson	(Lennox, McAdam)
Sept 17	Aberdeen	1-2	Latchford	McGrain	Lynch	Edvaldsson	MacDonald	McWilliams	Doyle	McAdam	Craig	Aitken	Wilson	(Doyle)
Sept 24	CLYDEBANK	1-0	Latchford	McGrain	Lynch	Edvaldsson	MacDonald	Aitken	Doyle	Glavin	McAdam 1	Burns	Wilson	(Dowie)
Oct 1	HIBERNIAN	3-1	Lachford	McGrain	Kay	Edvaldsson 1	MacDonald	Aitken	Glavin 1	Wilson	Craig 1	McAdam	Burns	
Oct 8	Partick Thistle	0-1	Latchford	Kay	Lynch	Glavin	MacDonald	Aitken	McLaughlin	McAdam	Craig	Burns	Wilson	(Edvaldsson)
Oct 15	ST MIRREN	1-2	Latchford	Kay	Burns	Edvaldsson	MacDonald	Munro	Wilson	McAdam 1	Glavin	Aitken	Conn	
Oct 22	Dundee United	2-1	Latchford	Aitken	Lynch	Glavin 1	MacDonald	Munro	Doyle	McAdam	Craig	Burns	Wilson 1	(Edvaldsson)
Oct 29	AYR UNITED	3-2	Latchford	Aitken	Lynch	Glavin 1	MacDonald 1	Munro	Doyle	Edvaldsson	McAdam 1	Burns	Wilson	
Nov 5	Motherwell	3-2	Latchford	Filippi	Lynch	Aitken	MacDonald 1	Munro	Doyle	McAdam	Craig 2	Burns	Wilson	
Nov 12	RANGERS	1-1	Latchford	Filippi	Lynch	Edvaldsson	MacDonald	Aitken	Doyle	Glavin	Craig	McAdam 1	Conn	(Wilson)
Nov 20	ABERDEEN	3-2	Latchford	Filippi	Lynch 1	Aitken 1	MacDonald	Munro	Doyle	Edvaldsson 1	Craig	McAdam	Conn	(Wilson)
Dec 10	PARTICK THISTLE	3-0	Latchford	Filippi	Lynch 1	Aitken	MacDonald	Munro	Doyle	Edvaldsson	McAdam 1	Craig	Conn	
Dec 17	St Mirren	3-3	Latchford	Filippi	Lynch 1	Edvaldsson	MacDonald	Aitken	Doyle	Glavin	McAdam 1	Craig 1	Burns	(Wilson, Dowie)
Dec 24	DUNDEE UNITED	1-0	Latchford	Filippi	Lynch	Aitken	MacDonald	Dowie	Doyle	Edvaldsson 1	McAdam	Craig	Conn	(Wilson)
Dec 31	Ayr United	1-2	Latchford	Filippi	Lynch	Aitken	MacDonald	Munro	Doyle	Edvaldsson 1	McAdam	Craig	Conn	(G McCluskey)
Jan 2	MOTHERWELL	0-1	Latchford	Filippi	Lynch	Glavin	MacDonald	Munro	Doyle	Edvaldsson	McAdam	Aitken	Wilson	(G McCluskey)
Jan 7	Rangers	1-3	Latchford	Filippi	Lynch	Aitken	MacDonald	Munro	Glavin	Edvaldsson 1	Craig	McAdam	Wilson	
Jan 14	Aberdeen	1-2	Latchford	Filippi	Lynch	Aitken	MacDonald 1	Munro	Glavin	Edvaldsson	G McCluskey	McAdam	Wilson	(Burns)
Feb 25	ST MIRREN	1-2	Latchford	Sneddon	Burns	Munro	MacDonald	Filippi	Edvaldsson	McAdam	McCluskey 1	Aitken	Conn	(Wilson, Casey)
Mar 4	Dundee United	1-0	Latchford	Sneddon	Dowie	Munro	MacDonald	Aitken	Edvaldsson	Craig	McCluskey	Burns	McAdam	(Filippi)
Mar 11	AYR UNITED	3-0	Latchford	Sneddon	Dowie	Munro	MacDonald	Aitken	Glavin 1	Edvaldsson 1	McCluskey	McAdam	Burns	
Mar 22	Motherwell	1-2	Latchford	Sneddon	Lynch	Munro	MacDonald	Aitken	Glavin	Edvaldsson	Craig 1	Dowie	McAdam	(Burns, Doyle)
Mar 25	RANGERS	2-0	Latchford	Sneddon	Lynch	Aitken	MacDonald 1	Dowie	Glavin 1	Edvaldsson	McAdam	Burns	Doyle	
Mar 29	Partick Thistle	4-0	Latchford	Sneddon	Lynch	Aitken	MacDonald 1	Dowie	Glavin	Edvaldsson	McAdam 1	Burns 2	Doyle	(Craig, Wilson)
Apr 1	ABERDEEN	2-2	Latchford	Sneddon	Lynch	Aitken	MacDonald	Dowie	Glavin 1	Edvaldsson 1	McAdam	Burns	Doyle	(McCluskey)
Apr 5	HIBERNIAN	2-1	Latchford	Sneddon	Aitken	Dowie	MacDonald	Burns	Glavin	Edvaldsson	McCluskey 2	McAdam	Doyle	
Apr 8	Clydebank	2-3	Latchford	Sneddon	Lynch	Aitken	MacDonald	Dowie	Glavin	Edvaldsson	McAdam	McCluskey 1	Burns 1	
Apr 12	Hibernian	1-1	Latchford	Sneddon	Burns	Aitken	MacDonald	Dowie	Glavin	Edvaldsson	McCluskey 1	McAdam	Doyle	
Apr 15	Hibernian	1-4	Latchford	Sneddon	Burns	Aitken	MacDonald	Dowie	Conroy 1	Edvaldsson	McCluskey	McAdam	Wilson	
Apr 17	CLYDEBANK	5-2	Latchford	Sneddon	Lynch	Aitken 1	MacDonald 1	Burns	Glavin 1	Edvaldsson 1	McAdam 1	Conroy	McCluskey	(Coyne)
Apr 22	PARTICK THISTLE	5-2	Latchford	Sneddon	Lynch	Edvaldsson	MacDonald	Conroy	McCluskey	Glavin 1	Craig 2	McAdam	Doyle 2	
Apr 26	Clydebank	1-1	Latchford	Sneddon	Lynch	Edvaldsson	MacDonald	Conroy 1	McCluskey	Glavin	Craig	McAdam	Doyle	(Mackie)
Apr 29	St Mirren	1-3	Latchford	Sneddon	Lynch	Edvaldsson	MacDonald	Aitken	Glavin 1	Mackie	McAdam	Conroy	McCluskey	(Craig)

LEAGUE CUP 1977

Aug 31	MOTHERWELL	0-0	Latchford	McGrain	Kay	Edvaldsson	MacDonald	Casey	Doyle	Lennox	Glavin	Burns	Wilson	
Sept 3	Motherwell	4-2	Latchford	McGrain	Kay	Edvaldsson	MacDonald	Casey	Doyle	Lennox	Glavin	Burns 1	Wilson 1	(Craig 1)
Oct 5	Stirling Albion	2-1	Latchford	Kay	Burns	Casey	MacDonald	Aitken 1	Doyle 1	Edvaldsson	Glavin	Craig	Lennox	(Dowie, G McCluskey)
Oct 26	STIRLING ALBION	1-1	Latchford	Kay	Lynch	Aitken	MacDonald	Munro	Doyle	Glavin	Craig	Burns	Wilson	(Conn, Mackie)
Nov 9	St Mirren	3-1	Latchford	McWilliams	Lynch	Aitken	MacDonald	Munro	Doyle	Edvaldsson 1	Craig 2	Conn	Wilson	(Glavin, Mackie)
Nov 16	ST MIRREN	2-0	Latchford	Mackie	Lynch	Edvaldsson	MacDonald	Munro	Doyle 1	Wilson 1	Craig	Aitken	Conn	(Lennox, McWilliams)
Mar 1	Hearts (N)	2-0 SF	Latchford	Sneddon	Dowie	Munro	MacDonald	Aitken	Wilson	Craig 1	G McCluskey 1	Burns	Conn	(Doyle)
Mar 18	Rangers (N) (aet)	1-2 F	Latchford	Sneddon	Lynch	Munro	MacDonald	Dowie	Glavin	Edvaldsson 1	G McCluskey	Aitken	Burns	(Doyle, Wilson)

SCOTTISH CUP 1978

Feb 6	DUNDEE	7-1	Latchford	Sneddon	Burns 1	Munro	MacDonald 1	Aitken	Glavin	Edvaldsson	G McCluskey 3	McAdam 2	Conn	
Feb 27	KILMARNOCK	1-1	Latchford	Sneddon	Aitken	Munro	MacDonald 1	Burns	Casey	Edvaldsson	G McCluskey	McAdam	Conn	
Mar 6	Kilmarnock	0-1	Latchford	Sneddon	Dowie	Filippi	MacDonald	Aitken	Edvaldsson	McAdam	G McCluskey	Burns	Wilson	

EUROPEAN CUP 1977-78

Sept 14	JEUNESSE D'ESCH	5-0	Latchford	McGrain	Lynch	Edvaldsson	MacDonald 1	McWilliams	Doyle	Glavin	Craig 2	Aitken	Wilson 1	(McLaughlin 1)
Sept 28	Jeunesse d'Esch	6-1	Latchford	McGrain	Kay	Casey	MacDonald	Aitken	Glavin 2	Wilson	Craig 1	Burns	Lennox	(Edvaldsson 2, J McCluskey)
Oct 19	SSW INNSBRUCK	2-1	Latchford	Aitken	Lynch	Edvaldsson	MacDonald	Casey	Doyle	Glavin	Craig 1	Burns 1	Wilson	(Conn)
Nov 2	SSW Innsbruck	0-3	Latchford	Aitken	Lynch	Glavin	MacDonald	Casey	Doyle	Edvaldsson	Craig	Burns	Wilson	

SCOTTISH LEAGUE 1978-79

Aug 12	Morton	2-1	Latchford	Filippi	Sneddon	Aitken	MacDonald 1	Edvaldsson	Doyle	Glavin 1	McAdam	Burns	Conn	(Casey)
Aug 19	HEARTS	4-0	Latchford	Filippi	Lynch	Aitken	MacDonald	Edvaldsson	Doyle	Glavin	McAdam 1	Burns 1	Conn 2	(Casey, Wilson)
Aug 26	Motherwell	5-1	Latchford	Filippi	Lynch	Aitken 2	MacDonald	Edvaldsson	Doyle	Glavin	McAdam 1	Burns	Conn 2	
Sept 9	RANGERS	3-1	Latchford	Filippi	Lynch	Aitken	MacDonald	Glavin	Doyle	Conroy	McAdam 2	Burns	McCluskey 1	
Sept 16	HIBERNIAN	0-1	Latchford	Filippi	Lynch	Aitken	Edvaldsson	Glavin	Conn	Conroy	McAdam	Burns	McCluskey	(Doyle)
Sept 23	Partick Thistle	3-2	Latchford	Filippi	Lynch 1	Aitken 1	MacDonald 1	Edvaldsson	Provan	Conn	McAdam	Burns	McCluskey	(Conroy)
Sept 30	ST MIRREN	2-1	Latchford	Filippi	Lynch 1	Aitken	Edvaldsson	Glavin	Provan	Conroy	McAdam	Burns	Conn 1	
Oct 7	Aberdeen	1-4	Latchford	Filippi	Sneddon	Aitken	MacDonald	Edvaldsson	Provan	Conroy	McAdam 1	Burns	McCluskey	(Glavin, Lennox)
Oct 14	Dundee United	0-1	Latchford	Filippi	Burns	Aitken	MacDonald	Edvaldsson	Provan	Conroy	McAdam	Conn	Lennox	(McCluskey, Mackie)
Oct 21	MORTON	0-0	Latchford	Filippi	Sneddon	Aitken	MacDonald	Edvaldsson	Provan	Conroy	McAdam	Burns	Lennox	(McCluskey)
Oct 28	Hearts	0-2	Latchford	Filippi	Lynch	Aitken	MacDonald	Edvaldsson	Provan	Conn	McAdam	Burns	McCluskey	(Mackie)
Nov 4	MOTHERWELL	1-2	Baines	Sneddon	Lynch	Aitken	MacDonald	Edvaldsson	Provan	MacLeod	McAdam 1	Burns	Conn	
Nov 11	Rangers *(N)	1-1	Baines	Filippi	Lynch 1	Aitken	MacDonald	Edvaldsson	Provan	MacLeod	McAdam	Burns	Doyle	
Nov 18	Hibernian	2-2	Baines	Filippi	Lynch	Aitken	MacDonald	Edvaldsson	Provan 1	MacLeod 1	McAdam	McCluskey	Doyle	
Nov 25	PARTICK THISTLE	1-0	Baines	Filippi	Lynch	Aitken	MacDonald	Edvaldsson	Provan	MacLeod	McAdam 1	Casey	Doyle	(Casey)
Dec 9	ABERDEEN	0-0	Baines	Filippi	Lynch	Aitken	MacDonald	Edvaldsson	Provan	MacLeod	McAdam	Burns	Doyle	(Conn)
Dec 16	DUNDEE UNITED	1-1	Baines	Filippi	Lynch 1	Aitken	MacDonald	Edvaldsson	Conn	MacLeod	McAdam	Glavin	Doyle	(Lennox)
Dec 23	Morton	0-1	Baines	Filippi	Lynch	Aitken	MacDonald	Edvaldsson	Provan	MacLeod	McAdam	Burns	Conn	(Lennox)
Mar 3	ABERDEEN	1-0	Latchford	McGrain	Lynch	Aitken	MacDonald	Edvaldsson	Provan	MacLeod	McAdam 1	Burns	Doyle	(Filippi)
Mar 17	Motherwell	2-1	Bonner	McGrain	Lynch	Aitken	MacDonald	Edvaldsson	Provan	MacLeod	Lennox 2	Burns	Doyle	(McAdam)
Mar 28	MORTON	3-0	Latchford	McGrain	Filippi	Aitken	MacDonald	Edvaldsson	Provan 1	Glavin 1	Lennox	Burns 1	Doyle	(McCluskey)
Mar 31	Hibernian	1-2	Latchford	McGrain	Filippi	Aitken	Edvaldsson	Conroy	Provan	Glavin 1	Davidson	Burns	Doyle	(McCluskey, Lennox)
Apr 4	Motherwell	4-3	Bonner	McGrain 1	MacLeod	Airken	Edvaldsson	Conroy	Provan	Lennox 1	Davidson 1	Burns	Doyle 1	(McCluskey)
Apr 7	PARTICK THISTLE	2-0	Latchford	McGrain	Lynch 1	Aitken	Edvaldsson	MacLeod	Provan	Conroy 1	Davidson	Burns	Doyle	
Apr 11	Dundee United	1-2	Latchford	McGrain	Lynch	Aitken	Edvaldsson	MacLeod	Provan	Conroy	Davidson 1	Burns	Lennox	(McAdam, McCluskey)
Apr 14	St Mirren	1-0	Latchford	McGrain	Lynch	Aitken	Edvaldsson	MacLeod	Provan	Conroy	Davidson	McAdam	McCluskey 1	
Apr 18	Hearts	3-0	Latchford	McGrain	Lynch	Aitken	Edvaldsson	MacLeod 1	Provan	Conroy 1	McAdam	Davidson	McCluskey	(Burns 1, Doyle)
Apr 21	Aberdeen	1-1	Latchford	McGrain	Lynch 1	Aitken	Edvaldsson	MacLeod	Provan	Conroy	Davidson	Burns	McCluskey	(Doyle, McAdam)
Apr 25	ST MIRREN	2-1	Latchford	McGrain	Lynch	Aitken 1	Edvaldsson 1	MacLeod	Provan	Conroy	Davidson	Burns	Doyle	
Apr 28	DUNDEE UNITED	2-1	Latchford	McGrain	Lynch 1	Aitken 1	Edvaldsson	MacLeod	Provan	Conroy	McCluskey	Burns	Doyle	

			1	2	3	4	5	6	7	8	9	10	11	SUBS
May 2	HIBERNIAN	3-1	Latchford	McGrain 1	MacLeod	Aitken	Edvaldsson	Conroy 1	Provan 1	Davidson	McCluskey	Burns	Doyle	
May 5	Rangers *(N)	0-1	Latchford	McGrain	MacLeod	Aitken	Edvaldsson	Conroy	Provan	Davidson	McCluskey	Burns	Doyle	(McAdam, Lynch)
May 7	Partick Thistle	2-1	Latchfield	McGrain	Lynch	Aitken	McAdam	MacLeod	Provan 1	Conroy	McCluskey 1	Davidson	Doyle	
May 11	St Mirren † (N)	2-0	Latchford	McGrain	Lynch	Aitken	McAdam	MacLeod	Provan	Davidson	McCluskey 1	Burns	Doyle	(Lennox 1, Mackie)
May 14	HEARTS	1-0	Latchford	McGrain	Lynch	Aitken	McAdam	Edvaldsson	Provan	Conroy 1	McCluskey	MacLeod	Doyle +OG	
May 21	RANGERS	4-2	Latchford	McGrain	Lynch	Aitken 1	McAdam	Edvaldsson	Provan	Conroy	McCluskey 1	MacLeod 1	Doyle	(Lennox)

* at Hampden † at Ibrox

LEAGUE CUP 1978

			1	2	3	4	5	6	7	8	9	10	11	SUBS
Aug 17	DUNDEE	3-1	Latchford	Filippi	Sneddon	Aitken	MacDonald	Edvaldsson	Doyle	Glavin 1	McAdam 2	Burns	Conn	
Aug 23	Dundee	3-0	Latchford	Filippi	Lynch	Aitken	MacDonald	Edvaldsson	Doyle 2	Glavin	McAdam	Burns	Conn 1	
Aug 30	Dundee United	3-2	Latchford	Filippi	Lynch	Aitken	MacDonald	Edvaldsson	Doyle	Conroy	McAdam	Burns	Conn	(Wilson)
Sept 2	DUNDEE UNITED	1-0	Latchford	Filippi	Lynch 1	Aitken	MacDonald 1	Edvaldsson	Doyle	Conroy 1	McAdam	Burns	Wilson	(McCluskey)
Oct 3	MOTHERWELL	0-1	Latchford	Filippi	Lynch	Aitken	MacDonald	Edvaldsson	Provan	Conroy	McAdam	Burns	Conn	(Glavin)
Oct 11	Motherwell	4-1	Latchford	Filippi	Burns	Aitken 1	MacDonald	Edvaldsson	Provan	Glavin	McAdam 2	Conroy	Conn	(McCluskey, Lennox 1)
Nov 8	Montrose	1-1	Baines	Filippi	Lynch 1	Aitken	MacDonald	Edvaldsson	Provan	Glavin	McAdam	Burns	McCluskey	(Casey)
Nov 15	MONTROSE	3-1	Baines	McGrain	Lynch 1	Aitken	MacDonald	Edvaldsson 1	Provan	Casey	McAdam 1	Doyle	Lennox	(McCluskey)
Dec 13	Rangers	2-3 SF	Baines	Filippi	Lynch	Aitken	MacDonald	Edvaldsson	Provan	Conroy	McAdam 1	Burns	Doyle 1	(Conn, Casey)

SCOTTISH CUP 1979

			1	2	3	4	5	6	7	8	9	10	11	SUBS
Jan 31	Montrose	4-2	Latchford	McGrain	Lynch 1	Filippi	MacDonald	Edvaldsson	Provan	MacLeod	McCluskey 3	Lennox	Doyle	
Feb 26	BERWICK RANGERS	3-0	Latchford	McGrain	Lynch 1	Aitken	MacDonald	Edvaldsson	Provan	MacLeod	McCluskey	Burns 1	Doyle	
Mar 10	Aberdeen	1-1	Latchford	McGrain	Lynch	Aitken	MacDonald	Edvaldsson	Provan	MacLeod	Conn	Burns	Doyle 1	
Mar 16	ABERDEEN	1-2	Latchford	McGrain	Lynch	Aitken	MacDonald	Edvaldsson	Provan	MacLeod	Conn	Burns	Doyle	(Lennox 1)

SCOTTISH LEAGUE 1979-80

			1	2	3	4	5	6	7	8	9	10	11	SUBS
Aug 11	MORTON	3-2	Latchford	Sneddon	McGrain	Aitken	MacDonald	McAdam	Provan 1	Conroy	McCluskey 1	MacLeod 1	Burns	(Lennox)
Aug 18	Rangers	2-2	Latchford	Sneddon 1	McGrain	Aitken	MacDonald	Edvaldsson	Provan	Conroy	McCluskey	MacLeod	McAdam 1	(Lennox, Doyle)
Aug 25	KILMARNOCK	5-0	Latchford	Sneddon	McGrain	Aitken	MacDonald	McAdam	Provan	Davidson 2	McCluskey 3	MacLeod	Doyle	(Lennox)
Sept 8	DUNDEE UNITED	2-2	Latchford	Sneddon	McGrain	Aitken	McAdam	Conroy	Provan	Davidson	McCluskey 2	MacLeod	Doyle	
Sept 15	Hibernian	3-1	Latchford	Sneddon	McGrain	Aitken	McAdam	Conroy 1	Provan	Davidson	McCluskey	MacLeod 1	Lennox 1	(MacDonald)
Sept 22	Aberdeen	2-1	Latchford	Sneddon	McGrain	Aitken 1	MacDonald	McAdam	Doyle 1	Conroy	Lennox	MacLeod	Burns	
Sept 29	ST MIRREN	3-1	Latchford	Sneddon	McGrain	Aitken	MacDonald 1	McAdam 1	Provan	Davidson	McCluskey	MacLeod 1	Doyle	(Lennox)
Oct 6	Partick Thistle	0-0	Latchford	Sneddon	McGrain	Aitken	Edvaldsson	Conroy	Provan	Davidson	McCluskey	MacLeod	Doyle	(Lennox)
Oct 13	DUNDEE	3-0	Latchford	Sneddon	McGrain	Aitken	MacDonald	McAdam 2	Provan	Doyle	McCluskey	MacLeod 1	Burns	(Lennox)
Oct 20	Morton	0-1	Latchford	Sneddon	Lynch	Aitken	MacDonald	McAdam	Provan	Lennox	McCluskey	MacLeod	Burns	(Conroy)
Oct 27	RANGERS	1-0	Latchford	Sneddon	McGrain	Aitken	MacDonald 1	MacLeod	Provan	Sullivan	McCluskey	Burns	McAdam	(Edvaldsson, Conroy)
Nov 3	Kilmarnock	0-2	Latchford	Sneddon	McGrain	Aitken	MacDonald	MacLeod	Provan	Sullivan	McAdam	Burns	Doyle	
Nov 10	Dundee United	1-0	Latchford	Sneddon	McGrain	Aitken	McAdam	MacLeod	Provan	Sullivan	Edvaldsson 1	Conroy	Lennox	
Nov 17	HIBERNIAN	3-0	Latchford	Sneddon	McGrain	Aitken	McAdam	MacLeod	Provan	Sullivan 1	Edvaldsson 1	Conroy	Lennox 1	
Dec 1	St Mirren	1-2	Latchford	Sneddon	McGrain	Aitken	McAdam	MacLeod	Provan	Sullivan	Edvaldsson	Conroy	McCluskey	(MacDonald 1, Lennox)
Dec 15	PARTICK THISTLE	5-1	Latchford	Sneddon	McGrain	Aitken	MacDonald 1	McAdam 2	Provan	Sullivan 1	McCluskey	MacLeod	Lennox 1	(Conroy)
Dec 22	MORTON	3-1	Latchford	Sneddon	McGrain	Aitken	MacDonald	McAdam 1	Provan	Sullivan 1	McCluskey	MacLeod	Lennox	(Doyle 1)
Dec 29	Rangers	1-1	Latchford	Sneddon	McGrain	Aitken	MacDonald	McAdam	Provan	Sullivan	Lennox 1	MacLeod	Doyle	
Jan 5	DUNDEE UNITED	1-0	Latchford	Sneddon	McGrain	Aitken	MacDonald	McAdam	Provan	Sullivan	Lennox	MacLeod 1	Doyle	(Edvaldsson)
Jan 12	Hibernian	1-1	Latchford	Sneddon	McGrain	Aitken 1	MacDonald	McAdam	Provan	Sullivan	Lennox	MacLeod	Doyle	
Jan 19	Aberdeen	0-0	Latchford	Sneddon	McGrain	Aitken	MacDonald	McAdam	Provan	Sullivan	Lennox	MacLeod	Doyle	
Feb 9	Partick Thistle	1-1	Latchford	Sneddon	McGrain	Aitken	MacDonald	McAdam	Provan	Sullivan	Lennox	MacLeod 1	Doyle	(Conroy)
Feb 23	DUNDEE	2-2	Latchford	Sneddon	McGrain	Aitken	MacDonald	MacLeod 1	Provan	Sullivan 1	Lennox	McCluskey	Doyle	
Mar 1	Morton	1-0	Latchford	Sneddon	McGrain	McAdam	MacDonald	MacLeod	Provan	Lennox	McCluskey	Casey	Doyle 1	
Mar 12	ST MIRREN	2-2	Latchford	Sneddon	McGrain	Aitken	MacDonald	McAdam	Provan	McCluskey 1	McGarvey	MacLeod	Doyle 1	
Mar 15	Kilmarnock	1-1	Latchford	Sneddon	McGrain	Aitken	MacDonald	McAdam	Provan	McCluskey	McGarvey	MacLeod	Doyle	(Lennox 1)
Mar 29	HIBERNIAN	4-0	Latchford	McGrain	MacLeod	Aitken	MacDonald 1	McAdam	Provan	Casey	McGarvey 1	Lennox 1	Doyle 1	(McCluskey, Burns)
Apr 2	RANGERS	1-0	Latchford	Sneddon	McGrain	Aitken	MacDonald	McAdam	Provan	Lennox	McGarvey 1	MacLeod	Doyle	
Apr 5	ABERDEEN	1-2	Latchford	Sneddon	McGrain	Aitken	MacDonald	McAdam	Provan	Doyle 1	McGarvey	MacLeod	Burns	(Lennox)
Apr 9	Dundee United	0-3	Latchford	Sneddon	McGrain	Aitken	MacDonald	McAdam	Provan	McCluskey	McGarvey	MacLeod	Lennox	
Apr 16	KILMARNOCK	2-0	Latchford	Sneddon	MacLeod	Aitken	MacDonald 1	McAdam	Provan	Lennox	McGarvey	Burns	Doyle 1	(McCluskey)
Apr 19	Dundee	1-5	Latchford	Sneddon	McGrain	Aitken 1	MacDonald	McAdam	Provan	Lennox	McGarvey	MacLeod	Doyle	(Burns)
Apr 23	ABERDEEN	1-3	Latchford	McGrain	MacLeod	Aitken	MacDonald	McAdam	Provan	Conroy	McCluskey 1	Burns	Doyle	(McGarvey)
Apr 26	PARTICK THISTLE	2-1	Latchford	McGrain	MacLeod	Aitken	McAdam 1	Conroy	Provan	Sullivan	McCluskey	McGarvey	Burns	
Apr 30	Dundee	2-0	Latchford	McGrain	MacLeod	Aitken	McAdam	Conroy 1	Provan	Sullivan 1	McCluskey	Burns	McGarvey	
May 3	St Mirren	0-0	Latchford	Sneddon	McGrain	Aitken	McAdam	MacLeod	Provan	Conroy	McCluskey	Burns	McGarvey	

LEAGUE CUP 1979

			1	2	3	4	5	6	7	8	9	10	11	SUBS
Aug 29	Falkirk	2-1	Latchford	Sneddon	Lynch	Aitken	MacDonald	McAdam	Provan 1	Davidson	McCluskey 1	MacLeod	Doyle	(Conroy, Lennox)
Sept 1	FALKIRK	4-1	Latchford	Sneddon	McGrain	Aitken	McAdam	Conroy 2	Provan	Davidson	McCluskey	MacLeod	Lennox 1	(Doyle 1)
Sept 26	Stirling Albion	2-1	Latchford	Sneddon	McGrain	Aitken	MacDonald	McAdam 1	McCluskey	Davidson	Lennox	MacLeod	Doyle 1	
Oct 10	STIRLING ALBION	2-0	Latchford	Sneddon	McGrain	Aitken	MacDonald	McAdam	Provan	Davidson	McCluskey	MacLeod 1	Doyle 1	(Lennox)
Oct 31	Aberdeen	2-3	Latchford	Sneddon	McGrain	Edvaldsson 1	MacDonald	Aitken	Provan 1	Conroy	McAdam	MacLeod	Doyle	(Lennox)
Nov 24	ABERDEEN	0-1	Latchford	Sneddon	McGrain	Aitken	MacAdam	MacLeod	Provan	McCluskey	Edvaldsson	Conroy	Lennox	(MacDonald)

SCOTTISH CUP 1980

			1	2	3	4	5	6	7	8	9	10	11	SUBS
Jan 26	RAITH ROVERS	2-1	Latchford	Sneddon	McGrain	Aitken	MacDonald	McAdam	Provan	Edvaldsson	Lennox 1	MacLeod	Doyle 1	(Conroy)
Feb 16	ST MIRREN	1-1	Latchford	Sneddon	McGrain	Aitken	MacDonald	McAdam	Provan	Sullivan	Lennox	MacLeod 1	Doyle	(McCluskey)
Feb 20	St Mirren (aet)	3-2	Latchford	Sneddon	McGrain	Aitken	MacDonald	McAdam	Provan	McCluskey	Lennox 1	MacLeod	Doyle 2	
Mar 8	MORTON	2-0	Latchford	Sneddon	McGrain	Casey 1	MacDonald	McAdam	Provan	McCluskey 1	Lennox	MacLeod	Doyle	
Apr 2	Hibernian (N)	5-0 SF	Latchford	Sneddon	McGrain	Aitken	MacDonald	McAdam 1	Provan 1	Lennox 1	McGarvey	MacLeod 1	Doyle 1	(McCluskey, Burns)
May 10	Ranges (N) (aet)	1-0 F	Latchford	Sneddon	McGrain	Aitken	Conroy	MacLeod	Provan	Doyle	McCluskey 1	Burns	McGarvey	(Lennox)

EUROPEAN CUP 1979-80

			1	2	3	4	5	6	7	8	9	10	11	SUBS
Sept 19	Partizan Tirana	0-1	Latchford	Sneddon	McGrain	Aitken	McAdam	Controy	Provan	Davidson	McCluskey	MacLeod	Lennox	(Doyle)
Oct 3	PARTIZAN TIRANA	4-1	Latchford	Sneddon	McGrain	Aitken 2	MacDonald 1	McAdam	Provan	Davidson 1	McCluskey	MacLeod	Doyle	(Lennox)
Oct 24	DUNDALK	3-2	Latchford	McGrain	Lynch	Aitken	MacDonald 1	McAdam	Provan	Davidson	McCluskey 1	MacLeod	Burns 1	(Lennox)
Nov 7	Dundalk	0-0	Latchford	McGrain	Aitken	McAdam	MacDonald	MacLeod	Provan	Conroy	Edvaldsson	Lennox	Burns	(Davidson)
Mar 5	REAL MADRID	2-0	Latchford	Sneddon	McGrain	Aitken	MacDonald	McAdam	Provan	McCluskey 1	Lennox	MacLeod	Doyle 1	
Mar 19	Real Madrid	0-3	Latchford	Sneddon	McGrain	Aitken	MacDonald	McAdam	Provan	Lennox	McCluskey	MacLeod	Doyle	(Burns)

SCOTTISH LEAGUE 1980-81

			1	2	3	4	5	6	7	8	9	10	11	SUBS
Aug 9	MORTON	2-1	Bonner	Sneddon	McGrain	Aitken	McAdam	Conroy	Provan	Sullivan	McGarvey	MacLeod 1	McCluskey 1	(Burns)
Aug 16	Kilmarnock	3-0	Bonner	Sneddon	McGrain	Aitken	McAdam	MacLeod	Provan	Sullivan 1	McGarvey 2	Burns	McCluskey	(Nicholas)
Aug 23	RANGERS	1-2	Bonner	Sneddon	McGrain	Aitken	McAdam	MacLeod	Provan	Sullivan	McGarvey	Burns 1	McCluskey	
Sept 6	PARTICK THISTLE	4-1	Bonner	Sneddon	McGrain	Aitken	McAdam	MacLeod 1	Provan	Sullivan	McGarvey 1	Burns	Nicholas 2	(McCluskey)
Sept 13	Hearts	2-0	bonner	Sneddon	McGrain	Aitken	McAdam	MacLeod	Provan 1	Sullivan	McCluskey	Burns	Nicholas 1	(Conroy)
Sept 20	AIRDRIE	1-1	Bonner	Sneddon	McGrain	Conroy	McAdam	Weir	Provan	Sullivan	McCluskey	Burns	Nicholas 1	(Doyle)
Sept 27	Aberdeen	2-2	Bonner	Sneddon	McGrain	McAdam	MacDonald	Conroy	Provan	Sullivan	McGarvey	Burns 1	Nicholas 1	(Doyle, MacLeod)
Oct 4	DUNDEE UNITED	2-0	Bonner	Sneddon	McGrain	Conroy	MacDonald	McAdam	McCluskey	Sullivan	McGarvey 1	MacLeod	Nicholas 1	
Oct 11	St Mirren	2-0	Bonner	Sneddon	McGrain	Aitken	MacDonald 1	McAdam	Provan	Sullivan	McGarvey	McCluskey	Nicholas	
Oct 18	Morton	3-2	Bonner	Sneddon	McGrain	Aitken 1	MacDonald	McAdam	Provan 1	Sullivan	McCluskey	Doyle	Nicholas 1	(MacLeod)
Oct 25	KILMARNOCK	4-1	Bonner	Sneddon	McGrain	Aitken	MacDonald	McAdam	Provan	Sullivan	McGarvey 2	Burns	Nicholas 2	
Nov 1	Rangers	0-3	Bonnor	Sneddon	McGrain	Aitken	MacDonald	McAdam	Provan	Sullivan	McGarvey	Burns	Nicholas	(McCluskey, Doyle)
Nov 8	ABERDEEN	0-2	Bonner	Sneddon	McGrain	Aitken	McAdam	Conroy	Provan	Sullivan	McGarvey	Burns	Nicholas	(McCluskey, Doyle)
Nov 15	Airdrie	4-1	Bonner	McGrain	Reid	Aitken 1	McAdam 1	Weir	Provan	McCluskey	McGarvey 1	Burns	Nicholas 1	

			1	2	3	4	5	6	7	8	9	10	11	SUBS
Nov 22	ST MIRREN	1-2	Bonner	McGrain	Reid	Aitken	MacDonald	McAdam	Sullivan	Weir	McGarvey	Burns	Nicholas	(McCluskey 1)
Nov 29	Dundee United	3-0	Bonner	McGrain	Reid	Aitken	MacDonald	McAdam 1	Sullivan	Weir 1	McGarvey	Burns	McCluskey	
Dec 6	Partick Thistle	1-0	Bonner	Sneddon	Reid	Aitken	MacDonald	McAdam	Sullivan	Weir	McGarvey	Burns	McCluskey 1	(Provan)
Dec 13	HEARTS	3-2	Bonner	Sneddon	Reid	Aitken	MacDonald 1	McAdam	Provan	Weir	McGarvey 1	Burns	McCluskey 1	
Dec 20	AIRDRIE	2-1	Bonner	McGrain	Reid	Aitken	MacDonald	McAdam 1	Provan	Weir	McGarvey	Burns	McCluskey 1	
Dec 27	Aberdeen	1-4	Bonner	McGrain	Reid	Aitken	MacDonald	McAdam	Conroy	Weir	McGarvey	Burns	McCluskey	(Provan, Nicholas 1)
Jan 1	Kilmarnock	2-1	Bonner	McGrain	Reid	Sullivan	McAdam	Aitken	Provan	Weir	McGarvey 2	Burns	Nicholas	
Jan 3	MORTON	3-0	Bonner	McGrain	Reid	Sullivan	McAdam	Aitken	Provan 1	Weir	McGarvey 2	Burns	Nicholas	
Jan 10	DUNDEE UNITED	2-1	Bonner	McGrain	Reid	Sullivan	McAdam	Aitken	Provan	Weir	McGarvey 1	Burns	Nicholas 1	
Jan 31	Hearts	3-0	Bonner	McGrain	Reid	Sullivan 1	McAdam	Aitken	Provan	Conroy	McGarvey 1	Burns 1	Nicholas	(McCluskey)
Feb 21	RANGERS	3-1	Bonner	McGrain	Reid	Sullivan	McAdam	Aitken 1	Provan	Conroy	McGarvey	Burns	Nicholas 2	
Feb 28	Morton	3-0	Bonner	McGrain	Reid	Sullivan	McAdam	Aitken	Provan 1	Conroy	McGarvey 2	Burns	Nicholas	
Mar 14	ST MIRREN	7-0	Bonner	McGrain	Reid	Sullivan	McAdam	Aitken 1	Provan	Conroy	McGarvey 3	Burns	Nicholas 1	(MacLeod, McCluskey 2)
Mar 18	PARTICK THISTLE	4-1	Bonner	McGrain	Reid	Sullivan 1	McAdam	Aitken	Provan	Conroy	McGarvey 1	Burns	Nicholas	(MacLeod 2)
Mar 21	Airdrie	2-1	Bonner	McGrain	Reid	Sullivan	McAdam	Aitken	Provan	MacLeod 1	McGarvey 1	Burns	Nicholas	
Mar 28	ABERDEEN	1-1	Bonner	McGrain	Reid	Sullivan	McAdam	Aitken	Provan	MacLeod	McGarvey	Burns	Nicholas	(McCluskey 1)
Apr 1	HEARTS	6-0	Bonner	McGrain	Reid	Sullivan	McAdam	Aitken	Provan 1	MacLeod 2	McGarvey 1	Burns	McCluskey 2	
Apr 5	Partick Thistle	1-0	Bonner	MacLeod	Reid	Sullivan	McAdam 1	Aitken	Provan	Conroy	McGarvey	Burns	McCluskey	(Nicholas)
Apr 18	Rangers	1-0	Bonner	McGrain	MacLeod	MacDonald	McAdam	Aitken	Provan	Conroy	McGarvey	Burns	Nicholas 1	
Apr 22	Dundee United	3-2	Bonner	McGrain	Reid	MacLeod 1	McAdam	Aitken	Provan	Conroy	McGarvey 1	Burns 1	Nicholas	
Apr 25	KILMARNOCK	1-1	Bonner	McGrain	Reid	Sullivan	McAdam	Aitken	Provan 1	MacLeod	McGarvey	Burns	Nicholas	
May 2	St Mirren	1-3	Bonner	McGrain	Reid	Sullivan	MacDonald	Aitken	Provan 1	MacLeod	McGarvey	Burns	Nicholas	

LEAGUE CUP 1980

Aug 27	Stirling Albion	0-1	Bonner	Sneddon	McGrain	Aitken	McAdam	MacLeod	Provan	Sullivan	McGarvey	Burns	McCluskey	(Conroy)
Aug 30	STIRLING ALBION (aet)	6-1	Bonner	Sneddon	McGrain	Aitken	McAdam	MacLeod	Provan 1	Sullivan 1	McGarvey	Burns 2	McCluskey	(Conroy, Nicholas 2)
Sept 22	Hamilton Academicals	3-1	Bonner	Sneddon	McGrain	Aitken	MacDonald	McAdam	Provan	Sullivan	Doyle 1	Burns 1	Nicholas 1	
Sept 24	HAMILTON AC	4-1	Bonner	Sneddon	McGrain	Aitken	MacDonald	McAdam	Provan	Sullivan	Doyle	Burns 1	Nicholas 1	(McGarvey 2)
Oct 8	Partick Thistle	1-0	Bonner	Sneddon	McGrain	Aitken	MacDonald	McAdam	McCluskey	Sullivan	McGarvey	MacLeod	Nicholas 1	
Oct 20	PARTICK THISTLE(aet)	2-1	Bonner	Sneddon	McGrain	Aitken	MacDonald 1	McAdam	Provan	Sullivan	Doyle	Burns 1	Nicholas	(Conroy)
Nov 12	Dundee United	1-1 SF	Bonner	McGrain	Reid	McAdam	MacDonald	Aitken	Provan	Weir	McCluskey	Burns	Doyle	(McGarvey, Nicholas 1)
Nov 19	DUNDEE UNITED	0-3 SFR	Bonner	McGrain	Reid	Aitken	McAdam	Weir	Provan	McCluskey	McGarvey	Burns	Nicholas	(Doyle, MacDonald)

EUROPEAN CUP-WINNERS' CUP 1980-81

Aug 20	DIOSGYOERI MISKOLC	6-0	Bonner	Sneddon	McGrain	Aitken	McAdam	MacLeod	Provan	Sullivan 1	McGarvey 3	Burns	McCluskey 2	(Nicholas, Doyle)
Sept 3	Diosgyoeri Miskolc	1-2	Bonner	Sneddon	McGrain	Aitken	McAdam	MacLeod	Provan	Sullivan	McGarvey	Burns	Nicholas 1	
Sept 17	POLITECHNICA TIMISOARA	2-1	Bonner	Sneddon	McGrain	Aitken	McAdam	MacLeod	Provan	Sullivan	McCluskey	Burns	Nicholas 2	(Conroy, Coyle)
Oct 1	Politechnica Timisoara	0-1	Latchford	Sneddon	McGrain	Aitken	MacDonald	McAdam	Provan	Sullivan	McGarvey	MacLeod	Nicholas	

SCOTTISH CUP 1981

Jan 24	Berwick Rangers	2-0	Bonner	McGrain	Reid	Sullivan	McAdam	Aitken	Provan	Weir	McGarvey	Burns 1	Nicholas 1	
Feb 14	STIRLING ALBION	3-0	Bonner	McGrain	Reid	Sullivan	McAdam	Aitken	Provan	Conroy	McGarvey 1	Burns 1	Nicholas	(McCluskey 1)
Mar 8	EAST STIRLING	2-0	Bonner	McGrain	Reid	Sullivan	McAdam	Aitken	Provan	Conroy 1	McGarvey	Burns	Nicholas	(MacLeod 1)
Apr 11	Dundee United	0-0 SF	Bonner	MacLeod	Reid	Sullivan	McAdam	Aitken	Provan	Conroy	McCluskey	Burns	Nicholas	(Doyle)
Apr 15	Dundee United	2-3 SFR	Bonner	MacLeod	Reid	Sullivan	McAdam	Aitken	Provan	Conroy	McGarvey	Burns	Nicholas 2	(Doyle)

SCOTTISH LEAGUE 1981-82

Aug 29	AIRDRIE	5-2	Bonner	McGrain	Reid	Aitken	Moyes	MacLeod	Provan	Sullivan	McGarvey 1	Burns 1	McCluskey 2	(Nicholas 1, McAdam)
Sept 5	Aberdeen	3-1	Bonner	McGrain	Reid	Aitken	McAdam	MacLeod	Provan	Sullivan	McGarvey 2	Burns 1	McCluskey	
Sept 12	MORTON	2-1	Bonner	McGrain	Reid	Aitken	McAdam 1	MacLeod 1	Provan	Sullivan	McGarvey	burns	McCluskey	
Sept 19	Rangers	2-0	Bonner	McGrain	Reid	Aitken	McAdam 1	MacLeod 1	Provan	Sullivan	McGarvey	Burns	McCluskey	
Sept 26	PARTICK THISTLE	2-0	Bonner	McGrain	Reid	Aitken	McAdam	MacLeod	Nicholas 1	Sullivan	McGarvey	Burns 1	McCluskey	(Moyes)
Oct 3	Dundee	3-1	Bonner	Moyes	Reid	Aitken	McAdam	MacLeod	Nicholas	Sullivan	McGarvey 1	Burns	McCluskey 2	
Oct 10	St Mirren	2-1	Bonner	Moyes	Reid	Aitken	McAdam	MacLeod	Nicholas 1	Sullivan	McGarvey	Burns	McCluskey 1	
Oct 17	DUNDEE UNITED	1-1	Bonner	Moyes	Reid	Aitken	McAdam	MacLeod	Nicholas	Sullivan	McGarvey	Burns	McCluskey 1	
Oct 24	Hibernian	0-1	Bonner	Moyes	Reid	Aitken	Garner	MacLeod	Nicholas	Sullivan	McGarvey	Burns	McCluskey	
Oct 31	Airdrie	3-1	Bonner	Moyes	Reid	Aitken	McAdam	MacLeod	Nicholas	Sullivan 1	McGarvey	Burns 1	McCluskey 1	
Nov 7	ABERDEEN	2-1	Bonner	Moyes	Reid	Aitken	McAdam	MacLeod	Provan	Sullivan	McGarvey 1	Burns	McCluskey 1	(Conroy)
Nov 14	Morton	1-1	Bonner	Moyes	Reid	Aitken	McAdam	MacLeod	Provan	Sullivan	McGarvey	Conroy	McCluskey 1	(Nicholas)
Nov 21	RANGERS	3-3	Bonner	Moyes	Ried	Aitken	McAdam 1	MacLeod 1	Provan	Sullivan	McGarvey 1	Conroy	McCluskey	
Nov 28	Partick Thistle	2-0	Bonner	Moyes	Reid	Aitken	McAdam	MacLeod	Provan 1	Sullivan	McGarvey	Conroy	McCluskey 1	(Nicholas)
Dec 5	DUNDEE	3-1	Bonner	McGrain	Reid	Aitken	McAdam	MacLeod	Provan	Conroy 1	McGarvey 2	Burns	McCluskey	
Jan 9	Rangers	0-1	Bonner	McGrain	Reid	Aitken	McAdam	MacLeod	Provan	Conroy	Nicholas	Burns	McCluskey	(Moyes, McGarvey)
Jan 30	Aberdeen	3-1	Bonner	McGrain	Reid	Aitken	McAdam	MacLeod 1	Sullivan	McStay 1	McGarvey	Burns	McCluskey 1	
Feb 2	HIBERNIAN	0-0	Bonner	McGrain	Reid	Aitken	McAdam	MacLeod	Sullivan	McStay	McGarvey	Burns	McCluskey	(Halpin)
Feb 6	Dundee	3-1	Bonner	McGrain	Reid	Aitken	McAdam	MacLeod 2	Sullivan	McStay	McGarvey 1	Burns	McCluskey	
Feb 20	PARTICK THISTLE	2-2	Bonner	McGrain	Reid	Aitken 1	McAdam	MacLeod	Halpin	McStay	McGarvey	Burns	McCluskey 1	(Conroy, Crainie)
Feb 27	Hibernian	0-1	Bonner	McGrain	Reid	Moyes	McAdam	MacLeod	McStay	Conroy	McGarvey	burns	McCluskey	(Crainie)
Mar 3	MORTON	1-0	Bonner	McGrain	Reid	Moyes	McAdam	MacLeod	Halpin	Sullivan	McGarvey 1	Burns	McCluskey	(Crainie)
Mar 13	St Mirren	5-2	Bonner	McGrain	Reid	Moyes	McAdam	MacLeod 2	Crainie	Sullivan 1	McGarvey	Burns 1	McCluskey 1	(McStay)
Mar 20	AIRDRIE	2-0	Bonner	McGrain	Reid	Aitken	Moyes	MacLeod	Crainie	Sullivan 1	McGarvey	Burns 1	McCluskey	(McAdam)
Mar 27	ABERDEEN	0-1	Bonner	McGrain	Reid	Aitken	McAdam	MacLeod	Crainie	Sullivan	McGarvey	Burns	McCluskey	(Moyes)
Mar 31	Dundee United	2-0	Bonner	McGrain	Reid	Aitken	McAdam	MacLeod	Crainie	Suillivan	McGarvey	Burns 2	McCluskey	(McStay)
Apr 3	Morton	1-1	Bonner	Moyes	Reid	Aitken	McAdam	MacLeod	McStay	Sullivan	Crainie 1	Burns	McCluskey	(Provan)
Apr 10	RANGERS	2-1	Bonner	McGrain	Reid	Aitken	McAdam	MacLeod	Provan	Sullivan	McAdam 1	Crainie 1	Burns	
Apr 14	Airdrie	5-1	Bonner	McGrain	Reid 1	Aitken 1	McAdam	MacLeod	Provan 1	Sullivan	McCluskey 1	Crainie 1	Burns	
Apr 17	DUNDEE	4-2	Bonner	McGrain	Reid 1	Aitken	McAdam	MacLeod	Provan 1	Sullivan	McCluskey 2	Crainie	Burns	
Apr 21	DUNDEE UNITED	3-1	Bonner	McGrain	Reid	Aitken	McAdam	MacLeod	Provan 1	Sullivan	McCluskey 2	Crainie	Burns	
Apr 24	Partick Thistle	3-0	Bonner	McGrain	Reid	Aitken	McAdam	MacLeod	Provan	Sullivan	McCluskey	Burns	Crainie 3	
May 1	HIBERNIAN	6-0	Bonner	McGrain	Reid	Aitken 1	McAdam	MacLeod 2	Provan	Sullivan	McCluskey 1	Burns 1	Crainie 1	
May 3	ST MIRREN	0-0	Bonner	McGrain	Reid	Aitken	McAdam	MacLeod	Provan	Sullivan	McCluskey	Burns	Crainie	
May 8	Dundee United	0-3	Bonner	McGrain	Reid	Aitken	McAdam	MacLeod	Provan	Sullivan	McCluskey	Burns	Crainie	(Moyes, McStay)
May 15	ST MIRREN	3-0	Bonner	McGrain	Reid	Aitken	McAdam 1	MacLeod	Provan	McStay	McCluskey 2	Burns	Crainie	

LEAGUE CUP 1981

Aug 8	ST MIRREN	1-3	Bonner	McGrain	Reid	Aitken	Garner	MacLeod	Provan	Sullivan	McGarvey 1	Burns	Nicholas	(McCluskey, Conroy)
Aug 12	St Johnstone	0-2	Bonner	McGrain	McAdam	Aitken	Garner	MacLeod	Provan	Sullivan	McGarvey	Burns	McCluskey	(Nicholas)
Aug 15	HIBERNIAN	4-1	Bonner	McGrain	Reid	Aitken	McAdam	MacLeod 2	Provan	Sullivan	McGarvey	Burns	Nicholas 2	(Moyes)
Aug 19	ST JOHNSTONE	4-1	Bonner	McGrain	Reid	Aitken	Moyes	MacLeod	Provan 2	Sullivan	McGarvey 1	Burns	Nicholas 1	
Aug 22	St Mirren	5-1	Bonner	McGrain	Reid	Aitken	Moyes	MacLeod 2	Provan	Sullivan	McGarvey	Burns	McCluskey 3	
Aug 26	Hibernian	4-1	Bonner	McGrain	Reid	Aitken	Moyes	MacLeod 1	Provan	Sullivan 1	McGarvey 2	Burns	McCluskey	

EUROPEAN CUP 1981-82

Sept 16	JUVENTUS	1-0	Bonner	McGrain	Reid	Aitken	McAdam	MacLeod 1	Provan	Sullivan	Nicholas	Burns	McCluskey	
Sept 30	Juventus	0-2	Bonner	Moyes	Reid	Aitken	McAdam	MacLeod	Provan	Sullivan	McGarvey	Burns	McCluskey	

SCOTTISH CUP 1982

Jan 23	QUEEN OF THE SOUTH	4-0	Bonner	McGrain 1	Reid	Aitken	McAdam	MacLeod	Halpin 1	P McStay	McGarvey 1	Burns	McCluskey 1	
Feb 13	Aberdeen	0-1	Bonner	McGrain	Reid	Aitken	McAdam	MacLeod	Sullivan	McStay	McGarvey	Burns	McCluskey	

Date	Opponent	Score	1	2	3	4	5	6	7	8	9	10	11	SUBS
Apr 12	Motherwell	2-2	Bonner	Traynor	Burns	Aitken	McCahill	Grant	Stark	McStay 1	Coyne	McGhee 1	Miller	(Walker, Fulton)
Apr 22	DUNDEE	2-1	Bonner	Grant	Rogan 1	Aitken	McCarthy	Burns	Stark	McStay	Coyne	McGhee 1	Miller	
Apr 29	Aberdeen	0-0	Bonner	Grant	Rogan	Aitken	McCarthy	Burns	Stark	McStay	Walker	McGhee	Miller	(Elliot)
May 6	HIBERNIAN	1-0	Bonner	Morris	Rogan	Aitken	McCarthy	Whyte	Grant	McStay	Miller 1	McGhee	Elliot	
May 13	St Mirren	1-0	Bonner	Morris	Rogan	Aitken	McCarthy	Whyte	Grant	McStay	Miller 1	McGhee	Elliot	(Coyne, Burns)

LEAGUE CUP 1988

Aug 17	AYR UNITED	4-1	Rough	Morris	Rogan	Whyte	McCarthy	Grant	Miller	McStay	McAvennie 1	Walker 2	Burns 1	
Aug 24	HAMILTON ACADEMICALS	7-2	Andrews	Morris	Rogan	Aitken	McCarthy	Whyte	Miller	McStay	McAvennie 2	Walker 2	Burns 1	(Stark 1, Archdeacon 1)
Aug 31	Dundee United	0-2	Andrews	Morris	Rogan	Aitken	McCarthy	Grant	Miller	McStay	McAvennie	Walker	Burns	(Stark, Whyte)

EUROPEAN CUP 1988-89

Sept 7	Honved	0-1	Andrews	Morris	Rogan	Aitken	McCarthy	Whyte	Grant	McStay	McAvennie	Walker	Burns	
Oct 5	HONVED	4-0	Rough	Morris	Rogan	Aitken	McCarthy	Whyte	Stark 1	McStay	McAvennie 1	Walker 1	Miller	(McGhee 1)
Oct 26	WERDER BREMEN	0-1	Bonner	Morris	Rogan	Aitken	McCarthy	Whyte	Stark	McStay	McAvennie	McGhee	Miller	(Burns, Walker)
Nov 8	Werder Bremen	0-0	Bonner	Morris	Rogan	Aitken	McCarthy	Whyte	Stark	McStay	McAvennie	McGhee	Burns	(Miller, Archdeacon)

SCOTTISH CUP 1989

Jan 28	DUMBARTON	2-0	Bonner	Morris	Rogan	Whyte	McCarthy	Grant	Miller	McStay	Walker 1	McGhee	Burns 1	(Stark, Baillie)
Feb 18	CLYDEBANK	4-1	Bonner	Morris	Rogan	Aitken	McCarthy	Grant	Stark 1	McStay	McAveninie 1	McGhee	Burns 2	
Mar 18	HEARTS	2-1	Bonner	Morris	Rogan	Aitken 1P	McCarthy	Grant	Stark	McStay	McAveninie	McGhee 1	Burns	
Apr 16	Hibernian	3-1 SF	Bonner	Grant	Burns	Aitken	McCarthy 1	Fulton	Stark	McStay	Walker 1	McGhee 1	Miller	
May 20	Rangers	1-0 F	Bonner	Morris	Rogan	Aitken	McCarthy	Whyte	Grant	McStay	Miller 1	McGhee	Burns	

SCOTTISH LEAGUE 1989-90

Aug 2	Hearts	3-1	Bonner	Morris	Burns	Aitken	Whyte	Grant	Galloway	McStay	Dziekanowski	Coyne 3(1P)	Fulton	(Walker)
Aug 19	DUNFERMLINE ATHLETIC	1-0	Bonner	Morris	Burns	Aitken	Whyte	Grant	Galloway 1	Mcstay	Dziekanowski	Coyne	Hewitt	
Aug 26	RANGERS	1-1	Bonner	Morris	Burns	Aitken	Whyte	Grant	Galloway	McStay	Dziekanowski 1	Coyne	Hewitt	
Sept 9	St Mirren	0-1	Bonner	Morris	Burns s/o	Aitken	Whyte	Grant	Galloway	McStay	Dziekanowski	Coyne	Hewitt	(Rogan, Walker)
Sept 16	Dundee United	2-2	Bonner	Morris 1	Rogan	Aitken	Whyte s/o	McCahill	Galloway	McStay	Dziekanowski	Coyne 1	Fulton	(Walker)
Sept 23	MOTHERWELL	1-1	Bonner	Morris	Rogan	Whyte	Elliott	Grant	Galloway	McStay 1	Dziekanowski	Coyne	Fulton	(Walker
Sept 30	Aberdeen	1-1	Bonner	Morris	Rogan	Aitken	Elliott	Whyte	Galloway	McStay	Dziekanowski	Walker	Miller 1	(Coyne)
Oct 4	HIBERNIAN	3-1	Bonner	Morris	Rogan	Aitken	Elliott	Whyte	Galloway	McStay	Dziekanowski 1	Walker 2P	Miller	
Oct 14	Dundee	3-1	Bonner	Morris	Rogan	Aitken 1	Elliott	Whyte	Galloway	McStay	Dziekanowski 1	Walker	Mathie	(Burns, Coyne 1)
Oct 21	HEARTS	2-1	Bonner	Morris	Burns	Aitken 1	Elliott	Whyte	Galloway	McStay	Dziekanowski	Walker	Mathie	(Miller, Coyne 1)
Oct 28	Dunfermline Athletic	0-2	Bonner	Morris	Rogan	Aitken	Elliott	Whyte	Galloway	McStay	Dziekanowski	Coyne	Miller	(Walker)
Nov 4	Rangers	0-1	Bonner	Morris	Burns	Aitken	Elliott	Whyte	Galloway	McStay	Dziekanowski	Coyne	Miller	(Walker)
Nov 18	DUNDEE UNITED	0-1	Bonner	Morris	Burns	Rogan	Elliott	Fulton	Galloway	McStay	Dziekanowski	Walker	Miller	(Grant, Hewitt)
Nov 22	ST MIRREN	1-1	Bonner	Morris	Rogan	Wdowczyk	Elliott	Whyte	Grant	McStay	Dziekanowski	Walker	Miller 1	(Galloway, Hewitt)
Nov 25	Motherwell	0-0	Bonner	Morris	Rogan	Wdowczyk	Elliott	Whyte	Grant	McStay	Dziekanowski	Walker	Miller	(Galloway, Hewitt)
Dec 2	ABERDEEN	1-0	Bonner	Morris	Wdowczyk	Aitken	Elliott	Whyte	Grant	McStay	Dziekanowski	Walker 1P	Hewitt	(Galloway)
Dec 9	Hibernian	3-0	Bonner	Morris	Wdowczyk 1	Aitken	Elliott	Whyte	Galloway	Grant	Dziekanowski 1	Walker 1	Hewitt	
Dec 16	DUNDEE	4-1	Bonner	Morris	Wdowczyk	Aitken	Rogan	Whyte	Grant	McStay	Dziekanowski 1	Walker 1	Hewitt	(Galloway, Miller 1)
Dec 26	Hearts	0-0	Bonner	Morris	Wdowczyk	Aitken	Elliott	Whyte	Galloway	McStay	Dzekanowski	Walker	Hewitt	(Grant, Coyne)
Dec 30	DUNFERMLINE ATHLETIC	0-2	Bonner	Morris	Wdowczyk	Aitken	Elliott	Whyte	Grant	McStay	Dziekanowski	Walker	Hewitt	(Miller, Coyne)
Jan 2	RANGERS	0-1	Bonner	Morris	Wdowczyk	Aitken	Elliott	Whyte	Grant	McStay	Coyne	Galloway	Miller	(Dziekanowski, Walker)
Jan 6	St Mirren	2-0	Bonner	Galloway	Wdowczyk	Aitken	Elliott	Whyte	Mathie	McStay	Dziekanowski 1	Fulton	Miller 1	(Hewitt, Walker)
Jan 13	Dundee United	0-2	Bonner	Morris	Wdowczyk	Galloway	Elliott	Whyte	Mathie	McStay	Dziekanowski	Fulton	Miller	(Walker)
Jan 27	MOTHERWELL	0-1	Bonner	Morris	Wdowczyk	Galloway	Rogan	Whyte	Miller	McStay	Dziekanowski	Walker	Fulton	(Coyne, Elliot D)
Feb 3	Dundee	0-0	Bonner	Morris	Wdowczyk	Galloway	Elliott	Whyte	Grant	McStay	Dziekanowski	Coyne	Rogan	(Walker, Fulton)
Feb 10	HIBERNIAN	1-1	Bonner	Morris	Wdowczyk	Galloway	Elliott	Whyte	Grant	McStay	Dziekanowski 1	Coyne	Fulton	(Miller, Walker)
Feb 17	Aberdeen	1-1	Bonner	Morris	Wdowczyk	Galloway	Elliott	Whyte	Grant	McStay 1	Dziekanowski	Coyne	Fulton	(Miller)
Mar 3	DUNDEE UNITED	3-0	Bonner	Morris	Wdowczyk	Galloway 1	Elliott	Whyte 1	Grant	McStay	Dziekanowski	Coyne	Miller 1	
Mar 10	HEARTS	1-1	Bonner	Morris	Wdowczyk	Galloway	Elliott	Whyte	Grant	McStay	Dziekanowski	Coyne 1	Miller	(Walker)
Mar 24	Dunfermline Athletic	0-0	Bonner	Morris	Wdowczyk	Rogan	Elliott	Whyte	Grant	McStay	Walker	Coyne	Creaney	(Fulton, Mathie)
Apr 1	Rangers	0-3	Bonner	Grant	Wdowzzyk	Rogan	Elliott	Whyte	Galloway	McStay	Dziekanowski	Coyne	Miller	(Fulton, Walker)
Apr 7	ST MIRREN	0-3	Bonner	Morris	Wdowczyk	Galloway	McCahill	Whyte	Grant	McStay	Walker	Coyne	Miller	(Elliot, Creaney)
Apr 17	Hibernian	0-1	Bonner	Morris	Wdowczyk	Galloway	Rogan	Whyte	Grant	McStay	Creaney	Walker	Fulton	(Miller, Dziekanowski)
Apr 21	DUNDEE	1-1	Bonner	Morris	Wdowczyk	Grant	Elliott	Whyte	Mathie	McStay	Miller	Walker	Fulton	(Rogan, Creaney 1)
Apr 28	Motherwell	1-1	Bonner	Galloway	Wdowczyk	Grant	Rogan	Whyte	Stark	McStay	Dziekanowski 1	Walker	Fulton	Milley, Creaney)
May 2	ABERDEEN	1-3	Bonner	Galloway	Wdowczyk	Grant	Rogan	Whyte	Stark	McStay	Dziekanowski	Walker 1	Fulton	(Miller, Creaney)

LEAGUE CUP 1989

Aug 16	Dumbarton	3-0	Bonner	Morris	Burns 1	Aitken	Whyte	Grant	Galloway	McStay 1	Dziekanowski 1	Coyne	Hewitt	(Walker, Rogan)
Aug 22	QUEEN OF THE SOUTH	2-0	Bonner	Morris	Rogan	Aitken	Whyte	Grant 1	Galloway	McStay	Dziekanowski 1	Walker	Hewitt	(Fulton)
Aug 30	Hearts*	2-2	Bonner	Morris	Burns	Aitken	Whyte	Grant	Galloway	McStay	Dziekanowski 1	Coyne	Hewitt	(Walker)
Sept 20	Aberdeen	0-1 SF	Bonner	Morris	Rogan	Aitken s/o	McCahill	Burns	Galloway	McStay	Dziekanowski	Coyne	Fulton	(Miller, Walker)

*won on penalties

EUROPEAN CUP-WINNERS' CUP 1989-90

Sept 12	Partizan Belgrade	1-2	Bonner	Morris	Rogan	Aitken	Whyte	Grant	Galloway 1	McStay	Dziekanowski	Coyne	Burns	(Walker)
Sept 27	PARTIZAN BELGRADE	5-4	Bonner	Grant	Rogan	Aitken	Elliott	Whyte	Galloway	McStay	Dziekanowski 4	Walker 1	Miller	

lost on away goals.

SCOTTISH CUP 1990

Jan 20	Forfar Athletic	2-1	Bonner	Morris 1P	Wdowczyk	Galloway	McCahill	Whyte	Mathie	McStay	Dziekanowski 1	Fulton	Miller	(Walker)
Feb 25	RANGERS	1-0	Bonner	Morris	Wdowczyk	Galloway	Elliott	Whyte	Grant	McStay	Dziekanowski	Coyne 1	Miller	(Walker)
Mar 17	Dunfermline Athletic	0-0	Bonner	Morris	Wdowczzk	Rogan	Elliott	Whyte	Grant	McStay	Dziekanowski	Coyne	Miller	
Mar 21	DUNFERMLINE ATHLETIC	3-0	Bonner	Morris	Wdowczyk	Rogan	Elliott	Whyte	Grant	McStay 1	Dziekanowski	Coyne 1	Miller 1	(Walker)
Apr 14	Clydebank	2-0 SF	Bonner	Morris	Wdowczyk	Galloway	Whyte	Fulton	Grant	McStay	Dziekanowski	Walker 2	Miller	
May 12	Aberdeen	0-0 F	Bonner	Wdowczyk	Rogan	Grant	Elliott	Whyte	Stark	McStay	Dziekanowski	Walker	Miller	(Coyne, Galloway)

(aet - lost 8-9 on penalties)

SCOTTISH LEAGUE 1990-91

Aug 25	Motherwell	0-2	Bonner	Morris	Wdowczyk s/o	Grant	Elliott	Whyte	Hayes	McStay	Dziekanowski	Walker	Collins	(McLaughlin, Miller)
Sept 1	ABERDEEN	0-3	Bonner	Morris	McLaughlin	Grant	Elliott	Whyte	Hayes	McStay	Dziekanowski	Nicholas	Collins	(Miller, Walker)
Sept 8	HIBERNIAN	2-0	Bonner	Grant	McLaughlin	Baillie	Elliott	Fulton	Miller 1	McStay	Dziekanowski 1	Walker	Collins	(Creaney, McCarrison)
Sept 15	Rangers	1-1	Bonner	Morris	Rogan	Grant	Baillie	Whyte	Miller	McStay	Dziekanowski	Walker	Collins	(Creaney)
Sept 22	HEARTS	3-0	Bonner	Grant	Rogan	Fulton	Elliott	Whyte	Miller 1	McStay	Dziekanowski	Walker	Collins	(Galloway, Creaney 1)
Sept 29	St Mirren	3-2	Bonner	Grant	Rogan	Fulton	Elliott	Whyte	Miller	McStay 1	Dziekanowski	Creaney 2	Collins	(Hewitt)
Oct 6	ST JOHNSTONE	0-0	Bonner (c)	Morris	Rogan	Fulton	Elliott	Whyte	Miller	Grant	Dziekanowski	Creaney	Collins	(Hewitt)
Oct 13	Dunfermline Athletic	1-1	Bonner	Grant	Wdowczyk	Fulton	Elliott	Rogan	Miller	McStay 1	Dziekanowski	Creaney	Collins	(Hewitt)
Oct 20	DUNDEE UNITED	0-0	Bonner	Grant	Wdowczyk	Fulton	Elliott	Rogan	Miller	McStay	Hewitt	Creaney	Collins	(Morris, Hayes)
Nov 3	Aberdeen	0-3	Bonner	Grant	Wdowczyk	Fulton	Elliott	Rogan	Galloway	McStay	Dziekanowski	Creaney	Collins	(Hayes, Miller)
Nov 6	MOTHERWELL	2-1	Bonner	McNally	Wdowczyk	Fulton	Baillie	Rogan	Miller	McStay	Coyne 2	Creaney	Collins	
Nov 10	Hearts	0-1	Bonner	Grant	Wdowczyk	Fulton	Baillie	Rogan	Miller	McStay	Coyne	Creaney	Collins	(Galloway, Dziekanowski)
Nov 17	ST MIRREN	4-1	Donner	McNally	Wdowczyk	Fulton	Baillie 1	Rogan	Miller 1	Grant	Nicholas	Creaney 1	Collins	(Galloway, Coyne 1)
Nov 25	RANGERS	1-2	Bonner	McNally	Wdowczyk	Fulton	Elliott 1	Baillie	Miller	Grant	Nicholas	Creaney	Collins	(Rogan, Coyne)
Dec 1	Hibernian	3-0	Bonner	McNally	Wdowczyk	Fulton	Elliott	Rogan	Coyne 2	Grant	Nicholas 1	Creaney	Collins	(Galloway)
Dec 8	Dundee United	1-3	Bonner	McNally	Wdowczyk	Fulton	Elliott	Rogan	Coyne 1	McStay	Nicholas	Creaney	Collins	(Grant, Britton)
Dec 15	DUNFERMLINE ATHLETIC	1-2	Bonner	Grant	Wdowczyk	Galloway	Elliott	Whyte	Miller	McStay	Coyne	Creaney	Collins	(Nicholas 1)
Dec 22	St Johnstone	2-3	Bonner	Grant	Wdowczyk	Fulton	Elliott	Baillie	Mathie	McStay	Nicholas	Coyne 1	Collins 1	(Morris, Dziekanowski)

			1	2	3	4	5	6	7	8	9	10	11	
Dec 29	HEARTS	1-1	Bonner	Morris	Wdowczyk	Grant	Elliott	Rogan	Mathie	McStay	Nicholas	Coyne 1	Collins	(Creaney, Dziekanowski)
Jan 2	Rangers	0-2	Bonner	Morris	Rogan	Grant	Elliott	Whyte	Creaney	McStay	Coyne	Walker	Collins	(Miller)
Jan 5	HIBERNIAN	1-1	Bonner	Morris	Rogan	Grant	Elliott	Whyte	Creaney	McStay	Coyne 1	Fulton	Collins	(Miller)
Jan 19	ABERDEEN	1-0	Bonner	Morris	Rogan	McNally	Elliott	Whyte	Miller	McStay	Coyne 1	Creaney	Collins	(Fulton, Walker)
Jan 30	Motherwell	1-1	Bonner	Morris	Wdowczyk	McNally	Elliott	Whyte	Creaney	McStay	Coyne	Dziekanowski 1	Collins	(Walker)
Feb 2	DUNDEE UNITED	1-0	Bonner	McNally	Wdowczyk	Grant	Elliott	Whyte	Mille	McStay	Coyne 1	Dziekanowski	Collins	(Hayes)
Mar 2	ST JOHNSTONE	3-0	Bonner	McNally	Rogan	Morris	Elliott 1	Whyte	Miller 1	McStay	Coyne 1	Creaney	Collins	(Mathie)
Mar 6	Dunfermline Athletic	1-0	Bonner	McNally	Rogan	Morris	Elliott	Whyte	Miller	McStay	Coyne	Creaney 1	Collins	
Mar 9	Hibernian	2-0	Bonner	McNally	Rogan	Morris	Grant	Whyte	Miller 2	McStay	Coyne	Creaney	Collins	(Wdowczyk, Hayes)
Mar 12	St Mirren	2-0	Bonner	Morris	Rogan	Grant	Wdowczyk	Whyte	Hayes	McStay	Coyne	Creaney 2	Collins	(Miller)
Mar 24	RANGERS	3-0	Bonner	Wdowczyk	Rogan 1	McNally	Elliott	Whyte	Miller 1	McStay	Coyne 1	Creaney	Collins	(Walker, Fulton)
Mar 30	MOTHERWELL	1-2	Bonner	McNally	Rogan	Morris	Elliott	Whyte	Fulton	Grant	Coyne 1	Walker	Collins	(Creaney, Britton)
Apr 6	Aberdeen	0-1	Bonner	Morris	Rogan	Wdowczyk	Elliott	Whyte	Miller	McStay	Coyne	Creaney	Collins	(McNally, Walker)
Apr 13	Dundee United	1-2	Bonner	McNally	Wdowczyk	Grant	Elliott	Whyte	Miller	McStay	Coyne	Nicholas	Collins	(Creaney, Rogan) +OG
Apr 20	DUNFERMLINE ATHLETIC	5-1	Bonner	Wdowczyk	Rogan	Grant	Elliott	Whyte 1	Miller	McStay	Coyne 2	Nicholas 2	Collins	(McNally, Mathie)
Apr 27	Hearts	1-0	Bonner	McNally	Wdowczyk	Fulton	Rogan	Whyte	Miller	McStay	Coyne	Nicholas 1	Collins	(Morris, Creaney)
May 5	ST MIRREN	1-0	Bonner	McNally	Fulton	Grant	Wdowczyk	Whyte	Miller	McStay	Coyne 1	Nicholas	Collins	(Baillie, Creaney)
May 11	St Johnstone	3-2	Bonner	McNally	Wdowczyk	Grant	Baillie	Whyte	Miller	Galloway 1	Coyne 1P	Nicholas 1	Fulton	(Creaney)

LEAGUE CUP 1990

Aug 22	AYR UNITED	4-0	Bonner	Morris	Wdowczyk	Grant	Elliott 2	Whyte	Hayes	McStay	Dziekanowski 2	Walker	Collins	(Hewitt, Miller)
Aug 29	Hamilton Academicals	1-0	Bonner	Morris	McLaughlin	Grant	Elliott	Whyte	Hayes	McStay	Dziekanowski	Walker	Collins	
Sept 5	QUEEN OF THE SOUTH	2-1	Bonner	Morris	McLaughlin	Grant	Elliott	Whyte	Hayes	McStay	Dziekanowski 1	Nicholas	Collins	(Miller 1, Walker)
Sept 25	Dundee United	2-0 SF	Bonner	Grant	Rogan	Fulton	Elliott	Whyte	Miller	McStay 1	Dziekanowski	Creaney 1	Collins	(Galloway, Walker)
Oct 28	Rangers (aet)	1-2 F	Bonner	Grant	Wdowczyk	Fulton	Elliott 1	Rogan	Miller	McStay	Dziekanowski	Creaney	Collins	(Hewitt, Morris)

SCOTTISH CUP 1991

Jan 26	Forfar Athletic	2-0	Bonner	Morris	Wdowczyk 1	McNally	Baillie	Whyte	Miller	McStay	Coyne 1	Dziekanowski	Collins	(Fulton)
Feb 26	ST MIRREN	3-0	Bonner	McNally	Rogan	Morris	Elliott	Whyte	Miller	McStay	Coyne 1	Creaney 1	Collins +OG	
Mar 17	RANGERS	2-0	Bonner	Wdowczyk 1	Rogan	Grant s/o	Elliott	Whyte	Miller	McStay	Coyne	Creaney 1	Collins	
Apr 3	Motherwell	0-0 SF	Bonner	Morris	Rogan	Wdowczyk	Elliott	Whyte	Miller	McStay	Coyne	Creaney	Collins	(Britton)
Apr 9	Motherwell	2-4 SF	Bonner	McNally	Rogan 1	Wdowczyk	Elliott	Whyte	Miller	McStay	Coyne	Creaney	Collins	(Britton) +OG

SCOTTISH LEAGUE 1991-92

Aug 10	Dundee United	4-3	Bonner	Morris	Rogan	Grant	Whyte	Wdowczyk	Fulton	Coyne 1	Cascaorino	Nicholas 1	Collins 2	(Galloway, Creaney)
Aug 13	Dunfermline Athletic	3-1	Bonner	Morris	Rogan	Grant	Whyte	Wdowczyk	Fulton	Coyne 1	Cascorino	Nicholas 2	Collins	(Galloway, Creaney)
Aug 17	FALKIRK	4-1	Bonner	Morris	Rogan	Grant	Whyte	Gillespie 1	Fulton	Coyne 2	Cascarino	Nicholas	Collins 1	(Galloway, O'Neil)
Aug 24	Aberdeen	0-1	Bonner	Morris	Rogan	Grant	Whyte	Gillespie	Fulton	Coyne	Creaney	Nicholas	Collins	(Wdowczyk, Galloway)
Aug 31	RANGERS	0-2	Bonner	Morris	Rogan	Grant	Whyte	Gillespie	Fulton	Coyne	Cascarino	Nicholas	Collins	(Galloway, Creaney)
Sept 7	ST MIRREN	0-0	Bonner	McNally	Wdowczyk	Galloway	Whyte	Gillespie	Miller	Fulton	Creaney	Cascarino	O'Neil	(Walker, Nicholas)
Sept 14	St Johnstone	0-1	Bonner	McNally	Wdowczyk	Grant	Galloway	Gillespie	Miller	Fulton	Creaney	Cascarino	Collins	(Whyte, Nicholas)
Sept 21	AIDRIE	3-1	Bonner	Morris	Wdowczyk	Grant	Whyte	Galloway 1	Miller 1	Fulton	Coyne	Nicholas 1P	Collins	(McNally)
Sept 28	Hibernian	1-1	Bonner	Morris	Wdowczyk	Grant	Whyte	Galloway	Miller	Fulton	Coyne	Nicholas 1	Collins	(McNally, Cascarino)
Oct 5	HEARTS	3-1	Bonner	McNally 1	Wdowczyk	Grant	Whyte	Gillespie	Miller	Galloway	Coyne	Nicholas 1P	Collins	(Cascarino 1, O'Neil)
Oct 8	Motherwell	2-0	Bonner	McNally	Wdowczyk	Grant	Galloway	Gillespie	Miller	O'Neil	Coyne 1	Nicholas 1	Collins	(Dziekanowski, Fulton)
Oct 12	DUNDEE UNITED	4-1	Bonner	McNally	Whyte	O'Neil	Galloway 1	Gillespie	Miller	McStay	Coyne 1	Nicholas 2	Collins	(Grant, Cascarino)
Oct 19	Falkirk	3-4	Bonner	Grant	Whyte	O'Neil	Galloway	McNally	Miller	McStay 2	Coyne	Nicholas	Collins 1	(Cascarino, Smith)
Oct 26	St Mirren	5-0	Bonner	Morris	Wdowczyk	Grant	Whyte	McNally	Miller	McStay 1	Coyne 2	Nicholas	O'Neil 1	(Fulton, Creaney 1)
Oct 30	ST JOHNSTONE	4-0	Bonner	McNally	Wdowczyk	O'Neil	Galloway	Whyte	Miller	McStay	Coyne 1	Nicholas 2	Collins 1	(Grant, Cascarino)
Nov 2	Rangers	1-1	Bonner	McNally	Wdowczyk	O'Neil	Galloway	Whyte	Miller	McStay	Coyne	Nicholas	Collins	(Morris, Cascarino 1)
Nov 9	ABERDEEN	2-1	Bonner	McNally	Morris	Galloway	Tony Mowbray	Gillespie	O'Neil	McStay	Coyne	Nicholas 1	Collins	(Creaney 1, Cascarino)
Nov 16	Hearts	1-3	Bonner	McNally	Galloway	Creaney	Mowbray	Gillespie	O'Neil	McStay	Coyne 1	Nicholas	Collins	(Whyte, Cascarino)
Nov 20	MOTHERWELL	2-2	Bonner	McNally	Whyte	Grant	Galloway	Gillespie	Miller	McStay	Coyne	Nicholas 2	O'Neil	(Creaney, Cascarino)
Nov 23	Airdrie	3-0	Marshall	McNally	Wdowczyk	Grant	Whyte	Gillespie	Miller	McStay	Coyne 1	Cascarino 1	Galloway	(Morris, Creaney 1)
Nov 30	DUNFERMLINE ATHLETIC	1-0	Marshall	McNally	Wdowczyk	Grant	Whyte	Gillespie	Cascarino	McStay	Coyne 1	Nicholas	Galloway	(Creaney)
Dec 4	HIBERNIAN	0-0	Marshall	McNally	Wdowczyk	O'Neil	Whyte	Gillespie	Cascarino	McStay	Coyne	Nicholas	Galloway	(Collins, Morris)
Dec 7	Dundee United	1-1	Marshall	McNally	Fulton	O'Neil	Whyte	Morris 1	Cascarino	McStay	Coyne	Nicholas	Collins	(Smith, Miller)
Dec 14	ST MIRREN	4-0	Marshall	O'Neil	Morris	Grant	Whyte	McNally	Cascarino	McStay	Coyne	Nicholas	Collins 1	(Miller, Creaney 2) +OG
Dec 28	Aberdeen	2-2	Marshall	Morris	McNally	Grant	Mowbray 1	Whyte	O'Neil	McStay	Coyne	Nicholas	Collins	(Fulton, Cascarino 1)
Jan 1	RANGERS	1-3	Marshall	Morris	McNally	Grant	Mowbray 1	Whyte	Galloway	McStay	Coyne	Cascarino	Collins	(Fulton, Creaney)
Jan 4	HEARTS	1-2	Marshall	Morris	McNally	Grant	Mowbray	Whyte	Galloway	McStay	Coyne	Cascarino	Collins 1	(Fulton, Creaney)
Jan 8	St Johnstone	4-2	Marshall	Morris	Wdowczyk	O'Neil	Whyte	Gillespie 1	Miller	McStay 1	Coyne 1	Creaney	Collins 1	(Fulton)
Jan 11	Motherwell	0-0	Marshall	Morris	Wdowczyk	O'Neil	Whyte	Gillespie	Miller	McStay	Coyne	Creaney	Collins	(Fulton, Cascarino)
Jan 18	Dunfermline Athletic	1-0	Marshall	Morris	Wdowczyk	O'Neil	Whyte	Gillespie	Miller	McStay	Coyne 1	Creaney	Collins	
Feb 1	FALKIRK	2-0	Marshall	Morris	Galloway	O'Neil	Whyte	Gillespie	Miller	McStay 1	Coyne 1	Creaney	Collins	(Fulton, Nicholas)
Feb 8	AIRDRIE	2-0	Marshall	Morris	Boyd	O'Neil	Whyte	Galloway	Fulton	McStay	Coyne	Creaney 2	Collins	(Miller, Nicholas)
Feb 22	Hibernian	2-0	Marshall	Morris	Boyd	O'Neil	Whyte	Gillespie	Miller	McStay	Creaney 1	Nicholas 1	Collins	(Fulton, Galloway)
Feb 29	Hearts	2-1	Marshall	Morris	Boyd	O'Neil	Whyte	Gillespie	Fulton	McStay	Coyne	Creaney 2	Collins	(Mowbray, Nicholas)
Mar 14	ABERDEEN	1-0	Marshall	Morris	Boyd	Fulton	Mowbray	Gillespie	Miller	McStay	Coyne	Creaney	Collins 1	(O'Neil)
Mar 17	MOTHERWELL	4-1	Marshall	Galloway	Boyd	O'Neil	Mowbray	Gillespie	Miller 1	McStay 1	Creaney 1	Nicholas 1	Fulton Collins	(Coyne)
Mar 21	Rangers	2-0	Marshall	Morris	Boyd	O'Neil	Mowbray	Whyte	Miller	McStay	Creaney 1	Nicholas 1	Collins	(Galloway, Coyne)
Mar 28	DUNDEE UNITED	3-1	Marshall	Smith	Wdowczyk	Gillespie	Mowbray	Whyte 1	Galloway	Grant	Creaney 1	Nicholas 1	Fulton	(Boyd, Coyne)
Apr 4	Falkirk	3-0	Marshall	Morris	Boyd	O'Neil	Mowbray	Whyte	Galloway	McStay	Creaney 1	Nicholas 1	Collins 1	(Fulton, Coyne)
Apr 8	St Mirren	1-1	Marshall	Morris	Boyd 1	O'Neil	Mowbray	Whyte	Galloway	McStay	Creaney	Nicholas	Collins	(Fulton, Coyne)
Apr 11	ST JOHNSTONE	3-2	Marshall	Morris	Boyd	Fulton 1	Mowbray	Whyte	Galloway	McStay	Creaney	Nicholas 2	Collins	(McNally)
Apr 18	Airdrie	0-0	Marshall	Morris	Boyd	Gillespie	Mowbray	Whyte	Galloway	McStay	Creaney	Nicholas	Collins	(Fulton)
Apr 25	DUNFERMLINE ATHLETIC	2-0	Marshall	Morris	Boyd	Fulton	Mowbray	Whyte	Miller	McStay 1	Creaney	Nicholas	Collins 1	(Galloway, Coyne)
May 2	HIBERNIAN	1-2	Marshall	Morris	Boyd	Fulton 1	McNally	Whyte	Miller	McStay	Creaney	Nicholas	Collins	(Coyne)

LEAGUE CUP 1991

Aug 21	Morton	4-2	Bonner	Morris	Rogan	Grant	Whyte	Gillespie	Fulton	Coyne	Creaney 2	Nicholas 2	Collins	(Galloway, Miller)
Aug 27	RAITH ROVERS	3-1	Bonner	Morris	Wdowczyk	Grant	Whyte	Gillespie	Fulton 1	Coyne	Creaney 1	Galloway	Miller 1	(McNally, Walker)
Sept 3	Airdrie (lost on penalties)	0-0	Bonner	Morris	Rogan	Galloway	Whyte	Wdowczyk	Miller	Fulton	Nicholas	Cascarino	Collins	(O'Neil, Creaney)

UEFA CUP 1991-92

Sept 18	GERMINAL EKEREN	2-0	Bonner	Morris	Wdowczyk	Grant	Whyte	Gillespie	Miller	Fulton	Nicholas 2(1P)	Cascarino	Collins	(McNally, Coyne)
Oct 1	Germinal Ekeren	1-1	Bonner	Morris	Wdowczyk	Grant	Whyte	Gillespie	O'Neil	Galloway 1	Coyne	Nicholas	Collins	(Fulton, Cascarino)
Oct 22	Neuchatel Xamax	1-5	Bonner	Grant	Wdowczyk	O'Neil 1	Whyte	McNally	Cascarino	McStay	Coyne	Nicholas	Fulton	(Creaney, Miller)
Nov 6	NEUCHATEL XAMAX	1-0	Bonner	McNally	Wdowczyk	O'Neil	Whyte	Galloway	Miller 1	McStay	Coyne	Nicholas	Collins	(Cascarino, Creaney)

SCOTTISH CUP 1992

Jan 25	MONTROSE	6-0	Marshall	Morris	Wdowczyk	O'Neil	Whyte	Gillespie	Miller	McStay	Coyne 3	Creaney 3	Collins	(Cascarino, Galloway)
Feb 11	DUNDEE UNITED	2-1	Marshall	Morris	Galloway	O'Neil	Whyte	Gillespie	Miller	McStay	Coyne 1	Creaney 1	Collin,s	(Fulton, Nicholas)
Mar 7	MORTON	3-0	Marshall	Morris	Boyd	Fulton	Mowbray	Whyte	Miller	McStay	Coyne	Creaney 2	Collins 1	(Galloway ,Nicholas)
Mar 31	Rangers	0-1 SF	Marshall	Morris	Boyd	O'Neil	Mowbray	Whyte	Miller	McStay	Creaney	Nicholas	Collins	(Galloway, Coyne)

SCOTTISH LEAGUE 1992-93

Aug 1	Hearts	1-0	Marshall	Morris	Boyd	Wdowczyk	Mowbray	Gillespie	O'Neil	McStay	Creaney	Nicholas	Collins	(Coyne, Miller)
Aug 5	Aberdeen	1-1	Marshall	Morris	Boyd	Wdowczyk	Mowbray	Gillespie	O'Neil	McStay	Creaney 1	Nicholas	Collins	(Whyte, Coyne)
Aug 8	MOTHERWELL	1-1	Marshall	Morris	Boyd	Wdowczyk	Mowbray 1	Gillespie	O'Neil	McStay	Creaney	Nicholas	Collins	(Miller, Coyne)
Aug 15	DUNDEE UNITED	2-0	Marshall	Boyd	Wdowczyk	Galloway	Mowbray	Gillespie	Miller	McStay	Payton	Creaney 2	Collins	(O'Neil, Coyne)

			1	2	3	4	5	6	7	8	9	10	11	SUBS
Aug 22	Rangers	1-1	Marshall	Boyd	Galloway	Grant	Mowbray	McNally	Miller	McStay	Creaney 1	Payton	Collins	(O'Neil, Slater)
Aug 29	Airdrie	1-1	Marshall	Boyd	Wdowczyk	Grant	Mowbray	Galloway	Miller	McStay	Payton 1	Creaney	Collins	(O'Neil, Slater)
Sept 2	ST JOHNSTONE	3-1	Marshall	Boyd	Wdowczyk	O'Neil	Mowbray	Galloway	Slater	McStay	Payton	Creaney 1	Collins 2	(McNally, Fulton)
Sept 12	HIBERNIAN	2-3	Marshall	Boyd	Wdowczyk 1	O'Neil	Mowbray	Galloway	Slater	McStay 1	Payton	Creaney	Collins	(Miller)
Sept 19	Falkirk	5-4	Bonner	Boyd	Wdowczyk 1	Grant	Mowbray	Gillespie	Slater	McStay	Payton 1	Creaney 2	Collins 1	(McNally)
Sept 26	PARTICK THISTLE	1-2	Bonner	McNally	Boyd	Grant	Mowbray	Gillespie	Slater	McStay	Payton 1	Creaney	Collins	(Miller, Galloway)
Oct 3	Dundee	1-0	Bonner	McNally	Boyd	Grant	Mowbray	Galloway 1	Vata	McStay	Slater	Creaney	Collins	(Payton, Fulton)
Oct 7	HEARTS	1-1	Bonner	McNally	Boyd	Grant	Mowbray	Galloway	Miller 1	McStay	Slater	Creaney	Collins	(Payton)
Oct 17	Motherwell	3-1	Bonner	McNally	Boyd	Grant 1	Mowbray	Galloway 1	Miller	McStay	Slater	Creaney	Collins	(Payton, O'Neil) +OG
Oct 24	AIRDRIE	2-0	Bonner	McNally	Boyd	Grant	Mowbray	Galloway	Miller	McStay 1	Slater	Payton	Collins 1	(Nicholas, Vata)
Oct 31	St Johnstone	0-0	Bonner	Galloway	Boyd	Grant	Mowbray	Gillespie	Miller	McStay	Slater	Creaney	Collins	(Payton)
Nov 7	RANGERS	0-1	Bonner	Galloway	Wdowczyk	Grant	Mowbray	Gillespie	Boyd	McStay	Slater	Creaney	Collins	(O'Neil, Nicholas)
Nov 11	Dundee United	1-1	Bonner	Galloway	Wdowczyk	Grant	Mowbray	Gillespie	Boyd	McStay	Slater	Creaney	Collins	(O'Neil, Nicholas)
Nov 21	FALKIRK	3-2	Bonner	Boyd	Wdowczyk	O'Neil 1	Mowbray	Gillespie 1	Slater	McStay	Creaney 1	Nicholas	Collins	(Payton, Vata)
Nov 28	Hibernian	2-1	Bonner	Grant	Boyd	O'Neil 2	Mowbray	Wdowczyk	Slater	McStay	Creaney	Nicholas	Collins	(Payton, Vata)
Dec 2	ABERDEEN	2-2	Bonner	McNally	Boyd	Grant	Mowbray	Wdowczyk	O'Neil	McStay	Slater 1	Creaney	Collins	(Payton, Vata 1)
Dec 5	Partick Thistle	3-2	Bonner	McNally	Boyd	Grant 1	O'Neil	Vata	Slater	McStay	Payton 1	Nicholas	Collins	(Creaney 1)
Dec 12	DUNDEE	1-0	Bonner	Boyd	Collins	Grant	McNally	Gillespie	Vata	McStay	Payton 1	Creaney	Slater	(McCarrison, Fulton)
Dec 19	Hearts	0-1	Bonner	McNally	Boyd	Grant	Mowbray	Gillespie	Vata	McStay	Payton	Slater	Collins	(Miller, Creaney)
Dec 26	DUNDEE UNITED	0-1	Bonner	McNally	Boyd	Galloway	Mowbray	Collins	Miller	McStay	Payton	Creaney	Slater	(Vata, Grant)
Jan 2	Rangers	0-1	Bonner	McNally	Boyd	Galloway	Mowbray	Collins	Miller	McStay	Payton	Creaney	Slater	(O'Neil, Grant)
Jan 23	Airdrie	1-0	Bonner	McNally	Boyd	Vata	Gillespie	Galloway	Slater	McStay	McAvennie	Coyne 1	Collins	(Creaney)
Jan 30	MOTHERWELL	1-1	Bonner	McNally	Boyd	Vata	Gillespie	Galloway	Slater	McStay 1	McAvennie	Coyne	Collins	(Payton)
Feb 3	ST JOHNSTONE	5-1	Bonner	McNally	Boyd	Vata	Wdowczyk 1	Galloway	Slater	McStay	McAvennie 1	Coyne 2	Collins 1	(Nicholas, Grant)
Feb 13	Aberdeen	1-1	Bonner	Boyd	Wdowczyk	O'Neil	McNally	Galloway	Slater	McStay	McAvennie	Coyne	Collins	(Vata, Payton)
Feb 20	PARTICK THISTLE	0-0	Bonner	Boyd	Wdowczyk	O'Neil	McNally	Galloway	Slater	McStay	McAvennie	Coyne	Collins	(Vata, Payton)
Feb 23	Dundee	1-0	Bonner	Boyd	Wdowczyk	Vata	McNally	Galloway	Slater	McStay	McAvennie	Payton 1	Collins	(Coyne)
Feb 27	Falkirk	3-0	Bonner	Boyd	Wdowczyk	Grant	McNally	Galloway	Vata	McStay	McAvennie 1	Payton 2	Collins	
Mar 10	HEARTS	1-0	Bonner	Boyd	Wdowczyk	Grant	McNally	Galloway	Slater	McStay	McAvennie	Payton 1	Collins	(Miller)
Mar 16	HIBERNIAN	2-1	Bonner	Boyd	Wdowczyk	Grant	McNally	Galloway	Slater	McStay	McAvennie	Payton 2	Collins	
Mar 20	RANGERS	2-1	Bonner	Boyd	Wdowczyk	Grant	McNally	Galloway	Slater	McStay	McAvennie	Payton 1	Collins 1	
Mar 27	Dundee United	3-2	Bonner	Boyd	Wdowczyk	Grant	McNally	Galloway 1	Slater	McStay	McAvennie 1	Nicholas	Collins 1	(Vata)
Apr 3	Motherwell	0-2	Bonner	Boyd	Wdowczyk	Grant	McNally	Gillespie	Slater	McStay	McAvennie	Nicholas	Collins	(Miller, Smith)
Apr 6	AIRDRIE	4-0	Bonner	Vata 1	Gillespie	Grant	McNally	Mowbray	Slater 1	McStay	McAvennie 1	Nicholas	Collins 1	(Miller, Smith)
Apr 10	St Johnstone	1-1	Bonner	Vata	Boyd	Grant	Mowbray	Gillespie	Slater	McStay	McAvennie 1	Nicholas	Collins	(Miller)
Apr 17	Hibernian	1-3	Bonner	Vata	Boyd	Grant	Mowbray	Gillespie	Slater	McStay	McAvennie	Nicholas 1	Collins	(Miller, Smith)
Apr 20	FALKIRK	1-0	Bonner	Smith	McQuilken	Grant	Vata	Galloway	Slater	McStay	McAvennie 1	Nicholas	Collins	(Miller)
May 1	ABERDEEN	1-0	Marshall	Smith	Boyd	Grant	Vata	Galloway	Slater	Fulton	McAvennie 1	Payton	Gray	(Miller)
May 8	Partick Thistle	1-0	Marshall	Smith	Boyd	Fulton	Vata	Galloway	Miller	McStay	McAvennie 1	Slater	Collins	(Wdowczyk)
May 15	DUNDEE	2-0	Marshall	Smith	Boyd	Fulton	Wdowczyk	Galloway	Slater	McStay 1	McAvennie 1	Creaney	Collins	(Grant, Miller)

LEAGUE CUP 1992

Aug 12	Stirling Albion	3-0	Marshall	McNally	Boyd	Galloway	Mowbray	Wdowczyk	O'Neil	Fulton	Creaney 2	Nicholas	Collins	(Grant, Coyne 1)
Aug 19	Dundee	1-0	Marshall	O'Neil	Boyd	Grant	Mowbray	McNally	Miller	McStay	Payton 1	Creaney	Collins	(Slater, Fulton)
Aug 26	Hearts	2-1	Marshall	Boyd	Wdowczyk	Grant	Mowbray	Galloway	O'Neil	McStay	Creaney 1	Payton 1	Collins	(Slater)
Sept 23	Aberdeen	0-1	Bonner	Boyd	Wdowczyk	Grant	Galloway	Gillespie	Slater	McStay	Payton	Creaney	Collins	(Miller, McNally)

SCOTTISH CUP 1993

Jan 9	Clyde	0-0	Bonner	Grant	Boyd	Wdowczyk	McNally	Galloway	O'Neil	McStay	Creaney	Slater	Collins	(Coyne, Miller)
Jan 20	CLYDE	1-0	Bonner	McNally	Boyd	Slater	Gillespie	Galloway	Miller	McStay	Payton	Coyne 1	Collins Grant	(Creaney)
Feb 6	Falkirk	0-2	Bonner	McNally	Boyd	Vata	Wdowczyk	Galloway	Slater	McStay	McAvennie	Coyne	Collins	(Grant, Payton)

UEFA CUP 1992-93

Sept 15	Cologne	0-2	Marshall	Boyd	Wdowczyk	Galloway	Mowbray	Gillespie	O'Neil	McStay	Slater	Creaney	Collins	(Grant, Nicholas)
Sept 30	COLOGNE	3-0	Marshall	McNally	Boyd	Grant	Mowbray	Galloway	Slater	McStay 1	Payton	Creaney 1	Collins 1	(Miller, Fulton)
Oct 20	Borussia Dortmund	0-1	Bonner	McNally	Boyd	Grant	Mowbray	Gillespie	O'Neil	McStay	Slater	Creaney	Collins	(Nicholas)
Nov 3	BORUSSIA DORTMUND	1-2	Bonner	Galloway	Boyd	Grant	Mowbray	Gillespie	Slater	McStay	Nicholas	Creaney 1	Collins	(Miller)

SCOTTISH LEAGUE 1993-94

Aug 7	Motherwell	2-2	Bonner	Boyd	Wdowczyk	Grant	McNally	Galloway	Slater 1	McStay	McAvennie 1	Creaney	Collins	(Nicholas, McGinlay)
Aug 14	HIBERNIAN	1-1	Bonner	Boyd	Wdowczyk	Grant	McNally	Galloway	McGinlay	McStay	McAvennie	Nicholas 1	Collins	(Payton, O'Neil)
Aug 21	RANGERS	0-0	Bonner	Boyd	Wdowczyk	Grant	McNally	Galloway	McGinlay	McStay	McAvennie	Nicholas	Collins	(Payton)
Aug 28	Partick Thistle	1-0	Bonner	Boyd	Wdowczyk	Grant	McNally 1	Galloway	McGinlay	McStay	McAvennie	Nicholas	Collins	(Payton)
Sept 4	ABERDEEN	0-1	Bonner	Boyd	Wdowczyk	Grant	McNally	Galloway	McGinlay	Vata	McAvennie	Nicholas	Collins	(Payton, Slater)
Sept 11	Raith Rovers	4-1	Bonner	Boyd	Wdowczyk	Grant	Mowbray	McNally	McGinlay	O'Neil	McAvennie	Nicholas 2	Collins	(Payton, 2 Slater)
Sept 18	DUNDEE UNITED	1-1	Bonner	Boyd	Wdowczyk	Grant	McNally	Galloway	McGinlay	McStay	Creaney 1	Nicholas	Slater	(O'Neil)
Sept 25	Hearts	0-1	Bonner	Boyd	Wdowczyk	Grant	Mowbray	McNally	McGinlay	McStay	McAvennie	Creaney	Slater	(O'Neil, Smith)
Oct 2	KILMARNOCK	0-0	Bonner	Gillespie	Boyd	Grant	McNally	Galloway	McGinlay	McStay	Payton	Creaney	Smith	(Wdowczyk, Nicholas)
Oct 6	St Johnstone	1-2	Bonner	Gillespie	Boyd	Grant	Mowbray	McNally	McGinlay	McStay	Creaney 1	Nicholas	O'Neil	(Byrne
Oct 9	DUNDEE	2-1	Marshall	Gillespie	Boyd	Grant	McNally	Galloway	Byrne	McStay	Creaney 1	Nicholas	Collins	(McGinlay 1, O'Neil)
Oct 16	Hibernian	1-1	Bonner	Gillespie	Boyd	Grant	Mowbray	McGinlay	Byrne	McStay	Creaney 1	Nicholas	Collins	
Oct 30	Rangers	2-1	Bonner	Gillespie	Boyd	Grant	Mowbray	McGinlay	Byrne	McStay	Creaney	Nicholas	Collins 1	(Payton, O'Neil)
Nov 6	PARTICK THISTLE	3-0	Bonner	Wdowczyk	Boyd	Grant	Mowbray	McGinlay 2	Byrne	McStay	Creaney	Nicholas 1	O'Neil	(Vata, McLaughlin)
Nov 9	Aberdeen	1-1	Bonner	Gillespie	Boyd	Grant	Wdowczyk	McGinlay	Byrne	McStay	O'Neil 1	Creaney	Collins	(Vata, Nicholas)
Nov 13	Kilmarnock	2-2	Bonner	Wdowczyk	Boyd	Grant	McNally	McGinlay 1	Vata	McStay	Creaney	Nicholas 1	O'Neil	(McAvennie)
Nov 20	HEARTS	0-0	Bonner	Gillespie	Boyd	Grant	Wdowczyk	McGinlay	Byrne	McStay	Creaney	Nicholas	Collins	
Nov 24	MOTHERWELL	2-0	Bonner	Gillespie	Boyd	Grant	Wdowczyk	McGinlay 2	Creaney	McStay	O'Neil	Nicholas	Collins	(Biggins)
Nov 27	RAITH ROVERS	2-0	Bonner	Gillespie	Boyd	Grant	Wdowczyk	McGinlay	Creaney	McStay	O'Neil	Nicholas	Collins 2	(Biggins, Vata)
Nov 30	Dundee United	0-1	Bonner	Gillespie	Boyd	Grant	Wdowczyk	McGinlay	O'Neil	McStay	Creaney	Nicholas	Collins	(Biggins, Galloway)
Dec 4	ST JOHNSTONE	1-0	Bonner	Gillespie	Boyd	Grant	Wdowczyk	McGinlay 1	Creaney	McStay	O'Neil	Biggins	Collins	(McAvennie)
Dec 11	Dundee	1-1	Bonner	Gillespie	Boyd	Grant	Wdowczyk	McGinlay	Creaney 1	McStay	O'Neil	Biggins	Collins	(McAvennie)
Dec 18	HIBERNIAN	1-0	Bonner	Gillespie	Boyd	Grant	Wdowczyk	McGinlay	Byrne	McStay 1	O'Neil	Biggins	Collins	(Nicholas, Galloway)
Jan 1	RANGERS	2-4	Bonner	Gillespie	Boyd	Grant	Wdowczyk	McGinlay	Byrne	McStay	O'Neil	Nicholas 1	Collins 1	(McNally, Biggins)
Jan 8	Partick Thistle	0-1	Bonner	Gillespie	Boyd	Grant	McNally	Galloway	Byrne	McStay	Creaney	Nicholas	Collins	(Mowbray, O'Neil)
Jan 11	Motherwell	1-2	Bonner	Gillespie	Boyd	Grant	Mowbray	McNally 1	Byrne	McStay	Nicholas	Collins	O'Neil	(Galloway, Creaney)
Jan 19	ABERDEEN	2-2	Bonner	Gillespie	Martin	McGinlay	Mowbray	McNally	Byrne 1	McStay 1	Biggins	Nicholas	Collins	(O'Neil, Galloway)
Jan 22	DUNDEE UNITED	0-0	Muggleton	Gillespie	Boyd	Grant	Mowbray	McNally	Byrne	McStay	McGinlay	Nicholas	Collins	(O'Neil)
Feb 5	Raith Rovers	0-0	Muggleton	Martin	Boyd	Mowbray	McNally	Byrne	Nicholas	McStay	McAvennie	McGinlay	Collins	(Gillespie, Biggins)
Feb 12	Hearts	2-0	Muggleton	Gillespie	Boyd	McNally	Mowbray	McGinlay	Byrne	McStay	Nicholas 2	Falconer	Collins	(O'Neil, Vata)
Feb 26	KILMARNOCK	1-0	Muggleton	Gillespie	Boyd	Martin	Mowbray	McNally	McGinlay	O'Neil	Nicholas	Falconer	Collins 1	(Byrne)
Mar 5	St Johnstone	1-0	Muggleton	McNally	Boyd	Martin	Mowbray	McGinlay	Byrne 1	McStay	Nicholas	Falconer	Collins	(Galloway, Gillespie)
Mar 19	Hibernian	0-0	Muggleton	McNally	Boyd	Martin	Mowbray	McGinlay	Byrne	McStay	Nicholas	Falconer	Collins	(Donnelly)
Mar 26	MOTHERWELL	0-1	Muggleton	Gillespie	Boyd	McNally	Mowbray	McGinlay	Byrne	McStay	Nicholas	Falconer	Collins	(Donnelly, O'Neil)
Mar 30	RAITH ROVERS	2-1	Muggleton	Martin	Boyd	Galloway	Mowbray	McGinlay	Byrne	McStay	Donnelly 2	Falconer	Collins	(McLaughlin, O'Neil)
Apr 2	Dundee United	3-1	Muggleton	Martin	Boyd	McNally	Mowbray 1	Galloway	McGinlay	Vata	Donnelly	Falconer 1	Collins 1	(McLaughlin, O'Neil)
Apr 6	DUNDEE	1-1	Muggleton	Martin	Boyd	McNally	Gillespie 1	McGinlay	Vata	McStay	Donnelly	Galloway	Collins	(McLaughlin)
Apr 9	HEARTS	2-2	Muggleton	Martin	Boyd	McNally	Gillespie	Nicholas	Vata 1	McStay	Donnelly	Falconer	Collins 1	(Galloway)
Apr 16	Kilmarnock	0-2	Muggleton	Galloway	Boyd	McNally	Gillespie	McGinlay	Vata	McStay	Donnelly	Falconer	Collins	(Nicholas)
Apr 23	Dundee	2-0	Bonner	Galloway	Smith	McNally	Wdowczyk	McGinlay 2	Martin	Nicholas	Donnelly	Falconer	Collins	
Apr 27	ST JOHNSTONE	1-1	Bonner	Smith	Martin	Wdowczyk	McNally	McGinlay	Nicholas	Galloway	Donnelly 1	Falconer	Collins	(O'Neil, McLaughlin)
Apr 30	Rangers	1-1	Bonner	Smith	Martin	Grant	Mowbray	McNally	McGinlay	Wdowczyk	Donnelly	Falconer	Collins 1	(Byrne, McLaughlin)
May 7	PARTICK THISTLE	1-1	Bonner	McNally	Wdowczyk	Mowbray	Smith	Falconer	McGinlay 1	Collins	Martin	Donnelly	Hay	(Grant, McLaughlin)
May 14	Aberdeen	1-1	Bonner	Smith	Martin	Wdowczyk	Mowbray	Gillespie	Hay	McGinlay	Donnelly 1	Falconer	Collins	(McNally, Byrne)

LEAGUE CUP 1993

			1	2	3	4	5	6	7	8	9	10	11	SUBS
Aug 10	Stirling Albion	2-0	Bonner	Boyd	Wdowczyk	Grant	McNally	Galloway	Slater	McStay	McAvennie 1	Nicholas	Collins	(McGinlay 1)
Aug 25	Arbroath	9-1	Bonner	Boyd	Wdowczyk	Grant	McNally 1	Galloway	McGinlay 1	McStay	McAvennie 3	Nicholas 1	Collins	(Payton 3, O'Neil)
Aug 31	AIRDRIE	1-0	Bonner	Boyd	Wdowczyk	Grant	McNally	Galloway	McGinlay	McStay	McAvennie 1	Nicholas	Collins	(Payton)
Sept 22	Rangers	0-1	Bonner	Boyd	Wdowczyk	Grant	McNally	Galloway	McGinlay	McStay	McAvennie	Creaney	Slater	(O'Neil)

SCOTTISH CUP 1994

			1	2	3	4	5	6	7	8	9	10	11	SUBS
Jan 29	Motherwell	0-1	Muggleton	Gillespie	Boyd	O'Neil	Mowbray	McNally	Byrne	McStay	McAvennie	McGinlay	Collins	(Biggins)

UEFA CUP 1993-94

			1	2	3	4	5	6	7	8	9	10	11	SUBS
Sept 14	Young Boys Berne	0-0	Bonner	Boyd	Wdowczyk	Grant	McNally	Galloway	McGinlay	McStay	Payton	Nicholas	Collins	(Creaney, O'Neil)
Sept 29	YOUNG BOYS BERNE	1-0	Bonner	Gillespie	Boyd	Grant	McNally	Galloway	McGinlay	McStay	Payton	Creaney	O'Neil	(Wdowczyk, Nicholas) +OG
Oct 20	SPORTING LISBON	1-0	Bonner	Gillespie	Boyd	Grant	Mowbray	McGinlay	Byrne	McStay	Creaney 1	Nicholas	Collins	(O'Neil)
Nov 3	Sporting Lisbon	0-2	Bonner	Gillespie	Boyd	Grant	Mowbray	McGinlay	Byrne	McStay	Creaney	Nicholas	Collins	(O'Neil)

SCOTTISH LEAGUE 1994-95

			1	2	3	4	5	6	7	8	9	10	11	SUBS
Aug 13	Falkirk	1-1	Marshall	Martin	Boyd	McNally	Mowbray	Grant	Galloway	McStay	Falconer	Walker 1	Collins	
Aug 20	DUNDEE UNITED	2-1	Marshall	Martin	Boyd	McNally	Mowbray 1	Grant	Nicholas	McStay	Falconer	Walker 1	Collins	(Donnelly (9) McGinlay (7))
Aug 27	Rangers	2-0	Marshall	Grant	Boyd	McNally	Mowbray	McGinlay	Galloway	McStay 2	Donnelly	Walker	Collins 1	(Nicholas (9) O'Neil (6))
Sept 10	Partick Thistle	2-1	Marshall	Grant	Boyd	McNally	Mowbray	McGinlay	Galloway	O'Donnell 2	Donnelly	Walker	Collins	(Nicholas (11) McLaughlin (7))
Sept 17	KILMARNOCK	1-1	Marshall	Martin	Boyd	McNally	Mowbray	McGinlay 1	Grant	McStay	O'Donnell	Walker	Collins	(Donnelly (2))
Sept 24	HIBERNIAN	2-0	Marshall	Galloway	Boyd	McNally	Mowbray	Grant	McGinlay	O'Donnell 1	Nicholas	Walker	Collins 1	(Donnelly (10) O'Neil (9))
Oct 1	Motherwell	1-1	Marshall	Galloway	Boyd	McNally	O'Neil	Grant	McGinlay	O'Donnell	Nicholas	Walker 1	Collins	(McStay (10) Falconer (9))
Oct 8	ABERDEEN	0-0	Marshall	Galloway	Boyd	McNally	O'Neil	O'Donnell	McGinlay	McStay	Donnelly	Walker	Collins	(Nicholas (10) Falconer (5))
Oct 15	Hearts	0-1	Marshall	Galloway	Boyd	McNally	Smith	Grant	O'Donnell	Mcstay	Donnelly	Walker	Collins	(Nicholas (8) Falconer (8))
Oct 22	FALKIRK	0-2	Marshall	Martin	Boyd	McNally	O'Neil	Grant	McGinlay	O'Donnell	Falconer	Nicholas	Collins	(Walker (2) Donnelly (9))
Oct 30	RANGERS	1-3	Marshall	Smith	Boyd	McNally	O'Neil	O'Donnell	Byrne 1	McStay	Donnelly	Walker	Collins (	(Falconer (2) Nicholas (7))
Nov 5	Dundee United	2-2	Marshall	Boyd	McKinlay	McNally	O'Neil	Grant	Byrne	McStay	Falconer	Walker	Collins 2	
Nov 9	PARTICK THISTLE	0-0	Marshall	Boyd	McKinlay	Mowbray	O'Neil	Grant	Byrne	Mcstay	Donnelly	Nicholas	Colloins	(McNally (9) J O'Neill (10))
Nov 19	Kilmarnock	0-0	Marshall	Boyd	McKinlay	McNally	O'Neil	Grant	O'Donnell	McStay	Falconer	Walker	Collins	(Donnelly (10))
Nov 29	Hibernian	1-1	Marshall	Boyd	McKinlay	McNally	O'Neil	Galloway	McLaughlin	McStay	Falconer	Walker	Collins	(Gray (11))
Dec 3	MOTHERWELL	2-2	Marshall	Boyd	McKinlay	Galloway	O'Neil	Grant	McLaughlin	McStay	Falconer 1	Walker	Gray	(Donnelly (7))
Dec 26	Aberdeen	0-0	Bonner	Boyd	McKinlay	Mowbray	O'Neil	Grant	McLaughlin	McStay	Hay	Walker	Collins	(Donnelly (9))
Dec 31	FALKIRK	2-0	Bonner	Boyd	McKinlay	Smith	O'Neil	Grant 1	McLaughlin	McStay	Hay	Walker 1	Collins	(Gray (3) Donnelly (9))
Jan 4	Rangers	1-1	Bonner	Boyd	Gray	O'Neil	Galloway	O'Donnell	Mc~Laughlin	McStay	Byrne 1	Walker	Collins	(Hay (9))
Jan 7	DUNDEE UNITED	1-1	Bonner	Boyd	Gray	O'Neil	Slavin	O'Donnell	McLaughlin	McStay	Byrne	Walker	Collins 1	(Hay (9) Falconer (10))
Jan 11	HEARTS	1-1	Bonner	Boyd	Gray	Galloway	Slavin	O'Donnell	Byrne	McStay	van Hooijdonk 1	McLaughlin	Collins	(Walker (9))
Jan 14	KILMARNOCK	2-1	Bonner	Boyd	Gray	McNally	Slavin	O'Donnell	McLaughlin	McStay	van Hooijdonk	Falconer 1	Collins 1	(Hay (7))
Jan 21	Partick Thistle	0-0	Bonner	Boyd	Gray	O'Neil	McNally	Grant	McLaughlin	O'Donnell	van Hooijdonk	Falconer	Collins	
Feb 4	Motherwell	0-1	Bonner	Boyd	Gray	O'Neil	McNally	Grant	O'Donnell	McStay	van Hooijdonk	Falconer	Collins	(McLaughlin (3))
Feb 11	HIBERNIAN	2-2	Bonner	Boyd	Gray	O'Neil	McNally	Grant	McLaughlin	O'Donnell	van Hooijdonk	Falconer 1	Collins 1	
Feb 25	Hearts	1-1	Bonner	McNally	McKinlay	O'Neil	Mowbray	Grant	McLaughlin	O'Donnell 1	van Hooijdonk	Falconer	Collins	(Walker (9))
Mar 5	ABERDEEN	2-0	Bonner	Boyd	McKinlay	O'Neil	Mowbray	Grant	McLaughlin	McStay	van Hooijdonk 2	Falconer	O'Donnell	(Collins (7))
Mar 21	Kilmarnock	1-0	Bonner	Boyd	McKinlay	Vata	Mowbray	O'Donnell	McLaughlin	McStay	van Hooijdonk	Falconer	Collins	(Walker 1 (10) Grant (7))
Apr 1	MOTHERWELL	1-1	Bonner	Boyd	McKinlay	Vata	Mowbray	O'Donnell	McLaughlin	McStay	van Hooijdonk	Walker 1	Collins	(Falconer (6))
Apr 15	Aberdeen	0-2	Bonner	Boyd	McKinlay	Vata	O'Neil	Grant	McLaughlin	McStay	Falconer	Walker	Collins	(Donnelly (10) O'Donnell (3))
Apr 19	HEARTS	0-1	Bonner	Vata	Boyd	O'Neil	Mowbray	Grant	McLaughlin	O'Donnell	Falconer	Walker	Collins	(Donnelly (10))
Apr 29	Falkirk	2-1	Bonner	Boyd 1	McKinlay	O'Neil	Mowbray	Grant	O'Donnell 1	McStay	Falconer	Walker	Collins	
May 2	PARTICK THISTLE	1-3	Bonner	Boyd	McKinlay	O'Neil	Mowbray	Grant 1	O'Donnell	McStay	Falconer	van Hooijdonk	Collins	
May 7	RANGERS	3-0	Bonner	Boyd	McKinlay	Vata 1	O'Neil	Grant	McLaughlin	McStay	van Hooijdonk 1	Donnelly	Collins	(O'Donnell (9) Falconer (10)) +OG
May 10	Hibernian	1-1	Bonner	Boyd	McKinlay	Vata	O'Neil	Grant	McLaughlin	McStay	van Hooijdonk	Falconer 1	O'Donnell	
May 13	Dundee Utd	1-0	Bonner	Boyd	McKinlay	Vata	Mackay	Grant	McLaughlin	McStay	van Hooijdonk	O Donnell 1	Collins	(Nicholas (7) Gray (6))

LEAGUE CUP 1994

			1	2	3	4	5	6	7	8	9	10	11	SUBS
Aug 16	Ayr United	1-0	Marshall	Martin	Boyd	McNally	Mowbray	Grant 1	Galloway	McStay	Falconer	Walker	Collins	(Donnelly (10))
Aug 31	Dundee	2-1	Marshall	Grant	Boyd	McNally	Mowbray	McGinlay	Galloway	McStay	Donnelly	Walker 1	Collins 1	(Nicholas (9))
Sept 21	DUNDEE UNITED	1-0	Marshall	Galloway	Boyd	McNally	Mowbray	Grant	McGinlay	McStay	Donnelly	Walker 1	Collins 1	(Nicholas (9) O'Neil (8))
Oct 26	Aberdeen	1-0 SF	Marshall	Smith	Boyd	McNally	O'Neil 1	Grant	Byrne	McStay	Donnelly	Walker	Collins	(McGinlay (7) Nicholas(10))
Nov 27	Raith Rovers	2-2* F	Marshall	Boyd	Galloway	McNally	O'Neil	Mowbray	Donnelly	McStay	Nicholas 1	Walker 1	Collins	(Falconer (9) Byrne (7))

*Raith won on penalties.

SCOTTISH CUP 1995

			1	2	3	4	5	6	7	8	9	10	11	SUBS
Jan 28	St Mirren	2-0	Bonner	Boyd	Gray	O'Neil	McNally	Grant	McLaughlin	O'Donnell	van Hooijdonk 1	Falconer 1	Collins	(Walker (10))
Feb 18	MEADOWBANK THISTLE	3-0	Marshall	McNally	McKinlay	O'Neil	Mowbray	Grant	McLaughlin	O'Donnell	van Hooijdonk 2	Falconer 1	Collins	(Walker (7) Craig (8))
Mar 10	KILMARNOCK	1-0	Bonner	Boyd	McKinlay	O'Neil	Mowbray	O'Donnell	McLaughlin	McStay	van Hooijdonk	Falconer	Collins 1	(Grant (6))
Apr 7	Hibs	0-0 SF	Bonner	Boyd	McKinlay	Vata	O'Neil	Grant	McLaughlin	McStay	van Hooijdonk	Walker	Collins	(Falconer (9))
Apr 11	Hibs	3-1 SFR	Bonner	Boyd	McKinlay	Vata	O'Neil	Grant	McLaughlin	McStay	Falconer 1	Walker	Collins 1	(Donnelly(10)O'Donnell 1(6))
May 27	Airdrie	1-0 F	Bonner	Boyd	McKinlay	Vata	McNally	Grant	McLaughlin	McStay	van Hooijdonk 1	Donnelly	Collins	(O'Donnell(10) Falconer(9))

* Celtic's home matches in League and Cup during the 1994-95 season were played at Hampden Park because of reconstruction at Celtic Park.

INDEX

Adams, Davie 25, 29
Aitken, Roy 111, 114, *115*, 118, 120, 124, 129, 131, 134, 136, 137, 140, 141
Allen, Willie 91
Andrews, Ian 139
Auld, Bertie *72*, 73, 79, 81, 83, 88, 91, *92*, 95, 96, 97, 98, 100, 101, 102
Baric, Otto 128, 129
Battles, Barney 21, 22
Bell, Jamie 17
Bennett, Alec 28
Biggins, Wayne 149
Blessington, Jimmy 17
Boden, Alec 62
Bonnar, Johnny 62, 63, 64
Bonner, Pat 119, 120, 121, *130,* 135, 137, 139
Boyd, Tom 143, 154
Bradford, Jock 41
Brady, Liam 118, *142,* 142, 143, 145
Bremner, Billy 97, 98
Brogan, Jim 100, 104, 106
Browning, Johnny 31, 54
Buchan, Willie 51, 53, 54, 55
Burns, Tommy 117, 119, 122, 123, 124, *125,* 127, 128, 129, 133, 134, 136, 137, 141, 148, *150,* 150, 152, 155, 157, *158,* 158
Burton, Liz 104
Burton, Richard 104
Busby, Matt 57, 59
Butcher, Terry *130,* 135
Cairney, Frank 117
Callaghan, Tommy 104, 106
Campbell, Johnny 17, 22, 23
Carruth, Joe 54, 55
Cascarino, Tony 143
Cassidy, Joe 36, 38, 39
Cassidy, Terry 145
Chalmers, Stevie 71, 72, *74,* 76, 77, 79, 80, 81, 82, 87, 90, *91,* 92, 93, 95, 101, 102
Chapman, Herbert 43, 44, 51
Charlton, Jack 97
Clark, John 78, 80, 82, 86, 102
Clarke, Allan 97
Claessen, Dr. Hubert 129
Clough, Brian 127
Coleman, John 12
Collins, Bobby 61, 63, 64, 66
Collins, John 141, 143, 149, *151,* 152, 154, 157
Connelly, George 92, 95, 97, 98, *101,* 104, 105, 110
Connolly, Paddy 39, 40, 42
Connor, Frank *122,* 127, 133
Conway, Dr. John 21
Cook, Willie 44, 56
Cooper, Terry 97

Craig, Alan 45
Craig, Billy 64
Craig, Bobby 70
Craig, Jim 76, 77, 79, *84,* 84, 86, 88, 92, 94, 95, 102
Craig, Joe 111
Craig, Tommy 133, 135, 143
Craigmyle, Peter 35, 39
Crainie, Danny 119
Creaney, Gerry 143
Crerand, Pat 72
Cringan, Willie 38
Crum, Johnny 52, 53, 55, 56, 57
Cruyff, Johan 101, 119, 120
Cunningham, Laurie 116
Dalglish, Kenny 92, 101, 104, 105, 106, *108,* 108, *110,* 110, 111
Davidson, Bobby 98
Davidson, Victor 101
Deans, John 'Dixie' 25, 105, 106
Delaney, Jimmy 52, 53, *55,* 55, 57, 59
Dempsey, Brian 144, 145, *147,*
Denny, Jim 103
Devlin, Tom 130
Di Stefano, Alfredo 115
Divers, John (1890s) 21, 22
Divers, John (1930s/40s) 52, *54,* 55, 56, 57, 59
Divers, John (1950s/60s) 67, 71, 73, 78
Dodds, Joe 31, 35, 54
Dolan, Mick 11
Donnelly, Simon 154, *155,* 156
Dorotheus, Brother 10
Doyle, Dan 13, 17
Doyle, Johnny 114, 116, 119
Dunbar, Mick 11, 12, 25
Dziekanowski, Dariusz 139, *140,* 140, 141
Elliott, Paul 139, 140, *141,* 141
English, Sam *46,* 46
Eusebio, 95
Evans, Bobby, *61,* 61, 63, 64, *66,* 67
Falconer, Willie 149, 157
Fallon, John 90, 93, 94, 95
Fallon, Sean 63, 69, 73, 101, 111
Farrell, James 145, 147
Fernie, Willie *58, 62,* 63, 67, 101
Gallacher, Hughie 38, 39
Gallacher, Patsy 30, 32, 34, 36, 38, 39, 40, 41, 42, *43,* 54, 59, 67
Gallacher, Tommy 59
Gallacher, Willie, 59
Gallagher, Charlie 73, 76, 83
Gallagher, Paddy 12
Galloway, Mike 139, 140
Geatons, Chic 44, 45, 46, 51, 57
Gemmell, Tommy 71, *76,* 76, 77, 78, 80, *82,* 82, 83, 84, 86, 87, 90, 92, 93, 94, 95, 96, 97, 98, 100, 101, 102, 106
Giles, Johnny 98
Gillespie, Gary 143

Glass, John 10, *11,* 12, 13, 21
Glavin, Ronnie 111, 113
Gloeckner, Rudi 77
Golac, Ivan 140
Grant, James 24, 26, 144
Grant, Peter 128, 134, 135, 140, 149, *156*
Grant, Tom 144, 145, 147
Gray, Stuart 156
Gribben, Jimmy 61
Groves, Willie 12, 14, 16
Haffey, Frank 70
Hamilton, Davie 25, 28
Hamrin, Kurt 93
Hannet, Josef *78*
Hasil, Franz 100
Haughney, Mike 64
Hay, David 92, 95, 97, 98, 99, *100,* 101, 104, 105, 107, 109, 110, 112, *122,* 124, 127, 129, 131, 133
Hay, Jimmy 27, 28
Hayes, Martin 141
Herrera, Helenio 78, 87,
Higgins, John 63, 69
Hodge, Johnny 22
Hogg, Bobby 51, 59
Hood, Harry 95, 103, 104, *106,* 106
Hughes, John 68, 70, 71, 72, 75, 78, 79, 82, 88, 89, 90, 91, 93, 95, 96, 97, *99,* 99, 100, 102
Hunter, George 60
James, Alec 39
Johnston, Mo 128, 130, 131, 133, 140
Johnstone, Jimmy *68,* 69, 70, 71, 72, 75, 76, 78, 80, *81,* 81, 82, 83, 86, 89, 90, 91, 92, 93, 95, 97, 98, 100, 101, *102,* 103, *104, 105,* 105, 106, 107, 108, 109, 110, 115, 156
Johnstone, Peter 32
Jordan, Joe 143
Kelly, James 9, 11, 12, 17, 21, 25, 29, 144
Kelly, Kevin 144, *145,* 145, 147
Kelly, Michael 144, 145, 147
Kelly, Sir Robert, 12, 31, 41, 57, 64, 71, 73, 78, *91,* 91, 95, 103, 105, 144
Kennaway, Joe 47, *55,* 57
Kienast, Reinhard 128, 129
Kindvall, Ove 99, 100
Latchford, Peter 118
Lawrence, Tommy 77
Lawton, Tommy 56, 57
Lennox, Bobby *73,* 73, 76, 77, *78,* 78, 79, *81,* 81, 88, 90, 91, 92, 93, 94, 95, 102, 103, 104, 105, 115
Lo Bello, Concetto 100
Loney, Willie 25, 49
Lorenzo, Juan Carlos 107, 108
Lynch, Andy *109*
Lyon, Willie 51, 54, 57
Macari, Lou 92, 101, 103, 104, 105, 109, 110, *144,* 147, 149, 150
MacDonald, Alex 114
MacDonald, Malky *54,* 55

MacDonald, Roddie 113, 118

MacKay, Duncan 68, 69

MacKay, Malky 156

MacLeod, Murdo 113, 114, 116, 118, 119, 120, 121, 122, 127, 128, *129,* 129, 131, 133, 134

McAdam, Tom *115,* 119, *126,* 127

McArthur, Danny 23

McAvennie, Frank *135,* 135, 136, *137,* 137, 139, 140

McAtee, Andy 31, 35, 38, 39

McAteer, Tom 31

McBride, Joe *77,* 80, 81, 82, 92, 93, 101

McCallum, Neil *9,* 11, 13

McCann, Fergus *147,* 147, 150, *152,* 157, 158

McCarthy, Mick 133, 135, 139

McClair, Brian 124, 127, *128,* 128, 130, 131, 133

McCluskey, George 114, *116,* 116, 117, 119, 120, 122

McColl, Jimmy 31, 32

McFadden, John 10

McFarlane, John 'Jean' 35, 39, 42

McGarvey, Frank 116, 118, 119, 120, 122, *123, 126,* 127, 128, 130

McGarvie, Eddie 38

McGhee, Mark 124, 133, 134, 136, 139

McGinn, Jack 130, 131, 142, 145, 147

McGonagle, Peter 51

McGrain, Danny 101, 105, 110, 111, 113, 114, 117, *118,* 118, 122, 131, 133

McGrory, Jimmy *34,* 34, 36, 38, 39, 40, 41, 42, 43, 44, 45, 48, 51, 52, *53,* 53, 54, 56, 57, 59, 67, 68, 71, 73, 104

McInally, Alan 128, 131, 133

McInally, Tommy 36, 41, 42, 43, 56

McKeown, Mick 12

McKinlay, Tosh 149, 156

McLaren, Jimmy 9, 12, 17

McLaughlin, Brian *155,* 156

McLaughlin, John H *10,* 10, 11, 15, 16, 21, 29

McLean, Adam 35, 38, 39, 40, 41, 42, 43

McLeod, Donnie 25

McMahon, Sandy 13, 17, 22, 23

McMaster, John 32

McMenemy, Jimmy 25, *27,* 28, 29, 31, 32, 49, 56

McMurdo, Bill 140

McNair, Alec 25, *26,* 30, 32 35, 38, 39, 49, 54

McNally, Mark *151*

McNee, Gerry 121

McNeill, Billy 70, 71, *73,* 73, 75, 76, 78, *79,* 83, *84, 85, 88,* 89, 93, 94, 95, 96, 100, *103,* 104, 105, 108, 110, *111,* 111, *112,* 112, 113, 114, 116, 117, 118, 120, 121, 123, 124, 131, 132, 133, *134,* 134, 135, 139, 140, 141, 142, 145

McPhail, Billy 64, 66, 67

McPhail, John 61, *62,* 63, 64

McStay, Jimmy 38, 40, 45, *47,* 51, 56, *57,* 57,

McStay, Paul 119, 120, *124,* 124, 127, 128, 129, 130, 131, 133, 134, 135, 136, 137, *138,* 138, 139, 140, 141, 143, 147, 149, *151,* 152, 155, 157, 158

McStay, Willie 38, 39, 41

Madden, John 11, 13

Maley, Tom 11, 12, 22, 25

Maley, Willie 11, 12, 13, 15, 16, 17, 20, 21, 22, 23, 24, 25, 31, 32, 36, 39, 42, 43, 44, 45, 46, 47, 49, 50, 54, 56, 59, 142

Malloy, Dan 13

Marshall, Gordon 154

Martin, Mick 143

Masopust, Josef 84

Matthews, Stanley 57, 69

Mazzola, Sandro 84, 105, 129

Meechan, Frank 64

Meechan, Peter 21

Meiklejohn, Davie 46

Mercer, Joe 56

Miller, Joe 136, 137, 139, 143

Miller, Willie 60

Mochan, Neil 63, 66, 67

Morris, Chris 133, 137

Morrison, Jock 51, 57

Mowbray, Tony *151*

Murdoch, Bobby 70, 72, 76, 77, 79, 81, *86,* 87, 88, 91, 93, *94,* 95, 98, *99,* 100, 104

Murphy, Frank 51, 55, 57

Murray, Steve 106

Napier, Charlie 44, 45

Nicholas, Charlie 117, 118, 119, *120,* 120, *121,* 121, 122, 123, 124, 133, 141, 143, 154

O'Donnell, Phil *151,* 157

O'Leary, Pierce 130

O'Neil, Brian 143, *144,* 154

Orr, Willie, 25, 27, 39, 42

Osorio, Rodolfo 91

Paterson, George 51, 57, 59

Peacock, Bertie 61, 63, *66,* 67

Picchi, Armando 87

Pieters Graafland, Eddie *96,* 100

Prati, Pierino 94

Provan, Davie 113, 117, 122, *123,* 127, 130, 133

Puskas, Ferenc 115

Queen, Tony 99, 111

Quinn, Jimmy 23, 24, 25, 28, 30, 31, *32,* 32, 42, 54, 56, 61, 105

Reid, Mark 120, 124, 127

Revie, Don 97

Reynolds, Jerry 13

Rivera, Gianni 93, 94

Roberts, Graham *135,* 135, 138

Rocco, Nereo 93

Rogan, Anton 136, 137

Rooney, Bob *86*

Roose, Leigh 29

Rough, Alan 139

St John, Ian 77

Sarti, Giuliano *82, 83,* 86, 87

Scarff, Peter 44, 45, 47

Schnellinger, Karl-Heinz 93

Shankly, Bill 77

Sharkey, Jim 64

Shaw, Charlie 32, 35, 38, 39, 41

Shepherd, Tony 135

Shevlin, Peter 39, 42

Simpson, Ronnie 78, *84,* 84, 86, 90, 91, 93, 95, 102

Sinclair, Graeme 120

Slater, Stuart 143

Slavin, Jim 156

Smith, David 145, 146, 147

Sneddon, Alan 116

Somers, Peter 25, 28

Souness, Graeme 134

Sprake, Gary 97, 98

Stanton, Pat 107, 111, 113, 133

Stark, Billy 133, 134, *135,* 136, 137, 139, 150

Stein, Jock 18, 61, 63, 64, *65, 66,* 69, 70, *71,* 73, 75, 76, 77, 78, 79, 80, 81, 82, 84, 86, 87, 89, *91,* 91, 92, 93, 94, 95, 96, 97, 98, 99, 100, 101, 102, 103, 104, 105, *107,* 107, 108, 109, 110, *111,* 111, 113, 117, 130

Stewart, Rod 152

Stielike, Uli 116

Stojkovic, Dragan 139

Taylor, Lord Justice 144

Thom, Andreas 152

Thomson, Alec 39, 40, 41, 43, 44, 51

Thomson, Bertie 44, 45, 47, 48

Thomson, John 34, *44,* 44, 45, *46,* 46, *47,* 47

Treytel, Eddie 100

Tully, Charlie *60,* 61, 62, 63, 64, 66, 67

van Hanegem, Wim 98, 99, 100

van Hooijdonk, Pierre *148,* 149, *156*

Vata, Rudi 149, *156*

Waddell, Andrew 121

Walfrid, Brother 9, 10, 12, 19

Wallace, Willie *80,* 81, 82, 83, 88, 90, 93, 95, 96, *98,* 100, 102

Walker, Andy 133, 134, *135,* 135, 136, *137,* 139, 140, 154

Walsh, Jimmy 63, 64

Weir, Jock 59

Wdowczyck, Dariusz 141

Weisfeld, Gerald 147

Welsh, Pat 12

White, Chris 144, 145, 147

White, Desmond 56, 103, *111, 122,* 123, 130, 144

White, Tom 33, 54, 56, 64, 144

Whyte, Derek 134

Williams, Evan 97, 100

Wilson, Harold 89

Wilson, Paul 106, *107,*

Wilson, Peter 40, 42

Wilson, Sammy 66

Woods, Chris 134, 135

Yeats, Ron 77

Young, Sunny Jim 32